CONTINUITY AND CHANGE

CONTINUITY AND CHANGE

The Harvest of Late Medieval and Reformation History

Essays Presented to Heiko A. Oberman on his 70th Birthday

EDITED BY

ROBERT J. BAST

AND

ANDREW C. GOW

BRILL

LEIDEN · BOSTON · KÖLN

2000

This book is printed on acid-free paper.

cover design by Titus Schulz
Arnhem, The Netherlands
typesetting by Elgraphic+DTQP
Schiedam, The Netherlands

Library of Congress Cataloging-in-Publication Data

Community and change : the harvest of the late medieval and Reformation
history : essays presented to Heiko A. Oberman on his 70th birthday / edited by
Robert J. Bast and Andrew C. Gow.
     p.   cm.
     Includes bibliographical references and index.
     ISBN 9004116338
     1. Reformation. 2. Church history—Middle Ages, 600-1500. I. Bast,
Robert James. II. Gow, Andrew Colin.   III. Oberman, Heiko Augustinus.
BR305.2 .C64 2000
270.5—dc21
                                                              00–041359
                                                              CIP

Die Deutsche Bibliothek - CIP-Einheitsaufnahme

Continuity and change : the harvest of late medieval and reformation
history ; essays presented to Heiko A. Oberman on his 70th birthday /
ed. by Robert J. Bast and Andrew C. Gow. – Leiden ; Boston ; Köln :
Brill, 2000
     ISBN 90–04–11633–8

ISBN   90 04 11633 8

PRINTED IN THE NETHERLANDS

CONTENTS

III. Exegesis and Interpretation

IV. Religious Life: Roots and Ramifications

Professor Heiko A. Oberman

PREFACE

"Continuity and Change", it might be charged, is one of those innocuous titles to which scholars turn by default when the muses refuse to inspire. Yet few epochs make a better case for such a rubric than the field of scholarship once defined as "Reformation History." Heiko Oberman came to maturity as a historian amongst a cohort of scholars still grappling with the great and abiding myth of the radical discontinuity of the Protestant Reformation from its medieval past — a myth equally useful for praise and blame. It is no small part of Oberman's prodigious scholarly achievement that in his studies on late-medieval philosophy, theology, and piety, on the Luther movement, the roots of antisemitism, the urban Reformation, on Calvin and the Reformed tradition (and those who know the true scope of his work will recognize at once the poverty of this sketch) he has shaken paradigms and challenged assumptions that stood for generations.

The chapters in this volume celebrate this extraordinary career, reflecting the uncommon breadth and range not only of Oberman's scholarship, but also of his friendships. Individually and collectively, the authors have tracked the debts incurred and the departures taken as Europe's peoples worked out some of the central problems of life and faith between the twelfth and the seventeenth centuries. We have picked our moment carefully, fairly optimistic that on his seventieth birthday, Heiko can be persuaded to lay down his pen, set aside his books, and interrupt for a few short hours a life of scholarly vitality that shows no sign of waning, long enough to celebrate it with us.

For encouragement, advice, and logistical support, the editors wish to express their gratitude to Thomas A. Brady, Jr., Susan Karant-Nunn, and Luise Betterton. Mr. Ivo Romein of Brill Academic Publishers provided sound counsel and congenial cooperation. Lara Brindle, J. Robert Falconer, and Derek M. Bast contributed greatly to the preparation of the indices. The University of Tennessee generously provided financial support with a grant from the EPPE fund for Exhibition, Performance, and Publication.

February, 2000

Robert J. Bast,   *Knoxville*
Andrew Colin Gow,   *Edmonton*

HEIKO OBERMAN'S DESERT HARVEST

Donald Weinstein *

It was a common supposition in the world of academe that Heiko Oberman's decision to accept a professorship at the University of Arizona (which had long been courting him) had as much to do with climate as with career. After loyally suffering Tubingen's damp for eighteen years, Mrs. Oberman needed warmer, drier airs for her arthritis. Toetie Oberman is everyone's favorite, and her husband's decision was applauded as a well-merited act of devotion and gratitude, but also widely regarded as a great sacrifice. How could this prolific scholar and teacher find happiness so far from the great libraries and research centers? And how could he make Reformation studies flourish in the desert? Would first-rate graduate students come to Tucson knowing they would have to compete for jobs with Ph Ds. from Harvard, Yale and Berkeley? Indeed, as the then Head of the Department of History, I was told by my counterpart at a major mid-western university: "Professor X, our Reformation historian, will retire in a few years time, but Oberman or no Oberman we won't be looking to the University of Arizona for his replacement!"

Happily, both Obermans have flourished in the Arizona climate. That Reformation studies have also blossomed was brought home to me recently in a very gratifying way. The chair of a search committee at that same mid-western university wrote to say that Professor X had just retired. Did we have any good entry-level candidates to replace him? Indeed we did. Students from European and American universities, unaffected by academic snobbery, have jumped at the chance to come to Tucson. They enter a program best described as baptism by full immersion, combining continuous, rigorous seminar training, close individual attention by Oberman himself and insistence upon genuine proficiency in Latin and the relevant modern languages. They are welcomed into the warm Oberman household where they enjoy fellowship with other students, members of the fam-

* Professor Emeritus, University of Arizona

ily and frequent scholarly guests and where they have access to the
fine Reformation book collection. With study abroad for dissertation
research a necessity, all have won Fulbright or other equivalent government fellowships. At this writing nine young men and women
have earned their Ph Ds. in the Oberman-founded Division for Late
Medieval and Reformation studies and all have found high quality
positions. Five more are at the dissertation stage. They and other
Division students have given numerous papers at professional meetings, published several articles and, so far, five books, with a number
of others on the way.

Oberman's uncompromising intellectual standards and inex-
haustible energy as scholar, teacher, mentor and administrator are
the bricks and mortar of the Division, but the edifice he has created is
no ivory tower. Rather he has made it a public resource, a kind of
Academy on the ancient model, an open place where scholars and
citizens meet and where learning and the exchange of ideas are
regarded as indispensable components of the good life, not as ends in
themselves. He gives unstintingly of himself in public lectures, adult
evening courses and discussion groups. The door to his office is open
to anyone — student, colleague, journalist or member of the lay
community — who seeks him out for public interviews or private
conversation, and an astonishing variety of people do. Clearly, the
gain is not all one-sided. Oberman seems to draw some of his fabu-
lous energy from such exchanges, and while few can match his zeal,
not to say genius, for public communication, he is an example to students and colleagues alike of the scholar's responsibility to society.

The doubts that buzzed over the academic grapevine as Heiko
Oberman proceeded to the *Reformationrein* American southwest have,
I think, been resoundingly put to rest. But the very success of the
Division raises another question: will the Oberman creation, shaped
by his private vision and so brilliantly reflecting his personality, survive without him? The question may be a bit premature because at
seventy Oberman is still very much in the thick of things where he
intends to be for some time to come. Nevertheless, I am confident
that the right answer is yes. However closely the Division is identified
with its founder, it is not identical with him, nor is it an extension of
his ego. Already a second distinguished Reformation historian, Dr.
Susan Karant-Nunn, has joined the Arizona faculty as Associate Professor of History and Assistant Director of the Division. Together she
and Heiko Oberman are writing a new chapter for it, and, like all

good history, this will be a story of both continuity and change. Oberman has built well; the edifice stands on its own. It has established a presence in, and tradition of, service to the University, the community and the world of Reformation scholarship which will take it well into this new millennium.

HEIKO OBERMAN AS MENTOR:
THE GRADUATE STUDENT BETWEEN
DOKTOR AND *VATER*

Robert J. Bast*

In 1985, the first full year of Heiko Oberman's tenure at the University of Arizona, the Division he would raise to such distinction was still young enough to accommodate students such as I was — raw, naïve, and undertrained. One of the many lacunae in my education was filled in my very first formal interview with Heiko (he the only man in Tucson wearing coat and tie in the summer heat), as my new mentor gravely defined and parsed the word *Doktorvater*. Though time has clouded the exact words spoken on that occasion, their effect remains vivid: this American didn't know whether to be relieved or alarmed by the layers of meaning evident in that slippery term, etymologically familiar, culturally so foreign.

In retrospect, both relief and alarm were entirely appropriate. As any of his students past or present can attest, Heiko expects much and pushes hard, and in those early years there was a great deal of ground to make up. Yet the demands of the *Herr Professor Doktor* were more than matched by the generosity and dedication of the *Vater*. Despite the extraordinary pressures of his own schedule of teaching, research, and writing; of correspondence, editing, fundraising and service to the academic community, to say nothing of his own private life, Heiko somehow managed to make time for each of his growing cadre of students in a way that those of us who now have our own can scarcely imagine. There were weekly sessions for each of us individually, time spent discussing our research or, more precious in hindsight, working line by line through a common primary source. It is one of Heiko's unique gifts that at such times, the pressures of schedule are firmly banished to the other side of the office door, and the text itself takes on such life and immediacy that the hour becomes a lively conversation between mentor, student, and author. Nor is any meeting complete until Heiko has inquired after morale, health,

---

* Associate Professor of History, University of Tennessee

family, and genuinely taken the measure of the human being whose present and future he has undertaken to shape. Such moments define what it means to be one of his students.

This personal dimension is carried over to the graduate seminar, in some respects the place where the heart and soul of the Oberman program are quintessentially manifest. The group assembles each week at Heiko's home in the foothills of the Catalina mountains (in our day, promptly at 7:00 p.m.), with the desert city spreading out below. Students take their places around the living room, and Oberman presides from his ornate, hand-carved chair (a family heirloom that the wags among us always suspected he favored not for its comfort but for its regal lines). Against the cool of the desert evening there is always a fire, and the dogs wander in and out freely, blithely ignoring the occasional Dutch rebuke. The evening begins with a brief survey of recent secondary literature, then progresses to a feast of scholarly discussion and analysis around a common primary source. Heiko aims high in his *sodalitas*: Augustine's *De Civitate Dei*, Luther's 1535 commentary on Galatians; the first edition of Calvin's *Institutes*, for example. Students take their turns each week leading the study of a prescribed chapter or segment, presenting summary and analysis, identifying problems of translation and interpretation, and proposing an agenda for the subsequent discussion. What follows is as good as graduate training gets: an inspired group debate on the nature and meaning of the text, the passions and personalities that crafted it, and its place in historical and historiographical context. Heiko presides over all of this with a light but expert hand, guiding but never dominating the discussion, willing to mix it up when his own interpretation is challenged, but doing so with unfeigned respect in which condescension has no part. There are a few rules, expressed in the aphorisms that have become so familiar to Heiko's students: "The phrase 'of course' has no place in the historian's vocabulary"; "the past is a foreign country". This is no arbitrary code: it is intended to combat presentism; to guard against that occupational hazard of our profession, the unconscious arrogance that comes with perfect hindsight; to drive home the Prime Directive of Heiko's program: *listen* to the sources.

Such evenings unfold in stages, punctuated by fortification from the largesse of the Oberman pantry that gives the lie to that malicious stereotype, the parsimonious Netherlander, and graced more often than not by the presence and insightful participation of Toetie

Oberman. In a second round, students present their own work: drafts of dissertation chapters, conference papers, grant proposals and the like. Group critique is frank and unsparing, yet offered up with collegial good will and to excellent effect. The hours pass — midnight often comes and goes without notice — yet Heiko seems to get livelier as they do, drawing energy from the proceedings themselves. This is all to the good, for it means that once the session is at a close, those with the stamina will join him on the veranda, drink copious amounts of his Heineken, and idle away another hour or so under the stars in unhurried and increasingly irreverent conversation.

Here too Heiko's unique gifts are at work, for the atmosphere he encourages fashions more than the artificial civility made necessary by the forced proximity and common purpose of graduate student life. Genuine friendships are built in that circle, and Heiko and Toetie contribute significantly to their construction. In the near decade of my own tenure in Tucson, we dozen or so students became something of a family — however dysfunctional, at times. We celebrated marriages, mourned their dissolution, rejoiced at births, wept at death. The Obermans unselfconsciously offered their home as a meeting place for this extended, ersatz clan, adjusting to the new customs and rituals of their adopted land with a bemused good will. In one of my fondest memories, Heiko trots around the bases of a hastily-constructed baseball diamond in his own backyard on a balmy Thanksgiving afternoon, still clutching a plastic bat, as half a dozen young children, their stomachs full to bursting with turkey, dressing, and (a modest concession to our hosts) the odd herring, run screaming wildly in hot pursuit.

Such moments have nothing to do with books, research, textual analysis, graduate training; nothing to do with the Harvest of Late Medieval Theology or Luther between God and the Devil or the Mystery of Calvin's Impact. They have everything to do with life, humanity, and the crafting of personal relationships. The celebration of Oberman's scholarly accomplishments, through this Festschrift, is justly deserved, the unparalleled merit of his works widely acknowledged, their author universally respected. Yet posterity should know, too, that Heiko Oberman was as good as his word: not *Doktor* only, but *Vater* to a generation of students who have gratefully contributed to the creation of this volume as a small token of their deep and enduring affection.

I. GOVERNANCE IN THEORY AND PRACTICE

CONFRONTING MARKET FREEDOM: ECONOMIC FOUNDATIONS OF LIBERTY AT THE END OF THE MIDDLE AGES*

Cary J. Nederman**

During the Latin Middle Ages, as in the modern world, the language of liberty was applied in a bewildering array of contexts. In part, this is due to the large variety of traditions concerning liberty available to the Middle Ages. For example, the urban conception of civic freedom, derived from antiquity, was transmitted by classical sources such as Roman Law and Cicero. Liberty in this sense pertains to the corporate rights that accrue to the citizens of a self-governing republic.[1] Christianity contributed a doctrine of liberty construed in terms of free choice, namely, the freedom to do God's will or to refrain from following divine ordinance. This is essentially a moral and personal conception of volition; it concentrates attention on the orientation of the individual's will.[2] The feudal structure of social as well as political relations generated a distinctive discourse of liberty defined as a sphere of action and judgement independent of the control and supervision of any superior authority. Out of such "territorial immunity" arises a principle of "inviolability," an exclusive and unabridgeable right of the lord to exercise power.[3]

These manifestations of freedom in the medieval world, and their application in theory as well as practice, have received wide attention from recent scholars. In particular, we now enjoy an enhanced appreciation of how the discourses of liberty arising from the Latin Middle Ages were received, restated, and transformed in modern Europe.[4] But one significant facet of the

---

*An earlier version of this paper was presented at the first National Convention of the Historical Society, Boston University, May 1999.

** Professor of Political Science, Texas A&M University

[1] Ch. Wirszubski, *Libertas as a Political Idea at Rome during the Late Republic and Early Principate* (Cambridge: Cambridge University Press, 1950).

[2] Albrecht Dihle, *The Theory of Will in Classical Antiquity (Berkeley: University of California Press, 1982).*

[3] Alan Harding, "Political Liberty in the Middle Ages," *Speculum* 55 (1980), 423-43.

medieval languages of liberty — the economic dimension — has been systematically overlooked in the literature. Doubtless, this reflects the more general assumption that medieval Europe was a "closed" economy, controlled by a small group of feudal nobles and urban oligarchs, and thus antagonistic to expressions of economic freedom. Moreover, it seems widely presumed, and certainly with some good reason, that the church functioned as a constraining force in the extension of liberalizing commercial values and practices. One need look no further than St. Thomas Aquinas's pronouncements about the evils of monetary exchange and economic profit-seeking to realize that key forms of economic freedom were commonly equated in the medieval mind with the road to vice and damnation.[5]

As is so often the case with broad statements about the Latin Middle Ages, however, these generalizations about medieval economic life and thought require some modification and qualification. Recent historical research has drawn attention to the evidence that Europe between roughly 1100 and 1300 underwent little short of a commercial revolution, reflected in rapid monetarization, market expansion, urbanization, and so forth.[6] By the end of the Middle

---

[4] See Edward Peters, "*Libertas Inquirendi* and the *Vitum Curiositatis* in Medieval Thought," Giles Constable, "Liberty and Free Choice in Monastic Thought and Life, especially in the Eleventh and Twelfth Centuries," and Robert L. Benson, "Libertas in Italy (1152-1226)," in George Makdisi, Dominique Sourdel, and Janine Sourdel-Thomine, eds., *La notion de liberté ay Moyen Age Islam, Byzance, Occident* (Paris: Les Belles Lettres, 1985), pp. 89-118, 191-213; Brian Tierney, "Freedom and the Medieval Church," John H. Munday, "Medieval Urban Liberty," H.G. Konigsberger, "Parliaments and Estates," and J.H. Baker, "Personal Liberty under the Common Law of England, 1200-1600," in R.W. Davis, ed., *The Origins of Modern Freedom in the West* (Stanford: Stanford University Press, 1995), pp. 64-202; and Cary J. Nederman, "Toleration, Skepticism, and the 'Clash of Ideas': Principles of Liberty in the Writings of John of Salisbury," in John Christian Laursen and Cary J. Nederman, eds., *Beyond the Persecuting Society: Religious Toleration Before the Enlightenment* (Philadelphia: University of Pennsylvania Press, 1998), pp. 53-70.

[5] St. Thomas Aquinas, *De regno*, II.3, in R.M. Spiazzi, ed., *Opuscula philosophica* (Turin: Marietti, 1954): "If the citizens devote their life to matters of trade, the way will be opened to many vices. Since the primary aim of traders is to make money, greed is awakened among citizens through the pursuit of trade. As a result, everything in the city will become vendable... Each person will work only for his own profit, despising the public good... In a city, civic life will of necessity be corrupted."

[6] See Lester K. Little, *Religious Poverty and the Profit Economy in Medieval Europe* (Ithaca: Cornell University Press, 1978); Richard H. Britnell, *The Commercialisation of English Society 1000-1500*, 2nd ed. (Manchester: Manchester University Press, 1996); and Britnell and Bruce M.S. Campbell, eds., *A Commercialising Economy: England 1068 to c. 1300* (Manchester: Manchester University Press, 1995).

Ages, central elements of economic organization were in place that would condition the emergence of capitalism during the Early Modern period. Indeed, the Roman church, so often regarded as a source of reaction in matters of material acquisition, has lately been touted by a group of economists as a paradigmatic instance of "an economic firm."[7] In sum, the economic life of medieval Europe was by no means so monolithic and "closed" as scholars have sometimes implied.

Still, one might reasonably ask, in the words of Lester K. Little, whether the economic morality promoted by medieval Christian theologians, philosophers, and lawyers was "so uncompromising ... that virtually any participation in the upper levels of the commercial economy involved the dangers of sin and conjured up visions of appalling punishments"?[8] In other words, it might be objected that the theory failed to keep pace with the practice up to the end of the Middle Ages, yielding a rejection in the abstract of those manifestations of economic liberty that occurred daily (and that perhaps even directly benefited the theoreticians who reviled them). This conclusion certainly appears warranted on the basis of the examination of the best recent scholarship concerned with economic freedom in medieval thought, found in the writings of Odd Langholm.[9] In his latest book, in particular, Langholm points out how medieval Latin schoolmen departed from their ancient and early Christian antecedents in their understanding of economic choice. Whatever their other differences, Aristotle, classical Roman law, and St. Augustine adopted an expansive notion of volition in connection with economic matters.[10] They shared the view, specifically, that actions taken under the pressure of "necessity" or "need" counted nevertheless as "free" rather than coerced. The only examples of "unfree" acts were those that arose from direct force or fraud. Hence, the logic of

---

[7] Robert B. Ekelund et al., *Sacred Trust: The Medieval Church as an Economic Firm* (Oxford: Oxford University Press, 1996). Also see John Gilchrist, *The Church and Economic Activity in the Middle Ages* (London: Macmillan, 1969).

[8] Little, *Religious Poverty and the Profit Economy*, p. 41.

[9] Odd Langholm, "Economic Freedom in Scholastic Thought," History of Political Economy 14 (1982), pp. 260-83; idem, *Economics in the Medieval Schools: Wealth, Exchange, Value, Money and Usury according to the Paris Theological Tradition, 1200-1350* (Leiden: Brill, 1992); and idem, *The Legacy of Scholasticism in Economic Thought: Antecedents of Choice and Power* (Cambridge: Cambridge University Press, 1998).

[10] For the following, see ibid., pp. 15-56.

pre-medieval teachings (though not necessarily their overt substance) seemed to justify mutual consent as an adequate standard of free action in the marketplace.

By contrast, Langholm argues that medieval scholastics consistently treated "need" as a limiting case of free exchange.[11] If the seller in a market relation possessed an item that the buyer required for his physical sustenance (say, water or bread), a form of compulsion was built into the economic interaction. Should the seller insist upon a price greater than that which would otherwise obtain (the ordinary market value), even in times of scarcity, he placed himself in mortal danger; independent mechanisms of supply and demand, let alone the explicit consent of the exchanging parties, were subordinate to the legitimate need of the buyer. Consequently, medieval schoolmen rejected the self-regulation of the marketplace as inadequate to protect the seller from the potential coercion that existed in every act of exchange. Some authors advocated strict price controls on victuals, while most simply concluded that the "common estimate" of value should form the thumb-nail guide for valid exchanges. In Langholm's view, however, the medieval schoolmen were united in their antipathy towards the position that only force and fraud constituted sufficient reasons to interfere in the consenting relationship between economic actors. Moreover, Langholm claims, the difference between medieval and pre-medieval economic perspectives on the nature of market liberty continues to shape discourses in the modern era, even into the twentieth century debates over the principles of neo-classical economics.[12]

Without question, Langholm's insights are valid for most of the literature that he surveys. It seems true that the mainstream of medieval thought set limits on economic liberty that derived from moral and theological, rather than strictly individual and voluntary, considerations. I wish to argue, however, that Langholm's account is incomplete, to the extent that he leaves out of his narrative thinkers who inherited and absorbed more directly the lessons of classical (by which I mean, ancient pagan and early Christian) economic doctrines, and who were thus more amenable to a market-driven conception of freedom. In the present essay, my attention will be focussed on two authors who fall clearly within the scholastic tradition: John of Paris, a Thomist who

---

[11] Ibid., pp. 59-136.
[12] Ibid., pp. 178-200.

attained the status of Master of Arts at the University of Paris, flourishing around 1300; and William of Pagula, an Oxford-trained canonist who spent much of his career as a parish priest in rural England during the early fourteenth century. I maintain that both John and William based their economic teachings on elements of the Roman legal tradition, which dispensed with any measure of value exogenous to the free operation of the market. Volition for the contributors to the *Corpus iuris civilis* formed a sufficient condition of a just exchange, a doctrine that Romanists expressed in the form of the maxim *Res tantum valet quantum vendi potest* ("A thing is worth the amount for which it can be sold").[13] The only circumstances in which the legal literature sanctions intrusion into the market and correction of an exchange are force and fraud. In turn, this doctrine was encapsulated in a maxim about property rights first found in the Code: *Quisque suae rei est moderator et arbiter* ("Everyone is the moderator and arbiter of his own goods").[14] Individuals are endowed with a full range of control over their property, designated by the term *dominium* (lordship, ownership), such that consent alone can be the mark of the legitimate alienation or transfer of one's possessions. When these two principles are fully embraced, the notion that moral precepts are relevant to the judgment of free market interactions is profoundly diminished, if not erased.

John of Paris

The reputation of John of Paris, and his major work of political theory, *De potestate regia et papali* (c. 1302), has formed a topic of considerable debate in recent years. On the one hand, Janet Coleman locates John's thought at the root of an intellectual tradition regarding private property and political power that culminates in the central chapters of that watershed of liberalism, John Locke's *Second Treatise of Government*. While Coleman acknowledges that the building blocks of *De potestate's* doctrine are largely conventional — in some cases directly adapted from the slightly earlier writings of Godefroid of Fontaines — she insists that the scenario he constructs is innova-

---

[13] *Digest* 13.1.14.pro, 36.1.1.16, and 47.2.52.29; see Langholm, *The Legacy of Scholasticism in Economic Thought*, pp. 32-38, 78.
[14] *Code* 4.35.21, 4.38.14; also *Digest* 41.1 passim. See Langholm, "Economic Freedom in Scholastic Thought," pp. 261-62.

tive in a manner that presages early modern natural rights theory.[15] By contrast, Odd Langholm's comparison of passages of *De potestate* with economic texts of the scholastic era, as well as with John's other works that comment on economic concerns, leads him to underscore the wholly conventional character of the former. John's views are "in fact a compound of Aristotle and Roman law," so that any associa- tion of them "with the tradition in early modern political theory whose most prominent exponent is Locke, is to demonstrate the full danger involved in anticipatory interpretation of ideas."[16]

As antithetical as these interpretations appear, there is an element of truth in each. Langholm is correct to emphasize John's debt to a range of commonplace sources, while Coleman is right to highlight the novelty of his combination of those materials. Yet both scholars miss some of the significance of John of Paris's creative synthesis. The central concern of *De potestate* is not to establish the indestructibility of "the private property of individuals or their natural rights to proper- ty" (Coleman); but neither is it entirely valid to say that John "never intended to raise as a separate issue the emancipation of individual property holders from either moral or legal authority" (Langholm).[17] The core of John's teaching about property and community, I main- tain, is to be found in his extension of the Roman law principle of economic liberty to the point of formulating a version of the doctrine of the primacy of the free market in relation to public affairs. To understand this, we must turn to the text of *De potestate*.

Whether or not *De potestate* was composed as a single treatise, and whether or not it bears some relation to the polemical conflict between the French King Philip IV and Pope Boniface VIII,[18] it takes as one of

---

[15] Janet Coleman, "*Dominium* in Thirteenth- and Fourteenth-Century Political Thought and its Seventeenth-Century Heirs: John of Paris and Locke," *Political Stud- ies* (1985), pp. 73-100; Coleman, "Poverty, Property and Political Thought in Four- teenth Century Scholastic Philosophy," in Christian Wenin, ed., *L'homme et son univers au moyen âge* (Louvain-la-Nueve: Éditions de l'Institut Supérieur de Philosophie, 1986), pp. 845-55.

[16] Langholm, *Economics in the Medieval Schools*, p. 393.

[17] Cf. Janet Coleman, "The Individual and the Medieval State," in Coleman, ed., *The Individual in Political Theory and Practice* (Oxford: Clarendon Press, 1996), p. 25 with Langholm, *Economics in the Medieval Schools*, p. 394.

[18] Janet Coleman, "The Intellectual Milieu of John of Paris OP," in Jürgen Miethke, ed., *Das Publikum politischer Theorie im 14.Jahrhundert* (Munich: Oldenbourg, 1992), pp. 173-206; Coleman, "The Dominican Political Theory of John of Paris in its Context," in Diana Wood, ed., *The Church and Sovereignty, c.590-1918* (Oxford: Basil Blackwell, 1991), pp. 187-223.

its main themes the differentiation of the types of rights over property that persons of various ranks and statuses (lay versus clerical conditions, secular versus ecclesiastical rulers) may claim. John sharply distinguishes throughout the work between *dominium* (lordship) and *iurisdictio* (jurisdiction), arguing that powers conferred by the former are primary and antecedent in relation to the latter. Thus, a political official (spiritual or temporal) may be able to judge in certain circumstances whether a member of the secular community is putting his property to an unjust use — that pertains to the realm of jurisdiction. But such judgement does not amount to a denial of the pre-existing ownership of the property nor of the rightful control over property exercised by its *dominus*. Rather, John declares, "the temporalities of laymen are not communal."[19] The earthly goods of non-clerics are rightfully apportioned by some means other than assignment by clergy or princes.

If the authority to use property does not in the first instance derive from a political/legal act or a moral/theological assessment, then whence does it arise? John gives a summary of his answer in Chapter III of *De potestate*:

> "Each is lord (*dominus*) of his own property as acquired through his own industry, therefore there is no need for a single person to dispense lay temporalities in common, since each is his own dispenser to do with his own at will (*ad libitum*)."[20]

This point is developed at greater length in Chapter VII:

> "The external goods of the laity are not granted to the community, as is ecclesiastical property, but are acquired by individual people through their own art, labor, or industry, and individual persons, insofar as they are individuals, have right (*ius*) and power and true lordship over them. And each person is able to order, dispose, dispense, retain, and alienate his own according to his will (*pro libito*) without injury to others, since he is lord. And therefore such goods do not have order and connection amongst themselves nor towards one common head who has them to dispose and dispense, since each one may order his things according to his will (*pro libito*). And therefore neither the prince nor the pope has lordship or the power of dispensing such things."[21]

---

[19] John of Paris, *De potestate regia et papali*, ed. Fritz Bleienstein (Stuttgart: Klett Verlag, 1969), p. 82. All translations from Latin in the following paper are my own.

[20] Ibid., p. 82.

[21] Ibid., pp. 96-97.

A disproportionate share of attention has been drawn by scholars to John's apparent statement of a labor theory of acquisition. Langholm is correct to note, however, that the appeal to *industria* is a fairly conventional move in medieval legal and scholastic literature, as is the claim that the individual is "dispenser" of his own goods.[22]

So in what way, then, is John's conception of property innovative or unique? The key, I believe, lies in the meaning of the penultimate sentence of the passage quoted. In an assertion for which I know no precedent in medieval writings, John denies any basis for the idea that earthly goods were a gift granted in the first instance by God to the human race as a common possession. The former reflected the view of St. Thomas and nearly every other schoolman (and indeed, John Locke, too). By contrast, John of Paris holds that one's lordship over temporalities owes nothing whatsoever to an interlocking system of property relations created artificially by a "just" division of the common. If this position is to be sustained, then private goods enter into some social setting only by an act of volition on the part of their proprietors. No person enjoys a pre-eminent moral claim the goods of another — even, presumably, in a case of pressing need. Property is antecedently private and individual, and takes on a communal bearing only by virtue of the will of its owner. Here is the *sine qua non* of a free market: individuals enter voluntarily with one another into an exchange relationship, the existence of which derives its entire legitimacy from the liberty of the participants. As John underscores at the close of Chapter VII of *De potestate*, "Each one disposes of his own as he wills."[23] The exercise of this freedom is in accordance with right and in itself harms no one.

But what about the jurisdiction enjoyed by rulers over the just and unjust uses of temporal goods? Does this not constitute a severe constraint on the liberty associated with private lordship over property? John is very precise in his construction of his explanation of the connection between individual property and the political/legal authority of church and secular ruler. Jurisdiction is rendered necessary by the entry of private proprietors into voluntary mutual relations with one another.

---

22 Langholm, *Economics in the Medieval Schools*, p. 393.
23 John of Paris, *De potestate regia et papali*, p. 98.

"For the reason that it sometimes happens that the common peace is disturbed on account of such external goods, as when someone takes that which is another's, and also at times because some people, who are excessively fond of their own, do not convey it according to what the needs and utility of the country require, therefore a ruler is instituted by the people to restrain such acts, in the manner of a judge discerning the just and the unjust, a vindicator of injuries, and a measurer of the just proportion owed to each for the common needs and utility."[24]

According to John, the temptation on the part of some to override the liberty of others, in conjunction with a failure of self-absorbed individuals to calculate and acknowledge the social costs of the profit they obtain by entering into reciprocal economic intercourse, comprise the only justifications for the jurisdiction of rulers. The "moral" limits that are imposed by government are those that arise directly from the failure of individuals to accept and act according to the principles of a market society. Moreover, only those who antecedently enjoy private property rights can authorize the appointment of a judge and executor over themselves and their goods. If something falls within my exclusive dominion, then only my consent can confirm jurisdiction over my property upon someone else. Granted that John's position is not quite an economic theory of political authority, he nonetheless recognizes that the exercise of individual free ownership forms the salient source of the friction and conflict that government is created to resolve.

The priority of liberty thus crucially informs the economic as well as political doctrines of *De potestate*. Holding to a conception of private property loosely derived from Roman law teaching, John of Paris proposes an extensive notion of the free sphere of individual action. The ability of government to fix limits on that realm of freedom requires direct and demonstrable harm to another — precisely the criteria invoked by classical Roman law. One's liberty to do with one's goods as one wishes is otherwise to be protected. No moral claim of dire need may properly constrain the terms under which one chooses to alienate (or to retain) property, since one's legitimate possessions derive from a wholly individual source and stand in no intrinsic or natural to the goods or rights of any other. Economic freedom is woven for John into the very fabric of human existence.

---

[24] Ibid., p. 97.

William of Pagula

One of the most extensive later medieval analyses of the political consequences of an economic conception of liberty may be found in two seldom examined treatises, whose authorship was once uncertain but is now safely ascribed to the English theologian, canonist, and parish priest William of Pagula. These twin tracts, commonly known by the collective title *Speculum Regis Edwardi III*, seem to have been composed in 1331 and 1332 respectively in order to alert the royal court of England to widespread discontent among the rural poor.[25] Although, for purposes of simplicity, I will treat the two texts as a single unit, it should be noted that the second recension is not simply a revision of the first. Rather, the former constitutes an entirely new treatise that restates essentially the same grievances as its predecessor, but develops its case in the larger context of royal administrative and fiscal practices. Yet in both versions, the argument is entirely directed to the hardships endured by the peasant population of the realm, that vast majority who lacked a literate political voice loud enough to be heard among magnates and royal officials.

The primary target of William's wrath in the *Speculum Regis Edwardi III* is the practice of royal purveyance, the alleged prerogative of the king to provide for his household and troops when touring the realm by confiscating local goods or purchasing them at a fixed, non-negotiable price. The practice of purveyance has roots in the customary powers associated with banal lordship,[26] but was seldom ever used by the English monarchy during most of the Middle Ages,

---

[25] They have been edited by Joseph Moisant, *De Speculo Regis Edwardi III* (Paris: J. Picard, 1891). Moisant, however, believed the tracts to be the work of Simon Islip, Archbishop of Canterbury, an attribution convincingly refuted by James Tait, "On the Date and Authorship of the Speculum Regis Edwardi," *English Historical Review*, 16 (1901), pp. 110-115. This misascription in no way detracts from Moisant's edition, which will be cited (with translations by the present author) according to the recension (either "A" or "B") and section number. The dating was first established by Tait, "On the Date and Authorship." It was confirmed, and the authorship of Pagula finally established, by Leonard Boyle, "William of Pagula and the *Speculum Regis Edwardi III*," *Mediaeval Studies*, 32 (1970), pp. 326-336. The circumstances of its composition have been analyzed by Cary J. Nederman and Cynthia J. Neville, "The Origins of the *Speculum Regis Edwardi III* of William of Pagula," *Studi Medievali*, 3rd series, 38 (1997), pp. 317-29.

[26] George Duby, *The Early Growth of the European Economy*, trans. H.B. Clarke (Ithaca: Cornell University Press, 1974), p. 172.

as the *Speculum* acknowledges.[27] Beginning around 1300, however, purveyance gradually came to be employed by the crown as a form of arbitrary indirect taxation.[28] To meet the growing costs of royal military activity costs, the king's array was sent into the countryside, where it could lay claim to provisions at a cheap rate or even for free. The consequences of purveyance were unequally distributed. It was often the moveable goods, and occasionally the labor power, of the peasantry that royal agents appropriated in their forays into rural villages. Purveyance struck mainly at the poorest of the crown's subjects.

Although there is some question whether William's attack on purveyance accurately reflects practices current in the early 1330s,[29] the issue at hand is not the historical factuality of his treatises. Rather, the present interest in the *Speculum Regis Edwardi III* derives from its reliance upon liberty in order to criticize contemporary economic policies. Given the focus of its complaints, William's work concentrates heavily the exchange relation, understood in terms of the nature and role of the market in the process by which money is given for goods. He seeks to defend the position that the royal use of purveyance constitutes an injustice, namely, theft — that is, a form of economic coercion — since the person subject to the exaction has no choice in the matter. Consequently, he needs to demonstrate a regulative principle for a properly ordered (i.e., non-coercive) system of price and value. To achieve this goal, he relies upon the model of the unconstrained marketplace.

William's account derives in fairly obvious ways from the Roman law view of market freedom. In the *Speculum Regis Edwardi III*, complete and unlimited liberty of exchange is rendered an explicit and seemingly absolute principle. In order to defend the proposition that the king and his servants are in effect guilty of robbery, William repeatedly and adamantly privileges volition. He begins with an idea, formulated in a largely convention manner, that each person "is lord (*dominus*) of his things, so that nothing is seized from his

---

[27] *Speculum Regis Edwardi III*, B 16.

[28] On the context for purveyance in later medieval English life, see A.B. White, *Self-Government at the King's Command* (Minneapolis: University of Minnesota Press, 1938), pp. 97-123 and J.R. Maddicott, *The English Peasantry and the Demands of the Crown, 1294-1341* (Oxford: Past and Present Society, 1975), pp. 15-16.

[29] See Nederman and Neville, "The Origins of the *Speculum Regis Edwardi III*," pp. 323-26.

goods against his will."[30] For William as for John of Paris, *dominium* connotes an exclusive realm of power over one's property with which no other individual may rightfully interfere. "In this world," William declares, "men ought to be free to do for themselves and theirs, according to their will."[31] In lordship and volition one encounters the twin principles that undergird the Roman law tradition of economic liberty.

Concomitantly, William draws the conclusion that robbery is an infringement of one's basic liberty, since lordship entails the freedom to do as one wishes with what one legitimately possesses. He asserts it as a universal and binding standard of conduct that "no goods should be seized against the will of their lords to whom they belong."[32] For anyone (even the king) to violate this constitutes an unjust act.[33] Theft, construed as the denial of the legitimate consent of the property owner, seems never to be justified, even in cases of extreme need. The will of the person who possesses goods is in all cases sovereign.

To condemn the impropriety of theft hardly seems an exceptional position to adopt. But William applies the doctrine to include compulsory exchanges of money for goods. Historically, the customary "privilege" of purveyance permitted the king's officials to buy whatever goods they required (as stipulated by the terms of their written commissions or patents) at a fixed rate. Only exceptionally did royal servants forego all payment, although such cases were known to occur. But William's point is that mandatory or enforced sale still constitutes a form of extortion or theft, inasmuch as it violates the lord's right to set his or her own price or to refrain from selling altogether.

> "If [royal servants] find the oats of any man, they say they wish to pay up to 3 pennies for a bushel of oats, even if it is worth 5 pennies; and if they find not oats but barley, they seize from the unwilling owner 1 bushel of barley for 3 pennies, even if it is worth 9 pennies.
>
> If, however, they do not find barley, but beans, they seize 1 bushel of beans for 3 pennies, even if 1 bushel is worth 12 pennies."[34]

---

[30] *Speculum Regis Edwardi III*, B 16.
[31] Ibid., A 5.
[32] Ibid., B 8.
[33] Ibid., A 1, B 44.
[34] Ibid., A 12.

Such actions are as much an affront to *dominium* as robbery, since the consent implied by one's lordship over an object is absolute and exclusive. Thus, as often as Edward III is admonished about the evil and injustice of taking his subjects' goods against their will, he is also warned "not to seize things for a lower price than the seller wants to receive."[35] The two points are indeed inseparable.

> "How can there be justice or equity these days, when something is bought for a lower price than the seller wishes to receive for it and when consent is constrained, inasmuch as buying and selling arise from the law of nations (*ius gentium*)? For where there is no consent, there is not sale but extortion, not justice but seizure, not equity but falsehood and iniquity."[36]

Likewise, should an individual not wish to sell her goods at all, William asserts that no political privilege can override or cancel that will, even if an adequate price is paid. William narrates a (possibly apocryphal) story of a "poor woman" from whom a royal servant forcibly purchases a hen, "from which she could have four or five eggs to keep her and her children." She is given "one denarius or at the most one and half denarii," yet "this poor woman did not want the hen to be sold for even three denarii."[37] It is as much a violation of freedom of ownership and exchange for the king's minions to demand the purchase of an item at a "fair" price as at one below the market level. The market relationship only exists when free contract is fully ensured. When the liberty to sell or not as one sees fit is curtailed, the consequence is the violation of one's property rights: objects are in effect taken by force, without the will or approval of their rightful owners. Insofar as purveyance violates the free and consensual operation of market exchange, the *Speculum* concludes, it is indistinguishable from theft.

It is important to highlight that William's defense of a market-based conception of liberty is proposed by him as an attack on the power and privileges of the political and economic elite. Given his insistence upon the primacy of liberty, the question naturally arises: What if the king refuses to lay aside the prerogative of purveyance, as the *Speculum Regis Edwardi III* insists he must do? What recourse exists for those whose rights to their property have been violated? The *Speculum* main-

---

[35] Ibid., B 20.
[36] Ibid., A 1.
[37] Ibid., B 43.

tains that the king's violation of the liberty of his subjects will result in danger to his own position. Edward III is cautioned that "there is no one in your kingdom more needy for love than you."[38] Such a thinly veiled threat is justified by William's assertion that the ruler who tramples the *dominium* of his subjects actually makes war on his own people. "Take heed, lord king, because without good counsel you make war every day," the *Speculum* advises, "taking the goods of many men when they are unwilling."[39] If there is no peace in the land because of the unjust practices of royal officials, then it is the king himself who causes the disturbance.[40] By disregarding the express volition of subjects, Edward III undermines the love that his subjects would otherwise afford him; he is to blame for the consequences.

These consequences are specifically identified by the *Speculum* as the rebellious behavior of the populace. The inference to be drawn is that a king who makes war on his people, and hence uses force in robbing them, may rightfully be opposed, just as one may repulse the force of a thief in order to protect oneself and one's goods. Sometimes, the intimation that rebellion provoked by the conduct of the royal curia may be justified is shrouded in vague terms. The *Speculum* warns Edward that "many evils may happen to you and your kingdom," as a result of which the king and his officials "will perish"; elsewhere, the king is advised, for lack of love, to expect the loss of his realm.[41] Such calamity will simply manifest the divine hand at work. "God will arouse war against you in which you will suffer great tribulation"; thereby "the Lord will free the English people from your hands more quickly than you think."[42] In these passages, the precise nature of the danger to royal safety, although of a violent character, is left unspecified. It is merely hinted that retribution for the king's violation of his subjects' lordship need not be confined to the afterlife, but may occur in the present world as well.

In other sections of the text, however, the threat to the unjust king is clearly explicated in terms of popular rebellion. The first recension of the *Speculum* likens the position of the unloved king within the kingdom to that of a head which cannot lead its own body: "Your

---

[38] Ibid., A 34.
[39] Ibid., B 37.
[40] Ibid., B 34-35.
[41] Ibid., A 10, A 18.
[42] Ibid., B 7, B 50.

people ... are not of one mind with you, although they seem to be of one body with you; and indeed, if they had a leader, they would rise up against you, just as they did against your father. Then in truth you would not have a multitude of people with you."[43] The lesson is stated here in no uncertain terms: if the monarch's subjects cannot rely upon their royal master, then they will not hesitate to replace him with someone whom they can love. His unmistakable point is that kings who "have extended their hand towards the goods and income of others" find that "the people rise up against them and they are almost wiped from the earth. And therefore be warned, and heed, lest you forget what happened to your father."[44] The persistent references to the unfortunate Edward II are painful reminders that recent precedent exists for the threats of revolt made by William.

In the *Speculum Regis Edwardi III*, then, the conception of market liberty given expression by Roman law sources is transformed into a compelling criticism of current political and administrative practices. The will of the property owner is so complete that any king who takes his subjects' goods without their consent — even by means of an enforced payment scheme — risks the loss of his legitimacy and the withdrawal of popular support. William of Pagula thereby takes the logic of economic liberty one step further down the trail that leads to the modern appraisal of political systems solely or primarily according to their economic consequences. Yet, as with John of Paris, William's thought remains solidly grounded in the intellectual uni verse of the Latin Middle Ages: he wraps his ideas in the language and doctrines of Christian teaching and of classical learning. But William is still able to mine from these sources lessons about the centrality of personal dominion over one's property that stand at a distance from the mainstream of medieval economic thought.

Conclusion

In the final chapter of *The Legacy of Scholasticism in Economic Thought*, Odd Langholm highlights the persistence in recent philosophical

---

[43] Ibid., B 11.
[44] Ibid., B 38.

and economic debates of the tension between unlimited and constrained conceptions of liberty. In Langholm's view, of course, the constrained idea of freedom constitutes a central contribution of medieval scholasticism to the modern world of economics. In the foregoing paper, by contrast, I have attempted to demonstrate how the present tension in economic theory in fact echoes a divergence of perspectives on the role of individual freedom and the nature of market relations almost seven centuries old. I do not deny Langholm's central historical thesis, namely, that scholasticism was overwhelmingly concerned with setting limits (moral, theological, and sometimes political) upon free market relations amongst individuals. The literature addressing usury, the just price, and analogous matters was far too extensive to suppose otherwise. My point, instead, is that medieval scholastics were not always so completely wedded to a constrained vision of economic liberty as has been supposed. In the cases of John of Paris and William of Pagula, we encounter two authors who, although possessing excellent scholastic credentials, provide intellectually compelling reasons to extend the sphere of economic freedom in a manner consonant with the more "libertarian" inclinations of their Roman law sources. I do not mean to impute "modernity" to the texts of John and William, however. As is clear from even a cursory glance at their writings, their conceptions of economic liberty remained imbedded in the religious and ethical concerns typical of the schoolmen. John and William certainly labor under assumptions fundamentally at odds with those operative in, say, Hobbes — or even Grotius or Locke.[45] Yet scholasticism ought not to be taken as so rigid that none of its adherents could endorse uncoerced and consensual market exchange as an adequate measure of economic freedom. John and William differ most notably from the main stream of scholastic thought in their apparent belief that political institutions and governments may appropriately be judged by the standard of economic well-being as well as in accordance with ethical and spiritual ends. Thus, the intellectual current followed by John and William culminates at the end of the Middle Ages in Fortescue's economic theory of the state — and beyond

[45] See Langholm, "Economic Freedom in Scholastic Thought," pp. 260-61; Langholm, *The Legacy of Scholasticism in Economic Thought*, pp. 139-77.
[46] On Fortescue, see Neal Wood, *Foundations of Political Economy: Some Early Tudor Views on State and Society* (Berkeley: University of California Press, 1994), pp. 44-69.

that, in the early stirrings of political economy during the sixteenth and seventeenth centuries.[46] John and William are not "anticipations" of modernity; rather, modern thinkers are simply "continuations" of patterns of thought and discourse that had their initial expressions in medieval Europe.

THE HOLY ROMAN EMPIRE'S BISHOPS ON THE EVE OF THE REFORMATION

Thomas A. Brady, Jr.*

"I have learnt that virtue without power is ridiculous, and that a Roman pontiff without the patrimony of the Church is nothing but a slave of kings and princes."[1]
— Enea Silvio Piccolomini (1405-1464) —

"[F]or Christian Kings are ... supreme pastors of their own subjects; and the Pope is no more but King and Pastor, even in Rome itself."[2]
— Thomas Hobbes (1588-1679) —

I. *The Reformation as a Medieval Event*

"The events of an entire millennium," wrote Leopold von Ranke in the 1830s, "infuse the conflicts ... between Catholicism and Protestantism, in the midst of both of which we still stand."[3] If that were true in Ranke's day, it is so no longer. The harsh world of the twentieth century cooled the ardor of ancient animosities, so that today we do not look back on the era of the Reformation as the dawn of modernity.[4] The Scottish theologian Alister E. McGrath has voiced a near consensus that "neither the events nor the ideas of the sixteenth century may be properly understood unless they are

---

* Professor of History, University of California, Berkeley
[1] Enea Silvio Piccolomini, *De gestis concilii Basilensis commentariorum libri duo*, edited by Denys Hay and W. K. Smith (Oxford: Oxford University Press, 1967), pp. 248, 250. I quote the translation from Paolo Prodi, *The Papal Prince — One Body and Two Souls: The Papal Monarchy in Early Modern Europe*, translated by Susan Haskins (Cambridge: Cambridge University Press, 1987), p. 13.
[2] Thomas Hobbes, *Leviathan or the Matter, Forme and power of a Commonwealth, Ecclesiasticall and Civil*, edited by Michael Oakeshott (Oxford: Oxford University Press, 1946), p. 382.
[3] Leopold von Ranke, *Deutsche Geschichte im Zeitalter der Reformation*, edited by Paul Joachimsen, 6 vols. (Munich: Drei-Masken-Verlag, 1926), vol. 1, p. 4.
[4] The shift has not gone unopposed. See Bernd Moeller in Berndt Hamm, Bernd Moeller, and Dorothea Wendebourg, *Reformationstheorien. Ein kirchenhistorischer Disput über Einheit und Vielfalt der Reformation* (Göttingen: Vandenhoeck & Ruprecht, 1995), pp. 8-10, 23.

seen as the culmination of developments in the fourteenth and fifteenth centuries."[5] For many scholars this shift popped into view, as
a ship suddenly makes the horizon, when Heiko A. Oberman published his landmark study of 1963, *The Harvest of Medieval Theology*. "It
is a curious — and dangerous — coincidence," he began, "that the
late medieval period is one of the least known in the history of
Christian thought *and*, at the same time, a period in the interpretation of which there are a great many vested interests."[6] Reformation
studies never looked back, and soon the historians of ideas and the
social historians, standing back-to-back, understood and attempted
to explain the Reformation as "the harvest of the Middle Ages."[7]

II. *Imperial Church and German Church*

When the Middle Ages and Reformation ceased to be understood
as contraries, the structures, forces, and events of the fourteenth, fifteenth, and early sixteenth centuries had to be reassessed in terms of
their futures as well as their pasts. The Holy Roman Empire, birth-
place and nursery of the Protestant Reformation, where the Reformation partly succeeded and partly failed, attracts attention especially to those features that scarcely had counterparts in Christendom's
other large kingdoms. One of the oldest and oddest of them is the
Imperial prince-bishopric.

All modern treatments of Imperial episcopacy in the fifteenth and
the first half of the sixteenth century emphasize both its aristocratic
social character in general and the regionally specific domination of

---

[5] Alister E. McGrath, *The Intellectual Origins of the European Reformation* (Oxford:
Basil Blackwell, 1987), p. 3. See also Euan Cameron, *The European Reformation*
(Oxford: Clarendon Press, 1991), p. 6: "the Reformation can only be understood in
terms of the late medieval world from which it grew and against which it rebelled.
Whatever the reasons for its political successes, the Reformation message began with
the late medieval Church and late medieval religion. . . ."

[6] Heiko Augustinus Oberman, *The Harvest of Medieval Theology: Gabriel Biel and Late
Medieval Nominalism* (Cambridge, Mass.: Harvard University Press, 1963), p. 1.

[7] I do not imply that this was the original intention of either Oberman or his
countryman, Johan Huizinga. A brilliant general interpretation from this point of
view is John Bossy, *Christianity in the West, 1400-1700* (Oxford and New York: Oxford
University Press, 1985).

[8] Lawrence G. Duggan, *Bishop and Chapter: The Governance of the Bishopric of Speyer to
1552*, (New Brunswick, N.J.: Rutgers University Press, 1978), pp. 119-120; Heribert
Raab, "Die oberdeutschen Hochstifte zwischen Habsburg und Wittelsbach in der

particular sees by particular groups of nobles and princely dynastics.[8] The most recent overview notes that in 1517, the year of Luther's 95 theses, twelve bishops who were princes born held seventeen sees, and among thirty-eight sees in the Empire's Rhenish-Danubian heartlands, only five were held by commoners.[9]

These men formed the leadership of what is variously called the "Imperial Church" (*Reichskirche*) or the "German Church," neither of which terms has much analytical value.[10] The Holy Roman Empire was not a "state" in any modern sense but a vast, flexible, and revisable web of relationships of lordship. Its rough shape could be described but, in some regions, not located precisely: chunks of the Kingdom of Burgundy had been falling away since the thirteenth century; the legal status of Imperial Italy possessed only intermittent political significance; the Bohemian kingdom's relationship to the Empire was a moot point; and the Empire's boundary on the northeast, where German colonization had far outrun the old Frankish kingdom's borders, defied definition.[11]

Modern scholars do not agree about which dioceses lay within the Empire and which did not.[12] It very much depends on the point in time. The bishopric of Geneva, for example, the diocese of which

---

frühen Neuzeit," *Blätter für deutsche Landesgeschichte* 109 (1973): 69-101; Eike Wolgast, *Hochstift und Reformation. Studien zur Geschichte der Reichskirche zwischen 1517 und 1648*, Beiträge zur Geschichte der Reichskirche in der Neuzeit, vol. 16 (Stuttgart: Franz Steiner Verlag, 1995), pp. 19-27; Anton Schindling, "Reichskirche und Reformation. Zu Glaubensspaltung und Konfessionalisierung in den geistlichen Fürstentümern des Reiches," in *Neue Studien zur frühneuzeitlichen Reichsgeschichte*, edited by Johannes Kunisch (Berlin: Duncker & Humblot, 1987), pp. 81-112.

[9] Wolgast, *Hochstift und Reformation*, pp. 20-21

[10] In his study of the expulsion of Imperial bishops from their cathedral cities, J. Jefferey Tyler writes imprecisely of "a German diocese," "the imperial church (*Reichskirche*)," "the German church," "German bishops," "the 'French' episcopal cities" (meaning the seats of the Empire's French-speaking dioceses). See his *Lord of the Sacred City. The Episcopus Exclusus in Late Medieval and Early Modern Germany*, Studies in Medieval and Reformation Thought, vol. 72 (Leiden: E. J. Brill, 1999), pp. 17 note 19, 203.

[11] Peter Moraw, *Von offener Verfassung zu gestalteter Verdichtung. Das Reich im späten Mittelalter 1250 bis 1490*, Propyläen Geschichte Deutschlands, vol. 3 (Berlin: Propyläen-Verlag, 1985), pp. 43-45.

[12] Compare the dioceses included and excluded by Erwin Gatz, ed., with Clemens Brodkorb, *Die Bischöfe des Heiligen Römischen Reiches 1448-1648. Ein biographisches Lexikon* (Berlin: Duncker & Humblot, 1996), pp. 778-847; Wolfgang Reinhard, "Die Verwaltung der Kirche," in *Deutsche Verwaltungsgeschichte*, edited by Kurt G. A. Jeserich, Hans Pohl, and Christoph von Unruh, vol. 1: *Vom Spätmittelalter bis zum Ende des Reiches* (Stuttgart: Deutsche Verlags-Anstalt, 1983), p. 154; and Georg May, *Die deutschen Bischöfe angesichts der Glaubensspaltung des 16. Jahrhunderts* (Wien: Mediatrix-Verlag, 1983), vii-xi. Tyler, *Lord of the Sacred City*, pp. 203-204, follows May.

belonged to the province of Vienne, came into union with the German kingdom (via the Kingdom of Burgundy) in 1032, and its bishop was regarded as a prince-bishop. Although the bishopric's Imperial ties began to loosen during the reign of Emperor Charles IV (r. 1346-1378), its bishop did not lose his standing as an Imperial estate until 1533.[13] The prince-archbishopric of Besançon had a similar history, but its archbishop lost his seat in the Imperial Diet only with the transfer of Imperial Burgundy to France around 1665.[14] There were altogether eight such "Latin bishoprics" (*welsche bistum*) — Besançon, Toul, Verdun, Lausanne, Geneva, Metz, Cambrai, and Liège — which in 1500 certainly belonged to the "Imperial Church" though they definitely were not "German."[15]

Other bishoprics were "German" in the sense that German-speakers had founded them and staffed them, but were not in the Empire, notably the entire province of Riga with its suffragan sees.[16] Their prince-bishops often possessed temporal authority, though it was shared with the Teutonic Order, but they were not Imperial bishops, and the fifteenth-century shift of power against the Order and in favor of the Kingdom of Poland made even the question of their "Germanness" moot.[17]

There were also dioceses whose bishops possessed no temporal authority and so did not belong to the "Imperial Church" in the usual meaning of term, though they doubtless lay in the Empire. Such sees were Breslau (province: Gniezno) and the new archbishopric of Prague (raised 1344 out of Mainz) and its suffragan see of Olomouc/Olmütz in Moravia, further, the southeastern sees of Laibach/Ljubljana (exempt), Pedena (province: Aquileia), and Vienna and Wiener Neustadt (both exempt), plus Schwerin (province: Bremen) on the Empire's northern border.

---

[13] Gerhard Köbler, *Historisches Lexikon der deutschen Länder. Die deutschen Territorien und reichsunmittelbaren Geschlechter vom Mittelalter bis zur Gegenwart*, 5th ed. (Munich: C. H. Beck, 1995), p. 194.

[14] Köbler, *Historisches Lexikon*, p. 58.

[15] They are listed in the assessments of 1431 and 1521 in Karl Zeumer, ed., *Quellensammlung zur Geschichte der Deutschen Reichsverfassung im Mittelalter und Neuzeit*, 2d ed. rev. (Tübingen: J.C.B. Mohr [Paul Siebeck], 1913), pp. 244, 313-314.

[16] Reinhard, "Die Verwaltung der Kirche," in *Deutsche Verwaltungsgeschichte*, vol. 1, p. 154, includes the province of Riga in the Empire's ecclesiastical organization around 1500.

[17] Köbler, *Historisches Lexikon*, pp. 114-115, 157, 472, 508-509, 537; Gatz, *Bischöfe 1448-1648*, pp. 791-792, 801-802, 823-824, 829 (Gatz omits Riga but not its suffragan sees).

It is difficult to say what "the German Church" might describe, because the very location of "Germany" was a sixteenth-century conundrum. Earlier, one spoke and wrote in the plural of "German lands," meaning regions where forms of German rather than Romance or Slavic tongues were spoken.[18] By 1500 "Germany" was catching on in both Latin and German, particularly in humanist circles. When the Nuremberg schoolmaster Johannes Cochlaeus (1479-1552) published his geography book in 1512, he wrote that "Germany" was bounded "on the south by Italy and Dalmatia, on the east by Hungary and Poland, on the north by the Baltic Sea and the North Sea, and on the west by France and the British sea."[19] His very generous estimate left the problem of Germany's precise location as a headache for future scholars.[20] The Netherlander Abraham Ortelius (1527-1598) gave up in disgust and noted with a sigh that "[Germany's] boundaries have been given differently by the various authors," while Matthias Quad (1557-1613), his German contemporary, concluded that "there is no country in all of Christendom which embraces so many lands under one name."[21] Sixteenth-century Saxons traveling westward still said that they were going "into the Empire," and popular usage permitted one to describe a Franche-Comtois, an Imperial subject but innocent of the German language, as "by heritage a German."[22] In the German lands of this era, it was quite uncertain "whether nation and fatherland meant different things."[23]

---

[18] This phrase was the usual term for the German-speaking lands until "Germany" emerged in the course of the sixteenth century. Ernst Schubert, *Einführung in die Grundprobleme der deutschen Geschichte im Spätmittelalter* (Darmstadt: Wissenschaftliche Buchgesellschaft, 1992), pp. 21-46; Georg Schmidt, *Geschichte des alten Reiches. Staat und Nation in der Frühen Neuzeit 1495-1806* (Munich: C. H. Beck, 1999), pp. 28-32.

[19] Johannes Cochlaeus, *Brevis Germanie descriptio (1512) mit der Deutschlandkarte des Erhard Etzlaub von 1512*, edited by Karl Langosch, Ausgewählte Quellen zur deutschen Geschichte der Neuzeit, vol. 1 (Darmstadt: Wissenschaftliche Buchgesellschaft, 1960), p. 66.

[20] Cochlaeus, *Brevis Germanie descriptio*, cap. IV, 1 (pp. 74/75).

[21] Quoted by Gerald Strauss, *Sixteenth-Century Germany. Its Topography and Topographers* (Madison: University of Wisconsin Press, 1959), p. 40; and James J. Sheehan, "What Is German History? Reflections on the Role of the *Nation* in German History and Historiography," *Journal of Modern History* 53 (1981): 1-23, here at 1-2.

[22] Karlheinz Blaschke, *Sachsen im Zeitalter der Reformation*, Schriften des Vereins für Reformationsgeschichte, no. 185 (Gütersloh: Verlagshaus Gerd Mohn, 1970), p. 126; Jacob Sturm of Strasbourg, referring to Nicholas Perrenot de Granvelle, in *Briefwechsel Landgraf Philipps des Großmüthigen von Hessen mit Bucer*, edited by Max Lenz, 3 vols., Publicationen aus den K. Preussischen Staatsarchiven, 5, 28, 47 (Stuttgart: S. Hirzel, 1880-91), vol. 1, p. 156 note 8.

[23] Schmidt, *Geschichte des Alten Reiches*, pp. 31-32.

The truth is that on the ecclesiastical map that showed Christendom in its provinces and dioceses, there appeared neither an "Imperial Church" nor a "German Church."[24] Many dioceses lay inside the Empire but belonged to provinces ruled from seats in other countries: Sitten/Sion (Tarantaise, 1510 exempt); Pedena, Trieste, and Trent (all Aquileia); Schleswig (Lund); and Cambrai (Rheims). Classification by language, too, yielded no clear boundaries, for sorting Imperial dioceses (excluding Imperial Italy) by spoken languages yields a variegated picture: 6 French, 3 mixed French/German, 3 Italian, 3 Italian/German, 1 Danish/German, and 7 Slavic/German. The list excludes Riga and its six suffragan sees, where German churchmen exercised spiritual authority over very mixed populations.

Summing up, it may make sense to speak of an "Imperial Church" in the sense of all of the prince-bishoprics and prince-abbeys, whose heads enjoyed the status of Imperial princes. The term "German Church," however, suggests a conformity of institutions with the national sentiments of German-speakers that had no foundation in fact.

III. *How Aristocratic was the Imperial Church?*

The recent publication of a biographical lexicon of the Empire's bishops between 1448 and 1648 provides for the first time a basis for a collective picture of them.[25] The work omits, true, a few sees that did long lie in the Empire, such as Cambrai, Geneva, and Besançon, and includes some that did not, such as Ermland, Kulm, Pomesanien, and Samland (though not Riga). It is not possible, therefore, to correct the lexicon's data to cover either all bishops within the Empire or all prince-bishops who sat in the Diet over the century studied here, 1450 to 1550. The resulting imprecision, however, is not great. Furthermore, for some bishops whose social origin is unknown, educated guesses have been made based on the information supplied. The analysis has also eliminated duplicates created by one person holding more than one see, either simultaneously or seri-

---

[24] Based on Gatz, *Bischöfe 1448-1648*, pp. 778-847.

[25] Gatz, *Bischöfe 1448-1648*. This volume, one of a series that is working its way back from the end of the Empire toward the Middle Ages, places the study of the Imperial episcopacy on an entirely new basis.

ally, but no distinction has been made between bishops who held sees in their own right and administrators or coadjutors of sees.

The following table is based on the careers of 405 persons who began to hold one or more sees between 1450 and 1550.

Table: Social Origins (Father's Status) of Bishops in the Holy Roman Empire, 1450-1550

	All Bishoprics	Prince-Bishoprics
Upper Nobles	87 (21.5%)	83 (25.8%)
Lesser Nobles	184 (45.4%)	160 (49.7%)
Burghers	93 (23.0%)	63 (19.6%)
Peasants	10 (2.5%)	6 (1.8%)
Unknown	31 (7.6%)	10 (3.1%)
TOTAL	405	322

The category of "upper nobility" includes members of the titled nobility from barons and counts through landgraves, margraves, counts palatine, princes, dukes, and ducal and royal bastards. "Lesser nobility" includes both Imperial and territorial untitled nobles; burghers" ranged from urban patricians down to a few artisan masters; and the "peasants" are mostly sons of leading village families. Together, the two categories of nobles, titled and untitled, who made up some 1.5% of the Empire's population in 1500,[26] make up exactly two-thirds (66.9%) of all bishops and just over three-quarters (75.5%) of all prince-bishops. The bishops from the upper nobility came mostly from a handful of great lay dynasties: the various Guelph lines in Brunswick, the Palatine Wittelsbachs, several Wettins from Saxony and Bavarian Wittelsbachs, margraves of Baden, a sprinkling of sons of a few other families, two Burgundian Valois and one Habsburg bastard.

Nobles, high and low, did dominate the Imperial episcopacy, and their share of the prince-bishoprics was greater than of all bishoprics. The commoners, 25.5% of all bishops and 21.4% of prince-bishops, made up half or nearly half the incumbents in groups of dioceses clustered in the two eastern corners of the Empire: Breslau, Ermland, Kammin, Kulm, Lübeck, Ratzeburg, Samland, and Schwerin in the

---

[26] Rudolf Endres, *Adel in der frühen Neuzeit*, Enzyklopädie Deutscher Geschichte, vol. 18 (Munich: R. Oldenbourg, 1993), p. 3.

northeast; Chiemsee, Gurk, Lavant, Seckau, Vienna, and Wiener Neustadt in the southeast. The whole province of Salzburg, indeed, offered better chances to commoners than did the provinces of Mainz, Cologne, Magdeburg, or Trier. The powerful bishoprics and archbishoprics in the old Imperial heartlands were the almost exclusive grazing grounds of the nobilities. The upper nobility dominated Cologne, Magdeburg, Mainz, Freising, Halberstadt, Hildesheim, Liège, Metz, Minden, Münster, Osnabrück, Strasbourg, and Utrecht; the lesser nobles enjoyed preference in Bamberg, Eichstätt, Havelberg, Meißen, Merseburg, Naumburg, Speyer, Trent, Worms, and Würzburg. Other sees, such as Trier, Augsburg, Basel, Constance, Passau, Regensburg, and Toul, saw incumbents from both sectors of the nobility.

The Imperial episcopacy was indeed heavily noble, and nearly twice as many of the bishops came from the lesser nobility as from the titled nobility. More surprisingly, it was also far more accessible to commoners than were the sees of its neighboring kingdom, France. Whereas slightly more than a quarter (25.5%) of all Imperial bishops between 1450 and 1550 came from the commons, the comparable figure for France under Francis I (r. 1515-1547) and Henry II (r. 1547-1559) was about 4%.[27] What explains this difference? It may be that King Francis I secured greater power over the Church in the Concordat of Bologna (1516) than Emperor Frederick III had in the Concordat of Vienna (1448). Probably so, but more important surely is the much weaker monarchy in the Empire. Maximilian I once joked that whereas he was a "king of kings," whose princely vassals did as they pleased, the French monarch was a "king of animals," whose subjects had to obey him.[28] The French kings of the sixteenth century enjoyed, indeed, extensive powers over the Church under the concordat, which they used to undermine the cathedral chapters' canonical rights to elect bishops and to promote nobles almost to the exclusion of commoners into their kingdom's sees.[29] The convergence of royal power and noble preferment lends plausibility to Perry Anderson's comment

---

[27] Frederic J. Baumgartner, *Change and Continuity in the French Episcopate: The Bishops and the Wars of Religion, 1547-1610*, Duke Monographs in Medieval and Renaissance Studies, no. 7 (Durham, N.C.: Duke University Press, 1986), pp. 31, 34.

[28] Hermann Wiesflecker, *Kaiser Maximilian I. Das Reich, Österreich und Europa an der Wende zur Neuzeit*, 5 vols. (Munich: R. Oldenbourg Verlag, 1971-1986), vol. 5, p. 5.

[29] Baumgartner, *Change and Continuity*, p. 32.

that "the Absolutist State was ... the new political carapace of a threatened nobility."[30]

The Imperial story is harder to read. Where pre-Reformation princes, notably the electors of Brandenburg and Saxony, managed to dominate bishoprics, the sees became near-monopolies of the territorial nobles.[31] This conforms to the French pattern. The Habsburg monarchs, however, operated in a different way. Emperor Frederick III (r. 1440-1493) acquired, mostly with papal approval, rights of nomination to most of the sees in his dynastic lands, and he secured the foundation of several new bishoprics — Laibach/Ljubljana (1463), Vienna and Wiener Neustadt (1469) — the latter pair at the expense of Passau. He shared with Salzburg nominations to the archbishopric's small suffragan sees (Lavant, Seckau, Gurk), to which he managed to promote his own choices. All in all, Frederick was amply rewarded for supporting the papacy against the rebel Council of Basel.[32] The pattern of royally influenced nominations to these sees, however, is quite ambiguous. Neither Frederick nor his successor, Maximilian I, seems to have favored noble candidates for the two sees they most closely controlled, Vienna and Wiener Neustadt.[33] The same was true of Emperor Charles V (r. 1519-1556), who nominated to Vienna Johann Fabri (1478-1541) and Friedrich Nausea (ca. 1496-1552), the sons respectively of an Upper Swabian blacksmith and an Upper Franconian cartright.[34]

IV. *Princes and Prince-Bishops*

If the bishop was the soul of his diocese, an Imperial prince-bishop, like the pope, possessed one soul and two bodies, one spiritual and one temporal.[35] The spiritual body was by far the elder, more stable, and better understood. Its union with *temporalia* — regalian

---

[30] Perry Anderson, *Lineages of the Absolutist State* (London: NLB, 1974), p. 18.

[31] Based on the lists and biographies in Gatz, *Bischöfe 1448-1648*.

[32] Wiesflecker, *Kaiser Maximilian I.*, vol. 5, p. 156.

[33] I say "ambiguous," because the absence in Gatz, *Bischöfe 1448-1648*, of information on the social background of any men promoted to these two sees suggests that most of them were commoners, because the possession of noble status is far more richly documented that its lack.

[34] Gatz, *Bischöfe 1448-1648*, pp. 175-177, 494-496. The study of Habsburg influence on episcopal appointments remains a desideratum.

[35] I take this image from Paolo Prodi, *The Papal Prince* (as in note 1)

rights and the lordship over lands, peoples, and castles — went back to the Ottonian age around 1000, that is, about the time when organization of the German kingdom into ecclesiastical provinces and dioceses had completed the shape it would largely retain for 800 years. The fusion of spiritual and temporal powers then acquired fixed legal form in the thirteenth century, when Emperor Frederick II raised the bishops to the rank of Imperial princes. Many of them expanded their temporal holdings during the following 200 years or so, but in the fifteenth century the initiative began to shift to the lay principalities. Originally patrimonial agglomerations of feudal, regalian, and dynastic rights, the territorial states that began to institutionalize during the fifteenth century seldom had significant roots as far back as the tribal duchies of post-Carolingian times.[36] Bavaria, Swabia, Franconia, and Saxony, it is true, continued to be called the "four pillars of the Empire," but, except for Bavaria, as homelands they continued to exist as figures of imagination rather than of power.[37]

So long as the lay dynasties ruled over collections of rights over lands, peoples, and incomes, which could be more or less easily disaggregated, the relative stability of episcopal *temporalia* caused them few problems. Early on, the antagonists of prince-bishops were not Imperial aristocrats but the burghers of their own cathedral cities, the first laymen to gain the ability to constitute institutionalized authority. One after the other, the prince-bishops of the Imperial heartlands in the south and west entered legal and military battles against their cathedral cities' burghers, who managed in many cases to force their bishop as an *episcopus exclusus* to leave the city and reside elsewhere in his territory. Some few, notably Würzburg, Bamberg, Eichstätt, and Passau, managed to retain rule over their cathedral towns, and others, such as Mainz in 1462, were able to retake it with force.[38] Only Freising's bishops never experienced an expulsion.

In the fifteenth century the initiative in forming institutions of governance began to shift to the lay dynasties, and from their creation of permanent institutions the classic German territorial state emerged. The process was guided not by an impersonal concept of

---

[36] E. Schubert, *Einführung*, pp. 196-202.
[37] Klaus Graf, "Das Land 'Schwaben' im späten Mittelalter," in *Regionale Identität und soziale Gruppen im deutschen Mittelalter*, edited by Peter Moraw, Zeitschrift für Historische Forschung, Beiheft 14 (Berlin: Duncker & Humblot, 1992), pp. 127-164.
[38] Tyler, *Lord of the Sacred City*, pp. 17-18.

state-building but by the need to manage concentrations of holdings
caused by numerous extinctions of aristocratic dynasties. The possibility of getting the resulting agglomerations of unrelated clusters of
rights under control depended on abandoning the primitive methods of aristocratic finance.[39] Princes did not abandon the repertory
of personal deeds, words, and gestures, of rituals, feuds, and marriage, and of genealogical display that configured the traditional
habitus of aristocratic politics, but they began to assemble people
who could supply them with the new practices — permanent offices,
fixed procedures, and regular record-keeping — that turned customs into permanent institutions.[40] Patrimonial lordship turned into
territorial governance when the people around the princes learned
how to "collect exactly and pay out effectively" (*recht einnemen und nue-
zlich guet ausgeben*).[41]

During the fifteenth century a new map, composed of dynastic territorial states, was developing as a permanent overlay on the much
older, stable map of the Empire as a Church arrayed into dioceses
and provinces. As clusters of resources to be managed, the Empire's
heartlands, with their large territories, many castles, and excellent
relations with the monarch, posed a serious problem to the great
dynasties, for the successful management of one episcopal election
did not normally bring permanent, institutionalized influence. The
strong reasons for wanting influence over elections did not just boil
down to the desire for episcopal incomes and lands.[42] Thoughtful

---

[39] Ernst Schubert, *Fürstliche Herrschaft und Territorium im späten Mittelalter*, Enzyklopädie Deutscher Geschichte, vol. 35 (Munich: R. Oldenbourg Verlag, 1996).

[40] Gert Althoff, "Ungeschriebene Gesetze. Wie funktioniert Herrschaft ohne
schriftliche fixierte Normen?" in idem, *Spielregeln der Politik im Mittelalter. Kommunikation
in Frieden und Fehde* (Darmstadt: Wissenschaftliche Buchgesellschaft, 1996), pp. 282-
304. How the new techniques might preserve and enhance traditional marks of aristocratic display is discussed with reference to the cult of lineage and the coming of
dynastic history by Jean-Marie Moeglin, *Dynastisches Bewußtsein und Geschichtsschreibung.
Zum Selbstverständnis der Wittelsbacher, Habsburger und Hohenzollern im Spätmittelalter*,
Schriften des Historischen Kollegs, Vorträge, no. 34 (Munich: Stiftung Historisches
Kolleg, 1993).

[41] Wiesflecker, *Kaiser Maximilian I.*, vol. 1, pp. 413-414, quoting a dedication to
King Maximilian penned in 1494 in a presentation copy of Engelbert of Admont's
De regimine principum. The earliest financial records of a lay prince come from Brandenburg in 1316-1317 and Brunswick-Lüneburg in 1324, and the earliest accounts from
the Teutonic Order in Prussia in 1399-1409. E. Schubert, *Einführung*, p. 197.

[42] See the discussion of this point by Robert James Bast, *Honor Your Fathers: Catechisms and the Emergence of a Patriarchal Ideology in Germany, 1400-1600*, Studies in
Medieval and Reformation Thought, vol. 63 (Leiden: E. J. Brill, 1997), pp. 167-185.

reformers and instructors of the faithful urged temporal rulers to act, seeing in them the rods God would raise up to smite the greedy, heedless clergy and restore the Church the prelates had ripped asunder.[43] For their part, fifteenth- and sixteenth-century Imperial princes often saw their own supervision of the clergy and the development of lay advocacy into princely *spiritualia* as fully justified by their responsibility for their subjects' spiritual welfare.

The old map of Imperial ecclesiastical jurisdictions, complicated by the growth of episcopal territories, posed formidable barriers to any Imperial prince who, heeding the fifteenth-century reformers' admonitions, aimed to extend his hand over the religious life of his lands. The consolidation of large dynastic states made temporal and spiritual authority less and less conterminous, for the leading states of the Wittelsbachs, Guelphs, Wettins, Hohenzollerns and Habsburgs stretched across parts of six, seven, or even ten dioceses.[44] Moreover, because each bishop's authority was guarded by his own *temporalia*, and because the electoral rights of chapters made permanent princely control of the sees impossible, efforts to influence elections, in which emperor and pope also freely mixed, posed a standing source of disruption and conflict.

The momentum in the fifteenth-century Empire lay nevertheless with the great dynasties, for over the course of 400 years the relationship between the two swords, spiritual and temporal, had been reversed. The emperors had once coordinated temporal with spiritual authority because of the superior, more stable character of the latter, and they thereby created the prince-bishoprics.[45] Now and in the future, the reversal of this process tended to reconfigure spiritual authority to an intensifying temporal power, thereby creating nascent

---

[43] Bast, *Honor Your Fathers*, p. 171, paraphrasing *The Reformation of Emperor Sigismund*.

[44] The Duchy of Bavaria lay in seven dioceses (Augsburg, Chiemsee, Eichstätt, Freising, Passau, Regensburg, and Salzburg); the Rhine Palatinate in seven (Mainz, Metz, Speyer, Strasbourg, Trier, Worms, and Würzburg); the County (since 1495 Duchy) of Württemberg in nine (Augsburg, Basel, Besançon, Constance, Speyer, Strasbourg, Toul, Worms, and Würzburg); and the two Saxonies in eleven (Bamberg, Brandenburg, Halberstadt, Magdeburg, Mainz, Merseburg, Meißen, Naumburg, Prague, Regensburg, and Würzburg). Anton Schindling and Walter Ziegler, eds., *Die Territorien des Reichs im Zeitalter der Reformation und Konfessionalisierung. Land und Konfession 1500-1650*, 7 vols. (Münster: Aschendorff Verlag, 1989-1997), vol. 1, p. 56; vol. 5, p. 8; vol. 5, p. 168; vol. 4, p. 8; vol. 2, p. 8.

[45] Karl Kroeschell, "Territorial Staatsbildung," in *Deutsche Verwaltungsgeschichte*, vol. 1, pp. 361-386; Wolgast, *Hochstift und Reformation*, pp. 29-82, 261-325.

territorial churches.[46] Unless halted or hindered, this process would subordinate spiritual to temporal authority, which is what happened in the Protestant territorial churches after the Reformation, but also in Catholic Bavaria. Luther's revolution may have accelerated, it did not create, this process. In 1508 Duke George (1471-1539) of Saxony boasted that over powers of every estate, "whether spiritual or temporal, whether of high, middling, or lower status," the prince stood "as their rightful direct lord, protector, advocate, judge, curator, and spokesman."[47] Everyone knew the saying attributed to a duke of Cleves-Jülich, "the Duke of Cleves is pope in his own lands."[48]

The intensification of territorial lordship during the fifteenth and early sixteenth centuries helps to explain why the prince-bishops and other prelates tended to support measures to promote pacification and order. Such forces lay behind the creation during the fifteenth century of the Imperial Diet, a parliament that from 1495 on moved to supply a new quality of law and order to the Empire. Prince-prelates were attracted to this promise, for the qualities that made them suitable to govern prince-bishoprics lessened their capacity for the military leadership and operations that still formed part of the repertory of an ideal German prince.

Whatever had been the functional relationship between the prince-bishop's two bodies in earlier times, by the fifteenth century it was becoming ever more difficult for a man to be both a very good bishop and a very good prince. To reformers of that day, the contradiction was clear enough. "Take a good look at how bishops act nowadays," declared the anonymous author of *The Reformation of*

---

[46] See Manfred Schulze, *Fürsten und Reformation. Geistliche Reformpolitik weltlicher Fürsten vor der Reformation*, Spätmittelalter und Reformation, new series, vol. 2 (Tübingen: J. C. B. Mohr [Paul Siebeck], 1991), esp. chap. 1; Jörn Sieglerschmidt, *Territorialstaat und Kirchenregiment. Studien zur Rechtsdogmatik des Kirchenpatronatsrechts im 15. und 16. Jahrhundert*, Forschungen zur kirchlichen Rechtsgeschichte und zum Kirchenrecht, vol. 15 (Cologne and Vienna, 1987). Curbing the temporal authority of the clergy was also practiced successfully in Central Switzerland. Peter Blickle, "Antiklerikalismus um den Vierwaldstättersee 1300-1500: Von der Kritik der Macht der Kirche," in *Anticlericalism in the Late Middle Ages and Reformation*, edited by Peter A. Dykema and Heiko A. Oberman (Leiden, 1992), pp. 115-132. This valuable case study shows that the central issue was temporal authority in the hands of clergy rather than of laymen, not some generalized sentiment about the "decline of the church." Willing confusion on this point is widespread.

[47] Quoted by Wolgast, *Hochstift und Reformation*, p. 24.

[48] Quoted by Wiesflecker, *Kaiser Maximilian I.*, vol. 5:157, who points out that this was a favorite saying of Duke Charles the Bold (d. 1477) of Burgundy.

Emperor Sigismund, composed around 1439 but first printed in 1476. "They make war and cause unrest in the world; they behave like secular lords, which is, of course, what they are... A bishop ought to take up permanent residence in the principal church of his diocese and lead a spiritual life there." He should be doctor of Scripture and theology, he should be salaried and not beneficed, and he should "conduct himself piously and honestly and have no worldly concerns."[49] Johann Geiler von Kaysersberg (1445-1510), Strasbourg's great cathedral preacher, told his burghers that a bishop was one "who serves the whole community," for "the Son of Man is come not to be ministered to but to minister."[50] Such unimpeachably orthodox churchmen did not think differently, merely less radically, than the German Hussites who had taught that "all priests should be poor and have nothing more than their daily bread."[51] Others thought more generously, and Friedrich Weygandt, a Mainz official who joined the Odenwald rebels in 1525, thought that while 100 gulden was a good annual salary for a priest, a bishop would require 1,000 gulden.[52]

The intensifying fifteenth-century critique of the Imperial prince-bishops sprang not from any theoretical objection to the fusion of spiritual and temporal power — burghers and princes alike believed that their authority possessed sacral legitimation and religious responsibilities — but from a perception that armored bishops harmed both the victims of their princely violence and the prestige and effectiveness of the Church. The resentment came to a head in

---

[49] *The Reformation of the Emperor Sigismund (c. 1439)*, in *Manifestations of Discontent in Germany on the Eve of the Reformation*, edited and translated by Gerald Strauss (Bloomington: Indiana University Press. 1971), p. 11.

[50] Johann Geiler von Kaysersberg, *Postille*, part II, 5, quoted by Léon Dacheux, *Un reformateur catholique à la fin du XVe siècle: Jean Geiler de Kaysersberg, étude sur sa vie et son temps* (Paris and Strasbourg: E. Delegrave, 1876), p. 544 note 2.

[51] Klaus Arnold, ed., *Niklashausen 1476. Quellen und Untersuchungen zur sozialreligiösen Bewegung des Hans Behem und zur Agrarstruktur eines spätmittelalterlichen Dorfes*, Saecula Spiritalia, vol. 3 (Baden-Baden: Verlag Valentin Koerner, 1980), p. 104.

[52] From Friedrich Weygandt's first reform program, in Günther Franz, *Der deutsche Bauernkrieg*, 7th ed. (Bad Homburg v. d. H.: Hermann Gentner Verlag, 1965), p. 198; an English translation in Tom Scott and Bob Scribner, eds./trans., *The German Peasants' War. A History in Documents* (Atlantic Highlands, N.J.: Humanities Press, International, 1991), pp. 259-264. For comparison's sake, a master artisan who worked for wages might be paid 50 gulden per year, and a nest egg of 200 fl. was considered "quite a lot of money." Walter Jacob, *Politische Führungsschicht und Reformation. Untersuchungen zur Reformation in Zürich 1519-1528*, Zürcher Beiträge zur Reformationsgeschichte, vol. 1 (Zurich: Zwingli-Verlag, 1970), pp. 102-103.

the wars of the mid-15th century, in which the Imperial free cities generally suffered at the hands of princes, both temporal and spiritual. In the Franconian theater of these struggles, a major aggressor was Dietrich Schenk von Erbach (ca. 1395-1459), who was elector and archbishop of Mainz from 1434 to 1459. [53] Though at first this sly politician strove for peace between the burghers and the clergy of Mainz, in the 1440s the city's burghers rose against his rule. The severity with which this armored prelate responded animates Ulrich Wiest's poem, "The Insolence of Ecclesiastical Princes." "O God, I call upon you in my grief," the poet prays,

"Wrecked lies the Christian ship upon the reef;
Come to our aid, grant us relief...
Not ours the guilt for bloody sword and mace
With which the bishops take the warrior's place.
Have patience with us. Recollect that you
Yourself called out, when mortal pain you knew,
'Forgive them, God, they know not what they do.'" [54]

The bishops, Ulrich sang, "...called our Christian state to lead, / Whose piety should grace the holy creed, / they are the first in warlike word and deed." He named Mainz, Eichstätt, and Bamberg as the sees whose bishops were ruining the Church:

"The faith that Fathers of our Church created,
Whose fervor centuries have not abated,
Is now, by wanton churchmen dissipated."

This state of affairs cannot go on much longer, for

"Prognostications make it all too plain:
Vengeance will come, and all the priesthood slain...
His patience ending, God will intercede
To break the bishops' wicked pride and lust
By fanning men's outrage into a gust
To blow the church itself into the dust."

---

[53] Gatz, Bischöfe 1448-1648, pp. 630-631.
[54] *Manifestations of Discontent*, edited by Gerald Strauss, pp. 100-103, from "Der geistlichen Fürsten Hoffart," in *Deutsche Volkslieder des Mittelalters*, edited by Fritz Kern, 2d ed. (Berlin, n.d.), pp. 369-372. My thanks to Robert Bast for bringing this poem to my attention. For other texts, see Albrecht Classen, "Anticlericalism in Late Medieval German Verse," in *Anticlericalism in the Late Middle Ages and Reformation*, pp. 91-114, here at pp. 99-101. Classen's valuable presentation of texts does not escape the tendency to confuse polemic with fact.

It is important to recognize that this poem is a polemic, a partisan piece composed amid strife over quite concrete issues, and that the most important issue was money. To burghers, the truly intolerable aspect of episcopal rule was the transformation of charity into finance. "The faithful don't give alms to see them spent," Wiest proclaims, "On vain unchristian pomp and merriment, / On lives that against God and Christ offend." Furthermore, the forecast of coming violence might be fulfilled symbolically rather than in the shedding of real blood. The prediction that "Vengeance will come, and all the priesthood slain" did not mean that people were prepared literally to slay their priests. Though this cry — "Kill the priests!" — was raised again and again, people did not seize opportunities to kill their clergy — as they sometimes did to kill the Jews.[55]

Still, the tempo and tone of anti-clerical and anti-episcopal polemic suggest that fifteenth-century tolerance for prince-bishops who behaved like the princes they were, instead of like the bishops they were, was growing thinner. This temper had to influence, in the longer run, the kinds of persons who were elected to the major sees. Not immediately, of course, and particularly not at Mainz, which sat in the cockpit of Rhenish princely politics. Dietrich Schenk von Erbach was followed by another warrior-archbishop, Count Diether of Isenburg-Büdingen (ca. 1412-1482), who was elected to the see of Mainz in 1460.[56] When the pope, to please Emperor Frederick III, reversed Diether's confirmation, the cathedral chapter elected Count Adolf of Nassau (ca. 1423-1475) in his stead.[57] The two archbishops called on their respective allies, and a civil war began in December 1461. When Count Adolf's forces captured the City of Mainz, he forced 800 burghers to leave the city without their goods and nullified Mainz's 200-year-old charter of liberties. Only after Adolf's death could Count Diether, freed of his long excommunication, resume his post as the head of the Empire's Church, senior elector, and ruler of one of the largest prince-bishoprics. A graduate of the University of Erfurt, upon regaining his see he founded in 1476 a university at Mainz. He remained every inch a prince, "one of the

---

[55] Arnold, *Niklashausen 1476*, pp. 101-102, 123; František Graus, "The Church and Its Critics in Time of Crisis," edited and translated by Dorothea A. Christ, in *Anticlericalism in the Late Middle Ages and Reformation*, pp. 65-81, here at pp. 74-76.

[56] Gatz, *Bischöfe 1448-1648*, pp. 330-332.

[57] Gatz, *Bischöfe 1448-1648*, pp. 4-6.

most belligerent figures ever to ascend the throne of Mainz."[58] In
that same year, 1476, he hatched the plan that led to the arrest and
judicial murder of the Drummer of Niklashausen, a poor shepherd
who drew tens of thousands to hear him tell how the Virgin Mary
spoke to him.

Diether's fierce, imperious nature contrasts dramatically with that
of his suffragan, Bishop Rudolf von Scherenberg (ca. 1401-1495),
who ruled the bishopric of Würzburg from 1466 until his death in
1495. Rudolf was neither a warrior-prelate, a big-spending sybarite,
or an aristocratic younger son forced into a cushy but dull alternative
career. He was the best bishop in living memory, the savior of
Würzburg as a religious enterprise.[59] Rudolf made peace with trou-
blesome neighbors; redeemed the crushing debt; curbed clerical
excesses, built new or restored ruinous parish churches, and mobi-
lized the printing press for religious work. In some things enlightened, in others — notably toward the Jews — not, Rudolf did make
a lasting impression. His virtues, wrote Wilhelm Werner von Zimmern (1485-1575) years later, "are impossible to praise sufficiently or
even to describe. Everything that adorns a pious, virtuous man in the
sight of God and the world, was found in superfluity in and around
him. He was, in addition a wise, talented, intelligent, and energetic
prince beyond compare."[60] In short, Rudolf seems to have been in
many respects a thoroughly pastoral bishop. But he was also a prince,
and it was Rudolf who in 1476 had the Drummer brought from
Niklashausen to the Marienberg, high above Würzburg, had him
condemned — probably by drumhead justice, as there is no record of
the trial — and consigned to the flames, finally stopping the hymn-
singing prophet's mouth.[61]

---

[58] Karl Siegfried Bader, quoted by Gatz, *Bischöfe 1448-1648*, p. 332.

[59] Gatz, *Bischöfe 1448-1648*, pp. 634-635. See Rudolf Zeissner, *Rudolf II. von
Scherenberg, Fürstbischof von Würzburg 1466-1495*, 2d ed. (Würzburg: Kommissions-Ver-
lag Buchhandlung Nikolaus Schneider,1952); Alfred Wendehorst, ed., *Das Bistum
Würzburg*, Teil 3: *Die Bischofsreihe von 1455 bis 1617*, Germania Sacra. Historisch-sta-
tische Beschreibung der Kirche des Alten Reiches, new series, vol. 13 (Berlin and
New York: Walter de Gruyter, 1978), pp. 21-49. His famous tombstone by Riemen-
schneider is often depicted, e.g., in *Würzburg. Geschichte in Bilddokumenten*, edited by
Alfred Wendehorst (Munich: C. H. Beck, 1981), plate 153.

[60] Wilhelm Engel, ed., *Die Würzburger Bischofschronik des Grafen Wilhelm Werner von
Zimmern und die Würzburger Geschichtsschreibung des 16. Jahrhunderts*, Veröffentlichungen
der Gesellschaft für fränkische Geschichte, series I: Fränkische Chroniken, vol. 2
(Würzburg: Kommissionsverlag Ferdinand Schöningh, 1952), p. 126.

[61] Arnold, *Niklashausen 1476*, pp. 113-123.

There is nothing unique or even unusual about this combination of pastoral virtues and princely severity in Rudolf von Scherenberg. Other able bishops of this time exhibit the same or similar combinations of episcopal and princely qualities. Johann von Dalberg (1455-1503), prince-bishop of Worms from 1482 to 1503, was one of the most highly educated bishops of his generation.[62] A graduate of Erfurt, he studied law at Pavia, where he also learned Greek and became rector, and at Heidelberg, where he was chancellor of the university, he sponsored humanist learning and drafted with his own hand the statutes of the Rhenish literary sodality. Like Rudolf von Scherenberg at Würzburg, Johann von Dalberg undertook numerous projects of clerical reform through visitations and synods and did much to repair the churches in the diocese of Worms. He was a forward-looking, learned reformer. But he was also a ruling prince, and he fought the burghers of his cathedral city tooth and nail, or, rather, interdict and outlawry, in a long, bitter struggle that made an irreparable breach between the burghers and their priests (the regular clergy sided with the burghers) and neatly primed them to greet Luther's movement with enthusiasm.

The annals of the Imperial Church before and after 1500 are filled with such figures, learned and devout bishops who administered stern justice and defended their rights against the laity and against rivals with all the weapons at hand. They led what John van Engen has called a fully mature church,[63] and they were as fully attuned to the aristocratic culture of the medieval governing classes as the ancient Church's bishops had been to the cultural habitus of late Roman civilization.[64] They were princes, but princes with a difference, their powers hedged around by two conditions of their office: the elective, non-heritable nature of their office, and the rights to co-governance of their cathedral chapters. The times, moreover, pressed them toward more serious occupation with their ecclesiastical duties. The experience of the diocese of Strasbourg may not be typical, but neither was it unique.[65] Count Palatine

---

[62] Gatz, *Bischöfe 1448-1648*, pp. 115-117.

[63] John Van Engen, "The Church in the Fifteenth Century," in Thomas A. Brady, Jr., Heiko A. Oberman, and James D. Tracy, eds., *Handbook of European History, 1400-1600. Late Middle Ages, Renaissance, Reformation*, 2 vols. (Leiden: E. J. Brill, 1994-95), vol. 1. pp. 305-330, here at p. 307.

[64] I owe this insight to Susanna Elm, my Berkeley colleague.

[65] Gatz, *Bischöfe 1448-1648*, pp. 16-17, 310-312, 608-609; Francis Rapp, *Réformes*

Ruprecht of Simmern (ca. 1416-1478), who held the see of Strasbourg from 1440 until 1478, never said Mass, wore lay garb and
sword, loved women and gambling, possessed neither miter nor
crozier, and left a reputation only as a "a most severe exploiter"
(*durissimus exactor*). His successor, Count Palatine Albrecht (1440-
1506), who ruled from 1479 to 1506, did celebrate Mass, prayed
and fasted, but at his funeral the cathedral preacher spoke of the
ideal bishop as a good shepherd but lost no word on Albrecht. The
Strasbourgeois were thus understandably astonished in 1508, when
the next bishop, Wilhelm von Honstein (1475-1541), arrived on
Corpus Christi to celebrate Mass in Strasbourg's cathedral, the first
bishop to do so in more than 150 years.[66]

Quite apart from the influence of the Council of Trent, the sixteenth-century incumbents of Mainz, Strasbourg, and many other sees
proved to be, on the whole, more concerned for their pastoral responsibilities, for learning, and for reform and discipline of the clergy than
their fifteenth-century predecessors had been.[67] The change is not to
be seen entirely as a reaction to lay and clerical criticism on religious
grounds, though this doubtless played a role. So did the rising taste for
"civilization" in the forms of learning, patronage of art, and esthetically
satisfying building at the princely courts, where, to an ever greater
degree, the nobles tended to acquire their educations.[68] Important,
finally, was the concentration of armed violence in the hands of the
Imperial lay princes. A single decree by King Maximilian and the Diet
of Worms in 1495 converted an ancient noble right — the feud — into
a criminal act: "We have abolished all publicly proclaimed feuds
throughout the Empire, and based on plenitude of Our Roman royal
power We forbid and abolish them by virtue of this mandate."[69]

---

et reformation à Strasbourg: Eglise et société dans le diocèse de Strasbourg (1450-1525), Collection de l'Institut des Hautes Études Alsaciennes, vol. 23 (Paris: Editions Ophrys,
1974), pp. 321-345, 347-370, 371-393.

[66] Thomas A. Brady, Jr., "Rites of Autonomy, Rites of Dependence: South German Civic Culture in the Age of Renaissance and Reformation," in *Religion and Culture in the Renaissance City*, edited by Steven Ozment (Kirksville, Mo.: Sixteenth Century Journal Publishers, 1989), pp. 9-24.

[67] The lists and biographies in Gatz, *Bischöfe 1448-1648*, allow this to be checked
rather easily.

[68] Rainer A. Müller, *Der Fürstenhof in der frühen Neuzeit*, Enzyklopädie Deutscher
Geschichte, vol. 33 (Munich: R. Oldenbourg, 1995).

[69] *Deutsche Reichstagsakten under Maximilian I.*, vol. 5, pp. 359-373, no. 334, here at p.
364.

V. *Creating the Holy Roman Empire*

The concentration of armed force in fewer hands occurred at the expense of the lesser nobles, whose feuding culture the princely states absorbed rather than suppressed.[70] It also disadvantaged, however, all of the ecclesiastical princes, whose temporal power tended increasingly to be dwarfed by the fewer but larger dynastic states. Their vulnerability came home to Franconian prince-bishops at mid-century, when Margrave Albrecht Achilles (1414-1486) of Brandenburg-Ansbach and his allies raged through the region. This situation reinforced the prince-bishops' spiritual responsibilities with a motive from the temporal side of their authority and encouraged them to support more law and order in the Empire. The way to order was to create institutions, a lesson the clergy knew better than any other group, including the burghers. At the beginning of the fifteenth century, the Holy Roman Empire possessed a monarchy and royal court and a defined body of electors, nothing more.[71] The major accomplishment of the next 100 years was the creation of the Imperial Diet, an assembly of the notables of the realm sitting in their own right and claiming to speak for "the Empire." This body, the Diet, produced between 1486 and 1521 a group of institutions through which the Empire would be governed for the next 300 years.[72] Indeed, it is not too much to say that through this activity the early modern Holy Roman Empire of the German Nation — a title first used in this form in 1486 — came into being.

The formation and the form of the Imperial Diet allotted great political weight to the prince-bishops. While as temporal lords they ruled collectively only over some 15-16% of the Empire's lands, in the Diet's politically important chambers they held their own in one

---

[70] This is the main argument of Hillay Zmora, *State and Nobility in Early Modern Germany: The Knightly Feud in Franconia, 1440-1567*, Cambridge Studies in Early Modern History (Cambridge: Cambridge University Press, 1997).

[71] Peter Moraw, "Wesenszüge der 'Regierung' und 'Verwaltung' des deutschen Königs im Reich (ca. 1350-1450)," in Peter Moraw, *Über König und Reich. Aufsätze zur deutschen Verfassungsgeschichte des späten Mittelalters*, edited by Rainer Christoph Schwinges (Sigmaringen: Jan Thorbecke Verlag 1995), pp. 73-88.

[72] Peter Moraw, "Versuch über die Entstehung des Reichstags," in Moraw, *Über König und Reich*, pp. 207-242.

and the upper hand in the other. Three archbishops occupied half the seats in the Diet's electoral chamber, while in the princes' chamber more than 50 lords spiritual — five archbishops and 46 bishops — outweighed the 30 or so lords temporal.[73] Moreover, each bishop had an equal vote, so that in this setting the petty holdings of Chur, Metz, Sitten/Sion, Constance, and Naumburg meant as much as the large territories of Würzburg, Bamberg, Salzburg, Münster, and Paderborn.

At the end of the century the bishops' potential force for reform became a reality. The point has often been made that, when the leaders of the churches dispersed after the failure at Constance and again at Basel of the reform of "head and members," the Imperial church's leaders were singularly unsuccessful in translating the general councils' agendas into local programs of reform. It is a point well taken, and the only truly adequate study of an Imperial diocese in this era, Francis Rapp's monumental work on Strasbourg, demonstrates brilliantly how episcopal reform foundered on the rocks of entrenched legal rights of the clergy, lay interference, and papal intervention.[74] Many other Imperial bishops, alone or with the collaboration of synods, undertook reforms in the post-conciliar era, with very modest long-term success. So modest, that Heiko A. Oberman has written of the "one hundred years of reform effort which had been keeping the Church in suspense and Germany seething ever since the Council of Constance (1414-18)."[75]

The (usually) unstated inference from this picture is that had the Empire's monarchs and ecclesiastical leaders accomplished more for reform during the post-conciliar age, the German lands would have undergone a non-revolutionary religious reformation comparable, perhaps, to that of England or even Castile. This is plausible, for the

---

[73] Wolgast, *Hochstift und Reformation*, pp. 19-20. See Reinhard, "Die Verwaltung der Kirche," in *Deutsche Verwaltungsgeschichte*, vol. 1, p. 154. I do not count the province of Riga, as he does, as belonging to the Empire. In addition to the prince-archbishops and prince-bishops, the grand masters of the Teutonic Order (since 1494) and the Knights of St. John sat in the Diet, and about 75 Imperial abbots and abbesses plus the provost of Ellwangen possessed a collective vote. One archbishop (Prague) and seven bishops possessed no temporal authority and, therefore, no seats in the Diet.

[74] Rapp, *Réformes et réformation à Strasbourg*.

[75] Heiko A. Oberman, *Luther. Menschen zwischen Gott und dem Teufel* (Berlin: Severin & Siedler, 1982), p. 33; English in *Luther. Man Between God and the Devil*, translated by Eileen Walliser-Schwarzbart (New Haven: Yale University Press, 1989), p. 23.

Imperial bishops' record as executors of Constance and Basel is not very impressive. On the other reform front, however, during the Imperial reform era they helped to equip the Empire with its first stable array of governing institutions.

One cannot expect to find behind the fifteenth-century Empire's reform impulses, which "never were laid to rest, ... and which despite decades of wrangling occupied the Diets again and again,"[76] a level of conceptualization or a continuous tradition of theorizing in any way comparable to contemporary thinking about the Church, whether conciliarist or papalist. The Imperial reform nevertheless did draw strength from the clerical culture and its ideas about institutions, representation, and power, which had been so greatly stimulated by the Western Schism (1378-1415), the Councils of Constance and Basel, and the vigorous survival of conciliarist loyalty and ideas in the Empire.[77] Reform of the Church and reform of the Empire were not two separate causes. In a tract he composed just before the Council of Constance opened, the German curialist turned conciliarist Dietrich von Niem declared that "it would be conducive to a reform of the temporal affairs of the Roman Church and the Empire if, insofar as possible, there were a firm and indissoluble league between the pope and the king or emperor."[78] An anonymous writer at Constance went further and applied the principles of ecclesiology

---

[76] Karl Siegfried Bader, "Kaiserliche und ständische Reformgedanken in den Reichsreform des endenden 15. Jahrhunderts," *Historisches Jahrbuch* 73 (1954): 74-94, here at p. 81; reprinted in Karl Siegfried Bader, *Ausgewählte Schriften zur Rechts- und Landesgeschichte*, vol. 1: *Schriften zur Rechtsgeschichte*, edited by Clausdieter Schott (Sigmaringen: Jan Thorbecke Verlag, 1984), pp. 464-484.

[77] Bader, "Kaiserliche und ständisches Reformgedanken," takes this almost for granted. Heinz Angermeier in "Die Reichsregimenter und ihre Staatsidee," *Historische Zeitschrift* 211 (1970), pp. 265-315, strongly opposed any connection and called the fifteenth-century reform writers mere scribblers, "[die] um ihrer politischen Zwecke willen nur den verschwommenen Konziliarismus wieder aufwärmten" (p. 270, and see also p. 298). He later came around to a much more positive view in *Die Reichsreform 1410-1555. Die Staatsproblematik in Deutschland zwischen Mittelalter und Gegenwart* (Munich: C. H. Beck Verlag, 1984), pp. 84-99.

[78] "Item bene expediret pro reformacione in temporalibus Romane ecclesie et imperii, quod fieret liga et confederacio fortissima et indissolubilis in quantum fieri posset, inter papam et regem vel imperatorem. . . ." *Acta ad ecclesiam in generalibus saeculi XV. conciliis reformandam spectantia / Quellen zur Kirchen Reformation im Zeitalter der großen Konzilien des 15. Jahrhunderts*, edited by Jürgen Miethke and Lorenz Weinrich, part I, Ausgewählte Quellen zur deutschen Geschichte des Mittelalters. Freiherr vom Stein-Gedächtnis-Ausgabe, vol. 38a (Darmstadt: Wissenschaftliche Buchgesellschaft, 1995), p. 268. See also E. Schubert, *Einführung*, p. 242.

— councils, elections, representation — to a projected reform of the Empire.[79]

A major peak of conciliarist thinking about the Empire in terms of the Church came with the great didactic analogy posed by Nicholas of Cusa (1401-1464) in Book III of his *De concordantia catholica*, which he composed in 1437-38 during the Council of Basel. Nicholas applied to the Empire such ecclesiastical principles as conciliar organization, consent, elections, and representation, and he also employed the church generally as a model for the institutionalization of the Empire.[80] He recommended forming a standing Imperial Governing Council to handle all Imperial business, a concept he based on the College of Cardinals and the General Council. He also suggested that similar councils be formed to administer the Empire's regions — "provinces," he called them — which mirrored the church's provinces and their synods.[81]

Although none of the reform proposals of the Diet between 1495 and 1521 refers or even alludes to Nicholas' proposals, his method of working from Church to Empire was not lost on the Imperial reformers when they came to think, as he had done, of providing the Empire with institutions for defense, taxation, justice, and law and order. When in 1495 the Diet discussed organizing sub-units, ecclesiastical provinces were actually suggested as administrative districts.[82] So feeble was the tradition of lay institutions of governance at this time that it was difficult even to think about the Empire except in terms of the Church. Later, with more experience, the planners

[79] The text is called "Advisamentum sacrorum canonum et doctorum ecclesiae catholicae de electione papae et cardinalium secundum exigenciam status ecclesiae modernae et quomodo huius sacri Constanciensis concilii habeatur brevi finis salutaris," in *Acta concilii Constantiensis*, 4 vols., edited by Heinrich Finke (Münster: Aschendorff Verlag, 1896-1928), vol. 3, no. 264. It is analyzed by Friedrich Hermann Schubert, *Die deutschen Reichstage in der Staatslehre der frühen Neuzeit*, Schriftenreihe der Historischen Kommission bei der Bayerischen Akademie der Wissenschaften, vol. 7 (Göttingen: Vandenhoeck & Ruprecht, 1966), pp. 90-96.

[80] Nicolai de Cusa, *De concordantia catholica libri tres*, edited by Gerhard Kallen, in *Opera omnia*, vol. 14 (Hamburg 1959), Book III, chaps. 1, 7, 12; English in *The Catholic Concordance*, edited and translated by Paul E. Sigmund (Cambridge: Cambridge University Press, 1991), pp. 215-216, 237-240, 248-249.

[81] Cusa, *De concordantia catholica*, book III, chap. xxv, para. 470; English in *The Catholic Concordance*, edited and translated by Paul E. Sigmund, p. 283.

[82] See the estates' proposal of 1495, in which the ten districts included the ecclesiastical provinces of Magdeburg, Salzburg and Aquileia, Besançon, and Bremen. *Deutsche Reichstagsakten unter Maximilian I.* (i.e., *mittlere Reihe*), vol. 5, edited by Heinz Angermeier (Göttingen: Vandenhoeck & Ruprecht, 1981), p. 336, no. 327.

dropped Church provinces in favor of corporate groupings of Imperial estates by region, which became the ten, later twelve, Imperial Circles, the early modern Empire's principal administrative, police, and military districts.[83]

To document the connections between ecclesiastical and Imperial reform would fill one of the truly glaring gaps in our knowledge of the pre-Reformation Empire. In the present state of our knowledge, the connections between Christian clerical culture and the Imperial reform are elusive and fragmentary. The threads seem nevertheless to have come together in the hands of one man, Count Berthold (1441-1504) of Henneberg-Römhild, since 1484 Archbishop and Elector of Mainz as the successor to Diether von Isenburg.

The recently published acts of the Imperial Diet of Worms in 1495 show that in all the reforms, the initiative lay with the Diet, not with King Maximilian, and that the leadership of the reform party lay from first to last with Berthold of Mainz.[84] Leopold von Ranke, who rediscovered Berthold, identified him as the man "who had framed the principal ideas and pressed the cause so far forward, and who refused to let it drop so easily."[85] Ranke awarded the palm of reform to Berthold, not to King Maximilian, and despite many subsequent challenges to this judgment, the acts of the Diets are revealing that Ranke was right.[86] To what degree

---

[83] Winfried Dotzauer, *Die deutschen Reichskreis (1383-1806). Geschichte und Aktenedition* (Stuttgart. Franz Steiner Verlag 1998).

[84] Gatz, *Bischöfe 1448-1648*, pp. 283-285. Missing from the literature there cited is Eduard Ziehen, *Mittelrhein und Reich im Zeitalter der Reichsreform 1356-1504*, 2 vols. (Frankfurt am Main: Selbstverlag, 1934-1937), vol. I, pp. 167-179, 198-218. The best modern study of Berthold is Karl Siegfried Bader, *Ein Staatsmann vom Mittelrhein. Gestalt und Werk des Mainzer Erzbischofs Berthold von Henneberg* (Mainz, 1955). The latest and most accurate review of Berthold's role in the Imperial Reform is by Christine Roll, "'Sin lieb sy auch eyn kurfurst . . .' Zur Rolle Bertholds von Henneberg in der Reichsreform," in *Kurmainz, das Reichserzkanzleramt und das Reich am Ende des Mittelalters und im 16. und 17. Jahrhundert*, edited by P. C. Hartmann, Geschichtliche Landeskunde, vol. 47 (Stuttgart: W. Kohlhammer, 1998), pp. 5-44, esp. p. 9 note 13.

[85] Ranke, *Deutsche Geschichte*, vol. I, p. 69.

[86] A little earlier (*Deutsche Geschichte*, vol. I, p. 68) Ranke had written: "Man muß sich wundern, daß man den Ruhm, die Reichsverfassung begründet zu haben, so lange und so allgemein dem Könige beigemessen hat, dem die Entwürfe zu derselben aufgedrungen werden mußten, und der dann deren Ausführung bei weitem mehr verhinderte als begünstigte." See Bader, "Kaiserliche und ständische Reformgedanken," pp. 471-472, who refers to Nicholas of Cusa as Berthold's "geistiger Lehrmeister" and writes that in Berthold's reform work "ja schließlich ein Stück jener Concordantia Catholica Wirklichkeit geworden [ist]." The contrary view is advanced by Wiesflecker, *Kaiser Maximilian I.*, vol. 2:175: Maximilian was "ein

Berthold and the men around him lay under the influence of earlier reform ideas and proposals, especially those of Nicholas of Cusa, remains an open question. It is nonetheless clear that at Worms the initial proposals of all of the great reform statutes came from the estates, not from the king. Furthermore, all the evidence speaks for a distinct lack of interest in general reform on the part of the leading lay princes.[87] That leaves the bishops and other prelates as probable members of Berthold's party. The Imperial bishops did support a program of reform, not of the Church but of its once shadowy twin, the Holy Roman Empire.

VI. *Governance by Priests in the Age of Reformation*

The early modern Holy Roman Empire was fashioned in part out of the substance of its oldest and most stable substructure, the Imperial Church, and out of the fusion of *spiritualia* and *temporalia* in the prince-bishoprics. The fashioning took place at a time when this kind of fusion was coming under ever heavier fire, both from reformers who wanted a more pastoral church and from critics who wanted more effective governments. As far back as Marsiglio of Padua (ca. 1296?-1343?), the call for a more spiritual Church with more pastoral leadership and the call for a stronger state had formed the two sides of a single coin.[88] This coin was not minted, as is often alleged, by the elimination of sacral authority but by its massive migration from spiritual to temporal lords. Thomas Hobbes' view, quoted at the head of this study, sums up the experience of his age.[89] "*Spiritualia* and *temporalia* were assimilated and fused in the new states," concludes Paolo

---

überzeugter Reformator," who "sei nur deshalb im Jahr 1495 diese Führungsrolle und der Sieg in Italien versagt geblieben, weil die in Worms versammelten Reichsstände ihm die gebührende Unterstützung versagt hätten."

[87] *Deutsche Reichstagsakten under Maximilian I.*, vol. 5, pp. 32, 68; E. Schubert, *Königtum und Landfriede im deutschen Spätmittelalter* (Munich: C. H. Beck, 1966), p. 531.

[88] J. A. Watt, "Spiritual and Temporal Powers," in *The Cambridge History of Political Thought, c. 350-c. 1450*, edited by J. H. Burns (Cambridge: Cambridge University Press, 1988), pp. 415-422.

[89] The most uncompromisingly extreme formulation of the principle, however, was not Hobbes' but Spinoza's. See Noel Malcolm, "Hobbes and Spinoza," in *The Cambridge History of Political Thought, 1450-1700*, edited by J. H. Burns (Cambridge: Cambridge University Press, 1991), pp. 530-560, and, in the same volume, Mark Goldie, "The Reception of Hobbes," pp. 589-615, here at pp. 610-615.

Prodi, "not only from a jurisdictional point of view but more particularly in the religious and cultural integration of their subjects, as a political and governing principle, until the affirmation of the *cuius regio, eius religio* ruled in the whole of Europe, Catholic and reformed, at the end of the wars of religion."[90] As a statement of the general shift of religious authority to temporal rulers, this is true, but it does not allow for the fact that not all of Christendom was ruled by such "new states."

The most obvious and most resistant exception was the Roman papacy. The popes' efforts to forestall a subordination of Church to State took the form of the transformation since 1450 of the lands of St. Peter into the Papal State, a miniature but precocious absolutist monarchy fused to a universalist spiritual power.[91] The long process of its gestation maximized the violent operations inherent in temporal lordship to a degree that famously provoked the fury of contemporary critics of rule by priests. To be sure, their criticisms drew something from the religious polemic "against bad priests who neglected God's Law," which found willing ears in all corners of fifteenth-century Christendom, though nowhere with greater consequence than in Hussite Bohemia.[92] The rise of the Papal State in the fifteenth and early sixteenth centuries also provoked, however, an especially trenchant, even savage, political critique. The formation of the Papal State clashed in Italy around 1500 with an ideal of the State of which Marsiglio had been but a precocious precursor.

The Florentines distinguished themselves in the service of this point of view. Niccolò Machiavelli (1469-1527) declared with tongue in cheek that ecclesiastical principalities "alone ... are secure and happy," because "their states are never taken away from [their rulers] as a result of not being defended; and their subjects do not object because they are not governed."[93] His countryman and contemporary, Francesco Guicciardini (1483-1540), minced no words in rendering, in his *History of Italy*, the classic judgment on the formation of the Papal State as the final wreckage of the ship of the Church on

---

[90] Prodi, *The Papal Prince*, p. 6.

[91] Prodi, *The Papal Prince*, pp. 1-16 and the formulation on p. 17.

[92] František Smahel, "The Hussite Critique of the Clergy's Civil Dominion," in *Anticlericalism in Late Medieval and Early Modern Europe*, pp. 83-90, here at p. 85.

[93] Niccolò Machiavelli, *The Prince*, chap. 11, here from *The Prince and Other Works*, translated by Allan H. Gilbert (New York: Hendricks House, 1964), p. 129.

the reef of temporal power. "On these foundations and by these means," Guicciardini wrote, "raised to secular power, little by little forgetting about the salvation of souls and divine precepts, and turning all their thoughts to worldly greatness, and no longer using their spiritual authority except as an instrument and minister of temporal power," the popes began to appear "rather more like secular princes than popes. Their concern and endeavors began to be no longer the sanctity of life or the propagation of religion, no longer zeal and charity toward their neighbors, but armies and wars against Christians, managing their sacrifices with bloody hands and thoughts..."[94] It is perhaps worth noting that the "secular princes" of Guicciardini's polemic were conceived in terms of Italian princes and European monarchs of his own day, plus the emperors in the humanists' recovered memory of ancient Rome. The State was sovereign — its inner configuration, republic or monarchy, was as secondary to the Renaissance writers as it had been to Marsiglio.

The critique of ecclesiastical lordship in the early sixteenth century nonetheless drew vital nourishment not only from the advance of theory and the experience of politics, but also from a change in religious sensibilities, according to which the lordship of priests was becoming increasingly repugnant. This sentiment, not political philosophizing, inspired Erasmus' (d. 1536) fierce diatribe against Pope Julius II (r. 1503-1513), who in the dialogue *Julius exclusus* arrives at heaven's gate expecting entry, only to be turned away by St. Peter, to whom Julius appears as a monster. Within twenty-five years of Julius' death, a recent study has noted, eight Imperial bishops would be excluded from their cathedrals.[95]

For all of that, however the general polemic against the lordship of priests also targeted the Imperial prince-bishoprics, their fate diverged markedly both from that of the papacy in particular and that of the clergy of Christendom in general. They, too, found their refuge in a state, but, given the political character of the Empire, not an absolutist one. German Protestant publicists, to be sure, deployed against them the common early modern attitude that government by priests was unnatural, detrimental to religion, and harmful to the

---

[94] Francesco Guicciardini, *The History of Italy*, translated and edited by Sydney Alexander (New York: Macmillan, 1969), book IV, p. 149.
[95] Tyler, *Lord of the Sacred City*, pp. 11-13.

body politic. Samuel Pufendorf (1632-1694) adjusted this view to local conditions in his book of 1667 on the Imperial constitution. He called the Catholic prince-bishops disturbers of the peace, for many of them "wear the helmet rather than the miter, and they do more to start wars and cause unrest among subjects than to spread piety."[96] This, of course, was generally untrue by his time.[97] His real objection to the Imperial prince-bishoprics was similar to Guicciardini's: fortified by royal endowments and backed by the pope, the bishops "had been able to free themselves wholly from temporal authority."[98] "Most people," Pufendorf concluded, "believe that the most deadly disease in the German Empire consists in so many of its subjects recognizing a foreigner as supreme lord." Pufendorf's is no longer the late medieval, religious argument — the lordship of priests is bad for religion — but the modern, political one — the lordship of priests blocks the absolute sovereignty of the State.

Neither in Pufendorf's time nor for another century was this apparent defect to be repaired. These decades, when the ravaged German lands healed their wounds and recovered their populations and wealth after the Thirty Years' War, proved a relatively good time for the prince-bishoprics. Perhaps in this age was coined the saying, "life is good under the crozier."[99]

---

[96] Samuel Pufendorf, *Die Verfassung des Deutschen Reiches*, translated by Horst Denzer (Stuttgart: Reclam, 1976), chap. 2, para. 10, p. 37.

[97] It is worth mentioning that the most obvious exception to this rule, Prince-Bishop Christoph Bernhard von Galen (r. 1650-1678) of Münster, invaded Gelderland and Overijssel with 20,000 men and English subsidies just as Pufendorf was writing this book. Jonathan Israel, *The Dutch Republic, Its Rise, Greatness, and Fall, 1477-1806* (Oxford: Clarendon Press, 1995), pp. 770-772.

[98] Pufendorf, *Verfassung*, chap. 3, para. 8, p. 51.

[99] Lutz Mackensen, *Zitate, Redensarten, Sprichwörter* (Wiesbaden: VMA-Verlag, 1981), p. 739, no. 8734: "Unterm Krummstab ist gut wohnen."
Keith Spalding, *An Historical Dictionary of German Figurative Usage* (Oxford: B. Blackwell, 1952-1999), p. 1558, notes this saying from 1716 but thinks it older. Johannes Agricola (1494-1566) collected a related (older?) form: "Unter dem krummen Stabe / unnd under den Graven ist gu(o)t wohnen," and added his comment: "Die Bischofe und Epte seind der krumme stab / Die Graven seind die sittsamen Herren / das mehrertail erlangen / Deßgleichen so warn die Bischofe und Epte / auch glimpflich / und nicht Tyrannen / Daher das Spruchwort erwachsen." Johannes Agricola, *Die Sprichwörtersammlungen*, edited by Sander Gilman, 2 vols., Ausgaben deutscher Literatur des XV. bis XVIII. Jahrhunderts (Berlin and New York: W. de Gruyter, 1971), vol. 2:122, no. 190.

LUTHER'S FIRST APPEAL TO SECULAR AUTHORITIES FOR HELP WITH CHURCH REFORM, 1520[1]

James M. Estes*

One of the few unquestioned certitudes of Reformation scholarship is that the Reformation in Germany found its typical institutional expression in *das landesherrliche Kirchenregiment*, that is, in churches established and organized in the imperial territories and subject to the territorial rulers as their earthly heads. A similarly unquestioned certitude is that the emergence of these Lutheran *Landeskirchen* was the culmination of a development that had begun well before the Reformation.[2] All this indisputable certainty can easily create the impression that the development of Lutheran territorial churches was foreordained by "the march of history" and thus all but automatic. It is therefore salutary to remember that it did not seem that way at all to those who were actually involved. The development of territorial churches before the Reformation had been difficult and controversial, and the continuation of that development in the sixteenth century, now complicated by religious schism, proved even more so. It took a whole generation of struggle against manifold obstacles, both theoretical and practical, to establish, organize, and secure the Protestant territorial churches that were governed by Christian magistrates whose responsibility for the establishment and maintenance of true religion had been adequately demonstrated by the theologians. It was not until 1535, after a decade and a half of struggle to keep thought abreast of sometimes turbulent change, that Philip Melanchthon, in the second edition of his *Loci communes*, succeeded in

* Professor Emeritus, Victoria College, University of Toronto
    [1] In the notes the following standard abbreviations have been used: LW = *Luther's Works*, ed. Jaroslav Pelikan, Helmut T. Lehmann et al., 55 vols. (St. Louis: Concordia Publishing House; Philadelphia: Fortress Press, 1955-1986); WA = *D. Martin Luthers Werke, Kritische Gesamtausgabe*, 60 vols. (Weimar: H. Böhlau, 1883-1980); WA-Br = *D. Martin Luthers Werke: Briefwechsel*, 15 vols. (Weimar: H. Böhlau, 1930-1978).
    [2] See Hans-Walter Krumwiede, "Kirchenregiment, Landesherrliches," in the *Theologische Realencyklopädie* (Berlin, W. De Gruyter, 1976-) 19:59-68. And for an excellent summary of developments before the Reformation, see Manfred Schulze, *Fürsten und Reformation* (Tübingen: J. C. B. Mohr [Paul Siebeck], 1991), esp. pp. 13-45.

giving the Lutheran doctrine of the *cura religionis* of Christian magistrates its characteristic and enduring formulation.[3] And it was not until the 1550s, after decades of effort that were interrupted and nearly undone by the Augsburg Interim (1548-1552), that the organization and administration of the territorial churches could achieve full development.[4] To examine in detail the experiences and the thinking of the reformers who took a leading role in these developments is to learn much about the way the Reformation actually happened and to discover how close the connection was between theology and the course of public events. This article is one small attempt at such an examination.

The emergence of *das landesherrliche Kirchenregiment* in Lutheran Germany owes at least as much to Martin Luther as it does to any other individual.[5] With the publication of the *Address to the Christian Nobility* in August 1520, he became the first of the reformers to issue a direct appeal to German secular authorities (in this case, the emperor and the imperial nobility in their capacity as the government of the Empire) to initiate an ecclesiastical reformation that would have to be

---

[3] The conviction that Christian magistrates should provide the reformation that the bishops had refused to provide was there from the beginning but, beginning in about 1530, the earlier emphasis on the establishment and enforcement of true doctrine and worship as the best way to maintain secular peace proved fallible in the course of controversy with opponents of "confessionalization" and was replaced with arguments that elevated the glory of God above secular peace and order as the aim of secular rule. See James M. Estes, "Erasmus, Melanchthon, and the Office of Christian Magistrate," *Erasmus of Rotterdam Society Yearbook Eighteen* (1998), 21-39; and idem, "The Role of Godly Magistrates in the Church: Melanchthon as Luther's Interpreter and Collaborator," *Church History* 67 (1998): 463-83.

[4] See, for example, the account of the organization of the territorial church in the Duchy of Württemberg in James Martin Estes, *Christian Magistrate and State Church: The Reforming Career of Johannes Brenz* (Toronto: University of Toronto Press, 1982), 59-80.

[5] Literature on this subject that is faithful to all the available evidence is astonishingly rare. The closest thing to it in English is W. D. J. Cargill Thompson, *The Political Thought of Martin Luther* (Brighton, Sussex: Harvester Press, 1984). Unfortunately, Professor Cargill Thompson did not live to revise his manuscript or supply it with notes, so the work must be used with some caution. Among recent German works, the most useful are Karl Trüdinger, *Luthers Briefe und Gutachten an weltliche Obrigkeiten zur Durchführung der Reformation* (Münster Westfalen: Aschendorff, 1975); and Wolfgang Sommer, *Gottesfurcht und Fürstenherrschaft: Studien zum Obrigkeitsverständnis Johann Arndts und lutherischer Hofprediger zur Zeit der altprotestantischen Orthodoxie* (Göttingen: Vandenhoeck & Ruprecht, 1988), especially pp. 23-73: "Luther's Obrigkeitsverständnis und die kursächsische Regierung unter Kurfürst Johann Friedrich [1534/35]." My own recently published thoughts on the subject are found in the articles cited in note 3.

carried out in defiance of Rome. In later years, after it had become clear that the focus of reform (pending some general settlement) was going to be the imperial territories rather than the Empire as a whole, Luther addressed similar appeals to the electors of Saxony and other territorial rulers. In so doing, he continued and exploited the long-established tendency of German ecclesiastical reformers to seek from Christian secular rulers the reforms that the clerical hierarchy either would not or could not provide. At the same time, however, Luther was, of all the reformers, the least comfortable with the idea of governmental responsibility for ecclesiastical and spiritual matters. As a result, it took him until the 1530s to achieve, with evident difficulty, the positive affirmation of secular responsibility for religious reform and church governance that his fellow reformers had achieved with ease in the early 1520s, and his arguments justifying governmental action in support of the establishment and maintenance of true religion were, from 1520 to the end of his life, the most complicated and tension-ridden of all those to come from the pen of any reformer.

My aim here is the limited one of examining, in more detail than has usually been the case, Luther's first appeal to secular authorities for help with the reform of the church, the planning and writing of which occupied him for several months in the spring and summer of 1520. There are two good reasons for this seemingly narrow focus. First, in making his case for secular intervention, Luther said a great deal that proved to be of fundamental importance not only for the development of his own thought on church and state in the years to come but also for that of his fellow reformers. Second, because the language that Luther employed in 1520 is occasionally vague and the arrangement of his material sometimes rather careless, it takes a detailed and careful examination of both the context and the content of the surviving texts to produce an accurate understanding of Luther's views and of their long-term significance. If one cannot possibly tell the whole story of Luther's contribution to the emergence of the territorial church in one brief essay, one can at least hope to make clear how much of the end was already present in the beginning.

Any assessment of Luther's appeal to "the Christian nobility" to play an important role in ecclesiastical reform has to begin with the fact that it was only after more than two years of public effort in behalf of such reform that Luther came to the conclusion that he would have to invoke the aid of princes and nobles. His first appeal was to the ecclesiastical establishment, whom he addressed in his capacity as a pastor responsible for the spiritual welfare of his flock and as an academic theologian with a sworn duty to combat errors and abuses in the church. Convinced that authentic Catholic truth about Christian penitence had been distorted and obscured by scholastic theologians, with disastrous consequences for simple believers, Luther voiced his protest in the *Ninety-Five Theses on the Power and Efficacy of Indulgences* (31 October 1517).[6] The *Theses*, as well as the succeeding works elaborating the position taken in them, were a challenge to theologians to restore theology to a sound basis and to responsible prelates to curb the abuses of the indulgence preachers. He took it for granted that the primary responsibility for ecclesiastical reform lay with the clergy, whose divinely appointed mission, he believed, was to nourish the people with the faithful preaching of the word and to remove all threats to their eternal welfare.[7] Only in the spring of 1520 did Luther abandon hope that bishops and prelates would provide reform and decide to appeal to secular princes to intervene to save a Christendom threatened by the malfeasance of the "Romanists."

Much to Luther's surprise and dismay, the defenders of the indulgence traffic, both in Germany and in Rome, made papal authority, rather than justification and penance, the dominant issue in the controversy unleashed by the *Ninety-Five Theses*. With varying degrees of sophistication, Luther's critics —John Tetzel, Sylvester Prierias, Cardinal Cajetan, John Eck, and others — identified the true church with the Roman Church and the Roman Church with the pope; elevated the authority of the pope above that of Scripture; asserted that popes and papally sanctioned councils cannot err; equated the practice of the church (e.g., the sale of indulgences) with the law of the church; and concluded that anyone who criticized any aspect of the church's teaching and practice with respect to indulgences had attacked the authority of the pope and was *ipso facto* a heretic. Faced with such arguments, Luther, whose inclination was to treat Scripture, the Fathers, popes, and councils as coordinate authorities in an

---

[6] Martin Brecht, *Martin Luther: Sein Weg zur Reformation, 1483-1521* (Stuttgart: Calwer Verlag, 1981), 173-230.

[7] Scott Hendrix, *Luther and the Papacy: Stages in a Reformation Conflict* (Philadelphia: Fortress Press, 1981), 1-32.

ecclesiastical consensus, increasingly found himself having to side with what seemed to him to be the clear teaching of Scripture against the erroneous teachings of popes, councils, and some of the Fathers. By the time of his famous debate with John Eck at the University of Leipzig in July 1519, Luther's study of Scripture and church history had led him to the conclusion that the Roman Church was only one possible manifestation of the true church, that papal authority was of human rather than divine origin, and that ultimate authority in the church rested not with popes or councils or Fathers but with Scripture alone.[8]

Theoretically, the door was still open to a reform that would leave the papacy and the traditional hierarchy intact but subject to the word of God and governing the church *de jure humano*. In the early months of 1520, however, during which (among other things) he read Lorenzo Valla's exposure of *The Donation of Constantine* as a forgery, Luther's already privately voiced suspicion that the Roman hierarchy was a tyranny in the service of Antichrist hardened into firm conviction, and he lost all hope that Rome would agree voluntarily to a genuine reform of any sort.[9] It was in these circumstances that Luther began to write of the need for secular intervention to clear the path to ecclesiastical reform. The earliest indication of his intention to appeal for such intervention is found in the *Treatise on Good Works*,[10] which was written in March/April 1520 and had appeared in print by 8 June.[11]

The *Treatise on Good Works* was a discussion of Christian ethics in the traditional form of a commentary on the Ten Commandments. As was customary, Luther divided the Decalogue into the First Table (commandments one through three), dealing with the duties of human beings toward God, and the Second Table (commandments four through ten), dealing with the duties of human beings toward one another. Following the same custom, he made the first com-

---

[8] Ibid., 32-94.

[9] Ibid., 95-107.

[10] *Von den guten Werken*, WA 6:202-76; LW 44:21-114. While consistently using the excellent LW translation of this and other works, I have occasionally made small adjustments in it in the interest of clarity and precision. In most cases, the change is the result of my insistence that the correct translation of *weltlich* is "secular" or (in some cases) "worldly," not LW's "temporal." Since I have in no case changed the actual meaning of the LW text, I have not felt it necessary to employ typographical or other devices to call attention to these adjustments.

[11] WA 6:196-97; LW 44:17-18.

mandment of the Second Table, "Thou shalt honour thy father and thy mother," the basis of his discussion of the duty of Christians to honour and obey not simply their own father and mother but also their "spiritual mother," the church, as well as secular authority.[12]

Luther's discussion of the obedience owed to "the spiritual authorities" is in fact a summons to resist those authorities because they have, by their misconduct, forfeited their right to be obeyed. Behaving like parents who foresake their children, they neither preach nor teach nor punish sin. Instead they devote themselves to "alien and wicked works," using the ban only against those who owe them money and selling dispensations, indulgences, parishes, bishoprics, and "everything else that was originally founded for the service of God throughout the world." Thus, while the wealth of the world is driven to Rome, church offices fall into the hands of the unlearned and the incompetent, the gospel is not preached, faith is destroyed, and Christendom goes "to wrack and ruin."[13] In these circumstances, "anyone who is able to do so" should help in whatever way he can. In particular it falls to kings, princes, and nobles, "for the benefit of Christendom and to prevent blasphemy and the disgrace of the divine name," to resist the pope and his crew. They must deal with the spiritual estate as they would with a father who has lost his senses and who, unless restrained and resisted, will destroy his children and heirs. There are those who think the matter should be referred to a general council, but councils are of no use, since they are so thoroughly under the control of "the Romans." Thus "it would be best — *indeed it is the only way left to us* — if kings, princes, nobles, cities, and communities would *take the first step* in this matter, so that bishops and clergy (*who are now afraid*) would have reason to follow."[14] Just what form this "first step" would take is not made clear.

Although Luther does not use the words *Not* or *Notstand*, it is clear that he is describing an emergency created by the failure of one of the pillars of Christendom, the clergy, to do its duty. In this emer-

---

[12] WA 6:250-65; LW 44:80-100. On the general subject of late-medieval catechisis centered on the Ten Commandments, with special emphasis on the use made of the Fourth Commandment, see Robert James Bast, *Honor Your Fathers: Catechisms and the Emergence of a Patriarchal Ideology in Germany, 1400-1600* (Leiden/New York/Köln: Brill, 1997). Bast's discussion of Luther concentrates on the reformer's views of patriarchy in the home (pp. 78-87) and in the church (pp. 122-310), though his views on patriarchy in the state get some attention as well (pp. 187-95).

[13] WA 6:255-57; LW 44:87-90.

[14] WA 6:256, 257-58; LW 44:88, 90-91 (emphasis added).

gency, the other pillar of Christendom, the secular authorities, is the only possible source of effective remedial action. At the same time, however, Luther's language indicates clearly that the task of the secular authorities is simply to get things started, to inaugurate the restoration of the proper functioning of spiritual government by bishops and clergy, not to exercise any sort of routine jurisdiction in the sphere of religion. Luther's discussion of secular authority and the obedience owed to it provides further evidence on this point.

For Luther, the duty of Christians to obey their secular rulers is established by the classic texts in the epistles of Paul and Peter (Rom. 13:1-7; Tit. 3:1; 1 Peter 2:13-14). Except in cases where governments command something clearly contrary to God's law, unquestioning obedience is owed them. Their office, however, is the purely secular one of protecting their subjects from temporal harm and punishing crimes like theft, robbery, adultery, gluttony, and drunkenness. This means that secular authority, even if it does wrong, cannot harm the soul but only one's body and possessions. For secular authority "has nothing to do with the preaching of the gospel, or with faith, or with the first three commandments." Whatever government does or does not do or believe, individual faith goes its way and does its job, "for I do not have to believe what the secular power believes." If, on the other hand, spiritual power does wrong, or merely neglects its duty, which is "to lead the people in faith to God," real disaster is the result. Thus, secular power "is but a very small matter in the sight of God" and not important enough to resist or disobey. But spiritual government "is an exceedingly great blessing and much too precious" in the sight of God for any Christian to suffer silently when it fails to do its duty. "Therefore, we must resist the spiritual power when it does not do right, and not resist secular power even when it does wrong."[15] This rather belittling description of secular authority, with its careful exclusion of that authority from the realm of faith and the first three commandments, is further indication that, even as Luther was contemplating the need for secular intervention in the normal sphere of spiritual government in order to rescue Christendom in a grave emergency, he was not prepared to assign to the secular office as such any direct or routine responsibility for the establishment and maintenance of true religion.

---

[15] WA 6:258-60; LW 44:91-3.

Neither, however, was Luther prepared to tolerate any diminution of the authority of secular government in its proper sphere of responsibility. In this connection it is noteworthy that his list of the "alien and wicked works" committed by the spiritual estate consists mostly of examples of the greedy and unscrupulous abuse of ecclesiastical authority to raise money.[16] In other words, a large category of ecclesiastical abuses consists of secular crimes committed by "spiritual" persons. Given Luther's definition of the office of secular authority as that of protecting its subjects against robbery, theft and other violations of the commandments of the Second Table, it would seem to follow that secular rulers, on their own initiative and in pursuit of their own divinely established responsibility, should take direct action against such abuses. And Luther's thinking is in fact already headed in that direction. Toward the end of his discussion of the fourth commandment, he briefly calls attention to the "knavery" of ecclesiastical judges and other episcopal and ecclesiastical officials who ban and fine poor people, harrassing them mercilessly until the last penny has been squeezed out of them. "This sort of thing should be prevented by the secular sword, since there is no other help or remedy."[17] The clergy, in other words, should prevent such things but, failing that, the secular authorities should exercise their responsibility to protect the property and security of their subjects.

In sum, the *Treatise on Good Works* shows that Luther saw Christendom in need of direct action by secular authorities to overcome an emergency that a negligent and corrupt clergy had caused but clearly could not deal with. Though vague about what that direct action should be, he distinguished clearly between those matters over which secular rulers had routine authority (secular crimes committed by clergymen) and those over which they did not (gospel, faith, and the first three commandments). His next treatment of these matters was not long in coming.

In mid-May 1520, while the *Treatise on Good Works* was still in press, the Leipzig Franciscan, Augustine Alveld, published a German pamphlet in defense of the the proposition that the pope in Rome has authority over all Christendom by divine right.[18] Enraged at the "rot-

---

[16] See p. 53, above.

[17] WA 6:262; LW 44:96.

[18] *Eyn gar fruchtbar vnd nutzbarlich buchleyn von dem Babtstlichen stul* ... See WA 6:280-81.

ten argument[s]" with which the Leipzig "blabbermouth" was poi-
soning the minds of laymen, Luther replied with *On the Papacy in
Rome, Against the Most Celebrated Romanist in Leipzig*,[19] the printing of
which had been completed by 26 June.[20] In his controversy with John
Eck the previous year, Luther had already argued that the papacy is
of purely human origin, that it is subject to judgment on the basis of
Scripture, and that it is possible (as in the case of the Greeks) to be
Christian without being subject to the authority of the pope.[21] All
these points are reiterated against Alveld.[22] More interesting in the
present context, however, is that in his refutation of Alveld, Luther
throws further light on the circumstances and the thinking that were
leading to his appeal to "the Christian nobility" to intervene in "spiritual" matters.

The pope and all his "Romanists," as Luther now calls them,
behave as if the papacy were the Antichrist and commit all kinds of
"spiritual and worldly knavery." They do not "feed the sheep," as
Christ commanded,[23] but prohibit the preaching of the gospel, allowing it and the Christian faith to collapse everywhere in the world."
Meanwhile, these "thieves, knaves, and robbers" burden Christendom with human laws designed to channel the wealth of the world to
Rome. They sell bishoprics, impose annates, annex parishes and religious foundations, peddle indulgences, and practice every other kind
of "robbery" and "extortion" they can think of. Since the pope does
not prevent this "blasphemous knavery," German princes and
nobles, out of concern both for the material welfare of their subjects
and for the honour of Christ, will have to do something about it. For
"the horrible disgrace of Christendom" has gone so far *"that there is no
more hope on earth except with secular authority."*[24]

Here, to an even greater degree than was the case in the *Treatise on
Good Works*, Luther makes clear that the pope and his "Romanists,"
who claim to possess an authority that is both absolute and higher
than any other, are not only bad pastors, and thus guilty of "spiritual

---

[19] *Von dem Bapstum zu Rome widder den hochberumpten Romanisten zu Leiptzck*: WA
6:285-324; LW 39:55-104.

[20] WA 6:281; LW 39:53.

[21] Hendrix, *Luther and the Papacy* (as in note 7), 81-89; Brecht, *Martin Luther* (as in
note 6), 285-95.

[22] See especially WA 6:321-22; LW 39:101-2.

[23] John 21:15-17.

[24] WA 6: 287-89, 308, 316, 322-23; LW 39:58-61, 84, 95, 102-03 (emphasis
added).

knavery," but also "thieves and robbers," and thus guilty of worldly or secular knavery. In neither case can a clergy subject to Rome provide reform. Thus hope lies with the secular authorities alone. Once again, however, Luther insists on the absolute secularity of secular authority. In the New Testament, he says, "no one is commanded by a clear word of God to exercise secular authority, even though no authority rises without God's hidden order. That is why St. Peter calls such governments human ordinances,[25] because they rule without the word of God, but not without God's help. Accordingly, they need not be godly."[26] Luther once again leaves unclear just what the "something" is that the incumbents of such authority should do to rescue Christendom from the Romanists.

In addition to this revisitation and limited elaboration of issues already dealt with in the *Treatise on Good Works*, the treatise *On the Papacy in Rome* includes a discussion of the meaning of the terms "Christendom" (*Christenheit*) and "Christian community" (*Christlich gemeyn*) that is of enduring significance for the development of Luther's thought on relations between church and state. Using "Christendom" and "Christian community" interchangeably with "church" (*Kirche*), Luther identifies three distinct meanings of the terms. According to the first, the only one that Luther finds rooted in Scripture, Christendom is "an assembly of all the people on earth who believe in Christ." It is not a physical assembly but rather a spiritual community of those who, in the words of St. Paul,[27] share "one baptism, one faith, one Lord" and "have no other head than Christ, even on earth." In other words, it is "the communion of saints" referred to in the Apostles' Creed. It is this spiritual unity alone, not physical location or external unity with Rome, that creates Christendom. As Christ himself said, "My kingdom is not of this world,"[28] and, even more clearly: "The kingdom of God does not come with external gestures, nor will anyone say, 'Lo, here it is' or 'There it is,' because the kingdom of God is within you."[29] Thus it is "a stinking lie" to say that Christendom is in Rome or that its head and power are there as a matter of divine order.[30]

---

[25] 1 Pet. 2:13.
[26] WA 6:318; LW 39:97.
[27] Eph. 4:5.
[28] John 18:36.
[29] Luke 17:20-21.
[30] WA 6:292-96; LW 39:65-69.

In addition to this scriptural way of speaking of "the holy church and of Christendom," there is a second way, according to which "Christendom is called an assembly in a house, or in a parish, a bishopric, an archbishopric, or a papacy." To this assembly belong the external forms of religion. In the Christendom so defined, bishops, priests, and members of religious orders are called the "spiritual estate," not because of their faith, for they may not have any, but because they have been externally anointed, wear distinctive vestments, and bear responsibility for the conduct of external worship. Although the words "spiritual" and "church," which refer only to the inner faith that alone makes true priests and Christians, are misused when applied to such externals, this manner of speaking has spread everywhere, producing the misconception that "such external glitter is the spiritual and true estate of Christendom or of the church." It is, however, only canon and human laws that call such externals "church" or "Christendom," not Scripture. It is therefore necessary to speak of two churches and to use two distinct names for them. The first church, the essential, basic, and true one, must be called "spiritual, internal Christendom," while the second, "which is man-made and external," must be called "physical, external Christendom." The former is governed by Christ alone, while the latter is ruled by canon law and by prelates — popes, cardinals, bishops, priests, etc. — whether they are true Christians or not. These two churches are, nevertheless, inseparable, like body and soul. For though it is possible to be a member of the external church without being a true Christian, that external church "never really exists without some people who are true Christians."[31]

According to a third way of speaking, it is not the Christian assembly itself that is called "the church" but rather "the houses that are built for worship." This has led to the buildings and other temporal goods of physical Christendom being called "spiritual" or "ecclesiastical" goods while the goods of laymen are called "worldly," even when they are better Christians and more truly spiritual than the clergy. The resulting pagan wrangles over the worldly goods that canon and human law have wrongly defined as "spiritual" goods have led to great confusion about the distinction between the spiritual and the physical church.[32]

---

[31] WA 6:296-97; LW 39:69-71.
[32] WA 6:297; LW 39:71.

From Luther's exploration of the various meanings of "Christendom" and "church," it is clear that, in his view, the true, inward church and the external, physical church, though intimately related, were not identical. Many of the features of the external, physical church that were in common parlance called "spiritual" were in fact matters of human origin and not in themselves an essential part of the inward, spiritual church. Moreover, many of the abuses committed by "the spiritual estate" were secular rather than spritual in nature. This understanding of what was and was not part of the true church would continue to be of fundamental importance long after its immediate use here as a weapon against the claims of the Roman church.

The content of the two treatises considered so far indicates that Luther's plan to invoke the intervention of secular government posed two difficult questions. The first one, already stated with reference to the content of the *Treatise on Good Works*, was that of the extent to which Christian secular government could in an emergency intervene in the routine jurisdiction of the clergy. The second question, posed more clearly in *On the Papacy in Rome*, was that of the extent to which any church or clerical establishment could retain independent control of human externals with no genuine status as "spiritual" matters. Do the external, man-made, secular aspects of church life belong under the control of a church competent to govern its own external affairs or do they belong by definition under the control of secular rulers equipped with a divine mandate to govern in all matters outside the internal realm of the spirit? The first question would be clearly posed and answered in the *Address to the Christian Nobility* while the second would be addressed only in part.

In the first week of June 1520, before *On the Papacy in Rome* had appeared in print, Luther received a copy of the *Epitoma responsionis ad Martinum Luther*, in which his old adversary in Rome, the Dominican Sylvester Prierias, defended papal absolutism with arguments that Luther found contemptible.[33] This appears to have been the last straw in Luther's encounter with the papacy. He immediately arranged for his own annotated version of Prierias' work to be published, complete with a sulphurous denunciation of the Rome of

---

[33] WA 6:325-26.

Antichrist and a formal farewell to it.[34] At the same time, he
announced to Georg Spalatin his intention "to issue a broadside
[*publicam schedam*] to [Emperor] Charles and the nobility of Germany against the tyranny and baseness of the Roman curia."[35] On
23 June he sent the manuscript to his close friend and Wittenberg
colleague, Nikolaus von Amsdorf, describing it to him as the product of their joint intention to address something to "the Christian
nobility of the German Nation" and soliciting Amsdorf's suggestions for improvement.[36] By mid-August the "broadside" had
grown into a major treatise and had been published under the title
*Address to the Christian Nobility of the German Nation Concerning the Reform
of the Christian Estate.*[37]

In the letter to Amsdorf that serves as the preface to the *Address*,
Luther summarizes with impressive brevity his reason for directing
an appeal to the nobility. "[I have] put together a few points on the
matter of the reform of the Christian estate, to be laid before the
Christian nobility of the German nation, in the hope that God may
help his church through the laity, since the clergy, to whom this task
more properly belongs, have grown quite indifferent."[38] The treatise
is, in other words, the product of Luther's continuing preoccupation
with the situation already addressed in the *Treatise on Good Works* and
On the Papacy in Rome. But it constitutes an advance over its predecessors in two major respects. First, rather than simply reiterate the gen-

---

[34] The planned publication is mentioned in letters of 7 June to Johann Heß and
Georg Spalatin (WA-Br 2:118, 120). By 13 June, the work was in press (ibid., 122),
and by the 26th the printing, as well as that of *On the Papacy in Rome*, had been completed (ibid., 130). The text is in WA 6:328-48.

[35] WA 6:120 (Luther to Spalatin, circa 7 June 1520): "Est animus publicam
schedam edere ad Carolum & totius germanie nobilitatem aduersus Ro[manae]
Curie tyrannidem & nequitatem."

[36] WA 6:404; LW 44:123. On 18 August, Philip Melanchthon wrote to Johann
Lange that Luther had been motivated to write the work by "certain persons whom
we both esteem highly" (*Melanchthons Werke in Auswahl*, ed. Robert Stupperich et al.,
7/1 [Gütersloh: Gerd Mohn, 1971]:87). Whether these "persons" included, in addition to Amsdorf and other university colleagues, members of the Saxon court, is not
clear. While it goes without saying that Luther learned much about imperial politics
and other matters from friends and acquaintances at court, Karl Bauer's argument
("Luther's Aufruf an den Adel, die Kirche zu reformieren," *Archiv für Reformationsgeschichte* 32 [1935]:167-217) that the *Address* was written at the instigation of members of the Saxon court rather than on Luther's own initiative fails for want of compelling evidence.

[37] *An den Christlichen Adel deutscher Nation von des Christlichen standes besserung*, WA
6:404-469; LW 44:123-217.

[38] WA 6:404; LW 44:123.

eral observation that Christian rulers must do "something," Luther calls on the emperor and the nobility to summon a church council. This means that his earlier fear of a council dominated by the pope and the Romanists[39] has given way to hope for a council free of such domination. Second, Luther now, for the first time, provides a coherent theological argument that both justifies governmental action in support of reform and carefully sets limits to that action.

This new degree of specificity about the nature and the extent of secular involvement in ecclesiastical reform may well have been inspired by the belief that effective governmental action was an imminent possibility. Certain features of the *Address* appear, at any rate, to have been designed to capitalize on what must have seemed to be a favourable political climtate in Germany at the time. It is striking, for example, that the title of the treatise is not *An die christlichen Obrigkeiten der deutschen Nation* (a title that would, with constitutional correctness, have included the governments of the imperial cities) but rather *An den christlichen Adel*, and that this exclusivity is duplicated in the opening salutation to the emperor and the nobility.[40] In the new emperor, Charles V, Luther was addressing not only a "young man of noble birth ... [who] has awakened great hopes of good in many hearts," but also a man with his own grievances against the Curia, which had tried desperately to prevent his election as emperor. It must have seemed reasonable to expect that Charles, like his medieval predecessors, would support reform and defend his subjects against exploitation by Rome. As for Luther's hopes concerning the nobility in general, he may have been influenced by offers of support received in the wake of the Leipzig Debate from the imperial knights Ulrich von Hutten, Franz von Sickingen, and Silvester von Schaumberg. Although there was no real alliance of aims or interests between Luther and these noble freebooters (whose propensity to violence he would in due course denounce), they seem to have given him a consciousness of political support outside Saxony that encouraged him in his determination to publish an appeal to the nobility.[41] In formulating the appeal, moreover, he took care to

---

[39] See above, p. 53.

[40] WA 6:405; LW 44:124.

[41] Brecht, *Martin Luther* (as in note 6), 353-54. Of the sources cited by Brecht, see especially WA-Br 2:162 (Luther to Johann Voigt, 3 August 1520): "Franciscus Sickingerus per Huttenum promittit tutelam mihi contra omnes hostes. Idem facit

incorporate into it a long catalogue of specific reforms similar to those in the traditional lists of German grievances against Rome, thus allying himself with the anti-Roman sentiment that was the common property of all the German princely courts, including those of the ecclesiastical princes.[42] If there was thus reasonable ground for hope that an appeal to the emperor and the nobility would evoke from them serious action in support of genuine reform, then it was important to be more specific than hitherto about the nature and the limits of such action.

The *Address* is divided into three sections. In the first, Luther attacks the "three walls" behind which the Romanists have shielded themselves from reform.[43] The second section,[44] which appears to have been part of Luther's original draft, is a brief discussion of measures needed to curb "Roman thievery and robbery," while the third,[45] which gives every indication of having been tacked on later, is the catalogue of traditional grievances referred to above. The most important section by far is the attack on "the three walls," in which Luther elaborates the view of the role of secular government in church reform to which he would adhere virtually without change for the remainder of the 1520s.[46]

The Romanists, says Luther, have cleverly built three walls around

---

Sylvester de Schawenberg, cum nobilibus Franciae, cuius literas pulchras habeo ad me. Nihil timemus amplius, sed iam edo librum vulgarem contra Papam de statu ecclesiae emendando: hic Papam acerrime tracto et quasi Antichristum."

[42] For many decades already, German officials had been compiling long lists of *gravamina* (grievances) about annates, papal usurpation of the right of appointment to German benefices, and a host of other curial expedients for "extorting" money from the Germans. The latest list of "*Gravamina* of the German Nation Against Rome" had been presented at the Diet of Augsburg in 1518, where Luther would have had direct access to them. The text, together with a related letter to emperor and estates by Erhard von der Mark, bishop of Liège, is in *Dr. Martin Luthers Sämmtliche Schriften*, ed. Johann Georg Walch et al., 15 (St. Louis: Concordia, 1899): 452-71.

[43] WA 6:406-15; LW 44:126-39.

[44] WA 6:415-27; LW 44:139-56.

[45] WA 6:427-69; LW 44:156-217.

[46] Despite the faults (including the wholesale omission of crucial evidence from the 1530s) that render it unacceptable as a general account of Luther's position on relations between church and state, Karl Holl's essay (1911) "Luther und das landesherrliche Kirchenregiment," reprinted in his *Gesammelte Aufsätze zur Kirchengeschichte* I (7th ed., Tübingen: Mohr [Siebeck], 1948):326-380, is still worth reading for its shrewdly perceptive analysis of the *Address to the Christian Nobility* and (despite overemphasis on the "congregational" element in Luther's thought) of developments in Luther's thinking during the remainder of the 1520s. Also instructive, though equally guilty of not getting beyond the 1520s, is Karl Müller, *Kirche, Gemeinde und Obrigkeit nach Luther* (Tübingen: Mohr [Siebeck], 1910).

themselves, with the result that no one has been able to reform them. The first wall is the claim that spiritual authority is above secular authority and that, therefore, secular authority has no jurisdiction over them. Though it takes Luther a while to make the point clear, this is the wall that protects the Romanists from action by the secular authorities against those ecclesiastical abuses that are in reality secular crimes. The second wall, the claim that only the pope may interpret Scripture, and the third, the claim that only the pope can summon a council, together make it impossible for Christian rulers to summon a council that will sit in judgment on the pope on the basis of Scripture and enact appropriate reforms. Luther's weapon against these three walls "of straw and paper" is the doctrine of the priesthood of all believers which, in the course of the attack on the first wall, he fully elaborates for the first time. The doctrine is too well known to require detailed summary here, but its practical implications need to be examined with some care.

Luther rejects as "pure invention" the traditional claim that Christians are divided into "the spiritual estate" (pope, bishops, priests, and monks) and "the secular estate" (princes, lords, artisans, farmers, and all other laypeople), with the former being more Christian and spiritual than the latter. All are, by virtue of baptism and faith, equally members of the spiritual estate and consequently all are priests. There is thus no difference in Christian status between laymen and priests, princes and bishops, religious and secular. Priests are simply those who minister to the community by exercising, on behalf of all, the priestly authority that is common to all. It is the call of the community, not episcopal consecration, that makes someone a priest. Only their office distinguishes clergymen from laymen. They are not, and cannot be, any more Christian than anyone else.[47]

By the same token, however, Christian secular rulers are not, and cannot be, any less Christian than anyone else. Indeed, since those who exercise secular authority have the same baptism, the same faith, and the same gospel as other Christians, it must be conceded that — like cobblers, blacksmiths, and peasants — "they are priests and bishops" and that "their office ... has a proper and useful place in the Christian community." Significantly, however, Luther here takes the opportunity to reassert the *equality* of all Christians. Bap-

---

[47] WA 6: 407-408; LW 44:127-8, 129-30.

tism, he says, makes of every Christian a priest, bishop, and pope, but it is not seemly that just anyone should exercise that office. "Because we are all priests of equal standing, no one must push himself forward and take it upon himself, without our consent and election, to do that for which we all have authority. For no one dare take upon himself what is common to all without the authority and consent of the community." In other words, emperors, princes, and other secular rulers have, by virtue of their baptism, *exactly the same authority in the church as other Christians*, no less than the others, but also no more.[48]

Given, then, that Christian secular rulers do not occupy a lower position on any hierarchical order of Christian status than do the clergy, there is no justification whatever for the old and long-disputed clerical claim to be "above" secular authority and consequently to enjoy exemption from the jurisdiction of the civil courts when they commit breaches of the civil law. Quite the contrary, in fact. When Paul said to all Christians, "Let every soul be subject to secular authority,"[49] he included the souls of the pope and all other clergymen in that subjection. Since, moreover, the office of secular authority is the divinely ordained one of punishing the wicked and protecting the good, it follows that pope, prelates, and all clergy are answerable to that authority for their manifold worldly wickedness. Secular rulers are no more prevented by supposed inferior status from doing their proper work vis-à-vis the clergy than are tailors, cobblers, stonemasons, carpenters, cooks, innkeepers, and farmers from supplying clergymen with clothes, shoes, housing, meat, and drink. If, therefore, the pope and his "mob" are guilty of robbing and defrauding Christians by collecting annates, selling bishop's *pallia*, peddling indulgences, or what have you, the secular authorities are free to exercise their office against them without hindrance. "Whoever is guilty, let him suffer."[50] In his catalogue of the "robbery, thievery, and skulduggery" inflicted on Germany by the pope and the Romanists — a catalogue much longer and more detailed in the *Address* than those in the treatises preceding it — Luther insistently and repeatedly drives home the point that both the emperor in particular and the princes and nobles in general have, by virtue of their status as secular

48 WA 6:408; LW 44:129.
49 Rom. 13:1.
50 WA 6:409-11; LW 44:130-33.

rulers, the right and duty to protect their subjects against such criminal behaviour.[51]

As for the second wall, Luther finds it "even more loosely built and less substantial than the first." The claim that the pope alone may interpret Scripture and that he is infallible in matters of faith is "an outrageous fancied fable" invented by the Romanists. The point here is not simply that the pope is subject to Scripture rather than the other way around, but also that the whole Christian community has the right and duty to judge the pope in the light of Scripture and reject the teachings of a heretical or unbelieving pope. Therefore, if it happens that the pope and his cohort are bad Christians and teach what is contrary to Scripture, ordinary Christians, who have been commanded to test and judge what is right or wrong in matters of faith, should side with Scripture against the pope and call the Romanists to account for their errors. To do so, however, they must have resort to a council, something against which the Romanists have erected their third wall.[52]

The claim of the Romanists that the pope alone can summon a council and confirm its decisions is a human regulation and thus valid only "as long as it is not harmful to Christendom or contrary to the laws of God." Therefore, if the pope deserves punishment at the hands of a council, the regulation giving him the sole right to summon a council is no longer valid.[53] In the past, many councils were called by persons other than the pope. Indeed, the most famous council of all, the Council of Nicaea, was called by Emperor Constantine, and later councils were convoked by other emperors. But for Luther the crucial matter is not that there is historical prece-

---

[51] Here are the two best and clearest examples from among many. WA 6:420: "Helt unnd gilt es, szo der Bapst des andern tags seiner erwelung regel und gesetz macht in seiner Cancelley, dadurch unszer stifft und pfrundt geraubt werden, da her kein recht zu hat, so sol es viel mehr gelten, szo der keyszer Carolus des andern tags seiner kronung regel und gesetz gebe, durch gantz deutsche landt keyn lehen unnd prfund mehr gen Rom lassenn kummenn durch das Baptsts Monat, und was hynein kummen ist, widder frey werde, unnd von den Romischen reuber erloszet, *da zu er recht hat von ampt wegenn seynis schwerdts*" (emphasis added). Ibid., 427-28: "Zum ersten, das ein yglich Furst, Adel, Stat, in yhren unterthanen frisch an vorpiet, die Annaten genn Rom zugeben, und sie gar abthue: dan der bapst hat...ein reuberey gemacht ausz den Annaten, zu schaden und schanden gemeyn deutscher Nation.... Szo ist die weltlich gewalt schuldig, zuschutzen die unschuldigen und weren das unrecht, wie sanct Pauls Ro. xiii. leret, und sanct Peter i. Pet. ij.... "

[52] WA 6:411-13; LW 44:133-36.

[53] WA 6:413.12-16, 414.4-18, 27-29; LW 44:136, 138.

dent for councils summoned by emperors but that *all Christians* have
the priestly right to summon a council if one is needed and the pope
refuses to call one. "*[W]hen necessity demands it*, and the pope is an
offense to Christendom, *the first man who is able should, as a true member
of the whole body*, do what he can to bring about a truly free council."[54] If, however, the right to summon a council in an emergency is
shared equally by all Christians, the ability to do so effectively is not.
"No one" — not cobblers, carpenters, stonemasons, or even Wittenberg theologians — "can do this [i.e., summon a council] so well as
the secular authorities, especially since they are also fellow-Chris-
tians, fellow-priests, fellow-members of the spiritual estate, fellow
lords over all things. Whenever it is necessary or profitable, they
ought to exercise the office and work [i.e., the office of government]
which they have received from God over everyone." They must not
stand by and do nothing simply because they do not possess routine
jurisdiction in the matter. In a human emergency — a fire in a city
or an enemy attack on it, for example — every citizen has the duty
to sound the alarm and summon the other citizens. The same is true
for an emergency in "the spiritual city of Christ." Honour and gratitude go to him "who makes known the presence of the enemy from
hell and rouses Christian people and calls them together" into a
council.[55]

The position that Luther has taken here has a complexity and an
inner tension that would never be completely eliminated from his
thought on the role of Christian magistrates in the church. It
involves a difficult and cumbersome distinction among (1) the routine authority that the prince exercises as political sovereign, (2) the
routine authority that the prince as baptized Christian shares equally with all other Christians, and (3) the special authority that the
prince as baptized Christian has in an emergency because he happens to be a prince. In making this distinction Luther remains true
to his conviction that the office of secular magistrate is the purely
secular one of preserving external peace and order and that church
reform is really the responsibility of the clergy exercising an authority delegated to them by the community of the faithful. To employ
the imagery used in the *Treatise on Good Works* but not repeated here
in the *Address to the Christian Nobility*, secular rulers are concerned only

54 WA 6:413.17-29; LW 44:136-37 (emphasis added).
55 WA 6:413.29-414.3; LW 44:137.

with matters pertaining to the Second Table of the Law; they have nothing to do with preaching the gospel, or with faith, or with the commandments of the First Table. Thus, even in an emergency, Luther cannot ask emperor and princes *as secular rulers* to exercise an authority in the church that they do not have. While he can ask them as secular rulers to deal with secular crimes committed by clergymen, he cannot ask them as secular rulers to call a church council. For that purpose, he has to address himself to emperor and princes in their capacity as individual Christians and participants in the priesthood of all believers and ask them to do what all Christians have the right and duty to do. In so addressing them, however, he invokes their status as secular rulers as justification for assigning to them *special* responsibility to act on behalf of their fellow Christians. They alone are the incumbents of an office that gives them authority over the whole community, which means that they alone have the wherewithal to bring into being the council that the pope and the Romanists are determined not to have.

It is thus clear that Luther was no believer in "Christian princes" in the sense of princes who hold office in a "Christian state" and who consequently have the routine obligation to establish and maintain true religion. There is here not even a hint that German princes should imitate the example of Old Testament kings who slew the prophets of Baal and restored true worship. And ancient Christian emperors are invoked as examples only in so far as they summoned councils; their destruction of pagan temples and their championing of orthodoxy against heresy goes unmentioned. Luther does, however, believe in Christian princes in the sense of Christians who happen to be princes and who thus can, in the context of a Christian community, use their princely authority to overcome an emergency in the church.[56] Though Luther does not say so, it seems clear that he expects the princes to do more than merely suggest or recommend attendance at a council. For their intervention to be effective, they will surely have to make free use of the power of the sword to compel participation in the council. It is equally obvious, however, that the job of the nobility is simply to "call" the council and see it through to

---

[56] The term "Notbischof" (emergency bishop) does not appear in Luther's works until 1539 and is used on only a few occasions in that year and in 1542. See James L. Schaaf, "Der Landesherr als Notbischof," in *Martin Luther und das Bischofsamt*, ed. Martin Brecht (Stuttgart: Calwer Verlag, 1990), 105-108.

a conclusion. It is job of the council, an ecclesiastical body, to deal with the internal affairs of the church.

This point is somewhat obscured by Luther's indication that his catalogue of specific reforms should be dealt with "either by secular authority or by a council,"[57] with no careful distinction drawn between the two. His intention, however, cannot be to say that it makes no difference whether reforms are enacted by a council or by secular rulers. His point, rather, is that all the needed reforms are "matters that ought properly to be dealt with in councils" and constantly tended to by the clergy but that, if councils and clergy fail in their duty, "ordinary people and the secular authorities" ought to take appropriate action.[58] Such action would consist either of direct governmental measures against ecclesiastical abuses that are secular crimes, or of the exercise, by the lay community under the leadership of its secular rulers, of the priestly right to deal with an emergency caused by the failure of the clergy in its spiritual responsibilities, or both. The aim is to restore the clergy to the normal exercise of its spiritual ministry, not to transfer any of their routine responsibility for spiritual matters and church governance to secular rulers.

There is, however, one passage in the catalogue of reforms in the *Address* where Luther does seem to call upon secular authority to intervene in spiritual matters. As he had already done in the *Treatise on Good Works* and in *On the Papacy in Rome,* Luther observes that the "barefaced robbery" of the Romanists is "ruinous to [both] the body and the soul of Christendom." In particular, the Romanists' practice of reserving German benefices for sale "to coarse, unlettered asses and ignorant knaves at Rome" not only enriches Rome at German expense but also undercuts the authority of German bishops and means that "the poor German people must do without competent and learned prelates and go from bad to worse." Thus, "for the salvation of the poor souls who perish because of this [Romanist] tyranny," the Christian nobility of Germany should decree that no further benefices be drawn into the hands of Rome, restore to German bishops the administration of German benefices, and pass legislation requiring that German bishops be confirmed in office, not by Rome

---

[57] This is the language used at the beginning of the third part of the treatise: WA 6:427; LW 44:156.

[58] This is the language used at the beginning of the second part of the treatise: WA 6:427; LW 44:156.

but, according to the decree of the Council of Nicaea, by the two nearest bishops or by the local archbishop. In this way they would show that "Germans do not intend to permit the holy name of Christ, in whose name all this knavery and destruction of souls goes on, to be scoffed at and scorned any longer, and that they have more regard for God's honor than for the authority of men."[59]

Since this is a question of the salvation of souls, the honour of God, and the constitution of the German church, rather than simply one of the protection of life and property, why does Luther assign responsibility to the nobility rather than to the council that he wants the nobility to call? It is inconceivable that someone who has just finished demonstrating at length that Christian rulers have no routine authority to summon a council could here be assigning them routine authority to supervise the German episcopate in the performance of their spiritual office. Luther's idea seems to be, rather, that the same kind of special intervention by Christian rulers that is necessary to the convocation of a truly free council will also be necessary to the restoration to the German bishops of their ability to exercise their spiritual office in the way that they should. Could a German episcopate subject to the tyranny of the Romanists be expected to participate effectively in a free council, pay attention to its decrees, or in any way provide genuine spiritual government? What Luther wants, then, is for Christian rulers to set the bishops free to do their proper work, not to take over that proper work for themselves. As he had put it in the *Treatise on Good Works*, if princes and nobles will "take the first step," bishops and clergy will "have reason to follow."[60]

There is one final issue to be dealt with. In the *Address*, Luther is clear that "in spiritual offices such as preaching and giving absolution" the clergy possess independent jurisdiction but that "in other matters" they are subject to secular authority.[61] He is, moreover, absolutely clear that those "other matters" include secular crimes committed by clergymen. But he neither poses nor answers the question of whether the category "other matters" also includes all the external, worldly matters of ecclesiastical life that, as he had explained in *On the Papacy in Rome*, are not an essential part of the

---

[59] WA 6:428.12-429.12; LW 157-58.
[60] See above, p. 53.
[61] WA 6:434.6-9; LW 44:165.

inward and spiritual church. The closest he comes to dealing with the
issue is in his recommendations concerning ecclesiastical courts. In
this connection, his main concerns are, first, that pope and bishops
should be more preoccupied with the scriptures, faith, and holy life
than with property and other secular matters, and second, that the
German nation should be "free and Christian again." He thus insists
that, as a general principle, "no secular matter" should be referred to
Rome but left instead to competent secular authority. With respect to
diocesan bishops' courts, he insists that they must deal exclusively
with "matters of faith and morals" and leave "matters of money and
property, life and honor" to the secular judges. Nevertheless, he continues, "it might be granted that cases concerning benefices or livings
be tried before bishops, archbishops, and primates," and that there
might be a national consistory court to exercise the appellate jurisdiction currently in the hands of Rome.[62] With respect to property and
goods, then, Luther's position is that it is a matter properly reserved
to the jurisdiction of secular government, which might concede to
church officials a degree of self-administration over the properties
from which clergymen derive their incomes. But he has nothing to
say about those externals, such as ceremonies and vestments, which,
as he had argued in *On the Papacy in Rome*, are intimately connected
with the spiritual office of preaching and teaching but are, at the
same time, not an integral part of the inward, spiritual church. He
would shortly argue that such matters, along with the appointment
and dismissal of pastors, were subject to the free choice of a Christian
community, a choice that could be exercised at the congregational
level if necessary.[63] But when the exercise of this right produced confusion and disorder in Saxony, Luther himself took the lead (1525-27)
in persuading the elector to institute a visitation that would impose
uniformity on the churches in his domains.[64] More about that
presently.

At the time of the publication of the *Address to the Christian Nobility*,
the entire development of the Lutheran territorial church and of the
thought that went with it still lay in the future. Though the details of
those later developments are beyond the scope of this article, a few

---

[62] WA 6:430-31; LW 44:160-61.

[63] See esp. *Das eyn Christliche versamlung odder gemeyune recht und macht habe, alle lere tzu
urteylen und lerer tzu beruffen, eyn und abtzusetzen, Grund und ursach aus der schrifft* (1523),
WA 11:408-16; and *De instituendis ministris Ecclesiae* (1523), WA 12:169-96.

[64] See Trüdinger, *Briefe und Gutachten* (as in note 5), 41-92.

observations about the lasting significance of what Luther said in 1520 are in order.

The most striking feature of Luther's first appeal to the German princes for help with ecclesiastical reform was his refusal to attribute to the secular office itself any authority at all in matters of faith or church governance. This is what dictated his convoluted argument that, in an emergency, princes who as princes have no authority to call a council have, as baptized Christians, not merely the same priestly right as other baptized Christians to call a council but rather, because they are princes, a special obligation to do so. Virtually all of Luther's fellow reformers would take the much simpler view that a Christian prince, both as prince and as baptized Christian, has the routine duty, not limited to emergencies, to supervise the establishment and maintenance of true religion. They were able to do this because they had come to the Reformation already committed to the conventional view, most recently and most cogently summarized by Erasmus, that the *respublica* itself is a religious entity whose ruler, the prince, has as his chief duty the establishment of true religion among his subjects, and that public peace and order depend on his performance of this duty.[65] What they learned from Luther about faith, the priesthood of all believers, the true church, the externals of religion, and magisterial responsibility for public peace and order, they adapted to this view.[66] Thus, while they agreed with Luther that the priesthood of all believers took authority away from the Catholic hierarchy and gave it to the Christian community as a whole, they took the view that the everyday exercise of that authority was best entrusted to "the foremost members"[67] and natural leaders of that community, Christian secular magistrates. And while they accepted without qualification Luther's view that matters of faith are beyond the authority of secular government and that the exercise of the Christian ministry belongs by right to the

---

[65] James M. Estes, "*Officium principis christiani*: Erasmus and the Origins of the Protestant State Church," *Archiv für Reformationsgeschichte* 83 (1992):49-72; id., "Erasmus, Melanchthon" (as in note 3) , 21-39.

[66] For a more detailed discussion of the way in which Luther's views were appropriated and adapted by those who had inherited the Erasmian view of the Christian state, see Estes, *Christian Magistrate* (as in note 4), 18-28.

[67] The phrase *praecipua membra ecclesiae* was first used by Melanchthon in 1537, though the idea is already present in 1520 in Luther's justification of the special obligation of princes, as baptized Christians who happen to be the incumbents of secular authority, to summon a council.

clergy, they also took seriously his view that the externals of religion
(including ceremonies and other external aspects of preaching and
the administration of the sacraments) are not part of the inward,
spiritual church. From this they drew the conclusion that such externals fall by definition under the authority of Christian secular rulers
who must, if they are to do their duty to maintain public peace and
order, imitate the example of the best Old Testament kings and early Christian emperors by establishing and maintaining true doctrine
and worship and abolishing false teaching and worship.[68] Christian
magistrates, in other words, are not the leaders of a merely human
enterprise who "need not be godly." They are, rather, the heads of
an entity established by God for the propagation of true religion and
who thus have a great deal to do with "gospel, faith, and the commandments of the First Table." Their role is in fact that of "custodi-
ans, with respect to external discipline, of *both* Tables of the Law."[69]
Although it took until 1535 to get this view of Christian magistracy
into its mature and lasting form,[70] it always had the advantage of the
relative simplicity that resulted from not requiring the prince to be
sometimes prince, sometimes Christian brother, and sometimes
both, as well as that of being in harmony with the territorial rulers'
own view of their office.[71] It was, moreover, especially in its mature
form, a view that could be supported with a great deal of (sometimes
strenuously interpreted) biblical evidence.[72]

The reasons for Luther's apparently unique belief in the absolute
secularity of secular authority, so out of harmony with the tradition

---

[68] For the development of Melanchthon's thought on these issues, see Estes,
"Erasmus, Melanchthon" (as in note 3), 29-38. For an important theological controversy over these issues, see *Whether Secular Government Has the Right to Wield the Sword in
Matters of Faith: A Controversy in Nürnberg in 1530 over Freedom of Worship and the Authority
of Secular Government in Spiritual Matters*, trans. and ed. James M. Estes (Toronto: Centre for Reformation and Renaissance Studies, 1994).

[69] Though this phrase was first used by Melanchthon in the second edition of his
Loci communes (1535), the idea it expresses was implicit in his thought as early as 1522.
See Estes, "Erasmus, Melanchthon" (as in note 3), 30-31.

[70] See note 3.

[71] See note 2.

[72] Particularly, though not exclusively, Old Testament texts commanding kings
and princes to serve the Lord and avoid his wrath by doing God's will and governing
in accordance with his law. Deut. 17:18-20, Ps. 2:10-12 (cf. Wisd. 6:1-6), Ps. 82, and
Isa. 49:23 became classic texts for this purpose. To the best of my knowledge,
Melanchthon and his colleagues began to use the last three of these texts only in
1530 or later, as part of the reworking of Lutheran thought referred to above in note
3.

that supplied the working assumptions of his fellow reformers, are difficult to pin down with certainty. There are grounds for suspecting that the original source was the influence of his Ockhamist teachers.[73] As we have seen, moreover, his own understanding of the doctrine of the priesthood of all believers dictated the conclusion that ultimate authority in the church belonged to all Christians equally, not to Christian princes or magistrates in particular. These theological motives were in due course reinforced by more practical ones. In the years immediately following the publication of the *Address to the Christian Nobility*, unhappy experiences with "godly" rulers produced a distrust and dislike of the German princes that reinforced his disinclination to attribute any responsibility for religion to the secular office itself.[74] For all these reasons (and, possibly, for others yet to be divined), Luther only slowly and reluctantly adopted a less cautious attitude toward princely intervention in the affairs of the church. In 1528, for example, his retroactive justification of his appeal to the Saxon elector to appoint a visitation commission (normally an episcopal responsibility) employed the same unwieldy arguments that he had used in 1520 to justify calling on the emperor and nobility to summon a church council. Once again he made the cumbersome dis-

---

[73] At all events, scholars have found in the political thought of William of Ockham some major emphases strikingly similar to the principal emphases in Luther's thought in the 1520s: namely, that secular authority is independent of spiritual authority and not necessarily Christian; that clergymen who commit secular crimes make themselves liable to secular jurisdiction; that secular rulers, who have no spiritual functions, are excluded from regular control of ecclesiastical affairs (though they have ultimate jurisdiction over the church's temporal goods); that, consequently, secular rulers may intervene in ecclesiastical affairs only in a grave emergency, and then only because they are Christian, not because they hold secular office. See Wilhelm Kölmel, *Wilhelm von Ockham und seine kirchenpolitische Schriften* (Essen: Ludgerus-Verlag Hubert Wingen, 1962), esp. pp. 167-70, 217-26; Arthur Stephen McGrade, *The Political Thought of William of Ockham: Personal and Institutional Principles* (Cambridge: Cambridge University Press, 1974), chapter 3.

[74] For example, in the name of their duty as "Christian princes," the emperor and the nobility of the German nation outlawed Luther and his followers in the Edict of Worms (May 1521) and ordered that his books be burned. Similarly, Luther's followers were harrassed and sometimes jailed by "godly princes" in the Habsburg Netherlands (1521-22) and in Albertine Saxony (1522-23), whose ruler, Duke George, also urged the Imperial Council of Regency to take harsh action against Luther's followers. These events left their mark on Luther's treatise *Von weltlicher Oberkeit, wie weit man ihr Gehorsam schuldig sei* (1523), with its sharp differentiation between secular authority and spiritual authority and its harsh denunciation of princes who interfere in God's kingdom by lording it over men's consciences. See Estes, "Godly Magistrates" (as in note 3), 471, esp. notes 18 and 23.

tinction between what the prince could and could not do as prince and what the prince could and should do as a Christian brother who happened to be a prince. By this time, however, the credibility of the distinction had been diminished by Luther's discovery that princely responsibility for the maintenance of public peace and order required that the elector impose conformity on those who did not voluntarily accept the new church order established by the visitation.[75]

Luther's problem was that his thought was tending simultaneously in two contradictory directions: on the one hand, toward a church free to regulate its own internal affairs without governmental interference (at least in all matters other than the management of its property), something that he would have liked but that circumstances did not allow; and, on the other hand, toward a church established under the patronage and protection of secular rulers, something that he needed but with which he was not really comfortable. By 1530 he had made up his mind in favour of the latter. His sense of the need for governmental protection for the newly established churches in Saxony and elsewhere against the twin dangers of Radical subversion on the one hand and Catholic restoration on the other, his growing confidence in the genuinely Christian character and motives of his own Saxon princes, and (probably) the cogency of the arguments of Melanchthon and others, led him to adopt a far more positive attitude toward the role of Christian magistrates in the establishment and maintenance of true religion. He stopped belabouring the distinction between the prince as prince and the prince as individual Christian, abandoned his limitation of princely intervention to emergencies, and described the highest duty of kings and lords as that of furthering the teaching of God's word, supporting the pastors and securing their freedom to preach, and warding off sects and false teachers.[76] At the same time, however, in his commentary on Psalm 101 (1535), the very work that included the most enthusiastic endorsement of the *cura religionis* of Christian princes that he would ever write, he pugnaciously reasserted his belief in the secularity of secular authority in language reminiscent of that used in 1520.[77] This

---

[75] WA 26:195-201 (Luther's preface to the published text of the *Unterricht der Visitatoren*, 1528).

[76] Estes, "Godly Magistrates" (as in note 3), 473-78.

[77] In 1535: "[T]he secular kingdom ... can have its own existence without God's kingdom... God made the secular government subordinate and subject to reason,

meant, first of all, that he still could not derive a princely obligation to support true religion from the nature of the secular office itself. He could only affirm, at great length and with considerable repetition, the right and duty of those extremely rare princes who are genuinely Christian and who are up to the task to serve God by maintaining true doctrine and worship and by abolishing heresy and idolatry. It also meant that he had to include a strenuous and not entirely convincing rebuttal of the perception that he was contradicting himself. Thus, even though he was now in virtually complete agreement with Melanchthon on the question of the religious duty of Christian magistrates, his stubborn refusal to acknowledge the existence of an intrinsically Christian state meant that the concision, clarity, and logical tidiness of Melanchthon's position always eluded him.[78]

What, then, was the significance of Luther's first appeal to secular authority for help with the Reformation in 1520? Most simply stated, it was that he used the doctrine of the priesthood of all believers to transfer authority in the church from the Roman hierarchy to the Christian community as a whole, a community that had secular princes and magistrates as its foremost members and natural leaders. This is what opened the door to everything that followed. Luther's initial hope that limited, short-term, emergency intervention by emperor and nobility would restore a reformed version of the existing hierarchy to its proper function of church governance soon gave way to the realization that the reform movement would have to enlist the help of territorial rulers to replace the old hierarchy with new institutions. Luther's hope that this too might be done on the basis of limited, short-term emergency intervention by secular rulers acting to sustain a church independent of their authority soon gave way to the realization that the need of the new territorial churches for protection from external threats and internal disorder was going to end in the

---

because it is to have no jurisdiction over the welfare of souls or things of eternal value but only over physical and temporal goods ... For this reason nothing is taught in the gospel about how it is to be maintained and regulated, except that the Gospel bids people to honor it and not oppose it." WA 51:238.28-29, 242.1-6.; LW 13:193, 198. And in 1520 (as cited on p. 57 above): "[N]o one is commanded by a clear word of God to exercise secular authority ... [Secular] governments [are human ordinances] that rule without the word of God ... Accordingly, they need not be godly."

[78] Estes, "Godly Magistrates" (as in note 3), 478-83.

extension and consolidation of the *landesherrliches Kirchenregiment* that was already more than a century old. Luther's refusal to believe in the working assumption of this development, namely that the secular office as such included responsibility for the establishment and maintenance of true religion, made it difficult for him to adjust to it or to find simple, straightforward arguments to justify it. His fellow reformers, on the other hand, blessed as they were with the concept of the Christian state in the form that Erasmus had given it, had a much easier time accepting and justifying magisterial authority over their new churches. It must not be forgotten, however, that a great deal of the theology to which Luther had already given expression in 1520 entered into that justification. It was his doctrine of the priesthood of all believers, his elaboration of the various meanings of "church," his identification of many "spiritual" abuses as secular crimes, and his definition of the externals of religion as human matters outside the realm of faith, that they used to vindicate the *cura religionis* of Christian magistrates. Their thought on this matter was just as authentically "Lutheran" as his, and his thought eventually became, in its own cumbersome and verbose way, the practical equivalent of theirs. If *das Kirchenregiment der evangelischen Landesherren* did not represent Luther's earliest and purest intentions, it nevertheless corresponded to his needs, and he contributed at least as much to its establishment as anyone else.

REFUGEES AND REFORM:
BANISHMENT AND EXILE IN EARLY MODERN AUGSBURG[1]

J. Jeffery Tyler*

I. *A Miserable Soul ("ein armer tropf")*

On the second day of 1599 a desperate woman opened the new year in court, facing two magistrates from the city council of Augsburg. She had already been in prison, awaiting her hearing for an unspecified amount of time.[2] Her interrogators probed for particular information; in response she identified herself as Sabina Hartmännin, originally from Augsburg and thirty years of age.[3] Queries continued about Sabina's criminal record, her destitution and ill health, illegal presence in the city and undesirable behavior. Sabina's replies exposed the nature and depth of her misery. Many of her answers reveal a life of begging and dissolute behavior, to which she had apparently turned in order to support herself and for which she had been previously expelled. Sabina had not eaten for two days and had planned to make a request for charitable assistance, but had been arrested beforehand.[4] She denied taking up a disreputable life in order to support herself.[5] At the end of her deposition Sabina Hartmännin threw herself on the

---

* Assistant Professor of Religion, Hope College

[1] I am grateful to Hope College for a Towsley Fellowship, which supported the research for this article; to Carl A. Hoffmann of the Universität Augsburg for his collegial assistance in the Stadtarchiv Augsburg and for access to his most recent work; to Roger Nemeth, Professor of Sociology at Hope College, for his generous guidance on the statistical data employed in this paper.

[2] "Actum Sambstags den 2 Januar anno 1599. Sabina Hartmännin von Augsburg Ist betlens halben Inn fronvest gelegt..." Stadtarchiv Augsburg (henceforth cited as StadtAA), Reichsstadt, Strafbuch des Rats 1596-1605, 68v, 3-5.

[3] "Sie haiß Sabina Hartmännin sei von Augsburg Ires alters 30 Iarn." Stadtarchiv Augsburg, Reichsstadt, Urgichten (henceforth cited as Urg.) 2 January 1599; on 21 September 1598 Sabina had previously appeared before the court and given her age as twenty-five; StadtAA, Reichsstadt, Urg. 21 September 1598.

[4] "... vnd sie getrug sich des betlens zubehelffen.... Sie sei hievor einmal betlens halben gezogen vnd hinauß gefürt worden.... In Zwen tag ... nichts zuo essen gehabt.... Vnd das almosen zubegern bis das sie etwas bekhommen, aber als bald desselben tags einzogen worden." StadtAA, Reichsstadt, Urg. 2 January 1599.

mercy of the court; the secretary recorded the content and tone of her plea:

> "She begged by God's will and grace for renewed access to the city especially because she is the child of a citizen. She was banished previously only because of her begging. Otherwise she will certainly perish, for of all the people she knows in her city (*heimat*) no one will give her anything. She wept bitterly and is a miserable soul (*ein armer tropff*)."[6]

Despite this desperate entreaty the magistrates ordered her expulsion from Augsburg and threatened her with physical punishment if she returned.[7]

The home city of Sabina Hartmännin had reached its financial and political apex by the time of her trial at the end of the sixteenth century. With a population of over 40,000 Augsburg had overtaken Nürnberg as the economic powerhouse of southern Germany, relying on the Fugger banking dynasty and the remarkable output of the city's textile industry as well as the renown of its armorers, gold and silversmiths; Augsburg was the city of imperial diets and often the beneficiary of the emperor's visitation and favor. The rule of an exclusively Protestant regime had endured for only a decade and

---

[5] "... aber sie hab nie vnzucht getriben." StadtAA, Reichsstadt, Urg. 2 January 1599.

[6] "Bitt vmb Gottes wille vnnd gnad wideröffnung der Statt sonderlich weil sie ein Burgers Kind darzu nur deß betlens hinauss geschafft worden. Dann sie sonsten verderben müeß weil sie Jedermann in ihr Heimat veisset vnd Ir also neimand nichts geben wölle. Hat bitterlich geweint vnd ist ein armer tropf." StadtAA, Reichsstadt, Urg. 2 January 1599.

[7] She received the sentence of *Stadtverweisung*; StadtAA, Reichsstadt, Urg. 2 January 1599.; "Sabina Hartmännin von Augsburg ist... heüt dato mit bethro nit mehr zu kommen ..." StadtAA, Reichsstadt, Strafbuch des Rats 1596-1605, 68v, 4-5.

Linguistic scholars have not yet discovered the nuances of the terminology of expulsion in Augsburg in the later Middle Ages or early modern period. Archival sources in Augsburg use *Stadtverbot, Stadtverweisung,* and *aus der Stadt geschafft* interchangeably. "Exile" might be used to denote expulsion of a citizen, while "banishment" might correspond to the removal of non-citizen residents and foreigners, but this is creative fiction, given the present state of scholarship. Even modern German is unclear at this point: "... in der Begrifflichkeit Stadtverweis, Ausweisung, Verbannung läßt sich keine klare definitorische Unterscheidung festmachen;" Carl A. Hoffmann, "Der Stadtverweis als Sanktionsmittel in der Reichsstadt Augsburg zu Beginn der Neuzeit," in *Neue Wege strafrechtsgeschichtlicher Forschung (Konflikt, Verbrechen und Sanktionen in der Gesellschaft Alteuropas. Symposium und Synthesen*, eds. H. Schlosser and D. Willoweit (Köln, Weimar, 1999), p. 198 (used by kind permission of Dr. Hoffmann prior to publication). In the end the author is left with a marvelous set of synonyms!

since the mid-sixteenth century Augsburg functioned as a bi-confessional city, tolerating Lutheranism and Roman Catholicism.[8]

Throughout this period a complex network of courts, magistrates, and civic officials monitored morality in the city while devoting remarkable personal attention to the malice and misgivings of the criminal and the poor. In fact, in the late fifteenth and early sixteenth centuries public officials had achieved a gradual and yet substantial reform of the judicial system, transferring significant legal power from the imperial official (*Vogt*), guilds (*Zünfte*), and a court of lower justice (*Einung*) to the city council (*Rat*) and new organs of oversight and interrogation. All significant criminal matters, including cases meriting banishment, were presented to magistrates of the city council, which also served as a final court of appeal. Members of the various assemblies of the *Rat* — the large council, small council, and thirteen (*Dreizehnerrat*) — appointed all lower judicial officials and served as interrogators; two magistrates were often listed as examiners (*auditores*) in the case files of the *Urgichten*. Minor judiciaries handled the lower jurisdictions, including the city court (*Stadtgericht*) over private claims, the punishment lords (*Strafherren*) over moral misdemeanors and violations of the Discipline Ordinance, and the marriage court (*Ehegericht*), which replaced episcopal oversight of marital disharmony and separation, paternity and guardianship.[9]

---

[8] The encyclopedic work on Augsburg in this period is Bernd Roeck's *Eine Stadt in Krieg und Frieden. Studien zur Geschichte der Reichsstadt Augsburg zwischen Kalendarstreit und Parität*, Schriftenreihe der historischen Kommission bei der Bayerischen Akademie der Wissenschaften 37 (Göttingen: Vandenhoeck und Ruprecht, 1989). For estimates of the changing population see Barbara Rajkay, "Die Bevölkerungsentwicklung von 1500 bis 1648," in *Geschichte der Stadt Augsburg von der Römerzeit bis zur Gegenwart*, eds. G. Gottlieb et al. (Stuttgart: Konrad Theis, 1984), pp. 252-8. The political prominence of Augsburg in the empire is sketched out by Winfried Schulze, "Augsburg 1555-1648: Eine Stadt im Heiligen Römischen Reich," in *Geschichte der Stadt Augsburg*, pp. 433-447. The guild structure, various industries, and financial enterprises during Augsburg's 'golden age' are described by Hermann Kellenbenz, "Wirtschaftsleben der Blütezeit," in *Geschichte der Stadt Augsburg*, pp. 258-301. On ecclesiastical and religious life in this bi-confessional city, see Paul Warmbrunn, *Zwei Konfessionen in einer Stadt. Das Zusammenleben von Katholiken und Protestanten in den paritätischen Reichsstädten Augsburg, Biberach, Ravensburg und Dinkelsbühl von 1548 bis 1648*, Veröffentlichungen des Instituts für europäische Geschichte Mainz, abendländische Religionsgeschichte 111 (Wiesbaden: Franz Steiner, 1983) and Herbert Immenkötter, "Kirche zwischen Reformation und Parität," in *Geschichte der Stadt Augsburg*, pp. 391-412.

[9] Carl A. Hoffmann, "Strukturen und Quellen des Augsburger reichsstädtischen Strafgerichtswesens in der ersten Hälfte des 16. Jahrhunderts," *ZHVS* 88 (1995),

Beneath the shimmering financial and political profile of Augsburg and behind the elaborate structures of its judicial system another city appears, including the destitute, criminal, and foreign defendants — those whose names and personal narratives typically did not merit tomes and treatises. But a remarkable display of their collective characteristics and fragmentary stories survive in court records. Moreover, the practice of exclusion reveals the social and religious values of this urban community, the views and behaviors inhabitants esteemed, the beliefs and expressions they prohibited, the residents they embraced and tolerated, the criminal and profane members they eliminated as a threat to civic order and godly society. Sabina Hartmännin emerges in her deposition in a series of roles threatening to Augsburg, but intriguing to the early modern historian. She was a beggar and prostitute, a citizen and refugee.[10] Sabina's identity and case is revealing as an example of civic exile, an area of research in legal, social, and religious history of late medieval and early modern Germany which has been generally overlooked and only most recently has received fresh scholarly attention. Carl A. Hoffmann has made a first, critical step into the survey and exploration of these issues in his study of banishment in Augsburg in the first half of the sixteenth century. He has begun the process of identifying the changing shape of penal law in Augsburg, the intensification of arrest and prosecution, the legal functions of expulsion, and the social norms exposed in this practice; thus far he has classified the forms of banishment in Augsburg, including those subjected to short-term, long-term (several years to a decade), and life sentences; others were expelled in combi-

---

67-81. Eugen Liedl provides a detailed introduction to legal procedure in Augsburg during the medieval (post 1276) and early modern periods: *Gerichtsverfassung und Zivilprozess der freien Reichsstadt Augsburg*, Abhandlungen zur Geschichte der Stadt Augsburg 12 (Augsburg: Hans Rösler, 1958). On the legal system as part of the larger civic government and the remarkable changes in the constitution during the sixteenth century, see Katarina Sieh-Burens, *Oligarchie, Konfession, und Politik im 16. Jahrhundert. Zur sozialen Verflechtung der Augsburger Bürgermeister und Stadtpfleger 1518-1618*, Schriften der Philosophischen Fakultät der Universität Augsburg: Historisch-sozialwissenschaftliche Reihe 29 (München: Ernst Vögel, 1986), pp. 28-40, 169-87; and Ingrid Bátori, *Die Reichsstadt Augsburg im 18. Jahrhundert. Verfassung, Finanzen und Reformversuche*, Veröffentlichungen des Max-Planck-Instituts für Geschichte 22 (Göttingen: Vandenhoeck und Ruprecht, 1969), pp. 30-34.

[10] The exile of elites has drawn the attention of scholars, especially regarding Italy; Randolf Starn, *Contrary Commonwealth. The Theme of Exile in Medieval and Renaissance Italy* (Berkeley: University of California Press, 1982); Susannah Foster Baxendale, "Exile in Practice: The Alberti Family In and Out of Florence 1401-1428," *Renaissance Quarterly* 44 (1991), 720-753.

nation with corporeal punishment or monetary fine; in some cases exile was not limited to a specific chronological term, but to the full payment of a debt.[11]

The case of Sabina Hartmännin offers tantalizing clues about the practices and policies of exclusion in late-sixteenth century Augsburg, and points us toward the data of specific archival sources and the implications of banishment for the ages of "Reformation" and "Confessionalization".

II. *Prostitutes, Beggars, and Weavers: the Data and Defendants of the "Urgichten" Collection of Augsburg*

The City Archive of Augsburg houses a number of remarkable collections for the study of banishment in the late medieval and early modern periods.[12] The *Urgichten* records are central to this study; in these documents the expulsion of Sabina Hartmännin and many oth-

---

[11] Hoffmann's survey also includes a quantitative analysis of banishment cases in Augsburg in the first half of the sixteenth century, the impact of expulsion on the exiled and their families, the implications of illegal return to the city, and the loss of honor associated with banishment; "Der Stadtverweis als Sanktionsmittel" (as in note 7, above), pp. 193-237. On banishment in late-medieval Augsburg see Adolf Buff, "Verbrechen und Verbrecher zu Augsburg in der zweiten Hälfte des 14. Jahrhunderts," *Zeitschrift des historischen Vereins für Schwaben* [hereafter *ZHVS*] 4 (1877), 160-231; and Karin Schneider-Ferber, "Das Achtbuch als Spiegel für städtische Konfliktsituationen? Kriminalität in Augsburg (ca. 1348-1378)", *ZHVS* 86 (1993), pp. 45-114. The state of scholarship as of 1978 in Germany regarding banishment from territory and city is summarized in H. Holzhauer, "Landesverweisung (Verbannung)," in *Handwörterbuch zur deutschen Rechtsgeschichte*, vol. 2 (Berlin: Erich Schmidt, 1978), pp. 1435-47.

Helmut Maurer has provided a detailed and innovative exploration of the spatial extent of banishment and the personal travails of exiles in Europe; "Erzwungene Ferne. Zur räumlichen Dimensionen der Stadtverweisung im Spätmittelalter," in *Grenzen und Raumvorstellungen (11.-20. Jh.) / Frontières et conceptions de l'espace (11e-20e siécles)*, ed. G. Marchal (Zürich: Chronos, 1996), pp. 199-122; for an Italian study, which includes primary documents, see Peter R. Pazzaglini, *The Criminal Ban of the Sienese Commune 1225-1310*, Quaderni die 'Studi Senesi' 45 (Milano: Dott. A. Giuffrè, 1979).

[12] Relevant collections include the following: *Achtbuch* (StadtAA, Reichsstadt, Schätze, Nr. 81), half of which is devoted to expulsions; it covers the period 1302-1528; exiles and banishments are recorded periodically in the *Ratsbücher* (StadtAA, Reichsstadt, Ratsbücher, by year and volume), beginning in 1392, and *Protokolle der Dreizehn* (StadtAA, Reichsstadt, Geheime Ratsbücher, Nr. 1-7) covering 1524-42; *Strafbücher des Rates* (StadtAA, Reichsstadt, Strafbücher des Rats), beginning in 1509 and listing the punishments decreed; *Suppliken* (StadtAA, Reichsstadt, Rat Suppliken), starting in 1513 and includes those seeking the lifting of banishment and the right to return to the city; Hoffmann, "Strukturen und Quellen des Augsburger

ers appear.[13] Moreover, the archival *Findbücher*, thc five volume Register of the Penal Court (*Register zum Strafamt*), provides immediate
access to crucial information about each case in the *Urgichten*, including name and date, and usually detailing the age, occupation (or
source of income), place of birth, and sometimes adding information
about marital status, offense committed, and punishment decreed.[14]
In particular, the Register identifies over seven hundred specific cases
relating to exclusion from the city. While nearly 90% end in banishment, about 10% indicate that expulsion has already occurred.[15] The
period 1564-1650 provides a more concentrated sample of banishment cases, covering the post-Reformation era through the Thirty
Years' War (1618-48).[16] Graph 1 shows the rate of expulsion from
1564 to the years after 1632 when the number of recorded cases
taper off.

A series of minor spikes appear in 1572/73, 1586, 1590, 1606, and
1621, while major increases are indicated in 1593-95, 1598-1600,

---

reichsstädtischen Strafgerichtswesen" (as in note 9, above), 82-98; other collections
contain cases resulting in expulsion and must be consulted practically page by page.

[13] The most likely definition of *Urgicht* is 'confession'; it's origins reach back to the
legal language of the fifth century (related in meaning to *confessio*) and to *urgiht*, *orgicht*,
and *gicht* in middle high German; in its medieval usage it assumes inquisitorial examination and the use of torture; W. Sellert, "Urgicht, Urgichtbücher," in *Handwörterbuch zur deutschen Rechtsgeschichte*, vol. 5 (Berlin: Erich Schmidt, 1998), p. 571.

Each surviving *Urgicht* or "case file" in Augsburg when complete contains the set
of questions asked, the answers of the defendant, and the verdict of the magistrates;
additional depositions and supporting documents may also be included.

[14] The Register inventories thousands of cases alphabetically by last name of the
defendant. As a result the Register provides swift access to cases when one already
has a specific individual in mind, but is less helpful in categorizing and assessing specific crimes, punishments, and general patterns of data. For a helpful description of
the collection with sample transcriptions, see Carl A. Hoffmann, "Strukturen und
Quellen des Augsburger reichsstädtischen Strafgerichtswesens" (as in note 9, above),
pp. 91-97.

[15] Three terms signified exclusion from the city as the court's verdict, comprising
most of the cases: *Stadtverweisung* (44.6%), *Stadtverbot* (43.5%), and *aus der Stadt geschaft*
(1.4%). 10.5% of the hearings indicated that an expulsion had already occurred;
individuals were brought before the court after their arrest within the city in violation of their sentence of banishment; some came to petition for lifting of the civic
ban, while others had just received such relief; in a few cases residents of Augsburg
are censured for housing the banished. On terminology for banishment and exile,
see n. 7 above.

[16] By defining this sample more narrowly it is possible to eliminate a few cases of
banishment from the data base, which are scattered sparingly over several decades:
five cases from 1524-41 and seven cases from 1658-1702; there are no cases of banishment entered in the collection between 1541 and 1564. This does not discount
exile in these periods but rather other records must be consulted.

GRAPH 1 - NUMBER OF EXPULSIONS

1564 - 1650

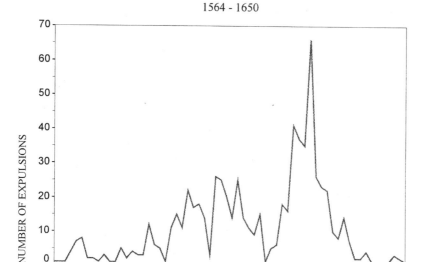

and especially from 1612 to 1618 with a peak of 66 cases in 1615. This preliminary survey of the *Urgichten* suggests that the pace of banishment was not consistent year to year.[17]

The arraignment of Sabina Hartmännin occurred precisely in the substantial spike between 1598 and 1600. Her case and identity expose other dimensions of banishment in Augsburg. She is one of 236 women appearing in the *Urgichten* collection who are driven out of Augsburg, 1564-1650. 465 male cases mark the gender majority during the period, but women make up nearly one third of the total. It cannot be said that such a decree was reserved exclusively for either gender nor that women were spared expulsion. Most intriguing in graph 2 is how often the lower female expulsion rate mirrors the higher male rate, especially in the peak years of 1598-1600 and 1612-18; banishment trends, when gender is considered, continue to

---

[17] Rates of expulsion analyzed here must be considered approximate, based in part on the survival of archival sources. In a fuller study of banishment in Augsburg, other collections must be studied with preference given to the *Strafbücher des Rats*, which unfortunately have not yet been adequately indexed.

GRAPH 2 - NUMBER OF EXPULSIONS

BY GENDER

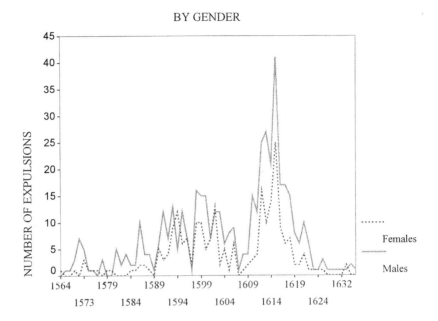

function in a similar relationship. Points of discontinuity, such as 1603, are particularly intriguing, when there are twelve male cases as compared to two for women. Overall the data confirms a trend identified by Carl Hoffmann in the first half of the sixteenth century: from 1511 to 1520, of those driven from the city, 67% were women; in contrast less than 30% of those banished from 1533-42 were women. The *Urgichten* Register suggests that rates for women continued at slightly over 30% throughout the later sixteenth and early seventeenth centuries, indicating a pattern consistent with the formal recognition of the Reformation in Augsburg in the 1530s and the continuing bi-confessional period from 1548 onwards.

In 1599 Sabina Hartmännin was one of ten women and sixteen men banished from Augsburg. At about twenty-five to thirty years old at the time of her hearing, Sabina was slightly over the median age of a refugee; over 50% of those expelled were twenty-four or younger and 75% were forty or under.[18] Nearing thirty and appar-

---

[18] The age of defendants was recorded in nearly 500 out of the 697 cases between 1564 and 1650. 16% of all defendants gave their age as between twenty-five and

ently not married, there is no evidence that Sabina had found gainful employment, nor that she received shelter from family, kin or friends. She had taken up more desperate measures. Indeed, in early 1599 magistrates focused on Sabina's disreputable lifestyle and poverty. They questioned her *vnzucht*, behavior which likely pointed to prostitution.[19] This is not surprising since she had appeared before the court only three months before in September of 1598 as a beggar and under suspicion of prostitution. As a destitute citizen Sabina had fallen ill and turned to the "Pilgrim's House" for care and recuperation. But after her departure from the charitable support of the city, she turned to unacceptable sources of income. She was arrested, imprisoned, and despite her desperate poverty, expelled from the city and its environs.[20] By January of 1599 she had been arrested for begging, prostitution, and violating her sentence of banishment. Magistrates recognized her continued descent into poverty and immoral living; they expelled her once again with the threat of corporeal punishment if she returned.[21]

---

thirty. As adults and seniors give their age there is a clear pattern in the data; statements of age are grouped in the years 30, 40, 50, 60, and 70; it appears that defendants were estimating their longevity; for example, 1 person indicated an age of thirty-seven, 4 an age of thirty-eight, 1 an age of thirty-nine, but 34 an age of forty, and only 1 an age of forty-three, and 3 at forty-four. Thus it may not be surprising that Sabina Hartmännin gave her age as twenty-five in 1598 and thirty in 1599.

Despite the percentage of those at twenty-four years of age, there are ninety-one depositions of those sixteen and under (18% of the cases) with one child as young as eight; thirty-nine gave their age as sixty or over (5% of the cases), with two at eighty and one at ninety-two; it cannot be said that banishment excluded the very young or the very old.

[19] "... aber sie hab nie vnzucht getriben." StadtAA, Reichsstadt, Urg. 2 January 1599. Lyndal Roper describes the connotations of *vnzucht*: "The force of the word *vnzuchtig* can hardly be caught in the English word 'undisciplined'. In essence a civil, moral term — the series of ordinances regulating citizens' moral behavior were *Zuchtordnungen* — *vnzuchtig* carried implications of disorder as well as sexual misbehavior, and it represented the antithesis of the *Zucht*, the moral order, which the Council wished to inculcate; *The Holy Household: Women and Morals in Reformation Augsburg.* Oxford Studies in Social History (Oxford: Clarendon Press, 1989), pp. 123-24.

[20] "Sabina Hartmännin von Augsburg ist etlich wuchen lang auf dem Pilgram hauß gelegen vnd Imm Irer Kranckhait curirt worden. Darüber hat sie sich aber auf das betlen vnd Inn das vnzüchtig leben begeben. Derowegen sie Im fronvest gelegt vnd heüt dato der Statt vnd Etter verwisen worden;" StadtAA, Reichsstadt, Strafbücher des Rats 1596-1605, 61r 16-19; see also StadtAA, Reichsstadt, Urg. 21 September 1598.

[21] See note 7, above. The case of Barbara Widenmännin suggests the fate that might have been in store for Sabina Hartmännin; Barbara appeared before the court on November 9, 1596; she was a twelve year old girl and not a native of Augsburg; she had been caught begging, was arrested, held briefly, and expelled. Barbara was apprehended and banished again on December 3, 1596, and then on three further

Sabina Hartmännin is numbered among over fifty-seven women whose connection to a life of prostitution figure in their interrogations and subsequent banishment, comprising 11% of all *Urgichten* cases in which "occupation" is known.[22] The fate of those souls who offered their bodies for remuneration in Augsburg during the sixteenth century is complex and intertwined both with the history of the Reformation and the decree of banishment. Until the 1530s Augsburg "supported" prostitution, monitoring an officially sanctioned city bordello; a brothel-keeper owned the premises, but the city might be liable for repairs. The brothel served distinguished guests of the city and provided an outlet for young, unmarried men and (albeit unofficially) the clergy, thereby protecting the honorable daughters and wives of the city. Furthermore, entrepreneurial prostitution outside the sanctioned brothel was also permitted to some extent, although civic prostitutes might be allowed to assault their "free" counterparts from time to time. On October 16, St. Gall's day, unofficial prostitutes, pimps, and procurers were driven from Augsburg in a form of ritual purification, although many returned in short order.[23]

The steady growth of a Protestant regime in Augsburg transformed policy regarding the practice of prostitution and expulsion.

---

occasions in 1597. After arresting and expelling her three times with threat of corporeal punishment between February and mid-May of 1598, the magistrates turned to more severe tactics. When Barbara appeared before them on 30 May 1598, she was whipped, and banished from Augsburg and its environs. Yet Barbara continued to return, repeating the cycle fifteen times by 20 April 1600; by her sixteenth birthday, Barbara had spent at least four years as a refugee, repeatedly arrested, interrogated, flogged, and expelled. Richard J. Evans has investigated a similar case in nineteenth century Germany; Gesche Rudolf was repeatedly arrested, imprisoned, punished, and banished from Bremen to such an extent that her attorney in 1822 calculated that her accumulated prison terms amounted to 18 years and she had been stroked with the cane 893 times; *Tales From the German Underworld. Crime and Punishment in the Nineteenth Century* (New Haven and London: Yale University Press, 1998), pp. 93-6.

[22] Source of income, whether from a legal occupation, begging or a life of crime, is indicated in 516 cases of those who were banished.

[23] Roper, *The Holy Household* (as in note 19, above), pp. 63-64, 89-92, 97-8. Public brothels had been a standard part of the civic European landscape since the midfourteenth century; official houses of prostitution first opened in Venice (1360), Toulouse (1363 or 1372), Dijon (1385), Frankfurt (1396), Nürnberg (1400), Florence (1403), Siena (1421), Munich (1433), Memmingen (1454), and Strasbourg (1469); Margaret L. King, *Women of the Renaissance* (Chicago: University of Chicago Press, 1991), p. 77.

In his study of the brothel in the later Middle Ages Peter Schuster describes the fifteenth century as "the century of the bordello;" *Das Frauenhaus. Städtische Bordelle in Deutschland (1350-1600)* (Paderborn: Ferdinand Schöningh, 1992), p. 57.

The "purification" of Augsburg, celebrated on St. Gall's day since at least 1302, last appears in 1536. Around 1532 the reforming magistrates of Augsburg closed the public brothel.[24] According to Lyndal Roper, the moral order of the city was reconfigured; public and unregulated prostitution increased. Those practicing the ancient profession and those taking advantage of such "services" were charged with adultery or fornication as opposed to prostitution. In the new civic legal system of Augsburg, interrogation of individuals replaced an annual day of corporate purgation. Civic authorities subjected prostitutes and their procurers in particular to torture and imprisonment, rituals of public shaming and corporeal punishment before final expulsion from the city.[25]

A life of prostitution offered grim and uncertain prospects in Augsburg, perhaps explaining in part the desperation of Sabina Hartmännnin. Licensed prostitution had been abolished; clandestine plying of the trade might lead to arrest, imprisonment, public humiliation and banishment. By 1599 other cities in southern Germany had pursued similar policies. Although it is not clear that the magistrates' suspicions regarding Sabina's moral character were justified, it is certain that she took up another form of public solicitation — begging. In both September of 1598 and January of 1599 Sabina was identified as a beggar in great social need. Similar to the association with prostitutes, she appeared once again in the company of the routinely banished. Beggars formed a sizeable population of those who were brought before the magistrates and whose sentences of banishment

---

[24] Hoffmann, "Der Stadtverweis" (as in note 7, above), p. 210. A prostitute hoping to find work in other cities near Augsburg would discover similar changes in legislation elsewhere. Brothels were officially closing in cities across southern Germany and the trend gradually crossed confessional lines: Nördlingen (1536), Kaufbeuren (1543), Schwäbisch-Hall (1553-54), Regensburg (1553), Nürnberg (1562), Bamberg (1568), Würzburg (1569), and Munich (1581); for the full list of German cities, see Schuster, *Das Frauenhaus* (as in note 23, above), pp. 182-84. Officially sanctioned prostitution continued in Italy; Merry E. Wiesner, *Women and Gender in Early Modern Europe*, New Approaches to European History (Cambridge: Cambridge University Press, 1993), p. 101; King, *Women of the Renaissance* (as in note 23, above), pp. 78-9.

[25] Roper, *The Holy Household* (as in note 19, above), pp. 112, 114, 119 n. 85, 127. Brutal punishment of those who violated their sentence of exile also occurred in Nürnberg: Barbara Wissnerin, a prostitute accused of theft and breaking and entering, had already been jailed and banished repeatedly; she was burned through the cheeks and two fingers were cut off; after being banished and arrested yet again she was executed by drowning; cited in Merry E. Wiesner, *Working Women in Renaissance Germany*, The Douglass Series on Women's Lives and the Meaning of Gender (New Brunswick: Rutgers University Press, 1986), p. 109.

were recorded in the *Urgichten*; nearly 29% of the defendants were either identified as beggars or charged with the crime. Graph 3 indicates the rate of expulsion for beggars who submitted to legal interrogation before their departure from the city;[26] the pattern of these expulsions show some striking and analogous peaks (1598 and 1615) when compared to the general trend of banishments in the period (see graph 1).

GRAPH 3 - NUMBER OF EXPULSIONS

BEGGARS

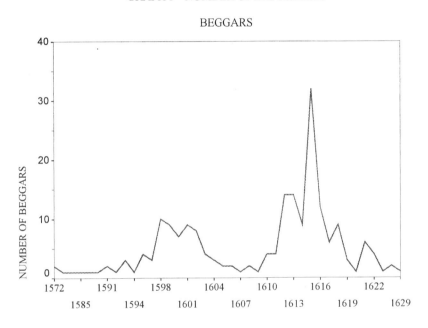

Note: numbers include all of those identified as beggars who are expelled as well as those cases in which the defendant is specifically banished for this crime in particular.

Similar to civic legislation regarding prostitution, regulation of poor relief and public begging had undergone considerable revision in Augsburg. Throughout the late fifteenth and sixteenth centuries magistrates drafted new *Ordnungen* to handle social problems related

---

[26] Since many foreign beggars were summarily driven from the city without their "day in court", it is likely that those who appear in the Urgichten have complex cases requiring magisterial intervention or review.

to a growing population. The *Bettelordnung* of 1459 forbade begging in homes and churches; the poor were allowed to solicit alms outside church sanctuaries. On feast days magistrates expected the entire family to beg together before the church; failure of the father to participate would lead to the expulsion of the whole family. Further revisions appear in the regulations of 1491, which were renewed in 1512 and 1519. Now "Begging Lords" (*Bettelherren*) were appointed to oversee the poor and their permission was required before one could commence seeking alms on the streets of Augsburg. In addition to the stipulations of 1459 beggars were required to wear a badge, indicating official permission and confirming their humble status in the community. In 1522 magistrates drafted yet another *Ordnung*, maintaining many of the former regulations, but revising the administration of poor relief to include six "Lords of Charity" (*Almosenherren*) and six assistants, who served for two year terms. These administrators not only monitored the conditions of the worthy impoverished through home visitations, but they also went house to house collecting money for poor relief. The approved poor could continue to beg in public while wearing the badge of permission; the law now restricted their solicitation to the street before their own parish church.[27]

Begging was never the same, however, after magistrates gave formal and full recognition to the Reformation in Augsburg in 1537. The *Ordnung* of 1541, which remained in effect until the Thirty Year's War, forbade public begging in the city. Those citizens and legal residents caught seeking alms publicly would be refused public assistance for one month; repeat offenders were expelled. Civic officials now delivered alms directly to the poor and such aid consisted of food, cloth, firewood, and kindling instead of money. The city was divided into thirds and the needy poor were expected to attend three prearranged worship services per year in their third of the city; home visits to check on the needs of the destitute occurred four times per year. Overall magistrates limited alms to those without personal resources. The elderly, sick, and disabled found succor; those able to work were removed from the registers of charity.[28]

---

[27] Claus-Peter Clasen, "Armenfürsorge im 16. Jahrhundert," in *Geschichte der Stadt Augsburg* (as in note 8, above), p. 337; and Clasen, "Armenfürsorge in Augsburg vor dem Dreißigjährigen Kriege," *ZHVS* 78 (1984), 67-9.

[28] Clasen, "Armenfürsorge im 16. Jahrhundert," pp. 337-8; Clasen, "Armenfürsorge in Augsburg" (as in note 27, above), 69-71.

Given Sabina Hartmännin's status as a burgher's daughter and her apparent destitution, by right she could have expected access to civic welfare. Thus, poor and sick, she recuperated from illness for one week in the Pilgrim's house. But after her departure Sabina's prostitution, begging, and banishment dissolved her rights of citizenship and disqualified her as a recipient of aid.[29] When she appeared in court three months later in violation of her sentence, Sabina referred to the unfortunate timing of her arrest; she was unable to follow through on her plan to seek alms.[30] But she was actually not eligible for civic welfare, and seems to have found a lack of compassion wherever she turned.[31]

As a suspected prostitute under the decree of banishment, Sabina could no longer seek assistance and in fact was present in the city illegally. In this way she had sunk to the level of foreign beggars, who had been forbidden from entering the city since 1541. Magistrates had turned to stern regulation, corporal punishment, enforced labor, and imprisonment, attempting to turn back the "begging plague" (*die Bettelplage*) which engulfed Augsburg on a daily basis. In a city of around forty thousand souls, which served as a center for regional markets and long distance trade, gate keepers and their "bounty hunters" (*Gassenknechte*), who were paid by the head for each foreign beggar apprehended, were not able to counter the wave of vagrant poor who daily infiltrated a city of wealth and opportunity.[32] Every month street monitors (*Bettelknechte*) expelled numerous beggars from the city; all forms of deterrence appear to have been unsuccessful; many of those expelled simply returned to Augsburg.[33]

As a banished beggar and suspected prostitute Sabina Hartmännin

---

[29] On the Pilgrim's House, see Claus-Peter Clasen, "Armenfürsorge in Augsburg," (as in note 27, above), pp. 100-1.

[30] "Sei erst am versheinen donnerstag ... das almosen zubegern bis das sie etwas bekhommen, aber als bald deselben tags eingezogen worden;" StadtAA, Reichsstadt, Urg. 2 January 1599.

[31] "... sie Jederman in ihr Heimat veisset vnd Ir also niemand nichts geben wölle..." StadtAA, Reichsstadt, Urg. 2 January 1599.

[32] During the later Middle Ages magistrates contended with mendicants and pilgrims as part of the begging population. In 1459 the city council had determined that beggars could remain from three to eight days in the city; those returning faced physical punishment; Clasen, "Armenfürsorge im 16. Jahrhundert," pp. 341-2; and Clasen, "Armenfürsorge in Augsburg" (as in note 27, above), 107-13.

[33] Calculation of the expulsion rate of beggars can only be approximate; Clasen is uncertain, but assesses the rate at 700 per month; "Armenfürsorge in Augsburg," (as in note 27, above), 112; Bernd Roeck estimates that around fifty foreign beggars per month were imprisoned or expelled throughout the first three decades of the seventeenth century; *Eine Stadt in Krieg und Frieden* (as in note 8, above), pp. 156-7. The

had forfeited her native rights as a burgher's daughter. But her case does raise an intriguing question about the treatment of citizens vis-à-vis residents. Is it logical to suppose that those with the status of burgher would be less likely to face banishment than residents who might be expelled at any moment without legal protection? Graph 4 supports this hypothesis in relationship to the *Urgichten* collection.

GRAPH 4 - NUMBER OF EXPULSIONS

BY RESIDENTIAL STATUS

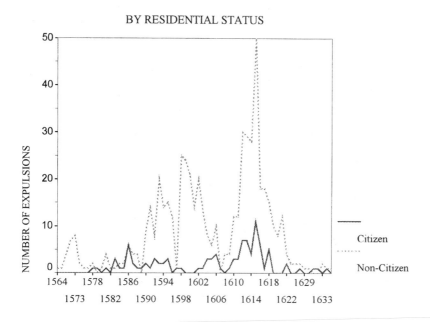

Note: "Non-citizens" include those with residential status in the city as well as illegal aliens.

strategy of the Augsburger magistrates was not unique, as Robert Jütte has noted: "Local authorities seldom used their legislative powers either to lock up the wandering or deviant poor (confinement) or to restrict their freedom to move within the municipal area (segregation). More often than not magistrates turned to the ancient remedy of expulsion. There was almost no town in early modern Europe which at one time or another did not prohibit begging and ordered the removal of all sturdy beggars and vagabonds;" *Poverty and Deviance in Early Modern Europe*, New Approaches to European History (Cambridge: Cambridge University Press, 1994), pp. 166-7; see also Jütte on civic expulsions, including from Augsburg: *Abbild und Soziale Wirklichkeit des Bettler und Gaunertums zu Beginn der Neuzeit: Sozial-, mentalitäts- und sprachgeschichtliche Studien zum Liber Vagatorum (1510)*, Beihefte zum Archiv für Kulturgeschichte 27 (Köln: Bohlau, 1988), pp. 34, 41, 42, 78, 84, 86.

There are occasional correlations, however, in the rate of expulsions, as in 1586. Furthermore, it is clear that developments around 1615, while having a profound effect on non-residents, also had a significant impact on citizens; the banishment of citizens rarely reaches comparable levels for non-residents, but paralleling trends, similar patterns of high and low expulsion rate, are apparent.

The case of a "poor soul" has directed our search through the *Urgichten* collection thus far; identified with beggars, harlots, and those in social distress (*soziales Elend*), Sabina Hartmännin was associated with offenses or conditions that lead to expulsion in over 60% of the cases in which the violation or circumstance of the defendant was recorded.[34] The magistrates of Augsburg handled many difficult cases, as recorded in the *Urgichten*, with a decisive and cost-effective solution — removal from the community. In addition to beggars and prostitutes, debtors, thieves, gypsies, and counterfeiters were expelled. Others were banished for trade with Jews, failure to pay civic fines, breaking the religious peace, use of a false name, instigation of unrest, and sale of forbidden books. When other legal records in Augsburg are consulted, further examples may be added. Lyndal Roper has shown that expulsion awaited couples who chose to live together outside of marriage; among those employed in the major trades of Augsburg, such as weaving, construction, or baking, entry into matrimony without trade rights or full citizenship meant banishment for the new couple; in fact, some young spouses were allowed to marry in Augsburg, but then were forced to depart due to the poverty of their new household. Those caught in adultery or unrepentant in their marital difficulties sometimes met a similar fate.[35] Carl Hoffmann has further identified

---

After the ordinance of 1541 forbidding public begging, magistrates not only faced the sheer number of beggars and the problem of civic surveillance, but also had to deal with some legal residents of Augsburg who commiserated with the foreign poor, taking beggars into their homes and establishments while sometimes physically hindering a civic official in order to enable a beggar to break free; Clasen, "Armenfürsorge in Augsburg," 110-11.

[34] The sample of cases in which circumstance or offense is identified is relatively small — 79 out of 711 cases — but the examples as background or causes of expulsion are illuminating.

[35] Roper, *The Holy Household* (as in note 19, above), pp. 137, 139, 169-77, 191-92, 194; Roper's excellent book also shows the degree to which the study of exile and banishment has been overlooked as an area of study in its own right; despite her reference to this punishment at least twelve times and in various sections of the text, there is no index citation for banishment, expulsion, or exile!

manslaughter, fraud, and religious deviance as "expulsory" offenses.[36]

A final dimension of the *Urgichten* collection merits consideration. Although prostitutes stand out in consideration of "occupation" and sources of income (11%), a clear majority of those appearing before the court and receiving a banishment sentence were employed in the service sector as well as in major trades and industries.[37] Male servants (2.3%), street vendors (2.4%), carpenters and builders (4.7%), maids (7.2%), and laborers (7.7%) make up a small, but significant part of the sample.[38] But the highest percentage of all categories belongs to the textile economy; males weavers and those employed in related professions account for 35% of the expulsion cases recorded in the *Urgichten*; women at work in the industry add 12% to the total, signifying that nearly one half of all exiles who were identified by their source of income, were employed in some occupation related to the textile industry. In the end this result may not be surprising since the weaving industry was by far the largest in Augsburg; journeymen and their sons totaled 1,152 in 1615 with a further 445 in related trades. Cycles of growth and recession in the economy of cloth production led to periodic decline in work followed later by demand for additional workers. In good times nearly half of those without taxable property were employed in the textile sector; over 30% of those city-wide without possessions were identified with weaving.[39] Striking as well is the rare appearance of more lucrative occupations in the *Urgichten* records; bankers, regional and international traders do not appear; only five gold and silversmiths and one medical doctor are brought before the court and expelled. Apparently the penal court to which the *Urgichten* attest, paid especial attention to the destitute, the prostitute, and the laboring poor. In the end, "Augsburg was not so much the city of the Fugger and the Welser, as the city of weavers."[40] The fate of a margin-

---

[36] Carl Hoffmann, "Der Stadtverweis," (as in note 7, above), pp. 202-03.

[37] Occupation/source of income are indicated in over two thirds of the sample — 516 of 711 cases; percentages are based on the 516 cases.

[38] Vendors included *Handler*, *Händlerin*, and *Hausierer*; among those accounted for in the carpentry and construction trades were *Zimmermänner*, *Kistler*, *Maurer* and *Maurergehilfe*, *Ziegeler* and *Ziegelerknechte*; Laborers designated included *Handarbeiter*, *Holzhacker*, *Kaminkehrer*, *Landesarbeiter*, *Spuler*, and *Tagelöhner*,

[39] Claus-Peter Clasen, "Arm und Reich in Augsburg vor dem Dreißigjährigen Krieg," in *Geschichte der Stadt Augsburg* (as in note 8, above), pp. 331-33.

[40] "Augsburg war nicht so sehr die Stadt der Fugger und Welser wie eine Stadt der Weber;" Claus-Peter Clasen, "Arm und Reich in Augsburg," in *Geschichte der*

al weaver often unravelled in this court. Given their poverty and precarious existence it may not be surprising that weavers were among
those banished most often. More intriguing is the annual rate (graph 5)
from 1572-1622, which displays the sharp rises and declines in the
pace of expulsion.

GRAPH 5 - NUMBER OF EXPULSIONS

WEAVERS

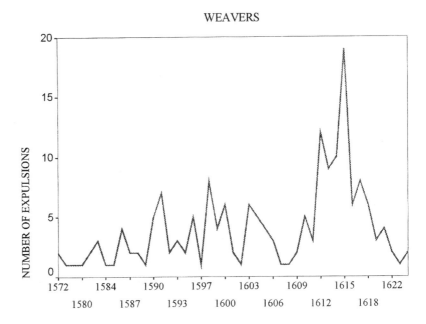

High points around 1598 and 1615 indicate the degree to which the
banishment data from the *Urgichten* may be shaped by the economic
fate of the weavers. Almost certainly defendants appear several times
in the overlapping categories of banishment, just as Sabina Hartmännin was identified as a beggar and prostitute. In 1615 there were six-
ty-six exiles recorded in the *Urgichten*, almost a third of whom were
weavers; almost forty of this sample were male along with over twenty-five women; beggars were noted in over thirty cases; citizens
appeared almost twenty-five times and non-residents peak at over

---

Stadt Augsburg (as in note 8, above), p. 334; see Clasen's exhaustive work on the weaving industry in Augsburg, including information on standards of living and poor
relief; *Die Augsburger Weber. Leistungen und Krisen des Textilgewerbe*, Abhandlung zur
Geschichte der Stadt Augsburg 27 (Augsburg: Hieronymus Mühlberger, 1981).

thirty-five. On the eve of the Thirty Year's War, a cataclysm during which the city of Augsburg lost more than half of its population,[41] magistrates were forcibly expelling the dignified and marginal at a remarkable rate. This civic policy mirrored the movement of peoples spawned by the religious turmoil of the sixteenth and seventeenth centuries.

III. *The Reformation as a "Refugee Movement"*

Legal records in Augsburg reveal the significance of banishment, a punishment applied to a variety of offenses throughout the later Middle Ages and Early Modern period. A cursory reading of the sources suggests that the convicted faced expulsion far more often than either imprisonment or execution. The seven hundred cases, nestled in the *Urgichten* collection, uncover a world in motion; citizens, residents, and foreign beggars marched outside the walls, left to rely on the availability of piecemeal work, the kindness of strangers, and the promise of return to the city. Month after month magistrates reshaped the urban population, defining its members by *Ordnungen* and interrogation, destitution and prostitution, citizenship and residence, inclusion and exclusion.

Against this background the impact of Reformation movements on the *stabilitas loci* of urban peoples is all the more striking. In the late twentieth century we have faced anew the remarkable transmigration of peoples, a series of "refugee movements" as residents are set in motion by opportunity, persecution, poverty, and war; in the last decade refugees have surged westward across borders no longer curtained with ideology and weapons of iron; in Bosnia and Kosovo, fugitives on all sides of the religious and ethnic divide have trekked for survival.

In 1984, five years before recent human migrations in Eastern Europe and the unravelling of the Soviet Union, Heiko A. Oberman presented his paper "Eine Epoche — Drei Reformationen" (One Epoch — Three Reformations) at a conference celebrating the five-hundred year anniversary of the birth of Ulrich Zwingli, reformer of Zürich. Oberman described a tripartite view of the six-

---

[41] Barbara Rajkay, "Die Bevölkerungsentwicklung," in *Geschichte der Stadt Augsburg* (as in note 8, above), p. 254

teenth century, identifying in addition to the "conciliar" and "civic", a third, revolutionary "Reformation of the Refugees", which burst through urban walls to countryside, territory, and kingdoms. In this migratory reform, which emanated from the Geneva of Calvin and was exemplified by the flight of Martin Bucer from Strasbourg to England, the experience of the refugee, summoned outside the city to homelessness and exile, became the primary carrier of revolutionary reform, forging a new, and more sympathetic relationship with the long-trekking Jews of Europe, and justifying active resistance to the opponents of the Gospel: "Those who did not take the long road into exile, but stayed home and cultivated the now very old dream of the sacred space within the city walls, were abandoned as mere fossils in the subsequent course of the Reformation."[42]

What Oberman has uncovered as a motivating force and programmatic vision in Calvinism, may well be broadened to capture a "refugee movement," or "refugee event," spawned by reformations throughout Europe. To those who looked on the status of refugee and trekker as a divine call and vision, it is critical to add many others who were compelled to life outside familiar borders and boundaries; some embraced movement, others were forced to flee. In Augsburg three patterns of expulsion are identifiable. First, in 1527 magistrates expelled around fifty Anabaptists, a policy repeated in 1531, 1533, 1545, 1546, 1550, 1562, and 1573, contributing to a wave of refugees and migrations which would spread throughout Europe.[43] Second, in 1537 the city council initiated city-wide religious reformation, abrogating the last vestiges of episcopal oversight in the city while ordering the

---

[42] Heiko A. Oberman, "One Epoch — Three Reformations," in H. A. Oberman, *The Reformation: Roots and Ramifications* (Grand Rapids: William B. Eerdmans, 1994), pp. 201-20, p. 220; the original German article: "Eine Epoch — Drei Reformationen," in *Zwingli und Europa. Referate und protokoll des Internationalen Kongresses aus Anlaß des 500. Geburtstag von Huldrych Zwingli von 26. bis 30 März 1984*, ed. P. Blickle, A. Lindt, and A. Schindler (Göttingen: Vandenhoeck und Ruprecht), 1985, pp. 11-26.

[43] Claus-Peter Clasen, *Anabaptism. A Social History, 1525-1618. Switzerland, Austria, Moravia and Central Germany* (Ithica and London: Cornell University Press, 1972), pp. 386, 388-192, 406-408; Clasen estimates that between 1525 and 1618 there were at least 12,522 converts to Anabaptism, affecting 2,088 villages and towns; in Augsburg there are records of 324 Anabaptists between 1525 and 1529, with further evidence of 126 from 1530-1618; *The Anabaptists in South and Central Germany, Switzerland and Austria, their Names, Occupations, Places of Residence, and Dates of Conversion: 1525-1618* (Goshen, Indiana: Mennonite Historical Society, 1978), pp. 9, 11, 15, 17-21, 26, 29-36.

departure of all clergy of the Roman Catholic Church, the confiscation of church properties, the closing of monasteries, and the reform of the convents.[44] These religious banishings — marking two very different sides of the confessional divide — were complemented by a third pattern, which reshaped civic policy in Augsburg. In the 1530s and 1540s the city council forbade all forms of prostitution and public begging, mandating the eradication of yet another segment of the urban population. The admonitions of Martin Luther, advising magistrates to outlaw prostitution and begging, while encouraging each commune to take care of its own poor, were reflected in civic policy in Augsburg.[45]

The full range and shape of this "Refugee Movement" is still to be discerned in and between cities, territories, and kingdoms throughout sixteenth and seventeenth century Europe. The haphazard migration of diverse peoples, embracing numerous and often opposing religious convictions and social identities, requires the scrutiny not only of the decisive decades, 1520-1550, but also the longer period of what has been termed the "age of Confessionalization", wherein the fate of the expelled are to be explored in terms of the Peace of Augsburg (1555), the shifting borders and broadsheets of confessionalism, and the strict application of social discipline. Most intriguing is the likely and as yet unexplored connection between the "Reformation of the Refugees", the refugees of the Reformation, and the longstanding exercise of exclusion, the usual banishment of the city's marked, marginal, and malicious peoples.

---

[44] On the expulsion of the clergy and bishop from Augsburg during the Middle Ages and sixteenth century, see J. Jeffery Tyler, *Lord of the Sacred City. The 'Episcopus Exclusus' in Late Medieval and Early Modern Germany*, SMRT 72 (Leiden: Brill, 1999), pp. 77-102, 179-185; on the reformation of the convents in Augsburg, see Lyndal Roper, *The Holy Household* (as in note 19, above), pp. 206-251.

[45] See *D. Martin Luthers Werke. Kritische Gesamtausgabe*, 60 vols. (Weimar: H. Böhlau, 1883-1980) 6, pp. 450f; 467.

PUBLIC SPACE. RESTRICTION OF NON-CALVINIST RELIGIOUS BEHAVIOR IN THE PROVINCE OF HOLLAND, 1572-1591*

James D. Tracy**

The religious settlement in the Dutch Republic has sometimes been accorded a uniquely modern status. Here — especially in the highly urbanized province of Holland — different Christian communities developed over the course of the seventeenth century a form of peaceful co-existence. The Dutch Reformed Church claimed a special place as what was called the "public" church,[1] sanctioned by the government; all houses of worship inherited from the medieval church were either placed at the disposition of the Reformed community, put to secular uses, or closed and eventually torn down. But Lutherans and Mennonites and Catholics — like the Portuguese Jews who settled in Amsterdam — were able to build appropriately decorated halls of worship within the walls of private houses. For this was a Republic fighting for its existence against Spain and the Spanish Inquisition, founded — according to a common opinion — on the principle of religious freedom. As was prescribed in the 1579 Union of Utrecht, which may be considered the founding charter of the new state, no citizen was to be molested on account of his beliefs.

This traditional conception of a uniquely tolerant and enlightened Dutch society has not stood up well under the scrutiny of more recent scholars. Hugo Grotius' suggestion that the ruling elites of Holland's cities formed their world view by reading Erasmus is now thought to have little or no foundation. The principle that civic freedom was

---

* A different version of this paper, "Begrenzter Dissens: die rechtliche Stellung der nicht-calvinistischen christlichen Gemeinden in Holland," was presented at a symposium on 'Dissent' held in Wittenberg, Germany, August 22-25, 199.

** Professor of History, University of Minnesota

[1] The earliest use I have found for this key term is in the record of the second national synod of the Reformed Church (Dordrecht, 1578), where the assembled dominees complain that "many blasphemers are to be found among those who visit the public churches (*openbare kerken*):" F. L. Rutgers, *Acta van de Nederlandsche Synoden des Zestiende Eeuw* (The Hague, 1889), 279. Parish churches (like town schools) were "public" in that they were subject to the control of civil authorities.

threatened by the dominance of any single creed, argued by Remon-
strant church historian Gerard Brandt (1626 — 1685), was not shared
by the town regents whose statecraft he professed to admire.[3] The
Dutch Revolt itself was not a popular uprising against foreign rule,
but a civil war in which one faction maintained itself in power on the
promise of keeping out the hated Spanish troops.[4] Revisionism has
sometimes gone too far. The thesis that the majority of the Dutch people were "Protestantized" only by a combination of social and political pressure, put forward by Pieter Geyl and L.J. Rogier, which made
the mistake of assuming that Calvinism could have no appeal of its
own, has not been confirmed by subsequent research.[5] There is, however, no doubt that the Reformed community embraced only a small
fraction of the population during the early decades of the Revolt — a
contemporary estimate of 10% in 1586 is now commonly accepted.[6]
Hence one may say in summary that if the Dutch Reformation settlement no longer seems uniquely modern, it is at least peculiar;
nowhere else in the Europe of this era did a government attempt to
build a new religious order on a Protestant church that included so
small a percentage of its citizens. This paper will explore one of the
most distinctive features of the Dutch settlement, that is, the less-than-

---

[2] See the comment of Cornelis Augustijn in M. E. H. N. Mout, H. Smolinsky,
and J. Trapman, eds., *Erasmianism: Ideal and Reality* (Amsterdam, 1997), 12.

[3] For Brandt, Christiane Berkvens-Stevlinck, "La Reception de l'*Historie der Reformatie* de Gerard Brandt et son Influence de la Conception de la Tolérance Hol-
landaise" in C. Berkvens-Stevelinck, J. Israel, and G.H.M. Posthumus Meyjes, *The
Emergency of Tolerance in the Dutch Republic* (Leiden, 1997), 131-140; for the connection
between civic freedom and religious pluralism, Brandt, *The History of the Reformation and
Other Ecclesiastical Transformations in and about the Low Countries* (4 vols.; London: T.
Childe, 1720-71), I, 30 (James Ford Bell Collection, University of Minnesota Library).

[4] Henk van Nierop, *Het Verraad van het Noorderkwartier. Oorlog, Terreur en Recht in de
Nederlandse Opstand* (Amsterdam, 1999).

[5] Pieter Geyl, "De protestanisering van Noord-Nederland," in his *Kernproblemen
van onze Geschiedenis: Opstellen en voordrachten 1927 - 1936* (Utrecht, 1937), 29-41; L. J.
Rogier, *Geschiedenis van het Katholicisme in Noord-Nederland in de 16e en 17e Eeuw* (2nd edition, 3 vols., Amsterdam, 1947). The latest assessment based on a careful local study
endorses one aspect of the Geyl-Rogier thesis (that the Reformed Church was most
successful where it had the support of the local government, and where Catholic
preaching was interrupted for a significant period of time): A. Ph. Wouters, P. H. A.
M. Abels, *Nieuw en Ongezien. Kerk en Samenleving in de Classis Delft, 1572 - 1622* (2 vols.,
Delft, 1994), I, 241.

[6] The most recent estimate for a particular locality is the study by Wouters and
Abels (note 5) of the *classis* of Delft, consisting of the city of Delft and the surrounding
rural area known as Delfland. For 1622, the authors estimate that (counting children
as well as adults) the Reformed community embraced 24.5% of the urban population, and 11.5% of the rural population: *Nieuw en Ongezien*, I, 229-239.

absolute restrictions on the religious activities of non-Calvinist Christian communities. This kind of unofficial toleration does not have
direct medieval precedents, but in keeping with the themes of this volume, it can be shown that the principles underlying the Dutch settlement were familiar, if in different contexts, to earlier generations of
Netherlanders. The discussion will first indicate the boundaries
between what Christian dissenters were permitted to do and what
they were not permitted to do, using as an example the *Resolutions* of
the provincial States of Holland[7] for the first two decades of the
Revolt, 1572 — 1591 (I). Recent Dutch scholarship has explained this
drawing of boundaries as an effort by civil authorities to control the
religious use of public space; the controls were new, but the concept of
public space and its implications were not (II.).

I.

In the early years of the Revolt the idea of a broad evangelical
"people's church" was not without its defenders. One sees this most
clearly at the *Jacobskerk* in Utrecht, under the leadership of Pastor
Hubert Duifhuis (d. 1581): here adults could decide for themselves to
approach the Table of the Lord, without the examination by the consistory (*kerkeraad*) that was obligatory in the Calvinist church order.[8]
But the *Jacobskerk* was an exception. From early on, the legislation of
the new state aimed at all levels — the towns, the provincial states,
and the States General — to secure official recognition for the
Reformed faith (*christelijke gereformeerde religie*). A sentence from a draft
treaty of union between the provinces of Holland and Zeeland (28
April 1576) may be taken as illustrative:

> "His Excellency [William of Orange, Stadtholder of both provinces]
> shall maintain and preserve the exercise of the reformed religion (*gere-
> formeerde religie*). He shall also provide that the exercise of all other reli-
> gions contrary to the Gospel shall cease and desist; but he shall not
> permit the individual person to be examined, burdened, injured, or
> hindered on account of his beliefs or his conscience."[9]

---

[7] *Resolutien van de Staten van Holland voor 1572* (278 vols., Amsterdam, 1793 - 1795),
hereafter abbreviated as *RSH.*
[8] Benjamin J. Kaplan, *Calvinists and Libertines in Utrecht* (Oxford, 1995).
[9] *RSH*, 1576, 67.

The boundary drawn here is between freedom of conscience, guaranteed for all, and the (public) exercise of religion, authorized only for the *gereformeerde religie*.

Leaders of the Reformed Church were not interested in having the *Heren Staten* create an established church in the usual sense of the term. Recent scholarship has emphasized the keen competition between Mennonites and Calvinists,[10] especially in the years before about 1600. Since the appeal of a more tightly disciplined community was drawing pious Calvinists into the Mennonite camp, Dutch Reformed churches formed the habit of limiting their recruiting to men and women whose neighbors vouched for their good character.

For their part, town magistrates and the deputies they sent to the provincial states were fully aware of the need for taking into account the sensibilities of non-Calvinist Christians — not to mention the considerable number of people who seem to have shown no interest in any church.[11] In 1581, preparing a new Instruction for William of Orange in keeping with the States General's decision to renounce allegiance to King Philip II of Spain, the States of Holland dropped the clause about seeing to it that the practice of other religious should cease and desist. Instead, the Prince was instructed "to maintain the practice of only the *gereformeerde evangelische religie.*"[12]

In this new order of things Dutch Lutherans had something of a privileged position, at least in the small Holland town of Woerden, which had embraced the Augsburg Confession during the 1550s, and was not persuaded to return to Catholicism by the bombardment organized by its overlord, the exiled Duke Erich of Braunschweig. In 1572 the rebel States of Holland formally recognized the Lutheran city council as continuing to exercise patronage rights over Woerden's parish church; the legal rights of the Reformed Church were recognized by having Reformed services in the castle church, with a preacher appointed by the States. But Woerden's Lutheran pastors did not easily accommodate themselves to the ordinances of an officially Calvinist state; for example, they insisted on recognizing King Philip II as the rightful sovereign of the Netherlands, despite the

---

[10] E.g., Joke Spaans, *Haarlem na de Refomatie. Stedelijk cultuur en kerkelijk leven, 1577 - 1620* (The Hague, 1989).

[11] A point stressed by Spaans (note 10) as well as by Wouters and Abels (note 5).

[12] *RSH*, 5 July 1581.

Republic's renunciation of allegiance in 1581.[13] The States had already stripped Woerden's town council of its patronage rights in 1580, but the Lutheran preachers appointed by the States were also dismissed when they ventured to speak against state policy from the pulpit. In addition, the town council was warned that Woerden's Lutherans should be content with their possession of the parish church; there must be an end to the molestation of burghers wanting to attend services at the castle church.[14]

One way of making life easier for non-Calvinist citizens was to prevent the Reformed clergy from gaining exclusive control over baptism and marriage, the essential rituals of family life. Under some pressure from civil authorities, church leaders agreed that for purposes of baptism the "public churches" were open to all Christians. The second national synod (1578) approved the principle that children of "people of the covenant" had a right to baptism, whether they were church members or not. The third national synod (1581) went a step further by decreeing that the part of the Reformed ritual in which parents and godparents were asked to swear to raise the child according to Reformed doctrine should be made optional.[15] In the case of marriage the States provided the alternative of civil matrimony.[16]

But Mennonites had no benefit from either of these concessions to non-Calvinists. In their view, baptism was not for children, and neither the church nor city hall could claim a monopoly in the blessing of Christian marriage. The *Resolutions* give no indication that the States were concerned to have local officials keep track of parents who did not have their children baptized; this represents a clear departure from the vigilance of Catholic authorities during the Habsburg era. The deputies did warn Mennonites in particular that they risked provoking "the wrath of God" if they presumed to live together as man and wife without the blessing of either a dominee or a burgomaster.[17] But they also seemed willing to make accommodations for productive citizens who happened to be Mennonites. In some

---

[13] One may note that dominees of the Reformed Church were also not allowed to contradict state policy from the pulpit; cf. *RSH* 27 March, 25 April, 7 May 1587.

[14] *RSH* 21 March 1575, 4 April, 13 June, 23 June, 13 September, 22 November 1580, 24 February 1581, 23 January, 19 February, 24 February 1582, 1 January 1583, 12 November, 17 December 1590.

[15] Wouters and Abels, *Nieuw en Ongezien*, I, 198-202.

[16] *RSH* 6 July 1580, 9 Mach 1589.

[17] *RSH* 9 March 1589.

parts of the Netherlands, the Mennonite refusal to swear oaths was penalized by law. In Groningen, for example, Mennonites were to be barred not only from official positions but also from trusteeships over private inheritances, unless they agreed to swear the appropriate oath. The States of Holland were somewhat more reasonable. When the village of Abbekerk requested permission to nominate Mennon-ites as candidates for the village council, the States declined the peti-tion, but offered the friendly suggestion that Mennonites could be proposed for membership in semi-public bodies, like the board that administered the property of orphans.[18] Here the deputies drew a clear boundary: Mennonites could be admitted to the preliminary stages of what was then understood as the *cursus honorum* for prospec-tive magistrates in towns and villages, but not to the magistracy itself.

There were really only two points on which the *Heren Staten* con-sistently took a hard line: there was not to be any public questioning of the religious order the authorities had decreed, and Catholic wor-ship was to be altogether forbidden by law, even in private. More than any other Hollander of these years, Dirk Volkertszoon Coorn-hert (1522 — 1590) tested the limits of the authorities' patience for public debate. Coornhert was at one time described as an "Erasmi-an," but it is now clear that his affinities were with the Spiritualists, including Hendrik Niclaes, founder of the Family of Love.[19] Coorn-hert sought an opportunity to prove, in open debate, that the Reformed Church's claim to purity of doctrine was not founded on scripture. The city government of Leiden, not exactly on good terms with the Reformed *classis* of Rijnland during these years, gave him an opportunity for doing so in 1579, but Coornhert wanted a wider forum. When he challenged two dominees from Delft (including the respected Arent Corneliszoon) to a debate before the States of Hol-land, the dominees were eager for a chance to give the lie to Coorn-hert's provocative contentions. The *Heren Staten* fixed a time and place for the confrontation, only to intervene after the first day and shut down the proceedings.[20] The deputies evidently considered it scandalous to allow Coornhert's challenge to go unanswered, but

---

[18] A. F. Mellink, S. Zijlstra, eds., *Documenta Anabaptistica* (7 vols., Leiden, 1991 -), VII, 232-234; *RSH* 6 September 1585.

[19] H. Bonger, *Leven en Werk van Dirk Volkertszoon Coornhert* (Amsterdam, 1978); H. Bonger et al., eds., *Dirk Volkertszoon Coornhert. Dwars, maar recht* (Zutfen, 1989).

[20] Bonger, *Leven en Werk van Coornhert*, 83-117.

scandalous in a different way to allow the debate to continue.

Dissidents within the Reformed Church[21] were not to disturb the public peace either. In 1582 certain unnamed dominees presented a petition to the States which defenders of the church (including the respected Hendrik van der Corput of Dordrecht and two other dominees) saw as offensive. Van der Corput and his colleagues asked that the petition be read in open session and the names of the petitioners made known, so as to squelch the scandalous rumors that were beginning to be bruited about. Some deputies (including those from staunchly Calvinist Dordrecht) agreed to this proposal, but the majority was of a different opinion. The offensive document was simply burned, never to be mentioned again.[22]

In 1588 the Lutheran pastors of Amsterdam presented a petition backed by the deputies of their city, which harbored a substantial German Lutheran community. The pastors asked that the *Heren Staten* authorize a colloquium to consider whether the Augsburg Confession was one of those religions indicated in the Union of Utrecht as "contrary to the Gospel" and therefore worthy of being suppressed, at least as far as public worship was concerned. It seems likely the deputies found this petition somewhat embarrassing. In any case they returned a gentle if negative reply: "since present circumstances do not permit any colloquies or public discussions, the petitioners are requested to keep silence, as they have done, until the *Heren Staten* shall determine otherwise."[23] Whether the deputies saw the Augsburg Confession as "contrary to the Gospel" may be doubted. But Lutherans were nonetheless not allowed to discuss their beliefs in a public forum.

Unlike other forms of Christian worship, Catholicism was prohibited by civil authorities at all levels not only in public, but also in private houses. That Catholics were singled out in this way reflected the needs of an incipient nation at war for its own survival. To begin

---

[21] To name the most important names: Carl Bangs, *Arminius. A Study in the Dutch Reformation* (2nd ed., Grand Rapids, Mich., 1985); on Caspar Janszoon Coolhaes, the preacher defended by Leiden's city government and opposed by his *classis*, H. C. Rogge, *Caspar Janszoon Coolhaes, de Voorloper van Arminius en de Remonstranten* (2 vols., Amsterdam, 1865); on the above-mentioned Hubert Duifhuis in Utrecht, Kaplan, *Calvinists and Libertines in Utrecht*; and on Hermannus Herbertszoon in Gouda, C. C. Hibben, *Gouda in the Revolt. Particularism and Pacifism in the Revolt of the Netherlands, 1572-1588* (Utrecht, 1983).
[22] *RSH* 15 February 1582.
[23] *RSH* 6 April 1588.

with, the new order in the Northern Provinces rested on an unspoken but clearly understood agreement between the ruling elite (many of whom were not Calvinist) and the Reformed Church. All governments of this era needed the blessing of a church, none more so that a new regime rebelling against an order long believed to be ordained by God. A church that could have blessed this government with greater enthusiasm for its war against Catholic Spain can scarcely be imagined. In return, the church demanded recognition of its privileged position in public law, and an outright prohibition of "popish idolatry." At the same time, authorities could not be certain of the political sympathies of the Catholic population. Many Catholics rallied to the Revolt, but others guarded silent hopes for a restoration of the legitimate monarchy, and some fled abroad to join in the fight against those who had usurped the king's rightful authority.[24] In these circumstances it was unthinkable that the government should countenance the public exercise of Catholic belief.

A group of influential Catholics from Haarlem learned this basic truth of Dutch life the hard way. Haarlem had adhered to the Revolt in 1577, on condition that the city's Catholic majority not be disturbed in the practice of their beliefs. But as in other cities,[25] such agreements had no meaning for fanatical Calvinists among the soldiery: in Haarlem's great parish church, the St. Bavokerk, "idols" were smashed and priests were driven out. The city government transferred the Bavokerk to the custody of Haarlem's Reformed congregation, and ordered the doors of all other churches barred. In 1581 a group of Haarlem Catholics, including men who had been magistrates and creditors of the central government before 1572, presented a petition to the *Heren Staten*. By right, they asserted, Haarlem's Catholics could lay claim to the Bavokerk; but in order to preserve the public peace — "despite the provocations of incendiary preachers" — they were willing to make do with the smaller Bakenessekerk. Like the petition from the unnamed dominees mentioned above, this request was burned and never mentioned again. But in this case burning was not enough, for the *Heren*

---

[24] See, for example, the discussion of Richard Verstegan from Guelderland (ca. 1550 - 1640) and his Catholic Book of Martyrs - *Theatrum Crudelitatum Haereticorum Nostri Temporis* (Antwerp, 1588) - in Van Nierop, *Het Verraad van het Noorderkwartier*, 257-261.

[25] E.g., in Delft in April 1573: Wouters & Abels, *Nieuw en Ongezien*, I, 274-275.

Staten took umbrage at the insulting reference to preachers appointed by their authority; they instructed Haarlem's magistrates that
those principally responsible for the petition were to be identified,
and "banned for four years from Haarlem and all other public
places in Holland."[26]

Only Catholic worship was prohibited by the *Heren Staten* under
pain of monetary fines, e.g. a hundred guilders for attendance at a
Catholic service, or for publication of "scandalous" mass- or prayer-
books.[27] But if the death sentences meted out by courts of the Habsburg era were not able to prevent the spread of Protestantism, these
milder penalties were no more effective at suppressing Catholicism,
especially after Sasbout Vosmeer of Delft organized the Holland Mission on a regular basis (1582). As in the reign of Charles V, North
Holland, with its maze of small streams and canals, was a favored
haunt for "sectarian" activity, save that it was now the Catholics
whose gatherings were labeled sectarian by the authorities. The dominees of this district forwarded their complaints to the *Heren Staten*:
"disgusting popish idolatry" was showing itself "right out in the
open" (*genoeg openbaar*), for as many as 2,000 people were said to have
gathered in broad daylight. In one North Holland village, a Jesuit
priest was said to have been accepted as the village schoolmaster; this
kind of insult to God's honor must never be permitted, "least of all in
a public (*openbare*) school in a Reformed land." To maintain God's
honor, the *Heren Staten* issued appropriate orders to local officers:
public gatherings must be prevented, priests must not be hired as
schoolmasters, the man who calls himself a bishop must be arrested,
and the stonework surrounding the well near the village of Bergen
must be torn down and taken away, to cut the roots of ancient superstition.[28]

No doubt the deputies understood well enough that mandates
would not make the problem go away. By around 1600, if not before,
Catholic communities were forming the habit of paying annual

---

[26] *RSH* 26, 27 May, 10 June 1581; it did not help the petitioners that the notorious Dirk Volkertszoon Coornhert (a native of Haarlem though not a Catholic) was
determined to be the author of the petition.

[27] *RSH* 24 July 1587, 9 March 1589.

[28] *RSH* 26 May 1582, 21 June, 17 September 1588; for North Holland in the
Habsburg era, Tracy, "Heresy Law and Centralization under Mary of Hungary:
Conflict between the Council of Holland and the Central Government over the
Enforcement of Charles V's Placards", *Archiv für Reformationsgeschichte* 73 (1982): 284-
307.

"recognition money" to the local sheriff, so as not to be harassed by periodic raids on their house-churches. Here too one may discern a boundary, though not one that was fixed by law. So long as Catholics kept their activities hidden from public view and paid off the sheriffs, neither the penal laws nor the complaints of local dominees were a source of great concern.[29]

II.

Among contemporary Dutch scholars, Willem Frijhoff has presented the clearest discussion of how Hollanders of a slightly later era understood the difference between public and private space, and what this distinction meant in religious terms. During the seventeenth century it was common for people even of modest means to hang paintings on the walls of their homes. When Dutch artists represented on their canvasses the interior spaces of homes, Frijhoff notes, the paintings they show on the walls of bedrooms often have a religious subject matter; but this is never the case for paintings shown adorning the walls of reception rooms or living room, where guests would be greeted. Using a collection of proverbs and amusing tales, Frijhoff draws out the implication that certain spaces — e.g., shops, or the passenger-barges that regularly plied important routes — were treated as "semi-public" spaces, where it was considered bad form to bring up religious controversies for discussion. The notion of "public" space was also shaped by light and darkness; by night, pious Catholics made treks along the old pilgrim paths, as they would not have dared to do during the light of day.[30]

Reading Frijhoff's conclusions back a few decades earlier, I would argue that one can best understand the religious legislation of the States of Holland during the early decades of the Revolt as an effort to control the religious use of public space. The *Heren Staten* erected what contemporaries called a "public church,"[31] that is, an ecclesiastical body that embraced all town and village parish churches that

---

[29] Christine Kooi, "Strategies of Catholic Toleration in Golden Age Holland," paper presented to a conference on 'Dutch Toleration in the Golden Age' (2 April 1999) at New York University, organized by Ronnie Po-Chia Hsia; a volume of the papers is to be edited by Prof. Hsia.

[30] Frijhoff, "Dimensions de la coexistence confessionelle," in Berkvens-Stevelink *et al.*, eds, *The Emergence of Tolerance*, 213-228.

were still used as houses of worship. The kind of dissent the gentlemen deputies would not countenance was any use of public space by
non-Calvinist communities. Public silence was imposed on Lutherans
and Mennonites, since any open discussion of their disadvantaged
status would call into question the rights of the *Heren Staten* to determine the religious order of the new state. A rather stricter public
silence was imposed on Catholics, because a discussion of their position would call into doubt not only the rights of the States, but also
the common claim of state and church that Holland was a
"Reformed land."

The idea that civil authorities should attempt to control religious
behavior in public but not in private represents a departure from
pre-Reformation precedents, at least at the level of legislation. The
Catholic governments of Holland's towns during the Habsburg era
often turned a blind eye to clandestine Protestant gatherings, but
the law of the land left no doubt that such activities were punishable, indeed (after 1529) punishable by death.[32] Yet the concept of
public space that the government now employed in dealing with
dissenters was in itself not so novel. For the clear distinction
between public and private behavior on which this policy depended, there are many medieval precedents, three of which may be
suggested here.

First, for all concerned with personal honor, insults that were
exchanged "in public" or "out in the open" had to be taken seriously. Honor in these centuries could be a matter of life and death, and
not just for dueling nobles; the ordinary man or woman who suffered his or her good name to be besmirched in public risked losing
a job, or losing credit with the lenders to whom common folk
turned in hard times. Just as preachers in thirteenth-century Italy
sought to reconcile the heads of feuding clans, Calvinist consistories
in Holland sometimes forestalled feuds by certifying for all and
sundry the good character of a party who considered himself
injured.[33] The *Heren Staten* also had a reputation to protect, and
they did so in part by ensuring that no one was allowed to contest

---

[31] See note 1.
[32] Tracy, "Heresy Law and Centralization."
[33] Florike Egmond, *Op het Verkeerde Pad. Georganiseerde Misdaad in de Noordelijke Nederlanden, 1650 1800* (Amsterdam, 1994), see the Index under "reputatie." Douglas Cat-
terall, "Community without Borders. Scots Migrants in Rotterdam, 1600 - 1690,"
Ph. D. Dissertation, University of Minnesota, 1998.

their authority to determine the proper order of worship for Holland.[34]

Second, the process by which social institutions came to be seen as public — that is, subject to supervision or control by town governments — is a familiar theme to historians of late medieval and early modern Europe. To take the example of poor relief, the charitable foundations established by pious bequests of the fourteenth or fifteenth century came under the control of boards appointed by town councils well before the centralizing reforms of the sixteenth century, whether Protestant or humanist in inspiration.[35] Humanist writers may also have been influential in creating a vocabulary to describe this process, as in Erasmus's dictum, "Sit schola publica aut nulla,"[36] meaning that parents should entrust their sons not to a schoolmaster subject to no authority, but to a school under the supervision of the city fathers.

Finally, and probably most relevant here, the idea that some things might be overlooked if done in private but not if done in public bears a strong resemblance to the ecclesiastical concept of public scandal. The traditional disciplinary practice of the Catholic Church depended at a number of points on circumstances of notoriety or reputation. In the church of the seventh century, public penitence was demanded of persons guilty of notorious sin, while those guilty of secret sins were allowed to confess in private to a priest. As church courts adopted the new inquisitorial procedure, beginning in the late twelfth century, judges were authorized to initiate proceedings against persons suspected of heresy solely on the basis of public repute (*fama*), without having to wait for an accuser to bring charges. To be sure, the use of ecclesiastical penalties by church courts evoked a good deal of resentment among lay people during the later medieval centuries, not least because excommunication was used most commonly as a penalty for non-payment of debt.[37]As much as anything else, churches in the

---

[34] For the concept of the honor of the ruler in seventeenth-century Germany, Wolfgang Weber, "Honor, fama, gloria. Wahrnehmungen und Funktionszuschreibungen der Ehre in der Herrschaftslehre des 17. Jahrhunderts," in Sibylle Backmann, Hans-Jörg Künast, Sabine Ullmann, B. Ann Tlusty, *Ehrkonzepte in der Frühen Neuzeit* (Berlin, 1998), 70-98.

[35] For Holland, Charles H. Parker, *The Reformation of Community. Social Welfare and Calvinist Charity in Holland, 1572 - 1620* (Cambridge, 1992).

[36] In his *Declamatio de Pueris Instituendis*, ed. Jean-Claude Margolin (Geneva, 1966).

[37] These examples are from Elisabeth Vodola, *Excommunication in the Middle Ages* (Berkeley, 1986).

Calvinist tradition claimed to offer a radical reform of church discipline. Yet the *classes* and consistories of the Reformed Church inevitably worked from a conceptual apparatus inherited from earlier centuries. To give but one example, adultery was seen as causing "scandal" only if the facts of the case had been bruited about. Thus one adulterous husband could rectify his standing with the church through a private conversation with the consistory, while another would be obliged to accuse himself of sin before the entire congregation.[38]

All of these circumstances shed light on the religious decrees promulgated by the States of Holland. With the exception of laws prescribing Catholic worship in private, the States made no effort to control religious behavior that could not be seen from the street. This is not to imply that anyone confused outward seeming and inner conviction. Rather, the deputies pursued an objective that would have been perfectly intelligible to responsible officials in earlier centuries. Exclusion of all sectarian activity from the public sphere was now seen as the minimum requirement for safeguarding the honor of the States, the honor of the church, and the honor of God.

---

[38] Herman Roodenburg, *Onder Censuur. De kerklijke tucht in de gereformeerde gemeente van Amsterdam, 1578 1700* (Hilversum, 1990), 131-133.

II. PRINT, PUBLICATION AND PIETY

FORGOTTEN BEST-SELLERS FROM THE
DAWN OF THE REFORMATION*

Michael Milway**

The title of this study hearkens to a collection of articles written by Heiko Oberman entitled *The Dawn of the Reformation*.[1] While book historians still use the phrase "eve of the Reformation" to refer to the period before 1517,[2] the more illuminating metaphor, dawn, "calls attention to that period of adumbration and clarification," in which reformers were "hindered and helped, enriched and infuriated,

---

* For their detailed and extensive comments on a previous draft of this article, I thank Paul Grendler (Chapel Hill), Bernard Roussel (Paris), Stephan Borgehammar (Uppsala), my colleagues at the Centre for Reformation and Renaissance Studies (Toronto), and the two editors of this volume.

** Curator, Centre for Reformation and Renaissance Studies, Victoria University in the University of Toronto.

[1] Heiko A. Oberman, *The Dawn of the Reformation: Essays in Late Medieval and Early Reformation Thought* (Edinburgh, 1986). I also draw on the title of Robert Darnton's pioneering investigation of eighteenth-century clandestine books, *The Forbidden Best-Sellers of Pre-Revolutionary France* (New York, 1995). I depart from his important lead, however, both in the period I examine and the explanation I offer for obscure best-selling authors. Darnton found that writers of illegal literature shrouded themselves in mystery. Daunted by the risk of discovery, indeed by the threat of penalty, they were architects of their own anonymity. Darnton, *Forbidden Best-Sellers*, 22, 60-66, 402 fn. 89. Three hundred years earlier, best-selling authors of the 1400s did nothing of the like. Even if obscure today — and many eminent medieval authors have become remarkably unfamiliar — this has nothing to do with illicit literature and secrecy. Book censorship was almost unheard of, let alone effective, during the fifteenth century. In 1479, Sixtus IV ordered the confiscation in Spain of Pedro de Gui's *Janua artis Raimundi Lulli*. In 1485 Berthold von Henneberg, archbishop of Mainz, issued a general decree in his diocese against books translated out of Greek or Latin into the vernacular, but did not prohibit specific titles or authors. In 1487 the papacy intervened officially for the first time against a specific title when Innocent VIII prohibited the 900 theses of Pico della Mirandola, a move that foreshadowed future *indices librorum prohibitorum*. Harsher still was the decree *Inter sollicitudines* issued by Leo X in 1515, which censored all translations from Hebrew, Greek, and Arabic into Latin, and from Latin texts into vernacular tongues. Yet if not lacking altogether, enforcement was the exception rather than the rule. In any case, none of these "prohibited books" were incunabular best-sellers. Condemnation did not help them reach that status.

[2] Sixteen book historians in one recent collection of articles take as their "point de départ théorique" the year 1517, "date traditionnelle de la mise en route de la Réforme." Jean-François Gilmont (ed.), *La Réforme et le livre* (Paris, 1990), 14; trans. Karin Maag, *The Reformation and the Book* (Aldershot, UK, 1998), 6. More subtle in

shaped and sharpened by the conflicting claims of mysticism, Augustinianism, nominalism and Renaissance humanism."[3] By divorcing 1516 from 1518, even if by metaphor alone — an image of night separating dusk and sunrise — we serve nothing but the ends of confessional history and reinforce the *ad hoc* temporal barriers that conceal channels of cohesion and stability. What follows investigates best-selling titles and authors from the fifteenth century. It is a statistical study of printing from 1455 to 1500 (see tables 1 and 2, pp. 141-142 below). Beyond what scholars have brought to light already about the formative years of printing history, this study shows that several market-establishing authors no longer receive even the slightest mention in handbooks and encyclopedias, let alone textbooks, having long been buried by neglect. A few top-selling titles have fared even worse. Hornbooks and primers, perhaps the two most reliable generators of revenue for Europe's first printers, have virtually all disappeared, victims of fragility.[4]

Alexander de Villa Dei's *Doctrinale* (ca. 1199) and Niccolò Perotti's *Rudimenta grammatices* (1473) are prime examples of forgotten bestsellers. Each sold better during the fifteenth century than any work by Cicero, Boethius, or Aquinas; and each became a centerpiece in controversy, a bone of contention between the *via antiqua* and the *via moderna*, between scholastics and humanists. Yet neither was written by a well known author if measured in footnotes and citations from today's literature.

In addition, this article indicates that those who funded the printing revolution by purchasing books were not first and foremost doc-

---

defining the frontiers of historical periods is the article by Henri-Jean Martin and Jeanne-Marie Dureau, "Années de transition: 1500 — 1530," in R. Chartier and H.-J. Martin (eds.), *L'Histoire de l'édition fraçaise*, Tome I: *Le livre conquérant: Du Moyen Âge au milieu du XVIIe siècle* (Paris, 1983), 217-225.

  [3] Oberman, *Dawn of the Reformation*, preface [v]. Almost a full century earlier, in a book by the same title, an English clergyman/historian Herbert Workman wrote: "My purpose is to trace the various influences and forces both within and without the Church, which produced the great revolution of the sixteenth century. At what hour 'dawn' begins is always a matter of dispute, and depends largely on local circumstances. But one thing is certain. A new day has begun long before the average worker has commenced his toil. So with the Reformation. The study of its causes cannot commence with Erasmus or Savonarola." Herbert B. Workman, *The Dawn of the Reformation*, I-II (London, 1901/02), I, vii.

  [4] Not only single copies but entire editions of incunabula have been lost, for example the *editio princeps* of Boiardo's *Orlando innamorato* (1484). No doubt many other editions have been lost for which we have no record. See Rudolf Hirsch, *Printing, Selling and Reading, 1450-1650* (Wiesbaden, 1974), 125 fn. 1.

tors, lawyers, and theologians. Neither were they wealthy nobles, book-hungry humanists, or eager university students. They were young schoolboys and common clergy. More than fifty years ago, in his classic study on *Medieval Texts and their First Appearance in Print*, E. Ph. Goldschmidt articulated the historical task taken up here: "We must form some general idea of the book-buying public that fifteenth-century printers had in mind as their potential customers." He also sounded a warning: "We must not lose sight of the fact that their requirements, not our curiosity, determined the selection [of the texts they printed]."[5] Goldschmidt identified seven categories of "the most promising sections of the reading public." Though broad in scope and instructive at one level, his categories are not, at least in the order he adopts, descriptive of the public he had in mind. His seventh category (schoolboys and their teachers) should have been his first; and his first category (university academics) should have come later.[6] Whatever the accuracy and implications of his interpretation, however, his directive was — and still is — worthy. We know remarkably little about the people who bought Europe's first printed books, their favorite authors, and their preferred titles.

Printers in Europe produced approximately 27,500 editions between the invention of movable type and the end of the fifteenth century (ca. 1455 —1500), the period examined in this study.[7] Their works ranged in format from single-page broadsheets to multi-vol-

---

[5] E. Ph. Goldschmidt, *Medieval Texts and Their First Appearance in Print* (London, 1943), 13-14.

[6] The seven categories are: 1) the universities with all their numerous members; 2) the clergy from rich bishops to poor vicars; 3) the monasteries and convents with their libraries; 4) the secretaries, ambassadors, judges, and bailiffs at court; 5) the feudal nobility; 6) the lawyers and physicians; 7) the schoolboys and their teachers. E. Ph. Goldschmidt, *Medieval Texts*, 14-15.

[7] The number 27,500 includes all books, pamphlets, and indulgences as long as the printed edition was made with moveable type, not produced as a block book. The real number of editions would be higher, but in some cases entire print runs have disappeared (see above, fn. 4). We now know of about 26,550 incunabular editions (see below, fn. 9). When all extant editions finally surface, incunabulists expect the number to be about 27,500. I use the word "edition" in line with Goff's practice. I do not count variations within one edition — often called "issues" — as separate editions. But I do count separate "printings;" and the difference between "number of printings" and "number of editions" is often great. For example, there are 105 "printings" of Aesop's *Fables*; but only 71 "editions," because Aesop's *Fables* was included once in an edition of the *Facetiae* by Poggius Florentinus, in three editions of the *Fabulae* by Laurentius Abstemius, and always as a key text in the popular *Octo auctores*. I rank best-sellers according to the number of printings, not the number of editions.

ume folio sets. Although no printed catalogue lists more than 60% of them,[8] the *Incunabula Short Title Catalogue* (ISTC), a British Library electronic database of fifteenth-century printing, records more than 95% of them, namely 26,550 editions.[9] A CD-ROM version of the database, the *Illustrated Incunabula Short Title Catalogue* (IISTC), opens access to realms of book history that until the advent of computer-aided research were all but unfathomable.[10] At once a case study of the IISTC and a quantitative analysis of best-selling incunabula, this article explores a new avenue to measure the size and preferences of the market. Mine is not the first statistical study of early books, though wider in scope than earlier research.[11] It is rather the first

---

[8] GW has 12,227 editions; Goff has 12,923 editions; and Hain has 16,299 editions. For a brief history of the study of incunabula, with a description of all important catalogues, see the classic study by Haebler, *Handbuch der Inkunabelkunde* (Stuttgart, 1925, 1966²), 6-32; trans. Alfred Pollard, *The Study of Incunabula* (New York, 1933; rpnt, 1967), 7-37.

[9] The ISTC was started by Lotte Hellinga in 1980 in the Incunabula Section of the British Library. Regarding the early years of the project see the conference volume, L. H. Hellinga and J. Goldfinch (eds.), *Bibliography and the Study of 15th-Century Civilisation*, British Library Occasional Papers 5 (London, 1987); and for a more recent if short report, see M. C. Davies, "The Incunabula Short Title Catalogue (ISTC)," *Bulletin of the Society for Renaissance Studies* 7 (1990): 1-7. The database now holds records for 28,360 editions. Only 26,550 of these refer to true incunabula, however, while the other 1810 refer to books once catalogued as incunabula but known today to postdate 1500.

[10] The plan to illustrate the ISTC on CD-ROM was started in 1994 as Project Incipit, a joint venture between the British Library, Primary Source Media, and several partner libraries. I have used the second edition (1998) of The *Illustrated Incunabula Short Title Catalogue* (IISTC), which contains the entire British Library ISTC, and about 20,000 digitized images of incunabula provided by partner libraries. Copyright for the database is owned by the British Library, for the CD-ROM by Primary Source Media, and for each image by the contributing institution. To date, the IISTC (2nd ed.) contains over 20,000 images of approximately 4000 different incunabular editions (i.e., about five images per edition). There is no plan to provide a complete text-version of each incunable, rather just enough information to distinguish one edition from another. That is to say, the IISTC is an electronic catalogue, not an electronic text edition of incunabula.

[11] Robert Steele based his analysis starting in 1903 on the 9,841 incunabula described in Robert Procter's *Index to the Early Printed Books in the British Museum* (London, 1888). Robert Steele, "What Fifteenth-Century Books Are About," *The Library*, 2nd ser. 4 (1903): 337-354; 2nd ser. 5 (1904): 337-358; 2nd ser. 6 (1905): 137-155; 2nd ser. 8 (1907): 225-238. John Lenhart based his analysis in 1935 on the 24,421 titles described in Copinger's *Supplement to Hain's Repertorium bibliographicum* (London, 1902). Lenhart, *Pre-Reformation Printed Books: A Study in Statistical and Applied Bibliography*, a special edition of *Franciscan Studies* 14 (1935), (New York, 1935), x. Beyond these two pan-European studies, there are also more focused regional investigations (see the various introductions to most volumes in the GW), and local studies (especially for major print centers including Paris and Venice). One important study compares

attempt to rank best-selling incunabula. While others have focused on what fifteenth-century books were about, I ask, using that knowledge, how popular they were, and for whom they were printed?[12]

The largest segment of the book-buying public was comprised of clergy, both secular and regular, men who purchased best-selling titles, including the *Stella clericorum*, and who bought popular authors, especially Andreas de Escobar († 1431) and Antoninus Florentinus († 1459). After Breviaries, Missals, and Bibles, the eleventh best-selling book of the fifteenth century was the *Manipulus curatorum*, a handbook for parish clergy written by Guido de Monte Rochen (ca. 1333) and printed 119 times (ca. 60,000 copies) from London to Rome and from Barcelona to Vienna.[13] It sold twice as many copies as Gratian's *Decretum*, three times more than Thomas Aquinas' *Summa theologiae*, and six times more than Boccaccio's *Decameron* or Augustine's *City of God*. Yet Guido de Monte Rochen and his manual for priests have long been overlooked by historians of the period.[14]

The second largest segment of the book-buying public embraced schoolboys who spent their money on required textbooks, including

---

Venice to Florence, Bologna, and Nuremberg. See Leonardas V. Gerulaitis, *Printing and Publishing in Fifteenth-Century Venice* (Chicago, London, 1976), esp. 57-159.

[12] Robert Steele divides his statistical analysis of incunablula into four topical catatories, based on "popular wants" [part 1, 337]: 1) theology and devotion; 2) law; 3) literature; and 4) science. He divides these "in accordance with such a classification as would have suggested itself to the mind of a contemporary" [part 4, 225]. Converting his hard numbers to percentages we get: 44% theology and devotion; 36% literature; 11% law; and 9% science. Steele shows his own literary preferences when he discusses these categories in a different order: 1) science; 2) theology and devotion; 3) law; and 4) literature. Steele, "What are Fifteenth Century Books About." John Lenhart, with only slight reserve, accepts Steele's figures as "a fairly good survey of the content of the fifteenth-century book production." Lenhart, *Pre-Reformation Printed Books*, 71.

[13] Print runs of incunabula were as small as 100 copies and as large as 2300 copies. To estimate the total number of copies for a given incunable, I assume, as do most researchers, an average print run of 500 copies. See Haebler, *Handbuch der Inkunabelkunde*, 142-145; Lenhart, *Pre-Reformation Printed Books*, 9-10; and Hirsch, *Printing, Selling and Reading*, 65-67. Others use a slightly higher average, see for example Frederick Goff, "Characteristics of the Book of the Fifteenth Century," in L. Hellinga and H. Härtel (eds.), *Buch und Text im 15. Jahrhundert. Book and Text in the Fifteenth Century*. Wolfenbütteler Abhandlungen zur Renaissanceforschung 2 (Hamburg, 1981), 27-34, here at 33.

[14] There is no article dedicated to Guido de Monte Rochen in any of the following reference works: *Dictionary of the Middle Ages; Dictionnaire de théologie catholique; Encyclopedia of the Renaissance, Lexicon des Mittelalters; Lexicon für Theologie und Kirche; Oxford Encyclopedia of the Reformation; Religion in Geschichte und Gegenwart; Theologische Realenzyklopädie*.

the *Doctrinale* by Alexander de Villa Dei, the number one best-selling author of the century, and the *Rudimenta grammatices* by Niccolò Perotti, the twelfth best-selling title of the century. Alexander sold twice as many books as Virgil or Savonarola, ten times more than Ficino or Dante, and twenty-five times more than William of Ockam or Gabriel Biel. Yet Alexander and his Latin textbook have gone the way of Guido and his handbook for clergy, steadily toward oblivion.[15] If any of these discoveries inspire moments of surprise, this study may pay its greatest dividend by reviving ghosts from the dawn of the Reformation, voices once compelling and ubiquitous, now remote and unfamiliar.

Not every best-selling incunable evokes surprise today. What follows serves in some cases only to fine-tune general impressions and widely held assumptions, some of which have been stated with more precision than the evidence allows. The statement by Roger Chartier that "the Book of Hours ... was incontestably the commonest of all books of religious practice," is almost accurate.[16] While more popular than Missals, Psalters, and Bibles in that order, they were second by a long shot to Breviaries. Other statements need serious amendment. E. Ph. Goldschmidt remarked, "it is neither unexpected nor particularly illuminating" to find that commentaries on Peter Lombard's *Sentences* — by Aquinas, Bonaventure, Scotus, and Biel — were "among the earliest, the most stately, and the most frequently reprinted of early printed books."[17] They were not. The most popular commentary on Lombard, the *Super quattuor libros Sententiarum* by Aquinas, was printed only fourteen times, not enough to make the top 200 best-seller list.

For many years, scholars have talked about best-sellers in both manuscript and early book culture. Anthony Grafton remarked that Leonardo Bruni's Latin translations of Greek classics, which survive in as many as 300 manuscript copies, were "literally best sellers before

---

[15] There is no article dedicated to Alexander de Villa Dei in any of the following reference works: *Dictionary of the Middle Ages; Dictionnaire de spiritualité; Dictionnaire de théologie catholique; Encyclopedia of the Renaissance, Oxford Encyclopedia of the Reformation; Religion in Geschichte und Gegenwart; Theologische Realenzyklopädie.*

[16] Roger Chartier (ed.), *Les usages de l'imprimé* (Paris, 1987); trans. Lydia Cochrane, *The Culture of Print: Power and the Uses of Print in Early Modern Europe* (Princeton, 1989), 139. Other sweeping claims about Books of Hours are even less accurate. One scholar calls them the "biggest best-seller" of the age: Janet Backhouse, *Books of Hours* (London, 1985, rpnt 1995), 3.

[17] Goldschmidt, *Medieval Texts*, 16.

printing."[18] Had I counted Bruni's Latin translations (75 printings of Greek classics and 41 printings of Italian works), and added those to his self-authored treatises (67 printings), he would have been number sixteen on my list of best-selling authors. Reinhold Kiermayr remarked that Sebastian Brant's *Ship of Fools* (*Das Narrenschiff*) "claimed a spot on the Western world's best-seller list for a few centuries."[19] If so, the fifteenth century was not one of them. With only 26 printings before 1501, it ranked only 136 on the best-seller list, a notable accomplishment nonetheless for a work first printed in 1494.[20] The point is that scholars have talked, and still talk, about late-medieval best-sellers without offering concrete figures and tangible bench-marks.[21] This study helps to fill that gap. The publishing history of incunabula still constitutes the most reliable index of a book's popular-ity and the most objective manifestation of the century's literary taste.[22] Not only did market conditions help dictate what incunabula were printed, but readers' tastes greatly affected those conditions.

Research Questions and Limitations

Any study of best-selling incunabula nevertheless confronts three problems at the outset. First, statistics of incunabula are less objec-tive than the word "statistics" might imply. An IISTC search for *Controversia de nobilitate*, under the author's name, Bonaccursius de Montemagno († 1438), will produce six records but not alert researchers to a collection called *Dialogi decem variorum auctorum* that

---

[18] Anthony Grafton, "The Importance of Being Printed," *Journal of Interdisciplinary History* 11 (1980): 265-286, here at 273-274.

[19] Reinhold Kiermayer, "On the Education of the Pre-Reformation Clergy," *Church History* 53 (1984), 7-16, here at 7.

[20] Sebastian Brant's *Ship of Fools* (*Das Narrenschiff*) holds a more prominent position as the 48th best-seller if we consider only those books printed during the last decade of the fifteenth-century.

[21] The term "best-seller" has long been used by eminent historians and bibliogra-phers of early book culture. See Hirsch, *Printing, Selling and Reading*, 67; Gilmont, *La Réforme et le livre*, 20.

[22] The kinds of archival evidence used by Robert Darnton to investigate literary taste in pre-Revolutionary France — namely wholesaler account books with detailed records of retail orders, supply shipments, and warehouse inventories — does not exist in sufficient quantity to study incunabula in similar fashion for any geographic region, let alone for all of Europe. Indeed, even for eighteenth-century France, Darnton's archival find in Neuchâtel is extraordinary and unparalleled. See above, fn. 1.

includes the *Controversia de nobilitate* as one of its nine dialogues; and to complicate matters Jean Miélot translated the Latin work into French as *Controversie de noblesse* while William Caxton used that French version for his English edition, appending it to Cicero's *Cato maior, sive de senectute*.[23] When every printing is really accounted for, we see that the *Controversia de nobilitate* appeared nine times rather than six. A discrepancy of three may not sound alarms, but a 33% margin of error should. Readers who search the IISCT "author" field for "Leonardus Brunus Aretinus" (most names are Latinized) will find 52 records, yet not discover that Bruni's works were incorporated into books authored by other writers (including the *Vita et fabulae* by Aesop, the *De amore* by Franciscus Florius, and the *Historiae Romanae decades* by Titus Livius), nor that the German version of Bruni's *De duobus amantibus*, a Latin translation of Boccaccio's vernacular *Decameron* IV.I, is found in the *Translationen etlicher Bücher* by Nicolaus von Wyle, nor that 75 printings of Bruni's translations still survive. In fact, as author, Bruni was printed 67 times rather than 52, enough of a difference to push him from number 77 on the list of best-selling authors to number 56. These figures do not include translations, because I assume that most readers were purchasing Aristotle, Plato, and Boccaccio, not Bruni, and I discount his prefatory letters for the same reason.[24] Statistics of this order deserve our utmost caution and scrutiny. They record extant incunabula, not every edition produced.[25] They do not distinguish between a flooded market and diminished interest.[26] They tempt us to assume that production rates followed market interests.[27] And they compel us to think that best-sellers were *ipso facto* important books.[28] Yet depending on one's values — then as today — best-sellers could be trivial or profound, mundane or revolutionary, worthless or commendable.

---

[23] Goldschmidt, *Medieval Texts*, 5.

[24] For best results when searching the IISTC, use the "all fields" option rather than the "author field" or "title field." Searching the "all fields" option will recover more records than may be relevant — e.g. the comment "not by Leonardus Brunus Aretinus" ISTC im00063600 — but these can be discounted on close record-by-record inspection.

[25] See above, fn. 4.

[26] A decrease in the number of Bibles printed during each of the last three decades of the fifteenth century (77, 62, 48 respectively) probably indicates a flooded market. A decrease in the number of printings of the *Ars minor* by Donatus during the same decades (133, 124, 109 respectively) while humanist grammars sold better each decade, probably indicates diminished interest.

Many humanists despised the most popular author of the fifteenth century, Alexander de Villa Dei. Among them was Aldo Manuzio, who regretted ever having to memorize the "stupid Latin verses" (*carmen ineptum*) written by Alexander.[29] Though ostensibly detailed and precise, best-seller lists of this order are at best impressionistic. They should not be studied under a microscope nor interpreted verbatim number for number.

Secondly, the modern technology that makes this investigation possible can jeopardize its value. Although facsimile editions are more affordable than genuine incunabula, they do not allow researchers to examine paper, ink, and bindings, key material evidence bequeathed to us from the past. Even though microtext editions permit libraries everywhere to collect incunabula in vast numbers, facilitating *sur place* comparative studies, the same format turns three dimensional artifacts into two dimensional projections. Notwithstanding the advantages of digitized texts that are cleaned up artificially, magnified readily, and sent around the world instantly, scanned books are no more material than an electron. Yesterday's unique libraries and special collections have become, thanks to modern technology, today's *bibliothèques imaginaires*, in the full sense of the double entendre: at our fingertips we can access a *dream library* rich beyond belief; but on our shoulders we have the burden of *imagination* simply to feel paper, smell mold, and see bindings. The vast coverage and immediate searchability of the IISTC facilitates new research, yet places incunabula into contexts that they themselves never knew. The first printers in Mainz worked for a relatively small cadre of

---

[27] Supply and demand marched to different paces often enough to bankrupt many a printer. See Hirsch, *Printing, Selling and Reading*, 61-77.

[28] Paul Grendler comments that "Niccolò Perotti wrote the second most important fifteenth-century grammar after Guarino's." Paul Grendler, *Schooling in Renaissance Italy: Literacy and Learning, 1300-1600* (Baltimore and London, 1989), 173. Although arguably the case — Guarino did write the first humanist grammar, and Perotti depended on it — "importance" requires qualification. In this case we might note that Perotti's grammar sold twice as many copies as Guarino's (117 and 53 respectively), and that Erasmus preferred, in an unhappy choice, Perotti's grammar to all others available. Erasmus, *De ratione studii*, in ASD I.2, 114.14-15; Eng. trans. *On the Method of Study*, CWE 24, 667.1618.

[29] "Equidem puero mihi, cum Alexandri carmen ineptum de arte grammatica memoriae madabam, non ita contigisse plurimum deleo." Aldus Manutius, *Rudimenta grammatices latinae linguae* (Venice, 1501), preface, A^r-A2^r; quoted here from Giovanni Orlandi (ed.), *Aldo Manuzio Editore. Dediche prefazioni, note ai testi*, I-II (Milan, 1975), I, 39-40, at 40.25-26.

largely local clients, mostly monastic libraries, while on the horizon
emerged a pan-European market with its vast network of presses,
warehouses, suppliers, shippers, smugglers, wholesalers, retailers,
peddlers, binders, purchasers, libraries and borrowers. Hardly aware
that the book market would one day embrace these the gargantuan
dimensions, early printers did not think to compile lists of pan-European best-sellers. This is our question, not theirs. [30]

Thirdly, even the phrase itself — best-selling incunabula — can
risk self-contradiction. According to Konrad Haebler, one-time dean
of fifteenth-century book history, the word "incunabula" refers primarily to the character (not age) of early books, namely to the aspect
of books when printing technology was still in its infancy, indeed, as
the term implies, yet in the cradle.[31] The German word *Wiegendrucke*
(cradle-printings) invokes the same metaphor. In conventional terms
that period runs from 1455 to 1500, even though the turn of the century changed precious little in printing history, except that Aldus
Muntius introduced italic type in 1501. The "last" incunable printed,
barely under the hammer on the final day of the century, was Anto-
nius Rampegollis, *Figurae Bibliae* (Venice: Georgius Arrivabenus, 31
December 1500), a book not particularly different from those printed
soon thereafter.[32] Accordingly, some early incunabulists confined
their bibliographies to books printed before 1480, while others
included books printed up to 1517.[33] Even today, Jean-François
Gilmont prefers a late date to mark the end of the cradle period of
printing, 1520 or 1540.[34] When scholars have ignored or rejected
1500 as a proper *terminus ad quem* to the incunabular period — a
mean or average date that indicates the end of an era — they have
thought of incunabula not as books belonging to a specific period but
as books that have not yet lost their traits of infancy (what Haebler

---

[30] The term "best-seller" dates from late nineteenth-century and originated in the
U.S. The first best-seller list (with six titles, as was standard for the first decade)
appeared in the *Kansas Times & Star* (25 April 1889).

[31] Konrad Haebler, *Handbuch der Inkunabelkunde*, 1-5.

[32] Hain 13689; ISTC ir00026000. "This is the sort of information easily pulled
out of the ISTC but difficult to discover by conventional methods." M. C. Davies,
"The Incunable Short Title Catalogue," 1.

[33] Haebler, *Handbuch der Inkunabelkunde*, 2-3.

[34] "La date de 1500, qui marque traditionnellement la fin des incunables, résulte
d'un choix malheureux. Le véritable passage à la maturité se situe pour l'imprimé
entre 1520 et 1540." Jean-François Gilmont, "L'imprimerie à l'aube du XVIe siècle," in idem (ed.), *La Réforme et le livre*, 19-28, here at 19.

calls *den echten Inkunabelcharakter*) and moved through what Gilmont terms *le véritable passage à la maturité*.[35] According to Haebler, to understand that change, we have to recognize that Europe's first printers expressed themselves as independent creative masters who sold their books directly to monastic libraries, whereas later printers became hired craftsmen employed by large publishing firms and international trade partnerships that aimed their books at private consumption. As printing technology moved from the artist's *atelier* to the entrepreneur's office, the business moved from a limited production of fine editions to a rigorous competition for market share, and incunabula lost their traits of infancy. This transition happened as early as 1480 in Venice and 1490 in Paris, but as late as 1550 in many provincial towns.[36] In these dangerously general terms, which do at least distinguish Gutenberg Bibles from Lutheran pamphlets, as well as the master creativity in the former from the hired craftsmanship in the latter, the idea of "best-selling incunabula" is an oxymoron. Europe's earliest printed books were not produced to be sold by the thousands. Today for the sake of convenience most incunabulists accept 1500 as a deserving compromise to mark the end of cradle-printings. Thus they associate incunabula more with a period than a character, and would see no conflict in the phrase "best-selling inclunabula." After all, common was the printer, especially late in the century, who sold books in massive quantity. Whether those goods were incunabula or books is a matter of historiographical perspective. I use "incunabula" to refer to books printed before 1501, as a temporal qualifier rather than a character judgment, and thus free myself to write of "best-selling incunabula," a phrase that would seem self-contradictory to Haebler.

Books for the Secular and Regular Clergy

The remainder of this study divides into two major sections, each dedicated to one of the two largest markets for incunabula, clergy and schoolboys subdivided further into catagories of literary genre: liturgical texts, *pastoralia*, grammar books. I have not established a table of best-selling genres because that would involve too many sub-

---

[35] Haebler, *Handbuch der Inkunabelkunde*, 3; Gilmont, "L'imprimerie," 19.
[36] Haebler, *Handbuch der Inkunabelkunde*, 4-5.

jective decisions and result in several artificial divisions. Are Bibles and Psalters a subcategory of liturgical texts or an independent genre of their own? Does the *Golden Legend* belong to *pastoralia* or to vernaculars readers for school children? It seems more prudent to discuss the content and characteristics of genres in prose than to try tabulating related data.

1. *Liturgical Texts.* Manuals used in the liturgy have not attracted the scholarly attention that one might expect of such phenomenal best-sellers because they record what is already known, widely accepted, and frequently recited. For better or worse, historians of ideas have always been more intrigued by the new and influential than by repeated iterations and slight variations of the tried and true. Yet at some level the social history of ideas must account for the popularity of books whether influential or unexamined, vintage or novel, original or redundant.[37] Among books used in the liturgy, we discover that printers of incunabula produced approximately 56,000 copies of the *Epistolae et evangelia*, 90,000 Bibles, 120,000 Psalters, 180,000 Missals, and 225,000 Breviaries.

The number one best-selling title of the fifteenth century was the Breviary.[38] Even though late-medieval Breviaries varied, I count them as one title, for each functioned as the Divine Office of the church, an official prayer-book for clergy that marked hours of the day, feasts of the saints, and seasons of the year.[39] The first uniform Breviary, promulgated by Pius V in the bull *Quod a nobis*, appeared in

---

[37] This is not to say that liturgy was stagnant in the late Middle Ages. One specialist observes that by the sixteenth century, "the Roman liturgy resembled a garden so overgrown with plants from different times and places (and with a few weeds as well) that the original design of the Mass and the Divine Office was somewhat obscured." Michael Kwatera O.S.B., s. v. "Roman Catholic Liturgy," in the *Oxford Encyclopedia of the Reformation*, II, 445. Nevertheless, intellectual historians have concentrated on important thinkers like Pierre d'Ailly, Bridget of Sweden, Dante, Duns Scotus, Avicenna, Ficino, William of Ockham, and Gabriel Biel, whose printed works combined (49, 40, 32, 31, 22, 21, 15 and 13 printings respectively, or 224 total) amounts to only half as many printings as the Breviary alone (449 total).

[38] Two dated still unsurpassed histories of the Breviary are: Pierre Batiffol, *Histoire du Bréviaire romain* (Paris, 1893); and Suitbert Bäumer, *Geschichte des Breviers* (Freiburg, 1895).

[39] Bibles, Psalters, Breviaries, Missals, and Books of Hours each differed somewhat as it moved from one edition to the next. But for the sake of this study, when gathering statistics for best-selling titles, I consider each of them as single titles. A New Testament printed without the Old is still a Bible. A Book of Hours even without the Seven Penitential Psalms is still a Book of Hours.

[40] On late sixteenth-century printings of the Breviary, see Robert Kingdon,

1568.[40] That edition remained largely unaltered until the recent *Liturgia Horarum* of 1970. Assuming a population of about 60 million people in Europe in late fifteenth century,[41] there was approximately one copy of the Breviary for every 270 people.[42] Since not every priest needed his own copy, especially in large monasteries and cathedral chapters where monks and canons shared property, we can assume that most rural parish clergy did have their own.

The fourth best-selling title of the century was the Missal. It prescribes words to be said and gestures to be performed by priests during the Mass. The first Missals appeared in manuscript in the ninth century then eventually superseded other medieval liturgical books, including the sacramentary (fixed prayers of the Mass), the antiphonary (chants sung by the choir), and the lectionary (readings from the Gospels and Epistles). By the thirteenth century, as Missals began to take a more definite shape, most of them had both an Ordinary (the *ordo missae*) and a Proper (divided further between the *proprium de tempore* and the *proprium sanctorum*). The Ordinary listed prayers and blessings for every Mass, while the Proper contained those unique to specific liturgical seasons or individual feast days. The printing press played a key role in standardizing the Missal. As large editions of identical Missals spread throughout Europe, the new technology replaced the old, and the textual variations permitted in manuscript culture slowly disappeared. The most common Missal was that used by the Roman curia (developed ca. 1200). In 1570 Pope Pius V promulgated a new authoritative edition, which with few and slight exceptions endured unaltered until the twentieth century.

Slightly less popular than Breviaries and Missals were Psalters and Bibles, the sixth and eighth best-sellers respectively. I count independant New Testaments as "Bibles," but do not include the quite different *Biblia pauperum*, popular in their own right as illustrated abridgments of scripture brought together with short explanations of biblical types. Bibles and Psalters were certainly read by lay people for study and devotion, as well as by clergy for reasons other than liturgy, but I discuss them here because priests read them daily at Mass, a

---

"Patronage, Piety, and Printing in Sixteenth-Century Europe," in D. H. Pinkney and T. Ropp (eds.), *A Festschrift for Frederick B. Artz* (Durham, 1964), 19-36, esp. 31-36.

[41] Jan de Vries, "Population," in T. Brady Jr., H.A. Oberman, J. Tracy (eds.), *Handbook of European History 1400-1600: Late Middle Ages, Renaissance and Reformation,* I-II (Leiden, 1994), I, 1-44, here at 13 (table 1).

[42] This does not include lost editions and manuscript copies. See above, fn. 4.

purpose and function that explains the huge demand for more printed copies. Priests also used the popular *Epistolae et evangelia* (number
thirteen on the list), a collection of passages from the Epistles and
Gospels to be read at Mass, one pericope from each category.[43] This
is how people actually heard scripture being read, key passages from
the life of Christ, from the parables, and from Paul's letters. The sim-
plest editions of the *Epistolae et evangelia*, less uniform even than Breviaries and Missals, were straight pericope-books, while others, more
complete, resembled *plenaria*, books that contained vernacular translations of the Epistles and Gospels followed by brief expositions of
difficult verses. If pericope-books were liturgical texts, *plenaria*
belonged more to the genre of *pastoralia*. They were used by preachers in their preparation of sermons. At least 56,000 copies of the *Epistolae et evangelia* appeared during the fifteenth century, and 85% of
those were printed in the vernacular (43 German, 28 Italian, 23
Dutch, 16 Latin, 1 Spanish, 1 Slavic), many of which were read pub-
lically on a daily basis. What is more, young children bought and
used them for school.[44] Their absence from the scholarly literature on
biblical literacy and vernacular Bible translations in late-medieval
and early modern Europe compels us to count the *Epistolae et evangelia*
as a forgotten best-seller from the dawn of the Reformation.

2. *Pastoralia.* The bishops who gathered for Lateran IV in 1215, more
than two centuries before the invention of movable type, mandated pastoral reform and, without knowing it, gave future printers of incunabula
one of their largest markets: *pastoralia* for priests. Leonard Boyle coined
the term *pastoralia* to designate a genre of works used to educate clerics
in their responsibility for the care of souls.[45] The decrees of the Fourth

---

[43] The *Epistolae et evangelia* vary considerably between editions. Some of them are
straight pericope-books. Others, somewhat more elaborate, can be called *plenaria*.

[44] Grendler, *Schooling in Renaissance Italy*, 280-281.

[45] "One may term aids of this kind ... *pastoralia* — a very wide term indeed, which
at its widest, embraces any and every manual, aid or technique, from an episcopal
directive to a mnemonic of the seven deadly sins, that would allow a priest the better to
understand his office, to instruct his people, and to administer the sacraments, or,
indeed, would in turn enable his people the readier to respond to his efforts in their
behalf and to deepen their faith and practice... There was precious little available by
way of *pastoralia* to the ordinary, run-of-the-mill priest in his *cura animarum* before about
1200." Leonard Boyle, "The Inter-Conciliar Period 1179-1215 and the Beginnings of
Pastoral Manuals," in F. Liotta (ed.), *Miscellanea Rolando Bandinelli Papa Alessandro III*
(Siena, 1986), 45-56, here at 46. Most of Boyle's articles pertaining to *pastoralia* are collected in Leonard E. Boyle, *Pastoral Care, Clerical Education and Canon Law, 1200-1400*,
Variorum Reprints (London, 1981); but see too his, "Summae confessorum," in *Les Gen-*

Lateran Council state that priests had to be capable "not only in the duty of preaching, but also in the hearing of confessions, and the imposition of penances,"[46] all of which created a need for instruction. As aids written for instruction, first in manuscript then in print, *pastoralia* set out in simple authoritative terms rudimentary instruction for priests on what to preach and how to administer the sacraments.[47] Whereas Boyle doubted "very much if any priest possessed much more than a *psalter* at any time before the late Middle Ages,"[48] that picture had changed by 1500. Most parish priests owned an array of *pastoralia*. From the top-fifty best-selling titles alone, we know that Europe's first print shops produced at least 80,000 manuals of confession and 90,000 pastoral handbooks.[49]

The *Manipulus curatorum* was written by a priest named Guido de Monte Rochen about 1333 and survives in 180 manuscript copies.[50]

---

res littéraires dans les sources théologiques et philosophiques médiévales: Définition, critique, et exploitation, Actes du Colloque international de Louvain-la-Neuve, 1981 (Louvain, 1982), 227-237; and "The Fourth Lateran Council and Manuals of Popular Theology," in T. J. Heffernan (ed.), *The Popular Literature of Medieval England* (Knoxville, 1985), 30-43.

[46] "... non solum in praedicationis officio, verum etiam in audiendis confessionibus et poenitentiis iniungendis ..." Canon 10, "De praedicatoribus instituendis," Lateran IV, in N. P. Tanner and G. Alberigo (eds.), *Decrees of the Ecumenical Councils*, I-II (London, Washington, D.C., 1990), I, 240.2-3.

[47] Based on the low literacy-rate of medieval priests, we can assume that the early literature of pastoral care, flourishing as it was during the thirteenth and fourteenth centuries, cultivated an audience of readers larger than priests alone. See Joseph Goering, *William de Montibus (c. 1140-1213): The Schools and the Literature of Pastoral Cure*, Pontifical Institute of Mediaeval Studies, Studies and Texts 108 (Toronto, 1992), 58-99, esp. 59-67. By the late fifteenth century, considerably more priests were literate; by some estimates as many as 50% of priests in southern Germany were university trained: see Bernd Moeller, "Frömmigkeit in Deutschland um 1500," *Archiv für Reformationsgeschichte* 56 (1965): 5-31, here at 26-28; and Kiermayr, "On the Education of the Pre-Reformation Clergy," esp. 15. Thus for the incunabular period we do not have to be as compelled as for the earlier period to look outside the priesthood when explaining the flood of printed *pastoralia*. Some priests as late as the end of the sixteenth century still refused to pray from a printed liturgical book, preferring instead handwritten copies. See Lenhart, *Pre-Reformation Printed Books*, 98 (though without documentation); cited by. Richard Cole, "The Reformation Pamphlet and Communication Processes," in H.-J. Köhler (ed.), *Flugschriften als Massenmedium der Reformationszeit. Beiträge zum Tübinger Symposium 1980*. Spätmittelalter und frühe Neuzeit 13 (Stuttgart, 1981), 139-161, here at 139; and J. L. Flood, "Le Monde Germanique" in Gilmont (ed.), *La Réforme et le livre*, 29-104, here at 32 fn. 8.

[48] Boyle, "The Inter-Conciliar Period," 45.

[49] The number of manuals of confession and pastoral handbooks would have been considerably higher had I counted more than just the top-fifty best-sellers.

[50] See Pierre Michaud-Quatin, s.v. "Guy de Montrocher," in *Dictionaire de Spiritualité*, vol. 6, cols. 1303f.; and Peter A. Dykema, "Conflicting Expectations: Parish Priests in Late Medieval Germany" (PhD dissertation, University of Arizona, 1998),

With 119 incunabular printings (ca. 60,000 copies), it ranks number eleven on the best-seller list. Because Guido shows considerable knowledge of canon law and quotes liberally from the church fathers and medieval theologians, scholars think he had a university education. He wrote his book for novice priests and titled it *Manipulus* because he wanted them to keep it close at hand. The first of three sections concerns six of the seven sacraments (leaving out penance) and devotes most of that space to the eucharist. This part of the book is a practical "how-to" guide on celebrating the Mass. The second section in 24 chapters is given to penance, treating in detail the topics of contrition, confession, and satisfaction. It instructs confessors in the art of making a thorough examination of a conscience by asking proper and probing questions, for which Guido relies heavily on medieval manuals of confession. The third and shortest section in four chapters is a brief summary of the Christian faith, a *Summario* or "catechism" of sorts with the Apostles' Creed, the Lord's Prayer and the Ten Commandments.[51] In a short discourse on the "etymology" of *sacerdos*, Guido remarks that priests should be literate so as to read the liturgy (*sacer dicens*), to administer the sacraments (*sacra dans*), to act as a spiritual guide (*sacer dux*), and to teach Christians the basics of faith (*sacer docens*).

Another pastoral handbook, the anonymous *Stella clericorum* (early 13th century), survives in 450 manuscripts and was printed 59 times during the fifteenth-century (ca. 30,000 copies), making it 42 on the best-seller list.[52] A short treatise of 23 chapters, the *Stella clericorum*

147-164. All the manuscript copies are listed in Horacio Santiago Otero, "Guido de Monte Roterio y el Manipulus curatorum," in S. Kuttner and K. Pennington, (eds.), *Proceedings of the Fifth International Congress of Medieval Canon Law* (Salamanca, 21-25 September 1976), Munumenta Iuris Canonici C-6 (Vatican City, 1980), 259-265.

[51] On the contents of Italian Renaissance *Summarii*, see Grendler, *Schooling in Renaissance Italy*, 343-345. The word "catechism" is a sixteenth-century term that refers to fundamental instruction in the Christian faith centered on the Apostles' Creed, the Lord's Prayer and the Ten Commandments. Sixteenth-century catechisms differ from their late-medieval ancestors (like this "catechism" in the *Manipulus Curatorum*) in style more than content. Sixteenth-century catechisms are generally, and more technically, dialogues between teachers and students, written as a series of questions and answers. See Robert J. Bast, *Honor Your Fathers: Catechisms and the Emergence of a Patriarchal Ideology in Germany, 1400-1600*, Studies in Medieval and Reformation Thought 63 (Leiden, New York, Cologne, 1997), passim, but esp. xiii fn. 7, and xvii with fn. 19.

[52] For the only recent edition, see Eric Reiter (ed.), *Stella clericorum*, Toronto Medieval Latin Texts (Toronto, 1997). For a list of surviving manuscripts and printed editions (though not complete), see Eric H. Reiter, "The *Stella clericorum* and Its

attracted a readership from Scandinavia to the Iberian Peninsula. The image of "morning star" in the title announces its focal theme of guidance, especially for priests. This explains why the book sometimes appears under the title *Stella sacerdotum*.[53] Compared to the *Manipulus curatorum*, it is less a practical guide in the administration of sacraments than an admonition to priests to live a moral life worthy of their high calling. The priestly vocation — namely caring for souls — is not to sport a crown, but to shoulder a burden.[54] Priests should acquire learning, develop eloquence, and practice upright living.[55] Instead of helping priests understand the theology of the liturgy or instructing them in the minute details of how and when to hold the host, the author reminds his priestly readers that their hands are like the Virgin's womb, for the Son of God is incarnate in both.[56] The concurrent success of the *Manipulus curatorum* and the *Stella clericorum* is due in large part to their differences: they are neither redundant nor at cross purposes. Priests had good reason to buy both.

They also had reason to purchase manuals of confession. The traditional ritual of Christian forgiveness comprises four key elements: contrition, confession, penance, and absolution. These mark steps through which baptized Christians, having sinned and fallen, must pass when being restored to grace. From the second to the seventh century, the dominant practice centered on canonical penance, which was both public and severe and imposed by a bishop instead of a priest. By the fifth century, as arduous penalties led Christians to delay their penance until the last minute, believing that dying sinners could be reconciled without major penitential exercises, penance became a gift to receive not just a duty to perform. By the end of the sixth century, another ritual of forgiveness emerged based on penitentials, short manuals of instruction that tallied specific sins with fitting tariffs and coached clergy in the art of helping penitents confess. In contrast to canonical penance, this ritual was essentially private

---

Readers: A Study of the Reception of Popular Theology in the Later Middle Ages" (PhD Thesis, University of Toronto, 1994), 280-312, 329-337.

[53] Eric Reiter (ed.), *Stella clericorum*, 4.

[54] "Cura enim animarum non debet esse honori sed oneri." *Stella clericorum*, 1.50-51.

[55] "Qvilibet pastor siui sacerdos tenetur in se habere tria, scilicet scienciam, eloquenciam, et bonam vitam." *Stella clericorum*, 5.1-2.

[56] "O veneranda sacerdotum dignitas, si digne et sacerdotaliter vixeritis, intra quorum manus uelut in utero Virginis Dei Filius incarnatur." *Stella clericorum*, 16.1-3.

(between confessor and penitent) but still severe, requiring three to seven years of bread and water for the sin of adultery. Until the thirteenth century, during which time penances became lighter and priests gained authority in their role, confession was thought necessary to forgiveness, but never declared universally obligatory until Lateran IV in 1215, when the decree *Omnis utriusque sexus* required yearly confession. In spite of the exaggeration in H. C. Lea's comment that it was "perhaps the most important legislative act in the history of the church," the decree did foster change relevant to the printing history of incunabula.[57] As the church integrated new ideas into old habits, a pastoral literature grew up around the need to instruct clergy. None of the great *Summae* for confessors became period best-sellers, being terrifically detailed, encyclopedic, and polemical. They include the first *summa* by Raymond of Peñaforte (ca. 1230), a Catalan canonist, as well as those by the Franciscan Angelus de Clavasio (1486), and the Dominican Sylvester Prierias Mazzolini (1514).

More popular were the shorter abridged manuals of confession. The two most sought after manuals, vastly different from each other in origin and content, hailed on the one hand from a canonist, Andreas Escobar († ca. 1430), and on the other from a Dominican archbishop, Antoninus Florentinus († 1459), better known as Antonino Pierozzi.[58] The *Modus confitendi* by Escobar, printed 89 times (ca. 45,000 copies), ranked number 22 on the best-seller list. A model examination of conscience to be used in preparation for confession, it was sold as a short work of six leaves. The *Confessionale — Defecerunt* by Pierozzi, so-called because of its incipit "*Defecerunt scrutantes scrutinio*," was printed 71 times (ca. 35,000 copies) and ranked number 30 on the best-seller list. It comprises a list of practical questions to guide penitents through the processes of examination and to help confessors impose appropriate penances.

3. *Sermon collections.* To equip priests as preachers, a generous selection of theoretical treatises and practical guides were available, including lexicons, *summae* of vitues and vices, collections of *exempla*, books on the *artes praedicandi*, and model sermons.[59] The *Legenda aurea*

---

[57] Henry Charles Lea, *A History of Auricular Confession and Indulgences in the Latin Church*, I-III (Philadelphia, 1896), I, 230.

[58] For the statistics gathered in tables one and two, I adopt the spelling of names used by the IISTC database, to facilitate further research. A search for "Pierozzi" for example produces nothing, not even a cross reference.

sanctorum by Jacopo da Varazze (Jacobus Voragine, † 1298) —
although read, too, by others in different contexts, including by
young children at school[60] — provided preachers with a survey of
saints lives organized, depending on which edition, into 180 chapters that followed the liturgical calendar. It was printed 150 times
(ca. 75,000 copies). Preachers used it together with other popular
handbooks to illustrate their sermons. They found similes, *exempla*,
parables, and proverbs gathered from nature, history, and the Bible.
They also depended on collections of printed sermons, available in
vast numbers, that modeled what they should say in the pulpit. Two
preachers appear on the list of best-selling authors based exclusively
on their published sermon collections. Although the Dominican
Johannes Herolt († 1468) did not produce any one collection popular enough to make the top-fifty list, at least under his own name,
the *Postilla Guillermi*, number eighteen with 98 printings (ca. 49,000
copies), was a near verbatim adaptation of Herolt's sermons.[61] This,
together with his other collections, made Herolt the twentieth best-
selling author of the century, ahead of Jerome, Seneca, Bernard of
Clairvaux, and Petrarch.[62] The Franciscan Roberto Caracciolo (†
1495) wrote six collections of sermons popular enough that he
became forty-fifth best-selling author, ahead of Boethius, Bruni, and
Valla.[63] Yet neither Herolt nor Caracciolo appear with even the
briefest biographical sketch in the *Dictionary of the Middle Ages,* the
Encyclopedia of the Renaissance or the *Encyclopedia of the Reformation.* Sev-
en other best-selling authors owe at least some of their popularity to
their model sermons, including Thomas Aquinas (fourth best-selling

---

[59] For much of the information in this paragraph, I have benefitted greatly by
reading an early draft of Stephan Borgehammar's forthcoming "Introduction" to
volumes 31-33 in the microfiche collection, *Incunabula: The Printing Revolution in Europe,
1455-1500* (Primary Source Media).

[60] See Grendler, *Schooling in Renaissance Italy*, 285.

[61] Catalogued under the name Guillermus, the sermons have been falsely attributed to Guilelmus Alvernus and Guilelmus Peraldus, who moreover get confused
with one another.

[62] Johannes Herolt's incunabular sermon collections include: *Sermones Discipuli* (51
printings), *Liber Discipuli de eruditione Christifidelium* (7 printings), *Sermones super epistolas
dominicales* (5 printings), *Quadragesimale Discipuli* (1 printing).

[63] Roberto Caracciolo's incunabular sermon collections include: *Sermones quadragesimales de poenitentia* (26 printings), *Le Prediche di Frate Roberto* (23 printings), *Sermones
de laudibus sanctorum* (18 printings), *Sermones de timore divinorum iudiciorum* (13 printings), *Sermones de adventu* (12 printings), *Sermones quadragesimales de peccatis* (6 printings).

author), Jean Gerson (seventh), Bonaventure (tenth), Albert the Great (eleventh), Jacopo da Varazze (eighteenth), Savonarola (twenty-third), and Johannes Nider (forty-seventh).[64] The year 1517 did not mark a mystifying paradigm shift in preaching or sermon literature, neither for its popularity nor for its frequency in print. Yet until the earlier period is better studied, we will not understand the extent of contrasts and continuities.

4. *Books of Hours*. If we allow for slight variations and count all printed *Horae* as one title, then Books of Hours were the century's second best-seller, a standard manual of popular devotion during the Middle Ages and Renaissance.[65] Used primarily by priests, when first introduced in the thirteenth century, and mostly for private devotion rather than pastoral care, Books of Hours eventually had a different audience. By the fifteenth century, printers targeted the laity. At their core, Books of Hours contain eight short services designed to be recited, not unlike the Divine Office of the Breviary, during different times of the day and night: Matins, Lauds, Prime, Terce, Sext, None, Vespers and Compline. These eight offices comprise the socalled Little Office of the Blessed Virgin Mary. In addition, most Books of Hours have a calendar of feast days, extracts from the Gospels, Hours of the Cross, Hours of the Holy Spirit, the Seven Penitential Psalms, the Office of the Dead, prayers to the Virgin, to the Trinity, and to various saints. Most fifteenth-century editions are in Latin, though sometimes even they contain short vernacular sections that correspond to shifts during the Mass from vocal prayer (Latin) to silent meditation (vernacular).[66]

Books for School Children

The second largest market for printers of incunabula was comprised of school children and their need for textbooks: hornbooks, primers, grammars, readers, catechisms, letter-writing manuals, and classical authors. These categories are not strict genres, for many of

---

[64] The sermons by Bernard of Clairvaux were read as devotional classics rather than used as homiletical models.

[65] See above, fn. 39.

[66] On the history of vocal and silent prayer, see Paul Saenger, "Books of Hours and the Reading Habits of the Later Middle Ages," in R. Chartier (ed.), *The Culture of Print: Power and the Uses of Print in Early Modern Europe* (Princeton, 1989), 141-173.

them can overlap in a single volume. For example the so-called "grammar" written by Aldo Manuzio and published in 1493, as revised in 1501, contains not only an invocation to Christ but also an alphabet table (typical of hornbooks), a list of syllables (common to primers), the Pater Noster, Ave Maria, Apostles' Creed, Ten Commandments, Salve Regina, several prayers, and a series of Psalms (not unlike catechisms).[67] Only after this "introduction" does Manuzio proceed to the basics of Latin grammar. Learning the alphabet and memorizing the Ten Commandments went hand in hand for both scholastic and humanistic grammarians. This observation led one recent historian to describe grammar as a moral art, and the masters who taught it, instructors in virtue.[68] Beyond the problem of defining genres is the equally difficult task of marking off disciplines. Although I refer to separate philosophies of education — the medieval *auctores* and the Renaissance *studia humanitatis* — clear borders do not divide them. Humanistic schoolmasters firmly rejected "logical" Latin grammars,[69] especially Alexander's *Doctrinale*,[70] and yet they generally retained Donatus for elementary grammar and Cato for novice readers. Finally, I divide all pre-university instruction into primary and secondary schools despite the fact that fifteenth-century models of education — parish, chapter, and cathe-

---

[67] Aldus may have written his grammar as early as 1487. See Kristian Jensen, "The Latin Grammar of Aldus Manutius and its Fortuna," in D. S. Zeidberg and F. G. Superbi (eds.), *Aldus Manutius and Renaissance Culture: Essays in Memory of Franklin D. Murphy*. Acts of an International Conference at Venice and Florence, 14-17 June 1994 (Florence, 1998): 247-285, here at 247. On "catechism" see above, fn. 51.

[68] The "fundamental social mission" of the grammar master, notes Paul Gehl in his recent study of Latin education in medieval Florence, was to inculcate urban lay elites with "classical and Christian Latin traditions." What is more, "elementary moral principles were included in the grammar classroom at all periods." He concludes, "Eventually, the Jesuit reformers of the sixteenth century swept away all moralizing in language education and gave us modern Latin, a philological rather than a philosophical construct, a skill and not a norm." Paul F. Gehl, *A Moral Art: Grammar, Society, and Culture in Trecento Florence* (Ithaca, 1993), 3-4, 240. Cf. Robert Black, "The Curriculum of Italian Elementary and Grammar Schools, 1350-1500," in D. R. Kelley and R. H. Popkin (eds.), *The Shapes of Knowledge from the Renaissance to the Enlightenment*, International Archives of the History of Ideas 124 (Dordrecht, Boston, London, 1991), 137-163, here at 138-140 and 153-54.

[69] On speculative grammar, see Jan Pinborg, "Speculative Grammar," in N. Kretzmann, A. Kenny, J. Pinborg (eds.), *The Cambridge History of Later Medieval Philosophy* (Cambridge, 1982; rpnt 1990), 254-269; and on logical grammar, see Terrence Heath, "Logical Grammar, Grammatical Logic, and Humanism in Three German Universities," *Studies in the Renaissance* 18 (1971), 9-64.

[70] Heath, "Logical Grammar," esp. 11-31, 41-63.

dral schools, public and private institutions, small *ad hoc* tutorials and large formal academies — do not all equally abide uniform simplification. Whichever path schoolchildren took between learning their ABCs and matriculating at university, however, they had to pass through both elementary and intermediate school curricula.

1. *Primary Schools.* The medieval curriculum for elementary education (ages five and six plus) relied on hornbooks for the ABCs, and primers for initial help in phonetics and reading.[71] Yet hornbooks and primers were fragile documents and often mistreated by their impatient users. Few if any survive from the fifteenth century.[72] Even so, archival evidence supports the assumption that children who graduated to Donatus had already learned their ABCs in hornbooks and primers. One schoolmaster near Pistoia, when ordering books in 1526 to sell to pupils, requested 20 hornbooks, 20 primers, and 6 grammars (namely Donatus).[73] If these early sixteenth-century figures from one Italian city at all indicate relative demand across Europe during the second half of the fifteenth century — and certainly more pupils learned the alphabet than studied Latin — then hornbooks and primers were Europe's most common incunabula, perhaps by a factor of two.[74] Without more evidence, we can never know for certain however.

The standard basic grammar was the *Ars minor*, attributed to Aelius Donatus (4th century). It existed virtually unchallenged for ten centuries as the first grammar for school children, one of the world's most tenacious best-sellers ever.[75] Indeed, the name Donatus was all but synonymous with grammar. Presses in Europe produced at least 284 incunabular printings (ca. 140,000 copies), making it number

---

[71] Andrew Tuer, *History of the Horn Book* (London, 1897; rpnt New York, 1979), passim. Grendler, *Schooling in Renaissance Italy*, 142-161.

[72] Grendler lists Hain 13532, *Psalterium puerorum*, as one "possible" incunabular primer. Grendler, *Schooling in Renaissance Italy*, 147 fn. 23.

[73] *"20 tavole di leggere, 20 salterii, 6 Donati."* As cited by Grendler, *Schooling in Renaissance Italy*, 32.

[74] The teacher ordered 3.3 times as many hornbooks and primers (20 each) as grammars (6). Since Donatus was printed 322 times, even in conservative terms we could thus expect at least 900 printings of hornbooks and primers (322 x 3.3 = 1063). The Breviary was printed 449 times: hence my estimate of "a factor of two".

[75] For the monumental critical edition, see Louis Holtz (ed.), *Donat et la tradition de l'enseignement grammatical. Étude sur l'Ars Donati et sa diffusion, IVe — IXe siècle* (Paris, 1981). For an English translation, see Wayland Johnson Chase (trans.), *The Ars Minor of Donatus: For One Thousand Years the Leading Textbook of Grammar*, University of Wisconsin Studies in the Social Sciences and History 11 (Madison, 1926).

five on the century's best-seller list. It teaches the parts of speech and
the main conjunctions and declensions. The late medieval work published in Italy, known by historians of grammar as *Janua* but not distinguished in most incunabula catalogues from the *Ars minor*, was
quite different.[76]

After Donatus, pupils advanced to Latin readers, the first of which
was the *Distichs* of Cato, printed 217 times in the fifteenth century (ca.
110,000 copies) and number seven on the century's best-seller list.[77]
Carrying the name Dionysius Cato but now attributed to Marcus
Porcius Cato the Censor († 149 BCE), the book includes a collection
of moral aphorisms influenced by ancient Greek and Roman texts,
compiled and augmented in the early Middle Ages. The fact that so
many pupils had to memorize the entire book explains why Cato's
moral sayings enjoyed such wide currency. Its importance both as a
Latin reader and a textbook for virtues was unrivaled, and the record
of its use would suggest that teachers accredited it with great success
on both counts. After working through Cato, children turned to other primary Latin readers, notably *Aesop's Fables* (number 16 on the
best-seller list, with 105 printings) and the *Ecloga* of Theodulus (number 62, with 46 printings). A popular metrical version of *Aesop's
Fables*, the *Aesopus moralisatus*, a best-seller on its own account (number
24, with 79 printings), if added to the prose version would boost that
classic to number eight on the best-seller list, just after the *Distichs* of
Cato.

2. *Secondary Schools.* The medieval curriculum for intermediate education, as for elementary education, boasted a standard grammar as
well as Latin readers, including some classical authors. The grammar
was Alexander's *Doctrinale*, used also by first-year university students
and number three on the century's best-seller list.[78] Written in verse
with 2,650 hexameter lines and printed at least 368 times (ca.
185,000 copies), it became the affliction of many a weary pupil.[79] It
took students beyond Donatus into the more complex realms of syn-

---

[76] See Grendler, *Schooling in Renaissance Italy*, 174-182. Even though the IISTC
identifies the author of the "*Ars minor (Rudimenta grammatices)*' as Donatus, I do not
count it (i.e. *Janua*) in my statistics for Donatus.

[77] For a Latin-English facing-page edition, see Wayland Johnson Chase (ed.), *The
Distichs of Cato: A Famous Medieval Textbook*, University of Wisconsin Studies in the
Social Sciences and History 7 (Madison, 1922).

[78] Heath, "Logical Grammar," 11.

[79] See the comment by Aldo Manutio, above at fn. 29.

tax, meter, and figures of speech. After a good grounding in the *Doctri-nale*, pupils could tackle intermediate readers, including two best-sellers. The *Facetus* (or *Liber faceti docens mores hominum*), a manual of good manners written in verse, ranked number 36 with 65 printings (ca. 32,000 copies), composed perhaps by John of Garland (early 13ᵗʰ c.). The *Floretus*, a short religious poem falsely attributed to Bernard of Clairvaux, was number 48 with 55 printings (ca. 27,000 copies). Not far behind were other authors from the popular reader-anthology entitled *Octo auctores*, itself printed 29 times but not enough to make the top 100 best-sellers. Beyond the five *auctores* already mentioned — the *Distichs* of Cato, *Aesop's Fables*, the *Facetus*, *Floretus*, and Theodulus' *Ecloga* — the remaining three included: Alanus de Insulis (Alain de Lille), *Doctrinale altum seu liber parabolarum*, a verse collection of aphorisms (number 55, printed 52 times); Pseudo-Bernard of Clairvaux, *De contemptu mundi*, a verse treatise on the state of world (number 58, printed 49 times); and Matthaeus Vindocinensis, *Tobias*, a verse treatise on virtue (number 104, printed 33 times). The most popular classical authors for intermediate medieval pupils were poets as well. The marketing success of Virgil's *Georgics* (number 15, printed 109 times) and his *Aeneid* (number 19, printed 96 times) owes much to the fact that teachers assigned them as textbooks. The same was true for *The Consolation of Philosophy* by Boethius, part verse and part prose, a popular reader for intermediate education (number 26, printed 75 times).[80]

Some medieval schools also taught *ars dictaminis*, the theory and practice of letter writing. Although normally a university subject, *ars dictaminis* could be studied in secondary schools by brighter pupils of sufficient means, many of them in preparation for careers as secretaries in the service of civic and religious authorities. They purchased and studied technical manuals of formulaic letter-writing, above all [pseudo-] Cicero's *Rhetorica ad Herennium* and his *De inventione* (with 34 and 15 printings respectively, neither on the top 100 list). Schoolmasters taught *ars dictaminis* in keeping with the principles of medieval logic and dialectics.

A rival pedagogy to *ars dictaminis* and the medieval *auctores* was the Renaissance *studia humanitatis*. In both primary and secondary

[80] On the curriculum of primary and secondary schools, see Grendler, *Schooling in Renaissance Italy*, 111-117, with detailed bibliography. Cf. Black, "The Curriculum of Italian Elementary and Grammar Schools," though he denies that there was a humanist revolution in grammar schooling before 1500 (esp. 138, 155).

schools, it relied on a curriculum drawn from prose more than poetry. Avid promoters of the *studia humanitatis* rejected medieval grammars. They defined grammar as the art of speaking and writing well as observed in the works of prose writers and poets, not as the science of speaking correctly and the logical analysis of language.[81] Although many humanistic teachers kept Donatus and Cato in their primary curriculum, they added Cicero and Terence for intermediate pupils while removing Alain de Lille, Theodulus, Matthaeus Vindocinensis, Pseudo-Bernard, Boethius, and Facetus. Cicero is the only author to have five titles on the top-fifty best-seller list, none of them manuals of *ars dictaminis*. Much of his late-medieval success is owing to humanistic school teachers who assigned his books as required reading.

The first Renaissance grammar was the *Regulae grammaticales* by Guarino of Verona (ca. 1418), written to replace the *Doctrinale* of Alexander. Printed 53 times and number 54 on the best-seller list, it deserves recognition more for its pioneering role than for its lasting popularity. A Renaissance grammar with more stamina on the best-seller list, the *Rudimenta grammatices* by Niccolò Perotti, was the century's twelfth best-seller with 117 printings, despite its late appearance on the market in 1473.[82] No other title experienced such phenomenal, quick, and widespread success,[83] almost 59,000 copies in 27 years.[84]

Dawn of the Reformation

Nothing so far in this study warrants the temporal qualifier in its title — dawn of the Reformation — for that era knows neither firm

---

[81] Isidore of Seville († 636) wrote, "Grammatica est scientia recte loquendi," whereas Niccolò Perotti observed in 1468: "Grammatica est ars recte loquendi recteque scribendi, scriptorum et poetarum lectionibus observata." As cited in Grendler, *Schooling in Renaissance Italy*, 162.

[82] Nicolaus Perottus, *Rudimenta grammatices* (Rome, 19 March 1473); Hain 12643; ISTC ip00300000. See W. Keith Percival, "The Place of the *Rudimenta grammtices* in the History of Latin Grammar," *Res Publicum Litterarum* 4 (1981): 233-263; and Wolfgang Milde, "Zur Druckhäufigkeit von Niccolò Perottis 'Cornucopiae' and 'Rudimenta grammatices' im 15. und 16. Jarhhundert," *Res Publicum Litterarum* 5 (1982): 29-42.

[83] 37 of the 117 printings came from outside Italy, including France, Germany, Spain and the Low Countries.

[84] 60,000 copies does not include the ca. 12,000 copies (23 printings) of the *Grammatica nova* by Bernardus Perger, an adaptation of Perotti so close to the original that some bibliographers group the two together.

beginning nor absolute end, let alone the same precise boundaries attributed to the period of incunabula. Indeed, whereas my statistics focus on books printed before 1501, that very limitation, though necessary for practical reasons, skews the picture of literary tastes at the "Dawn of the Reformation". The market for some authors is exaggerated: Donatus was printed 374 times between 1455 and 1500. For others, the opposite is true: Erasmus appeared only 3 times between 1495 and 1500. Yet Erasmus and Donatus were both best-selling authors at the dawn of the Reformation. Improved electronic research tools will one day allow scholars to collect bibliographic data for both the fifteenth and sixteenth centuries at once, and my figures will need adjusting. But until then, whereas the dawn of the Reformation did at least in part fall to the years 1455-1500, printing statistics from those years are the most complete and reliable metric of the popularity of books that publicized, challenged, and swayed "the conflicting claims of mysticism, Augustinianism, nominalism and Renaissance humanism."[85] After three centuries of prominent and ubiquitous use, Alexander's *Doctrinale* gradually ceded pride of first place to grammars less steeped in medieval dialectics and more in tune with Renaissance rhetoric.[86] While scholastic grammarians disliked the novelty in Perotti's grammar, humanistic grammarians protested the Aristotelian logic in Alexander's. At the University of Tübingen the transition was complete by 1531.[87]

The first harbinger of change came in 1496, when the Augustinians in Tübingen (one year before Johann von Staupitz arrived) petitioned the faculty of Arts (one year after Gabriel Biel had died) to accept students who had learned their Latin in grammars written by Italian humanists, not Alexander. In no ambiguous terms, the university complied, noting that students could be taught in fact "more suitably and fully" in newer grammars, specifically the *Grammatica nova*, than in "Alexander's long drawn-out asides."[88] *Grammatica nova* is

[85] Oberman, *Dawn of the Reformation*, as above, fn. 3.

[86] Heath, "Logical Grammar," esp. 11-31, 41-63.

[87] Oberman, "Headwaters of the Reformation," 67 fn. 107. For a more detailed examination of the climate of heated debate in Tübingen at the turn on the century, see idem, *Werden und Wertung der Reformation*, Spätscholastik und Reformation 2 (Tübingen, 1977, ²1979), esp. 17-55; trans., *Masters of the Reformation* (Cambridge, Mass., 1981), 15-44.

[88] The Faculty of Arts noted that Augustinians "in exercitio grammaticali comodosius et compendiosius completuri quam per illam longam digressionem Alexandri

Perger's popular adaptation of Perotti's *Rudimenta Grammatices*.[89] That same year, Heinrich Bebel, an inspiring advocate of grammatical reform, arrived in Tübingen as professor of rhetoric. He and his students, including Jacob Henrichmann (law), Johannes Altenstaig (theology), and Johannes Brassicanus (rhetoric) all began to condemn Alexander's *Doctrinale*, urging the use of Perotti's grammar in its place. The controversy flared and in 1505 the Faculty of Arts had to insist on Donatus and Alexander as required texts, a dire if conciliatory attempt to re-establish order. As the fight continued, humanist grammars eventually won the day. According to a visitation report of 1531, Alexander and Donatus were no longer being read. In the *via moderna*, students preferred Johannes Brassicanus, and in the *via antiqua*, Aldus Manutius.[90]

Heiko Oberman has shown in every chapter of his oeuvre that in order for scholars to grasp the Late Middle Ages, Renaissance, and Reformation, they have to discern all three periods as united and examine each as it overlaps the next, all the while tolerant and perceptive enough to see a "waxing harvest" where others perceive but a "waning autumn."[91] The cradle period of printing belongs to all three periods, indeed, even to the Reformation during its dawn. As Oberman noted in his Heineken Lecture of 1996: "Today late medieval history and the era of Renaissance and Reformation have been reunited, and the once magical shift in the year 1500 is left only to preoccupy the collectors of rare incunabula."[92] Although it must be added that many incunabula were once anything but rare, having been sold in tens of thousands of copies, if today they seem obscure, that could be due to the harsh, non-discriminating elements of nature, but it is also, at least in some cases, the fault of our selective,

---

edoceantur, utpote per certas regulas artis grammatice in unum quam brevissime redactas, que grammatica nova dicitur, aut alia consimilis una cum autore aliquo per declinationes et latinitates, continuando huiusmodi exercitium sicut in bursa." Universitätsarchiv Tübingen XV, 17; fol 35ʳ, quoted here from Johannes Haller, *Die Anfänge der Universität Tübingen 1477-1537*, I-II (Stuttgart, 1929), II, 82.

[89] See above, fn. 84. Cf. Heath, "Logical Grammar," 29.

[90] "Alexander et Donatus non leguntur apud modernos, sed legitur Brassicanus in M[odernorum] et Aldus in Realium," Universitätsarchiv Tübingen I, ir, fol. 10ʳ, quoted here from Haller, *Die Anfänge der Universität Tübingen*, II, 183.

[91] Heiko A. Oberman, *The Harvest of Medieval Theology: Gabriel Biel and Late Medieval Nominalism* (Cambridge Mass., 1963; Durham, 1983).

[92] Heiko A. Oberman, "The Devil and the Devious Historian: Reaching for the Roots of Modernity" (30 September 1996), *in KNAW / Heineken Lectures 1996*, Royal Netherlands Academy of Arts and Sciences (Amsterdam, 1997): 33-44, here at 34.

feeble memory. Once famous authors and popular titles have become forgotten best-sellers. Without having closely heeded Goldschmidt's admonition to remember that people's needs in the fifteenth century, not our curiosity, determined their preferences,[93] our keen interest in nobility and humanism, however valid, has helped us understand the role that princes assumed as patrons, and humanists as printers, in the book industry. But it has also obscured from us the crucial function that simple clergy and young schoolboys served by helping fund that revolution. Our loyal search for the pedigree of profound ideas has helped us fathom the incongruous assertions of humanists and scholastics, the *via antiqua* and the *via moderna*. But it has likewise eclipsed for us the vital segment of that same fifteenth-century intellectual climate that depended on best-selling hornbooks and primers, popular *pastoralia*, notable sermon collections, and the famous *octo auctores*.

[93] See above, fn. 5.

Best-Selling Titles (1455-1500) Table 1

	Title	Author	Total Printings
1	Breviarium [Romanum, etc.]		449
2	Horae: [Ad usum Romanum; includes the Officium BMV]		404
3	Doctrinale	Alexander de Villa Dei	368
4	Missale [Romanum, etc.]		359
5	Ars minor [not including "Janua"]	Donatus, Aelius	284
6	Psalterium		239
7	Disticha de moribus	Cato, [pseudo-] Dionysius	217
8	Biblia [not including Biblia pauperum, and Aurea biblia]		178
9	Legenda aurea sanctorum	Jacobus de Voragine	150
10	Bucolica	Vergilius Maro, Publius	138
11	Manipulus curatorum	Guido de Monte Rochen	119
12	Rudimenta grammatices [w/o Perger, Grammatica nova]	Perottus, Nicolaus	117
13	Epistolae et evangelia		112
14	Elegantiolae	Datus, Augustinus	110
15	Georgica	Vergilius Maro, Publius	109
16	Fabulae [not including Aesopus moralisatus, see below]	Aesopus	105
17	Comoediae	Terentius Afer, Publius	103
18	Postilla super epistolas et evangelia	Guillermus [adapted from J. Herholt, Sermones]	98
19	Aeneis	Vergilius Maro, Publius	96
20	Mirabilia Romae		93
21	Super arboribus consanguinitatis	Andreae, Johannes	91
22	Modus confitendi	Andreas de Escobar	89
23	Ars moriendi		80
24	Aesopus moralisatus [metrical version of Fabulae]	Aesopus [metrical version by Anonymous Neveleti]	79
25	Institutiones	Justinianus	77
26	De consolatione philosophiae	Boethius	75
27	Summulae logicales	Johannes XXI, Pont. Max.	74
28	Imitatio Christi	[Thomas à Kempis?] [Dionysius Carthusiensis? Gerardus de Vliederhoven?]	72
29	Cordiale quattuor novissimorum		71
30	Confessionale: Defecerunt scrutantes scrutinio	Antoninus Florentinus [Antonino Pierozzi]	71
31	De officiis	Cicero, Marcus Tullius	68
32	Paradoxa Stoicorum	Cicero, Marcus Tullius	68
33	Epistolae Heroides	Ovidius Naso, Publius	67
34	Cato maior, sive de senectute	Cicero, Marcus Tullius	67
35	Super [primo/secundo/tertio] digesti [novi/veteris]	Bartolus de Saxoferrato	66
36	Liber Faceti docens mores hominum	Facetus	65
37	Regula: Dominus quae pars	Remigius	65
38	Laelius, sive de amicitia	Cicero, Marcus Tullius	65
39	Fiore di virtù		62
40	Vita Terentii [as prefaced to Terentius, Comoediae]		62
41	De duobus amantibus	Pius II, Pont. Max. [Aeneas Sylvius Piccolomini]	62
42	Stella clericorum		59
43	Epistolae ad familiares	Cicero, Marcus Tullius	59
44	Meditationes vitae Christi	Bonaventura, S	58
45	Vita	Aesopus	58
46	Liber sextus decretalium	Bonifacius VIII, Pont. Max.	58
47	Vitae sanctorum patrum	Hieronymus	56
48	Floretus	Pseudo-Bernardus Claravallensis	55
49	Expositio hymnorum		54
50	Lucidarius	[derived from a text by Honorius Augustodunensis]	54

Best-Selling Authors (1455-1500) Table 2

	Author	Total Printings
1	Alexander de Villa Dei	383
2	Donatus, Aelius [not including "Janua"]	336
3	Cicero, Marcus Tullius	333
4	Thomas Aquinas	259
5	Bartolus de Saxoferrato	252
6	Augustinus, Aurelius	251
7	Gerson, Johannes	210
8	Sixtus IV, Pont. Max. [Franciscus, Cardinalis de Rovere]	204
9	Justinianus	202
10	Bonaventura, S	199
11	Albertus Magnus	192
12	Innocentius VIII, Pont. Max. [Giovanni Battista Cibo]	188
13	Andreae, Johannes	187
14	Aesopus	186
15	Cato, [pseudo-] Dionysius	184
16	Aristoteles	176
17	Vergilius Maro, Publius	175
18	Jacobus de Voragine	175
19	Ovidius Naso, Publius	164
20	Herolt, Johannes [including the Postilla of "Guillermus"]	164
21	Pius II, Pont. Max. [Aeneas Sylvius Piccolomini]	161
22	Hieronymus	160
23	Savonarola, Hieronymus	141
24	Antoninus Florentinus [Antonino Pierozzi]	140
25	Perottus, Nicolaus	140
26	Datus, Augustinus	131
27	Garlandia, Johannes de	129
28	Terentius Afer, Publius	123
29	Seneca, Lucius Annaeus	121
30	Guido de Monte Rochen	119
31	Bernardus Claravallensis [may included Pseudo-Bernardus]	110
32	Maximilian I	105
33	Mancinellus, Antonius	103
34	Petrarca, Francesco	101
35	Ubaldis, Baldus de	101
36	Johannes XXI, Pont. Max. [Petrus Hispanus]	100
37	Andreas de Escobar	97
38	Peraudi, Raimundus, Commissary	96
39	Guarinus Veronensis	94
40	Vegius, Maphaeus	90
41	Tartagnus, Alexander	88
42	Faber de Budweis, Wenceslaus	87
43	Remegius	86
44	Baptista Mantuanus	84
45	Caracciolus, Robertus	80
46	Boethius	78
47	Nider, Johannes	78
48	Boccaccio, Giovanni	77
49	Nicolaus de Lyra	77
50	Sulpitius Verulanus, Johannes	73

HANDBOOKS FOR PASTORS: LATE MEDIEVAL MANUALS FOR PARISH PRIESTS AND CONRAD PORTA'S *PASTORALE LUTHERI* (1582)

Peter A. Dykema*

A common, indeed stereotypical, image in late medieval and early modern religious discourse is that of the ignorant, lazy, greedy and lecherous cleric.[1] This critique grew sometimes out of lay frustration with clerical privileges and in other instances was the result of the distance between the workaday world of peasants and urban artisans on the one hand and clerics on the other. In such situations lay clichés blossomed because clerics, whether priests or pastors, were not well integrated into wider communities. The medieval Catholic church itself contributed to the development of the stereotype through repeated canons and decrees, diocesan statutes and bishops' pastoral letters bemoaning the failure of priests to conform to clerical ideals of comportment.[2] Open and widespread criticism of the late medieval clergy has provided many historians, already beginning in the sixteenth century, with evidence to support a "corruption thesis", whereby clerical failings and the resultant resent-

---

* Lecturer in History, University of Arizona

[1] For the pan-European phenomenon of the stereotype in the Middle Ages, see Paul Lehmann, *Die Parodie im Mittelalter* (Munich, 1922; rev. ed., Stuttgart, 1963) and František Graus, *Pest — Geissler — Judenmorde. Das 14. Jahrhundert als Krisenzeit* (Göttingen, 1987; rev. ed., 1988), 86-93, 144-53; for Italy, see Silvana Seidel Menchi, "Characteristics of Italian Anticlericalism," in *Anticlericalism in Late Medieval and Early Modern Europe*, ed. Peter A. Dykema and Heiko A. Oberman, Studies in Medieval and Reformation Thought 51 (Leiden, 1993), 271-81; for Germany in the early Reformation, see Hans-Christoph Rublack, "Anticlericalism in German Reformation Pamphlets," in *Anticlericalism*, 461-89 and for the seventeenth century, Rublack, "'Der wohlgeplagte Priester'. Vom Selbstverständnis lutherischer Geistlichkeit im Zeitalter der Orthodoxie," *Zeitschrift für Historische Forschung* 16 (1989): 1-30.

[2] Canons 7, 14-17 and 63-66 of the Fourth Lateran Council addressed the proper behavior of clerics; *Conciliorum Oecumenicorum Decreta*, ed. Giuseppe Alberigo and others (3rd ed., Bologna, 1973; henceforth *COD*), 237, 242-43, 264-65. Two later canons incorporated into many diocesan statutes and bishops' letters were the Constance decree on the life and dress of clerics (*COD*, 449) and the Basel canon on concubines (*COD*, 485-87); see my dissertation "Conflicting Expectations: Parish Priests in Late Medieval Germany," (University of Arizona, 1998), 85-103, 108-112, 134.

ment among the laity explain the outbreak of the Reformation.[3]

One of the primary flaws in most forms of the corruption thesis has been the failure to describe in detail what exactly was expected of the clergy at the end of the Middle Ages. Lacking full identification of these expectations, it is difficult to measure the degree to which priests, monks and bishops either met them or fell short. Another shortcoming, pointed out by Heiko Oberman, is that an over emphasis on the negative aspects of the stereotype often "has distorted and disguised the underlying programmatic call for renewal."[4]

This essay will examine one such effort to renew the church: the late medieval and early modern program to educate, train and professionalize the secular parish clergy by providing pastors with simple guidebooks and manuals to ensure correct teaching, proper administration of the sacraments, and responsible management of the parish. I will first focus on fifteenth-century manuals for parish priests and then turn to an analysis of the *Pastorale Lutheri*, a late sixteenth-century Lutheran handbook for preachers and pastors. This study will afford a fitting perspective from which to assess continuity and change over a wide chronological scope as it investigates, for both the late medieval and late Reformation contexts, the targeted readership for the handbooks, the goals of the authors, the structure of the texts, the definitions given for pastoral care and the prescribed duties of the priest, pastor and preacher.

I. *Late Medieval Manuals for Parish Priests*

Responding to parish clergy "hammering at the gates of theology for solid food" and inspired by the agenda of the Fourth Lateran Council (1215) to improve pastoral care, canonists and theologians worked vigorously in the thirteenth through fifteenth centuries to produce a wide array of instructional literature known collectively as *pastoralia*.[5] Among

---

[3] For a concise description and rejection of this corruption thesis, see Hartmut Boockmann, "Das 15. Jahrhundert und die Reformation," in *Kirche und Gesellschaft im Heiligen Römischen Reich des 15. und 16. Jahrhunderts*, ed. Hartmut Boockmann (Göttingen, 1994), 9-25.

[4] In his preface to *Anticlericalism in Late Medieval and Early Modern Europe*, ix.

[5] A succinct and expert introduction to this literature is Leonard E. Boyle, "The Fourth Lateran Council and Manuals of Popular Theology," in *The Popular Literature of Medieval England*, ed. Thomas J. Heffernan (Knoxville, 1985), 30-43. The "hammering ... for solid food" statement was made by Robert Courson in 1207; Boyle, 33.

the most important species in this wide genre are guides to hearing confession, catechisms, compendia to canon law, and manuals for parish priests.[6]

The category "manuals for parish priests"[7] includes dozens of titles which first appeared in manuscript form but then burst forth in hundreds of editions following the invention of the printing press. The technology offered by Gutenberg and his fellow printers allowed for the wide distribution of those texts preferred by bishops and reform theologians (especially significant for the German fifteenth century were Jean Gerson and Nicholas of Cusa) as well as the favorites of the marketplace. Some of the manuals were undeniably best-sellers. The *Manipulus curatorum* by Guido de Monte Rocherii[8] was printed in 119 editions all over Europe during the second half of the fifteenth century, six editions between 1483 and 1493 in Strasbourg alone; the *Cura pastoralis*, a study guide for the episcopal examination prior to ordination, was brought out in 48 editions in the years from 1492 to 1529.[9] The impact of other titles was more localized but, when promoted by church officials, could have been profound nonetheless. For example, the *Summa rudium* was only printed three times, yet all three editions were issued in 1487, the year after an episcopal synod at Augsburg

---

[6] Penitential manuals dominated the early production of *pastoralia* due to Lateran IV's distinctive understanding of penance, whereby the priest hearing confession was called to examine circumstances and discern clearly the condition of the penitent's soul. Thus he was enabled to act as judge, doctor and counselor in the application of penance rather than merely as a dispenser of pre-set punishments. See Martin Ohst, *Pflichtbeichte. Untersuchungen zum Bußwesen im Hohen und Späten Mittelalter* (Tübingen, 1995), 50-138 and Thomas Tentler, *Sin and Confession on the Eve of the Reformation* (Princeton, 1977), 22-27. For early catechisms, see Robert James Bast, *Honor Your Fathers: Catechisms and the Emergence of a Patriarchal Ideology in Germany, 1400-1600*, Studies in Medieval and Reformation Thought 63 (Leiden, 1997), 3-13.

[7] See my "Conflicting Expectations." The following pages summarize part II, "Instruction and Expectations: The Praxis of Pastoral Care," 118-246. Friedrich Wilhelm Oediger addresses the manuals briefly in chapters 3, 6 and 7 of his *Über die Bildung der Geistlichen im späten Mittelalter* (Leiden, 1953); for manuals in England, see Eamon Duffy, *The Stripping of the Altars: Traditional Religion in England 1400-1580* (New Haven, 1992), 53-87, 209-32.

[8] *Editor's note:* one of a number of variants for the writer also known as Guido de Monte Rochen, on whom see above, 117.

[9] See "Conflicting Expectations," appendix A, "Manuals for Parish Priests: Printing and Reception History," 303-13. Guido wrote his handbook in 1333. It was praised by Gerson and recommended by synods at Geneva (1435, 1445) and Basel (1503); it also survives in 180 manuscripts, a large proportion of which were produced in Germany during the middle decades of the fifteenth century. See also the contribution elsewhere in this volume by Michael Milway, which I have not yet been able to consult.

had recommended the text for the parish clergy of the diocese.[10]

These handbooks helped to standardize the basic training of the parish priest, directing it toward a vocational profile which combined the aura of the cultic priest with a professional ideal increasingly espoused from the Fourth Lateran Council onward. Usually written with the uninitiated or "simple" priest in mind, these are practical primers replete with do's and don'ts, step-by-step instructions and advice for the everyday tasks faced by the parish priest. When the unexpected occurred, these manuals gave the priest necessary information to troubleshoot, resolve the problem, and reduce the spiritual risk. Summarizing the most important conclusions of sacramental theology and canon law, these guides were conceived as delivery systems, providing the priest with authoritative answers while also providing the historian with valuable information on the possible reception and creative application of scholastic thought in the daily affairs of a cleric responsible for pastoral care. Surely it was often the case that, alongside the necessary liturgical volumes, such a manual would have been the only book or manuscript on a priest's shelf.[11]

A defining characteristic of the manuals for parish priests is their target audience: the literate yet inexperienced cleric.[12] Guido de Monte Rocherii composed his handbook for the instruction of "neophyte" priests, choosing to write it in a modest but useful style since

---

[10] Another example of local support for a manual is that for Johannes Auerbach's *Directorium curatorum*. Written in 1420 and printed much later in just three editions, it was recommended repeatedly by synods in Eichstätt (1434, 1447), Brixen (1449, 1453) and Augsburg (1452, 1469, 1486, 1506, 1517). Copies have survived from many south German and Austrian parishes, leading Hartmut Boockmann to suggest that monastic houses affiliated with the Melk-Tegernsee observant reform may have distributed copies to all their incorporated parish churches; "Aus den Handakten des Kanonisten Johannes von Urbach (Auerbach)," *Deutsches Archiv für Erforschung des Mittelalters* 28 (1972): 497-532.

[11] For patterns of handbook ownership, see "Conflicting Expectations," 229-30.

[12] While it is true that not all clerics were literate, the simple Latin of the manuals would not have proved an obstacle to most parish priests or vicars by the late fifteenth century. At that time the number of priests in the diocese of Constance, for example, who had attended university was approaching 40% and still more had some kind of formal education. This, however, says little about their training for parish ministry. Only a minority of those attending university studied theology and fewer still had experience in ways to apply book-learning to pastoral practice: exactly the gap the manuals sought to fill: "Conflicting Expectations," 224-33. For a recent review of scholarship on the education of clerics throughout Europe, see Erich Meuthen, "Zur europäischen Klerusbildung vom 14. bis zum 16. Jahrhundert," in *Mediävistische Komparatistik*, ed. Wolfgang Harms et al. (Stuttgart, 1997), 263-94.

his goal was not to achieve eloquence but rather to advance the soul.[13] The *Summa rudium* begins by noting the confusion, doubt and errors wrought by contradictory voices among the canon lawyers. As the acquisition of truly authoritative volumes would prove too expensive, the author chose to produce his small *Summa* for the needs of the "simple" priest, simple not because of a deficit in intelligence but due to a lack of experience ("simplicium et minus peritorum sacerdotum").[14]

Canonists and theologians wrote the manuals for parish priests in an effort to bolster pastors in their responsibilities. A lack of experience in pastoral issues could prove dangerous, since in the sacraments the eternal destiny of souls was at stake. Priests who were unprepared or poorly trained could bring grave calamity upon their flock as even the slightest careless lapse in the ordained rites could render the sacraments void. The *Manuale parrochialium sacerdotum* points to the challenges faced by a priest going about his duties, warning against the naivete or sheer ignorance that could endanger not only the souls of his parishioners but his own eternal salvation as well.[15] The tract guides its user through holy dilemmas; how to prevent sacrilege and avoid divine jeopardy. What must a priest know about emergency baptisms? What ought he do when the consecrated wine is spilt or an insect is found in the chalice? A well conceived guide could provide the otherwise untutored priest with the necessary confidence to fulfill his sacred duties and assuage his appropriate fears about offending God. A good manual was trustworthy so long as its clerical reader stuck to the text![16] The manuals for parish priests

---

[13] "Hec ergo attendens et vigili meditatione perpensans sequens opusculum de instructione neophitorum curatorum composui rudi quidem stilo, sed utili non curans de verborum ornatum sed de animarum commodo et profectu." *Manipulus curatorum* (Strasbourg, 1483), a3.

[14] "Quia varia dicta sanctorum et contrariae opiniones doctorum legentibus perplexitates et dubia pariunt, materias curtas prolixant, errores et fastidium generant, studium solicitum egerunt et pro libris comparandis exigunt pingues expensas, Ideo ad utilitatem et ad informationem simplicium et minus peritorum sacerdotum hanc summula Rudium cum diligencia conportare curavi." *Summa rudium* (Reutlingen: J. Otmar, 1487), a2.

[15] "Quoniam ex quorundam simplicium ignorantia sacerdotum aliquando quedam sunt que vergere possunt in suarum et aliorum periculum animarum hoc eis sub brevitate notavimus, non ut ipsi occasione istorum in alique obligentur de novo sed ut his que agere debent simpliciter informentur." *Manuale parrochialium sacerdotum* (Strasbourg, ca. 1485), 2. This manual could have been written as early as the mid-thirteenth century but was still quite popular in the fifteenth and sixteenth, published twenty times in the Empire 1483-1514.

[16] "Unde sine formidine et scrupulo conscientie quilibet ignarus et simplex sacer-

were meant to fill the breach, to prevent spiritual malpractice by providing the simple priest with a bulwark against the perils of pastoral care.

Given the central place of the sacraments in the official liturgy of medieval Catholicism, it is not surprising that all the manuals for parish priests here studied address the sacraments and how to celebrate them correctly, sometimes paying special attention to penance. The *Manipulus curatorum* is divided into three parts. The first pertains to six of the seven sacraments, leaving penance to comprise the second major portion. The third sets forth the articles of faith and the best way the priest can convey them to his parishioners. The structure of the *Summa rudium* is similar. Following a treatment of the Trinity and the Catholic Creed, as well as the Ten Commandments and the works of mercy, there is found a substantial section on six of the sacraments. An explication of the seven vices and virtues appears next and forms the transition to the extensive discussion on the many aspects of penance: confession, interrogation of penitents, reserved cases, excommunication, absolution, indulgences and the discretion of the confessor.[17] Also ordered around the seven sacraments, the *Manuale parrochialium sacerdotum* differs in that it essentially consists of a lengthy warning to priests against inadvertently profaning the sacred, and, should they do so, instructions on how to rectify the damage. Included as well is a section on attendance at diocesan synods and chapters on appropriate clerical behavior (avoid taverns, refrain from wearing pointed shoes), clerical immunities, fasting and feast days. Ulrich Surgant's *Manuale curatorum* is distinctive in that it includes a large and comprehensive treatment of preaching.[18] The first half of the work constitutes an *ars praedicandi*, addressing such issues as the parts of a good sermon, how to apply authorities, the rule of simplicity, and proper pronunciation. The second book of Surgant's manual puts these rules into practice by interspersing

---

dos hunc libellum leget qui ratione evidentissime autoritatis et stili simplicitatis potest vocari Summa rudium Autentica et sibi formiter adhereat." *Summa rudium*, a2.

[17] In their form and in the topics they address, the *Manipulus curatorum* and the *Summa rudium* are similar to the structure of early English manuals for parish priests; see W. A. Pantin, *The English Church in the Fourteenth Century* (Notre Dame, 1962), 195-218.

[18] Surgant was a parish priest in Basel and four times university rector there; his *Manuale curatorum* was first published in 1503. Jürgen Konzili, "Studien über Johann Ulrich Surgant (ca. 1450-1503)," *Zeitschrift für schweizerische Kirchengeschichte* 69 (1975): 265-309; 70 (1976): 107-67, 308-88; 71 (1977): 332-92.

instructions on various aspects of pastoral care with sample Latin, German and even occasionally French sermons illustrating the issue at hand.

Essentially a study guide for the episcopal examination a candidate for the priesthood was to pass in order to be ordained, the *Cura pastoralis* presents the historian with a clear statement of the knowledge and skills expected of the priest as he entered his pastoral charge. The *Cura* begins with the statement "the care and guardianship of souls is burdensome and vexing to whom it has been entrusted inasmuch as he is to watch over human souls so that they not perish but may be saved."[19] The text then defines the cure of souls according to four meanings of *sacerdos*. The priest is called *sacerdos* because he celebrates the mass, thus he proclaims sacred words (*sacra dicens*). Likewise he administers the sacraments and is a giver of holy things (*sacra dans*). In hearing confession, the priest is a holy leader (*sacer dux*) and must therefore distinguish between what is sin and what is not. Finally, priests are the instructors of the people since they teach sacred truths (*sacra docens*). These four etymologies emphasize the divine gifts granted to the priest by virtue of his ordination.[20] Following an interpretation dating back to the late thirteenth century, the author of the *Cura* then elaborates on the four meanings of *sacerdos* by associating each with a set of tasks and human abilities. As celebrant the priest must pronounce correctly and understand what he says in the mass; as minister of the sacraments he must know their material, form, how they are liturgically administered, and their effect; as judge of the conscience he must distinguish between types of sin and know what acts of satisfaction to impose; and as teacher he must grasp the fundamentals of the faith, which in the late fifteenth century generally meant a basic knowledge of the Creed, the Ten Commandments, the *Ave Maria* and the Lord's Prayer.[21] Together the etymologies and

---

[19] "Cura est onerosa atque sollicita custodia animarum alicui commissa, ut animas hominum custodiat, ne pereant sed potius ut salventur." *Cura pastoralis pro ordinandorum tentamine collecta* (Basel: M. Lamparter [1510]), A ii. The *Cura* may have been written in the 1420s; see "Conflicting Expectations," 190-91. The definition, attributable to the *Summa aurea* of the thirteenth-century canonist Hostiensis, also appears as the answer to the question 'what is the care of souls?' in both Surgant's *Manuale curatorum* (81ᵛ) and Michael Lochmaier's *Parochiale curatorum* (Hagenau: H. Gran, 1498; first publ. in 1493 or 1495), a3.

[20] The four meanings are taken from the seventh-century theologian John of Damascus and are found in Guido's *Manipulus curatorum* as well (a 3ᵛ).

[21] *Cura pastoralis*, A ii-iiᵛ; *Manipulus curatorum*, a 3ᵛ. The tasks and duties stem from

elaborations offer a vivid job description for the late medieval priest in charge of pastoral care. Not only vivid, it is also an accurate job description for the time.

Throughout the Middle Ages various commentators pointed to a basic, yet critical mass of knowledge required for the priesthood. Well aware that a chantry priest need not have the same experience or erudition as the rector of a large parish but that both should know more than a layman, canonists and theologians specifically defined the requirements for each grade of cleric and priest. In order to be ordained to the priesthood, the candidate had to be able to read Latin out loud and understand what he read, to sing and read notes, to discern the most common forms of sin, administer the sacraments properly, teach the creeds, and to calculate the dates of feast days. These requirements are essentially the same as those put forth in the *Cura pastoralis* and Guido's *Manipulus curatorum*.

In a sermon to a council at Rheims in 1408, Jean Gerson stated that those to be nominated to the care of souls ought to know the Ten Commandments, the articles of faith, and the material, mode and formula for each sacrament. In his instructions for a parish visitation written in the same year, he directed that it was necessary to determine whether the priest knew how to sing and read the liturgy, knew and understood the commandments and seven deadly sins so that he could castigate sinners in his flock, and finally, whether or not the priest owned some booklet or guide in which all this information was written.[22] Exactly this information, and the required book as well, could have been provided by any of the manuals for parish priest studied here.

These fifteenth-century primers are not primarily devotional or theological, but deal with the practical matters of the clerical life. Praxis, often liturgical praxis, is always in the forefront. At a time

---

the *Summa de bono* compiled by the Dominican, Ulrich Engelberti; Oediger, *Bildung der Geistlichen*, 55-56. On the variety of ways "fundamentals of the faith" could be interpreted in the Middle Ages and sixteenth century, see Bast, *Honor Your Fathers,* 6-23.

[22] "Sermo de vita clericorum," in *Opera omnia*, ed. Louis Ellies Du Pin, 5 vols. (Antwerp, 1706; repr. Hildesheim, 1987), 2:576-84, 579; *De visitatione praelatorum et de cura curatorum*, in *Oeuvres complètes*, ed. Palémon Glorieux, 10 vols. (Paris, 1960-1973), 8:47-55, 50. Similar questions are found in Nicolaus of Cusa's visitation instructions for Brixen (1455), a visitation guide for Freising (1475), and Ulrich Surgant's own comments on visitations in *Manuale curatorum*, 125-125ᵛ; see "Conflicting Expectations," 181-86.

when most parish clerics received their field training in the form of an apprenticeship with an experienced priest or vicar, the flood of *pastoralia* produced by the end of the fifteenth century was to supply literate — but inexperienced — priests with reliable resources to address relevant questions and solve problems, thus marking an important step towards the professionalization of the parish clergy. Although they did not claim to teach canon law, they listed what was most necessary: the rights, privileges and immunities of the cleric. They did not offer a tightly argued theology of the sacraments but set forth their proper administration, often providing the most detailed advice on penance and confession. They taught how to calculate the liturgical year, how to maintain a parish, and how a curate should dress and behave himself. While it is important to realize that these handbooks represent a significant effort to standardize and professionalize the parish ministry, it is also clear that they continued to promote the sacramental role of the priest and his cultic function. Throughout the manuals, the stress is on the liturgy, the sacramental rites, and on the priest as celebrant. By combining the aura of the cultic priest with the training of the competent pastor, the manuals for parish priests established one key set of ecclesiastical expectations, thus helping to shape the demands placed upon clerics responsible for pastoral care.

II. The "Pastorale Lutheri"

To move from the Catholicism of the late fifteenth century to Lutheranism in the late sixteenth century is to seek to leap across a wide canyon with many complex side fissures. The early evangelical movement of the 1520s was at its most radical when it rejected the validity of the church's sacramental system as a necessary means of grace and sought to abolish the clerical estate controlling that system. Yet the transition from ordained priest to called pastor (or to a true priesthood of all believers) was by no means an easy one. The enthusiasm of the early Reformation decades, when convinced individuals made choices to support or reject religious change, did not always result in structural change. Scholarship of the past twenty-five years has called into question an older view that the Protestant Reformation was a great transforming event in European history, pointing instead to limited success or even failure of reform goals, and stressing continuity in social and mental structures from late medieval to early modern times and across the confessional spectrum. The relevance of this discussion for the present study can be shown by the persistence in the sixteenth century of the same conditions which motivated the production of manuals for parish priests in the fifteenth century: pastors assigned to the care of souls lacked the appropriate experience; although sometimes well-educated, they were not necessarily trained in the specifics of pastoral care. Studies of clerical education in early modern Lutheran territories have shown that young pastors were isolated from lay society during their years of instruction, rarely studied theology at university, were trained in a disputational style that had little application for vernacular sermons to rural parishioners, and had only the slightest exposure to the practical details of running a parish.[23] Leading clerics of the time recognized these shortcomings and sought to provide advice to young pastors frustrated in their vocation. Clearly there was still a market for handbooks addressing pastoral care.

Conrad Porta (1541-1585), a theologian and pastor from Eisleben in County Mansfeld, compiled the *Pastorale Lutheri* in 1582 in order to provide young and inexperienced pastors in the region sure advice concerning their duties in preaching and pastoral care. A collection of and commentary upon excerpts from Lutheran writings, primarily those of Luther himself, the *Pastorale Lutheri* has as its primary concern the promotion of correct doctrine and the rejection of spurious teachings.[24] This is no surprise given its immediate context. The heirs of Luther's Reformation had been fighting over his legacy for the previous thirty years, culminating in the compromise "Formula of Concord" of 1577 and its inclusion in the *Book of Concord* in 1580. County Mansfeld was dominated by 'Gnesio-Lutherans' in that party's strug-

---

[23] Bruce Tolley, *Pastors and Parishioners in Württemberg during the Late Reformation 1581-1621* (Stanford, 1995), 24-63; Luise Schorn-Schütte, *Evangelische Geistlichkeit in der Frühneuzeit. Deren Anteil an der Entfaltung frühmoderner Staatlichkeit und Gesellschaft. Dargestellt am Beispiel des Fürstentums Braunschweig-Wolfenbüttel, der Landgrafschaft Hessen-Kassel und der Stadt Braunschweig* (Gütersloh, 1996), 159-226; and an even more widely comparative study by Schorn-Schütte, "The Christian Clergy in the Early Modern Holy Roman Empire: A Comparative Social Study," *Sixteenth Century Journal* 29 (1998): 717-31.

[24] *Pastorale Lutheri, das ist: Nuetzlicher und noetiger Unterricht, von dem fuernemsten stuecken zum heiligen Ministerio gehoerig, und richtige Antwort auff mancherley wichtige Frage, von schweren ... Casibus ... Fuer anfahende Prediger ... zusammenbracht, und auff beyderley Edition aller seiner buecher ... gerichtet,* 1ˢᵗ ed. (Eisleben: Petri, 1582); 2ⁿᵈ ed. (Eisleben/Leipzig: Petri/Grosse,

gles against the "Philippists" and was likewise the backdrop for a bitter split within the Gnesio-Lutheran front during the late 1560s and 1570s.[25] Although a larger effort is not explicitly mentioned in the *Pastorale*, Porta's work can be seen as part of an attempt by Mansfeld's clerical leadership to introduce doctrinal clarity and liturgical uniformity into the county's ecclesiastical affairs following the promulgation of the *Book of Concord*. The Mansfeld consistory held synods in 1580 and 1586 and, in the latter year — the same year the second edition of the *Pastorale* came off the presses — they approved both a new church ordinance and a revised ritual book for the county's preachers.[26] Hieronymus Mencel, the consistory's superintendent, certainly appreciated Porta's efforts. Noting that the *Pastorale* provided careful and complete solutions to many of the most difficult questions faced by the pastor, Mencel declared in his preface to the first edition that he would recommend the text to all the pastors in the county.[27]

1586) = *Verzeichnis der im deutschen Sprachgebiet erschienenen Drucke des XVI. Jahrhunderts* (Stuttgart, 1983ff; henceforth *VD 16*), L3563. All citations are to this 2nd edition. This essay concentrates on Porta's own voice in the *Pastorale* but notes as well Porta's use of Luther's works. Porta was working on the expanded second edition when he died in 1585. Hieronymus Mencel, the superintendent for Mansfeld, arranged for its publication with an appended treatise previously published by Porta: *Von Kirchenguettern und gemeinen Almosen, und rechtschaffener verwaltung derselben* (Eisleben/Leipzig: Petri/Grosse, 1584), this appears on folios 409-482 of the 1586 *Pastorale*. The *Pastorale* was published once more in the sixteenth century, in 1591 (Eisleben: Hoernig) = *VD 16*, L3576. Porta's other writings include a catechism and a handbook on the religious training and proper comportment of girls (*Jungfrawen Spiegel*); see *VD 16*, P4333-4345.

I owe a debt of gratitude to Margaret Mola of Tucson, Arizona, for allowing me to study her copy of the 1586 *Pastorale*, a family heirloom.

[25] Robert Kolb, "Dynamics of Party Conflict in the Saxon Late Reformation: Gnesio-Lutherans vs. Philippists," *Journal of Modern History* 49 (1977): D 1289-1305. The Formula of Concord brought broad agreement among Lutherans but did not end all disputes, especially in Mansfeld; see Kolb, "The Flacian Rejection of the Concordia: Prophetic Style and Action in the German Late Reformation," *Archiv für Reformationsgeschichte* 73 (1982):196-216. Both articles are reprinted in Kolb's *Luther's Heirs Define His Legacy: Studies on Lutheran Confessionalization* (Aldershot/Brookfield, 1996).

[26] *Die evangelischen Kirchenordnungen des XVI. Jahrhunderts*, ed. Emil Sehling, vol.2/2 (Leipzig, 1904; repr. Aalen, 1970), 179-87; 197-215 for the ordinance; 215-48 for the ritual, written by Hieronymus Mencel already in 1580.

[27] "Aber diß Pastorale hat darinne den fuerzug, das es nach dem Goettlichen Worte, von allen stuecken des heiligen Kirchenamptes, fuernemlich und am meisten Doctoris Martini Lutheri meinung trewlich fuehret und anzeucht, viel schwerer Punct und faelle, die gar offt im heiligen Kirchenampte fuerfallen, richtig und reichlich mit Lutheri worten erkleret, auch viel verworrener handel und streit deutlich entscheidet." Preface to the 1st ed., bb iiii; Mencel's promise to recommend the text to the pastors further on the same page. From Mencel's preface to the 2nd ed., a ii: "Und weil er dasselbe auff die manchfeltigen felle, welche sich bey unserm heiligen

Porta sought as well to place his handbook in a wider context. Well aware his *Pastorale* stood in a long and venerable tradition of pastoral manuals, Porta felt he must justify the publication of yet another work; especially a compendium.[28] In doing so, he confirmed the powerful influence Martin Luther continued to hold over his followers forty years after his death. Porta's explanation entails three points. Whereas other writers are bland and confusing, Luther is always passionate and clear, saying in a paragraph what others only say in pages. Secondly, since most pastors cannot afford to purchase all of Luther's writings, the *Pastorale* is intended to eliminate this disadvantage and ensure that they have available the necessary knowledge to fulfill their calling.[29] Finally, by turning to the words of the Wittenberg reformer directly, the preacher may avoid the shrill rants of half-witted know-it-alls claiming to teach orthodox doctrine — surely a reference to the intramural debates among the Lutheran parties.[30]

Porta intended the *Pastorale* to serve the young and inexperienced cleric and to provide these raw preachers with solutions to the tough problems they would face each day. Porta perceived himself as the seasoned *veteranus*, sharing his knowledge with pastors unsure of their responsibilities, just as Paul did in his pastoral letters to Timothy and Titus.[31]

Ministerio wuenderlich pflegen zuzutragen, gerichtet, und viel noetiger, schwerer und gefehrlicher Fragen, mit sonderlicher bescheidenheit unnd fuersichtigkeit, wol, richtig und deutlich entscheiden, hat er damit vielen leuten, sonderlich aber den Kirchendienern, nuetzlich gedienet."

[28] Porta mentions Ambrose, *De dignitate sacerdotali*; Augustine, *Homilia de pastoribus*; Jerome, *De vita clericorum et sacerdotum*; Gregory the Great, *De cura pastorali*; the canons and decretals *De vita et honestate clericorum*; Bucer, *Von der geistlichen Seelsorge*; Erasmus Sarcerius, *Pastorale oder Hirtenbuch* (first published in 1562) and Nicolaus Hemmingius, *Pastor sive pastoris optimus vivendi agendique modus* (first published in 1565); cc iv and cc iii.

[29] *Pastorale*, dd i. The intention to help out poor clerics is mentioned in a number of the late medieval manuals, for example, the *Summa rudium*.

[30] Porto's handbook seeks to avoid the "unzeitige gespey und geschrey, etlicher halbgelerter alzu nasenweiser Klueglinge und Sonderlinge." *Pastorale*, cc iii-iiiv.

[31] His audience is not the "hochgelarten, lang geuebten und erfahrnen Predigern, Sondern den jungen und anfahenden" (dd i) and his purpose is to show "wie sich junge und ungeuebte, ja wol auch zimliche alte und erfahrne Prediger, in schweren und sorglichen Casibus, so fast teglich im H. Predigtampte und sonderlich in grossen Kirchspielen und Gemeinen fuerzufallen pflegen, verhalten sollen." *Pastorale*, cc iii. Note that *causae* are here defined as common problems, not as exercises in academic sophistry. For the comparison to Paul, see cc iv. The reader of the *Pastorale* was warned, however, not to apply Porta's or Luther's advice too rigorously, especially in cases when established church ordinances contradicted the *Pastorale*, or when circumstances demanded another response (dd iiv).

Writing and compiling his handbook in a time of great confessional strife, the pastor from Eisleben was well aware of the ramifications
of the struggle. Years earlier, Luther had exposed the pope as the
antichrist, revealed the gospel, and opened the way to right worship
in word and sacrament, yet Porta anguishes that these advances are
threatened in his own time by the machinations of the Devil, the lies
of the papists, the arrogance and insolence of the "Schwermer und
Rottengeister," and feuds among the Lutherans.[32] The eternal conflicts and disputations are caused by those who truly do not know the
fear of God.[33] The *Pastorale* does not pull any punches in the warning
it gives to pastors: the world despises the true preacher and wishes
only to insult him.[34] Porta expects no grand success for the evangelical movement. Quoting Luther with approval, he states that if a pastor were to have merely two or three godly parishioners, be they even
children, he should thank God for such grace, for, as Luther put it,
"we live here nowhere else but in the devil's graveyard, as if among
haughty dragons and snakes."[35] Humble though his expectations for
success may be, so is his conviction firm that the preacher must
remain true to the gospel and fight for correct doctrine: the on-going
survival of Luther's true reform hangs on this point.

"There is no more prized treasure on earth nor anything more

---

[32] These enemies of the Gospel appear throughout the *Pastorale*, here one exemplary list: "Der Sathan, die alte Schlange und Teuffel; Die Tyrannen, als der Tuer-
cke, Bapst und andere Verfolger und Bluthunde; Schwermer oder Ketzer und Rottengeister; Falsche Brueder und Apostatae oder Mamelucken." 190-190ᵛ. See also
Mencel's foreword to 1ˢᵗ ed (bb i - iv), and chapters I.2, VI.4-20, XXI, XXIII and
XXIV.

[33] "Wo aber Gottes furcht nicht ist, da ist das ewige fragen, disputiren, gruebeln,
excusiren, difficultiren, refutiren, declariren, protestiren und consultiren on auffho-
eren." *Pastorale*, 407; cf. Johann Valentin Andreae's similar complaint a generation
later, in Tolley, *Pastors and Parishioners*, 39-40.

[34] "Die Gottlosen Epicurer halten die Prediger fuer ihre Spotvogel, Liedlein, fuer
ein Fluch, und Fegopffer, fuer die geringsten und verachtesten leute, fuer lose Pfaf-
fen, etc." *Pastorale*, 6; cf. chapter XXI, "Vom Widerstande und Creutze des
rechtschaffenen Prediger."

[35] "... denn du lebest doch hie nichts anders denn in des Teuffels Mordgruben,
und als unter eitel Drachen und Schlangen." *Pastorale*, 379ᵛ; *WA* 45: 709.13-14, cf.
WA 19: 72-75. The recipient of this *Festschrift* is the leading expert on Luther's pes-
simistic outlook regarding the success of the church in this world. See Heiko Oberman, *Luther: Man Between God and the Devil* (New Haven, 1989), esp. 264-71 and "Martin Luther: Forerunner of the Reformation," in Oberman, *The Reformation: Roots and
Ramifications* (Edinburgh, 1994), 23-52. For apocalyptic themes later in the sixteenth
century, see Robin Bruce Barnes, *Prophecy and Gnosis: Apocalypticism in the Wake of the
Lutheran Reformation* (Stanford, 1988).

noble in this life than a truly devoted pastor and preacher." With this citation from Luther's published sermon, "Why children must be sent to school," Porta begins his description of the dignity and duties of the pious pastor.[36] Foremost are the tasks of the office pertaining to the soul, whereby the pastor, through the power of the Word, releases his parishioners from sin, death and the Devil, and brings them to eternal life.[37] But likewise crucial are his great works in the world: upholding the authorities, keeping the peace, teaching obedience and discipline and advising men and women of every estate how they ought to conduct themselves in their own God-given offices.[38]

Among all of these tasks, however, it is clear that Porta gives prime position to those duties involving preaching, that is, the doctrinally correct and thus sometimes thankless preaching of the gospel. "Pastor" is quickly replaced by "preacher" in Porta's chapter headings as he passionately addresses the trials, tribulations and tasks of the servant of God's Word.[39] When, after 200 folios, the *Pastorale* moves first to the "external" behavior of the preacher ("Eusserlichen Leben und Wandel") and then to advice on the proper administration of the sacraments, Porta turns from vital exhortation to clinical guidance, from empowering rhetoric to legalistic advice. The core of Conrad

---

[36] "Es ist kein trewer Schatz, noch edler ding auff Erden, und in diesem Leben, denn ein rechter trewer Pfarher oder Prediger." *Pastorale*, 1ᵛ; cf. *Ein Sermon odder Predigt, das man solle kinder zur Schulen halten* (1530), in *D. Martin Luthers Werke. Kritische Gesamtausgabe. Abteilung Schriften* (Weimar, 1883ff; henceforth *WA*), 30/2: 533.25-7. The *Pastorale* is divided into 32 chapters, each with sub-sections. Porta begins the body of his manual with chapter one, "Von des heiligen Predigampts Wirdigkeit und Hoheit, in Gottes Reiche, und fuer seinem Angesichte," section one, "Was ist ein fromer Pfarherr oder Prediger und wofuer soll man denselben halten."

[37] Porta provides a whole series of quotations from Luther here, dividing what belongs to the office of pastoral care into those tasks regarding "das ewige leben" or "wercke gegen die seelen" and the duties addressing "das zeitlich leben" or "wercke gegen der wellt." Among the former include the office-holder's call to preach, teach, hear confession, bind and loose, baptize, administer the sacrament, console, warn, admonish, resurrect the dead and heal the blind, deaf, and lame. *Pastorale*, 1ᵛ-2; *WA* 30/2: 527.19-24, 535.26-29.

[38] "Denn ein Prediger bestetigt, sterckt, und hilfft erhalten alle Obrigkeit, allen zeitlichen Friede, stewret den Auffruehrtschen, lehret Gehorsam, Sitten, Zucht und Ehre, unterricht Vaterampt, Mutterampt, Kinderampt, Knechtampt, und Summa, alle Weltliche Empter und Stende." *Pastorale*, 3; cf. *WA* 30/2: 537.26-30.

[39] Although the Protestants did bring a distinctive stress to the preaching duties of the pastor, there is solid evidence of the growing importance of preaching in late medieval religious life: see above for Surgant's 1503 sermon-oriented manual for parish priests; for the increasing popularity of endowed preacherships in the fifteenth century, see Michael Menzel, "Predigt und Predigtorganisation im Mittelalter," *Historisches Jahrbuch* 111 (1991): 337-84.

Porta's message to his young and experienced readers alike is clear: the *Predigeramt* and the preacher fulfilling its demands are the means chosen by God to bring to completion his plans for humanity.

Chapter IX of the *Pastorale* concludes Porta's long study of the duties of the preacher. It begins with the question: "What more should a servant of the Word do, after he, through his sermons and related pastoral care, has taught, condemned, consoled, encouraged and warned the people?"[40] This list, supplemented with prayer, summarizes the obligations laid upon the office of preacher. Through these activities the preacher relies on the Word of God to clarify the gospel, correct false teachings, edify immature Christians, and bring peace to the desolate. Even these activities can be further grouped into two relational tasks: the preacher faces the people to teach them what is godly and proper and then turns to God to ask that they all do what is right and good, and thus might achieve the victory.[41]

III. *The "Pastorale Lutheri" and Late Medieval Manuals for Parish Priests*

1. *Doctrinal purity and ritual purity*

The *Pastorale* emphasized that the preacher's fundamental task is to preach and teach correctly the basics of evangelical theology. The best preachers are expected to be fully grounded in the Bible, it is the core of their preparation. They will meditate on the words prayerful-

---

[40] "Was sol denn ein Deiner des Worts mehr thun, wenn er in der Predigt und sonsten geleret, gestraffet, gestroestet, vermanet und gewarnet hat?" *Pastorale*, 186. I have expanded "und sonsten" into pastoral care related to preaching because the structure of the manual makes this very clear. The titles of chapters V-IX present the components of the preacher's office: teaching ("Vom Leren"), condemnation of false doctrine and godless living ("Vom Straffen"), consolation of anguished sinners ("Vom Trosten"), encouragement and admonishment of believers ("Vom Vermanen und Warnen"), and prayer ("Vom Beten"). Other aspects of pastoral care, the sacraments, marriage, care for the poor and sick, and administration of the parish are treated later in the treatise and are clearly not granted the same weight by Porta.

[41] *Pastorale*, 186. The preacher is to pray for himself and his parishioners yet against his enemies. Porta provides seventeen sample prayers to use against the opponents of the gospel: Satan, Turks, papists, persecutors, heretics, *Schwärmer*, and false brethren; *Pastorale*, 190-95ᵛ. For the two-fold task of the preacher, *coram hominibus* and *coram Deo*, in Luther's writings, see Harald Goertz, *Allgemeines Priestertum und ordiniertes Amt bei Luther* (Marburg, 1997), 64-7 with reference to a number of citations Porta may have had in mind here.

ly and then go out and experience the Word as they practice their vocation.[42] But no matter the level of their preparation, the *Pastorale* advised preachers to avoid sermons on the most difficult passages in the Bible (Daniel and Revelation) and to stick to the material addressed in Luther's *Large* and *Small Catechism*, including the Ten Commandments, the Lord's Prayer and the Creed. Solid knowledge of these basic statements of Christian faith and life is what the laity requires. The pastor must present the teachings to them in words, images and examples which they will understand, repeating themes and vocabulary until a topic is grasped and only then moving on to something new.[43] The goal is for the inexperienced preacher to be able to preach confidently and accurately on the key doctrines of the evangelical faith: justification by faith, law and gospel, and the important differences between the two.[44]

The emphasis on correct doctrine seen throughout the *Pastorale* can be best understood by a close contextual reading of chapter VI, "Vom Straffen." This chapter, the longest in the handbook at forty folios, directs most of its attention toward the identification and rejection of false doctrine. Porta calls his readers to use their sermons both like bread and the sword,[45] to nourish their listeners' faith and to beat back heretical teachings. After a quick round of well-known "heretics", among them the pope, his bishops, Jews, Turks and "Mohammedans," Porta turns to a specific theological problem, one to which he devotes nearly twenty-five folios. At issue was whether original sin is an accident or the substance of the fallen

---

[42] Based on advice given by Luther and Caspar Huberinus; *Pastorale*, 30[v] and 32-33[v].

[43] *Pastorale*, 39, 40, 48. Because the catechetical literature provides reliable resources for orthodox sermons, Porta offered references to additional materials, including his own catechetism, the *Layenbibel* (1578). The need for sermons to match the ability of the audience to comprehend had long been realized by medieval commentators; see for example *De eruditione predicatorum* by Humbert of Romans (after 1263) and Surgant's *Manuale curatorum*, already discussed. On the need to teach via rote memorization, see the frustrated reflections of the mid-fifteenth-century chaplain and writer, Johannes Wolf, as related in Bast, *Honor Your Fathers*, 23-30.

[44] *Pastorale*, 57. Porta then lists less important theological themes with appropriate references to Luther's writings as well as key passages from Luther's commentaries on the Bible. Here the question could be raised whether such references would really have been helpful to the average pastor. Porta's two lists take up twelve folio pages. Given that Porta intended his *Pastorale* for pastors with little experience and few resources, it is doubtful that many would have taken his advice and copied for themselves a Lutheran systematic theology or a commentary on all of the scripture.

[45] "nehren und wehren"; *Pastorale*, 79.

human creature, the latter position argued by Matthias Flacius Illyricus and his supporters and rejected in the *Pastorale*. This debate, an outgrowth of the earlier synergist controversy over the contribution of the human will to conversion, split the Gnesio-Lutheran party in the 1570s.[46] The ramifications went far beyond a theological debate in Porta's home county of Mansfeld, as some of Flacius' supporters, including one count of Mansfeld, were driven out of the region by military forces in 1575 and again in 1578. The leader of the anti-Flacians was none other than Porta's mentor, the county's superintendent, Hieronymus Mencel. The sections of the *Pastorale* addressing the accident-substance debate reveal the tensions of the late 1570s just as the emphasis on correct doctrine throughout the handbook reflects the theological confusion among Lutherans prior to and even after the adoption of the Formula of Concord in 1577. It is no accident that Porta dedicated his guide to six Lutheran abbots from the region around Magdeburg, Braunschweig and Wolfenbüttel, praising them for their support of right doctrine and the *Book of Concord*.[47]

The concern with correct doctrine is, of course, not absent from the late medieval manuals. They do prescribe a clear, if basic, understanding of the Creed, commandments and sacraments. But by Porta's time the doctrinal stakes had been raised. In an era of confessional heterodoxy, his most-pressing goal was to prevent error. If the late medieval manuals protected the priest from the perils of pastoral care by ensuring ritual purity and avoiding sacrilege, the *Pastorale* protected the Lutheran preacher from false teachings by securing adherence to the true Lutheran dogma set by the *Book of Concord*.[48]

2. *The Ten Commandments*

The manuals for parish priests reflect the increased importance of the Decalogue for the catechetical and moral theology of the

---

[46] Kolb, "Dynamics of Party Conflict," 12-16.

[47] *Pastorale*, cc iv[v].

[48] In chapter XV, "On serving the sacrament" (277[v]-299) the only section in the *Pastorale* dealing with the eucharist, Porta gives few instructions how to officiate or how to carry out the liturgical rituals. Rather his concern is to delineate those who are eligible for the sacrament and those who must be barred from it. Such decisions are made based upon the doctrinal beliefs of the recipient; the ritual purity of the celebrant is replaced by the doctrinal beliefs of the recipient.

Late Middle Ages. The *Summa rudium* has an extensive section on the commandments while the other manuals employ them as rubrics in their detailed sections on penance, displacing the older emphasis on the seven deadly sins.[49] Robert Bast has argued that the growing authority of the Ten Commandments continued unabated into the Reformation era as Protestant religious and political leaders pursued an evangelical ordering of family, church and state according to divine precepts.[50] The testimony of the *Pastorale* affirms Bast's findings. In no less than five of his thirty-two chapters, Porta arranges his argument according to the commandments: to call upon pastors to use discernment in consolation since only by taking into account the specific law having been violated can the deceit of the Devil be dispelled; to categorize the weaknesses of faith and behavior into which believers commonly fall; to characterize the virtues and sins most commonly found among preachers; to expose the arrogance of false preachers; even to regulate the behavior required for extended residency at the hospital and poor house in Eisleben.[51]

3. *The Burden of Pastoral Care*

The portrait of preachers gleaned from the pages of Porta's *Pastorale* is of men authorized by their call but despised by their parishioners, hounded by the Devil and challenged at every turn by false teachers. In his chapter on condemnation of false doctrine and godless living, Porta warns his readers that parishioners will not take kindly to denunciations issued from the pulpit. Unrest in the community will most likely be the result. The people will complain that the pastor is acting as a lord and they will in turn condemn not only him but also his wife and children, bringing shame to the *Pfarrhaus*. Despite this gloomy forecast of the ramifications, Porta urges his readers on to fulfill their duty: the preacher is not subject to the wishes of peasants and

---

[49] The thirteenth-century *Manuale parrochialium sacerdotum* uses the seven deadly sins; cf. Bast, *Honor Your Fathers*, 32-45.

[50] *Honor Your Fathers*, 78-104, 122-45, 186-234.

[51] *Pastorale*, 122-59 ("Vom Trosten"), 159-85 ("Vom Vermanen und Warnen"), 197-200ᵛ, 395ᵛ-399ᵛ, 446-449ᵛ. For example: a resident at the *Spital* could find work at another farm not owned by the *Spital* only if he had the permission of the hospital administrator; to do otherwise would be a breach of the fourth commandment. Here the *Spital* functions as a residential parent (*in loco parentis*). Porta also ordered his *Jungfrawenspiegel* according to the commandments.

lords but is subject to God and his commands.[52] Elsewhere, Porta notes that the churches of his day are falling into chaos; some parishes have no pastors, and in others the church buildings themselves lie in ruin. All this is described as part of the Devil's plan to rid the land of schools and churches before his days of rule are over. No one is happily willing to support the church anymore, in contrast to the time under the 'papists'. Pastors are constantly accused of being greedy and must defend themselves against such calumnies.[53]

The picture is far different in the late medieval manuals where the priest is always at the center. Conflict is muted because in the explanation of the priest's ritual activities, the parishioners are only dimly present. They are the objects — even indirect objects — of the priests actions while the Devil is nowhere to be found. Priests described in the manuals are set apart through their ordination and enjoy just freedoms and privileges. Although there are passages in the *Manuale parrochialium sacerdotum* addressing greed and avarice among the clergy, it is assumed that certain priests have indeed purchased their benefice or regularly charge non-traditional fees for pastoral care. Such practices are condemned with the goal of correcting real shortcomings; there is no echo of lay complaint against clerical privilege.[54] In the late medieval manuals the burden of pastoral care is the threat of liturgical sacrilege and the ensuing punishment of God. Porta, on the other hand, reveals real frustration and bitterness. He describes the life of a pastor as being under constant siege: such is the burden of pastoral care in the late Reformation.

With the benefit of hindsight, the historian can see how in the 1570s and 1580s Europe was pushed into yet another cycle of religious crisis, characterized by strict and clear distinctions between confessional lines.[55] Despite the clarity brought by the Formula of Concord, Conrad Porta prepared his handbook against a chilling

---

[52] *Pastorale*, 110ᵛ-114.

[53] *Pastorale*, 410ᵛ; see also chapters XX, XXI, and XXXI: "Von Unterhaltung und Besoldung der Prediger," "Vom Widerstande und Creutze des rechtschaffenen Prediger," and "Was fuer schwere Straffen uber die ienigen ergehen werden, welche die Kirchenguetter zu sich reissen, oder mit denselben und der gemeinen Almosen ubel umbgehen?" For the standard complaint of clergy that parishioners consider them to be greedy, see Schorn-Schütte, "Christian Clergy," 725-26.

[54] *Manuale parrochialium sacerdotum*, 7-7ᵛ; cf "Conflicting Expectations," 217-20.

[55] R. Po-chia Hsia, "The Structure of Belief: Confessionalism and Society, 1500-1600," in *Germany: A New Social and Economic History*, vol. 1, *1450-1630*, ed. Bob Scribner (London, 1996), 355-77, 361.

backdrop created by recent conflicts against the Philippists and amongst the Gnesio-Lutherans, the Saint Bartholomew's Day massacre in France and resurgent Catholicism throughout Europe: chilling but not surprising. Conrad Porta was convinced that the Devil was on the loose, spinning his webs of deceit while godly pastors were rejected and scorned by the people. With his *Pastorale Lutheri*, Porta staked his claim on the promises of God and the ultimate victory of true doctrine.

There are clear similarities between the late medieval manuals for parish priests and the *Pastorale Lutheri*. Both were conceived as inexpensive resources for the pastor lacking experience in the duties of his charge. Both stress practical advice about the core duties of the pastor, and both describe his relationship with the laity: how he is to serve them, what he must teach them. But there are fundamental and deep differences. The late medieval handbooks present the ideal priest as an ordained doctor of the soul, expert in penitential circumstances, and reliable in liturgical practice. Conrad Porta's vision presents a pastor and preacher called into battle; he must follow God's demands yet is attacked by the Devil and held in contempt by the godless. Whereas the primary thrust of the manuals for parish priests was to prevent sacrilege and promote ritual purity, the *Pastorale Lutheri* sought to promote doctrinal purity, beat back the Devil and prevent error.

PROTESTANTISM, PUBLICATION AND THE FRENCH WARS OF RELIGION: THE CASE OF CAEN

Andrew Pettegree*

In the years after 1555 the French Protestant church experienced a period of vast growth.[1] From the foundation of the first recognisably Calvinist congregations in this year to the outbreak of the French religious wars a short seven years later, the Huguenot movement had recruited as many as one million members, organized in over one thousand churches: at its height probably a quarter of the urban population of France. The growth of Protestantism in turn stimulated (and at least partly, was stimulated by) a large increase in vernacular Protestant printing. The new congregations were hungry for religious writings of all kinds: works of instruction and consolation, prayer books and handbooks of congregational worship, polemic against the established Catholic church. The market in Protestant publishing expanded rapidly to meet this demand.

What is less frequently remarked upon is that this development also entailed a change in the nature and location of the Protestant printing presses. In the years before the most rapid expansion of the Huguenot movement French Protestant publishing had been entirely dominated by Geneva.[2] The well-resourced publishing industry in Calvin's home town had grown up as a result of Protestant emigration from France, and for much of the 1540s and 1550s its output was sufficient to satisfy the needs of the small evangelical groups

---

* Prossfeor of History and Director, The St Andrews Reformation Studies Institute, St Andrews, Scotland.

[1] The general literature on the French Protestant movement is now reasonably copious. See especially, N. M. Sutherland, *The Huguenot Struggle for Recognition* (New Haven, 1980), Mark Greengrass, *The French Reformation* (Oxford, 1987), Mack Holt, *The French Wars of Religion* (Cambridge, 1995). It is a pleasure to acknowledge here the help I have received from other members of the French book project group in the St Andrews Reformation Studies Institute, and from those libraries which are enlightened enough to permit reproductions from their early printed books. Without such reproductions work of this sort would be impossible.

[2] Robert Kingdon, *Geneva and the Coming of the Wars of Religion in France, 1555-1563* (Geneva, 1956). Francis Higman, *Piety and the People. Religious Printing in French, 1511-1551* (St Andrews Studies in Reformation History, 1996). Idem, *Censorship and the Sorbonne* (Geneva, 1979).

within the kingdom. The results of the Genevan monopoly were by and large beneficial. In particular, it was important that the body of works published in Geneva during these years, heavily but not exclusively dominated by Calvin's own writings, were characterized by a definite doctrinal coherence. Thus the closely controlled Genevan industry helped bring order and give intellectual shape to the nascent French movement; indeed, at this stage, before the formation of a national church, the ideological coherence of the printed propaganda emanating from Geneva was one of the movement's strongest cards.[3]

However, as the French Huguenot movement began to attract ever larger numbers of adherents towards the end of the 1550s, the Genevan monopoly served the movement less well. For many different reasons — problems of supply, economy, and speed in satisfying demand — it became urgently necessary to establish presses closer to the market. Thus the rapid growth of Protestant congregations in France in these years stimulated in turn the growth of a native French publishing industry.

For all that, the conditions that stimulated the growth of Protestantism did not entirely remove the constraints under which the industry had previously operated. With the solitary and unusual exception of the Marot/Bèze Psalter, the publication of Protestant works within the kingdom of France was never officially authorized.[4] Even as they responded to the commercial opportunities presented by the growth of this new market, French publishers still had to be aware that they were engaging in what remained an illegal activity. Mindful of these considerations, few printers who worked within France were prepared to place their names and place of work on Protestant works. Even during the years 1560-1565, the high point of the French Protestant movement in terms of both numbers and confidence, only a small proportion of the Protestant works printed with-

---

[3] For the regulation of the Genevan printing industry see Hans Joachim Bremme, *Buchdrucker und Buchhändler zur Zeit des Glaubenskämpfe* (Geneva, 1969); R. Crahay, 'Censure Romaine et censure Genevoise au XVIeme siècle', in *Les Églises et leurs institutions au XVIeme siècle* (Montpellier, 1978), pp. 169-191.

[4] E. Droz, 'Antoine Vincent, la propagande protestante par le psautier', in Gabrielle Berthoud (ed.), *Aspects de la propagande religieuse* (Geneva, 1957), pp. 276-93. The peculiar circumstances which permitted de Bèze to obtain this authorization are discussed in Geneviève Guilleminto-Chrétien, 'Le contrôle de l'édition en France dans les années 1560: la genèse de l'édit de Moulins', in Pierre Aquilon and Henri-Jean Martin (eds.), *Le livre dans l'Europe de la Renaissance* (Paris, 1988), p. 382.

in France actually bear the name of the printer and place of publication.

The high proportion of Protestant works published anonymously makes it extremely difficult to reconstruct with any certainty large parts of this Protestant publishing network. The extent of the involvement of printers in the established centres of Lyon, and particularly in Paris, remain largely undisclosed. However, modern typographical analysis permits some of the mysteries of this anonymous printing to be unlocked, and the resources of the Sixteenth Century French Book project, currently in progress in the Reformation Studies Institute at the University of St Andrews, will in due course make possible the identification of many of the printers involved in this secretive industry.[5] The project, which is attempting a systematic survey of all religious books published in France during the sixteenth century, has located a high proportion of the surviving copies of these enigmatic works, and work has now begun in identifying printers and locations. What follows is the first full attempt to reconstruct the history of the most important provincial centre of Protestant printing within France: that of Normandy, heavily centered upon Caen, the second city of the province.

Historically, Normandy was one of the parts of France in which Protestantism had secured some of its earliest adherents.[6] Prosperous, densely populated and well-connected through trade to the outside world, Normandy was bound to find adherents of the new doctrines among its more than usually mobile population. A number of its citizens were among the early martyrs of Protestantism within France, and there is evidence that Calvin's books were circulating in the province from the early 1540s. As Calvinist congregations began to form within France, the towns of Normandy seemed especially eager to embrace the new doctrines. A visitor to the famous Guibray fair in 1560, one of the most important and best attended fairs in France, found the whole event a ferment of evangelical agitation. Enthusiasts

---

[5] Information on the book project is published in an annual report, available from the director on demand, or via the Institute's website.

[6] For Normandy Protestantism see Philip Benedict, *Rouen during the French Wars of Religion* (Cambridge, 1981); Maryélise Suffern Lamet, 'Reformation, War and Society in Caen, 1558-1610' (University of Massachusetts, Ph.D., 1978). An article based on this unpublished dissertation is also useful: idem, 'French Protestants in a position of strength. The Early Years of the Reformation in Caen, 1558-1568', *Sixteenth Century Journal*, 9, 1978, pp. 35-55.

for the new religion moved through the stalls chanting evangelical songs, and openly confronting Catholics who stood in their way.[7] In Rouen, the provincial capital, during 1560 and 1561 Protestant zealots repeatedly sought confrontation with outraged members of the local Catholic congregations, defying the orders for restraint issued by an increasingly desperate town council.[8]

But at least in Rouen Calvinism had met with local resistance: in Caen even this seems barely evident. Here, the penetration achieved by the Huguenot movement was rapid and complete. The foundation of a Calvinist church in 1558 was followed by a wave of iconoclastic incidents, which met with little resistance. A local source noted in 1560 the distribution of pamphlets "containing a statement of their faith against the Holy Sacrament of the altar and the power of the pope and of the priests."[9] The news of the massacre of Vassy stimulated a co-ordinated campaign of image-breaking and destruction in the churches and monasteries of Caen, after which Mass was no longer celebrated. The town's Protestant allegiance was sealed by a visit towards the end of the first war by the Protestant army led by the Admiral Coligny, accompanied by Théodore de Bèze, who conducted a communion service and baptisms for the local congregation. Caen's experience was mirrored by a chain of smaller towns in lower Normandy stretching up into the Cotentin peninsula, including St Lô, Bayeux and Cherbourg. Given that a high proportion of the local nobility had also declared their allegiance to the new religion, Lower Normandy was in many respects fast becoming a Protestant stronghold.

These were apparently ideal conditions for the growth of a local Protestant printing industry. The ubiquity of the Protestant congregations and the high degree of support among both the local nobility and civic elites seemed to promise relative security; the growth of the congregations (at its height, a third of the population of Caen) created buoyant demand; there was, moreover, a local tradition of printing on which to build. In fact, the origins of Protestant printing in the province are shrouded in a mystery of a slightly discreditable nature.

---

[7] Nathanaël Weiss, 'Une mission à la foire de Guibray: Lettre d'un ministre Normand à Calvin, août 1561', *Bibliothèque de la Société d'Histoire du Protestantisme Français* (hereafter *BSHPF*), 28 (1879), pp. 455-64.

[8] Benedict, *Rouen*, ch. 2.

[9] "...contenant leur foi et créance contre le St. Sacrement de l'autel et puissance du pape et des prêtres." Lamet, 'Reformation in Caen', p. 160.

Some years ago, the distinguished bibliographer Jean François Gilmont, then compiling a bibliography of the Genevan printer Jean Crespin, noted the appearance of Crespin's trademark printing device, the anchor and serpent, on a number of works which appeared not to have emanated from his press. In fact, he concluded, these books were not Genevan at all, but the work of an anonymous printer in Normandy whom he identified, with a fine dramatic touch, as the "Fausseur Normand" — the Norman Forger.[10] It is now possible to identify this printer with a fair degree of certainty as Pierre Philippe of Caen. Works bearing the counterfeit anchor device are printed with the same materials as other books now identified as those of Philippe's press. Indeed, since this connection has been made it is possible to identify the Caen press as one of the busiest Protestant printing houses operating within the borders of France during these years.[11]

The first question to be addressed in investigating Philippe's work is why he made use of a counterfeit version of Crespin's printing device in this way. The initial motive must undoubtedly have been concealment. Philippe's first work as a Protestant printer was published in 1559, when the Protestant community in Normandy was emerging from the shadows, but when open adherence to the new doctrines was still perilous.[12] A printer, with his fixed equipment, was especially vulnerable to retribution if his handiwork was identified: this explains why at this stage Philippe supplied his work not only with the camouflage of a Genevan mark, but with a false place of printing. Yet Philippe was still using the Genevan mark in 1562, when conditions were very different and the same considerations would no longer apply. In this year he published two editions of Ratramnus' *Traité du corps et du sang de Jesus Christ*, one bearing the anchor mark, and one not.[13] In these circumstances, the decision to

---

[10] J.-F. Gilmont, *Jean Crespin. Un éditeur réformé du XVIe siècle* (Geneva, 1981), pp. 101-5. See also idem, *Bibliographie des Editions de Jean Crespin, 1550-1572* (2 vols., Verviers, 1981).

[11] A partial listing of Philippe's works is attempted in Pierre Aquilon, *Bibliographie Normande. Bibliographie des ouvrages imprimés à Caen et à Rouen au seizième siècle* (Répertoire bibliographique des livres imprimés en France au seizième siècle, fasc. Hors série, 1992) (hereafter *RBN*), pp. 320-25. The identification of Philippe as the 'fausseur Normand' together with the discoveries made in the course of this investigation will more than treble the number of works that can be attributed to his press.

[12] Francesco Negri, *Tragedie du roy franc-arbitre* [Villefranche = Caen, Philippe], 1559. Gilmont, *Crespin Bibliographie*, 59/9*.

[13] Gilmont, *Crespin*, p. 104. Idem, *Crespin Bibliographie*, 62/4***.

persist with the Genevan mark was probably commercially led. Members of the congregations, long used to purchasing books from Crespin's press, regarded the Genevan mark as a certification of quality. Genevan facsimiles therefore possessed a certain authority in the marketplace, which local printers were keen to exploit.

This fact explains why so much of the Protestant publishing produced in Normandy in these years was Genevan both in the choice of books and their style. In this respect Philippe most certainly led the way. The initial letters that decorate his books are locally re-cut imitations of alphabets familiar from the works of the Genevan printers Estienne and Crespin. And in addition to the famous Crespin anchor, Philippe also employed a version of the printer's device of another Genevan printer, Jean Durant, on an edition of a popular small tract, the *Sommaire recueil des signes sacrez*, in 1561.[14]

Philippe's editions clearly enjoyed a considerable commercial success. Fuelled by the rapid expansion in the local congregation after 1560, Philippe's presses turned out a growing number of editions, including many of the most popular texts of the new movement: the *Baston de la foi* of Guido de Brès, Bartholemy Causse's *Vrai Bouclier de la foi* and a new French translation of Luther's *On the Freedom of a Christian*.[15] As he prospered, so his works became more costly and ambitious. In 1562 Philippe published a fine folio edition of Calvin's *Institutes*, the only one published outside the large printing houses of Geneva and Lyon.[16] But even this was not the most ambitious of Philippe's ventures, for in this same year he also brought to the press a pirated version of the English Geneva Bible.[17] This was a very large undertaking, and not just because of the technical difficulties of publishing in a foreign language. A work of this size would have absorbed the whole energies of his pressmen for at least two months, and involved a considerable investment in terms of capital and labor. The fact that such an ambitious venture could be undertaken (and this was not the only

---

[14] Copy in the Paris, Bibliothèque de la Société d'Histoire du Protestantisme Français, Rés. 9051. This is one of five editions of this small anonymous work (sometimes attributed to Théodore de Bèze) published in 1561. Philippe was responsible for two, one with, and one without the Durant-style mark; *RBN* (Philippe), no. 5 for this second version.

[15] *RBN* (Philippe), nos. 1, 3.

[16] J.F. Gilmont and R. Peter, *Bibliotheca Calviniana. Les oeuvres de Jean Calvin publiés au XVIe siècle* (2 vols., Geneva, 1991-94), 62/7.

[17] Gilmont, *Crespin*, p.103. STC 2095.

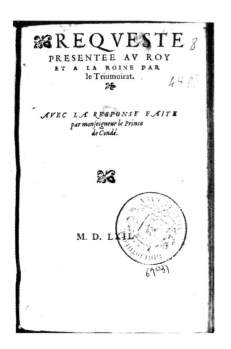

Fig 1: Requeste presentee au Roy [Caen, Le Chandellier], 1562.
(Caen, Bibliothèque Municipale)

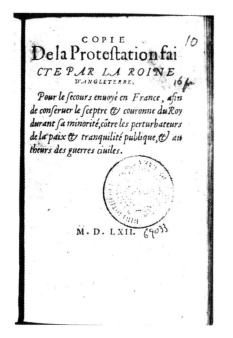
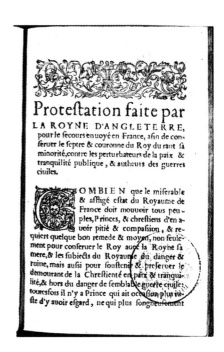

Fig 2: Copie de la Protestation faicte par la Roine D'Angleterre
[Caen, Philippe], 1562. (Caen, Bibliothèque Municipale)

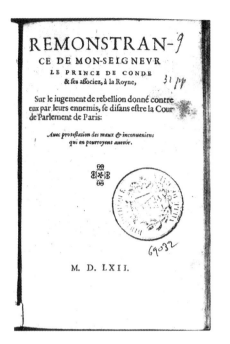

Fig 3: Remonstrance de Monseigneur le Prince de Condé
[Caen, Mangeant], 1562. (Caen, Bibliothèque Municipale)

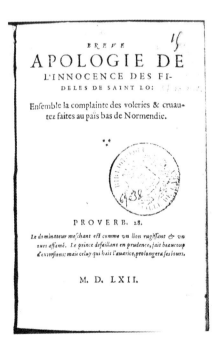

Fig 4: Breve apologie de l'innocence des fideles de Saint Lo
[Caen, Mangeant], 1562. (Caen, Bibliothèque Municipale)

Fig 6: Title Page woodcut from La Bible. St Lô [=Caen], Mangeant, Auber and Le Cordier, 1562, (Edinburgh, New College)

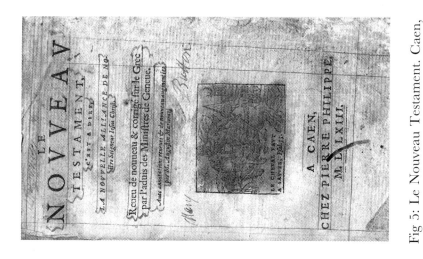

Fig 5: Le Nouveau Testament. Caen, Philippe, 1563, (Glasgow, Private Collection)

Fig 7: Reconstructed alphabet from Mangeant Bible

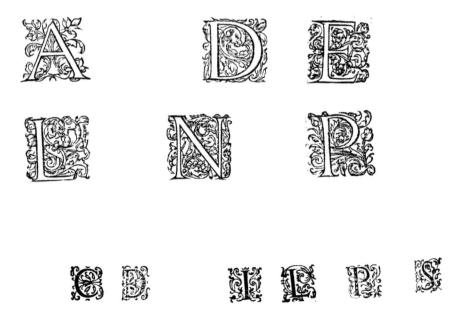

Fig 8: Reconstructed alphabet from Philippe New Testament

such book to be published locally, as we shall see) demonstrates that the Protestant printing industry in Normandy commanded considerable capital resources. Certainly demand for Protestant books was by this stage sufficient to sustain not only Philippe but also several other new publishers.

The best known of these other newly emerging publishing businesses was that run by Pierre Le Chandellier. The more cautious Le Chandellier began printing only in 1562, after the edict of January had given the Protestant congregations a degree of legal protection. In this and following years Le Chandellier turned out a number of substantial works for the use of the Protestant congregations, including a New Testament, at least three editions of the psalms, and the popular works of Causse and de Brès.[18] In the newly relaxed climate almost all of the works are signed, and are easily identified by his distinctive initial letters. But it is now becoming clear that Le Chandellier also published works that he was less anxious to identify as his own. A recent discovery in the municipal library at Caen has thrown a whole new light on the operations of several of the more respectable Caen printing houses.

This single bound volume contains seventeen small ephemeral tracts from the years 1560-63.[19] Most are extremely rare: some indeed known in no other surviving copy. All are of a wholly different character from the works discussed above, being examples of the short political manifestos issued in increasing numbers during these years by local Calvinist congregations and the movement's national leadership. None carry the name of their printer, but typographical analysis reveals the involvement of at least three of the Caen printers: Philipppe, Le Chandellier and a third printer yet to be discussed, Simon Mangeant.

A number of these tracts are manifestos published by the major Normandy congregations, including an appeal to the Queen mother, Catherine of Medici, from the inhabitants of Rouen and a defense of the congregation of St Lô against the accusation that they had been responsible for the local outbreaks of iconoclasm.[20] The publication

---

[18] *RBN* (Le Chandellier), nos. 1, 1*, 4, 5, 6, 7.

[19] Caen, Bibliothèque Municipale, Rés. A. 1565.

[20] *Elegie de la Royne mere du Roy envoyee par les citoyens de Rouen*, n.p. [=Caen, Philippe], n.d. [1562]; *Breve apologie de l'innocence des fideles de Saint Lo*, n.p. [=Caen, Mangeant], 1562. Caen, Bibliothèque Municipale, Rés. A. 1565/12, 15. See Figs. 1,4.

of such works on a Normandy press is not surprising, though the fact that congregations in these places both turned to printers in Caen, rather than having them printed in their own towns is worthy of note. This would have been for very different reasons in the two cases. St Lô was yet to establish a printing press; Rouen, in contrast, has a long-standing publishing industry, but the poisoned relations between Protestants and Catholics within the city made the publication of evangelical works a perilous undertaking. Consequently, only a very small number of Protestant works were ever printed in Rouen, and then only in conditions of great secrecy.[21]

Interesting as these local works are, as striking in this Caen collection is the presence of a selection of the manifestos issued by the Huguenot military leadership under the aegis of the Duc de Condé, here re-issued with Caen imprints (Fig. 3). These manifestos originally emanated from the press of Éloi Gibier in Orléans, who published several editions of the twenty tracts that make up the corpus of the Condéan manifestos in a series of highly recognizable quarto editions.[22] The Gibier editions were extremely popular and widely disseminated, and it has not previously been recognized that Condé's manifestos may also have been reprinted on other presses within France: in this respect the discovery of these small octavo Normandy editions is an event of some importance. In fact, the Condéan tracts were more widely disseminated even than this. There is evidence of other French, possibly Parisian reprints of some of the more popular works,[23] and the pamphlets achieved contemporary translations in at least two other European vernaculars, English and German.[24]

---

[21] The best documented Protestant printing house was that of Abel Clémence, whose output has now been largely reconstructed by the researches of Clutton and Gilmont. *RBN*, pp. 361-3. The bookseller Florent Valentin was also briefly involved in the Protestant book trade: an edition of the Marot/Beze psalms bearing his name survives in the Bibliothèque de la Société d'Histoire du Protestantisme Français in Paris (Rés. 12155). Interestingly this edition, possibly printed locally, also uses a replica of the printer's marks of Jean Durant of Geneva (see above, n. 14). For the beginnings of printing in St Lô see below.

[22] Louis Desgraves, *Éloi Gibier, Imprimeur à Orléans, 1536-1588* (Geneva, 1966). J.-F. Gilmont, 'La première diffusion des "Mémoires de Condé" par Éloi Gibier en 1562-1563', in Aquilon and Martin, *Le livre dans l'Europe de la Renaissance*, pp. 58-70.

[23] Paris, Bibliothèque de France, LB 33.116C, LB 33.64cC/D, LB 33.65.

[24] *Declaration made by Condé of the causes which have constrained him to take on the defence of the King's authority*, London, Rowland Hall for Edward Sutton, 1562. Oxford, Bodelian Library 8o O 67 (1) Th. contains no fewer than nine of these English translations of the Gibier tracts. German edition of the *Declaration* recorded in the cata-

It is interesting to ask why these Normandy editions were published without the name of the printer. After all, all three printing houses were printing other works during these years with their names attached, and these editions would have been as recognizably their work to interested contemporaries as they are to modern bibliographers. The decorated initial letters used at the opening of the text in all but a couple of these tracts (on sig. A2r) are extremely distinctive. In this respect, the disguise of anonymity is pretty threadbare: there is no real attempt by the printers to disguise their workmanship. In fact, it was an open secret that Caen's Protestant printers were turning out political tracts of this nature. In July 1563 Théodore de Bèze, by now returned to Geneva, informed Heinrich Bullinger in a letter that that one of the most important of these works, Coligny's defense against the charge of complicity in the assassination of the duc de Guise, had been published in Normandy.[25]

What then is the purpose of the printers' discretion? It seems that what may have been intended here is not so much anonymity in the usual sense as 'deniability'. The printers may have been governed by the need to be mindful of the sensitivities of their friends and allies on the Caen city council. Philippe, Mangeant and Le Chandellier were all leading figures in the city's new Protestant establishment. Pierre Philippe was the most actively involved, apparently serving as elder of the Calvinist congregation from the beginning of the congregation's surviving records in 1562 through to 1569.[26] Both Mangeant and Le Chandellier were also committed church members, bringing their children for baptism and attending the church's services. The fact that Le Chandellier's daughter Sara was sponsored at her christening by the 'honorable homme M. Gieffroy Le Laboureur, principal du collège du Boys', the local Latin school, suggests his own influential connections.[27]

The ties of friendship and the business associations which connected the Caen printers to the city's governing council, itself heavily infiltrated by members of the Calvinist congregation, would have

---

logue of the former Staatsbibliothek Berlin, Staatsbibliothek, Flugschr. 1562/21 (a collection dispersed or destroyed in the Second World War).

[25] *Correspondence de Théodore de Bèze*, ed. Henri Meylan et. al., (12 vols., Geneva, 1960-), vol. IV, no. 276.

[26] C.E. Lart, *The Registers of the Protestant Church at Caen, vol. 1: Births and Marriages, 1560-1572* (1908), pp. 13, 30, 132, 162, 333, 393, 485.

[27] Lart, *Registers*, pp. 57,127, 388, 423 (Le Chandellier).

made them fully aware of the political constraints within which the community was obliged to operate. Whereas the Calvinist publishers were prepared to own responsibility for uncontroversial works for congregational worship, the publication of the more incendiary political tracts without acknowledgement of local provenance made it easier for the council to avoid having to take official cognizance of their existence. The same strategy was followed quite consciously by the Genevan city authorities, who on several occasions authorized publication of works potentially offensive to other neighboring powers on the specific condition that Geneva was not mentioned on the title-page: a clear breach of their otherwise rigorously enforced procedures.[28] There is no evidence that the Caen authorities were directly involved in this way, but the discretion shown by the city's printers certainly seems to have been appreciated. In 1564, when the religious climate in the city (as nationally) had altered quite considerably, and Protestants no longer enjoyed the freedoms of two years before, the local authorities could comment that "the printers and booksellers of this city print and publish many suspect and scandalous books, in which neither the name of the author nor of the printer appears", for all the world as if this had come to their attention for the first time.[29]

The Caen publisher most heavily committed to the publication of the Condéan tracts was the third member of the triumvirate of leading Protestant printers, Simon Mangeant.[30] The discovery of these political works is particularly interesting in his case, for otherwise Mangeant's stock in trade consisted entirely of editions of the New Testament and the Marot/Bèze psalms.[31] Between them Caen's printers accounted for a high proportion of the numerous editions of both works known to have been published in France during these years. To some extent this breach of the previous Genevan monopoly on these works was known of and approved in Geneva. Théodore de Bèze had himself orchestrated the publication of the complete psalm edition by a large number of different printers within France: this was the only realistic way to meet the huge demand for this cornerstone of congre-

[28] Bremme, *Buchdrucker*, pp. 79-86.

[29] '...les Imprimeurs & libraires de cette ville, impriment & mettent en verité plusieurs livres suspects & scandaleux & ausquels n'est escrit le nom, ou l'autheur, ou de l'imprimeur.' Lamet, 'Reformation in Caen', p. 292.

[30] Caen, Bibliothèque municipale, Rés. A. 1565/9, 14, 15, 16. See Figs. 3, 4.

[31] RBN (Mangeant), nos. 2-6.

gational worship. But the Normandy editions of both the New Testament and the Psalter had their own distinctive characteristics, being supplied with a particularly full apparatus of glosses and supporting materials.[32] In the Psalter these were the work of the distinguished pastor, Augustin Marlorat, by 1561 established as the leading figure of the Rouen church, and later a tragic victim of the Catholic vengeance which followed their repossession of the city in 1563.

Mangeant published four editions of the psalms and New Testament in as many years — a sure indication of the buoyant demand for these texts at this time. He was also the leading figure in the consortium responsible for the only full edition of the French Calvinist Bible published in Normandy during these years.[33] A complete Bible was obviously a publishing enterprise of a different order from the small books which were the stock in trade of most jobbing printers of the day, and to finance it Mangeant went into partnership with two other figures in the Caen publishing industry, Henry Auber and Louis Le Cordier.[34] The Bible was published in 1562 with the address, 'Saint Lô' (Fig. 6).

Why the three Caen publishers involved should have opted to claim this as a product of a St Lô printing house is something of a mystery. It is almost certainly not printed there — the printing materials are clearly those of Mangeant's Caen office, and it would have made little sense to transport these materials the 40 miles to St Lô to print a single book. No other book is known to have been published in St Lô before Thomas Bouchard established a small printing house there in 1564.[35] One possible solution is that even though the Bible was printed in Caen, the financial backing for the project came from the wealthy St Lô Calvinist community. This would certainly have been an extremely expensive book to finance, occupying as it would have done Mangeant's press for up to four months work.[36]

---

[32] Bettye Chambers, *Bibliography of French Bibles. Fifteenth- and Sixteenth-Century French-language editions of the Scriptures* (Geneva, 1983), nos. 280, 281, 292, 316, 336, 338, 353.

[33] Chambers, *Bibles*, no. 292. I have examined the fine copy in the library of New College, Edinburgh.

[34] On Auber and Le Cordier, *RBN*, p. 365.

[35] RBN (Bouchard). A Claudin, 'Les origines de l'imprimerie à Saint Lô en Normandie', *Bulletin du Bibliophile*, 1894.

[36] This calculation is based on the size of the book, and the number of impressions that could be taken from a press in a single day. See here especially J-F. Gilmont, 'La Fabrication du Livre dans la Genève de Calvin', in Jean-Daniel Candaux and Bernard Lescaze (eds.), *Cinq siècles d'imprimerie genevoise* (Geneva, 1980), pp. 89-96.

The end product of these endeavours was certainly a book of which all concerned could have been proud: a rich folio, lavishly decorated with initial letters and the fullest possible repertoire of the maps and technical diagrams, which were all that the Calvinist churches were prepared to permit by way of illustration.[37] The woodcuts for the maps were shared with Pierre Philippe's pirated English Genevan Bible of the same year, but for the title-page the printers commissioned a new and striking decorative woodcut: a landscape dominated by a tree from which Absolom dangles from his hair. The surrounding motto draws the lesson: "Le meschant sera surprins par ses iniquitez, et sera apprehendre par les cordes de son peche" [The sinner will be overtaken by his iniquities, and hanged by the rope of his own sins].

This choice of decorative illustration is itself interesting. The Absolom theme is very rare in the context of such woodcut art: I know of only one other example outside of a Bible text illustration, in an English pamphlet of the Edwardian period entitled 'the hurt of sedition'.[38] The adoption of such a theme in the French context might seem a little rich for a church which had grown in flagrant defiance of the law, particularly in Normandy where the progress of the Huguenot congregations (particularly in both Caen and St Lô) had been accompanied by frequent violent attacks on Catholic church property. The use of such a design is perhaps an indication that by 1562 the Huguenot leadership was confident that their movement was passing into a new stage: from insurgency to new Protestant establishment. In such a context an appeal for the preservation of law and the social order would have seemed entirely appropriate.

More generally, the publication of so large a number of books for Calvinist congregational worship is itself a sign of the vitality and strength of the churches in Lower Normandy at this stage of the religious conflict. Even with the conclusion of the first war in 1563, which brought considerable restrictions to the congregations' freedom of worship in many towns in France, the Huguenot strongholds

---

[37] Catherine Delano-Smith and Elizabeth Morley Ingram, *Maps in Bibles, 1500-1600. An Illustrated Catalogue* (Geneva, 1991), 1.3.1/2, 2.3/3, 3.1/3, 5.2/3, 6.2/3.

[38] STC 5109-5110 (3 ed.s of 1549). The authorship of this work is attributed to Sir John Cheke. It was one of a number of works on a similar theme published in the wake of the popular uprisings of the summer of this year. I am very grateful to Vivienne Westbrook who first drew this woodcut to my attention.

of Lower Normandy remained largely insulated from its effects. In contrast to the provincial capital, Rouen, which was forcibly returned to Catholic control in 1563, Caen's Protestant community at first remained firmly in control, ignoring all restrictions on the number of Protestant churches laid down by the peace of Amboise, and allowing the re-establishment of Catholic worship within the city only with the greatest reluctance. The Norman congregations could not however ignore the rapid downturn in the church's fortunes elsewhere in France. A hint of this is contained in a new title-page woodcut design commissioned by Mangeant's former partners Auber and Le Cordier, and used for the first time for an edition of the Marot/ Bèze psalms published in 1564.[39] This shows a figure representing truth combating two warriors in the form of beasts, one tonsured, with the motto: 'Verité est à la fin victorieuse' [Truth wins out in the end]. The band separating the upper and lower levels has the less confident tag: 'Il ne faut aquiescer à homme quelconque contre la verité' [One must never give way to any man when truth is at stake], a sentiment that reflects the pressures under which Huguenots now operated in many parts of France. Bound with the only surviving copy of this work, in the library of Magdalen College (Cambridge), is a previously unrecognized edition of the French Confession of Faith, also emanating from the Caen printing shop of Auber and Le Cordier. Reflecting the new temper of the times, the Confession is here published with an extended (and apparently new) preface, protesting against the outrages which are now committed against members of the Reformed congregations within the kingdom of France.[40]

Catholic control of Caen was restored in 1568, in the wake of the short second war. But even now, relations between the faiths were significantly better than in many parts of France. The new Catholic majority in the city council was careful to avoid vindictiveness and reprisals, and on the whole relations between the faiths continued to be harmonious. This was possibly a constructive response to the discretion and moderation with which the former Protestant establish-

---

[39] Cambridge, Magdalen College: A-21-29.

[40] *Confession de foy*, n.p. [=Caen, Auber & Le Cordier], 1564, sig. A2r: Les poures fideles qui sont involement diffamez, & affligez par le royaume de France, à cause qu'ils desirent de servir purement Dieu, sans se polluer aux superstitions de la Papulté, à tous ceux qui leur voudont prester audience. Cambridge, Magdalen College: A-21-29/2.

ment had exercised their supremacy after the takeover of power in 1562; or it may simply have been the case that the Calvinists remained such a formidable presence at all levels of city life that any more aggressive action would have been counter-productive. The change in circumstances did require some adaptation on the part of Caen's Protestant printers. Although most continued to work, they now retreated into the discretion that had characterized their publications before the Calvinist takeover. Both Mangeant and Le Chandellier also gave increasing attention to the publication of Latin scholarly books for the local university community.[41]

This local tradition of relative harmony even survived the terrible events that followed the St Bartholomew's Day Massacre in 1572. In Caen the city authorities worked effectively to prevent a local bloodbath. The city letter books preserved in the local departmental archive contain a fascinating document, a letter from the king requiring the city fathers to arrange for the local re-publication of the official tract explaining the reasons for Coligny's murder.[42] A copy of the prototype version published by Jean Dallier in Paris was enclosed, and still survives carefully filed along with the letter.[43] But there is no evidence that the Council ever took any steps to follow the King's instructions: in the local context it would certainly have been incendiary and counter-productive. The contrast with events in Rouen is again instructive. Here news of the massacre in Paris prompted Rouen's Catholics to turn on the remnants of the once powerful Calvinist congregation in their midst. Several hundred people were hunted down and killed; many thousands of their badly intimidated brethren adjured the faith rather than lose their lives.[44] In Rouen there were still scores to settle from the brief period of Calvinist supremacy in 1562; in Caen, it seems that both sides valued the relatively good relations that had been maintained between the confessions enough to take steps to protect the newly vulnerable congregation from reprisals.

---

[41] RBN (Le Chandellier), nos. 21, 23, 26-30, (Mangeant), nos. 8-12.

[42] Caen, Archives départementales du Calvados, 1 B 3, fols. 142-3. On other occasions the Caen council carried out very dutifuly instructions to make proclamation of local edicts, as is proven by the printed copies of locally printed proclamations preserved in the same letter-book.

[43] *Declaration du Roy, de la cause et occasion de la mort de l'Admiral, & autres ses adherens & complices, dernierement advenue en cette ville de Paris*. Paris, Jean Dallier, 1572.

[44] Benedict, *Rouen*, ch. 5.

Nevertheless, something had to be done to remind Protestants that the old dispensation was at an end, and significantly it was the Calvinist printing community who were singled out. The town council now set in train a formal visitation of the shops of three of the leading Protestant figures in the industry, Pierre Philippe, Etienne Thomas and Pierre Le Chandellier. The brief account of this investigation, discovered in the Caen archive by my student Alexander Wilkinson, makes fascinating reading, because there are clear hints that even this punitive raid may have been an elaborate charade staged with the collusion of those involved.[45] The commissioners arrived at Le Chandellier's shop to find the proprietor absent; his wife was left to display the stock. The official record shows nothing more sinister than a blameless selection of classical works and university textbooks. However, on the outside flyleaf there is a note of other texts found in a different room, including forty copies of Calvin's Commentary on Paul and "several books of the format [used] in the Reformed churches."[46]

The Calvinist publishers seem to have taken the lesson to heart. Although both Le Chandellier and Mangeant remained in business, they confined their work largely to blameless Latin texts. When Le Chandellier ventured once more into Protestant publishing later in the decade, he reverted once again to the stratagem of using false addresses.[47] But it was important that the Protestant presses survived even in this debilitated form, for in the last decade of the century Caen's presses would find a new role as loyal supporters of the authority of the former Protestant champion, Henri de Navarre. Here again the city deliberately took a divergent path from that of Rouen, a stubborn stronghold of the Catholic League. Caen was briefly rewarded for its loyalty with the transfer of the local parlement from Rouen until the provincial capital capitulated and recognized the inevitability of Henry's victory.

During the brief heyday of Protestant publishing within France, Caen's small printing shops turned out a total of around sixty Protestant books. It is a small but significant group, second only in size to the output of the mighty Lyon publishing industry, which also gave

---

[45] Caen, Archives départementales du Calvados, 1 B 3, fols. 150-53.
[46] "...plusieurs livres de format des églises Reformées." Idem, fol. 151.
[47] *RBN* (Le Chandellier), nos. 22 ('Zurich'), 25 ('Basqueville').

Protestant publishing a relatively free rein during these years. The popularity of these local editions, many of which were printed several times over in a short space of years, is an indication of the extent of the commitment to the new faith in the towns of Lower Normandy during these years. It was very important for these large and well-organized congregations that there existed a reliable local supply of books, given the cost of transporting bulky goods from either Lyon or Geneva. As Caen's room for maneuver diminished, its role passed to La Rochelle, the new publication and distribution center in the west of France.

The role of La Rochelle is well established; the place of Caen in the annals of French Protestant printing much less so. The emergence of Caen's role from out of the shadows points to the value of research which combines bibliographical investigation with searches in local archives: the same techniques will undoubtedly reveal much that is not presently known about Protestant printing in Lyon and Paris. Within the purely bibliographical sphere, this case study also suggests certain conclusions that have a general application for the study of vernacular Protestant printing in France. Even with the often anonymous or unattributed works such as those identified here, the general concept of anonymity requires some refinement. There is a great difference between work published without mention of printer or place of publication, but clearly recognizable as the work of a particular print shop, on the one hand, and, on the other, books published without any distinguishing marks whatsoever. The works of the Caen printers fall generally into the first category —which is what of course has permitted them to be identified here — as do most of the works printed in Lyon. In both places printers felt sufficiently safe from reprisal to own their handiwork, at least implicitly. Many of the anonymous editions published in Paris, however, are very much in the second category. Works of this sort may be the work of jobbing printers, new to the trade, but often their physical characteristics and workmanship suggest rather that these are books by accomplished printers who have deliberately removed any identifying features in order to avoid reprisals. Printers were well aware that the authorities often investigated illegal or incendiary works by carrying them round print shops and asking members of the trade to identify the culprit.[48] In the very different environment of fiercely Catholic Paris, an inopportune use of a distinctive decorative initial might have meant signing one's own death warrant.[49]

Secondly, this investigation of the output of the Caen publishing houses suggests that even in a developing market there was still room for a high degree of specialization. This operated both at the level of individual printers, and between printing centers. Even when printers were printing exclusively religious and Protestant works, which seems to have been the preference of most of Caen's printers, they confined their output to distinct sub-categories within the whole field of Calvinist writings. Caen's printers published no examples of the scathing satirical pamphlets, many of them in verse form, which were so popular with the Protestant congregations. Works of this sort dominated the output of the Lyon printer Jean Saugrain, one of the major new forces to emerge during the years when French Protestantism was at its most ebullient.[50] That Caen printers avoided these popular and lucrative works may have been part of a self-denying ordinance intended to preserve harmony in the local community. If this was so it may have helped them avoid the bloody retribution that was the fate of printers in both Paris and Lyon when the balance of the local religious struggle turned against them.

---

[48] This was a technique used quite widely in Europe, including the tightly regulated Netherlandish and English printing industries.

[49] In July 1560 the Parisian printer Martin L'Homme was executed for having been found in possession of a stock of copies of François Hotman's anonymous attack on the Cardinal of Lorraine, *Le Tigre de France*.

[50] I am currently engaged in a study of the output of Saugrain's print-shop.

III. EXEGESIS AND INTERPRETATION

TRISTITIA AND THE FEAR OF HELL IN MONASTIC REFLECTION FROM JOHN CASSIAN TO HILDEMAR OF CORBIE

Alan E. Bernstein*

Among the legacies of the ancient world is a complex mixture of culturally defined concepts of death that competed and overlapped. The most significant change, largely completed by the time of the closing of the New Testament canon, was one in which "moral death" replaced "neutral death." That is, neutral death, with its all-embracing underworld, which separated the dead from the living, yielded to moral death, with an afterlife that segregated the wicked from the good.[1] "Inner death," a new variant, arose with the passing of political unity from Latin Europe and the simultaneous growth of monasticism. Since, in Christianity, the true difference between life and death appears only in the other world (eternal life versus eternal death), physical death began to serve as a model for life. It is in this context that one reads about death to the world, mortification, and other metaphors that applied death to life or rather to a certain (monastic) way of life.[2]

* Professor of History, University of Arizona

[1] For a full discussion, see my book, *The Formation of Hell: Death and Retribution in the Ancient and Early Christian Worlds* (Ithaca, NY: Cornell University Press, 1993). What follows examines a theme I will pursue farther in a sequel devoted to belief in hell during the early Middle Ages.

[2] For other works that consider views of death in late antiquity and the early Middle Ages, see Peter Brown's two lectures under the collective title "The End of the Ancient Other World": I. "Gloriosus Obitus: Death and Afterlife, 400-700 A.D." and II. "The Decline of the Empire of God: From Amnesty to Purgatory" in *The Tanner Lectures on Human Values* 20 (Salt Lake City: University of Utah Press, 1999), 21-50 and 51-85. The second of Brown's lectures has also been published with modifications as "Vers la naissance du purgatoire: Amnistie et pénitence dans le christianisme occidental de l'Antiquité tardive au Haut Moyen Age," *Annales. Histoire. Sciences Sociales* 52, no. 6 (1997), 1247-1261. See also Frederick S. Paxton, *Christianizing Death: The Creation of a Ritual Process in Early Medieval Europe* (Ithaca: Cornell University Press, 1990); Arno Borst, "Three Studies of Death in the Middle Ages," in *Medieval Worlds: Barbarians, Heretics and Artists in the Middle Ages*, tr. Eric Hansen (Chicago: University of Chicago Press, 1992), 215-243; Éric Rebillard, *In Hora Mortis: Évolution de la pastorale chrétienne de la mort aux IVe et Ve siècles*. Bibliothèque des écoles françaises d'Athènes et de Rome 283 (Paris: Boccard, 1994); Patrick Geary, "Exchange and

One change that accompanies the early medieval, Christian inversion of death occurs in the function of hell. If the only true death is damnation, and physical death leads the righteous to eternal life, then hell itself would seem to become less menacing. Yet, because one can only be saved in humility, hell moves not away, but nearer, as this paper will attempt to show. Though the monks' search is for God, humility prevents any satisfaction with spiritual progress or confidence that the goal will be attained. Instead, the religious must focus on the immensity of his or her faults, which seem to drag one so far from God that hell seems dangerously near. Thus humility demands that the monk simultaneously accept hell as a possible fate and respect it as the source of a salutary fear prompting repentence. For, as the authors examined below were fond of observing, "Fear of God is the beginning of wisdom" (Ps. 110 [111].10 cf. Prov. 9.10). This dread could be transcended, they said, quoting 1 John 4.18: "Perfect love drives out fear."

The anxiety that prompted these two statements inspired varied and tenacious traditions. In the monastic context of the early Middle Ages, these emotions combined with the pursuit of humility. These two concerns, humility and fear, blend at the point where the healthy fear of God warns ascetics not to become satisfied with their humility but rather to consider themselves vile, useless, and unworthy: worms in God's eyes.[3] This tradition, largely from Psalms, emerges anew in the Gospels, in the writings of John Cassian, in the Rule of St. Benedict, and Benedict's Carolingian interpreters Smaragdus of St. Mihiel and Hildemar of Corbie.[4] In monastic reflection, these considerations made hell a welcome sanction, the fate of those who abandon or neglect their ascetic calling. The unstated assumption in this view of things is the argument that the punishment for evading healthy disci-

---

Interaction Between the Living and the Dead in Early Medieval Society," in *Living with the Dead in the Middle Ages* (Ithaca: Cornell University Press, 1994), 77-92.

[3] On fear as an aspect of medieval and early modern religious feeling, see: Jean Delumeau, *Sin and Fear: The Emergence of a Western Guilt Culture, 13th-18th Centuries*, tr. Eric Nicholson (New York: St. Martin's Press, 1990 [1983]); idem, *La Peur en Occident, XIVe-XVIIIe siècles: une cité assiégé* (Paris: Fayard, 1978); Piero Camporesi, *The Fear of Hell: Images of Damnation and Salvation in Early Modern Europe*, tr. Lucinda Byatt (University Park: Pennsylvania State University Press, 1990 [1987]).

[4] For example, Ps. 72[73].22: "Ad nihilum redactus sum"; Ps. 21[22].7: "Ego sum vermis et non homo," which are cited in connection with the sixth and seventh rungs of the Ladder of Humility in the Rule of St. Benedict and taken up in the commentaries thereon, discussed below.

pline is to endure its rigors after death. This view of hell's deterrent function reveals important aspects of monastic psychology and the experience of living under a rule. Conversely, the monastic analysis of fear, especially as it derived from institutional discipline, affected the depiction of hell.

1. *Cassian*

John Cassian (360-435) put it succinctly in the first book of his *Conferences*. Although life in the flesh makes it virtually impossible to succeed completely, the goal of the monk, he said, is to keep the mind's eye firmly fixed on the highest good. He can be hindered by God's efforts to try him, or the attacks of demons, or his own weakness, specifically by the influence of the flesh.[5] Lust for the flesh leads directly to vices.[6]

In the *Institutes*, Cassian considers the vices individually. Because they affect the will's resolve to resist the flesh, two are of particular importance: sadness (*tristitia*) and sloth (*acedia* or *accidia*). Before analyzing these vices in turn, it would be wise to note that Cassian's inventory of eight vices did not survive unchanged through the Middle Ages. Gregory the Great (d. 604) shortened the list. In the process, he blended *acedia* into *tristitia* and in the regions under Roman influence until the eleventh century, the two became one.[7]

Sadness may arise out of other vices: from anger over a pleasure that escapes us, lust for some gain beyond our reach, or some other

---

[5] *Conlationes*, 4.6-8; ed. Michael Petschenig, CSEL 13 (Vindobonae: C. Gerold, 1886), 100-103.

[6] *Conl.* 4.11.2; p. 105, lines 14-15: "[I]ntestinum cotidie intra nos geritur bellum, dum concupiscentia carnis, quae praecipitanter fertur ad vitia ...."

[7] Morton Bloomfield, *The Seven Deadly Sins*. ([East Lansing:] Michigan State University Press, 1967 [1952]), 72. Gregory folded *vana gloria* or *iactantia* into *superbia* as one sin, blended *acedia* into *tristitia* and added *invidia*. The relevant passage is in his *Moralia in Job* 31.45 treating Job 39.25. Bloomfield, 69-72 and 356, notes 24 and 25. Siegfried Wenzel speculated that Gregory sacrificed *acedia* because it was too specifically a desert illness for his Western audience and too specifically a monastic concern for the Christian community at large. *The Sin of Sloth: Acedia in Medieval Thought and Literature* (Chapel Hill: University of North Carolina Press, 1960), 24-27. Like Wenzel, Christoph Flüeler stresses the literal roots of *acedia* in the situation of hermits in the Egyptian wilderness. When Gregory abandons *acedia* for *tristitia*, his list of derivative vices nonetheless overlaps with Cassian's so that their original relationship remains transparent. "Acedia und Melancholie im Spätmittelalter," *Freiburger Zeitschrift für Philosophie und Theologie* 34 (1987), 379-398 at 380 and notes 6-8.

frustrated expectation. Sometimes, sadness may afflict us and we may be depressed *(deprimimur)* at the instigation of the Devil *(Inst.* 9.4). One form of sadness is useful, however, in that it causes us to take stock of our lives and to correct what is wrong *(Inst.* 9.10). This type of sadness illustrates the perspective of Ecclesiastes 7.5[4] "The heart of the wise is in the house of mourning *(tristitia)*; but the heart of fools is in the house of mirth." The other form of sadness leads not to repentance but to despair *(desperatio animae)* such as that of Cain after his fratricide or Judas after his betrayal *(Inst.* 9.9). "It causes one to behave like a madman or a drunk; it breaks and crushes him beneath a penal despair."[8] Or again, this form of sadness voids the spiritual life; "it is full of rancor, fruitless grieving, and penal despair."[9] Cassian's use of "penal" to describe the despair to which those depressed by sadness are prey illustrates the central theme of this paper.[10] From Cassian on, monastic reflection proposed a continuity linking uncorrected psychological conditions, in this case the vice of *tristitia*, to the impenitent's penal condition in the next life. Thus Augustine referred to the spiritual suffering of hell as "fruitless repentance" — the result of neglecting discipline in this world and therefore experiencing it in the next, where it can no longer be avoided, no matter how ardently one repents.[11] Thus, except for the sadness that consists of grief for sin, we must banish it from our hearts, as if *tristitia* were the same as lust, avarice, or anger. Like them, it leads to despair and thence to death *(Inst.* 9.12). A soul afflicted by sadness is of no more value than wormridden lumber, fit only for the fire *(Inst.* 9.1). No one could miss this allusion to Matt. 3.10 and 7.19 ("Every tree that does not bear good fruit is cut down and thrown into the fire") and its evocation of hell's flames.

---

[8] Jean Cassien, *Institutions cénobitiques.* 9.1.12-14; ed. Jean-Claude Guy. Sources chrétiennes 109 (Paris: Les Éditions du Cerf, 1965), 370: "[U]elut amentem facit et ebrium sensum frangitque et obruit desperatione poenali."

[9] *Inst.* 9.11.12-13; p. 378: "[P]lena rancore et maerore infructuoso ac desperatione poenali."

[10] Cassian's use of "poenalis" is much stronger, I think, than that suggested by the French *pénible* (as Guy), meaning "difficult" or "painful." There is a specific continuation in the next world of suffering imposed for a disorder bordering on insubordination. Hence the suffering is specifically punitive.

[11] *De ciuitate Dei, libri XXII*, 21, 9, lines 34-36; Corpus Christianorum, Series Latina 48 (Turnhout, Belgium: Brepols, 1955), 775: "[C]orpore sic dolente animus quoque sterili paenitentia crucietur."

Cassian defines *acedia* as the Greek equivalent of "taedium" or "anxiety of heart" *(anxietas cordis)*. *Acedia* borders on *tristitia* but applies more specifically to hermits and especially those who live in the desert, where it attacks them most fiercely in the heat of mid-day. Psychologically, *acedia* is spiritual paralysis. It deprives the stricken monk of his resolve, makes him feel he has mistaken his calling, and achieved no spiritual benefits from his ascetic training. Now his cell disgusts him and he yearns to leave it and socialize with the other monks or he retreats there into constant sleep (hence "sloth," for this inactivity, though, clearly, the English term does not cover enough of this complex disturbance). He becomes a distraction or, worse, a bad influence on his fellows *(Inst.* 10.2-3).

But monastic vocation is part of a battle against the devil, and *acedia* is desertion from service. "And so the warrior of Christ becomes a fugitive and a deserter from the campaign."[12] The terms are military: the monk is a warrior of Christ *(miles Christi)*, who fights *(decertare)* in a struggle *(agon)*. The mental disorder which undermines him disturbs the community's social order. It becomes insubordination, even treason, and the melancholy monks are to be shunned, even discharged as rebels, traitors *(contemptores, contumaces)*.[13] They should be deprived of companionship,[14] of communal meals.[15] The community's correction of the monk who has surrendered to *acedia*, and thus become a deserter, will threaten him with fear for his life now, and so elicit the possibility of punishment in the afterlife. This dire association will return him to salutary discipline *(Inst.* 10.12).

Tristitia and *acedia* bear other vices as well. From *tristitia* come *rancor, pusillanimitas, amaritudo, desperatio*. From *acedia* come *otiositas, somnolentia, inportunitas, inquietudo, peruagatio, instabilitas mentis et corporis, uerbositas, curiositas (Conf.* 5.16). Of these terms, *amaritudo* will have the most significant future in the literature to be examined here, though *desperatio* also plays a role. These terms from Cassian's analysis of vice recur in discussions of hell's spiritual torments.

---

[12] *Inst.* 10.3; p. 388-90: "[I]ta militiae suae fugitiuus ac desertor Christi miles effectus." Cf. Ibid., 10.21.5, lines 48-50; p. 420: "Quos etiam inordinatos ac rebelles notat [Paulus], ab his studiosos quosque segregari praecipiens."

[13] *Inst.* 10.7.8 – 10.12.1; pp. 398-406. Cf. ibid., 10.19.18-19; p. 414: "[C]ontra eius scilicet interdictum otiosus eum non sine reatu peccati contumaciaeque praesumens."

[14] *Inst.* 10.16; p. 410, line 19: "publica ... segregatione."

[15] *Inst.* 10.12 line 15; p. 406: "... eis interdicens substantiam."

The crucial aid in the struggle against these vices is humility. Cassian's prescribed path to humility was to have immense influence. Both the Rule of the Master and the Benedictine Rule adapt it. The starting point he offers is the fear of God, which in turn provokes the cleansing of vices and the cultivation of virtues (*Inst.* 4.39.1-3). To encourage humility further, Cassian provides some Guides to Thought, *"cogitationum principia"* (*Inst.* 4.37.10-11). These principles emphasize two interrelated themes: meek acceptance of hardship, which Cassian calls "vilitas," and self-humbling (*Inst.* 4.39.2). Arranged as a series of steps, they inspired the Ladder of Humility developed by Benedict of Nursia in his Rule and his anonymous source, the Rule of the Master. In particular, I wish to stress this one: "present yourself like an evil and useless worker," because the term "useless" recalls the fate of the servant in Matt 25.30: "Cast the useless servant into outer darkness, where there will be weeping and gnashing of teeth" (cf. Matt. 24.51) and it complements the infernal fate of the wormridden lumber cast into the fires of Matt. 3.10 and 7.19, referred to above. For those who succced, however, Cassian describes this advantage:

> "Once [humility] is truly attained, it will immediately guide you across its highest step to the charity which has no fear, through which all that you considered previously not without suffering fearfulness, you will begin to regard without any labor, as if naturally, not out of the contemplation of punishment or out of any fear, but out of the love of the good itself and delight in the virtues."[16]

Cassian is contrasting earlier to later conditions; what had been done from fear is now done from charity. Yet Cassian does not consider fear the exclusive motivation in the early stages of development; he says only that the religious then performs good works *not without* some deterrent threat. Nor did the religious conform exclusively out of love. In this bundle of mixed emotions, as humility increases, love drives out fear along the lines suggested by 1 John 4.18. It is important to see how the authors to be considered describe the negative goad. For Cassian, the terms are "pain of fear-

---

[16] *Inst.* 4.39.3, lines 27-33; p.180: "Quae cum fuerit in ueritate possessa, confestim te ad caritatem, quae timorem non habet, gradu excelsiore perducet, per quam uniuersa, quae prius non sine poena formidinis obseruabas, absque ullo labore uelut naturaliter incipies custodire non iam contemplatione supplicii uel timoris ullius, sed amore ipsius boni et delectatione uirtutum."

fulness," which evokes punishment but does not name it, and "punishment" and "fear," again, without naming the object, destination, or condition to be feared. The Rule of the Master and the Benedictine Rule use a similar construction, but name Gehenna as the source of the fear.

Cassian expresses this internal tension between fear and love, avoidance of vice, and the pursuit of virtue in another way, drawing on Luke 17.20-21:

> "Inside us, indeed, there can be nothing other than ... friendship with either the vices or the virtues, through which we prepare either the kingdom of Christ or of the devil.... Consequently, if the kingdom of God is inside us, and the kingdom of God consists of justice and peace and joy, whoever abides in these qualities is doubtless in the kingdom of God, whereas those who occupy themselves in injustice and discord and sadness [*tristitia*], are established in the kingdom of the devil and in hell and in death [*in regno diaboli et in inferno ac morte*] (*Conf.* 1.13.2-3)."

Failure to eradicate these vices, then, makes one friends with the devil and leads to hell.

2. *The Rule of the Master and of Benedict*

Though Cassian clearly sees hell as the destination for those who tolerate vice, Gehenna and fear of its fires appear much more prominently in the Benedictine tradition. In order to understand this point, however, it is necessary to consider the slightly earlier, anonymous Rule of the Master (RM), which became so close a model for the better known and far more influential Rule of St. Benedict (RB).[17] In his Prologue, the Master clearly sets forth two alternatives. If one obeys

---

[17] It would go beyond the scope of this paper to pursue the other monastic rules, for men and women, that circulated in the West between Cassian, Benedict of Nursia, and Benedict of Aniane. Timothy Fry offers a good overview in *The Rule of St. Benedict in Latin and English with Notes* (Collegeville, Minn.: The Liturgical Press, 1981), 42-64. Useful surveys appear also in Rosamond McKitterick, *The Frankish Kingdoms under the Carolingians* (London and New York: Longman, 1983), 109-124; C. H. Lawrence, *Medieval Monasticism*, 2nd ed. (London and New York: Longman, 1989 [1984]), 1-85. See also the magisterial Friedrich Prinz, *Frühes Mönchtum im Frankenreich* (München: R. Oldenbourg: 1965). For the relationship of the Rule of the Master to the Benedictine Rule, see Fry's synthesis, 69-90 and in particular, *La Règle de Saint Benoît*, ed. A. de Vogüé et Jean Neufville, 7 vols. Sources Chrétiennes 181-186 [vol. 7 published independently](Paris: Les Éditions du Cerf, 1971-72) at Vol.1, pp. 245-314.

his Rule, one attains "eternal glory with the saints."[18] Conversely, should one not fulfill the precepts he offers, one finishes "in the eternal fire of Gehenna with the devil."[19] In his Prologue, too, Benedict emphasizes hell as he recommends submission to monastic discipline for all who "flee the pains of Gehenna and wish to attain eternal life."[20] Gehenna is the most unequivocal term for hell.[21] Both the Master and Benedict surpass Cassian in explicit references to Gehenna.

Following the lead of Cassian, the RM lists principles of good living, a Holy Craft (*ars sancta*), among which we find number 51, which advises: "Cultivate a horror of Gehenna" (*Gehennam expavescere*, 3, 51). Benedict, too, provides Tools of Good Works (*instrumenta bonorum operum*), which include the same principle (RB 4, 45). The RM's Chapter 10, 7 describes the famous Ladder of Humility. On that ladder ascent occurs by self-humbling (*humilitate*), and descent occurs by self-exaltation (*exaltatione*), and Benedict adopts the same ladder (RB 7). It is important to note in passing the scriptural basis for this opposition, the biblical flair for humbling the haughty. Isaiah announces the turning of the tables: "Sublimes humiliabuntur" (10.33) and Luke provides a cyclical paradox: "Every one who exalts himself will be humbled, and he who humbles himself will be exalted" (14.11 and 18.14).[22] These biblical passages draw their rhetorical force from antithesis; they state no quantitative formula claiming, for example, that one is humbled to the extent that one had overreached. In the early Middle Ages, writers ventured to calibrate these differences.[23]

The Rule of the Master and the Rule of St. Benedict, therefore, order the monk's life around humility. External discipline, particularly obedience to the abbot, for which "fear of Gehenna" is a prominent reason (RM 7, 3 cf. RB 5, 3), furthers the monk's internal, spiritual ascent.

---

[18] *La Règle du Maître*, Prologue, 20, ed. Adalbert de Vogüé. Sources Chretiennes 105 (Paris: Editions du Cerf, 1964): "ad aeternam cum sanctis gloriam."

[19] RM, Prologue, 21: "in aeternum ignem gehennae cum diabolo."

[20] RB, Prologue, 42: "[F]ugientes gehennae poenas, ad vitam volumus pervenire perpetuam."

[21] For an effort to distinguish the various synonyms for hell, see my *Formation of Hell*, chapters 8 & 9, *passim*, and esp. pp. 228 and 282.

[22] Other examples: Ps. 87.16; Job 22.29; Matt. 23.12; James 4.10; 1 Peter 5.6.

[23] Peter Brown correctly attributes calibration to Gregory the Great. "The End of the Ancient Otherworld, Lecture I. Gloriosus Obitus," 37. For two examples, see below, note 40 and note 43.

According to the RM, "the disciple scales the first step of humility on the ladder to heaven if, always placing the fear of God before his eyes so that he may ever flee complacency and always be mindful of all that God has commanded, he always turns over in his mind how Gehenna burns those who despise the Lord by their sins and that which eternal life has prepared for those who fear God."[24] Benedict's variations are minor (RB 7, 11). Then, if he also renounces his own will and perverse thoughts, he will be a "useful brother" (*utilis frater* RM 10, 19; RB 7, 18). The association of these ideas combines another echo of Matt. 25.30 and the "outer darkness" for the useless brother with another unambiguous reference to Gehenna as a deterrent.

On the twelfth step, the Master and Benedict urge that even here, at the pinnacle, the monk should "consider himself guilty of his sins at all times and picture himself already present at the terrible judgment" that is to come (RM 10, 84; RB 7, 64). The twelfth step does not threaten damnation, but the immanence of judgment opposes any self-satisfaction in the monk's humility.

In concluding the discussion of humility, the RM and the RB sum up the spiritual progress accomplished via the twelve steps with a statement that resembles Cassian's, but which is more specific about the nature of the fear. First, the RM.

> "Therefore, when the disciple has ascended all these steps of humility, he will be well advanced up the ladder of this life in the fear of God, and will soon attain that perfect love of the Lord which expells the fear through which all that he had previously obeyed not without dread he will begin to accomplish without any effort, as if naturally, out of long training, no longer through the fear of Gehenna, but through the love of that good training itself and delight in the virtues."[25]

Benedict varies the language slightly.

---

[24] RM 10-11: "Primum itaque humilitatis gradum in scala caeli ascendit discipulus, si timorem Dei sibi ante oculos semper ponens, obliuionem omni hora fugiat et semper sit memor omnia, que praecepit Deus, ut quomodo et gehenna contemnentes Dominum de peccatis incendat, et uita aeterna quid timentibus Deum praeparet, animo suo semper reuoluat."

[25] RM 10, 87-90: "Ergo his omnibus humilitatis gradibus a discipulo perascensis, uitae huius in timore Dei bene persubitur scala et mox ad caritatem illam Domini peruenientes, quae perfecta foris mittit timorem, per quam uniuersa, quae prius non sine formidine obseruabas, absque ullo labore uelut naturaliter ex consuetudine incipiet custodire, non iam timore gehennae, sed amore ipsius consuetudinis bonae et delectatione uirtutum."

"Therefore, when the monk has ascended all these steps of humility, he will soon attain that perfect love of God which expels the fear through which all he had previously obeyed not without dread he will begin to accomplish without any effort, as if naturally, out of long training, no longer from the fear of Gehenna, but from the love of Christ, and from that good training itself and from delight in the virtues."[26]

The core of this analysis is Cassian's, but the Master and Benedict explicitly name Gehenna as the source of the fear without which one might not turn to Christ. As in Cassian, the formulation "non sine formidine" implies that an important part (but not all) of the benefit achieved comes from the removal of a negative motivation. Whereas there is no fear in perfect love, not everything was done from dread even prior to attaining that state.

In the Ladder of Humility put forward by the Rule of the Master and adopted by Benedict, then, hell appears positively, as a stimulus *nearly* indispensable to undertaking monastic discipline, because the fear of God, along with fear of Gehenna, is the first rung on the ladder of humility. Ninth-century commentators on the Benedictine Rule, such as Smaragdus of St. Mihiel and Hildemar of Corbie, will further expand this positive function of hell.

Fear of God and of Gehenna is only the first step. Reaching pure love is a long process. The vices are certainly obstacles, particularly *acedia* and *tristitia*. Whereas the Master and Benedict are virtually interchangeable on the substitution of *caritas* for fear, Benedict is far more attuned than the Master to the dangers of *tristitia*. His sensitivity emerges in the chapters concerning excommunication. Here, *tristitia* comes to the fore.

In the RM, an insubordinate disciple threatens the house's order. He is a demonic tool. The Master prescribes a formal denunciation followed by an intimidating tirade. The offender is a rebel, another Judas. The abbot portrays the culprit before the awful divine judgment and recoiling from the ridicule the blessed will heap upon him as he departs with the goats to damnation (RM 13, 15). Then the

---

[26] RB 7, 67-69: "Ergo, his omnibus humilitatis gradibus ascensis, monachus mox ad caritatem Dei perveniet illam quae perfecta foris mittit timorem; per quam universa quae prius non sine formidine observabat, absque ullo labore velut naturaliter ex consuetudine incipiet custodire, non iam timore gehennae, sed amore Christi et consuetudine ipsa bona et delectatione virtutum." Based on the Latin in Fry's bilingual edition, the translations are nonetheless my own.

wayward monk will be exiled from the common table and sentenced to menial work in isolation, where no brother will offer any comfort. Guilt will be his only consolation.[27] When an excommunicated monk seeks to return, the repentant brother is to prostrate himself and, from the floor, deliver a long prescribed speech in which, among other things, he beseeches the abbot to behave like the shepherd who left ninety-nine sheep to find one wanderer (after Matt. 18. 12-13, cf. Luke 15. 4), and to forgive him. The abbot then reproaches the monk for his fault. Finally the brothers pray for him. The monk then prays to God directly and, finding evidence of divine mercy in Scripture, begs forgiveness. At last, by the ceremony of washing the hands of his brothers, he is reintegrated into the community (RM 14).

By and large, in his discussion of excommunication (RB 23-27), Benedict follows the order of topics of the RM, but condenses the treatment considerably. What differs most is the tone. It is not the suppliant excommunicant who begs the abbot to show mercy, but Benedict as author of the Rule who stipulates that he must. The abbot, in particular, is to counsel the backslider wisely and energetically, lest he lose one of his sheep. Senior monks are to comfort the wavering brother in private and urge him to make satisfaction by returning to humility and "to console him lest he be caught up in even deeper sadness" (*tristitia*), soothingly paraphrasing 2 Cor 2.7 rather than some harsher texts (RB 27, 3).[28] The RM has no counterpart to this gentleness with regard to excommunicates.

Another contrast will help elucidate this difference in approach. In describing the abbot, both the Master and Benedict say that he occupies in the monastery the place of Christ and that his name, "abba" means "father" (RM 2, 2-3; RB 2, 2-3). Unlike the Master, however, Benedict continues by encouraging monks to take up the commitment to the religious life, so that they may be spared divine justice, a force Benedict compares to two dangers: an angry father who would disinherit his sons and a dread lord who would condemn his evil servants to eternal punishment (RB Prol., lines 6-7). This series of authority figures, Christ, abbot, and father, is the key to *tristitia*'s profound ramifications in RB 27. *Tristitia* appears to be a mis-

---

[27] RM 13, 49: "Sit ubique solus et ei sola culpa solacium."
[28] Marian Larmann, "*Contristare* and *Tristitia* in the RB: Indications of Community and Morale," *American Benedictine Review* 30 (1979), 159-174. The author is primarily concerned with the avoidance of *tristitia* at the "horizontal level," as a concern for harmony between the brothers. For the passage quoted here, see 167.

alignment of the monk with these authorities. This condition could be aggravated by undue harshness from the abbot, the one closest in physical proximity to the monk.[29] Because Benedict so respects the dangers of *tristitia*, he urges the abbot not to worsen a bad situation.[30] Benedict (and not the Master) makes avoidance of *tristitia* into something more than an individual battle against vice, but rather like Cassian's discussion of *acedia*'s dangers, he regards it as an institutional necessity, because *tristitia* threatens collective morale. Given the danger of *tristitia* to the psychological fabric of the monastery, it is not difficult to see why it would enter speculation about the other world.

3. *Isidore of Seville*

Beyond Cassian's influence on the Rule of the Master and on Benedict, Isidore of Seville (560-636) provided another perspective on the patristic tradition. Isidore forged a crucial link between patristic psychology and the spiritual torments of Gehenna. Though Cassian had explained that *acedia* and *tristitia* would *lead* to hell, Isidore declared them, or their subordinate disorders like bitterness (*amaritudo*), characteristic of the spiritual state of the damned in hell. In his *Sentences* he said: "The punishment of the damned in Gehenna is twofold: *tristitia* burns the mind, and fire burns the body."[31] Isidore applies "tristitia," a term from monastic psychology, to the punishments of hell. This procedure is not surprising, since Isidore believed the Greeks did it, too. In his *Etymologies*, he derives *tristitia* directly from the underworld. The river Styx, he

---

[29] Confirmation occurs in Benedict's Prologue, which describes those enrolled in the monastery as taking up arms to fight under Christ the king (another image of authority, RB Prol. 3), whom the monks do not wish to distress *(contristari)* by their evil actions (RB Prol. 5).

[30] RM gives *tristitia* little attention. (See Larmann, 168-69.) RM 5 is a list of vices. Neither *tristitia* nor *acedia* appears. They are replaced by *pigritia*, "laziness." The vices come from the Devil, and those who fail to uproot them will receive the "Gehenna of perpetual fire."

[31] San Isidoro, *Los tres libros de las "Sentencias."* Biblioteca de Autores Cristianos. Santos Padres Españoles 2 (Madrid: La Editorial Catolica, 1971) book 1, cap. 28, §1; p. 299: "Duplex damnatorum poena est in gehenna, quorum et mentem urit tristitia, et corpus flamma." Note that this quotation continues: [The action of the flame and of tristitia is] "iuxta vicissitudinem, ut qui mente tractaverunt quod perficerent corpore, simul et animo puniantur et corpore."

says, "gets its name from *stygeros*, that is from *tristitia*, in that it causes people to be sad or because it generates sadness."[32] There is thus
a direct link between the psychological state of sadness and the
nature of the underworld.

Back in his *Sentences*, Isidore provides a developed but concise summary of doctrine on penance. He recounts struggles within the mind
as it laments past sins, fears future punishment, and hopes for eternal
reward. He refers to an "inner shame" which "already punishes the
penitent by his own judgement in repenting."[33] Cassian had referred
to this phenomenon as the good form of *tristitia*; Isidore calls it "bitterness" (*amaritudo*). Because of the way it will be taken up in the ninth
century, I wish to stress the element of inner struggle that Isidore des-
ignates by this term. Here it is a good stimulus, like the fear of
Gehenna in the Benedictine Rule. Of *amaritudo* Isidore says: "Bitterness causes the soul to repent, to examine its deeds more carefully,
and to remember, in weeping, the gifts of God that it has spurned.
Indeed, there is nothing worse than to recognize one's guilt without
weeping."[34] To neglect this discipline, Isidore says, "to scorn repentance and to remain in guilt is to descend into hell after death."[35]
Sidestepping *amaritudo* becomes contempt and entails damnation.
What you avoid now, you endure later.

4. *Smaragdus and the brush with hell*

This function of *amaritudo* was important also to Smaragdus of St.
Mihiel, a comparatively little-known figure active in the circle of
Benedict of Aniane and at the courts of Charlemagne and Louis the
Pious. He was made abbot of Castellion in 800 and of Saint-Mihiel

---

[32] "Styx *apo tou stygeros*, id est a tristitia, dicta, eo quod tristes faciat vel quod tristiti-
am gignat." Isidorus Hispalensis, *Etymologiarum sive Originum Libri XX*, ed. W. M.
Lindsay, 2 vols. (Oxford: Clarendon, 1911) 14.9.6.

[33] *Sent.* 2.12.5; p. 328: "[Q]uando id, quod se admisisse recolit interius erubescit,
suoque iudicio paenitendo iam punit."

[34] *Sent.* 2.13.4; p. 329: "Amaritudo paenitentiae facit animum, et sua facta subtil-
ius discutere, et dona Dei, quae contempsit, flendo commemorare. Nihil autem peius
quam culpam agnoscere, nec deflere."

[35] *Sent.* 2.14.2; p. 333: "[C]ontemnere paenitentiam, et permanere in culpa,
descendere in infernum post mortem est." Similarly, ibid.: "Ergo peccare ad mortem
pertinet, desperare vero in infernum descendere," and ibid.: "Perpetrare flagitium
aliquod mors animae est...."

on the Meuse in 814; he lived until past 825.[36] In 817, in conjunction with the reforming synod of Aachen, he wrote what is considered to be the earliest surviving commentary on the Benedictine Rule.[37]

Smaragdus blended his understanding of *amaritudo* into "affliction" (*afflictio*), a discipline crucial to the monk's self-humbling. But before examining that shift, it would be opportune to see how he valued Benedict's concern for the *tristitia* of the excommunicated monk. With exaggerated punishment the resultant *tristitia* can be "greater and deeper than ... before the offense."[38] *Tristitia* can devour and swallow the wayward religious.[39] These verbs of consumption recall the function of the hellmouth. Thus Smaragdus underlines Benedict's concern that excessive punishment increase the offender's *tristitia* and so render him useless to the community.

Beyond the risk of paralysis from *tristitia*, there is the contemplative's obligation to scrutinize his behavior and combat his evil thoughts. In this connection, Smaragdus is best understood by combining his explanations of Benedict's 72 Tools of Good Works, which he calls the Precepts of the Spiritual Craft, with the Rungs of the

---

[36] On Smaragdus, see: F. Rädle, "Smaragdus v. St-Mihiel," *Lexikon des Mittelalters*, 7 (1995), 2011-2012; Réginald Grégoire, "Smaragde," *Dictionnaire de Spiritualité* 14 (1990), 959-61; J. Leclercq, "Smaragdo," *Dizionario degli Istituti di Perfezione* 8 (1988), 1583-84; Pio Paschini, "Smaragdo," *Enciclopedia Cattolica*, 11 (1953), 819-20; David Barry, "Smaragdus of St. Mihiel and his Commentary on the Rule of St. Benedict," *Tjurunga* 36 (1989), 3-9; Joyce Hill, "Aelfric and Smaragdus," *Anglo Saxon England* 21 (1992), 203-237; Alain Dubreucq, "Smaragde de Saint-Mihiel et son temps: Enseignement et bibliothèques à l'époque carolingienne," *Mélanges de la bibliothèque de la Sorbonne* 7 (1986), 7-36; Jean Leclercq, "Smaragdus," translated by John J. Mellerski, in *Introduction to the Medieval Mystics of Europe*, ed. Paul Szarmach (Albany: SUNY Press, 1984), 37-51; Fidel Rädle, *Studien zu Smaragd von Saint-Mihiel*, Medium Aevum: Philologische Studien 29 (Munich, 1974); W. Witters, "Smaragde au moyen âge: la diffusion de ses écrits d'après la tradition manuscrite," *Etudes ligériennes d'histoire et d'archéologie médiévales*, ed. R. Louis (Auxerre, 1975); Henri Robas, "Étude sur Smaragde, abbé de Saint-Mihiel," *Mettensia* 6 (1909-12); André Wilmart, "Smaragde et le psautier," *Revue Biblique* 31 (1922), 350-59.

[37] The commentary attributed to Paul the Deacon is actually by Hildemar of Corbie, whom I discuss below. It dates from 845-50. See Wolfgang Hafner, *Der Basiliuskommentar zur Regula S. Benedicti. Ein Beitrag zur Autorenfrage karolingischer Regelkommentare*. Beiträge zur Geschichte des alten Mönchtums und des Benediktinerordens 23 (Münster: Aschendorff, 1959), 97.

[38] Smaragdus, *Expositio in Regulam S. Benedicti* cap. 4, item 50; edd. Alfredus Spannagel & Pius Engelbert. Corpus Consuetudinum Monasticarum 8 (Siegburg: F. Schmitt: 1974), 27,3; p. 227, lines 20-21: "maiorem et profundiorem quam antea habuit quando deliquit."

[39] Ibid., line 21: "*Absorbeatur* dicit, id est devoretur vel deglutiatur."

Ladder of Humility. Thus, Precept number 50, and Rung 5 on the Ladder of Humility both concern confessing evil thoughts. Following Isidore, Smaragdus calls the mental anguish that arises from opposing evil thoughts *amaritudo*. Quoting Gregory, he says it cleanses the mind of the base thoughts it has conceived. Moreover, using a quantitative formula, the sooner the penitent opposes evil thoughts, the sooner grace intervenes and the conflict is resolved:

> "For the weaker the ties between evil thoughts and their effects in action, the more quickly they are dissolved. And [God] shows how easily he grants grace when this happens. Thus repentance does not advance to anguish (*cruciatus*), but [instead] a conceptual affliction cleanses the mind as quickly as mental iniquity pollutes it."[40]

Like Isidore, Smaragdus insists that those who surrender to evil thoughts go to hell, where they suffer anguish (*cruciatus*) forever. According to this line of reasoning, barring the danger of complacency, the monk should voluntarily accept the temporary anguish of bitterness in the cloister in order to escape the unending anguish of damnation in hell.

Smaragdus mentions *cruciatus* again as he considers Benedict's precept 45 that the monk should always fear Gehenna. Indeed, *cruciatus* is his generic term for the sufferings of hell. He says: "[In hell] all the damned are thrown to suffer anguish (*cruciandi*).... What enlightens is not felt there, but only what causes anguish (*cruciat*). All that is there brings neither light nor joy, but is full of darkness, grief, and anguish (*cruciatibus plena*).[41] Anguish, then, is the general condition of hell. Those who avoid the bitterness (*amaritudo*) of monastic discipline, by failing to confront their faults, endure its pain as *cruciatus* in hell, later, forever.

---

[40] Smaragdus, 4, 50; p. 131, lines 3-10, quoting Gregorius Magnus, *Regula Pastoralis* 3.29; *Patrologiae cursus completus, Series latina*, ed. J.-P. Migne (Paris, 1844-64), 77, 109C: "Misericors enim deus eo citius peccata cordis abluit, quo haec exire ad opera non permittit; et cogitata nequitia tanto citius solvitur, quanto ad effectum operis districtius non ligatur; et quam super haec sit facilis venia ostendit: Qui dum se adhuc promittit petere, hoc quod se petere promittebat obtinuit, quatenus quia usque ad opus non venerat culpa, usque ad cruciatum non perveniret poenitentia, sed cogitata adflictio mentem tergeret quam tantummodo cogitata iniquitas inquinarat."

[41] Smaragdus, 4, 45; p. 126, lines 17-18 and 127, lines 6-9: "Illuc enim omnes cruciandi proiciuntur dampnati.... Ibi enim non sentitur quod inluminat, sentitur tamen quod cruciat, et omnia quae ibi sunt sita non luce vel gaudio referta sed tenebris, doloribus et cruciatibus sunt plena."

To recapitulate briefly, then, *cruciatus* becomes the evil end of a series of associated psychological states. *Acedia* withdraws the monk from all ascetic activities, including, for example, the good form of *tristitia*. This salutary *tristitia* comes from disgust with one's evil thoughts and healthfully brings confrontation with one's guilt. *Amaritudo* comes near to being a synonym for this introspective confrontation with one's own base desires, a self-analysis (aided by confession) that purges the consequences of their arising. Failure to undergo this discipline in life brings it on after death. For Isidore of Seville, it is *tristitia* that overcomes the souls who postponed it too long. For Smaragdus, the *amaritudo* avoided in life becomes *cruciatus* in death. The overlap between these terms is functional: they have to do with confronting guilt. They are not synonymous, but they are related through their connection to the willingness required of religious persons to address their faults.

Confessing one's base thoughts voids them of guilt, says Smaragdus, but the confession itself requires humility. Cassian taught that humility requires acceptance of hardship and self-humbling. Smaragdus develops this theme farther: humility entails cultivating a sense of being despicable, unworthy, and evil, feeling oneself deserving only hell. As much as the monk may strive for humility, he can take no satisfaction from it, because he does not know how his work will be received by Christ. Instead, as Cassian and the RM and RB recommend on the Sixth Step of the Ladder of Humility, he should "consider himself a bad and unworthy worker."[42] Thus in the pursuit of humility, one must consider oneself not only liable to damnation, but virtually damned.

Smaragdus prepares his reader for this approach in his introduction to Chapter 7, the presentation of the Ladder of Humility. "The more precious one is to oneself, the baser he is to God; the baser he is to himself on account of God, the more precious he is to God."[43] The

---

[42] Smaragdus, 7, 49; p. 184, line 28 – p. 185, line 3: " Ideo monachus operarium iudicat se malum, quia quomodo opus eius recipiatur nescit a domino. Operamur enim nos exterius, sed quomodo opus a domino recipiatur nescimus interius. Ideo indignum se iudicat, quia sicut 'non sunt condignae passiones huius saeculi ad futuram gloriam quae revelabitur in nobis,' ita non sunt digna quamvis sint bona opera nostra ad conquirendam gloriam vel praemia sempiterna." Cf. Smaragdus, 7, 65; p. 191, lines 13-14: "Qui etiam si quid boni tua gratia largiente fecero, quo fine hoc faciam quave a te districtione pensetur, ignoro."

[43] Smaragdus, 7, 4; p. 163, lines 22-24: "Tanto ergo fit quisque vilior deo, quanto pretiosior sibi; tanto pretiosior deo, quanto propter [*ed.*: per] eum vilior sibi ...." Cf.

point of this apparent self-deprecation emerges when Smaragdus comes to the worm of Psalm 21[22].7 ("But I am a worm, and no man"). As the last shall be first, so the vile worm feeds on the wood and becomes pure. "The worm seems to be more humble and more vile than all the beasts. But the worm feeds on a Wood that proves to be purer the frailer it is. To this the monk may be compared, for the more he is despised and considered weak and vile, the holier and purer he is before God."[44] By means of this allegory, Smaragdus shows that the descent of humility into apparent baseness and abjection reverses itself and ascends. It is at the moment of recognizing one's fitness for damnation that one attains humility and heaven opens up. As Smaragdus put it: "let us humble ourselves for glory"[45] This is the strategy of Christian reversal.[46]

At this point, one senses that the contemplative has reached bottom, because Smaragdus begins to shift from an emphasis on one's own worthlessness to urge humility as a source of strength.[47] "Humility, that glorious culmination, attains Jerusalem."[48] Or again: "whereas pride

---

Gregorius Magnus, *Moralia in Job* 18.38, line 2, ed. M. Adriaen, Corpus Christianiorum, Series Latina 143A (Turnhout, Belgium: Brepols, 1979-81), p. 924: "[T]anto unaquaeque anima fit pretiosior ante oculos Dei, quanto prae amore ueritatis despector fuerit ante oculos suos." Or again, line 9: "Tanto ergo fit quisque uilior Deo quanto pretiosior sibi; tanto pretiosior Deo quanto propter eum uilior sibi: quia humilia respicit et alta a longe agnoscit."

[44] Smaragdus, 7, 52; p. 186, lines 8-12: "Vermis enim humilior cunctis animantibus esse videtur et vilior. Nutritus enim vermis ex ligno quanto fragilior, tanto esse probatur et purior. Cui comparatur monachus, qui quanto in hoc saeculo fuerit dispectior, infirmus et vilior, tanto apud deum sanctior invenitur et mundior." Smaragdus's taste for these biblical paradoxes is apparent, as he paraphrases 1 Cor 1.25; 1 Cor. 1.27; and 1 Cor 3.19 at Smaragdus 7, 50; p. 185, lines 6-7: "Apud saeculum enim istum se iustus cognoscit stultum, ut inveniatur sapiens apud deum."

[45] Smaragdus 7, 65; p. 191, line 8: "[H]umiliemur ad gloriam." In his commentary on Luke 18.14, Bede uses this same phrase. In contrast to those who promote themselves to ruin, "let us," he says, "humble ourselves to glory." *In Lucae Euangelium Expositio* 5,18 line 1184; ed. D. Hurst. Corpus Christianorum, Series Latina, 120 (Turnout, Belgium: Brepols, 1960), 325.

[46] The term is my own, but I draw here on a seminal discussion by Gerard E. Caspary, *Politics and Exegesis: Origen and the Two Swords* (Berkeley: University of California Press, 1979) esp. Chapter 3, "Hermeneutical Interlude," pp. 102-124. No summary can do justice to his intricate exposition, but in brief, Caspary outlines a "Christian grammar" structured by polarities distributed along four tensions: ethical, hierarchical, lateral (central vs. peripheral), and temporal.

[47] See Francis F. Seeburger, "Humility, Maturity, and the Fear of God: Reflections on RB 7," *American Benedictine Review* 46, 2 (1995), 149-168, esp. at 160, where he compares this Benedictine view of humility to the way an alcoholic reverses direction after "bottoming out."

[48] Smaragdus 7, 54; p. 187, line 5: "Humilitas enim ista Hierusalem tangit glo-

thrusts one down to Tartarus, humility raises one to Heaven."[49] The nadir of guilt, self-humbling, and worthlessness becomes the *fastigium*, the pinnacle of heaven. The nadir and the zenith interact and nearly correspond: "Humiliemur ad gloriam!"

As I have reflected on Smaragdus' exposition, I have been drawn to mathematical figures. He puts the approach to hell, at least in contemplation and in the sense of self-accusatory guilt, so close to the approach to heaven, that I have imagined him changing the Ladder of Humility into a circle or a wheel, on whose circumference hell and heaven occupy adjacent points. More accurate, perhaps, is the image of a parabola, which descends downward, in negative territory, through self-abasement to a certain point, the moment of believing oneself fit only for hell, when, crossing the axis, all that had been negative becomes positive, and what had been a descent becomes an ascent. The points at either end of the curve, however, remain apart and will never meet. This image would trace the account of the passage from fear to love expounded by Cassian and reiterated by the Master and Benedict. It would move, however, from Christian grammar to Christian mathematics.

The fear of hell in the *Commentary* of Smaragdus comes from an experience known to conscientious monks. It is the fear of eternal consequences should monks fail to lighten the burden of vices, to relieve the guilt that accumulates over unconfessed sins. Smaragdus expressed this link between hell and guilt when he used *afflictio* to connect Isidore's *tristitia* (a term that Cassian also used in this sense) with anguish (*cruciatus*), its consequence in the next world.

5. *Hildemar of Corbie: timor servilis, timor castus*

Whereas Smaragdus emphasizes the monk's liability to hell as a part of his worthlessness and almost seems to consider the lip of the hellmouth as a springboard to heaven, Hildemar of Corbie emphasizes the polar opposition between hell and heaven through the repulsive and attractive forces of two different kinds of fear. Hildemar was a

riosa fastigia." Quoting Cassiodorus, *Expositio Psalmorum in Ps.* 118, 71; ed. M. Adriaen, Corpus Christianorum, Series Latina 98 (Turnhout, Belgium: Brepols, 1958), 1087, lines 1201-1202.
[49] Smaragdus 7, 54; p. 187, line 6: "Nam sicut superbia mergit ad tartarum, ita ista tollit ad caelum."

monk of Corbie from 821 or 826 until 841, when he went to Italy to reform a house in Brescia, then Civate. He died around 850 and wrote his *Commentary on the Benedictine Rule* probably in the last five years of his life.[50] As Hildemar sums up the Ladder of Humility, he elaborates on the theme taken from 1 John 4.18 and developed ever since Cassian, that, at the pinnacle of this development, charity displaces fear. His discussion distinguishes between *timor servilis*, base fear, dread of negative consequences such as Gehenna, and *timor castus*, pure fear, respect for divine judgment, awe. This distinction was known to Augustine. The Bishop of Hippo considered *timor castus* to be as different from *timor servilis* as fear of punishment is from love of justice.[51] Yet Hildemar brings the two much closer together and makes them interact.

It might at first seem that Hildemar proposes a steady progression from *timor servilis* on the first rung to *timor castus* on the twelfth. For example, he sighs as he notes that the apostles and martyrs were accustomed to have *timor castus* directly, but monks in general attain charity only through a combination of both fears. "An interval of servile fear" is required.[52] Paraphrasing the RB, Hildemar continues: "Before, the monk was not able to maintain perfect, chaste love without effort or the fear of Gehenna, but afterwards, it comes almost naturally...."[53] It seems Hildemar can apply "castus" interchangeably to both fear and love (*amor*).

---

[50] For Hildemar see. Louis Galllard, "Hildemar," *Dictionnaire de Spiritualité* vol. 7, part 1 (1969), 521-22; G. Bernt, "Hildemar v. Corbie," *Lexikon des Mittelalters* 5 (1990), 15-16; Klaus Zelzer, "Überlegungen zu einer Gesamtedition des früh-nachkarolingischen Kommentars zur Regula S. Benedicti aus der Tradition des Hildemar von Corbie," *Revue Bénédictine* 91, 3-4 (1981), 373-82; idem, "Von Benedikt zu Hildemar: Die Regula Benedicti auf dem Weg zur Alleingeltung im Blickfeld der Textgeschichte," *Regulae Benedicti Studia* 16 (1987), 1-22; idem, "Von Benedikt zu Hildemar: Zu Textgestalt und Textgeschichte der Regula Benedicti auf ihrem Weg zur Alleingeltung," *Frühmittelalterliche Studien* 23 (1989), 112-130; Mayke de Jong, "Growing up in a Carolingian Monastery: Magister Hildemar and his Oblates," *Journal of Medieval History* 9 (1983), 99-128.

[51] *In Iohannis Euangelium Tractatus* 43,7 ed. R. Willems, Corpus Christianorum, Series Latina, 36 (Turnhout, Belgium: Brepols, 1954), 375: "Est timor seruilis, et est timor castus; est timor ne patiaris poenam, est alius timor ne amittas iustitiam." I wish to thank Fred Paxton for this reference and for his advice on an earlier version of this paper.

[52] Hildemar, *Expositio Regulae ab Hildemaro Tradita*, ed. Rupertus Mittermüller (Ratisbon, New York, Cincinnati: Frederick Pustet, 1880), 269: "Utinam, o Deus, sicut illi sancti jugiter hunc castum meruerunt habere timorem, nos per intervallum timorem servilem mereamur habere!"

[53] Hildemar, 269: "[A]nte perfectum amorem castum, non poterat ille monachus sine timore gehennae vel laboris custodire, postea quasi naturaliter...."

Hildemar's view of the twelfth rung, however, is complicated. He recapitulates the whole Ladder of Humility with two rhetorical questions that juxtapose the first step with the twelfth. Why did Benedict say that the first stage of humility is the fear of God? And why in describing the twelfth rung, the consummation of perfect *caritas*, did Benedict admonish: "One must consider oneself guilty (*reum*) of one's sins *at all times*" (*reum se* omni hora *aestimet de peccatis suis*)? Hildemar answers by adding a complication not present in Benedict. Though surely Benedict hoped to avoid complacency on the twelfth rung, Hildemar, elaborates: "Benedict knew that a man can fall even from the height of perfection, if, before becoming completely confirmed (*solidatus*) in divine charity, that is, in *timor castus*, he should take pride in himself."[54] Here Hildemar emphasizes the evocation of the first step implicit in the term "guilty" (*reum*) and the allusion to the Last Judgment by stating: "[Benedict] therefore mentions fear in this very twelfth step, because *timor servilis* is necessary to protect virtue precisely when the person applying [that virtue], is passing into *timor castus*."[55]

Although on the twelfth rung one may eventually experience only *timor castus* and reach perfect charity, Hildemar clearly insists that the two fears are mixed, at least temporarily, even there, until the transition is completed.

> "Before [attaining perfect charity] the monk may [occasionally] possess *timor castus*, but not perfectly, because he is accustomed to be overcome by *timor servilis*. And from this, one may know that sometimes *timor servilis* and sometimes *timor castus* leads to the good, because sometimes this happens by the love of God and sometimes by the fear of Gehenna, that is, through tears and all the rest."[56]

Tears, contrition, repentance are left behind no more than *timor servilis*. One senses in Hildemar how many reverses impede the monk striving for humility.

Only after Hildemar has interpreted Benedict as fortifying *timor*

---

[54] Hildemar, 266: "[P]osse cadere hominem etiam de summa perfectione, si, antequam solidatus fuerit in caritate divina, i.e. in casto timore, superbierit."

[55] Hildemar, 266: "[I]deo etiam in isto gradu duodecimo mentionem timoris fecit, quia timor servilis adeo est necessarius, ut tegat virtutem, quam operatur quis, donec transeat in castum timorem."

[56] Hildemar, 268-269: "[A]nte monachus habeat castum timorem, sed tamen non perfecte, quia superabatur a timore servili; nam in hoc potest cognoscere, quod aliquando timore servili aliquando timore casto, quia aliquando amore dei, aliquando timore gehennae agit bonum, i. e. lacrimas et reliq[ua]."

castus with *timor servilis* does he discuss Benedict's statement paraphrasing Cassian to the effect that one transcends the twelfth step
"not so much from the fear of Gehenna as through the love of
Christ." Benedict rightly mentions Gehenna, Hildemar explains, following Cassian, "because after attaining pure love, one functions not
by the fear of Gehenna, but by the love of Christ ... and love of the
virtues."[57] Thus, for Hildemar, Gehenna and the fear of hell are so
crucial to the monk's progress that he includes interaction between
timor servilis and *timor castus* even on the twelfth rung, at the last instant
before *timor castus* fades into perfect charity. This blend of the mean-
est and the noblest forms of fear constitutes a structural parallel to the
interaction that Smaragdus had sensed between the consciousness of
guilt and liability to hell at the extreme of humility (at once a nadir
and a zenith) and, at the other extreme, attainment of the culmination, the *fastigium*, of the Heavenly Jerusalem.

The two fears encompass a ladder that guides the religious, but
even its lowest rung is below the reach of an excommunicate. When
the Rule enjoins moderation in dealing with an excommunicated
monk, "lest he be absorbed in a greater *tristitia*," following Cassian,
Hildemar sees the fate of Judas as a negative example. "For when he
ought to have repented for the evil he committed, Judas lost his bear-
ings *(oblitus est sui)* and was sucked in. He hanged himself in a noose
through excessive sadness."[58] This obsession with sadness, or despair,
should not befall wayward monks lest, like Judas, they perish eternally.[59] For Hildemar, it was *tristitia* as despair that blocked the path of
Judas to repentance. In such a situation, even *timor servilis* is a step up.
When *tristitia* prevents access to even the most basic fear of God,
damnation results.

---

[57] Hildemar, 269: "[P]ost perfectum castum amorem non per timorem gehennae,
sed amore [amore: Mittermüller prints "timore"] Christi et consuetudine ipsa bona
et dilectione virtutum."

[58] Hildemar, 357: "*ne abundantiori tristitia absorbeatur:* sicuti Judas absorptus est; ille
enim cum debuerat agere poenitentiam de malo, quod fecit, oblitus est sui et absorptus est, prae nimia tristitia laqueo se suspendit."

[59] Hildemar, 357: "Hanc vero absorptionem, i.e. desperationem voluit cavere S.
Benedictus,... ne frater prae nimia tristitia desperet et sibi aliquid mali, sicut Judas
fecit, inferat et in aeternum pereat...."

Conclusion

Monastic thinkers from John Cassian to Hildemar of Corbie addressed a broad range of psychological phenomena. From *accidia* to *tristitia* to *amaritudo* to *afflictio*, however, there is no straight line of development. What unites these moods is their connection to spiritual danger and their termination in hell. For *acedia*, the relationship is direct: remain slothful, go to hell. For *tristitia*, the situation varies. *Tristitia* as woe, as paralysis, resembles *acedia*. *Tristitia* as despair prevents atonement and damns. *Tristitia* as concern over one's sins, like contrition or repentance, is a positive force, like revulsion from evil. But Isidore linked these two meanings: if one does not sorrow over one's sins, that other *tristitia*, anguish, encumbers the damned spirit forever. Cassian derived *amaritudo* from *tristitia*, but for Smaragdus it became a catalyst in his penitential psychology, where it elicits the *afflictio* that cleanses the penitent soul. *Amaritudo* and *afflictio* are emotional states to be cultivated by the virtuous, those willing to accept a difficult spiritual discipline. Those who evade this treatment plunge into hell and endure these pains forever. Hildemar's analysis of the progression from *timor servilis* to *timor castus* intersects this traditon of cultivated sorrow as the introspective religious, ascending the ladder of humility, imagine themselves, with Smaragdus, more and more liable to damnation, echoing the Master and Benedict: "reum se omni hora ... aestimet."

Smaragdus confirms the tradition, traceable back through the Master and Benedict to Cassian, that knowledge of one's own worthlessness is necessary to humility. Ascetics cultivating humility must regard themselves as worms, useless workers, unworthy before God. Worthlessness includes liability (*reatus*) to hell. It is through this frank encounter with damnation that heaven looms nearer. This confrontation with hell is one variety of what I choose to call "inner death." One is tempted to compare this approach to hell in monastic introspection to the *Descensus* in which Christ, too, traversed the underworld as if in a necessary step towards heaven. With the ordeal of his brush with hell safely passed, the ascetic's, *timor servilis* becomes *timor castus*. The pit of guilt, an inner death, becomes the path to rebirth and eventually to heaven. Though that final step is not attainable by human means alone, it is the final change by which *caritas* displaces *timor castus*. Moreover, because the renunciation required to develop humility is both difficult and necessary, these writers contended that damnation was a just consequence for those who avoided the encounter. In this way the writers examined here made *acedia*, the unwillingness to undergo this trial, portend and then, in *tristitia, amaritudo, afflictio,* and *cruciatus,* become the psychological fate of the damned.

SAPIENTIA JUDAEORUM:
THE ROLE OF JEWISH PHILOSOPHERS IN SOME SCHOLASTIC THINKERS[1]

Bernard McGinn*

In 1517 the Renaissance scholar Luigi Ricchieri distinguished three forms of Judaism in his *Lectionum antiquarum*: Talmudic Judaism, which he described as heretical; Philosophical Judaism, which he discounted as late in origin; and finally Kabbalistic Judaism, the oldest and truest form, originally revealed to Moses.[2] This Renaissance tripartite view of Judaism had deep roots in the Christian Middle Ages.[3] Its ultimate source, I believe, can be traced to the most popular anti-Jewish work of the Middle Ages, the *Dialogi contra Judaeos* of the convert Petrus Alfonsi, written about 1110.[4] Petrus's work represents a new stage in the history of Christian encounter with Judaism, not least because of the ample knowledge

* Professor of History and Historical Theology, University of Chicago Divinity School

[1] I am happy to contribute this essay to a *Festschrift* in honor of my friend, Heiko Augustinus Oberman, whose research has done so much to enrich our understanding of the history of Jewish-Christian relations in the medieval and early modern periods. Although the "ecumenical" philosophical dialogue studied here did not contribute to any broad social amelioration, let alone toleration, of the Jews in medieval Europe, it does show that the "collective anamnesis" of Christian attitudes toward the Jews which Heiko Oberman has called for (*The Roots of Anti-Semitism* [Philadelphia: Fortress, 1984], 16) remains an ongoing task.

[2] *Ludovici Caelii Rhodigini Lectionum Antiquarum Libri XVI* (Basle: Froben, 1517, Bk. VI, cap. 1 (p. 251): "Observavimus igitur triplici calle Hebraeorum doctrinam incedere. Quippe aut ad Talmuticos recurrunt, aut ad Philosophos, aut ad Cabilistas. Talmutica haeresis initia ducere animadvertitur non vestusta admodum, ut quae annis paulominus ducentis post Christum ab Hebraeis adversum nos consarcinata deprehendatur. Qui vero Philosophibus rationibus Bibliae arcana explicare adorti sunt, principe inter eos Aegypto Mose, Averrois tempora non praecedunt, a cujus interitu non aguntur plus minus anni trecenti ac triginta. Tertia superest Cabala omnium vetustissima, et verax in primis. Quando ab optimo maximo Deo Moysi insinuatam, constans opinio est."

[3] See Bernard McGinn, "Cabalists and Christians: Reflections on Cabala in Medieval and Renaissance Thought," *Jewish Christians and Christian Jews*, edited by R. H. Popkin and G. M. Weiner (Amsterdam: Kluwer, 1994), 11-34.

[4] There is a poor edition of the *Dialogi* in J.-P. Migne, ed., *Patrologia Latina* (hereafter PL) 157:507-650. On Petrus see John Tolan, *Petrus Alfonsi and His Medieval Readers* (Gainesville, etc.: University Press of Florida, 1993), chaps. 2 and 5 on the *Dialogi*.

he had of his former faith. Petrus attacked Talmudic Judaism for irrationality and for breaking with biblical traditions, a starting point for the opposition to the Talmud that was to lead to its burning as a heretical book at Paris in 1248. Petrus was also aware of Jewish medieval philosophy, especially that of Saadia Gaon (d. 942), whose thought he uses in arguing for the reasonableness of the concept of creation and which he also critiques in defending the Trinity.[5] Finally, Petrus employed a proto-Kabbalistic work, the *Secreta secretorum*, to show that esoteric Judaism had knowledge of the Trinity of divine Persons in the Godhead.[6] This observation was the beginning of the trajectory of thought that found confirmation for the deepest Christian mysteries in Kabbalah.

Luigi Ricchieri, a scholar but not a philosopher, dismissed Jewish philosophy because of its relative newness in relation to the antiquity of the Kabbalah, but four centuries earlier Petrus Alfonsi had engaged Saadia in philosophical debate. Petrus's option points the way toward the attitude taken toward Jewish philosophy among many scholastics, especially in the thirteenth century. If we can take these three strands of Judaism as a heuristic tool for understanding late medieval intellectual attitudes toward the Jews, then it is possible to say that the condemnation of the Talmud as a species of heresy represents the worst aspects of Christian misunderstanding and persecution of Jews, while the growing interest in esoteric Judaism that eventually produced Christian Kabbalah may be seen as a species of co-opting Judaism for a Christian agenda, namely, proving that belief in the Trinity and in Christ as Redeemer had been the "inner" truth of Judaism since the time of Moses. It is the purpose of this essay to suggest that it was in the philosophical encounter between Judaism and Christianity that we can find something more like a true conversation of traditions, one in which a measure of mutual respect, if not always agreement, is visible.

The importance of this philosophical dialogue should not be exaggerated. If we wish to characterize it as in some way "ecumenical," it was scarcely so in the sense of leading to anything like greater toleration of Judaism as a religion or Jews as a group in society. The basic

---

[5] See *Dialogi* VI-XII.

[6] The identity of this work remains under discussion. For one attempt to determine its possible contents, see Alfred Buchler, "A Twelfth-Century Physician's Desk Book: The *Secreta Secretorum* of Petrus Alfonsi Quondam Moses Sephardi," *Journal of Jewish Studies* 37(1986):206-12.

attitude of Western Christians to other religions was well summarized in the passage from the *Chanson de Rolande* (line 1015): "*Paien unt tort e chrestiens unt dreit*" — The Christians are right, and the pagans are wrong. Jews were often viewed as even *more* wrong than pagans, as the terrible pogroms, expulsions, and other forms of repression make clear. Nevertheless, the growth of knowledge in the twelfth and thirteenth centuries, and especially the expansion of the scholastic method for doing theology, was accompanied by an insatiable hunger for the scientific and philosophical nourishment that Western Europeans recognized had originated in ancient Greece, but that in recent centuries was more amply present in Islam and Judaism than in the West. And so a major effort to translate and to assimilate the wisdom of alien traditions was undertaken in the twelfth and thirteenth centuries. Although this assimilation was largely a matter of books and had little, if any, impact on day-to-day relations between Christians and Jews, the respect that we see among some scholastic thinkers for the intellectual contributions of Jews and Muslims marks a new moment in the evolution of Christian thought.

In the scholastic encounter with non-Christian thought the greatest attention was given to the translation and study of Aristotle as a basic resource for the ongoing task of reconciling reason with faith. Here, it is important to note that thirteenth-century scholastics, unlike Luigi Ricchieri, did not think that forms of non-Christian philosophy should be dismissed merely because they were modern. On the Islamic side, Avicenna (d. 1037) and Averroes (d. 1198) are the prime examples of recent philosophers whose views were accorded great respect and played an important role in Scholasticism. Though the use of Jewish philosophers was more restricted, it was by no means negligible.

Four Jewish philosophers were known to the scholastics.[7] Two of these, Philo and Isaac Israeli, were of relatively minor moment;[8] but

---

[7] The role of Jewish philosophers in Scholasticism has been studied for over a century. Still important is the detailed research of Julius Guttmann, especially *Die Scholastik des dreizehnten Jahrhunderts in ihren Beziehungen zum Judentum und zur jüdischen Literatur* (Breslau: Marcus, 1902).

[8] Philo appears to have been known indirectly through citations in the Fathers, mostly Origen, Ambrose, and Jerome. Isaac Israeli's *Book of Definitions* and *Book on the Elements* were translated by Gerard of Cremona and cited by a number of scholastics, but cannot be said to have had a major influence. See Alexander Altmann and S.M. Stern, *Isaac Israeli. A Neoplatonic Philosopher of the Early Tenth Century* (Oxford: Clarendon Press, 1958).

the other two, Solomon Ibn Gabirol and Moses Maimonides, had real significance for the schoolmen. Let me say a brief word about each of them before trying to suggest how their thought was utilized and what the dialectic of agreement/disagreement and understanding/misunderstanding we find in these medieval encounters may have to tell us.

Gabirol (d. 1058) is one of those Jewish thinkers who masked his identity so well that Christians never realized he was a Jew. His philosophical *summa*, the *Fons Vitae (Mekkor Hayim)*, deliberately eschews any Jewish identifying themes, so that medieval Christians took him to be either a convert from Islam or an Arab Christian.[9] Still, even if his Christian readers had known the true identity of *Avicebrol* or *Avencebrol*, as they usually called him, there is no reason to think that they would not have continued to read him, not least because he had composed one of the most systematic and interesting attempts to harmonize Neoplatonic metaphysics with the creationist belief common to Jews, Christians, and Muslims. Although the encounter of Latin scholastics with Gabirol was often reduced to a few key issues, especially universal hylomorphism (i.e., the teaching that all created reality is a composition of form and matter) and the plurality of substantial forms in individual beings, it was symptomatic of Christian emphasis on the importance of rethinking Neoplatonic philosophy in the light of biblical revelation.[10]

Maimonides's *Guide of the Perplexed (Moreh Nevukhim)* completed about 1190, though decidedly more Aristotelian in its philosophical background, was scarcely needed as an introduction to Aristotelianism by the time it was translated into Latin c. 1230-40 as the *Dux neutrorum*.[11] Its wide use by many schoolmen testifies not only to the

---

[9] For an edition of the *Fons Vitae*, see *Avencebrolis Fons Vitae ex Arabico in Latinum translatus ab Iohanne Hispano et Domenico Gundisssalino*, ed., Clemens Baeumker (Münster: Aschendorff, 1892-95. *Beiträge zur Geschichte der Philosophie des Mittelalters* 1.2-4). The best general study is that of Jacques Schlanger, *La philosophie de Salomon Ibn Gabirol: Étude d'un Néoplatonisme* (Leiden: Brill, 1968).

[10] Christians, of course, could look back to previous examples of systematic attempts at wedding Neoplatonism and Christianity, such as the *corpus dionysiacum* of c. 500, and John Scottus Eriugena's *Periphyseon* of the late ninth century.

[11] The *Guide* was originally written in Arabic and first translated into Hebrew in 1204 by Samuel Ibn-Tibbon. It will be cited here in the translation of Shlomo Pines, *Moses Maimonides. The Guide of the Perplexed*, 2 vols. (Chicago: University of Chicago, 1963). At least two partial Latin versions survive, along with a complete text based on the later Hebrew translation of al-Harizi. A form of the Latin translation was printed in Paris in 1520 under the title *Rabbi Mossei Aegyptii Dux seu Director dubitantium*

respect they had for Maimonides as a philosopher, but also to their sense that he was a kindred spirit to the scholastic attempt to integrate faith and reason in a synthesis that would be at once philosophically cogent and religiously effective. Thomas Aquinas, for example, expressly paid tribute to Maimonides's effort to fashion an agreement *(concordare)* between Aristotle and sacred scripture, even when he disagreed with him.[12]

The extent to which various scholastic authors were able to engage in a fruitful discussion with Jewish philosophers like Gabirol and Maimonides, I suggest, is based in large part upon how they viewed the relation of philosophy and theology, or reason and faith. Scholastic views about the relation of faith and reason varied widely.[13] In what follows I would like to illustrate something of the range of the encounter with Jewish philosophy through a glance at three modes of conceiving the status of philosophy found among some of the pre-eminent scholastics of the thirteenth century.

The first option is that expressed by Bonaventure. The Franciscan doctor argued that there were two distinct forms of philosophy — one the product of reason, the other a philosophy based upon the

---

aut perplexorum, but in the absence of a modern critical edition it is difficult to know how this early printing relates to the versions used by Albert the Great, Aquinas, Eckhart, and others. On the history of the Latin versions, see Wolfgang Kluxen, "Literargeschichtliches zum lateinischen Moses Maimonides," *Recherches de théologie ancienne et médiévale* 21(1954):23-50; "Maimonides und die Hochscholastik," *Philosophisches Jahrbuch der Görresgesellschaft* 63(1955):151-65; "Die Geschichte des Maimonides im lateinischen Abendland als Beispiel einer christlich-jüdischen Begegnung," *Miscellanea Mediaevalia 4. Judentum im Mittelalter*, ed. Paul Wilpert (Berlin: De Gruyter, 1966), 146-66; and "Maimonides and Latin Scholasticism," *Maimonides and Philosophy*, edd. S. Pines and Y. Yovel (Dordrecht: Nijhoff, 1986), 224-32. The most recent survey of the influence of the Latin Maimonides can be found in Kurt Ruh, *Geschichte der abendländische Mystik. Band III. Die Mystik des deutschen Predigerordens und ihre Grundlegung durch die Hochscholastik* (Munich: Beck, 1996), 45-56.

[12] E.g., Thomas Aquinas, *Summa theologiae* Ia, q.50, a.3 (hereafter abbreviated as *STh*).

[13] The institutional and intellectual complexities of the relation between philosophy and theology have been studied in two important papers published in *Knowledge and the Sciences in Medieval Philosophy. Proceedings of the Eighth International Congress of Medieval Philosophy (S.I.E.P.M.)*, edd. Monika Asztalos, John E. Murdoch, Ilkka Niiniluoto (Helsinki: Acta Philosophical Fennica, Vol. 48, 1990). The essay of Tullio Gregory, "Forme di conoscenza e ideali di sapere nella cultura medievale" (11-71), provides a broad overview of models and ideals of knowledge and science in the medieval period down to the fourteenth century, while that of John Marenbon, "The Theoretical and Practical Autonomy of Philosophy as a Discipline in the Middle Ages: Latin Philosophy, 1250-1350" (262-74), concludes that "regarded as disciplines, [medieval] *philosophia* and modern philosophy bear little resemblance" (273).

metaphysics found in revelation. Though Bonaventure respected the first form of philosophy, he was primarily interested in the second, and therefore he had little interest in engaging Jewish philosophers. The second option was found among those scholastics (both Franciscans and Dominicans) who sought to establish an independent space for a philosophy based on rational demonstration and to show, as far as possible, the harmony between this natural philosophy and Christian revelation. These thinkers, especially Albert the Great and his pupil Thomas Aquinas, were ready to engage the Jewish philosophers on the level of reason — utilizing, adapting, and often disagreeing with them in a form of ecumenical dialogue. Finally, a third approach can be found in Meister Eckhart. Eckhart, like John Scottus Eriugena before him, made no distinction between the content of what philosophy might attain and what theology taught (though philosophy and theology differed according to their mode of teaching). Eckhart was open to a deeper assimilation of Jewish thought precisely because of this fusion of philosophy and theology.

Let us begin with the first option. As has been shown by John Quinn and Zachary Hayes, Bonaventure held that there were two levels of the relation between reason and faith and therefore two forms of philosophy.[14] Since both reason and faith come from God, there can be no incompatibility between them. Therefore, the Seraphic Doctor recognized the existence of a philosophical science that made use of reason (a natural power, but one with a connatural connection to the divine ideas) in order to arrive at truths about God and the world. Nevertheless, this form of philosophy, especially in fallen humanity, often went astray, in Bonaventure's view, and thus was in need of the guidance of faith to avoid error. But Bonaventure was more interested in a second level of philosophy, one which draws reason up into faith and makes use of the rational power to construct a properly Christian metaphysics which the theologian employs as an integral part of his task to understand and defend the truths of revelation. The core of this latter form of philosophy is well expressed in a text from the first of the *Collations on the Hexaemeron* where Bonaven-

----

[14] See John F. Quinn, *The Historical Constitution of St. Bonaventure's Philosophy* (Toronto: PIMS, 1973); and Zachary Hayes, "Christology and Metaphysics in the Thought of Bonaventure," *Celebrating the Medieval Heritage. A Colloquy on the Thought of Aquinas and Bonaventure*, edited by David Tracy, *The Journal of Religion. Supplement* 58(1978), S82-S104.

ture analyzes seven ways in which Christ is the center, or *medium*, of all things. The first of these is Christ as the *medium metaphysicum*, i.e., the center of *Christian* metaphysics. This is how he puts it:

> "This is the *medium metaphysicum* that leads back [to God], and this is our whole metaphysics — emanation, exemplarity, consummation — that is, to be illuminated by spiritual rays and to be led back to the Highest Source.
> And thus you will be a true metaphysician."[15]

Bonaventure was not oblivious to the importance of the first, or natural, form of philosophy. He did insist, though, that the essential principle which any form of natural metaphysics must recognize in order to be true and useful for theology was that of exemplarity, the natural preparation (what the scholastics called the "obediential potency") for the recognition of the Word as the exemplar of all things in Christian metaphysics. Hence Aristotle, while helpful as a logician and naturalist, was a bad metaphysician because of his attack on Plato's Ideas, and thus, in Bonaventure's view, a serious danger to Christian teaching. In his broadside against Aristotle in Collation 6, Bonaventure praises the good natural metaphysicians of exemplarity, namely, Plato, Plotinus, and Philo, "the most learned of the Jews" (*disertissimus Iudaeorum*), who, following Jerome, he took to be the author of the book of Wisdom.[16]

Bonaventure was forced to engage Aristotle, Averroes, and Avicenna because they were so large — and for him so dangerous — a part of scholastic education. He did not have to engage Jewish philosophers in the same way. Aside from one possible mention of Isaac Israeli,[17] as well the praise directed to Philo, he was oblivious to Jewish thinkers. It is difficult to think that he did not know of Maimonides, because his teacher, Alexander of Hales, was one of the first to use the Jewish philosopher. Similarly, although Bonaventure was an adherent of the doctrine of universal hylomorphism of which Gabirol was the major philosophical proponent,[18] he never mentions

---

[15] *Collationes in Hexaemeron* 1.17 (*Sancti Bonaventurae Opera Omnia* 5:332b): "Hoc est medium metaphysicum reducens, et haec est tota nostra metaphysica: de emanatione, de exemplaritate, de consummatione, scilicet illuminari per radios spirituales et reduci ad summum. Et sic eris verus metaphysicus."

[16] *Coll.* 6.2-7 (5:360-62). The passage citing Wisdom 7:25-26 and 29 is found in 361b-62a.

[17] *In I Sententiarum* d.7, art.1, quaest.1 (*Opera* 1:134).

[18] See, e.g., *In II Sententiarum* d.3, a.1, q. 1; and d.17, a.1, q.2 (*Opera* 2:89-91, 413-16).

Gabirol's *Fons Vitae* in defending this position.[19] The Franciscan's distinctive view of the two forms of metaphysics helps explain this absence of dialogue with Judaism.

In Albert the Great and especially in his pupil Thomas Aquinas we encounter a different view of the relation of faith and reason. As Etienne Gilson noted, Albert was the first scholastic to recognize the difference between patristic thought and the new philosophical learning and thus to insist that "theology was specifically distinct from philosophy and that faith was a mode of cognition specifically other than natural reason."[20] For Albert and Thomas, reason and natural philosophy, because they were based upon evidence, had a measure of independence in relation to theology, the science of God made available by faith.[21] In Albert, the degree of freedom is remarkable and perhaps even problematic,[22] while Thomas sought to subordinate and assimilate philosophy (especially but not solely Aristotelian philosophy) in service of *sacra doctrina*. In order to accomplish this Aquinas often had to stand Aristotle on his head. I will suggest that he did much the same with Maimonides, even when he agreed with him.

The fact that Albert and Thomas gave philosophy more inde-

---

[19] For a discussion of Bonaventure's teaching on this point, see Quinn, *Historical Constitution*, 219-319, and 845.

[20] Etienne Gilson, *History of Christian Philosophy in the Middle Ages* (New York: Random House, 1955), 278. For a more detailed study of the relation of philosophy and theology in Albert, see Édouard Wéber, "La relation de la philosophie et de la théologie selon Albert le Grand," *Archives de philosophie* 43(1980):559-588.

[21] Both Aquinas (see *STh* Ia, q.1, a.1) and Albert (e.g., *Summa theologiae* Ia, tr.3, q.13, m.3) held that there were truths, such as the Trinity, that surpassed reason and could only be known by revelation. In concert with all thirteenth-century scholastics, they agreed that *theologia* was a *scientia*, and they were pioneers in identifying the subject matter of theology as God. While Aquinas argued that *theologia*, or *sacra doctrina* as he preferred to call it, was primarily a speculative science (Ia, q.1, a.4), Albert was closer to Augustine and most Franciscans in his definition of *theologia*: " ...theologia scientia est secundum pietatem, hoc est, quod non est de scibili simpliciter ut scibile est, nec de omni scibili, sed secundum quod est inclinans ad pietatem" (*Summa theologiae* Ia, tr.1, q.2). On thirteenth-century understandings of the nature of theology, helpful background can be found in Ulrich Kopf, *Die Anfänge der theologischen Wissenschaftstheorie im 13. Jahrhundert* (Tübingen: Mohr, 1974). The best study of Thomas's understanding of *sacra doctrina* remains Gerald F. Van Ackeren, *SACRA DOCTRINA. The Subject of the First Question of the "Summa theologica" of St. Thomas Aquinas* (Rome: Catholic Book Agency, 1952).

[22] Though Albert insists on the compatibility of faith and reason, in his thought the two often seem to be almost independent trajectories. See the discussion in Loris Sturlese, *Die deutsche Philosophie im Mittelalter. Von Bonifatius bis zu Albert dem Grossen 748-1280* (Munich: Beck, 1993), 342-50.

pendence than Bonaventure had cut both ways. On the one hand, it meant that they were more committed to actual philosophical work, though always within the broader context of their commitment as theologians. This commitment is evident not only in the numerous commentaries they wrote on Aristotle, but also in the way they strove to incorporate philosophical argumentation into their theological writings. In an age when most scholastics accepted Augustine as the ultimate master of all learning, both philosophical and theological, Albert was bold enough to say that despite the bishop of Hippo's authority in theology, he did not have an equal position in medicine or in natural philosophy.[23] On the other hand, both Albert and Thomas Aquinas were engaged in the critical appropriation of what reason could discover for the purposes of Christian faith and practice. In contrast to the philosophical fideism of the radical Aristotelians, they were happy to learn from the philosophers, but were also always prepared to judge. Thomas tended to disagree politely, always willing to give a benign interpretation where possible. Albert was more testy in his critiques and comments.

Albert made selective use of Maimonides in his efforts to create a corpus of philosophical and scientific works for the training of theologians. He also often criticized the Jewish sage.[24] For example, he rejected Maimonides's identification of the angels with the Aristotelian separate intelligences,[25] and he felt that the discussion of prophecy in the *Guide* did not leave enough room for the role of supernatural *gratia* in the various forms of prophesying.[26] In other

---

[23] See *In II Sent.* d.13, a.2, in *Beati Alberti Magni Opera Omnia*, ed. S.C. Borgnet (Paris: Vives, 1895), Vol.28:247: "Unde sciendum, quod Augustino in his quae sunt de fide et moribus plusquam Philosophis credendum est, si dissentiunt. Sed si de medicina loqueretur, plus ego crederem Galeno, vel Hippocrati; et si de naturis rerum loquatur, credo Aristoteli plus vel alii experto in rerum naturis."

[24] The most detailed study of the role of Maimonides in Albert's thought is Jacob Guttmann, "Der Einfluss der maimonidischen Philosophie auf das christliche Abendland," *Moses ben Maimun. Sein Leben, seine Werke und sein Einfluss*, edd. W. Bacher, M. Brann, D. Simonsen, and J. Guttman (Leipzig: Fock, 1908), 153-75.

[25] See, e.g., *Summa theologiae* IIa, tr.2, q.53, m.3; *De causis et processione mundi* Ia, tr.4, cap.7. Eckhart alone among the scholastics accepted Maimonides's view in this matter; see, e.g., *Expositio Libri Genesis* n.116 (LW 1:273), and *Expositio Libri Sapientiae* n.12 (LW 2:333). All citations from Eckhart refer to *Meister Eckhart. Die deutschen und lateinischen Werke* (Stuttgart and Berlin: Kohlhammer, 1936-; LW= *Lateinischen Werke* and DW= *Deutschen Werke*).

[26] For texts and a discussion, see Guttmann, "Der Einfluss," 169-75.

places, especially in his treatment of arguments for and against the eternity of the world in Book 8 of his *Commentary on the Physics of Aristotle*, he made considerable use of Maimonides's *Guide* 2.14 in countering seven philosophical proofs for the world's eternity.[27] Even more importantly, in mustering his philosophical argument against the necessitarianism of Greco-Arabian thought (i.e., its teaching that the world is a necessary product of the First Cause), Albert utilized Maimonides's position on the importance of the Divine Will in creation (e.g., *Guide* 2.19). As he put it in *Physics* 8, tr.1, chapter 13: "The knowledge of this problem [i.e., whether the world is eternal] depends on the knowledge of another, which is, whether caused beings flow from the First Cause through necessity of nature or through the will's choice, and this can be known only through First Philosophy."[28] (This principle was also to be crucial in the creation theology of his student, Thomas Aquinas.)

Albert the Great's use of Maimonides is a good example of what might be called piecemeal appropriation; his encounter with Gabirol is an even better example of a critical dialogue.[29] It is not that the Dominican was too much an Aristotelian to appreciate the Neoplatonism of the Jewish sage. Rather, as recent studies have shown, Albert's metaphysics of "flowing" (*fluxus*), especially as set forth in his *De causis et processu universitatis* — a paraphrase, commentary, and expansion of the Proclean *Liber de causis* — was a mixture of Platonic and Peripatetic elements.[30] Albert devoted three chapters in this work to an attack on the fundamental principles of the *Fons Vitae*.[31]

---

[27] See *Physica* VIII, tr.1, cap.11; cf. *In II Sent.* d.1, art.10; and *Summa theologiae* IIa, tr.1, q.4, m.2, a.5.

[28] *Alberti Magni Physica*, ed. Paul Hossfeld (Westphalia: Aschendorff, 1993. *Opera Omnia* IV.II. Libri 5-8), 575: "Dependet autem scientia hujus problematis a scientia alterius, quod est, utrum per necessitatem naturae fluunt entia causata a prima causa vel per electionem voluntatis, et illud sciri non potest nisi per primam philosophiam."

[29] For what follows see the more detailed treatment in Bernard McGinn, "Ibn Gabirol: The Sage Among the Schoolmen," *Neoplatonism and Jewish Thought*, ed. Lenn E. Goodman (Albany: SUNY, 1992), 77-110, and the literature cited there.

[30] See especially Edward Booth, *Aristotelian Aporetic Ontology in Islamic and Christian Thinkers* (Cambridge: Cambridge University Press, 1983), chap. 5; and Alain de Libera, *Albert le Grand et la philosophie* (Paris: Vrin, 1990), chap.IV.

[31] See *Alberti Magni. De causis et processu univeritatis a Prima Causa*, ed. Winfried Fauser (Westphalia: Aschendorff, 1993. *Opera Omnia* XVII, Par II), Liber I, tr.1, cap.6; tr.3, cap.4; tr.4, cap.8 (ed., 13-14, 39-40, 55-58). Liber I, tr.1, cap.5 contains a detailed exposition of Gabirol's views. This new critical edition lists 160 references to Gabirol in the work, as compared with only 14 references to Maimonides.

Although he has harsh words about the work, he obviously had read it carefully and found Gabirol's particular synthesis of Neoplatonism worthy of detailed study and incisive refutation. Indeed, Gabirol's most acute readers among the schoolmen were often not his propo-nents, such as his translator, the Spanish archdeacon Dominicus Gundissalinus, or William of Auvergne who praised him as the "omnium philosophantium nobilissimus," but those, like Albert and Thomas, who read him to refute him.[32]

What did Albert find wrong about Gabirol's Neoplatonic synthe-sis? Like many scholastics, Albert objected to Gabirol's teaching about universal hylomorphism and the plurality of substantial forms in existing beings. With considerable acuity, however, the Dominican *magister* penetrated beyond these much-discussed teachings back to the premises of Gabirol's metaphysic. The Jewish philosopher based his system on two fundamental principles of Neoplatonic meta-physics. The first is the principle of mediation (i.e., that two extremes cannot be related apart from a mediating principle), the second is the principle of coinherence (i.e., that is, as the Middle Platonist Nume-nius once put it, "all in all, but in each according to its nature"). To these he joined a third principle, the axiom that the Absolute One can only produce a duality. "The Creator of all things," he said, "ought to be one only, and the created should be different from him. Hence, if the created were only matter or only form, it would be assimilated to him and there would not be a medium between them, for two is after one."[33] In employing these principles to forge a syn-thesis between Jewish belief in an omnipotent creator God and a Neoplatonic universe constituted by coinherent levels of the emana-tion of the fundamental binary pair of matter and form, Gabirol emphasized the role of the Divine Will *(Voluntas creatrix)* as the ulti-mate medium between God and the dual creation. (For Gabirol this *Voluntas* takes the place of the *Logos* of Philo.)

Albert's opposition to Gabirol is rooted in two essential aspects of his own thought: his metaphysics of God as the *immediate* creator of all

---

[32] The Dominican, Berthold of Moosburg (c. 1300-c. 1365), quite possibly a stu-dent of Eckhart, forms an exception in his extensive use and appropriation of Gabirol, as suggested below.

[33] *Fons Vitae* IV.6 (ed. Bauemker, 222): "...quia creator omnium debet esse unus tantum, et creatum debet esse diversum ab eo, unde si creatum esset materia tantum aut forma tantum, assimilaretur uni, et non esset medium inter illa, quia duo sunt post unum."

things, including particulars; and his stress on the role of the Divine Intellect in creation. (The latter rests upon both traditional Christian teaching about the Logos, as well as Aristotle's principle that the will is always specified to activity by the intellect.)[34] Albert argued that Gabirol's principles of mediation and coinherence compromised a free and direct divine creation,[35] and that his teaching on the Divine Will threatened Christian teaching — and good philosophy — about the intelligibility implanted in the universe by its Creator. This also led him to attack Gabirol's dictum that from a source that is simply One something that is two must flow according to the order of nature. According to Albert, Gabirol was wrong to contradict the axiom (thought to go back to Aristotle) that held that "from what is one only what is one can come to be." The Dominican scornfully noted that denying the principle of "one from one" was held by no other philosopher save "Avicebron in *The Fount of Life*."[36]

Thomas Aquinas's use of both Gabirol and Maimonides was extensive. According to the research of Father Vansteenkiste, Thomas refers to the former 23 times by name and to Maimonides by name 76 times and at least another 10 times implicitly.[37] In the case of Maimonides and Aquinas we even have a rare example of an interchange that went both ways, because Italian followers of Maimonides later translated parts of Aquinas's *Summa theologiae* into Hebrew.[38] Like his teacher Albert, Thomas's attitude toward Gabirol

---

[34] As the *De causis et processu* lib.I, tr.3, cap.4 shows, Albert denies that the Divine Intellect requires the mediation of an inferior will-principle to create the world, a position which does not contradict the emphasis on God's freedom in creating noted above.

[35] This, of course, is not to say that Albert did not accept the full panoply of the levels of being worked out by the Greco-Arabian "Peripatetics." But he understood it in the light of the Dionysian immediacy of divine action on all levels–the unique and direct causality of the *fluens principium*.

[36] *De causis et processu* lib.I, tr.4, cap.8. Albert was mistaken in this, because Maimonides, following al-Ghazzali, had also questioned the "one from one" axiom (see *Guide* 2.22). For a study, consult Arthur Hyman, "From What is One and Simple only What is One and Simple Can Come to Be," *Jewish Neoplatonism*, 111-35. Most medieval authorities cite the axiom as given by Aristotle, but its explicit formulation first occurs in al-Farabi and Avicenna.

[37] C. Vansteenkiste, O.P., "Autori Arabi e Giudei nell'opera di San Tommaso," *Angelicum* 37(1960):336-401.

[38] See Giuseppe Sermoneta, "Pour une histoire du thomisme juif," *Aquinas and Problems of his Time*, ed. by G. A. Verbeke and Daniel Verhelst (Leuven-The Hague: Peeters, 1976), 130-35; and "Jehudah ben Moseh ben Daniel Romano, traducteur de saint Thomas," *Hommage à Georges Vajda*, ed. G. Hahon and C. Touati (Louvain: Peeters, 1980), 231-62.

was mostly negative, as can be seen in the many detailed refutations he made of Gabirol's arguments for universal hylomorphism and plurality of forms.[39] His use of Maimonides was more extensive, more complex, and continues to elicit different evaluations.[40] A number of interpreters have emphasized the agreement or at least convergence of the views of these two great thinkers, but I will suggest a different perspective. To be sure, there are important aspects of Thomas's philosophical positions, such as the proofs for the existence of God, especially the third way (*STh* Ia, q.2, a.3), as well as his attacks on views claiming to demonstrate the eternity of the universe (e.g., *STh* Ia, q.46, a.1), where the Dominican was happy to employ arguments adapted from Maimonides. Aquinas's dialogue with Maimonides was always a productive one for him, both in what he accepted and what he rejected.[41] Nevertheless, Maimonides's attempt to bring together faith and philosophy seems to have been more significant for the Angelic Doctor in helping him to clarify where he differed from the Jewish thinker than in leading him to common positions. Both thinkers sought to relate reason and faith, but they did so within different religious contexts and in different ways. Hence, Thomas frequently disagrees with Maimonides, though always with respect. Even more revealing is the fact that when he agrees with Maimonides he often does so within a the context of making a point that "stands Maimonides on his head," so to speak. In a brief presentation I can do no more than to give one example of each procedure, starting with the "benign reversal" appropriation.[42]

---

[39] See especially *In II Sent.* d.3, q.1, a.1; *De ente et essentia* 5; *Summa contra Gentiles* 2, 50; *De substantiis separatis* 5-8; *De spiritualibus creaturis* a.3; *STh* Ia, q.50, a.2, and q. 66, a.2. Thomas also attacked Gabirol's view of the plurality of substantial forms; see, e.g., *In II Sent.* d.12, q.1, a.4; *De sub. sep.* 6; *De spir. creat.* aa.1 and 3; *Quaest. de anima* q.6; *In II de anima*, lect.1; *Quodlibet* XI, q.5, a.5; and *STh* Ia, q.66, a.2. One of Thomas's most extensive encounters with Gabirol occurs in *STh* Ia, q.115, a.1, where he discusses the activity of bodies. The best work on Thomas's encounter with Gabirol is Fernand Brunner, *Platonisme et Aristotelianisme. La critique d'Ibn Gabirol par Saint Thomas d'Aquin* (Paris-Louvain: Éditions Béatrice-Nauwelaerts, 1964).

[40] The literature is large and uneven. A number of important articles can be found in *Studies in Maimonides and St. Thomas Aquinas*, Selected with an Introduction and Bibliography by Jacob I. Dienstag (n.p.: KTAV, 1975). Among recent important works, see especially Avital Wohlmann, *Thomas d'Aquin et Maimonide. un dialogue exemplaire* (Paris: Du Cerf, 1988); and *Maimonide et Thomas d'Aquin. Un dialogue impossible* (Fribourg: Editions Universitaires, 1995).

[41] Wohlman, *Thomas d'Aquin et Maimonide. un dialogue exemplaire*, 321, aptly describes Maimonides as "un interlocuteur privilégié."

[42] Had space allowed, in the category of direct disagreements it would be interest-

In *Guide* 1.33-34 Maimonides discussed why the truths of divine
science are hidden under the parables of the Torah. They have been
hidden, he says, "because at the outset the intellect is incapable of
receiving them." Maimonides goes on to spell out five reasons for
this, based both on the difficulty of the secrets and on the minds and
characters of humans, "that prevents the instruction of the multitude
in the veritable methods of speculation and that prevents their being
taught to begin to grasp the essences of things as they are."[43] Maimonides's point is to underline the esotericism of divine science —
"these matters are for the few solitary individuals of a very special
sort, not for the multitude" (1.34). Thomas Aquinas quotes Maimonides's five reasons three times in the course of his writings, but to
quite a different effect.[44] The most revealing treatment is found in his
Exposition on Boethius's De Trinitate, an early discussion of the relation
between faith and reason written about 1258-59. Here Thomas cites
Rabbi Moses within the context of a non-Maimonidean distinction
between two kinds of truths about God: natural truths which can be
known, at least potentially, by all humans,[45] and strictly supernatural
truths which can only be known through divine grace.[46] With regard
to the revelation of natural truths, Aquinas emphasizes that they are
taught by faith precisely in order to make them accessible to all, as
far as possible, rather than as a means of restricting them to an intellectual elite — "Hence, lest the multitude of humans were to remain
empty of divine knowledge, humanity was divinely provided with the

---

ing to pursue Thomas's critique of Maimonides's denial that the universe was created for humanity (*quod finis creationis caeli sit homo*) in *In IV Sent.* d.48, q.2, a.3, ad 6,
responding to *Guide* 3.13 and 25. See Hans Liebeschütz, "Eine Polemik des Thomas
von Aquin gegen Maimonides," *Monatsschrift für Geschichte und Wissenschaft des Juden-
tums* 80(1936):93-96.

[43] These quotations from *Guide* 1.33 are taken the Pines translation, *Moses Maimonides. The Guide of the Perplexed*, 1:71-72.

[44] See *In III Sent.* d.24, a.3, q.3, sol. I; *Expositio super Librum Boethii De Trinitate* q.3,
a.1; and *De Veritate* q.14, a.10. For comments on these texts, see P. Synave, "La
révélation des vérités divines naturelles d'après Saint Thomas d'Aquin," *Mélanges
Mandonnet*, 2 vols. (Paris: Vrin, 1930) 1:327-70; and Ruedi Imbach, "*Ut ait Rabbi Moyses*: Maimonidesche Philosopheme bei Thomas von Aquin und Meister Eckhart,"
Collectanea Franciscana 60(1990), 105-06.

[45] See *Sancti Thomae de Aquino Expositio super Librum Boethii De Trinitate*, ed. Bruno
Decker (Leiden: Brill, 1965), q.3, a.1 (p. 111): Ad quorum quaedam plene
cognoscenda possibile est homini pervenire per viam rationis etiam in statu huius
vitae.

[46] The same distinction is at the basis of Aquinas's argument for the necessity of
sacra doctrina in *STh* Ia, q.1, a.1.

way of faith."[47] So, the reasons that Maimonides sees for restricting truth to the few are adapted by Thomas Aquinas as arguments for the fittingness of revealing truth to all.

To illustrate an example of disagreement, consider Aquinas's ongoing discussion with Maimonides on the proper form of language about God.[48] Both thinkers were in fundamental agreement that the human mind cannot know what God is — there is no quidditative knowledge of God, in Aquinas's language.[49] God remains *penitus ignotus*, "totally unknown."[50] Both thinkers also recognize the important role that the *via negationis*, the way of negation, plays in the strategies by which religious persons continue to speak about the mystery that they can never comprehend. In his early works, Aquinas sometimes suggests that negation is the best way of speaking about God. In the *Exposition on Boethius's De Trinitate* q.6, a.3, for example, a continuing progression of negations denying that predications drawn from created realities can belong to God creates a "logical space" within which we "understand" ever more clearly what God is not.[51] Nevertheless, in his final treatment of the matter in *Summa theologiae* Ia, q.13, a.2, Aquinas explicitly disagreed with Maimonides and argued for the priority of eminent predication over negative statements as the most effective way of speaking about God. In Thomas's doctrine of eminence by way of analogy the negative element remains central, in that we cannot know the way in which the names we use apply to God (*modus significandi*), but this does not prevent our affirmation that what the names signify (*id quod significant*) belongs most truly to the Blessed One.[52] The difference

---

[47] Ibid. (p. 112): Unde ne multitudo hominum a divina cognitione vacua remaneret, provisa est ei divinitus via fidei.

[48] This aspect of the encounter between Aquinas and Maimonides has been much discussed. For a perceptive treatment, see David Burrell, *Knowing the Unknowable God: Ibn-Sina, Maimonides, Aquinas* (Notre Dame: University of Notre Dame Press, 1986); and "Aquinas and Maimonides: A Conversation about Proper Speech," *Immanuel* 16(1983):70-85. Cf. Wohlmann, *Thomas d'Aquin et Maimonide. un dialogue exemplaire*, chap. IV.

[49] See John F. Wippel, "Quidditative Knowledge of God According to Thomas Aquinas," *Graceful Reason. Essays in Ancient and Medieval Philosophy Presented to Joseph Owens* (Toronto: PIMS, 1983), 273-99.

[50] Thomas Aquinas, *Summa contra Gentiles* 3.49: "...penitus manet ignotum." See Anton C. Pegis, "Penitus Manet Ignotum," *Mediaeval Studies* 27(1965):212-26.

[51] *Expositio super Librum Boethii*, q.3, a.3 (pp. 220-23). Compare this with, e.g., *In I Sent.* d.8, q.1, a.1, ad 4; and *Summa contra Gentiles* 1.14 (though later in this *summa*, in 1.30-35, Aquinas indicates his preference for analogy and the *via eminentiae*).

[52] See *STh* Ia., q.13, a.3. This key distinction was used by Aquinas throughout his works; e.g., *In I Sent.* d.35, q.1, a.1, ad 2; *De Pot.* q.7, a.2, ad 7; *Summa contra Gentiles* 1.30.

is a real one that has effects in many areas of their thought that cannot be pursued here.[53] We might summarize the divergence this way. According to Aquinas, we cannot *know* God, but we can make positive predications about him that are true, not metaphorical, though we cannot grasp *how* they are true. For Maimonides, we can neither *know* God *nor* make positive predications about him that are true. The only true statements about him are negations; even the actional attributes drawn from scripture are finally only metaphors.[54]

Not all scholastics agreed with Thomas Aquinas's rejection of Maimonides's position on the primacy of negative predication, even in his own Dominican order. Meister Eckhart, though elusive, is in some ways closer to Maimonides than he is to Thomas.[55] In order to understand how Eckhart could appropriate the Jewish philosopher's thought in areas where other Christians questioned or rejected it we need to begin with Eckhart's understanding of the relation of philosophy and theology. Aquinas carefully distinguished between the natural truths about God that could be explored by reason and strictly supernatural truths, such as the Trinity and the Incarnation, which reason could never attain on its own. *Sacra doctrina*, founded on revelation, taught both kinds of truths and therefore contained both a

---

[53] Wohlman, *Maimonide et Thomas d'Aquin. Un dialogue impossible*, 191, puts it well: "L'opposition fondamentale entre la théorie des attributs négatifs et la doctrine de l'analogie, suffirait à manifester la différence radicale entre nos deux auteurs à l'interieur d'une conviction également affirmée de la transcendence de Dieu. La réflexion ontologique et l'expression philosophique portent déjà la marque d'attitudes religieuses inconciliables."

[54] See *Guide* 1.52-53, etc. It should be noted that Gabirol is in agreement with Maimonides here: there is no *sapientia* regarding God the *essentia prima*; see *Fons Vitae* 5.40 and 43 (ed. Bauemker, 329 and 388). On the actional attributes, see Seymour Feldman, "A Scholastic Misinterpretation of Maimonides' Doctrine of Divine Attributes," *Maimonides. A Collection of Critical Essays*, edited by Joseph A. Buijs (Notre Dame: University of Notre Dame Press, 1988). Feldman shows that the scholastics generally misunderstood Maimonides' view on actional attributes, but I do not think that this is the case for the late Aquinas in *STh* Ia, q.13, a.2.

[55] On the relation between Eckhart and Maimonides, see Joseph Koch, "Meister Eckhart und die jüdische Religionsphilosophie des Mittelalters," *Jahresbericht der Schleschischen Gesellschaft. Philosophisch-psychologische Sektion* 101(1928):134-48; Hans Liebeschütz, "Meister Eckhart und Moses Maimonides," *Archiv für Kulturgeschichte* 54(1972):64-96; B. McGinn, "Introduction," *Meister Eckhart. Teacher and Preacher* (New York: Paulist Press, 1986), 15-30; Niklaus Largier, "*FIGURATA LOCUTIO*. Hermeneutik und Philosophie bei Eckhart von Hochheim und Heinrich Seuse," *Meister Eckhart: Lebensstationen-Redesituationen*, edited by Klaus Jacobi (Berlin: Akademie, 1997), 303-32; and Yossef Schwartz, "'*Ecce est locus apud me*'. Maimonides und Eckharts Raumvorstellung als Begriff des Göttlichen," *Raum und Raumvorstellungen im Mittelalter. Miscellanea Mediaevalia 25* (Berlin: De Gruyter, 1998), 348-64.

philosophical and a doctrinal theology. Meister Eckhart rejected this distinction.

In his *Commentary on John*, Eckhart notes that because all truth proceeds from the same source there can be no conflict between what we find in nature and in scripture, a position common to all scholastics. But Eckhart interprets this in an unusual way, holding that all the truths of the three forms of science — theological, natural, and moral — are present, though in different modalities, in philosophy, in the Old Testament, and in the New Testament. "Moses, Christ, and the Philosopher teach the same thing, differing only in the way they teach, namely as worthy of belief [Moses], as probable or likely [Aristotle], and as truth [Christ]."[56] Eckhart's position at first glance may look like a form of specifically Christian metaphysics close to that of Bonaventure, one holding that the truths revealed by Christ enable the philosopher-theologian to understand the Trinitarian and Christological basis of reality. But the Dominican seems to be saying something else — a more daring claim that Aristotle and other philosophers, not least Maimonides, knew and taught what Aquinas would have called supernatural truths, whether they clearly recognized this or not. Of course, Eckhart knew that philosophers made mistakes, and he often criticized erroneous philosophical views,[57] but he thought that precisely as a rational discipline philosophy was not limited to what Aquinas would call natural truths about God.

It is actually the converse of this bringing together of philosophy and theology that was most important for the German Dominican. After all, Eckhart was primarily a *magister theologiae*, a scriptural exegete, and a preacher. Most of his technical scholastic works are scriptural commentaries designed to provide material for preaching. Paradoxically, however, they take the form of philosophical commentaries, following

---

[56] *Expositio sancti Evangelii secundum Iohannem* n.185 (LW 3:155): "Idem ergo est quod docet Moyses, Christus et philosophus, solum quantum ad modum differens, scilicet ut credibile, probabile sive verisimile, et veritas." It is interesting to note that Eckhart cites Maimonides's observation (*Guide* 2.23) that Aristotle's teaching about the supralunar world is only *verisimile*.

[57] In his Latin works, as far as I can determine, Eckhart never criticizes Maimonides, though in discussing the different kinds of law he says that Aquinas's division (*STh* IaIIae, q.99, a.4) is more rational and clearer than that of Maimonides in *Guide* 3.36 (cf. *Expositio libri Exodi* n.230). Kurt Ruh, *Geschichte* 3:55, notes that in his German Sermon 71 (DW 3:217-18; cf. DW 3:403) Eckhart does criticize the view that the soul resides in the heart, a position held by Maimonides, though he does not mention him by name.

the model of Maimonides. Thus, he says that the purpose of the *Commentary on John* is "to explain what the holy Christian faith and the two Testaments maintain through the help of the natural arguments of philosophers."[58] In the prologue to the second of his commentaries on Genesis, *The Book of the Parables of Genesis*, he explicitly introduces Maimonides as his guide to the parabolical interpretation of scripture, one that does not intend to *prove* the philosophical truths found in scripture (that is the function of the systematic parts of his unfinished *Opus Tripartitum*), but that seeks "to show that what the truth of holy scripture parabolically intimates in hidden fashion agrees with what we prove and declare about matters divine, ethical, and natural."[59]

The Bible, then, contains the whole of philosophy, though its parabolical character means that it does not *demonstrate* philosophy in the scientific sense. But scriptural commentary can serve as the instrument for the creation of a philosophico-theological exposition of the deepest mysteries of God, nature, and ethics. This fact appears to have become more and more clear to Eckhart during and after his second period teaching as regent master in Paris (1311-13). Hence, in his late exegetical works, the influence of Maimonides comes more and more to the fore, as Eckhart, in what Niklaus Largier has described as an "hermeneutical turn" sought to create a new form of *philosophia spiritualis* in which reason negates itself in attaining awareness of the identity of ground between God and the soul.[60]

Eckhart used Maimonides throughout his exegesis, but nowhere more than in the *Commentary on Exodus*, where the Jewish philosopher is the most cited authority — more than Aristotle, Aquinas, and even Augustine![61] The Dominican employs *The Guide* for many pur-

---

[58] *Expos. sec. Ioh.* n.2 (LW 3:123).

[59] *Liber Parabolorum Genesis* n.4 (LW 1:454): " Primum est, quod non est putandum, quasi per talia parabolica intendamus probare divina, naturalia et moralia ex parabolis; sed potius hoc ostendere intendimus, quod his, quae probamus et dicimus de divinis, moralibus et naturalibus, consonant ea quae veritas sacrae scripturae parabolice innuit quasi latenter." In the *Expositio libri Exodi* n.211 (LW 2:178) he makes the same point again: "...sacra scriptura plerumque sic narrat historiam, quod etiam tenet et innuit mysteria, docet etiam rerum naturas, mores instruit et componit."

[60] Largier, *FIGURATA LOCUTIO*, 316-32; and "Intellekttheorie, Hermeneutik und Allegorie: Subjekt und Subjektivität bei Meister Eckhart," *Geschichte und Vorgeschichte der modernen Subjektivität*, edd. Reto Luzius Fetz, Roland Hagenbüchle and Peter Schulz (Berlin: de Gruyter, 1998), 460-86.

[61] The *Expos. Ex.* can be found in LW 2:1-227 and has been translated in *Meister Eckhart. Teacher and Preacher*, edited and translated by Bernard McGinn (New York: Paulist Press, 1986), 41-146. By my calculation, in this work Eckhart cites Mai-

poses.[62] The most important use of Maimonides for core themes of Eckhart's thought is to be found in the "Treatise on the Names God" that takes up a considerable part of the commentary.[63] Here Eckhart engages in a threeway discussion with Thomas Aquinas and Maimonides, one in which he stands both authorities on their heads to construct his own theory of language about God.

Eckhart's "Treatise" is complex and at first glance inconsistent in places. Although the German Dominican cites Maimonides's arguments for the pre-eminence of negative predication extensively and generally hews to a strictly apophatic line,[64] there are passages in the treatise where he uses Aquinas's language of analogy and thus seems to maintain some kind of priority for the *via eminentiae*.[65] Is Eckhart confused? I would argue, rather, that he is employing features of both the Jewish sage and his Dominican predecessor to create a new

---

monides 85 times, Augustine 77, Aquinas 73, and Aristotle 49 times. Among other philosophical works, the *Liber de causis* is cited 13 times, Avicenna 12, Gabirol 3, and Averroes and al-Ghazzali each once. The "Verzeichnis der von Meister Eckhart zitierten Autoren" in LW 2:675-77, has a somewhat different tally, noting 169 references to Maimonides, explicit and implicit, and 109 to Augustine. Although the identification of implicit sources is partly subjective, it is remarkable that both these tallies have Maimonides more prevalent than Augustine in the *Expos. Ex.*. This preponderence does not appear to be the case in Eckhart's other Old Testament commentaries.

[62] Among the most extensive employments are the frequent citations of *Guide* 3.9, 22-23, 25 and 33, in discussing the commandment against coveting (Ex. 20:17) in *Expos. Ex.* nn.196-204 and 214-19.

[63] *Expos. Ex.* nn.34-78 and 143-84 (LW 2:40-82 and 130-58). A translation can be found in *Meister Eckhart. Teacher and Preacher*, 53-70, and 90-102.

[64] Large sections of *Expos. Ex.* nn. 37-44 and 171-84 are taken directly from the *Guide* 1.50-63.

[65] Two texts stand out. (1) After rejecting any real distinction of attributes in God and thus siding with Maimonides against Aquinas in *Expos. Ex.* n.58, Eckhart goes on to say in n.61: "Nec tamen propter hoc vanae sunt aut falsae huiusmodi attributiones distinctae, eo quod ipsis aliquod vere et reale in deo respondet" (LW 2:66). What is this *aliquod vere et reale*? Taking a hint from the *Expositio libri Sapientiae* nn.144-57 (LW 2:481-94), I would suggest that it is the dialectical *unum* as capable of doing all things (*cum sit una, omnia potest*). But power to do all things, in Eckhart as in Maimonides (*Guide* 1.52-53), might be best conceived of as an actional attribute, i.e., one which really says nothing about God himself. (2) In *Expos. Ex.* n.78, at the conclusion of his discussion of the role of positive predications (nn.73-78), Eckhart cites Thomas's famous distinction (see *STh* Ia, q.13, a.3, and *Summa contra Gentiles* 1.30) between the substance of the perfections signified (e.g., goodness, truth, life, etc.), which really does belong to God, and the *modus significandi*, which we always draw from our way of knowing creatures. However, Thomas used this distinction to argue for the legitimacy of an analogical language of *esse* while Eckhart employs it within the context of his dialectical understanding of *esse* as the *negatio negationis*. For more on the *via eminentiae*, see, e.g., nn.35 and 178.

dialectical form of God-language. Briefly, its structure goes some-thing like this.

(1) Maimonides is right to deny that all "dispositions," that is, predicates ascribed to God based on what we know, "even if they are perfections in us, are no longer so in God and are not more perfect than their opposites" (n.44).

(2) But *esse indistinctum*, the absolute existence revealed in Exodus 3:14, is not a name or *dispositio* based on the being of creatures (because we know only particular beings, what Eckhart called *esse hoc et hoc*).[66]

(3) Therefore, from the divine perspective of *esse indistinctum*, "no negation, nothing negative belongs to God, except for the negation of negation which is what the One signifies when expressed negatively" (n.74). The conclusion indicates that language drawn from creatures as *esse hoc et hoc* must be rejected — it tells us nothing about God. But the language of *esse indistinctum* can and must be predicated of him in positive fashion.

Eckhart's language of indistinction, however, is not the kind of analogical and eminent predication we find in Thomas Aquinas. It is a form of dialectical language and therefore is best manifested through the affirmation that God is the indistinct or absolute One. If, as David Burrell has argued, in Thomas Aquinas divine simpleness (*simplicitas*) is to be conceived of not as an attribute of God, but as a formal feature of divinity,[67] that is, as the foundation for all predicat-ing and not a mere instance of it, then it would seem that indistinc-tion plays an analogous role in Eckhart's God-language, though in a dialectical manner. The dialectical logic of *unum/esse indistinctum* is the norm of all language about God.

In defending this way of talking about God in a key passage in the *Commentary on Exodus*, Eckhart appeals explicitly to both Maimonides and Gabirol, along with a Christian authority, Boethius. As he puts it:

> "No difference at all is or can be in the One, but 'All difference is below the One,' as it says in the *Fountain of Life*, Book 5 [23]. 'That is truly one in which there is no number,' as Boethius says [*On the Trinity* 2]. And Rabbi Moses [*Guide* 1.51], as mentioned above, says that God

---

[66] It is clear from passages found in nn.40, 44, 48, 51, 53, 74, 158, and 161-69 that *esse indistinctum* is not a *dispositio*.

[67] Burrell, *Knowing the Unknowable God*, chap. 3, especially 46-47.

is one 'in all ways and according to every respect,' so that a 'multiplicity either in intellect or in reality,' is not found in him. Anyone who beholds the number two or who beholds distinction does not behold God, for God is one, outside and beyond number, and is not counted with anything."[68]

Although Eckhart did not make as much use of Ibn Gabirol as he did of Maimonides, it is interesting to see him cite both Jewish sages in this passage as resources for his theology of the Indistinct One.[69]

Eckhart's fellow Dominican Berthold of Moosburg, who shared the Meister's view of the full conformity of philosophy and theology,[70] was remarkable for his extensive use of the Jewish Neoplatonism of Gabirol. Berthold's *magnum opus*, the massive *Commentary on the Elements of Theology of Proclus*, now in the process of being edited, is perhaps the most "Gabirolean" of all scholastic works.[71] Further study may help reveal more about the relationship between Berthold's Eckhartian perspective on the relation of philosophy and theology and his openness to Jewish philosophy in the person of Solomon Ibn Gabirol.

---

[68] *Expos. Ex.* n.58 (LW 2:64-65): "In uno autem nulla prorsus cadit nec cadere potest differentia, sed omnis 'differentia sub uno' est, ut dicitur De fonte vitae l. V. 'Hoc enim vere unum est, in quo nullus numerus est,' ut ait Boethius. Et Rabbi Moyses, ut supra dictum est, dicit quod deus est unus 'omnibus modis et secundum omnem rationem,' ita ut in ipso non sit invenire aliquam 'multitudinem in intellectu vel extra intellectum,' l. I c. 50. Qui enim duo vel distinctionem videt, deum non videt. Deus enim unus est, extra numerum et super numerum est nec ponit in numerum cum aliquo."

[69] Eckhart cites the same *auctoritas* from *Fons Vitae* 5.23 *(omnis differentia sub uno est)* in *Expo. Io.* n.389 (LW 3:332). He also appeals to Gabirol's doctrine of God as one in *Expos. Gen.* n.27 (LW 1:205), citing a text from *Fons Vitae* 5.24. For a survey of the role of Gabirol in Eckhart, see Fernand Brunner, "Maitre Eckhart et Avicébron," *Lectionum Varietates. Hommage à Paul Vignaux (1904-1987)* (Paris: Vrin, 1991), 133-52. There is one other place where Eckhart quotes Maimonides and Gabirol together. This appears in his comment on Ex. 33:23 *(Expos. Ex.* n.281 [LW 2:225-26], citing *Fons Vitae* 1.4 and *Guide* 1.58).

[70] Berthold has only begun to attract significant attention over the past two decades. For a survey of his thought and the literature about him, see Alain de Libera, *La mystique rhénane d'Albert le Grand à Maître Eckhart* (Paris: Éditions du Seuil, 1994), 317-442. De Libera studies Berthold's view of the relation of philosophy and theology on 319-26.

[71] The extent of Berthold's use of the *Fons Vitae* will be evident to anyone who peruses the two volumes of his commentary on Proclus's *Elements of Theology* that have thus far appeared in the *Corpus Philosophorum Teutonicorum Medii Aevi*. See *Berthold von Moosburg. Expositio super Elementationem Theologicam Procli*, edd. Maria Rita Pagnoni-Sturlese, Loris Sturlese, and Burkhard Mojsisch (Hamburg: Meiner, 1984-). In Vol. VI, 1, containing Propositions 1-13, the Index auctoritatum lists 77 references to Gabirol, while Vol. VI, 2, containing Propositions 12-34, lists 68.

The text from the Exodus commentary cited above was not peripheral to Eckhart's teaching. The fact that it was included as article 23 of the Papal Bull *In agro dominico* (giving Maimonides the unusual distinction of being condemned as a "Christian" heretic) shows that it is crucial for understanding Eckhart's distinctive form of God-language.[72] For Eckhart, God alone is really One; all that is below him "incurs the guilt of distinction" and difference (n.58) — the "metaphysical fall" characteristic of many forms of Neoplatonism. Any distinction of attributes in God comes totally from the side of our intellect and is not to be found in the *Unum* whose distinction (i.e., transcendence) is his very indistinction, that is, his absolute unity in himself and with all things. As Eckhart put it in his *Commentary on Wisdom*: "Everything which is distinguished by indistinction is the more distinct the more indistinct it is, because it is distinguished by its own indistinction. Conversely, it is the more indistinct the more distinct it is, because it is indistinguished by its own distinction from what is indistinct."[73] Maimonides's apophaticism provided an important basis for the negative pole of this dialectic, just as Aquinas's stress on the eminence of *esse* did for the positive pole. But Meister Eckhart appropriated both forms of God-language within the context his own theory about language's relation to God.

These test cases illustrating the dialogue between Jewish philosophers and Christian schoolmen show us both the achievements and the limitations of such philosophical conversations. Bonaventure had no need of Jewish philosophy, while Albert and Aquinas found Gabirol and Maimonides stimulating discussants who helped them

---

[72] Eckhart defended the truth of this passage both at the Cologne and Avignon trials. In adhering to this teaching about the absolute unicity of God, Eckhart broke with Aquinas (see, e.g., *ST* Ia, q.13, aa.2-4), and also with those, like Giles of Rome in his *Errores Philosophorum*, who singled out Maimonides's refusal to admit "aliquam multitudinem nec re nec ratione" in God as his fundamental error. The first four of the fourteen errors Giles ascribes to Maimonides deal with the lack of multiplicity in God. See *Giles of Rome. Errores Philosophorum*, edited by Josef Koch and translated by John O. Reidl (Milwaukee: Marquette University Press, 1944), 58-60.

[73] *Expos. Sap.* n.154 (LW 2:490): "...omne quod indistinctione distinguitur, quanto est indistinctius, tanto est distinctius; distinguitur enim ipsa indistinctione. Et e converso, quanto distinctius, tanto indistinctius, quia distinctione sua indistinguitur ab indistincto. Igitur quanto distinctius, tanto indistinctius; et quanto indistinctius, tanto distinctius, ut prius." Translation from *Eckhart. Teacher and Preacher*, 169. For more on this dialectical notion of the One, see Bernard McGinn, "Meister Eckhart on God as Absolute Unity," *Neoplatonism and Christian Thought*, ed. Dominic O'Meara (Albany: SUNY, 1982), 129-39.

think through their own approaches to philosophy and theology. This is especially evident in the dialogue between Maimonides and Aquinas, an encounter that continues to spark intellectual interchange between Jews and Christians today. Less studied, but no less challenging for contemporary discussion, was the way in which Eckhart used Jewish philosophers, primarily Maimonides. Given his optimistic view of the unity of philosophy and theology, Eckhart could make more positive use of Maimonides than other scholastic thinkers had, but he did so from his own perspective and for his own purposes. (The same appears to be true in the case of Berthold of Moosburg's use of Gabirol, but this remains to be studied.)

Philosophical dialogue, however, had little or no effect on the growing antipathy and hatred toward the Jews in the late Middle Ages. But as we look back over the history of the relations between the two faiths from our vantage point at the end of the second millennium of the Common Era, these forms of philosophical ecumenism show that there were some moments of genuine discussion and positive appreciation even in the centuries prior to rise of Enlightenment critiques of religious intolerance. Today, as we seek out more substantial grounds, both philosophical and theological, for solidarity between the two faiths these past witnesses are still worth pondering.

CHRISTIAN COLONIALISM:
LUTHER'S EXEGESIS OF HEBREW SCRIPTURE

Andrew Colin Gow*

I. *Colonizing the Past*

In colonial hegemonic relationships, the colonizer attempts to control access to the inheritance of cultural and other legacies. One means of doing so is to deny the validity of, say, an aboriginal religion; another is to prevent individuals or cultural groups from learning and appropriating their heritage. The goals can vary from promoting assimilation to mainstream society to exercising control over subjects who cannot be assimilated.[1] Colonial approaches to the past of subordinate or minority groups, as Siân Jones has recently argued in an eminently practical context, generally produce "the critical scrutiny of a minority group's identity and history by the dominant society, rather than vice versa, ultimately perpetuating the relations of power between groups".[2] Medieval Christian attitudes toward Judaism were consistently "colonial" in regard both to Jewish existence and to Jewish tradition, especially concerning biblical texts. Nicholas Donin, Peter Schwartz (Petrus Niger)

---

* Associate Professor of History, University of Alberta
[1] The burgeoning genre of "post-colonial" theory and the literature on related themes, nowhere more hegemonic than in literature studies, has produced a vogue for the study of colonial relationships from this theoretical angle. Although most historians are indifferent to this and other dominant approaches in other humanities departments, those working on actual colonial topics have been quick to appreciate and appropriate for their own use the theoretical implications (and claims) of post-colonial studies. Thomas Metcalf, for instance, has argued that "throughout the late nineteenth century, the British sought to comprehend, and thus control, the colonial peoples and their past." "Architecture and the Representation of Empire: India, 1860-1910", in: *Representations* 6 (Spring 1984), 37-65; 40. This quasi-Foucauldian model provides a useful way to conceptualize the process whereby Christian Hebraists, often aided by Jewish converts to Christianity, sought to comprehend and thus control the Hebrew Scriptures. Roger Chartier has provided a helpful model and an analysis of the process of cultural appropriation in *Cultural history: between practices and representations*, trans. by Lydia G. Cochrane (Cambridge, UK: Polity Press, 1988).
[2] *The Archaeology of Ethnicity. Constructing Identities in the Past and Present* (London/New York: Routledge, 1997), 142.

and many others argued that Talmudic Judaism was a corruption of the true religion of Israel, and thus that contemporary Jews were no more the legitimate seed of Abraham than Christians were; perhaps even less so.[3] Confiscating and burning the Talmud, under the aegis of Donin or of the Cologne Dominicans, were acts of colonial dominance made conceivable by Christian hegemony over "truth", Judaism and Jews themselves. Not merely oppression, then, but appropriation, redefinition and delegitimization have been central strategies in traditional (and some contemporary) Christian dealings with Jews and Judaism. Without wishing to suggest that Christianity has sinned against Judaism by interpreting Hebrew Scripture differently than Jews do, I would like to suggest that it might be useful to consider the extent to which Christian exegetes need to deny the validity of Jewish understanding of Hebrew Scripture in order to justify either Christianity itself or Christian attitudes toward Judaism. Thus, I will propose both historical and theological evaluations of a number of crucial moments in Christian exegesis of Hebrew Scripture.

II. *Supercession and Appropriation*

The standard Christian trope that characterized Judaism as past, as superseded, certainly was no medieval invention, but dates from the first centuries of Christian community and canon formation.[4]

---

[3] See Peter Schwartz (Petrus Niger), *Der Stern Meschiach* (Esslingen: Conradus Feyner, 1477). In *The Archaeology of Ethnicity*, Jones notes: "[M]inority groups are subjected to a relentless discourse which requires them, in one form or another, to possess a traditional homogeneous culture and identity stretching back in a continuous fashion into the past." (142). She notes that many groups will necessarily fail to clear this excessively high ontological hurdle. There seems to be a long tradition of such scrutiny, reaching back into pre-colonial European encounters with 'Others'. Jones' ideas also elucidate part of the motivation behind some of the recent attempts to show that Ashkenazic Jews descend largely from Turkic groups such as the Khazars. An even more radical version of this impulse can be found in the ideas of the 'British Israelite' movement (and its counterparts among current-day white supremacists), which claims that the British are the true sons of Abraham's covenant (b'rit-ish, 'covenant man') and the Jews are merely interlopers (or worse, the spawn of Satan).

[4] Robert Chazan, *Medieval Stereotypes and Modern Antisemitism* (Berkeley: University of California Press, 1997), 102ff, and see the literature cited on page 162, note 14; Rosemary Radford Ruether, "The *Adversus Judaeos* Tradition in the Church Fathers: The Exegesis of Christian Anti-Semitism", in: *Essential papers on Judaism and Christianity in conflict, from late antiquity to the Reformation*, ed. by Jeremy Cohen (New York: New

The church Fathers were forced to deal extensively and intensively with the issue of Jewish Scripture and Jewish "rejection" of Jesus as Messiah. In the Middle Ages, the popular and widespread depiction in two and three dimensions of the victorious Church triumphing over the defeated Synagogue (often shown as blind-folded or blinded, holding a broken spear) made clear, in public, the relationship between Christian and Jewish faiths in the past and in the present.[5] Seeking to comprehend, and thus to control the Hebrew Scriptures was part of the same project that sought to discredit Jewish religion, Biblical learning, and exegesis. Medieval Christian exegesis pointed beyond the "literal" or historical sense to the allegorical, mystical and eschatological (or *heilsgeschichtlich*) Christian senses of the Christian and Hebrew scriptures. Medieval theology in the west continued and intensified early Christian attitudes to Judaism as having been superceded by Jesus, the Gospels, and hence, by Christianity.[6]

However, in the high Middle Ages, the Victorines recognized the validity of Jewish exegesis in literal interpretation and developed the search for the literal sense of Scripture as the foundation of all the other, "higher-order" senses. Although few exegetes in this tradition bothered to learn Hebrew, many recognized and copied the rabbinical references they found in Andrew of St. Victor and, later, in Nicholas of Lyra. Protestant theologians — Luther first and foremost — called for a return to Scripture as the first priority of Christian knowledge and as the source of faith. Luther's dictum *sola scriptura* produced a renewed emphasis on *biblical* texts (to the relative exclusion of the Fathers and Doctors), especially on the Christian Scriptures. This in turn called attention to Jewish understandings of Hebrew Scripture. While "Scripture alone" was the central principle

York University Press, 1991), 174-189; Alan Davies, ed., *Antisemitism and the Foundations of Christianity* (New York: Paulist Press, 1979); Rosemary Radford Ruether, *Faith and Fratricide. The Theological Roots of Anti-Semitism* (New York: Seabury Press, 1974); Beryl Smalley, *The study of the Bible in the Middle Ages.* 3rd ed., rev. (Oxford: Basil Blackwell, 1983).

[5] See Wolfgang Seiferth, *Synagogue and Church in the Middle Ages; Two Symbols in Art and Literature,* trans. by Lee Chadeayne and Paul Gottwald (New York: Ungar, 1970); for a study of this theme in literature, see Friedrich Ohly, "Synagoge und Ecclesia. Typologisches in mittelalterlicher Dichtung", in: *Schriften zur mittelalterlichen Bedeutungsforschung* (Darmstadt, 1977), 312-337.

[6] For the medieval period, see Bernard Blumenkranz, "The Roman Church and the Jews", in: Cohen, ed., *Essential papers*, 193-230.

of Luther's exegesis, it did not necessarily mean Scripture *first*,[7] as we shall see in what follows.

Luther believed that the meaning of Scripture is clear, univocal, open and simple,[8] thus not subject to endless debate and dissection. This point was usually directed against the Catholic "tradition of the Church," but it also served to discredit (often intricate and complex) rabbinical and Talmudic exegesis. While Luther was certainly not the only Protestant reformer interested in the Hebrew Scriptures — Calvin wrote many volumes of commentary on them as well —, his treatment of the "Old Testament" and of Jewish exegesis is by far the best known and most cited within the academy and beyond. For this reason, Luther's interpretation of Hebrew Scripture will receive the lion's share of attention in this brief study.

The debate over the context of Luther's utterances, late and early, concerning Jews and Judaism, moved in the 1970s and '80s from theological to broader readings, yet the *method* of Luther's exegesis has received little attention in recent years.[9] The beginning point of this contribution to the analysis and evaluation of Luther's exegesis of Hebrew Scripture is Wilhelm Maurer's view that the primary subject of Luther's later treatises (in terms of sheer volume and in terms of emphasis) is the correct interpretation of Hebrew Scripture — and this is a crucial insight whether or not one seeks to separate Luther's later *theological* work from his civic politics.

Luther's late works are essentially theological and must be read

---

[7] Karl Holl has formulated the problem sharply as a case of circular thought: "One must possess the Spirit in order to understand the Word, but it is the Word alone through which one attains to the Spirit. Through the Word and only through the Word is it possible to penetrate to the heart of the matter [die Sache; cf. *res*!]; but on the other hand, one must come into contact with the heart of the matter, with God and Christ, in order to understand the meaning of the words" (my translation). "Luthers Bedeutung für den Fortschritt der Auslegungskunst", in: *Gesammelte Aufsätze zur Kirchengeschichte*, vol. 1, 'Luther' (Tübingen, 1923), 544ff., 567.

[8] "Scriptura [...] ipsa per sese certissima, facillima, apertissima, sui ipsius interpres, omnium omnia probans, iudicans et illuminans." (Holy Scripture [is] on its own most definite, simple, open, its own interpreter, testing, judging and elucidating all things). *Assertio omnium articulorum M. Lutheri per bullam Leonis X. novissimam damnatorum*, in: *D. Martin Luthers Werke. Kritische Gesamtausgabe*, 60 vols. (Weimar: H. Böhlau, 1883-1980) [hereafter *WA*] 7,97,23.

[9] See Mark U. Edwards, Jr., "Against the Jews", in: Cohen, ed., *Essential papers*, 345-37; Heiko A. Oberman, *The Roots of Anti-Semitism in the Age of Renaissance and Reformation*, trans. James I. Porter (Philadelphia: Fortress Press, 1984); Wilhelm Maurer, "Die Zeit der Reformation", in: *Kirche und Synagoge*, ed. by. Karl-Heinrich Rengstorf and Siegfried von Kortzfleisch (Stuttgart, 1968), vol I, 363-452.

theologically. Yet Maurer insists that any deep "theological insights"[10] contained in Luther's treatise *Against the Jews and their Lies* cannot be "saved" or separated from their virulently antisemitic context.[11] Thus, any artificial, often confessionally motivated attempt to extract time-less theological nuggets from the dross of Luther's gross prejudices (at least as revealed in his late writings on the Jews and Judaism) is both anachronistic and fundamentally harmful to Jewish-Christian rela-tions. Maser notes that Luther's writings on the Jews are essentially nothing other than treatments of the relevant much-debated passages from the Bible.[12] Central to Luther's approach to Judaism throughout his career and especially in the late treatises was the entirely conven-tional belief that Judaism had been replaced, superceded, by Chris-tianity.

Among the "reformers", supercession was not exclusive to Luther by any means. John Calvin, for instance, preached concerning Deuteronomy 12:

> "The ceremony [of sacrifice] belonged to the time of the Law: today we are content with the truth, and we know, since our Lord Jesus Christ has appeared to us, that we no longer need a material temple to be able to say that God is with us."[13]

Yet "supercession" does not exhaust Christian attitudes to pre-Chris-tian Biblical contents and figures. The patriarchs and prophets are frequently claimed by Christian interpreters as precursors, even as members of the *communio sanctorum*,[14] especially after the thirteenth

---

[10] Wilhelm Maurer, *Kirche und Synagoge. Motive und Formen der Auseinandersetzung der Kirche mit dem Judentum im Laufe der Geschichte* (Stuttgart, 1953), 47.

[11] Peter Maser, "Luthers Schriftauslegung im Traktat 'Von den Juden und ihren Lügen' (1543). Ein Beitrag zum 'christologischen Antisemitismus' des Reformators", in *Judaica* 29 (1973), 71-84, 149-167; 72ff.

[12] Maser, "Luthers Schriftauslegung", 152.

[13] "La ceremonie en estoit du temps de la Loy: auiourd'huy contentons-nous de la verité, et cognoissons, puisque nostre Seigneur Iesus Christ est apparu, qu'il ne faut plus de temple materiel pour dire que Dieu est avec nous [...]." *Ioannis Calvini opera quae supersint omnia*, ed. G. Baum, E. Cunitz, E. Reuss (Brunswick: C.A. Schwetschke, 1863ff.) [hereafter *Calvini opera*], 27, 174, Sermon 81.

[14] An example from the 1482 fresco cycle in the dome of the cathedral at Siena demonstrates the tension inherent in such depictions. Arrayed around the dome, forty-two prophets and patriarchs make up the highest place in the cycle of images in the cathedral. Each figure is crowned with a halo, recalling the medieval custom of including these Hebrew Bible figures in the litany for All Saints' Day. See Friedrich Ohly's discussion of these figures in his study "Die Kathedrale als Zeitenraum", in: *Schriften zur mittelalterlichen Bedeutungsforschung* (Darmstadt, 1977), 171-273; 228-229.

century. Not merely triumph and supercession of the old by the new, but appropriation and refiguration are apparent in standard Christian uses (artistic, liturgical) of Hebrew figures such as the patriarchs and prophets. Yet we will also see that texts are more slippery than it might appear from these preliminaries, and close exegesis can both use and refute Jewish readings of Scripture to make polemical points. Crucial to a better understanding of medieval and Reformation-era Christian exegesis of Hebrew Scripture is a sense not only of *why* it was done as it was, but also *how*.

III. *'Qui notitiam rei non habet, illum notitia nominis non sublevabit'*

Martin Luther disagreed strongly with Jewish interpretations of Scripture and built his objections into both his exegetical works and his religio-political polemic. In claiming the Hebrew Bible as well as the New Testament not just for Christian readers, but for Christian truth, Luther was continuing an unbroken tradition of medieval exegesis that was Christological, polemical, and supercessionist.[15]

Of the voluminous literature on anti-Judaism and anti-Semitism in the early modern period — the final era of mass "ethnic cleansing" (from Spain) and repeated expulsions from western Europe — a fairly large proportion of the total is devoted to studying the eschatological and pastoral goal of converting as many Jews as possible to Christianity.[16] Late in Luther's life, reports of Christian "judaizing" or

Ohly's overly neat distinction between the sibylls, representing the "Old Time" (in the floor) and the other images in the church, which are otherwise from the Christian Scriptures, representing the "New Time", fails at this crucial juncture: both the sibylls (specifically the Tirburtine sibyll) and the patriarchs/prophets functioned as precursors to Christianity in medieval theology, and as authorities in their own right: the much-cited formula "teste David cum Sibylla" demonstrates the conceptual and functional closeness of these groups. See Bernard McGinn, *Visions of the End. Apocalyptic Traditions in the Middle Ages* (New York: Columbia University Press, 1979), 20. Richard Emmerson notes that during the Middle Ages the Sibylline Oracles, whether Christian in origin or not, were often considered to have been divinely inspired: *Antichrist in the Middle Ages: a study of medieval apocalypticism, art, and literature* (Seattle: University of Washington Press, 1981), 47.

[15] See, for example, Jeremy Cohen, "Traditional Prejudice and Religious Reform: The Theological and Historical Foundations of Luther's Anti-Judaism", in: Sander Gilman and Steven Katz, eds., *Antisemitism in Times of Crisis* (New York: New York University Press, 1991), 81-102.

[16] On the eschatological content of Luther's attitude toward Jews and Judaism,

even conversion to Judaism all over Europe, from the Czech lands to Poland, impelled him in 1538 to write *Against the Sabbatarians*,[17] in which he attempted to win back "new" Jews by characterizing Judaism as dead, superseded.[18] As Stephen Burnett has recently argued, following in Heiko Oberman's footsteps, Luther was far more afraid of Jewish biblical interpretation than of the evil that could be wrought by actual Jews themselves: Jews could not really harm Christians except with "falsehoods" concerning the Scriptures.[19] Civic toleration was the line Luther preached until late in his life: Oberman argues that Luther's attitude toward real Jews, right up until the publication of *On the Jews and their Lies* (1543),[20] was that they were to be tolerated so long as they did not missionize, did not attempt to hold public office or interfere with Christians. From the 1543 pamphlets on, and in his tract *An Admonition against the Jews*, a short treatise appended to his last sermon (February 15th, 1546), Luther counsels Christian magistrates no longer to tolerate not so much the *practices* of Jews as their *attitudes and beliefs*, because the latter were dangerous to Christian belief and blasphemous. Those who refused to convert were to be expelled. Naturally, any remaining synagogues and Jewish holy books were to be destroyed.[21] As Oberman

---

see for example chapter 17, "The Jews at the End of Time", of Oberman's *The Roots of Anti-Semitism*, 118-122. The recent literature on Luther and the Jews includes a number of monographic treatments, e.g. Johannes Brosseder, *Luthers Stellung zu den Juden im Spiegel seiner Interpreten. Interpretation und Rezeption von Luthers Schriften und Äusserungen zum Judentum im 19. und 20. Jahrhundert vor allem im deutschsprachigen Raum* (Munich, 1972) and a volume edited by Heinz Kremers, *Die Juden und Martin Luther—Martin Luther und die Juden: Geschichte, Wirkungsgeschichte, Herausforderung* (Neukirchen, 1985). Among older studies, Joachim Rogge's article "Luthers Stellung zu den Juden", in *Luther* 40 (1969), 12-24 and Reinhold Lewin, *Luthers Stellung zu den Juden. Ein Beitrag zur Geschichte der Juden in Deutschland während des Reformationszeitalters* (Berlin, 1911; reprint Aalen, 1973) deserve to be read carefully.

[17] *Wider die sabbather an einen guten Freund* (1538), WA 50, 312-337.

[18] *Ibid.*, WA 50, 313, 12-15. See Oberman, *The Roots of Antisemitism*, 118-119.

[19] Stephen Burnett, "Reformation-Era Christian Hebraism at a Crossroads: Martin Luther, Sebastian Münster, and the Proper Use of Jewish Biblical Commentaries", a paper presented at the Sixteenth Century Studies Conference, Toronto, October 1998, the complete text of which was generously made available to me by the author.

[20] *Von den Juden und ihren Lügen*, WA 53, 417-552. 1543 also saw the publication of the pamphlets *Vom Schem Hamphoras* (WA 53, 579-648) and *Von den letzten Wurten Davids* (WA 54, 28-100). In the latter, Luther argues, against rabbinical exegesis of the Hebrew Bible, that Hebrew Messianic prophecies refer to Jesus.

[21] The latter recommendations are found in *On the Jews and their Lies*, WA 53, 522ff. See Oberman, *The Roots of Anti-Semitism*, 121. The late treatises against the

has argued repeatedly and in the face of considerable opposition, none of this is to suggest that the "earlier" Luther, say of the mission-izing 1523 pamphlet *That our Lord Jesus Christ was a born Jew*,[22] was actually "friendly" toward Jews and then in his dotage decided to hate them: on the contrary, his attitudes to Jews and Judaism throughout his career as reformer are based more on his opposition to Jewish understandings of Scripture than on his reaction to flesh-and-blood Jews.[23]

Crucial to Luther's views on Jewish exegesis of the Hebrew scrip-tures is Luther's Christology, the core of Luther's theology because Luther's notion of the *scopus* of Scripture is closely tied to the expe-rience of salvation. Jesus is the *scopus* of Scripture: "Everything in Scripture is everywhere about Christ alone."[24] As the antisemitic Erich Vogelsang put it, hitting the mark — for all the wrong rea-sons — "For Luther, the 'Jewish question' [*Judenfrage*] is first and last the question of Christ".[25] Furthermore, to Luther, scriptural exegesis is always easy and straightforward because the result is pre-determined by the truth of Christ: "Take Christ out of the Scrip-tures and what more will you find in them?"[26] If read through Christological lenses, the Hebrew Bible (understood as the Old Testament) prophesies the advent of Jesus as Messiah. This is, of course, scarcely novel: it is part of the Gospel foundation of tradi-

---

Jews were used by the Nazis to great effect: see, for example, Walther Linden, *Luthers Kampfschriften gegen das Judentum* (Berlin: Klinckhardt, 1936) and other items cited by Maser, "Luthers Schriftauslegung", 83, note 6.

[22] *Daß Jesus Christus ein geborner Jude sei. WA* 11, 307-336.

[23] E.g., Oberman, *The Roots of Anti-Semitism*, 128, note 26; Oberman claims that on the other hand, many specialized studies, such as Peter Maser's article "Luthers Schriftauslegung" are marred by a concentration on the later pamphlets as though they were representative of Luther's views in general. This does not quite do justice to Maser's solid but repetitive survey. Luther's attitude to the Jews as reported by Nazi propaganda relies almost exclusively on the late pamphlets (e.g., Martin Sasse, ed., *Martin Luther über die Juden: Weg mit ihnen!* (Freiburg, 1938); there is no space here for a broader bibliography). The literature tends to fall into neat camps: either Luther 'woke up' to 'Jewish perfidy' (imagined or actual); or he was always against either Judaism or Jews. There has been strong reaction to Oberman's distinction and sense that Luther's attitude is continuous; however, none of these reactions stands up to close scrutiny. See also my discussion *infra* of the term *alma* in the 1523 treatise.

[24] "Universa Scriptura de solo Christo est ubique." *WA* 46, 414,15; cf. *WA* 53, 468,28. See Volkmar Herntrich, "Luther und das alte Testament", in: *Lutherjahrbuch* 20 (1938), 93-124, esp. 96ff.

[25] *Luthers Kampf gegen die Juden* (Tübingen, 1933), 9.

[26] 26 "Tolle Christum e scripturis, quid amplius in illis invenies?" *WA* 18, 606,24; cf. Maser, "Luthers Schriftauslegung", 155.

tional Christianity.[27] Yet one wonders if being a Christian necessitates dismissing practically all Jewish exegesis of the Hebrew Bible, especially of its prophetic materials and references. This would seem to have been the case for Luther in particular and for Christians in Luther's time in general. Luther is *adding* nothing to traditional Christianity when he reads Hebrew Scripture Christologically. As Jeremy Cohen has recently shown, Luther brought little that was new to his exegesis of the Hebrew Bible.[28] Yet his readings of Scripture are uniquely powerful and have exercized a very considerable influence on Lutheranism and on Protestant theology as a whole.

Luther asserted unequivocally, in accordance with the tradition of the Gospels, Fathers and Doctors, that the Christian Bible was the correct guide and lens through which to read the Hebrew Scriptures. Informally, he disqualified Jewish exegesis on the grounds that Jews are "the greatest enemies of the Bible".[29] In the introduction to *On the*

---

[27] As David Steinmetz trenchantly opined in response to an earlier version of this paper delivered at the Sixteenth Century Studies Conference (Toronto, October 1998), accusing Luther of reading the Hebrew Bible in this way is merely to accuse him of being a Christian. However, there is a difference between a *divergent* reading of Hebrew Scripture and a hostile blanket *disqualification* of Jewish exegesis, as Uwe Bauer argues (q.v. *infra*).

[28] "Traditional Prejudice and Religious Reform", 83.

[29] "Die Juden meinen, wir mussen von inen die bibliam studirn. Ja wol! Solten wir bibliam lernen ab eis, qui sunt summi hostes bibliae? Ich sehe wol, wo unser Hebrei hinaus wollen. Sie wolten gern, das wir unser neu testament solten vorliern und das niemer hetten. Drumb sehe ein ittlicher auff dasselbige uleissig. Das wirt in das alte wol lernen vorsthen. Wenn Moses sagt von dem Christo, so nem ich in an; sonst soll er mir nichts sein. So sagt Christus: in Moses und propheten de me scriptum est." (The Jews say that we should study their Bible. Yes indeed! Should we learn about the Bible from them, who are the greatest enemies of the Bible? I see all too well what our Hebrews want. They would be happy if we were to lose our New Testament and have it no more. So everyone should take special care to [study] it diligently. It will teach him well to understand the Old [Testament]. When Moses speaks of Christ, I accept him; otherwise he is of no interest to me. Thus says Christ: It is written about me in Moses and the prophets.) Martin Luther, *Tischreden. Kritische Gesamtausgabe*, ed. by Karl Drescher, 6 vols. (Weimar, H. Böhlaus Nachfolger, 1912-21), 5, 220, 25-31 (5535), winter 1542-43. In 1546, he calls the Jews "Gottes worts Feinde" [enemies of God's word] because they interpret Scripture differently: *WA* 53, 436,11). Calvin was similarly hostile about Jewish exegesis, referring in this case (not surprisingly) to Isaiah 7,14: "Locus satis notus est ac celebris, cap. 7,14: sed Iudaei pro solita sua malitia eum [Isaiah's prophecy, his *vaticinium*] depravant..." (The passage is well enough known and famous, chapter 7, verse 14: but the Jews, by their usual ill-will distort [Isaiah's prophecy]...) *Commentarius in Harmoniam Evangelicam*, Matthew I, *Calvini opera*, 45, 66.

Jews and their Lies, he wrote: "It is not my intention to quibble with the Jews or learn from them how they interpret and understand Scripture, as I know all that very well already. Even less do I seek to convert the Jews, as that is impossible."[30] However, between reading the prophets and psalms Christologically and accepting only Jewish readings of the same material there is a huge gulf; one that might have room for alternatives. This is not to suggest that Luther should or could have thought differently about Jewish exegesis; only that his ideas had a history, were contingent; that their partialness might have had some important consequences; and that present-day Christians and Jews might need to revisit these questions.

Writing about anti-Jewish interpretations of Psalm 1 in the works of Luther and in modern German Protestant exegesis, Uwe Bauer has paved the way for a respectful Christian understanding of Jewish exegesis of the Hebrew Bible.[31] According to Bauer, Protestant readings of the Hebrew Bible since Luther have too often read Christian contexts into Hebrew texts, failed to respect Jewish religious sensibilities and exegesis, and contributed materially to anti-Judaic attitudes in Protestant communities. The same might well be said about most Christian exegesis of Hebrew Bible texts *before* the Reformation, but the reasons and techniques used relate to slightly different goals. Protestant exegesis has frequently aimed at opposing Jewish "law"[32] to "grace" and to the Gospels; and at equating Mosaic "Law" with Roman "legalism".[33] Thus, Luther's approach to Jewish Scripture

---

[30] "Es ist mein furhaben nicht, das ich wollte mit den Jüden zancken oder von jnen lernen, wie sie die Schrifft deuten oder verstehen, Ich weis das alles vorhin wol. Viel weniger gehe ich damit umb, das ich die Jüden bekehren wolle, Denn das ist unmüglich." *WA* 53, 417,20. The last sentence betrays, of course, a very different agenda from the hopeful missionary one pursued in the 1523 treatise *That Jesus Christ was a born Jew*.

[31] Uwe F. W. Bauer, "Anti-Jewish Interpretations of Psalm 1 in Luther and in Modern German Protestantism", in: *The Journal of Hebrew Scriptures* [ISSN 1203-1542], available on-line at http://www.ualberta.ca/ARTS/JHS/Articles/article8.htm#t2

[32] *Lex* is a tendentious traditional translation of *torah*, which is more accurately rendered as guide, path. Luther's typological distinction between unfulfillable 'Law' and gracious Gospel—not his invention but characteristically his by dint of insistence—makes his understanding of Jewish 'law' more useful for polemical purposes than accurate for theological or scholarly ones.

[33] In *On the Jews and their Lies*, Papists, *Schwärmer* and Muslims often form one conglomerate of error, misled by Satan, unwilling to understand Scripture as Luther does; the same has been observed by Reinhold Lewin for the conglomerate Turks, Jews and the Pope in other of Luther's writings: Bauer, *Luthers Stellung zu den Juden*, 48, note 7.

was bound up not only with Christian imperatives regarding Christology, but also with inner-Christian debates regarding authority, ritual, liturgy, grace and the path to salvation. If the "unfulfillable" demands of Roman "legalism" were merely half-digested Jewish "Law", all the more reason to insist on grace as the blade that cuts the Gordian knot. Taking either a Christian polemic view of Talmudic observance or the priestly emphasis (post-Babylonian or Second Temple period) on ritual observance and purity as representative of a single Jewish "theology" [sic], and ignoring prophetic[34] and many later rabbinic preferences for an ethics-based observance, is one way to depict Judaism as "legalistic", especially if the prophetic passages that urge personal and ethical observance are interpreted Christologically and not in their historical Hebrew context.

If knowledge is power, to speak with the modern French philosopher, how much more so was knowledge of the Bible and of what it "really" meant a central form of religious truth, cultural capital and political might in the pre-modern world? Reformation "Biblicism" has received much attention from scholars interested mainly in what was new about Protestant approaches to biblical texts and their uses.[35] But the continuity between medieval and early modern uses of biblical texts as the best-authorized inspired source of religious truth, cultural capital and political legitimation has received rather less attention.[36]

---

[34] E.g., Jeremiah 31:31 ff.

[35] Part of the blame must be assigned to Protestant triumphalist readings of late-medieval piety and atttitudes to the Bible. One of the main culprits is the venerable Jaroslav Pelikan, who insists that Luther's translation "liberated the Bible", e.g. most recently in: *The reformation of the Bible, the Bible of the Reformation: a catalog of the exhibition by V. R. Hotchkiss and D. Price.* New Haven: Yale University Press; Dallas: Bridwell Library, 1996. On Reformation 'Biblicism', see David C. Steinmetz, ed., *The Bible in the Sixteenth Century* (Durham: Duke University Press, 1990).

[36] See Michael Milway's entry "German Bible Translations" in the *Encyclopedia of the Renaissance* (forthcoming) for an idea of the wealth of German Bible translations available before the Reformation. Milway's count of incunabula (published before 1500) elsewhere in this volume shows that the second-largest genre of text published in book form before the Reformation (after liturgical handbooks, missals and breviaries) consisted of Biblical texts, glosses, and translations—over 800 editions! The existing literature on the medieval Bible (e.g., Beryl Smalley, *The study of the Bible in the Middle Ages* [3rd ed., rev. Oxford: Basil Blackwell. 1983], P. Riché and G. Lobrichon, eds., *Le Moyen Age et la Bible* [Paris: Beauchesne, 1984. (= La Bible de tous les temps, 4)], and W. Lourdaux and D. Verhelst, eds., *The Bible and Medieval Culture* [Louvain: Louvain University Press, 1979]) ignores the fifteenth century almost entirely. The few works on this topic are quite old, e.g. Franz Falk, *Die Bibel am Ausgange des Mittelalters, ihre Kenntnis und ihre Verbreitung* (Cologne: Bachem, 1905) and Erich Zimmermann, *Die deutsche Bibel im religiösen Leben des Spätmittelalters* (Potsdam: Akademische Verlagsgesellschaft Athenaion, 1938).

Luther participated in the "medieval" (or rather, traditional) attitude concerning the true meaning of Scripture and lost no opportunity to describe Jewish exegesis and understanding of Scripture as dead, lifeless, lacking in Spirit, sterile, enslaved to the letter. His animosity spilled over into his attitude to one of the few medieval scholars whose work he used and cited with approval on occasion, Nicholas of Lyra,[37] partly because Lyra often drew from Jewish exegesis to help make sense of difficult passages.[38] According to an old Latin-school saw, *"si Lyra non lyrasset, Lutherus non saltasset."*[39] It is true that Luther often danced to a tune that Lyra had composed two hundred years earlier, but Luther used some fancy footwork and did not hesitate to skip a beat when the music offended him.

Nicholas of Lyra has long been reputed the foremost medieval defender, in the tradition of Andrew of St. Victor and the Victorines, of the literal interpretation of scripture — as the basis on which all 'spiritual' interpretation must be founded in order to be accurate. For this reason he has also been seen as the central link in the chain that unites medieval and historical-critical scholarship.[40] The literal approach meant that spiritual interpretations of Hebrew scriptures had to depend on careful textual analysis of the Hebrew originals. As James Morey has noted in his ground-breaking work on Peter Comestor:

> "The point to make here is that Christian doctors, confused over some obscure Biblical verses, turned to their Hebrew counterparts for an explanation not only as the *Glossa* took form but also in the later twelfth (with Peter) and fourteenth (with Nicholas) centuries."[41]

Luther was able to read Hebrew Scripture in a way that took Hebrew terms seriously and literally in their original context, if it suited his polemical or confessional purposes. When he did so, he was

---

[37] In *On the Jews and their Lies*, Luther mentions Lyra a number of times: *WA* 53 417,24; 476,17; 480,1; 482,22; 489,10; 498,28.

[38] Luther saw in Lyra's understanding of the literal sense as the historical-factual one the danger of succumbing to Jewish exegetical methods; Maser, "Luthers Schriftauslegung", 159.

[39] If Lyra had not played his lyre, Luther would not have danced [to the tune].

[40] A. Kleinhans, *Lexikon für Theologie und Kirche*, vol. 7, col. 992f: Lyra was "der beste Exeget des späteren Mittelalters und der Ring, der die Exegese des Mittelalters mit der der Neuzeit verbindet."

[41] Peter Morey, "Peter Comestor, Biblical Paraphrase and the Medieval Popular Bible", in *Speculum* 68,1 (January 1993), 6-35; 14.

able to rely on a rich tradition of medieval undertandings *ad litteram* of important Biblical texts. Hugh's, Comestor's and Lyra's literal readings of the Noah's ark story were central to later-medieval and early modern understandings and depictions of the ark *per se*,[42] aside from all allegorical, tropological or eschatological significance, and to Luther's extremely straightforward reading *ad litteram* of the description of the ark as a *teva*, or box, in Gen. 6-9. Luther attempted to close debate on the ancient and perennial subject of what the ark might have looked like, how big it must have been to hold seven pairs of each of the clean animals and one pair each of all the others, how the manure and food might have been handled, etc. In both academic lecturing and public preaching on Genesis, he cuts discussion off with the *sententia* that the ark was not a boat, nor should it be called an "ark" (*Arche*) henceforth, but a box — "ut ein sargk", like a coffin.[43] And so it was depicted in early Luther Bibles and Protestant propaganda, with the commanding title "Der kaste(n) Noe" (Noah's box).[44] This decisive break with a long pictorial tradition in which the ark was generally represented as a boat or a building on a boat is both a new development conditioned by text-centered Reformation exegesis *and* the logical extension of the medieval tradition of literal

---

[42] This topic will be treated in a separate article currently in preparation. See, for example, Peter Comestor, *Historia scholastica*, "[...] habuit enim quinque cameras, quas Augustinus etiam, praeter sentinam dicit ibi fuisse [...]. Una enim camerarum erat stercoraria, altera apothecaria, et super haec mansionem erat alia tracamerata. Laterales camerae erant una immitium, altera mitium animalium, media hominum, et avium." *Patrologiae cursus completus, Series latina*, ed. J.-P. Migne (Paris, 1844-64), 198, 1083. This was perhaps the most influential description of the ark in the Middle Ages, and certainly one of the most widespread; Lyra follows it closely in his *Postilla perpetuae*.

[43] "Audistis, quomodo deus omnipotens iratus fuit ob mundi nequitiam et praecepit Noe edificare arcam, quia volebat perdere mundum. Iam videbimus edificium arcae et quae fuerit fides Noe, 3° quid hec significent. De longitudine etc. dicit textus, praesertim exprimit personas, quae erant 8. Arca est latina dictio, nos germani proprie kasten oder lange laden. [...] Hoc torserunt huc, quod Christum haben wollen drauß machen. Er ist schlecht vier ecken gewest sine tecto, ut ein sargk. [...] Velim, in mundo esset mos, ut kast vocaretur, non arca. Haec est edificatio." *Predigten über das erste Buch Mose, gehalten 1523/24*, *WA* 14, 188.

[44] In *Das alte testament Deutsch* (Wittenberg, 1523), the ark has "Der kaste Noe" painted on the roof; this image was reprinted in the Strassburg Bible of 1524. Another chest-ark appears in *Die fünff Buch Mose des alten testaments teutsch* (Augsburg, 1523) and is reprinted in the 1537 Ingolstadt Bible. Thomas Wolff's Basel reprinting of 1524 contains this woodcut by Hans Holbein the Younger of "Noah's chest". See Phillip Schmidt, *Die Illustration der Lutherbibel 1522-1700. Ein Stück abendländische Kultur und Kirchengeschichte* (Basel: Verlag Friedrich Reinhardt, 1962), 159.

exegesis. The effect was to break with centuries of artistic and official exegesis in the interest of Biblical accuracy and truth. It is worth noting that Luther explicitly rejects Christological readings of the ark/"box" itself as a *figura* of Christ because he feels they are overdrawn and not warranted by the text. Lyra's influence on Luther was definite and commanding, but as one recent commentator has argued, perhaps a bit less straightforward than the image of Luther dancing after the Pied Piper suggests.[45]

Lyra's insistence, in the tradition of the school of St. Victor, on literal meaning did not exclude an interest in the spiritual meaning of Scripture. After completing his close reading *ad litteram* of the entire Bible in his monumental *Postilla super totam bibliam* (1322-1331), he composed a much briefer *Postilla moralis* (or *mystica*, 1334-1339). However, his main concern was to establish the literal meaning of words and language: the "sensus literalis seu historicus", which must be correct for the other senses to be findable. For the Hebrew Bible, he followed the Hebrew and Aramaic texts, and called frequently on Jewish exegetes, especially Rashi (rabbi Shlomo ben Yitchak, 1040-1105).[46] The historical sense, meaning what the author meant when he wrote it down, and the *sensus literalis* may not be quite the same, but they were close enough for Nicholas. Knowledge of this fundamental building block of truth was meant to place the exegetical enterprise on a firm foundation, not to undermine it. However, as we will see, asking Jews, especially learned commentators like Rashi, for their understanding of particularly thorny passages, often opened the way for destabilizing readings of texts that had been invested with Christian certainty — all the more so since they were unclear either in the original or in the Vulgate, and frequently in both.

Martin Luther interpreted Biblical texts in light of contextual clues ("*sola* fide") and according to traditional Christological methods[47] as

---

[45] T. Kalita, *The Influence of Nicholas of Lyra on Martin Luther's Commentary on Genesis* (Diss. Catholic University of America), Washington, 1985 (UMI 8515077).

[46] See Franz Böhmisch, "Raschi und Nicolaus de Lyra in der Auslegung der Genesis" (www.ktf.uni-passau.de/mitarbeiter/boehmisch/lyra.html), Passau 7.2.1995.; see also H. Hailperin, *Rashi and the Christian Scholars* (Pittsburgh, 1963).

[47] Linking the 'clarity' issue to inspired reading of Scripture, Luther wrote: " Si de interna claritate dixeris, nullus homo unum iota in scripturis videt, nisi spiritum Dei habet, [...] Spiritus enim requiritur ad totam scripturam et ad quamlibet eius partem intellegendam." (If you should speak of [Scripture's] inward clearness, no man would see even a single letter in Scripture unless he has the spririt of God, ... For the Spirit is needed to understand all of Scripture and any part of it whatsoever.) *WA* 18, 609,55.

foreshadowing the coming of Jesus of Nazareth as Messiah.[48] Christological readings of Hebrew Bible texts rarely coincide with Jewish
interpretations; and in Luther's case, Christ-centered readings had
a directly polemical function that colonized and appropriated
Hebrew Bible texts. For example, in his 1523 treatise *That our Lord
Jesus Christ was a born Jew*, Luther was especially adamant about the
famous passage in Isaiah (7, 14): "A young woman is with child,
and she will bear a son, called Emmanu El ['God-with-us']." Jewish
exegetes generally understand the word *alma* to mean a young girl
who has reached child-bearing age, not a virginal maiden.[49] Along
with many other Christian interpreters before and after his time,
Luther understood *alma* to mean a virgin or maiden, and thus, by
prefiguration, Mary, mother of Jesus,[50] and he condemns Jewish
opposition to this interpretation as "childish and shameful", the
result of Jews' being "pugnacious about words" and "hanging so

---

[48] By way of comparison, to Calvin, the meaning of Isaiah 7 is entirely self-evi-
dent, and the words need no explanation except as they relate to the Christological
interpretation: *Institutio religionis christianae* (1536), cap. 2, 'de fide': "Deplorata res
erat, nisi maiestas ipsa Dei ad nos descenderet, quando ascendere nostrum non erat.
Ita Dei filius factus est nobis Immanuel, id est, nobiscum Deus (Ies. 7)." (The matter
[humanity's fallen state] was hopeless if the very majesty of God would not descend
to us, since it was not in us to ascend to him. And so God's Son became for us
Immannuel, that is, God with us.) *Calvini opera* I, 1-251, 65. Calvin in fact goes so far,
in his second sermon on Deuteronomy 12, V,3-7 (Wednesday, October 2nd, 1555)
as to say that the prophet Isaiah "named" Jesus "Emmanuel": "[...] car nostre
Selgneur Iesus n'a point prins en vain le nom d'Emmanuel: comme il est ainsi nom-
mé par le Prophete Isaie, c'est à dire: Dieu avec nous." ([..] for our Lord Jesus Christ
did not use the name Emmanuel in vain: for he is thus named by the Prophet Isaiah,
that is to say: God with us.) *Calvini opera* 27, 174.

[49] On *alma*, meaning a young woman who has attained the age of fertility, see
Yehoshua Gitay, *Isaiah and his Audience. The Structure and meaning of Isaiah 1-12* (Assen:
Van Gorcum, 1991), 139, and 257 note 33; and Abraham Ibn Ezra (1092-1167) on
Isaiah, in *The commentary of Ibn Ezra on Isaiah*, ed. and trans. by M. Friedländer, 2 vols.
in one (New York: P. Feldheim, 1873-77), 42. The only parallel in canonical Hebrew
Scripture is Prov. 30,18-19: "Three things there are which are too wonderful for
me,/four which I do not understand:/the way of the vulture in the sky,/the way of a
serpent on the rock,/the way of a ship out at sea,/the way of a man with a girl."
[*v'derech gever b'alma*]. *The New English Bible* (Oxford: Oxford University Press, 1970),
786. This hardly suggests virginity. According to the commentary of Joseph Jensen,
O.S.B., and William H. Irwin, C.S.B., on 'Isaiah', *alma* "is not the technical term for
virgin (*betula*). This is best understood as a wife of Ahaz; the child promised will guarantee the dynasty's future [...] and for that reason can be called Immanuel ("with us
is God")". *The New Jerome Biblical Commentary*, eds. Raymond E. Brown, S.S., Joseph
A. Fitzmyer, S.J., and Roland E. Murphy, O.Carm. (Englewood Cliffs, NJ: Prentice
Hall, 1990 [1968]), 229-248; 235.

[50] *Dass Jesus Christus ein geborner Jude sei*, WA 10, 320-323.

244 ANDREW COLIN GOW

hard on the letters".[51] Luther appeals to what he believes his readers will recognize as a Christological rendering and translation of
this passage in the gospels of Matthew and Luke. Luther's argument concludes with an understanding of the rough translation of
alma as *magd* [maid] in German, and appeals to German, not
Hebrew semantic fields:

> "And if I was to have told Isaiah how to express himself here, he
> would have said, in accordance with my advice, not 'bethula', but
> 'alma', because 'alma' is more fitting here than 'bethula'. It is also
> clearer if I say 'See, a maid [magd] is pregnant', than 'a virgin
> [jungfraw] is pregnant'. For virgin [jungfraw] can mean many things,
> including a woman of fifty or sixty years, unable to bear a child. But
> maid means a young woman, nubile, fertile and virginal, such that not
> only her state of virginity, but also her youth and fertile body is meant.
> For this reason in German, [female] young people are generally called
> maids [meyde] or maiden-folk and not virgin-folk."[52]

This desperate attempt to make the Hebrew mean what it does not
say suggests that Isaiah was right to avoid the clear technical Hebrew
term for a *virgo intacta* in order to make the meaning clearer! Luther
drives the point home by insisting on the correctness of the *German*
idiom he has chosen to translate the Hebrew:

> "So the text of Isaiah is most precisely translated into German as 'See,
> a maid is pregnant'. That these are the words in Hebrew, no Jew who
> otherwise [generally] understands Hebrew and German will deny me,
> for we Germans do not say '*concepit*, the woman has conceived'. The
> preachers made such [bad] German from the Latin [text]. But the
> German man, and the mother tongue, say: The young woman 'goes
> pregnant' or 'goes heavy' or is pregnant."[53]

---

[51] "Und weyl sie denn ja so wort kriegisch sind und an den buchstaben so hart
hangen, [...]. Aber es ist kindisch und schimpfflich, so mit wortten sich behelffen
[...]." *WA* 11, 322.
[52] "Und wenn ich hette sollen Isaiam heyssen reden, so must er myr eben geredt
haben, wie er geredt hat, nicht 'Bethula', sondern 'Alma' sagen, denn 'Alma' sich
besser hie her schicket denn 'Bethula'. Es lautt auch deutlicher, wenn ich sage: 'Sihe,
eyne magd gehet schwanger' denn 'eyne jungfraw gehet schwanger'. Denn jungfraw
ist eyn wytleuffiges wort, das auch wol eyn weybs bilde seyn mag von funffzig,
sechzig jaren, tzur frucht untuchtig. Aber magd heyst eygentlich ein jung weybs bild,
das manbar, tzur frucht tuchtig und unverruckt ist, das es nicht alleyn die
jungfrawschaft, szondern auch die jugent und fruchtbarn leyb mit begreyffe. Also
heyst man auch auff deutsch gemeyniglich das junge volck Meyde odder meyde volck und nicht jungfrawen volck." *WA* 11, 322-323.
[53] "So ist nu das gewißlich der text Isaie auffs aller eygentlichst verdeutscht: 'Sihe

Luther's translation *is pregnant* [present tense] is correct. His further arguments are circumstantial, based as much on German as on Hebrew usage and rely, in the final analysis, on his certainty that the virgin birth must have been foretold rather than on textual evidence (i.e., context, semantic field, attested usage). For present purposes, the actual semantic field of the Hebrew word *alma* or the meaning of the passage[54] at the time of Isaiah is less important than Luther's method of interpreting it.[55] The usefulness and validity of the Hebrew Bible to Luther depended on its (supposed) prefiguration of Christian truth.[56] Luther insists on knowing the meaning of the Isaiah passage in a way that excludes Jewish readings, thus appropriating it for Christian truth and denying any other meaning it might have. Grammatical accuracy intended to provide a literal understanding of the earthly application of a particular passage especially provoked Luther's ire.

Finally, Luther was able to read Hebrew scripture in a way that admitted the original Hebrew meaning but attacked Jewish exegesis of the passage nonetheless. As Maser has examined Luther's exegesis of a number of prophetic passages in some detail, it is apposite to treat a passage that might not appear on the Christological radar.

---

eyne magd geht schwanger'. Das diß die wort auff Ebreisch sind, wirt myr keyn Jude leucken, der anders Ebreisch und deutsch verstehet, denn wyr deutschen sagen nicht: 'concepit, das weyb hatt empfangen'. Die Prediger haben aus dem latin solch deutsch gemacht. Sondern so spricht der deutsch man und mutter tzunge: Das weyb gehet schwanger adder gehet schweer odder ist schwanger." *WA* 11, 323.

[54] The passage is in the present tense and refers in its original context to the short span of time in which the threat to Jerusalem from the two kings besieging it would be lifted: by the time a young woman, who *is now* pregnant, has given birth. Although later Jewish readings of this passage admit of a Messianic interpretation, that is far from being a firm consensus. I am endebted to my colleague Francis Landy for help with this passage.

[55] Peter Maser has argued much the same point concerning Luther's exegesis of a number of classical Messianic prophecies (as seen from the Christian perspective, at least). Gen. 49,10; 2 Sam. 23,2-5; Jer. 33,17-36; Hag. 2,6-9; Dan. 9,24. Maser, "Luthers Schriftauslegung", 78-82; 149-150.

[56] Similarly, in discussing Gen. 49,10 ("The scepter will not depart from Judah, until Shiloh comes"), Luther reads history as determining the interpretation of prophecy (Herod replaced the Sanhedrin after he destroyed them, thus uniting secular and legal power in a way that contradicted Luther's exegesis of 'scepter', so it must have been time for the Messiah to come); and regarding the question of whether or not it is possible to determine the year in which Messiah was born (*WA* 53, 454,2), Luther tells his reader to read the history books and see if it has not yet happened and been completed; as Maser notes: "Die Verheissung bestimmt den Geschichtsverlauf, und dieser bestätigt die Verheissung!" ("Luthers Schriftauslegung", 79).

As an example, the *sensus literalis seu historicus* of a passage to which Rashi, Lyra and Luther all devoted a certain amount of attention, the angel's speech to Hagar concerning her fate and that of the son she is bearing, Ishmael (Gen. 16, 12), bears closer examination.

Lyra glosses the first four words of the Vulgate version of this passage ("Hic erit ferus homo...") as follows: "Hic erit ferus homo. In Hebreo habetur Silvester homo diligens nemora et venationes, quia factus fuit iuuenis sagittarius."[57] "Silvester" is a mistranslation of the Hebrew word *pere*, wild ass or onager.[58] Only reading Rashi's paraphrase ("loving the woods and the hunt") into the word *pere* could possibly produce "silvester".[59] Indeed, Lyra followed Rashi very closely in glossing the Hebrew word *pere* (pe resh aleph) as "woodsman, hunter (literally, loving the wilderness and the hunt) as he will have been raised to be a bowman from his childhood on".[60] Lyra reads the text somewhat differently from mainstream Jewish tradition and from the Vulgate, using the Latin word *silvester* (woodsy and therefore by extension wild) to render the Hebrew word for onager or wild ass. Lyra did, nonetheless, take the main part of his commentary from Rashi. Lyra seems to have gone looking for a Hebrew interpretation of the odd word *pere* and the colourless translation *ferus* in the Vulgate, and found it in Rashi, whose further description was the origin of the mistranslation *silvester/silvestris* that creeps into later texts, though not the Vulgate.[61]

---

[57] He was a wild man. In Hebrew (!) he is called "woodsy", a man loving the woods and hunting, as he was trained as an bowman in his youth. Nicolaus de Lyra, *Postilla super totam Bibliam* I, Straßburg 1492 (reprint Frankfurt a/M: Minerva GmbH., 1971), Fiii[v], lemma x. The Hebrew *pere* does not mean "woodsy" or *silvester* or anything similar.

[58] See C. F. Keil and F. Delitzsch, *Commentary on the Old Testament in ten volumes*, Vol. I: *The Pentateuch*, trans. James Martin (Grand Rapids, MI: William B. Eerdmans, 1983 (reprint)), 220; vol. IV: *Job*, by F. Delitzsch, trans. Francis Bolton (Grand Rapids, MI: William B. Eerdmans, 1982 (reprint)), 331.

[59] *Chumash with Targum Onkelos, Haphtaroth and Rashi's Commentary*, Hebrew text and trans. by Rabbi A.M. Silberman (Jerusalem: Silbermann Family, 5745; orig. London: Shapiro Valentine and Co., 1934), vol. 'Bereshith', 64: *pere adam* means "One who loves the hunt and open spaces to hunt wild animals...". This Rashi justifies with a cross-reference to Gen. 21,20, where Ishmael is described as abiding in the desert and becoming an archer; here, Rashi describes Ishmael thus: "He used to live in the desert and rob travellers." (*ibid.*, 90).

[60] Note x to Genesis 16: "Hic erit fer[us] ho[mo]. In Hebreo h[abetu]r Silvester ho[mo] dilige[n]s nemora & venat[i]o[n]es. Q[uia] fact[us] fuit iuuenis sagittari[us], ut h[abetu]r i.xxi.c." Nicholas of Lyra, *Postilla super totam Bibliam*, 4 vols., Straßburg, 1492; vol. I, Fiii (v) (Reprint Frankfurt a.M.: Minerva GmbH., 1971).

[61] E.g., Gutenberg's 42-line Bible (Mainz, 1454-55) prints the Vulgate text "Hic erit ferus homo...", as does the Catholic Louvain Bible of 1547.

Luther's *Lectures on Genesis* were delivered as classroom lectures between June 1535 and November 1545, and thereafter edited from students' notes in a process that casts some doubt on Luther's direct authorship of certain passages. In discussing the passage about Hagar that we have already mentioned, the angel's curse on Ishmael, Luther delivers a sharp critique of Nicholas of Lyra's use of rabbinic exegesis and scholarship.[62] That Luther himself was speaking in this passage is clear from a direct first person (plural) reference to "our German translation of the Bible" (see *infra*) and from polemical references to his old opponents Erasmus and Sadoleto. In his reading of this passage, Luther railed against Jewish "inability to grasp" what Luther considered the true meaning of Scripture.

Luther's reading of this passage was unique. First, he started with a different text than the Vulgate's "Hic erit ferus homo". Luther's read "Is erit homo silvestris".[63] This translation seems to rely on Lyra's gloss! It may well be that Luther was furnishing his own Latin translation of the Hebrew as he went, as it deviates sharply from the Vulgate in most passages, and is closer in structure and diction to the Hebrew text. Yet at this crucial juncture, Luther's text follows Lyra and Rashi, not the Hebrew or even the Vulgate. As we shall see, Luther knew that the Hebrew word *pere* means onager, and at the same time dismissed it, seeking justification for his translation from outside the passage. As Koffmane pointed out in his introduction to volume 42 of the Weimar Edition, Luther was no longer lecturing for other doctors and fellow scholars, but for the undergraduates so that they could, one day, say they had heard Luther lecture. Granted, then, his main concern was not careful exegesis so much as dogmatics and the importance of certain passages for pastoral work and preaching. As Koffmane, a superintendant of the Lutheran church, put it, "Luther never tires of drawing on the breadth and depth of his experience to direct the attention of his young listeners to the religious and ethical truths of Scripture."[64]

---

[62] See Jaroslav Pelikan, Introduction to vol. 2 of *Luther's Works*, ed. Jaroslav Pelikan (Saint Louis, MO: Concordia Pub. House; Philadephia: Fortress Press, 1955-1986), p. x; and Introduction to *LW* 8, p. ix.

[63] *WA* 42, 595, 27.

[64] G. Koffmane, Einleitung, *WA* 42, ix: "Viel wichtiger sind die oft sehr langen dogmatischen Erörterungen. Er hat die Hörer oft auf die Wichtigkeit einer Stelle für Predigt und Seelsorge aufmerksam gemacht. Die religiösen und ethischen Wahrheiten der Schrift aus der Fülle seiner Erfahrungen heraus den Jüngeren ans Herz zu legen wird er nicht müde."

Biblical truth and not the Biblical text itself seems to have been at the
centre of Luther's enterprise in these lectures, as Koffmane admits.
Luther himself declined at least once when asked after an interruption
due to ill health to continue the lectures, saying: "I have been giving
only a rough and approximate reading, meant as a means to give others the occasion to start thinking."[65]

In his lecture on Genesis, Luther attacked Jewish understanding of
Hebrew Scripture:

> "The Jews' nonsensical talk proves that they know nothing about
> things sacred. Yet they convince great men, such as Lyra, and in our
> own time men who are well versed in their language and give great
> credence to their empty talk.
>   But this happens to the Jews because they have lost the knowl-
> edge of the heart of the matter. For knowledge is of two kinds: some
> concerns what the word itself means; some concerns the subject mat-
> ter. He who does not understand the heart of the matter will never be
> uplifted by knowing the meaning of mere words."[66]

Luther continues:

> "The same thing is happening to the Jews, for they grasp nothing but
> the meaning of the words; they have completely lost sight of the heart
> of the matter. [....] but where there is no knowledge of the heart of the
> matter, knowledge of the meaning of words is useless."[67]

I have translated *res* as "the heart of the matter" in certain places
because 'subject' is too weak: Luther is talking about the "*real* thing",
the fundamental or underlying reality as opposed to its mere verbal
signifier. Not knowing precisely what the original words mean, but
approaching them in the right spirit are the key to understanding the
Scriptures, according to this vision of exegesis.[68]

---

[65] Lauterbach's diary for May 29, 1538, p. 88: "est tumultuaria et imperfecta lec-
tio, qua aliis do ansam cogitandi"; cited by Koffmane, *WA* 42, Einleitung, x.
[66] "Nugae Iudaeorum [...] arguunt eos nihil scire sacrarum rerum, et tamen
trahunt secum magnos viros, sicut Lyram, et nostro tempore viros in ipsorum lingua
doctissimos qui tales nugas saepe admirantur. Accidit autem hoc Iudaeis ideo, quia
amiserunt cognitionem rei. Notitiae enim duplices sunt: alia, quid nominis: alia, quid
rei. Qui notitiam rei non habet, illum notitia nominis non sublevabit." *Vorlesungen
über 1. Mose* 16:12, *WA* 42, 596, 11-17.
[67] "Idem Iudaeis evenit, nihil enim habent, nisi cognationem, quid nominis: rem
prorsus amiserunt. [...] ubi autem notitia, quid rei, non est, ibi notitia, quid nominis
frustra est." *WA* 42, 598, 19-20.
[68] See Friedrich Hahn, "Luthers Auslegungsgrundsätze und ihre theologischen

These passages are a discursive interjection, a drawing of lessons from a discussion of the Arabs, the descendants of Hagar and Ishmael; and they are an outburst against "Jewish" methods and contexts for interpreting Scripture. The connection of these general remarks to the topic is tenuous at best. Luther had quibbled a few lines earlier with the Jewish translation of the word *pere* (pe resh aleph) as "onager", pointing rather to the adventitious similarity between *pere* and "our" Latin word *ferus*:[69] "The Jews translate this word as onager. What kind of animal that is, I do not know; after all, I have never seen one!"[70] He then points out: "However, in my German translation of the Bible I have understood the word to mean wild, as in *ferus*."[71] In this, then, Luther follows the Vulgate.

Luther's first comment on this passage is: "This description properly concerns the Arabs, who never stay in any single place. Rather, they carry everything with them on wagons, and live mainly by theft."[72] He claims that the Arabs, Ishmael's descendants, are a wild people who have no portion of land allotted to them, no home or fixed abode, who sleep under this tree one night, and under another the next, living by robbery and banditry, caring not at all for cities, laws or the institutions necessary to the good order of human societies — they are wild indeed.[73] In effect, Luther is trying to determine or to prove *a posteriori* his reading of the word *pere* from what he takes to be the current condition of the Arabs.[74]

Voraussetzungen", in: *Zeitschrift für systematische Theologie* 12 (1935), 165-218; esp 167: " Die Theologie geht der Einzelexegese voraus; erst res, dann verba!" (Theology preceeds precise exegesis: first the *res*, then the *verba*!).

[69] "Vocabulum (PERE) est fere nostrum, ferus." *WA* 42, 595, 31.

[70] "Iudaei exponunt pro onagro: Id quale animal sit, nescio. Non enim vidi." *WA* 42, 595, 32

[71] "Nos autem in translatione nostra Germanica Bibliorum pro nomine generali exposuimus 'Wild', ferum." *WA* 42, 595, 32-34.

[72] "Haec descriptio proprie ad Arabes pertinet qui nullo certe in loco consistunt. Sed omnia sua secum in plaustris vehunt, et ex rapina fere vivunt." *WA* 42, 595. Cf. Rashi on Gen. 21,20, *supra*, note 60: Ishmael robbed travellers!

[73] "Primum igitur vides Ismaelem non habere certam et fixam terrae portionem, sicut Abrahamum, cuius posteritati diserte promittitur terrae Canaan.

Mores igitur et ingenium Ismaelis vere est contra omnes. Alii enim manent in certis civitatibus aut pagis, Ismael autem solitudines amat, est ferus et errabundus, hodie sub hac arbore, cras sub alia cum familia sua vivit: sicut hodie Arabes et Trogloditae, qui, ut Breytenbach scribit, licere sibi iure putant, ut ex rapinis et latrociniis vivant.

Hoc significat Angelus, cum vocat (*Pere*) silvestrem hominem, qui non curabit civitates, non leges, non instituta necessaria ad societatem generis humani conservandam." *WA* 42, 595, 35 – 596, 5.

[74] The parallel to the myth of the Wandering Jew and the Jewish diaspora as punishment for deicide is too clear to ignore.

In this context, the word *pere* means wild or savage by extension, from its root meaning "wild ass". This is reasonable and does not do actual violence to the original text. Luther insists that the angel means by this that Ishmael (and by current definitions, Arabs) will be a wild man, who cares nothing for towns, laws, nor the core human institutions. Luther's problem is that he thinks Jews pay too much attention to the precise animal named, the onager or wild ass, which inhabits the Middle East. However, Rashi does nothing of the sort! Luther is interested only in the comparison of Ishmael to a wild thing — whatever kind of animal it might be, and is not at all interested in the *thing* itself. From *pere* to *silvestris* ("woodsy", "forestière") is a long stretch, as onagers certainly do not and did not live in forests; and Luther is unwittingly relying, uncritically, on Lyra and ultimately on Rashi for this word. Perhaps more important is that Luther uses material external to the text to provide the context that determines the meaning of the passage.

Of course Luther had never seen a middle-eastern wild ass; but one may be permitted to ask how many Arabs he had seen and how much of "Arabia", and of course there is the question of how Ishmael came to be understood as the progenitor of the Arabs, when Hagar was an Egyptian — for which we have no space here. In addition, it is unclear whether or not his reference to Lyra is meant to critique Lyra's gloss of this passage in the *Postilla* or Lyra's method in general — though the point is much the same in either case.

IV. *The Heart of the Matter*

The text analysis I have attempted illustrates the difference between Luther's method of exegesis in this lecture in particular — and his use of context in general — and Lyra's much more "historical" literal method based on the interpretation of individual words and passages. Luther is impatient with readings of Scripture that do not proceed from a knowledge of "Christian truth", and this leads him to play rather fast and loose with sacred texts that he, by his own standards, might have been expected to interpret more carefully. At the end of his remarks on this passage, Luther launches an attack both at learning that is not governed by the *res* of correct faith and at opponents of Reformation doctrine, adding:

"Whenever Erasmus, a man whose learning and eloquence was just about miraculous, began to speak about justification or matters of faith, he stammered miserably and talked nonsense; but in discussing other matters he had great success."[75]

Erasmus serves here as lightning rod for Luther's impatience with religious interpretive frameworks other than his own; this is why Erasmus is dragged, from some distance, into a discussion in which he otherwise plays no part. And as I have noted above, Luther amply demonstrated his belief that disagreeing with Jewish readings implied a condemnation of Roman Catholic ones as well.

Luther's attitude toward literal interpretation is at best ambiguous, and differs considerably both from his idea of Jewish exegesis and from Lyra's method as Luther understood it. That he often misunderstood his dancing master was amply shown by Thomas Kalita in a brief technical dissertation on Luther and Lyra in 1985.[76] Lyra actually posited a double literal interpretation, according to which the word in the Bible has one plain meaning, but the thing to which it refers can have other, symbolic or spiritual meanings. This suggests an alternative method for Christians to read Hebrew Scripture that does not do direct violence either to the text itself or to historical and contemporary Jewish readings.[77]

To make Christian sense of the Hebrew Bible, Luther relied not on the symbolic meaning of the things to which Biblical texts referred, but on the context of "true faith," which would guide the interpreter to a proper understanding of Scripture based not so much on knowing the meanings of individual words as on knowing "the heart of the matter." This necessarily involved the rejection of Jewish exegesis and in many places of Lyra's methods as well — which was not surprising, giving Lyra's frequent reliance on rabbinical learning to make sense of difficult grammar and vocabulary.

More important than his relationship with Lyra in this context is Luther's attitude toward the proper method of determining the real meaning of Scripture: no amount of Hebrew grammar or knowledge

---

[75] "Erasmus, homo ad miraculum usque eruditus et facundus, quoties de iustificatione et rebus fidei loqui incipit, miserrime balbutit et ineptit: in aliis rebus explicandis foelicissimus." *WA* 42, 596, 20-23.

[76] See above, n. 45.

[77] Luther in fact prohibits "double exegesis" as Heinrich Bornkamm pointed out in *Luther und das Alte Testament* (Tübingen, 1948), 223f., thus opening a gulf between his reading of Scripture and modern historical-critical analysis.

of special vocabulary could make up for a lack of the proper Christian perspective. In interpreting the "Old Testament", the "heart of the matter" was Christian truth, not skill in Hebrew. Calvin, as we have seen, shared many of Luther's certainties, including this one, concerning Judaism and Jewish interpretation of Scripture.

What are we to make of Luther's rather disjointed lecturing, in which contradiction, backwards logic, anti-Judaic doctrine and anti-Arab prejudice vied for space? Are these simply the ramblings of a crotchety old man, or can we claim some measure of representativity for them? Are they separable from his theology because they occur largely in teaching and homiletic contexts? We know from his remarks on Jewish exegesis and Hebrew scholarship that Luther did not trust Jews with their own holy books. He made a desperate attempt to show that *alma* meant virgin in Isaiah 7,14. He was not wrong about the additional figurative meaning of *pere*, but that he picked so minor a point on which to stake a critique both of Lyra and of Jewish exegesis suggests that the matter was an extremely pressing one for him. In teaching the next generation of pastors, Luther was willing to use whatever material fell into his hands to drive home the point that only the *res* of Christian faith provided access to the true meaning of the Hebrew Bible. The consequences of this method coupled with his calls for the conversion or expulsion of Jews from German towns and territories had both immediate and long-term effects — on Jewish communities, on Lutheran theology, and on Christian-Jewish relations in Germany.

The approach to Hebrew Scripture common to Luther and Calvin, finally, is an attempt to deny the validity of Judaism, based as it is on particular readings of Scripture; and taken with Luther's attitude to Jewish learning as a whole, part of a colonial campaign to prevent Jews from teaching and learning about Scripture in ways consonant with Jewish beliefs and traditions.

CALVIN AND THE GREEK FATHERS

Irena Backus*

It would be inappropriate to consider Calvin as a patristic scholar and to imagine that his theology represented any kind of patristic Renaissance. Calvin was no Erasmus and there is no evidence that he considered patristic writings as a "golden river" to be contrasted with the "shallow runnels" of scholasticism.[1] The object of the present study is to examine the role played in Calvin's works by the extremely limited corpus of Greek Fathers that was known to him. Several studies have already been devoted to the broad topic of "Calvin and the Fathers", since the appearance of Luchesius Smits' magisterial Saint Augustin dans l'oeuvre de Jean Calvin,[2] and R. J. Mooi's *Het kerk-en dogmahistorisch element in de werken van Johannes Calvijn.*[3] Unfortunately, those two works set the tone for the way "Calvin and the Fathers" were to be studied and all works on the topic that appeared subsequently have tended either to examine Calvin's use of one Father, be it Augustine, Eusebius of Caesarea, Cyprian or Bernard of Clairvaux,[4] or else evaluate quotations from several Church Fathers (and other authors) in one or more of Calvin's works.[5] This study

---

* Professor of History, Institut d'histoire de la Réformation, Université de Genève

[1] On Erasmus and the Church Fathers cf. Erika Rummel. *Erasmus' Annotations on the New Testament. From Philologist to Theologian.* Toronto: University Press, 1986, 53; Jan den Boeft, "Erasmus and the Church Fathers". In *The Reception of the Church Fathers in the West.* Edited by I. Backus. Leiden: Brill, 1997, 537-572; Irena Backus, "Erasmus and the Spirituality of the Early Church". In *Erasmus' Vision of the Church.* Edited by Hilmer Pabel. (Sixteenth Century Essays and Studies, vol. 33). Kirksville, Mo.: Sixteenth Century Journal Publishers, 1995, 95-114.

[2] 2 vols., Assen: van Gorcum, 1956, 1958.

[3] Wageningen: H. Veenman 1965.

[4] J. M. J. Lange van Ravenswaaij. *Augustinus totus noster. Das Augustinverständnis bei Johannes Calvin.* Göttingen: Vandenhoeck und Ruprecht, 1990; Irena Backus. "Calvin's Judgement of Eusebius of Caesarea. An Analysis". *The Sixteenth Century Journal* 22 (1991): 419-437; Anette Zillenbiller. *Die Einheit der Katholischen Kirche. Calvins Cyprianrezeption in seinen ekklesiologischen Schriften.* Mainz: Philip von Zabern, 1993; Anthony N. S. Lane. *Calvin and Bernard of Clairvaux* (Studies in Reformed Theology and History, N.S., Number one). Princeton, N.J.: Princeton Theological Seminary, 1996.

[5] Johannes van Oort. "John Calvin and the Church Fathers". In *The Reception of the Church Fathers in the West,* 661-700; Anthony N. S. Lane. "The Sources of Calvin's Citations in his Genesis Commentary". In *Interpreting the Bible. Historical and Theo-*

adopts a somewhat different approach in that it sets out to show how Calvin handles the Greek Fathers in five different genres of writing, the five being a preface, marginal annotations, a biblical commentary, a work of anti-Trinitarian polemic, and a work of dogmatic theology (i.e. the *Institutes*). As exhaustivity can hardly be attained within the limits of a short essay, we shall naturally confine ourselves to examining representative samples of exegesis, polemics and dogmatics. As for the other two genres, there is so far no record of Calvin writing a preface to or annotating any Church Father other than John Chrysostom.

1. *The Preface to the Homilies of John Chrysostom (1540?)*

The origins and the purpose of Calvin's unpublished and unfinished preface to the Homilies of Chrysostom[6] are quite unknown. Baum, Cunitz and Reuss date the piece provisionally at 1540 although that date can only be considered as approximate.[7] However, given Calvin's insistence in the preface on the organisation of the Early Church as model for the Church of his own day, it is not unlikely that it was written in Strasbourg under the influence of Bucer.[8] Other characteristics of the piece, notably its insistence on Chrysostom's qualities as preacher, are perhaps due to the influence of Erasmus. It is not at all clear which homilies of Chrysostom Calvin intended to translate into French, or indeed why the preface is in Latin. Baum, Cunitz and Reuss who published the text on the basis of Geneva MS. fr. 145 fol. 160 r.-v. presume that it was intended to

---

logical Studies in Honour of David F. Wright. Leicester: Intervarsity Press, 1997, 47-96; A.N.S. Lane. *John Calvin, Student of the Church Fathers.* Edinburgh: T. & T. Clark, 1999.

[6] CO 9: 831-838.

[7] Ian Hazlett confirms this on paleographical evidence in his "Calvin's Latin Preface to his Proposed French Edition of Chrysostom's Homilies: Translation and Commentary". In *Humanism and Reform. The Church in Europe, England and Scotland, 1400-1643. Essays in Honour of James K. Cameron.* Edited by James Kirk. Oxford: Blackwell, 1991, 129-150, esp. 132-133 (Hereafter referred to as: *Hazlett*).

[8] The idea that the history of the Early Church should show pastors of Bucer's time how to run a parish was indeed a distinctive feature of the Strasbourg Reformation so much so that the Strasbourg Church ordinances of 1534 dictated that every parish library should contain a copy of Eusebius-Rufinus' *Historia ecclesiastica* and of Cassiodore's *Historia tripartita*. Cf. Martin Bucer and Matthew Parker. *Florilegium patristicum*. Edited by Pierre Fraenkel. Leiden: Brill, 1988, XV.

validate Calvin's endeavours as translator among the learned and wonder why the Genevan reformer, given his linguistic skills, should have felt the need for that type of apology.[9] Ian Hazlett sees the preface as a preliminary draft, which was to be translated later into French.[10] The venture never came to anything and represents Calvin's unique attempt at patristic edition.

It is not difficult to see why Calvin should have felt the need to justify it, if one reads the opening of the preface with the minimum of care and attention: Calvin was simply worried that the novelty of his venture would make him the butt of criticisms . "For I see", he states, "that as is almost always the case with anything new, there will be some who will not only criticise my efforts as vain, but who will think that they are to be condemned outright as being of too little use to the Church".[11] A typical example of public outcry in matters of ecclesiastical innovation was the criticism of vernacular translations of the Bible, which gradually turned into approval and even enthusiasm.[12] Indeed Calvin's chief argument for publishing Chrysostom in the vernacular is that if the common people is not to be deprived of the word of God, then it is not to be denied working tools which can be used to gain a true understanding of

---

[9] CO 9: LXV: "Homiliarum Chrysostomi versionem gallicam meditatus est Calvinus, nisi omnia nos fallunt, vel antequam Gallia excesserit, vel omnino antequam ipse Nouo Testamento commentariis illustrando animum applicuerit. Certe in praefatione sua quae sola exstat proposoti testis, neque ea integra et absoluta, concionatorem illum celeberrimum eo maxime nomine commendat quod suos labores plebi inscripsit, cuius commodis vernacula translatione facta ipse quoque huius autor inseruire voluit. Ex qua declaratione facile tu efficies illum nihil simile adhuc tentasse, quo vulgi necessitatibus e scriptura sacra priuatim erudiendi prospiceret. Vbi tamen mireris eum praefationem suam quasi excusatione apud doctiores opus fuisset, latine conscripsisse. Typis illa nunquam descripta est. Exstat autoris autographon in bibliotheca Geneuensi Cod. 145 fol. 154 seq. [!] sine inscriptione propria. Legitur tamen in fronte titulus ab antiqua manu additus hic: 'Praefatio in editionem Homiliarum Chrysostomi a D. Caluino meditatam, quae tamen no exstat. Interponit hic suum tum de Chrysostomo, tum de aliis quos illi comparat ecclesiae doctoribus iudicium apposititie".

[10] Cf. *Hazlett*, 130-131.

[11] CO 9: 831: "Video enim quod in rebus nouis euenire fere solet, quosdam non defuturos qui laborem hunc meum non modo superuacuum contemnant, sed etiam vt parum vtilem ecclesiae repudiandum prorsus censeant." Cf. *Hazlett*, 138.

[12] CO 9: 831: "Indignum enim facinus esse putabant plebeiis hominibus promulgari Dei mysteria quae tam diu apud sacerdotes et monachos suppressa fuerant. Neque enim videbatur aliud id esse quam sacrarium Dei sublata omni reuerentia profanari. Atqui inter eos quoque, quibus id tantopere displicebat, videmus nunc omnes eiusmodi querimonias in gratulationes conuersas esse." Cf. *Hazlett*, 139.

it.[13] Although nothing came of his Chrysostom translation, it seemed to be, at least in its conception, part of a larger plan to make the works of the Fathers available in the vernacular in so far as they helped the faithful understand the Bible. Calvin chose Chrysostom first and foremost because, like the Genevan reformer and several other Church Fathers, he abided by Paul's rule of communicating God's mysteries to the common people. Calvin here echoes to some extent Erasmus' praise of Chrysostom's popular oratory in the latter's preface to his 1530 edition of the Church Father.[14] However, whereas Erasmus' concerns are predominantly aesthetic (Chrysostom spoke beautifully in a popular idiom), Calvin's tend to be of a didactic and civic nature: it is a preacher's duty (enjoined by Paul) to address himself as clearly and articulately as possible to as wide an audience as possible. Calvin's position here seems somewhat paradoxical: he advocates eloquent appeal to the largest possible number in an unfinished Latin preface to a non-existent French translation of unnamed homilies by Chrysostom !

Equally paradoxical appear to be Calvin's strictures on Chrysostom's linguistic deficiencies:

> "These homilies combine various elements but it is the interpretation of Scripture that holds pride of place, a subject in which — so it is agreed by all men of sense — none of the ancient authors whose writings are still extant today can better him [Chrysostom], especially when he treats of the New Testament. A lack of knowledge of Hebrew, however, made it impossible for him to excel equally in the Old."[15]

While Calvin's basic point is perfectly sound — Biblical exegesis can claim to be authoritative only when backed by a sound knowledge of the relevant languages — his tone does appear exaggeratedly dogmatic given that he himself, to the best of our knowledge, only ever

---

[13] CO 9: 832: "Iam vero, si aequum est plebem christianam non spoliari Dei sui verbo, neque deneganda sunt ei instrumenta quae ad veram eius intelligentiam vsui sint futura." Cf. *Hazlett*, 141.

[14] Cf. Allen, *Ep.* 1800, ll. 110-130.

[15] CO 9: 834: "Sunt autem homiliae, quae quum variis partibus constent, primum tamen in illis locum tenet Scripturae interpretatio, in qua Chrysostomum nostrum vetustos omnes scriptores qui hodie exstant antecedere nemo sani iudicii negauerit. Praesertim vbi nouum testamentum tractat. Nam quominus in veteri tantum praestaret, obstabat hebraicae linguae imperitia." Cf. *Hazlett*, 144.

had recourse to the Latin translation of the works of John Chrysostom, published by Chevallon in Paris in 1536.[16]

It is not unlikely that Calvin's linguistic exigencies were less strict when it came to translating Bible commentaries than they were when it came to translation of the Bible itself. If Calvin intended to produce a French translation of Chrysostom based only on the Latin version, then it might be argued that he advocated a hierarchy of knowledge of Hebrew and Greek: indispensable for preachers who wanted to correctly interpret and translate the Bible, the two languages were not essential for preachers (including Calvin himself) who wished to have access to ancient commentaries on it. It is worth noting here that, as has been shown by A.N.S. Lane, Calvin did not collate the 1540 Latin translation of Basil of Caesarea (by Janus Cornarus) with any of the existing Greek editions and was perfectly happy to cite from the Latin in his *Reply to Pighius* published in 1543.[17]

In spite of this apparent lack of linguistic rigour, Calvin was perfectly aware of the distinction between the Greek and the Latin Fathers, and devotes two paragraphs of the preface to considering the two corpora, each comprising six names: Tertullian, Cyprian, Hilary, Jerome, Ambrose and Augustine for the Latins; Chrysostom, Origen, Athanasius, Basil, Cyril of Alexandria and Gregory of Nazianzus for the Greeks. Theophylactus is seen by Calvin (rightly) as an imitator of Chrysostom — "nihil habet laude dignum quod non a Chrysostomo sumpserit." Although, following the Erasmian patristic canon, he names only six/seven Greek Fathers in his sole venture into patristics, Calvin is aware that the corpus could be extended by adding later Fathers. However, he considers them not worthy of discussion.[18]

---

[16] We shall be analysing Calvin's manuscript annotations in his copy of the edition further on. Cf. Alexandre Ganoczy and Klaus Müller. *Calvins Handschriftliche Annotationen zu Chrysostomus. Ein Beitrag zur Hermeneutik Calvins.* Wiesbaden: Franz Steiner Verlag, 1981. Referred to hereafter as: *Ganoczy/Müller.*

[17] Cf. A. N. S. Lane. "Calvin and the Fathers in Bondage and Liberation of the Will". In *Calvinus sincerioris religionis vindex.* Edited by W. H. Neuser and B. Armstrong (Sixteenth Century Essays and Studies, vol. 36). Kirksville, Mo.: Sixteenth Century Journal Publishers, 1997, 67-96. For information on the relevant Greek and Latin editions of Basil cf. Irena Backus. *Lectures humanistes de Basile de Césarée. Traductions latines (1439-1618).* Paris: Études Augustiniennes, 1990, 29-54, 211-258.

[18] CO 9: 834: "Plures recensere nihil opus est, de quibus controuersia esse nulla potest." Cf. *Hazlett,* 144. On the Erasmian patristic canon see den Boeft (as in note 1).

What interests Calvin are the Fathers of the first five centuries. Disregarding rather cavalierly the editions of Irenaeus, Gregory of Nyssa, Justin Martyr, Ignatius of Antioch, which were already available, Calvin takes Chrysostom as the apex of Greek patristic achievement and declares that he cannot be compared to many other Fathers seeing as "among the Greeks there was no one before him or even in his time whose writings are available today, with the exception of Origen, Athanasius, Basil and Gregory". Origen, according to Calvin, does nothing but obscure the clarity of Scripture with his eternal allegories, while Athanasius, Basil and Gregory did not leave sufficient Commentaries to enable a comparison — the two Cappadocians having shown more skill in rhetoric than in tasks of a didactic nature. In the century immediately following, only Cyril is worth a mention "second only to Chrysostom but not able to compete with him," together with Theophylactus who has "nothing to commend him other than what he took from Chrysostom".

The corpus of Greek Fathers in what was never to become Calvin's unique venture into patristics can thus be reduced to Chrysostom and even he, as Calvin shows in the second part of his preface, is to be read with caution. Wishing his readers to derive the greatest possible benefit from Chrysostom's writings but without in any way challenging the Greek Father's status as a "faithful servant of Christ", Calvin emits the following caveats: too much weight given to good works at the expense of election, too much emphasis on human free-will, inadequate emphasis on grace. Chrysostom is not to be blamed excessively for this: Christian religion with its emphasis on the incapacity of man to do any good at all goes against all philosophical precepts; already in Chrysostom's time there was no shortage of philosophers who used the fatalistic aspect of Christianity to discourage people from adopting it. There were equally many wicked and licentious men within the Church who used determinism as a pretext not to improve when admonished by their pastors. It was to strike a balance between these two pressure groups that Chrysostom made so many unclear statements about the relationship between grace and free-will. These slips, concludes Calvin, should be forgiven but in no way perpetuated.

Chrysostom as a Greek Father, representative of the Antioch School of Biblical exegesis, would have been quite unknown to Calvin and his contemporaries. The condemnation of Antiochene christology by the Council of Ephesus in 431 did not impinge upon the 16th century image of the bishop of Constantinople. Chrysostom's ascetism and his aspirations to the angelic life, which Calvin did know and which his readers would have expected him to criticise (or, for that matter, Chrysostom's relations with the empress Eudoxia) receive not so much as a mention. Does the reference to philosophers suggest that Calvin was aware of Pagan influences on Greek theology and exegesis in their full subtlety ? More likely, depicting Chrysostom as responding to pressures from both advocates of free will and determinists, Calvin is thinking of his own difficulties and pressures he himself had to endure. He hopes, implicitly, to resist them better than Chrysostom did. No representative of any "Golden Age", the bishop of Constantinople is portrayed in Calvin's preface as an ally from the past. What makes him an ally is his attention to the Bible and the very fact that he lived in the past. For, Calvin concludes:

> "If we want the best for the well-fare and salvation of the Church, we will find no better guide, in my opinion, than to adopt the discipline of the Early Church [...]."[19]

2. *Calvin's Annotations in his copy of Chrysostom*

It is along those two parameters — status of the Bible and Church discipline — that we should interpret Calvin's annotations or more precisely, underlinings, in his copy of Chrysostom rather than look for how they relate to chief points of Calvin's theology, as their editors, Ganoczy and Müller, have attempted.[20] One glance at the underlinings suffices to show that what captured Calvin's attention were statements to do with the status of the Bible and its immediate, practical or ecclesiological applicability on the one hand, and remarks on the discipline and running of the Early Church on the other. A few examples of each type of underlining or annotation will suffice here.

Gen. 3,21: *Fecitque Iehova Deus Adae et vxori eius tunicas pelliceas et induit eos.*

---

[19] CO 9: 838: "Nam si volumus ecclesiae saluti bene consultum, nulla reperietur magis idonea ratio, mea quidem opinione, quam si disciplinae normam a veteri ecclesia petamus...". Cf. *Hazlett*, 150.

[20] Cf. note 16, supra.

Calvin underlined most of Chrysostom's Commentary on that passage and indeed it suited his purpose admirably. The bishop of Constantinople makes two basic points: the Lord in his mercy made fur coverings for Adam and Eve so as to cover up the very bodies that had sinned and to remind us to lead godly and austere lives. Secondly, inveighing against people (women in particular) who dress too luxuriously, he notes that clothing was a necessary consequence of the original sin, and should therefore be regarded as a sign of it.[21] The entire passage was carefully underlined by Calvin. Ignoring completely Chrysostom's interests in the ascetic life, which was what oriented the Church Father's interpretation of Genesis 3, Calvin was to make his teaching on clothing very much his own. In his Commentary on Genesis, Calvin simply paraphrases Chrysostom's teaching, omitting all reference to God's mercy, when he comments on the passage in question:

> "By this clothing God wanted the first men [...] to note their corruption and so to remember their sin. It is not to be denied that at the same time he wanted to provide us with an example so that he would accustom us to dressing modestly and with as little ostentation as possible."[22]

In his Sermons on Genesis (1559) Calvin goes a step further and emphasizes God's design with great vehemence: animal skin being a squalid, evil-smelling object, had more dignity than man in his fallen state which it was intended to portray. It was also to serve as an example to Christians to dress modestly.[23] The Genesis passage on the expulsion from Paradise was found by both Chrysostom and Calvin to contain very similar potential for immediate, practical

---

[21] Cf. *Ganoczy/Müller*, 70-71: "Quia propter transgressionem poenae mortis reus erat factus protoplastus opusque habebat veste quae confusionem tegeret, pelliceas fecit vestes, quo docuit nos vt mollem et dissolutam vitam fugiamus [...] Quare, dic obsecro, corpus ita ornas et gaudes eiuscemodi amictu ? Non cogitas quod pro magno supplicio, propter transgressionem, tegmen hoc excogitatum est ?".

[22] CO 23: 78: "Voluit ergo Deus in tali habitu primos homines non secus ac prius in nuditate, conspicere suam foeditatem atque ita pecccati reminisci. Interea negandum non est quin exemplar nobis proposuerit, in quo nos ad frugalem ac minime sumptuosum vestitum assuefaceret."

[23] Sermon 19, Bodley, fol. 105v.: "[...] mais quoy qu'il en soit, Dieu nous monstre quelz nous sommes, quand il prefere la peau des bestes brutes, à tout ce que nous avons de dignité en nous, dont nous sommes ainsi enflez d'orgueil." Cf. Max Engammare. "Le paradis à Genève. Comment Calvin prêchait-il la chute aux Genevois ?" *Études théologiques et religieuses* 69:3 (1994): 338. Engammare ibid. considers Calvins' insistence on animal skins as punishment an idea original to Calvin. In fact it is already implicit in Chrysostom's Commentary on Genesis.

application to their respective problems as preachers. However, Calvin was not naïve and knew full well that certain passages of Chrysostom's Commentaries, however apt they may have appeared, needed to be noted but could not be integrated into his own exegesis. The best example of this is probably Chrysostom's admonition to his audience to read the Scriptures, which takes the form of an excursus in his Commentary on John 1,14 *Et Sermo caro factus est et habitauit in nobis*. Calvin read the excursus very carefully and underlined the most pertinent passages, such as this one, twice or even three times, once horizontally, twice vertically:

> "What is it that I ask from you ? That on one day per week or at least on Saturday, you take the trouble to read the Gospel lessons which you should look at before hearing these sermons, repeat them frequently at home, investigate their meaning diligently, note everything that is clear and unclear [...]".[24]

Calvin's Commentary on John was written in 1552.[25] Trinitarian problems took priority over moral exhortations and naturally there is no trace of the Chrysostom passage in Calvin's own exposition of John 1,14. However, there can be no doubt that it influenced Calvin's own conception of the Bible and its practical applications in general.

As for underlinings that are to do with the government and discipline of the Early Church as model of the Church of Calvin's own time, we shall confine ourselves to one example which occurs in the 60th Sermon *Ad populum Antiochenum*:

> "The table was not of silver and the cup was not of gold, the very cup out of which Christ gave his own blood to the disciples: yet both those things were precious and awesome, because they were filled with spirit. If you want to honour the body of Christ, do not despise his nakedness, do not honour him here with silk clothes, if, outside, you are going to neglect him dying of cold and exposure."[26]

---

[24] *Ganoczy/Müller*, 100: "Quid igitur a vobis contendim ? vt vna dierum in hebdomade, vel saltem sabbato, curae vobis sit euangelicas legere lectiones, quas ante has conciones in manibus habere, domi frequenter repetere, earum diligenter sensum disquirere, quid clarum, quid obscurum sit adnotare velitis [...]."

[25] *In Euangelium secundum Johannem Commentarius pars prior*. Edited by Helmut Feld (*Ioannis Calvini Opera exegetica*, 11:1). Geneva: Droz, 1997. Cited hereafter as: Calvin, *In Ioh.*, ed. Feld.

[26] *Ganoczy/Müller*, 152: "Non erat illa mensa tunc ex argento nec aureus calix, ex quo sanguinem proprium Christus suis dedit discipulis; preciosa tamen erant illa omnia et tremenda, quoniam erant spiritu plena. Vis Christi corpus honorare, ne nudum eum despicias; nec eum hic quidem sericis honores vestibus, extra vero gelu et nuditate pereuntem contemnas."

Chrysostom, true to his principles, incites his hearers to perform concrete good works which are directly inspired by an act of faith: any
poor man whom they would care to help is Christ.[27] At the same
time he attempts to inculcate an austerity of life that would help
Christians living in the world draw a little nearer to the ideal of the
vita angelica. In other words, the passage when read in context advocates those very good works that Calvin warned his readers against in
the unfinished preface. However, taken out of context, the passage
does bear resemblance to a critique of Roman Catholic practices
common in Calvin's time. Read with those critiques in mind, it could
legitimately be taken as a warning issued by the fourth-century
Church against an excessively ornate celebration of the Mass. The
austere model of Church office was the one also adopted by the Early
Church — that was the lesson Calvin chose to draw from 60th Sermon *Ad populum Antiochenum*.

As was noted by Ganoczy and Müller,[28] Calvin did also cite passages of Chrysostom, notably in the *Institutio*, that he had neither
underlined nor annotated in his edition of the Church Father's
works. A typical example is *Inst.* 4,12.5, where the Genevan
Reformer, insisting on the necessity of admonition and excommunication, cites Chrysostom's authority as sufficient for excommunicat-
ing all stubborn offenders, even if they are rich and powerful:

> "Those who have power of administering the sacrament, if knowingly
> and willingly they admit someone who is unworthy and whom they
> should by right have refused, they become thereby guilty of sacrilege
> as if they were giving the Lord's body to the dogs. That is why
> Chrysostom severely upbraids priests who do not dare exclude anyone
> because they live in fear and trembling of the great and the powerful.
> "You will be held accountable for his blood" [Ez. 33,8] he says. If you
> fear men, they will laugh at you, but if you live in awe of God, then
> men too will be in awe of you."[29]

---

[27] On this cf. e.g. Ivo auf der Maur, *Mönchtum und Glaubensverkündigung in den
Schriften des heiligen Johannes Chrysostomos*. Freiburg: Universitätsverlag, 1959.

[28] *Ganoczy/Müller*, 22-25.

[29] *Inst.* 4, 12.5: "Verissimum est enim, eum, cui commissa est dispensatio, si sciens
ac volens indignum admiserit quem repellere iure poterat, perinde reum esse sacri-
legii acsi corpus Domini canibus prostitueret. Quamobrem Chrysostomus grauiter
inuehitur in sacerdotes, qui dum magnorum potentiam formidant, neminem audent
arcere. Sanguis, inquit, e manibus vestris requiretur [Ezech. 3.d.18, et 33.c.10]. Si
hominem timetis, ille vos deridebit; sin Deum, eritis hominibus quoque ipsis venera-
biles". The quotation comes from Chrysostom, *In Matth.* 82 (83).

What Ganoczy and Müller do not note is that this quotation from Chrysostom was added in 1543, two years after the institution of the Consistory and the rule of exclusion from the Lord's Supper of stubborn offenders. The bishop of Constantinople and his use of Ezekiel 33,8 was judged to be of sufficient authority.[30] This application of Chrysostom's problems to the problems he would have been facing himself is an interesting instance of the Genevan Reformer reading and re-reading the Chevallon edition of Chrysostom and using the bishop of Constantinople's pronouncements on discipline as a blueprint for his own.

Chrysostom was to Calvin a source of extremely useful information about the discipline of the Early Church, and as such could be adopted wholesale. Moreover, Chrysostom's way of using the Bible held great attraction for the Genevan Reformer. However, one must guard against overinterpreting the annotations and underlinings in his own copy of Chrysostom: they serve only as a rough guide to the way Calvin read the Church Father and many were never to resurface explicitly in Calvin's works, while other, non-annotated passages did. Even given this caveat, the Genevan Reformer's use of Chrysostom is remarkably coherent and, in contrast to his use of many other Church Fathers, not primarily oriented by the demands of inter-confessional polemics.

3. *Polemics and Dogmatics: Trinity and the Free Will*

What of the other Greek Fathers? The minuscule corpus mentioned in the Chrysostom preface was to expand to include the ante-Nicene Fathers: Justin Martyr, Ignatius of Antioch and Irenaeus under the pressure of diverse controversies, notably Trinitarian and Lutheran. Even the much-maligned Origen was periodically to assume a certain amount of status. The discussions with Servetus, his contention that the Trinity was basically an unfortunate invention of the First Council of Nicaea and his use of the ante-Nicene Fathers to support it made Calvin and the Genevan ministers rethink their position in those same terms, as is shown i.a. by the French version of the *Defensio orthodoxae fidei* [...] *contra errores*

---

[30] Cf. e.g. T. H. L.Parker. *John Calvin: A Biography*. London: Dent, 1975, 82-89.

Serveti,[31] entitled *Declaration pour maintenir la vraye-foy de la Trinité*.[32] In the vernacular version of the work, the presence of the patristic argument is as strong as in the Latin version. Both sides of the dispute are given: Servetus having put forward a form of monarchianism, Calvin cited several propositions extracted from *De Trinitatis erroribus* and the *Restitutio christianismi* so as to show the full enormity of Servetus' errors, notably his conception of the second Person of the Trinity as an image of the man Jesus Christ in the Godhead. It was to defend his conception of Person and to show that his doctrines were in line with the pure, i.e. the ante-Nicene Church,[33] that Servetus had recourse to a mass of proof-texts from Tertullian, Irenaeus and "Clement St. Peter's disciple", i.e. the *Pseudo-Clementine Recognitions*, whose authenticity he naturally did not question. It is not clear whether Servetus knew that Irenaeus was a Greek writer and whether the fact was of any significance to him. It is sufficient here to discuss one of the proof-texts to show the specificity of Servetus' use of Irenaeus:

> "The first passage is to be found in book four, chapter 17, page 216 and 217: the Jews were remiss not recognising him who spoke in human guise to Abraham, Aaron and Moses, saying he was the Son of God, the Word of God, that is, Jesus, who had formed man in his image and who was the image of God. Irenaeus shows clearly that there was a human person in the Word and an effigy of man, in the semblance of which Adam's flesh was fashioned [...]."[34]

The page references show that Servetus (and indeed Calvin) was referring to Erasmus' second edition of Irenaeus, published in Basel by the Heirs of Froben in 1528. The passage referred to is *Adu. haer.* 4,7.4, according to modern numbering, where Irenaeus criticises the Jews for imagining that God the Father could be known without

---

[31] Cf. Rodolphe Peter, Jean-François Gilmont. *Bibliotheca calviniana. Les oeuvres de Jean Calvin publiées au 16e siècle.* I: *Écrits théologiques, littéraires et juridiques.* Geneva: Droz, 1991, no 54/6. Cited hereafter as: *Peter/Gilmont*.

[32] Cf. *Peter/Gilmont* I, no. 54/5.

[33] *Declaration*, 1554, 109: "J'ay dict que la seconde Personne en la Deité a esté iadis ainsi nommée, pource que c'estoit vne montre ou representation de l'homme Iesus Christ. Lequel desia par hypostase subsistoit en Dieu et reluisoit visiblement en la Deité. Or pource que ce moyen de personne est incognu à Caluin et que toute la chose quasi en depend, i'ameneray icy les passages des anciens docteurs qui prouueront mon intention."

[34] *Declaration*, 1554, 112: "Le premier est au liure quatriesme, chapitre 17, page 216 et 217, les Iuifs ont failli ne cognoissans point celuy qui a parlé en figure humaine à Abraham, Aaron et Moyse, estre le Fils de Dieu, la Parolle de Dieu, à

God the Word as it was the latter who spoke to Abraham in human guise in Gen. 18,1. Irenaeus' doctrine of the Trinity was certainly not fully developed. However, it is important to bear in mind that the passage is cited by Servetus out of context. As is well-known, book four of *Aduersus haereses* is a plea for the unity of the Old and the New Testament against Marcion and the Gnostics who attempted to introduce an unknown God the Father so as to replace the God of the Old Testament. In 4,7.4 Irenaeus puts the Gnostics on par with the Jews whose theology is equally partial in recognising only the Old Testament at the expense of the New. If Irenaeus had monarchianist tendencies, they certainly stemmed from his desire to show the unity of God against the system put forward by the Gnostics; at no stage did he envisage the second Person of the Trinity as an image of the man Christ in the Godhead.

Although Servetus' reading of Irenaeus was tendentious, the Spaniard's appeal to the ante-Nicene Fathers constituted a grave danger, as it risked leaving Calvin with the (relatively) late first Council of Nicaea as the sole non-Scriptural guarantor of the doctrine of the Trinity. The ante-Nicene Fathers had to be wrested back — that was the object of the second part of the *Declaration*, entitled *Brieve Refutation des erreurs et impiétés de Michel Servet présentée par les ministres de l'Eglise de Geneve à Messieurs du Conseil comme il leur auoit esté commandé*, the group of "ministres" being headed by Calvin himself.[35] It was not difficult for Calvin and his colleagues to refute Servetus' interpretations of Irenaeus. Point one just cited was curtly dismissed, all it meant was that it was Jesus Christ (as pre-existent logos) who spoke to Old Testament Patriarchs in human shape — there was absolutely nothing to suggest that there was an effigy of man in the Godhead.[36] But Calvin's and his associates' prime concern was not to refute particular arguments but

---

savoir Iesus qui auoit formé l'homme à son image et qui desia estoit la figure de Dieu. Irenée monstre manifestement qu'il y a eu vne personne humaine en la Parolle et vne effigie de l'homme à la semblance duquel la chair d'Adam a esté formée [...]".

[35] The last page contains a list of "ministres et pasteurs de l'Eglise de Geneue qui ont approuué ce liure et y ont souscrit". The names are those of : "Iean Calvin, Abel Pouppin, Iaques Bernard, Nicolas des Gallars, François Bourguoin, Nicolas Petit, Remond Chauuet, Matthieu Malesian, Michel Cop, Iean Pirer, Iean de sainct André, Iean Baldin, Iean le Feure, Iean Macard, Nicolas Colladon".

[36] *Declaration*, 1554, 134: "Veu que le premier lieu ne contient autre chose sinon que c'estoit Iesus Christ qui a anciennement parlé aux Peres en figure d'homme, Seruet argue brutalement en tirant de la ie ne scay quel fantosme eternel d'vn homme".

to show that, contrary to Servetus' claims, the Trinity was not an invention of Athanasius and the Fathers of the Council of Nicaea, and that Irenaeus, Tertullian, Justin and Origen did not only teach "une disposition de la Trinité".

Their defence was convincing although, curiously, neither Origen nor Justin was mentioned explicitly in the body of the ministers' reply (no doubt because neither had been actually cited by Servetus). The most space was given over to Tertullian and Irenaeus; Clement of Rome was dismissed as forgery (on the basis of the Pseudo-Gelasian *Decree*) and the ministers took great pleasure in reminding Servetus that one of his most often invoked mentors, Ignatius of Antioch, "whoever he was",[37] did not at all bear out the Spaniard's teaching and very clearly put forward the doctrine of the pre-existent Logos. Recovering the ante-Nicene Church in the Antitrinitarian dispute boiled down to recovering Tertullian for the Latin Fathers and Irenaeus for the Greeks. Tertullian and Irenaeus also resurfaced in the controversy with Valentino Gentile in 1561. Indeed, Gentile too argued that the doctrine of the Trinity was an unfortunate invention of the Council of Nicaea and attempted to appeal to the two chief ante-Nicene doctors. The parallel with Servetus did not escape Calvin, who condemned it in no uncertain terms:

> "As I do not want to repeat myself, the readers, if they so wish, may learn from reading my refutation of Servetus how hard that sordid impostor tries to get Irenaeus to side with him. He tries to do the same with Justin Martyr and yet we could not wish for a more illustrious patron of our teaching [...]"[38]

However, it would be naïve to suppose that Irenaeus and Justin, once recovered for the defence of the orthodox doctrine of the Trinity, play a crucial role in Calvin's exposition of the dogma in the *Institutes* of 1559 (1.13) although Irenaeus does, as we shall see, play *a* role.

---

[37] *Declaration*, 1554, 140-141: "Nous sommes aussi esbahis comment Servet enseuelit icy Ignace, duquel il a tousiours faict son aduocat, se tenant bien fierement asseuré de luy. Or quel qu'il soit cestuy-là qu'on a intitulé Ignace, il dit en la page 22, Epistre aux Magnesiens, que Christ a esté engendré du Pere deuant les siecles. Aux Philippiens, pa. 30 il dit que ce passage de Salomon se doit rapporter à Christ, d'autant qu'il est Dieu et Parolle diuine, à sauoir: di moy son nom ou le nom de son Fils."

[38] *Expositio impietatis Valentini Gentilis*, 1561, CO 9: 371: "Quia nolo actum agere, cognoscent lectores, si volent, ex refutatione Serueti quam stolide Irenaeum in suas partes trahere conetur foetidus hic impostor. Eadem est Iustini ratio, quo nullus doctrinae nostrae luculentior patronus nobis optandus est."

There, refuting all possible heresies, Calvin takes the Biblical text of Hebrews 1,3 as his starting point prior to defining the difference between *essentia* and *hypostasis*. Calvin is acutely aware of the problems of translating Greek terminology into Latin but does not think that there is a fundamental difference of teaching between the Latin and the Greek Church. However, he does insist that the doctrine of the Trinity is biblically based and he cites numerous passages from the Old and the New Testament to support this contention.

Patristic testimonies, such as they are, are post-Nicene and relatively few in number. Where the Fathers are of help, irrespective of whether they are Greek or Latin, is in sections devoted to the problem of how to talk about the difference between the three persons of the Trinity: the Father, the Son and the Holy Spirit. Calvin begins with a brief definition drawn from Gregory of Nazianzus' *Sermo de baptismate* and then, as we shall see, moves through several patristic testimonies. Irenaeus is only of secondary importance.

> "A distinction between the Father and the Word and the Word and the Spirit can be established from the Scriptures. The greatness of this mystery, however, shows us what piety and care should be exercised when discussing this matter. I find these words of Gregory of Nazianzus very much to my liking 'I cannot think of one [Person of the Trinity] without immediately being overwhelmed by the splendour of the three; on the other hand, I cannot conceive of the three without immediately being brought back to their unity'."[39]

The choice of Gregory of Nazianzus is by no means arbitrary, given that it was the Cappodocian's teaching that helped restore the Nicene Faith prior to the Council of Constantinople in 381, during which Gregory was appointed bishop of Constantinople (an honour he declined). Calvin cites the passage in Greek already in the 1539 edition of the *Institutes*. Where did he get it from? Most likely from the 1516 Aldine edition of 16 *Orations* of Gregory, either directly or via an intermediate source. He obviously judged the statement of suffi-

---

[39] *Inst.* 1,13.17, CO 2: 104: "Rursum et quaedam Patris a Verbo, Verbi a Spiritu distinctio Scripturis demonstratur. In qua tamen excutienda, quanta religione ac sobrietate versandum sit, ipsa mysterii magnitudo nos admonet. Ac mihi sane vehementer istud Gregorii Nazianzeni arridet: οὐ φθάνω τὸ ἕν νοῆσαι, καὶ τοῖς τρισὶ περιλάμπομαι οὐ φθάνω τὰ τρία διελεῖν, και εἰς τὸ ἕν ἀναφέρομαι: 'non possum vnum cogitare quin trium fulgore mox circunfundar nec tria possum discernere quin subito ad vnum referar" [Gregory of Nazianzus, *Oratio* 40.41 (*de baptismate*), MPG 36: 417-418].

cient importance to cite in Greek together with his own translation.[40]

Gregory of Nazianzus echoed Calvin's own uncertainty about how to talk about the three Persons of the Trinity but the question remained open. Should one use analogies from the material, human world ? Calvin notes that Fathers such as Augustine among the Latins and Cyril of Alexandria among the Greeks sometimes adopted that approach but not without specifying that there was a vast difference between the human and the divine. On the authority of several of Augustine's works and that of Cyril's *De Trinitate*,[41] Calvin therefore decides to dispense with that approach and goes back to the Bible: Romans 8,9 and 2 Peter 1,21 show clearly (to his mind) that the Son proceeds from the Father and that the Holy Spirit proceeds from both. The problem of the three Persons thus settled and his and Gregory's problem partly solved, Calvin turns to the question of their common nature (*natura*). Basing himself on John 14,10 (*ego in Patre et Pater in me*), Calvin asserts that there is no difference of essence (*essentia*) between Persons: the Son's essence is in the Father's and vice versa. It is only their properties — the Father begetting, the Son begotten — that are distinct. One text by Augustine (in fact Alcuin) and two by Cyril of Alexandria provide Calvin with all the proofs he needs.[42]

Gregory of Nazianzus' problem to do with the simultaneity of the three and the one is solved with the help of the Scripture, Augustine and Cyril of Alexandria. Although our prime concern here is to show Calvin's attitude to and use of the Greek Fathers, one cannot but be struck by the fact that Calvin, when he has recourse to *testimonia*,

---

[40] *Gregorii Nazanzeni Orationes lectissimae* XVI. [Opera M. Musuri editae]. Venetiis in aedibus Aldi et Andreae Soceri, 1516, 172v.-203r. The first Greek edition of Gregory's *Opera omnia* came out in 1550 from the presses of Johannes Herwagen, Basel. Cf. *Catalogus translationum et commentariorum.* Edited by P. O. Kristeller, F. E. Cranz, V. Brown et alii. Washington, D.C.: Catholic University of America Press, 1960, vol. 2, *Gregory of Nazianzus*, 77-82, and Irena Backus. *La Patristique et les guerres de religion en France. Étude de l'activité littéraire de Jacques de Billy (1535-1581) O.S.B., d'après le MS. Sens 167 et les sources imprimées.* Paris: Études Augustiniennes, 1993, 88-103.

[41] *De Trin. dial.* 3, MPG 75: 600. *Inst.* 1,13.18, CO 2: 105. Calvin used the 1528 Basel (Andreas Cratander) edition of the works of Cyril of Alexandria.

[42] *Inst.* 1,13.19, 105-106. "Siquidem in vnaquaque hypostasi tota intelligitur natura, cum hoc, quod subest sua vnicuique proprietas. Pater totus in Filio est, totus in Patre Filius, quemadmodum ipse quoque asserit: ego in Patre et Pater in me [Ioh. 14,10] nec vlla essentiae differentia seiungi alterum ab altero scriptores ecclesiastici concedant." (Aug. Hom. de temp. 38 [= Alcuin, *De fide sanctae Trin.* lib. 1-2, MPL 101: 13-25], Cyril, *De Trin. dial.* 7 [MPG 75: 1075], 3 [MPG 75: 787]).

tends to cite both representatives of the Latin and of the Greek Church. This would suggest firstly that he is strongly dependent on the Fathers as *auctoritates* (isolated testimonies made to converge into one doctrine) and secondly that he sees the Christendom of the first five centuries as united a contrast with his own era.

But to return to our earlier point, what has happened to Irenaeus and Tertullian recuperated with such vigour against the contentions of Servetus ? No ante-Nicene Father plays a central part in the elaboration of the doctrine of the Trinity in the *Institutes*. In the expository part of the work, Calvin simply provides Biblical substantiation for the non-Biblical Nicene doctrine. However, the ante-Nicene Fathers, notably Irenaeus (and Tertullian), are cited extensively when Calvin comes to refute those of his heretical contemporaries who do not see the Son as God.

> "That they accumulate so many passages out of Irenaus where he asserts that the Father of Christ is the sole and eternal God of Israel, is either due to shameful ignorance or to total wickedness. They could not have noticed that that holy man dealt with and fought fanatics who said that the Father of Christ was not that God who had once spoken through Moses and the prophets but goodness knows what spectre come into being as result of the ruin of the world."[43]

Referring obliquely to *Adu. haer.* 3,19.2, the Genevan Reformer notes that the Father is called God whereas the Son is called God "absolutely". Calvin's reading of that passage is by no means innocent and his attempts to make Irenaeus conform to the Nicene doctrine of the pre-existent Logos appear heavy-handed. While Irenaus does indeed stress the unity of God of the Old and the New Testament, his concern in book three is primarily to rehabilitate the material creation (which the Gnostics associated with the Demiurge). Therefore, while not denying the Son's divinity, he insists first and foremost on the manifestation of that divinity in the human and therefore material Jesus. This aspect of Irenaeus' Trinitarian doctrine was not at all suitable for defence of the Nicene teaching, and that is

---

[43] *Inst.* 1,13.27, CO 2: 114: "Quod multos locos accumulant ex Irenaeo vbi patrem Christi asserit esse vnicum et aeternum Deum Israel, vel pudenda inscitia est, vel summa improbitas. Animaduertere enim debuerant sancto viro negotium et certamen fuisse cum phreneticis, qui patrem Christi negabant illum esse Deum qui per Mosen et prophetas olim loquutus fuerat, sed nescio quod spectrum e labe mundi productum."

no doubt the reason why Calvin in the *Institutes* could not accord the bishop of Lyon the same normative status as he accorded Gregory of Nazianzus or Cyril of Alexandria. In the same way, Justin Martyr is referred to very briefly as one of the most ancient Fathers, "[qui] nobis autem per omnia suffragatur" [44] while Ignatius of Antioch's *Epistles* are dismissed as an outright forgery, Calvin's view of them having always been negative.[45] Calvin's condemnation of Ignatius, which was to be echoed nearly a century later by Jean Daillé, was largely due to the fact that since 1498 only the Long Recension of the *Epistles* was available and this contained several interpolations as well as four spurious pieces. In the climate of confessional tensions it was simpler for Calvin to confine the entire corpus to the realm of the apocrypha.[46]

In his exposition of the doctrine of the Trinity in the last edition of the *Institutes*, Calvin's main point of reference was the Bible which he attempted to harmonise first and foremost with the pronouncements of Augustine and only secondly with the Greek post-Nicene Fathers. While conscious of the problems of terminology when translating from Greek into Latin, Calvin did not see the Greek Fathers he referred to as members of an alien Orthodox Church but as representatives of an United Christendom. The ante-Nicene Greek Fathers play a less important role; only Irenaeus is forced, rather unsuccessfully, into the role of a forerunner of the doctrine of Nicaea and Constantinople.

4. *Free will. Calvin's Treatise against Pighius and the Institutes*

In his treatment of the doctrine of the Trinity, Calvin ably chose such Greek Fathers as could serve his purpose. The problem, howev-

---

[44] *Inst.* 1,13.29, CO 2: 116.

[45] *Inst.* 1,13,29, CO 2: 116: "Ignatium quod obtendunt, si velint quidquam habere momenti, probent apostolos legem tulisse de quadragesima et similibus corruptelis. Nihil naeniis illis quae sub Ignatii nomine editae sunt putidius."

[46] The authentic *Epistles* of Ignatius are those to the Ephesians, Magnesians, Trallians, Philadelphians, Smyrnians and Polycarp. Those are the letters cited by Eusebius and Theodoret. A Latin version of the seven genuine but interpolated letters, together with four spurious ones, was first published by Jacques Lefèvre d'Etaples in 1498. It was accepted *in toto* by Roman Catholic writers and rejected by Calvin and his disciples. The short Recension of Ignatius' *Epistles* (without the letter to Polycarp) was first published by J. Ussher in 1644.

er, was quite different when it came to free will as only Augustine was found to be satisfactory. As was pointed out by A.N.S. Lane in a recent article, in the 1539 *Institutes* Calvin claimed that with the exception of Augustine, the early Fathers were so confused, vacillating and contradictory on the subject of free choice that almost nothing could be determined with certainty from their writings.[47]

Pighius attempted to refute this claim in *De libero arbitrio* to which Calvin replied in 1543. The Greek Fathers invoked were Pseudo-Clement of Rome (*Recognitiones*), Irenaeus, Basil, Origen and Chrysostom. Calvin made considerable efforts to "win back" Irenaeus, claiming that he attributed free will to the unfallen man.[48] Curiously enough, Calvin also wrested back Origen (denying that the Alexandrian's doctrine of free will was excessive, although admitting that it was unclear[49]) and Basil who was magically made to conform to Calvin's own position.[50] Paradoxically, only Chrysostom, so respected by Calvin as bishop and Biblical teacher, escaped rehabilitation.[51]

Needless to say, the *Institutes* passage remained unchanged. Calvin cannot be seen as completely inconsistent given that it is Chrysostom and not Origen or Basil whom he judges to be the most explicit expositor of the iniquitous doctrine of free will in the *Institutes*. *Inst.* 2,2, entitled *Hominem arbitrii libertate nunc esse spoliatum et miserae seruituti addictum*, is constructed very differently to chapter 1.13 on the Trinity in which Calvin added Patristic quotations so as to give a Nicene meaning to a collection of Biblical passages. Here, Calvin starts off by criticising ancient philosophers for according too much importance to the doctrine of free will; he then moves on to the Fathers, all of whom, with the exception of Augustine, are found more or less wanting. The bulk of the Biblical quotations in support of bondage of the will come at the very end of the chapter, where they are often accompanied by quotations from Augustine. Sections 4-9 are ostensibly devoted to the critique of the Fathers, most of whom have tried to accommodate the teaching of Pagan philosophy

---

[47] A. N. S. Lane, "Calvin and the Fathers in *Bondage and Liberation of the Will*". In *Calvinus sincerioris religionis vindex*, 67-96, esp. 67. Cf. also John Calvin. *The Bondage and Liberation of the Will: A Defence of the Orthodox Doctrine of Human Choice against Pighius*. Edited by A. N. S. Lane, tr. G. I. Davies. Grand Rapids, Mi.: Baker Bookhouse, 1996. Cited hereafter as: *Lane/Davies*.

[48] *Lane/Davies*, 71; CO 9: 282.

[49] *Lane/Davies*, 70; CO 9: 280-281.

[50] *Lane/Davies*, 75-77; CO 9: 284-286.

[51] *Lane/Davies*, 79-80; CO 9: 287-288.

to the Scripture, partly so as not to become the laughing stock of philosophers and partly so as not to force humankind into a sort of fatalistic inactivity. Chrysostom, cited several times, is considered by Calvin to have been particularly remiss in granting too much importance to human powers, although nearly all ancient doctors are unclear.

As is his wont in the *Institutes*, Calvin cites selected brief passages from each Father to support his case. Four excerpts from Chrysostom were cited to show his exaggerated respect of free will, one from the *Homilia de proditione Judae* and three from the *Homilies on Genesis*. (Needless to say, none of the three excerpts was ever underlined by Calvin in his own copy of Chrysostom). Calvin's method of citing the Fathers bears more than a superficial resemblance to the *auctoritates* method although frequently, as here, Calvin's aim is diametrically opposed to that of e.g. Bonaventure:[52] his *auctoritates* are either an argument to be demolished, as happens to be the case with Chrysostom, or an argument corroborating a Biblically-based doctrine such as that of the Trinity.

As in the case of the Trinity, so when discussing free-will, Calvin is acutely conscious of the distinctions between the Greek and the Latin terminology but in this instance he insists that there is no underlying unity of subject-matter:

> "Those who vaunted themselves as the disciples of Christ used too philosophical a language to talk about this matter. The term free will never ceased to be used by the Latins as if humans were unfallen to this day. The Greeks were not ashamed to use a much more arrogant term; they speak of power over oneself as if man had ever had power over himself."[53]

Man had free will before the fall but not power over himself. Calvin does not pursue the concept of αὐτεξούσιον but insists on finding a definition of *liberum arbitrium*. He chooses Origen's definition in *De principiis* 3 (1.3, GCS 22,197), "the capacity of human reasoning to distin-

---

[52] On this cf. Jacques-Guy Bougerol. "The Church Fathers and *Auctoritates* in Scholastic Theology to Bonaventure". In *The Reception of the Church Fathers in the West*, 289-335.

[53] *Inst.* CO 2: 189: "Nimis ergo philosophice hac de re loquuti sunt qui se Christi iactabant esse discipulos. Nam quasi adhuc integer staret homo, semper apud Latinos liberi arbitrii nomen extitit. Graecos vero non puduit multo arrogantius vsurpare vocabulum; siquidem αὐτεξούσιον dixerunt, ac si potestas suiipsius penes hominem fuisset."

guish between good and evil" as being the most similar to Augustine's (in fact Hugh of St. Victor's). Calvin takes this definition as his point of departure with a view to elaborating upon it: "a human being does not have the free will to do *good* unless he is helped by special grace of God which is granted to the elect only, through regeneration".[54] Thus qualified, Origen's definition shrinks to attributing to human powers the capacity to discern and do evil. Having thus demolished the Greek Fathers in the person of Origen and especially his beloved Chrysostom, Calvin seems to feel he has gone too far and cites a passage from Chrysostom's (in fact Pseudo-Chrysostom's) *Homilia prima in aduentu* where the Greek Father supposedly says that man is not merely a sinner by nature but is nothing but sin,[55] together with several passages from late Augustine which also stress man's total sinfulness. He could, he adds, multiply quotations from the Fathers (including Chrysostom and Origen, it is implied) that show human nature to be intrinsically evil but he does not wish to be accused of citing only those passages that serve his purpose.[56]

The latter comment is revealing not just of Calvin's bad faith — after all he had cited numerous passages showing that the Greek Fathers overvalued free-will — but also of his method of working with Patristic literature. He read the Fathers by picking out passages, and more often than not, passages that served his purpose. However, he never abandons the Fathers, particularly the Greek Fathers, and even after severely criticising them in the section on free-will, he ends on a positive note:

"Nonetheless I will say this: although they sometimes exceed all measure in exalting free will, they alwàys aim to turn man away from trust-

---

[54] Calvin found "Augustine's" definition ("non ab eo [Origene] variat Augustinus quum docet facultatem esse rationis et voluntatis qua bonum eligitur gratia assistente, malum ea desistente") in Peter Lombard's *Sentences* 2, dist. 24,3 or in a commentary on the *Sentences*. Cf. Hugh of St. Victor, *Summa sent.* 3,8, MPL 176: 101 and O. S. 3: 246. *Inst.* 2,2.6, CO 2: 190: "Hoc si recipitur, extra controversiam erit non suppetere ad bona opera liberum arbitrium homini nisi gratia adiuuetur, et gratia quidem speciali, qua electi soli per regenerationem donantur."

[55] *Inst.* 2,2.9, CO 2: 193: "Quid illud Chrysostomi, quod omnis homo non modo naturaliter peccator, sed totus peccatum est ? Si nihil boni nostrum est, si homo a vertice ad calcem totus est peccatum, si ne tentare quidem licet quantum valeat arbitrii facultas, qui iam inter Deum et hominem laudem boni operis partiri liceat ?". For the Pseudo-Chrysostom's *Homilia 1 in aduentu* cf. OS. 3:252, note 2.

[56] *Inst.* 2,2.9, CO 2: 193: "Possem eiusmodi formae permulta ex aliis referre, sed nequis cauilletur me seligere sola ea quae causae meae seruiunt, quae autem aduersantur, callide praeterire, ab hac recitatione abstineo."

ing in his own powers, so as to teach him that all his virtue resides in God."[57]

5. *The Presence of Greek Fathers in Calvin's' Commentaries. The Example of the Johannine Prologue*

What we have called the *auctoritates* method of using the Fathers, be they Greek or Latin, applied to the *Institutio* and to polemical treatises but not so much to Biblical exegesis. In Calvin's Commentaries the Fathers were very rarely referred to explicitly, but this does not mean that they were not used. We shall now evaluate Calvin's use of the Greek Fathers, especially Cyril, in his *Commentary on the fourth Gospel*, and more particularly the Johannine Prologue. Cyril, although hardly ever mentioned explicitly, is found on closer inspection to be omnipresent, much more so than the modern editor's notes would lead us to believe. Thus at *John* 1,1, commenting on the phrase *In principio*, Calvin states: "Therefore Augustine rightly draws our attention to the fact that this beginning is without a beginning".[58] The modern editor notes quite correctly that the only possible source for this statement is not Augustine but Cyril who says ad loc. that the beginning here has no beginning but is infinite and incomprehensible.[59]

Regarding the phrase *sermo erat apud Deum*, Calvin says that it would be absurd for the Evangelist to say that [the Word] was always with God, if the Word were not a distinct person in the Godhead; the phrase thus constitutes (still according to Calvin) a refutation of Sabellius.[60] There is no editorial note here, but turning to Cyril we can isolate the same point from his more diffuse comments on the passage. Cyril says: "By saying that 'the word was with God' he shows that the Son was an individual being existing by himself".[61]

---

[57] *Inst.* 2,2.9, CO 2: 193: "Audeo tamen hoc affirmare, vtcunque nimii interdum sint in libero arbitrio extollendo, hunc tamen illis propositum fuisse scopum, vt hominem a virtutis suae fiducia penitus auersum, in Deo vno fortitudinem suam repositum habere doceant."

[58] Calvin, *In Ioh.*, ed. Feld, 13-14: "Recte ergo Augustinus principium hoc, cuius nunc fit mentio, principio carere admonet."

[59] MPG 73: 26.

[60] Calvin, *In Ioh.*, ed. Feld, 14: "Absurde enim diceret Euangelista semper cum Deo vel apud Deum fuisse nisi propria quaedam illi subsistentia in Deo foret. Ergo ad refellendum Sabellii errorem valet hic locus quia ostendit Filium a Patre differre."

[61] MPG 73: 31.

Still in the same verse, commenting on *et sermo erat Deus*, Calvin comments: "since God is one, it follows that Christ is of the same essence with the Father and yet different in some respect".[62] Again, there is no editorial note indicating the possible source for this statement, but there is no doubt that the source is Cyril who states *ad loc.*: "not only was the Word with God but he was God so that through the fact of his being with God, he can be recognised as being different from the Father, and believed to be the Son subsisting independently, and through the fact of being God he can be seen to be consubstantial [...]".[63]

Calvin's reliance on Cyril in the Johannine Prologue does not prevent him from (tacitly) opposing the Alexandrian's punctuation of John 1,3 (full stop after *sine ipso factum est nihil*).[64] Cyril is also present in other chapters of Calvin's Commentary. Thus it is interesting to note that at John 6,63 Calvin criticises Chrysostom for referring *caro non prodest quicquam* to the Jews' carnal understanding and so demarcates himself from Martin Bucer who follows Chrysostom although he does not explicitly mention the Jews. Calvin takes the phrase to refer to Christ's flesh, eaten carnally without true faith. Although he does not name his sources, they are obviously Augustine and Cyril.[65]

Conclusion

Our enquiry into Calvin's use of the Greek Fathers has not been exhaustive. However, it has been full enough to enable us to reach certain conclusions.

It is obvious that Calvin was interested in a small corpus of Greek Fathers (although he was not particularly concerned to read them in their original language) and that he saw them as part of the ancient United Christendom. It is significant that he never seriously raised the *Filioque* question. In his polemical works and in the *Institutio* where he cites the Fathers following, at least stylistically, the mediaeval *auctoritates* method, he makes sure that he gives his readers excerpts from

---

[62] Calvin, *In Ioh.*, ed. Feld, 15: "*Et sermo erat Deus.* Iam quum vnicus sit Deus, Christum eiusdem esse cum Patre essentia et tamen in aliquo differre sequitur."
[63] MPG 73: 39.
[64] Calvin, *In Ioh.*, ed. Feld, 16-17.
[65] Calvin, *In Ioh.*, ed. Feld, 223.

the Greek and the Latin Fathers whatever the issue. He is also acutely aware, as we saw, of differences in terminology and of the difficulties attendant upon translating Greek Trinitarian terms into Latin.

Never a patristic scholar, Calvin was nonetheless a keen reader
and user of a limited corpus of the Greek Fathers, with a greater
interest in the post-Nicene than the ante-Nicene representatives of
the Early Greek Church, Irenaeus constituting the sole exception.

No Greek Father was ever adopted wholesale but no Greek Father
(not even Origen) was ever rejected out of hand, so long as no real
doubts were cast upon the authenticity of his writings. As his annotations in his copy of Chrysostom show, Calvin needed the intellectual
and moral backing of the Greek Church for his ideas on Church discipline and one cannot imagine what his doctrine of the Trinity
would have been like had he not read Cyril.

Although his sole venture into patristic scholarship came to nothing, there is no doubt that at some stage in his career he entertained
the notion that the educated faithful should read the Bible with the
aid of patristic commentaries translated into the vernacular. However, several characteristics of the Greek Fathers were either disregard-
ed or disparaged by Calvin. Allergic to philosophy (while fond of citing ancient philosophers), he criticised any attempt to integrate it into
Christian thought, which meant i.a. that Biblical allegory was confined to outer darkness; spirituality, asceticism and monasticism, present in the works of Chrysostom, Gregory of Nazianzus, Basil of Caesarea and others, were completely ignored.

Calvin's Early Greek Church was thus a very partial Church,
strangely reminiscent of his own conception of theology and Church
organisation[66].

---

[66] An earlier version of this paper was delivered at the 7th International Congress
of Calvin Research in Seoul (S. Korea), August, 1998. I am grateful to A.N.S. Lane
for his remarks on that first version.

IV. RELIGIOUS LIFE: ROOTS AND RAMIFICATIONS

THE SAYINGS OF THE FATHERS:
AN INSIDE LOOK AT THE NEW DEVOUT IN DEVENTER

John Van Engen*

The New Devout formed communes in ordinary houses on ordinary streets, first in Deventer and Zwolle in the 1380s, then in market towns throughout the Ijssel river valley and the county of Holland. A passerby might see them in the street going to market or to church, even look in on them; interested townspeople attended "collations" held in the vernacular; clients came round to order manuscripts, prepared for a fee. Within these towns and neighborhoods, however, the New Devout counted as neither lay townspeople nor professed religious, and they acted as neither guildsmen nor ordinary clerics. They set themselves up as "private religious," "private" because they took no vows and were bound to no public ecclesiastical corporation, "religious" because they imposed on themselves a life of intense devotion. The tenor of life in each household depended significantly, more so than in a house under a rule, on the quality of its individual members and its leadership, for the Devout lived, strictly speaking, freely. To guide that life, accordingly, they drew up, ingeniously and quite self-consciously, written aides: "exercises" and "proposals" to direct individual religious practices, "customaries" to govern collective practices, "lives" to memorialize Brothers and Sisters at death, and "devotional tractates" in number and variety to nourish the inner life. Devout households, though independent in principle, over time formed loosely bound networks: heads of houses formed links and considered common policies by way of an annual assembly, men served in the more numerous women's houses as confessors, and both Sisters and Brothers kept steady ties to the regular branch of their movement, the Canons and Canonesses of Windesheim. Still, they recognized no common rule, no required corpus of readings, no superior or general chapter.

All this has invited protracted historical dispute. Almost from the

* Professor of History, University of Notre Dame

inception of the Modern Devotion, certainly since its demise, and
especially from the nineteenth century onwards, historians have
made strong claims, sometimes contradictory, about the nature and
import of the Devout movement. Studies since the 1960s have sought
to place them more carefully and convincingly in their own societies,
to understand them as pursuing their own purposes more than agendas of the sixteenth century. While a new synthetic approach may
now be overdue, local studies still have much to contribute. This
essay presents a single work from a single house, an unedited quire
from the first household of Brothers, a text almost entirely overlooked
until now, partly because its script is so difficult, partly because historians have not adequately considered texts in this genre. The quire is
filled with "*dicta*" or "sayings," presented here in an appended edition. These entries, on close reading, offer an immediate record,
sometimes nearly stenographic, of spiritual conversation inside the
household, a mirror to the inner life and teachings of men at Deventer struggling to embody the New Devotion two generations into the
movement. This founding household, called the Heer-Florens House,
had organized informally in the 1380s, acquired its own house and
property on the present Striksteeg in 1391, and expanded the house
in 1441 to allow for more Brothers.[1] The text presented here appears
to date from the later 1440s, or about 1450. Its fifty-five sayings allow
a fascinating glimpse, an "insider's view," into this first house of
Brothers, and by implication into Devout life more generally in the
mid-fifteenth century.

The set of sayings edited and studied here, the *Dicta patrum*, is preserved and transmitted in two forms, the presumed "original," a single quire in Brussels, Royal Library, 8849-59, ff. 67-76 (here = MS
B), then in a revised and polished version two generations later, preserved in The Hague, Royal Library, 128 G 16, ff. 166r-175r (here =
MS A). Both manuscripts originated in the Heer-Florens House in
Deventer, and both are miscellanies, that is, made up of various
works and quires subsequently bound together, MS B gathered as a
single unit around 1501, MS A about 1518/20.[2] Originally, these

---

[1] Basic on the formation of the house remains: C. van der Wansem, *Het ontstaan en
de geschiedenis der Broederschap van het Gemene Leven tot 1400* (Leuven 1958). See now
Anton Weiler, *Volgens de norm van de vroege kerk* (Nijmegen 1997), pp. 4-25.

[2] I am foregoing an elaborate description or apparatus, since I have long codico-
logical studies of both manuscripts in progress. Both are complex miscellanies, falsely
or confusingly bound at present. For basic orientation on MS B, see M. Carasso-

sayings were entered into a single quire duodecimo in size (the "hand-sized" format favored for devotional volumes), which consisted of ten folios or five bifolios of coarse paper. This quire (subsequently bound into what became MS B) must have been handled independently for a generation or more, with its smudged front and back leaves. A working set of notations, not a finished text, it is overall in poor condition, shows a lack of order and rubrication, and was written in a difficult script (one key reason, perhaps, why this text has gone unedited and unstudied). The title on its first folio, *Dicta patrum*, is written in a broader hand and darker ink, added later, possibly by the original scribe, more likely by the later compiler of the codex. The original scribe simply started in writing on the first folio, without explanation, and eventually left the last four folios blank. The first two or three folios show a relative consistency of script, perhaps indicating the work of a single initial writing campaign, especially the first eight items. Thereafter, sayings were written in several at a time, sometimes even singly, towards the end in an ever broadening hand. Each saying was set off, in the left margin, with a simple paragraph marker (corresponding to a distinct number in the edition). In the outer margin, many were denoted with a thematic rubric (given in brackets in the edition).

The hand in this quire is that of Brother Peter from Hem near Hoorn (1424-1479), longtime librarian of the Heer-Florens House in Deventer.[3] His hand is known from two other extant works, a *vita* of Geert Grote, founder of the New Devout, which now forms the first quire in MS B, and the *Vitae fratrum* of the Brothers at Deventer, which now forms the opening quires of MS A.[4] Brother Peter's own life was memorialized in a *vita* written by a disciple named Albert of Lübeck, this too extant in a single copy (also a single quire) now part of MS A.[5] Like so many other Brothers, Peter Hoorn, a leading figure in the house during his lifetime, first came to Deventer for school-

Kok, *Repertorium van verhalende historische bronnen uit de middeleeuwen* (The Hague 1981), n. 204, pp. 227-29 (with further references), and *Manuscrits datés conservés en Belgique, Tome V: 1481-1540* (Brussels 1987) no. 656 (pp. 42-43), with nn. 668, 678, 679, 680

[3] I had come to this judgement independently through my work with manuscripts from the house in Deventer, and was pleased to see it expressed now by two other manuscript scholars: Karl Stooker and Theo Verbeij, *Collecties op Orde: Middelnederlandse handschriften uit kloosters en semi-religieuze gemeenschappen in der Nederlanden*, 2 vols. (Leuven 1997), 2.115.

[4] Carasso Kok (n. 2 above) nn. 347, 348, pp. 375-77.

[5] Carasso-Kok (n. 2 above) no. 105, p. 130.

ing in the 1430s, was attracted to the Devout, entered their House in 1442, and died there in 1479 at age fifty-five. Intelligent and able enough that professed religious attempted to recruit him away,[6] he ardently defended the Devout way of life and remained loyal to it until his death.[7] Though he served for thirty years or more as house librarian (not the same position as *scriptor*), the *vita* reports that his was a poor hand for writing[8] — amply demonstrated by the quire containing these *dicta*. Peter Hoorn nonetheless could, and did, work laboriously to achieve legibility in the standard *bastarda* script when copying out the texts of the *vitae*. This quire of *dicta*, written less carefully, must represent something closer to a personal notebook.

After Peter Hoorn's death in 1479, someone, perhaps another librarian, saved this quire, no doubt owing to its general interest for the entire household. In the 1510s this or another Brother, recognizing its import but also its poorness of hand and sloppiness of language, resolved to produce a polished copy. The scribe deserves attention in his own right (in another essay), for he copied a variety of materials central to the house's life, both *vitae* and *dicta*, eventually adding this work of his own to a set of quires already in existence which began with Peter Hoorn's copy of the *Vitae fratrum* — all this then making up MS A. Of those materials this scribe saw fit to add to the *vitae*, a disproportionate number consisted of *dicta*: those of Brother John Hattem (d. 1485), of the "fathers," of Florens Radewijns, and of Thomas of Kempen (actually a part of his *Imitatio Christi*). Whether

---

[6] "Et tanto amore domui nostre et exerciciis est colligatus, ut nunquam post ingressum per inconstanciam uacillaret; sed si aliquando siue monachi siue quicumque alii eum ad alium ordinem siue uite modum niterentur attrahere, non sine rubore ab ipso recedebant. Omnium enim qui se a domo nostra retrahere conabantur manus pii zeli dente momordit." *Vita Petri Hoorn*, ed. Gerhardus Dumbar, *Analecta seu vetera aliqua scripta inedita* (Deventer 1719), p. 149.

[7] "Cordialiter ualde dilexit non solum domum nostram sed eciam totum statum nostrum. Quapropter non potuit equanimiter tolerare si quid contra honorem aut domus nostre aut tocius status diceretur uel fieret; sed aut uerbis, si commode posset, aut scriptis, si uerbis non posset, utrumque nitebatur defendere. Et multum, eciam usque ad extremum uite sue, anxiabatur, si aliquando domui nostre aliquod periculum, et maxime spirituale, uidebatur imminere." *Vita Petri Hoorn*, ed. Dumbar pp. 154-55.

[8] "Ceterum quamquam ualde graue et laboriosum sibi esset opus scripture, eo quod tremulam et minus aptam haberet manum scribendi, et presertim in hyeme quando pre frigiditate articulorum manus, quos naturaliter frigidos habuit, nonnunquam penna ex inualidis manibus scribentis prosiliit. Ipse tamen propter hoc nec scribere omisit nec ad ignem recurrit, sed requisita penna, quomodo ualuit, opus scripture consummauit. Et nunquam se ad alia officia facienda ordinari postulauit, sed usque ad mortem scriptor permansit." *Vita Petri Hoorn*, ed. Dumbar p. 151.

or not he knew that the original quire containing the *Dicta patrum* stemmed from Peter Hoorn (he probably did), this Brother-scribe smoothed out the language in re-copying, and provided a title, *Quedam dicta patrum*. Of the fifty-five items in Peter Hoorn's original collection, this Brother reproduced forty-one of them, some literally, more often in a polished or abbreviated form. His series corresponds to the original set as follows: 1-5, 11-13, 17, 20-23, 6-9, 25-30, 33-35, 38-43, 45-48, 50-53, 55, 9, 10. His re-ordering of items 6-10 is best grasped as a result of copying. In the original, these items came on the verso or back side of the first folio, and extended (unusually) to the top margin of the second folio — and must, for some reason, have been passed over initially. For the purposes of this essay, this version, though also transcribed below, is significant only as testimony to the continuing vitality of these *dicta* in the house in the 1510s.

What Brother Peter intended upon starting this quire is not entirely clear. At the head of the first folio is a rubric "*de bonis*," but in fact only the first saying concerned the house's goods. The first eight sayings treat key Devout themes (privileges, recruits, study, stewardship, prayer), and the next go on to priesthood, the sacrament, and copying. These were, inevitably, the central themes for a Devout household; but if there was any notion of system, it vanished soon enough. Yet this quire cannot be understood entirely as an occasional notebook for jotting items down randomly. Some sayings come as a series on a related theme (say, chastity). More crucially, in the copying, repeated words and/or erasures indicate that he must at times have been copying from another work or an even rougher draft. Perhaps this quire was, just as it appears, a personal notebook for gathering up "sayings of the fathers," memorable spiritual teachings by senior members of the community. This also fit with his interest in the *vitae* of house members. But this may also represent a stray quire from his personal "*rapiarium*" or scrapbook of spiritual teachings. All Brothers were encouraged to keep them. Most were constructed of loose quires and odd scraps of rough paper (in this case, five bifolios, an unusual size), and most also disappeared once a brother died, unless they were of unusual spiritual or devotional interest, as in the case of Gerlach Peters. This quire, whatever its origin, purpose or context, was not filled to the end, its last four folia left blank. Notably, none of the sayings recorded here involve, or are attributed to, rector Egbert (1450-83) or the procurator John of Hattem (1448-85), influential figures in the house's life after 1450. Just as strikingly, Dirk of Herxen,

rector at Zwolle (1409-57) and widely acclaimed as the leading
Devout figure in this era, appears only once indirectly [12],[9] and not
as a teacher—perhaps an indication of how independent each household could be. The sayings in this quire fit, in short, the 1440s. Peter
Hoorn entered the House in 1442 at age eighteen. In his twenties,
looking back to the founders, he was himself becoming immersed in
their ways and teachings. Either he gave up collecting after Godfrey's
death in 1450, or started another quire for the 1450s and afterwards,
which is not preserved.

For living members of a household as well for their heirs, "sayings"
comprised all the stories and proverbs they told among themselves,
sometimes as the exhortation of a senior "father," sometimes a word
that emerged from common discussion, sometimes an individual
word one to another. Some were startling and brief, as this one on
the priestly office: "The Brothers of our house of Father Florens having come together on one occasion, Father Godfrey said to them, 'I
say to you, Brothers or Sisters, what I heartily feel. I would wish that
I was blinded in both eyes, and remained so until death, and thus
would never have come to the priesthood'" [9]. Or the rector might
return from a visit to another house and tell a long story as a kind of
exemplum, such as about apostasy [16]. Or it could be a personal
exchange, this one elicited by Peter himself: "I once asked a certain
man, 'If you were young and healthy, what would you want most to
give yourself to, and how?' And he said to me, 'I am a poor man with
a weak head. But our fathers gave themselves most to breaking their
own wills'." [4] Each "saying," whether a pithy response or a long
story, offered a "word" that touched Brothers or Sisters in their struggle to live the Devout life. Taken together, the fifty-five entries scrib-
bled by Peter Hoorn into this quire signal the living importance of
"sayings" (*dicta*) as a genre central to the experience and teachings of
the New Devout. If devotional manuals and exercises set out the ideal or the plan, sayings articulated their working out, language closer
to actual practice: what was said to foster the devout life, in what
tone or manner, on what occasion. Beyond individual exercises,
house customaries, and collective lives, such admonitory and proverbial words deeply informed the tone of religious life in a household.
Reports of such words, passed along or written down as individual
sayings or as whole sets, inscribed as precedents the collective ideal,

---

[9] To lighten the apparatus, the sayings will be referred to by number in brackets.

marking-out this distinctive way of life. If new members of a household, like Peter, or wearied and aging members, were ever to capture
or re-capture the excitement of the "fathers," they had to make these
sayings their own, absorb this in-house spiritual wisdom.

Oral communication strongly marked these sayings, even if, now,
a loose quire of written notices must be our point of departure. Yet it
is possible still to overhear the buzz of spiritual wisdom. Several sayings open anecdotally, that 'so-and-so said that so-and-so once said'.
Four of these [38, 41, 43, 51] take the telling right back to the house's
founder, Florens Radewijns, by way of two or three intermediaries.
Another [53] involves the rector who succeeded Florens, Amilius
(1400-04). Still another [35] offers an oral report, by way of two
intermediaries, of something that originated at nearby Windesheim.
Sometimes the communication was private, one Brother to another,
reported now by Peter or at second- or third-hand. Often it was collective, whether coming out of exhortation or group discussion.
When MS A (f. 156r) reproduced the sayings of John of Hattem, it
did so under the rubric "*quedam dicta et exhortationes eiusdem.*" A senior
Brother might "exhort" to a variety of audiences: fellow members of
the household, young students, Sisters in women's households,
laypeople gathered for a collation. While few or no collations, at least
at Deventer, got recorded as "sermons," the teachings often got
passed on as "sayings," the proverbial and memorable points. Further, and most importantly, this communal environment fostered
group discussion. Spiritual questions were "moved" (the preferred
verb), with the results handed on as a "saying" coming out of a "collation" [18, 41]. Thus when a venerable former rector visited the
house, "he and our Brothers coming together, it was moved, among
other topics, 'what is perfect mortification or renunciation'" [12].
The brothers "came together" [9, 21] on a variety of occasions, on
Sunday afternoons, especially during Lent [16, 33, 34], on Corpus
Christi day [11] and *kermis* [54], also when a visiting "father" stopped
through the house [7,12]. Further, the *dicta* themselves became
objects of reflection and discussion [42] at many opportunities, especially while relaxing at their farm site outside Deventer after bloodlet-
ting [20, 35, 42], or when the heads of households gathered (*communi
conuentu fratrum*) [29], or as part of mutual edification and admonition
on subjects as diverse as Lent or mortification or contemplation.

Of the fifty-five sayings entered into this quire, six certainly [7, 27,
38, 43, 44, 55] and five possibly [5, 13, 14, 15, 40] involved Peter

Hoorn himself. In the very last [55] he said simply, "when I was once alone with Rector Godfrey at Diepenveen," and that echoes one reported earlier [9]. Once [27] he reports that "Peter of Amsterdam told me"; twice [38, 43] that "Brother Dirk told me"; and another time [44] that "I asked a certain brother." Many sayings are addressed "to us," meaning the Brothers at the house in Deventer. Others, out of propriety or humility, take a more anonymous stance. One [7] uses the third person, that "Father Pe" made a request which provoked a saying directed to the entire household. In another [5] Ontgher of Hoorn, head of the house for students, speaks "to a certain person," possibly Peter. In two sayings [13, 14] "a certain brother" is reported to ask about the work of copying, something, as noted, troubling for Hoorn — the exchange probably originally involving Peter himself. In another [15] Rector Godfrey warns a "certain brother" about persistence in his vocation, adding a horrific story about "apostasy." Rival religious did try to recruit Peter Hoorn, probably early during his stay at the house, when Godfrey was still rector and profession as a regular was altogether thinkable for a promising cleric like Peter, then in his 20s. On another occasion [40] a "certain brother" asked Rudolph about "externals," clothes, food, and the like. The anonymity adopted here is consistent with the humility practiced in Devout writing, and may not in every occasion have meant Peter himself. But it may hint that he foresaw or imagined this material made available to others. A possible eleven sayings, one-fifth of the total, reveals that the collection, while pertaining to the whole house and society, had a special connection to Peter Hoorn himself.

Sayings appeared from the beginning of the Devout movement, written down early as bearers of this form of life. When Thomas of Kempen described the "fathers" of the movement in his "dialogue for novices" around 1440, based partly on his own and his brother John's personal experiences in Deventer much earlier in the 1390s-1400s, he also copied out, as appendices to these "lives," selections from such "sayings," testimony to their original vision.[10] Later scribes sometimes chose to excerpt only the sayings, producing independent clusters of them in "florilegia"-style manuscripts. There also existed,

---

[10] For examples from Geert Grote, Florens Radewijns, and Lubbert see Thomas of Kempen, *Dialogus noviciorum*, ed. M.J. Pohl, *Opera Omnia* (Freiburg 1922), 107-09, 198-210, 260-67.

as an altogether independent transmission, a lengthier version of the sayings attributed to the founders Geert Grote and Florens Rade-wijns, this possibly Thomas of Kempen's own source, known from a lost manuscript copied in the Heer-Florens house.[11] Further, beyond the "Sayings of the Fathers" (*Dicta patrum*) edited and presented here, the same manuscript (MS B) contains sayings attributed to the early and influential Devout priest, Johannes Brinckerink (d. 1419) and to the longtime procurator (1448-85) of the Heer-Florens House, John of Hattem,[12] both texts also still unedited, the second partly repro-duced in MS A.[13] Indeed the "sermons" or collations attributed to Johannes Brinckerinck, and alluded to in one of the sayings [6], most scholars now agree, were built up from "*dicta*" taken down by the Sis-ters and later put together as whole pieces.[14] In yet another case, probably from the 1470s, the Brothers at Deventer excerpted from their own *Vitae fratrum* to make up a set of exempla-like sayings orga-nized around specific spiritual topics.[15] All this pertains only to the founding house in Deventer. Careful investigation doubtless will turn up more.

The origins of "*dicta*" among the Devout must be sought in the two worlds that came together in the making of "private religious." Proverbs formed a significant part of the everyday lay world, pepper-ing language with a kind of folk wisdom—a subject known but understudied among medievalists.[16] Indeed Latin proverbs often entered vernacular writing in the later middle ages, and presumably

---

[11] The rubric in the manuscript was, apparently: "Incipiunt aliqua uerba notabilia domini Florentii et magistri Gherardi magni." See J.F.Vregt, "Eenige ascetische tractaten, afkomstig van de Deventersche Broederschap van het Gemeene leven, in verband gebragt met het Boek van Thomas a Kempis De Navolging van Christus," *Archief voor de Geschiedenis van het Aartsbisdom Utrecht* 10 (1882), pp. 427-72.

[12] See now my "Managing the Common Life: The Brothers at Deventer and the Codex of the Household (The Hague, MS KB 70 H 75)," in *Schriftlichkeit und Lebens-praxis im Mittelalter*, ed. Hagen Keller, Christel Meier and Thomas Scharff (Munich, 1999), pp. 111-69

[13] MS B, ff. 44r-55r, 266r-267v.

[14] P.F.J. Obbema, "Brinckerinck en Jan van Schoonhoven," in: *Codex in Context*, ed. Chr. de Backer (Nijmegen 1985), pp. 277-87.

[15] I first edited this collection: "The Virtues, The Brothers, and the Schools: A Text from the Brothers of the Common Life," *Revue Bénédictine* 98 (1988) 178-217; which was then further interpreted by Heiko Oberman, "Die Gelehrten die Verkehrten: Popular Response to Learned Culture in the Renaissance and Reforma-tion," in: *Religion and Culture in Renaissance and Reformation*, ed. Steven Ozment (Kirksville, MO 1989), pp. 43-62.

[16] Though little researched as yet in Middle Dutch, this topic may be pursued in the volume of essays edited by J. Reynaert, *Wat is wijsheid?* (1994)

ordinary speech as well. The Dutch language, moreover, is, still today, exceptionally rich in proverbs and idiomatic expressions. It was, for many of the Devout Brothers and Sisters, the form of speech that came most readily to a person's tongue in everyday life. For clerical men among the Devout, Latin was to be the first and ordinary religious language; yet at times the recorders of these sayings, and those whom they recorded, also went over into the vernacular without hesitation [20, 21, 41]. Devout households, approached from this vantage point, did exactly as other civic households, managed the ways and byways of life with a set of memorable expressions or short stories, guides to conduct and decision-making ready at the tongue and easily understood.

But there was a second source. The Devout understood their way of life as restoring the ideals of the Gospel, but no less significantly of the Desert Fathers. The *Vitaspatrum*, whether in Cassian's *Collations* or in the translated Latin forms of the *Verba seniorum*, ranked nearly at the top of Geert Grote's self-imposed reading list, indeed just after the Gospels, before other books of the Bible. Cassian or the *Verba seniorum* would remain at the top of reading lists right down through the subsequent history of this movement, and be translated into Middle Dutch by the Devout.[17] The Desert Fathers, as was plain to read, were also, many of them, though angelic exemplars of the Christian life, not "professed" in the strict sense. Most influentially, they dispensed their spiritual wisdom overwhelmingly in the form of "sayings." An apt word, a probing response, a telling story, a puzzling expression — this was the stuff of spiritual wisdom. So too for the New Devout, this was the supply of wisdom from which they hoped to live themselves and in which to form others. Thus, the sayings generated in Devout households, and passed down to Devout heirs, brought two forms together, quite simply, the proverbs of the street and the wisdom of the desert, the lay and the religious, the vernacular and the Latin.

---

[17] Geert Grote's remarkable *Conclusa et proposita, non uota* appear as an appendix to his *vita* in Thomas of Kempen, *Dialogus noviciorum*, ed. M.J. Pohl, *Opera Omnia* (Freiburg 1922) 7.97. Whether that rubric came from Master Geert or from Thomas, it became highly influential through this transmission, the only form in which it circulated. On the normative influence of his list, and on these reading lists in general, the basic work is now: Thomas Kock, *Die Buchkultur der Devotio moderna: Handschriftenproduktion, Literaturversorgung und Bibliotheksaufbau im Zeitalter des Medienwechsels* (Frankfurt 1999), pp. 111-47.

For a young Peter Hoorn, only in his twenties, the sayings he chose to enter into this quire came predominantly from "fathers," those whom he regarded as the spiritual elders in their movement. In the quire itself, and in the copying, there is no apparent ordering with respect to persons, and only a slight one with respect to themes. The point lay in the sayings themselves, each an independent treasure of spiritual wisdom. Twenty-one of the fifty-five, or two-fifths, are attributed to Godfrey Thorn of Moers, longtime rector of the House (1410-50), whose *vita* Peter Hoorn would himself write not long after 1459. There he described Godfrey, the man who introduced him to religious life, as "profound and succinct" in giving counsel on matters of conscience,[18] though perhaps too easily overcome by piety and charity as a disciplinarian — this perhaps congruent with one saying [10] in which the rector worried about his responsibility in the confessional. Yet, he might "slap" younger members of the community after they made confession — this a veiled reference to Hoorn himself.[19] Godfrey ruled, notably, only during Peter Hoorn's first eight years in the House, between his 18th and 26th year, a time when he was likely intensely open to spiritual teaching. Peter's own *vita* reported an especially close and intense bond between them.[20] At the very beginning of Godfrey's *vita* Peter Hoorn cited explicitly two of the more forceful sayings he had entered into his collection [55, 52] — the first coming out of their personal interaction, now passed on as said "*cuidam familiariter.*"[21] The *vita* further reports a saying [= 11, but especially 28] that presents Godfrey's view on what puts the Brotherhood spiritually at risk.[22] Yet, many more sayings plainly circulated than Peter Hoorn earlier had entered into his quire, *dicta*-like remarks reported throughout the *vita*. So the quire of

---

[18] "Profundus erat et succinctus in consiliis suis, circa talia dumtaxat que conscienciam tangunt". *Vitae fratrum*, ed. Dumbar, p. 116.

[19] *Vitae fratrum* ed. Dumbar, p. 119. Compare *Vita Petri Hoorn*, ed. Dumbar, p. 149.

[20] "Eumque nouicius esset pre aliis iuuenibus diligentissime a rectore domus ammoneri et exercitari postulauit, et quod peciit impetrauit. Nam Dominus Gotfridus pro tunc rector domus nostre, piis eius uotis annuens, eum pre ceteris frequenter aspere corripuit, sepe coram aliis humiliauit, alapas eciam aliquando in priuato ad maxillas dedit. In quibus omnibus paciens fuit, et nunquam contra rectorem murmurauit; quin pocius presumebat se diligi quod merebatur argui. Nec fefellit eum opinio ista, quia dominus Gotfridus eum pre aliis affectuose diligebat, et infirmatus libenter eum habuit in seruicio suo, sciens eum ad omnia promptum esse, nec posse in officiis caritatis fatigari." *Vita Peteri Hoorn*, ed. Dumbar, p. 149-50.

[21] *Vitae fratrum*, ed. Dumbar, p. 115.

[22] Ibid, p. 117.

dicta from about 1450 was not a simply a source-book for the *vita* a decade later. Such sayings must have passed around orally and come to mind as Peter wrote this *vita*, or were written down in a quire no longer preserved.

Thirteen of the fifty-five sayings, just over one-fifth, come from Rudolph of Muiden, the second most senior Brother in the House, procurator for many years (1420s-1448), then father-confessor for Sisters at the Master Geert's house several blocks away. Peter also eventually wrote his *vita*, about 1460, but with no direct quotation of the sayings. Especially in the 1440s, Rudolph's presence would have loomed large inside the house. He too, as a young man, moved from the schools in Deventer into the household of the Devout, but earlier. He saw Florens in 1398, just after the household had survived an inquisitorial investigation and an attack of plague; he joined about 1402. One year before his death in 1459 he began to write a memoire of the House, which evolved into, as many of these did, a set of *vitae*.[23] Peter Hoorn subsequently took this work over, re-copied it in what is now the beginning quircs of MS A, and himself added *vitae* for Godfrey, Rudolph, and later brothers into the 1470s. Rudolph was remembered here, by Peter Hoorn about 1460, as devoted to the household, its members, and their ways. Though a man of few words, he carried great authority. When he gave counsel or offered sayings, Peter noted, we all listened. He spoke his views, then kept silent if others objected or argued another view.[24] At mealtimes, Peter recalled, his words were few, and he spoke rather about the deeds and sayings than about other writings.[25] Peter's *vita* of Rudolph is richer and more engaged in many respects than his treatment of Godfrey; yet there are only occasional echoes of the *dicta* Peter had earlier copied into his quire.

The balance of the sayings come from various Devout figures, especially two. Henry Wetter served as the first rector of the house at Alberghen (1407-37/38), after beginning as procurator in the house

---

[23] Carasso-Kok (n. 2 above), no. 361, pp. 393-94.

[24] "In consiliis et dictis suis tante fuit auctoritatis, quod ipso loquente omnes auscultaremus. Quocirca habuit hunc morem, quod requisitus plane et breuibus uerbis dixit sentire suum. Quando autem aliquis contrarie arguebat, ipse humiliter tacebat, nec ullo modo dictum uel consilium suum defendere siue statuere satagebat." *Vitae fratrum*, ed. Dumbar, p. 131.

[25] "Et fuit sermo eius parcus sub prandiis et cenis, et pocius de patrum factis et dictis quam de scripturis...." Ibid. 130

at Zwolle. After his resignation, he lived on as a Brother in the Devout community (d. 1466), also after his house went over in 1448 to the Windesheim canons.[26] He visited the house in Deventer on more than one occasion, and was plainly regarded as one of the venerable worthies, a founding father. Peter Hoorn recorded six sayings attributed to him [7, 12, 29-32], the first of these requested by Peter himself as a "memorial word," lest he not return to them again (in fact, he lived on some twenty more years).[27] Another six of these sayings [21-26], all on the subject of chastity, are attributed to Henry of Gouda (d. 1410), a Brother from the house in Zwolle who acted as founder and father-confessor for the Sisters in Arnhem, the residential town for the dukes of Gelderland. This Henry also figured as a founding father, though obviously long dead in the 1440s. At least the first saying [21] reached Peter by way of Rector Godfrey. Whether he had also passed on the remainder, or another person in the House, or (less likely) these were already written down somewhere, is hard to know. In Peter Hoorn's quire they were copied in at the same time (ff. 69v-70r), with the same pen and ink. Still another Henry, not easily identifiable, visited the house, and left behind two striking sayings [36,37]. Notable, in other words, is the presence of an extended community. While most sayings derive from the two senior and authoritative figures in the house, "fathers" from throughout the movement chanced to come through the house and pass on their own store of proverbial wisdom.

To reduce a proverbial culture to a set of systematic teachings would violate its essential nature, turn *dicta* into devotional tractates or methodical exercises. For private religious constructing lives, alone in their rooms and together in the household, books and routines centrally shaped how they lived as individuals and what they were meant to be about as a collective. The ordered day which the Devout imposed on themselves, the ordered prayers, ordered reading and meditation — this is what first strikes readers of their exercises and customaries, even their devotional books. But historical imagination

---

[26] See now Weiler (n. 1 above), pp. 77-81 for the extensive literature on Henry and Alberghen.

[27] If the situation in this saying [7] may be read literally, then the text has a mistake. Henry ruled for thirty-one years, not twenty-one. For Peter to have been present and put the question, the date must be after 1442, thus a good five years since Henry's resignation.

must not allow this scene to become rigid, lifeless. For the religious life within these households, for all the inherent tensions between personal spiritual aspirations and a communal life, the *dicta* must be listened to, especially, though this becomes hard in a short interpretive essay, for their proverbial quality, their flash of insight, their ability to capture a moment. Take, for instance, the Brothers' sense of place in the world, as those withdrawn from the world and yet not fully, at least not in recognized legal or religious categories. Tricus or Dirk (d. 1443), a Brother from the earliest days, whom Peter Hoorn revered as a source, reported a word from Henry Bruyn, an even earlier Brother (d. 1398), who had spent much of his time copying in his room [45]. When someone peered into his room and saw how pleasant it was, Brother Henry quipped: "This room is my Holland, my Brabant, my Diocese, my Gelderland." In one sweeping gesture this former merchant named off the regional political principalities, only to declare his identity and allegiance as now contained entirely in a private room within a communal household, a cell where amidst writing and devotion a new sense of fatherland had emerged.

Or, take *kermis*, the feast of church dedication, a civic holiday in later medieval northern towns. Rather than to process in the street, behind the canons and the parish priest and alongside fellow citizens, Godfrey had all the brothers crowd into his room. Our *kermis* (*dedicatio nostra*), he said, is to call to mind how we got to this particular place, by what means and under what circumstances, and to consider what spiritual progress we have known in actual deed. If anyone finds himself negligent, he must ring the bells of his heart, to renew and to re-establish within his heart his intentions (*proposita*) — even as the people in town are now recalling the city's spiritual founders and patrons, Willibrord and Lebuin. Rudolph thereupon chimed in behind Godfrey: But we have our patron present now and the relics of the saints are processing before us, that is, if we find, after passing ourselves in review, that we have acted well. And for this our calling we must give God thanks [55]. These men, not parishioners hearing an exhortatory sermon at mass during *kermis*, not professed religious being reminded of their vows, not townspeople processing through town once a year to honor local patron saints, had, in joining a Devout household, privately dedicated themselves within a self-made religious community. While fellow townspeople celebrated the founding of their parish, the Devout gathered to renew and internalize their personal feast of church dedication. As with any good saying, a person's sense of things had to be transformed in a flash: not a civic *kermis* but a personal *dedicatio*.

But what sort of person could undertake such a project, and why? What historians have debated for a century, Rudolph put succinctly in a saying by way of commenting on the qualities looked for in new members [2]. With respect to the body, future Devout needed, he observed, the physical strength to sustain a rigorous way of life, lest one or another's frailty lower the expectations and change customs for the entire household. With respect to the soul, they needed a certain disposition of spirit (*inclinati*) towards this abject and humble estate, towards the care and managing of young people, and towards a will to cultivate the virtues (*inclinati ad despectum statum humilitatis nostre et tractum puerorum et uoluntas emendandi mores*). Each trait requires unpacking, especially the first and third. As to the second, among the important tasks which Brothers fashioned for themselves, beyond acting as community models and spiritual guides, as father-confessors to Sisters, and as copyists, was the oversight of young men in the schools, much of it involving moral and spiritual training, some of it teaching.[28] They took it for granted, at least at Deventer with its important school and household for students; but they carried it out mostly in separate households, and defended it only occasionally in treatises. In these sayings this task rarely comes up, less than allusions to their guidance of Sisters. So while an important consideration in recruitment, at least for the house in Deventer, it did not get at the inner life of the household as such.

Devout households had, at least initially and for about two generations, no "status," in either sense. Operating as neither laity nor the professed, living in communal poverty and supporting themselves with jobs neither clerical nor urban, they could claim no recognized "estate" (*status*), in the medieval sense. They also enjoyed, most of them clerics in minor orders and with no good clerical posts, no status in the metaphorical sense. Parents, we know from the *vitae*, objected vigorously to sons "seduced" into joining these households, thus foregoing any chance of securing an important church post or a place in a distinguished religious order. This peculiar sense of status, or no

---

[28] This is still inadequately studied, but see G. Epiney-Burgard, "Die Wege der Bildung in der Devotio Moderna," in: *Lebenslehre und Weltentwürfe im Übergang von Mittelalter zur Neuzeit,* ed. H. Boockmann-B. Moeller-K. Stackmann (Göttingen 1989), pp. 181-200.

status, of a despised inbetween estate in medieval society, of pursuing only humility, textured the tone of these sayings throughout. For it situated, nearly always indirectly, the context within which an action or virtue transpired or was imagined — their room as their province, their calling as a personal *kermis*. Anyone who chose to join, who gave up all their private goods and their ambitions in behalf of a devout commune, had to face up to this early on. They needed, as Rudolph put it, the disposition of soul for an "abject estate." And yet, or perhaps for that very reason, Henry of Alberghen was remembered to say [29] in a general meeting of Brothers (an early *colloquium?*) that his view on the matter was simple, that a man should persevere until death in the house at Deventer, and this be recognized as the "common good" (*communis bonus*), the standard. Godfrey immediately added that whoever did so in heartfelt obedience would take wing from this world (*auolaret*) without purgatory. What more telling word could there be? What more compelling reassurance about this way of life?

The New Devout lived, at least into the mid-fifteenth century, with a sense of the fragility of their community, of a need for constant attentiveness to sustain this way of life, a memory of troubles and losses in early days. When Brother Peter once got off alone with the rector outside their house — he would have been in his twenties —, he asked privately about the "future success of our house." One can sense his anxiety. Godfrey, then already aged, in office for nearly forty years, conceded that he was just then thinking about that very thing [55] — if there was a further response, Peter did not record it. Several sayings take as their central motif that such and such an action will endanger the household (*immineret*), spell its ruin [2, 46], a notion that seems never far from their minds, echoed also in the *vitae* (see n. 7 above). Only a few such considerations are institutional. The first recorded [1] employed etymological wordplay to warn against thinking much about privileges for their way of life, since good practices thereby disappear: "privileges" meaning "deprived law" (*priui-legium dicitur quasi 'priuans legem'*). In fact the Devout were quite prepared to seek and invoke privileges as required to defend their way of life.[29] But this word-play planted resistance in Devout minds to the

---

[29] See now my "Privileging the Devout: A Text from the Brothers at Deventer," in: *Roma, magistra mundi, Itineraria culturae medievalis: Mélanges offerts au Père L.E. Boyle à l'occasion de son 75ᵉ anniversaire* (Louvain-la-Neuve 1998), pp. 951-63.

very thing professed orders and civic guilds strived for everyday: written documents to guarantee their rights. As in civic households, prudent stewardship was the key. The Brothers were much edified, Peter
reports [7], by a word from Henry of Alberghen most worthy of
remembrance (*Verbum memoria dignissimum... memoriale relinquo*). In
twenty-one years (thirty-one?) as head of his house, he had never
spent "one penny," which he could not openly account for before the
entire household. Every town-father or guildsman or householder
(Geert Grote's father had served as treasurer in Deventer for a time)
would have felt the force of that story, but so too did all these Brothers who had committed their lives and goods to a jointly-held household.

   Even more worrying was attrition. A horrific story, possibly told
first to Peter himself, related the awful end of someone found "incon-
stant," as Peter Hoorn's rubric labeled it [15: see n. 6 about himself],
a man utterly convinced he was headed for hell because he had left a
"good congregation," the ordinary word for a household. Another
[16] told of a layman associated with a house of canons who strayed
into drunkenness and sex and then left the house to marry, his sins
exposed by the Virgin whose robe was thereby stained. On another
occasion, as the Brothers sat round after one of their regular blood-
lettings and spoke Dutch (*dixit ipse teutonice*), a real sign of relaxing
[20], Rudolph set a "puzzle" for them, a phrase he had found crude-
ly written into one of the spiritual scrapbooks (*rapiarum*): 'Here and
not elsewhere, thus and not otherwise, now and not sometime'.
These proverbial words should spring to mind, Rudolph finally
explained, whenever a Brother hears about the wonders of religious
life elsewhere, in a Carthusian house or among the Canons Regular
(two of the significant paths into orders for the Devout). Then a man
should say in his heart: this house and no other, these exercises and
no other way, this path acted upon now and not improved upon
tomorrow. The catchy phrase (*hic et non alibi, sic et non aliter, nunc et non
alias*) worked in this case to stabilize those Devout tempted by visions
of a grander religious life in some professed house. For a man like
Peter, sought by recruiters, the phrase could even function as a kind
of mantra, effectively a self-made vow. Because there was no vow, no
legal bond, and in some sense less public shame in apostasy, the reso-
lution to stay in a household had to come from within, and had constantly to be reinforced.

   If members of a household imaged their lives as on the edge, abject, inbetween, always at risk, what religious end did this serve? The central feature of their lives was the re-shaping of their moral and spiritual selves, what they referred to as "progress in the virtues" and saw as related to the "will," a person's core intentionality. Henry of Albergen, echoing in his own way Rudolph's first and third traits, says that the heart of the matter is to live and die in this humble state, to seem a person of no worldly account: *oportet qui uilis et despectus et contemptus mori et uiuere et nullius reputacionis apparere* [12]. Thus one saying, echoing a common teaching, but delivered in this case to Peter personally, reduced it all to a simple end: the whole point, according to the fathers, was to "break your own will" [44]. Our enterprise is nothing if we do not pursue humility, Florens said [38]. According to the fathers, our whole enterprise, says Rudolph, is "mortification" [39]. Concretely, they should expect to wear handed-down clothes, patched and re-patched [41], and simply to say "thanks" for whatever food they received, good or bad [40]. When one "father" tried to express exactly what this might mean for a Brother or a Sister, he put it this way: all consisted in not hiding anything from a father-confessor, not acting without permission of a rector, ever aiming to purify the "intentions" associated with any act [30]. However much this appears to reiterate what might be said in a professed house, it is directed toward people not under vow, who are to attain a state of pure intentions and transparent humility as a private act of inner volition carried out in a freely formed household. Brother Peter recorded another version [45] focused upon the acts of someone living in such a self-made religious community, in this case an example attributed by re-telling to the venerable Henry Bruyn (d. 1398). Such an ideal brother will love his cell as his homeland, be dedicated almost exclusively to the holy writings and a good book above a good horse, enjoy engaging in spiritual conversation or holding a collation, be pleased to celebrate the divine office frequently, never say anything evil about anyone and never anything behind someone's back not said to his face, and prefer to spend his time in copywork. This is that commune for reading, writing, meditating, and conversing which the Devout imagined as ideal, reduced here to six concrete and memorable points against which any brother could measure himself.

These households were mixed, overwhelmingly clerical but of all ranks, with a fair number of laymen and only a select number of priests, those chosen by the community for ordination to serve the community's ends, not a status or privilege in its own right. Very striking, in the *vitae* but even more so in these *dicta*, is their deep ambivalence and reluctance about the priestly office. At one level this is abject humility working itself out, a sense of unworthiness to handle the Body and Blood of Christ. Godfrey issued a pointed saying to the effect that our community is so failing, so lacking in progress, because we do not adequately prepare ourselves for the reception of communion and we so lukewarmly say our office [28]. This can come at times with a heavy weight of scrupulosity, which is driven home by another of his striking sayings. Whenever someone died for whom he had served as father-confessor, Godfrey says aloud, he is invaded by a certain "horror" that he might have missed something, to the person's eternal detriment [10]. Yet, something more is at work here, a deep fear of the pride and arrogance assumed to go with clerical office. Such sentiments were widespread in the town streets all about them, and ambition was virtually bred into these clerics, certainly expected of them in the schools preparing them for clerical posts. Godfrey accordingly gave as his "counsel" that a person should never in any way presume to pursue the priesthood [9] — as, in the house, Brothers could not put themselves forward. All this was, in a sense, a sanctioned or admissible form of that anticlericalism rampant in late medieval towns.[30] But it could verge toward an anti-sacerdotalism sometimes ascribed to the New Devout, which simmered steadily within the entire community, Geert Grote himself remaining a deacon. In another of his pointed declarations, Godfrey says that the priesthood "devours virtue," and drags after it a "long red tail" [52]! On his deathbed Father Florens, after whom the house was named, declared, so this saying fixed it, that he wished he had never touched a chalice [51]. Amilius, his successor (1400-04), is remembered with one pithy remark, that entering the priesthood is often an occasion for sin [53]. Rector Godfrey (1410-50) is cited repeatedly, in the *dicta* and the *vita*, as saying he was half-blind when he entered the priesthood, and wished he had lacked both arms and both legs so he could have been excused from it [55, 9]. Godfrey issued yet another memorable word: Without a great and violent fortitude and a special gift of the Spirit, a man will only decline in virtue after entering the

---

[30] See my "Late Medieval Anticlericalism: The Case of the New Devout," in *Anticlericalism in Late Medieval and Early Modern Europe*, ed. Peter Dykema-Heiko Oberman (Studies in Medieval and Reformation Thought 51, Leiden 1993), pp. 19-52.

priesthood [52]! Or again, in his own voice: I am a thousand times more fearful of the sins I committed after becoming a priest than those done before [9]. The steady drumbeat of these sayings could only pound into the Brothers fear and wariness before the priestly office, not entirely unlike that of their lay neighbors, and a sense that religious virtue must be pursued principally in another way.

As they tended to perceive the priesthood as power and privilege, so they grasped learning as aimed mostly at ambition and pride. In a house where copying and reading and writing and meditating upon books loomed larger in practice and emphasis than in any imaginable urban household, sayings worked to impress upon Brothers the proper end of this activity: devotion and prayer. Study is good, Rudolph remarked, when it kindles remorse and prayer, but better when you hardly know how to begin studying without praying first [4]. Ontgher of Hoorn, leader of the boys' house, noted that he could lead collations best — something almost every Brother in theory might be called upon to do — when he studied a little and then gave himself over to prayer. If he scrambled his mind with much studying, he found that he hardly knew what to say, even if he had prepared [5]. John Brinckerink claimed that he wrote "collations" only for himself, that is, as part of his personal religious regime, though in fact they became famous, especially among the Sisters [6]. What danger to our household, Rudolph remarked, if we give up reading the guides to devotional and religious life, and picked up instead intellectual tractates and the sermons of schoolmen [3]. All this hammering away at intellectual work powerfully recalls the opening sayings in the opening book of Thomas of Kempen's *Imitation of Christ*, for they were actually borne of the same milieu. These men were mostly "clerical" in the basic medieval sense, literate and oriented in the schools toward the posts which learning opened up, indeed drawn from schools into these households. Though such sayings could easily become anti-intellectual in their extreme, their purpose in practice, and in context, was to cut off that temptation which lay nearest to hand for clerics who spent their day with books, that is, making intellectual work an end in itself or a step to fame or to promotion, not the means to devotional exercise. The Devout thus attempted to restructure and to re-think the "book-learning" enterprise. Hence Godfrey's advice to a brother who found the copying difficult, probably Peter himself. What could you want to do more pleasing to God than to write out the Holy Writings? — though he added that it must be combined with charity and obedience [14]. He further suggested that this Brother imagine himself as a knight going into battle, mounting the writing stool as his horse, with parchment as his shield and the quill his lance [13]. Over against all clerical pride and ambition, they had rather to practice "perfect mortification," to live and die, also in their copywork and their spiritual notebooks, as a complete nobody in the world. "You all know that, I hope," Henry says to the Brothers at Deventer. But in monasteries and households, he went on, "I can hardly find any such." And: "I hope I can find four here." [12].

Over against pride in priesthood or in learning, the Devout held up "fraternal charity," mutual respect and concord within the house. Disparate individuals choosing to live a communal life in close urban quarters — this was not easy, and they knew it. Godfrey reportedly quipped that he could bear a father-confessor falling asleep while hearing confessions in their house, so long as the man found the Brothers chaste and in mutual charity [27]. To single out these two virtues, in a group that tended toward scrupulosity, and to do so with a humorous word, deserves note, and must have struck a chord. One Lent, after discussion, they decided that each should, as their penance that season, bear with complete equanimity whatever they found hardest to put up with, without admonition from others and without improper excuses [33]. During another Lenten Sunday afternoon discussion, the rector encouraged each to "convert to interiority." This he explained as meaning there was to be no rancor or suspicion among them, only a striving for heartfelt mutuality and unity [34]. As ever in this inbetween state, the paradigm for mutuality, though not far from that of a professed religious house, had to come from their own invention. Brothers or Sisters were, importantly, to "admonish one another" — the main check on frayed relations. This could sound frightful in a small community. Yet, Rudolph said, its proper exercise could drive away "bitterness of heart" and that it stood in place of a chapter of faults. One early Brother observed that the House would perish without it [46]. The meaning is clear. Several sayings presume latent tensions between individual and community aspirations in a communal household. Without mutuality, without a certain bearing with one another (even as Lenten penance), without an opportunity for mutual admonition, the household could explode. Yet sayings could also register encouragement. One visitor claimed to find the Brothers so "mature, humble, and compelling" that it

completely overwhelmed his interior as he stood in reverence outside
before the bake-ovens; coming into their presence was like approaching a palace [37].

The Devout remained in some sense free individuals, each with his
own room. The heart of the matter, religiously speaking, was for
each brother or sister to cultivate the virtues and the interior life,
alone in his cell/room before the eyes of God. Here they made their
own choices, about their time, their reading, their own spiritual
scrapbook, their personal spiritual program or exercises. Rudolph
thought, for instance, that after completing their evening prayers
they would do better to stay in their room and do something good
rather than wander out and get busy in something dubious [47]. But
this was a choice. Many Brothers, going back to Geert Grote, took
inventory of themselves and their faults at night. But it was better,
Rudolph observed about himself, sometimes not to start, because you
would never get on to anything else [50] — a word of spiritual warning in an atmosphere thick with intensity and scrupulosity. Directing
the will toward the inner self with such intensity could generate distress. Take prayer, the heart of religious life. Godfrey expressed his
firm personal belief that heartfelt prayer never returns empty, always
accrues grace, whether or not it is felt. But it is easier, he notes, when
someone feels the grace poured in in response [8]. For men who had
set themselves apart for prayer, but not as professed and public intercessors, worry about their personal prayer regimen, and its effectiveness, must have eaten away at their confidence at times.

Or take chastity. As men and women not under vow, yet committed to chastity, set apart in households and yet still moving in an
urban world, restraining the urges of the flesh demanded unflagging
attention. Stories impressed upon them that even men ninety years
old could fall, that old men never lost their wandering eye or their
desire, that victory over the flesh came, if at all, only to aging hump-
backs [21]. Indeed those truly keeping watch over their chastity could
never be secure, always guarding their eyes and the other senses [25].
The Devout saw sex as rampant among the young they served in the
schools and met in the streets: Very few young people in their day,
either men or women, one said, managed to keep their chastity — so
few, common folks would hardly believe it [23]. One "father"
quipped to a certain woman he knew, probably associated in some
way with the Devout, that she would never be satisfied with a hundred men. Later, as he prophesied, they found her as a public prosti-

tute in Deventer [24]. These stories, edgy, fearful, even mean-spirit-
ed, bespoke their situation, uncloistered men who could never be
quite sure about themselves or the other members of their household.
Strikingly, when Peter later wrote the *vita* of Godfrey and praised his
chastity he did so with this odd hedge: their rector went to the grave
a pure virgin, without knowledge of a woman, he said, he was virtually certain[31] — an affecting realism about human nature and an
urban environment, or scrupulosity, or both.

As they had to guard their chastity while living in an open urban
environment, so they had to guard against earthly desire in every
way. The passions, Godfrey taught, should be imagined as chains
that bind, and no one should imagine himself to rise above others on
this score [17] — a pointed jab at hidden desires or latent self-right-
eousness. Henry of Albergen noted the obvious about song and lyric,
that they moved people in a variety of ways. For him it darkly
warned of death, but the former rector at Zwolle, he noted, had to
leave town at times to escape their effects [31]. This same Henry,
when visiting in Deventer, used to walk to the gate of the city and
look up the IJssel River toward Zutphen, then think to himself that
all this, like the moving river itself, will pass away [32]. With this
poignant observation, Peter noted, we were admonished toward contempt for the world. Such sayings could seize upon common experiences — songs, city streets, a moving river — only to teach abstinence in their midst, a disciplining of the senses. In an act of self-
indictment, one father noted that he preferred reproach for his public
faults, however minor, rather than for his hidden sins, however large
[36]. Whatever their degree of virtue, this tension could never be
released if the community was to be sustained. Rudolph noted that
their "whole business" was simply mortification [39]. But these days,
if the Brothers gathered to "move" any topic in common, he lament-
ed, it always pertained in some way to their greater convenience or
comfort (*commoda*).

These sayings reveal a community living on the edge, the Devout
having constantly to fashion and discipline themselves in order to distinguish their lifestyle from that of worldly neighbors without suc-

---

[31] "Castitatem similiter ualde zelabat in omnibus, et fratribus nostris et extraneis.
Qui eciam immunis est a domino reseruatus ab omni muliere in omni uita sua et, ut
credo ex uerisimili coniectura [!], obiit purus uirgo." *Vitae fratrum*, ed. Dumbar, p.
118.

cumbing to the security and privilege of vows and a rule. This is what
Peter Hoorn caught in the buzz of these sayings, what he wrote down
as a permanent memorial in this quire, perhaps as a part of his own
personal scrapbook and interior development during his early days in
the House, perhaps as a repository of teachings to pass along within
the house to later generations. At a superficial level, the sayings may
seem to iterate common medieval teachings about virtue, chastity,
humility, abstinence, contentedness — the Devout never claimed to
aim for novelty. Yet while claiming only to restore good old teachings, they brought many distinctive accents, for instance, in their attitudes toward the priesthood and their unrelenting, self-imposed interiority. Above all, these sayings disclose, in extraordinary fashion, the
inner dynamics of a self-made religious commune: how they sustained an urban household dedicated to a rigorous life of common
virtue, how they turned spiritual teachings buried in monastic tractates into proverbs in Latin or Dutch, how they turned their own
companions, departed or still alive, into sources of memorialized wisdom. Life and wisdom lay in the proverbial word, the saying that
captured Devotion in practice, spiritual life in tension. In discovering,
or re-discovering, the role of the "saying" in a spiritual community,
the Devout, though mostly anxious about themselves and their
charges, found a form that was to have an extraordinary future. For
The Imitation of Christ, one of the most influential of early modern religious books, appealed from this same experience. That book is really
four pamphlets, each pamphlet made up in fact of numerous sayings,
de-contextualized and re-organized under thematic rubrics, but sayings all the same, which in private reading individuals could then lift
out in order to re-contextualize in almost any setting, be it a religious
cloister or a lay household. The Devout, as "private religious" committed to a life in their cells and in their household, faced up to and
mastered the religious dynamic of the in-between state.

APPENDIX: A WORKING EDITION OF THE *DICTA PATRUM*

This appendix offers first a working edition of the *Dicta patrum* as found in MS B (Brussels, Royal Library, MS 8849-59). For a full critical edition, a few cruxes would need still to be resolved in reading this difficult hand. In this edition the marginal notations in the manuscript have been entered in brackets below the relevant saying. The numbering of these sayings, in arabic numerals, is my own. For purposes of comparison, and for the continuing reception of these sayings roughly seventy years later (probably about 1518/20), I have also transcribed the text as it appears, revised and polished, in MS A. Each saying there is provided a number in roman numerals corresponding to its original in MS B in arabic numerals.

Dicta patrum[1]
<De bonis>[2]

[1] Item, conuenerunt aliquando fratres, et dixit dominus G[odefridus] pater noster: Non quereremus multa priuilegia in communibus consuetudinibus nostris; hoc enim modo leges et bone consuetudines solent perire, unde et priuilegium dicitur quasi 'priuans legem'.
<De non querendis priuilegiis>

[2] Item, dixit dominus Rodolphus: Duo debemus in suscipiendis nouiciis attendere principaliter. Primo, ut satis sint[3] fortes et apti in corpore et naturali complexcione. Unde dixit idem: Non esse faciliter nobis acceptandum inde nullomodo aliquem qui non sufficeret ad communes labores et obseruancias consuetudinum domus nostre, quia non solum tales quibus oportet indulgi in cibis et quibusdam laboribus sunt suis preuelegiis[4] contenti. Verumeciam cum possunt uel audent, trahunt et pro posse alios uel totam communitatem ad huiusmodi, et sic ex talium accepcione immineret domui nostre pro tempore graue periculum. Secundum, ut sint apti in anima, ut uidelicet sint inclinati ad despectum statum humilitatis nostre et tractum puerorum et uoluntas emendandi mores.
<De hospiciis uel nouiciis>

---

[1] This title was inserted at the head of the quire/first folio in a bold hand and darker ink, sometime later, possibly by the same hand, that is, by Peter Hoorn

[2] This rubric was written by the original hand, that is, Peter Hoorn's, at the top of the first folio. In practice, as a title rubric, it would seem to apply only to the first saying.

[3] *satis* written twice, the second corrected to *sint*.

[4] priulgiis *er. et scripsit* preuelegiis.

[3] Item, dixit sepius idem Rodolphus: O quid putatis, fratres, imminebit tunc domui domini Florencii cum ad hoc ueniret quod fratres *Profectus religosorum, Horologium, Meditaciones Bernardi*, et similes deuocionis libros[5] abiciant et contempnant uel paruipendant, et *Sermones Iordani* uel consimiles intellectuales et predicatorios assumant. Puto uere quod contingeret ei sicud pater sanctus Franciscus uidit sibi ostendi in statua cum capito aureo et collo argenteo etcetera. Illud et ipse suis fratribus predixit. Unde dixit idem R[odolphus] qualiter pater noster dominus Amilius habuit in uoto (nescio quociens in anno) studere *Profectus religiosorum*.
<De studio librorum intellectualium non pro affectu>

[4] Item, dixit idem R[udolphus]: Puto quod tunc aliquis bene studet, quando ita studet quod accenderet ad compunctionem et oracionem, et uix scit ultra studere quin oporteat prius orare.
<De studio bono>

[5] Item, dixit aliquando cuidam Ontgerus Hoirn[6]: Quando modicum studui et post hoc dedi me aliquo tempore ad oracionem, uel exercitaui me in aliqua deuocione, paratus sum loqui cum pueris uel aliis de quacumque materia spirituali sicut michi occurrit. Quando uero obrui intellectum multis scripturis et diutino studio, non affectatus oracione uel alia aliqua deuocione, uix inuenio quid dicam, eciam in multis preuisus.
<De studio pro pueris uel aliis>

[6] Item, dixit Rodulphus de Iohanne Aernem,[7] quia dixit aliquando nunquam se aliquid scripsisse pro collacionibus aliis faciendis sed solum propter se, quamuis ipse ualde multa scripsisse cognoscitur.
<De non colligendo pro aliis>

---

[5] These three titles refer, respectively, to a portion of David of Augsburg's *De exterioris et interioris hominis compositione*, Henry of Susa's *Horlogium sapientiae*, and one of the devotional texts ascribed in the later middle ages to Bernard. This corresponded to a "program" of reading relatively common throughout the Devout movement, which went back to Geert Grote himself. See now Thomas Kock, *Die Buchkultur der Devotio moderna: Handschriftenproduktion, Literaturversorgung und Bibliotheksaufbau im Zeitalter des Medienwechsels* (Frankfurt 1999) 111-47, and Nikolaus Staubach, "Von der persönlich Erfahrung zur Gemeinschaftsliteratur: Entstehungs- und Rezeptionsbedingungen geistlicher Reformtexte im Spätmittelalter," *Ons geestelijk erf* 68 (1994) 200-28.

[6] Little is known about Ontgher Hoorn, except that in mid-century he became a leading figure in the house for students established by the Brothers at Deventer. The reference here would be to his role in holding "collations" for these young men.

[7] This is John Brinckerink (d. 1419), one of the founding figures in the Deventer community, and father-confessor in later years to the Sisters at Diepenveen. His collations, or versions of them, exist still in Middle Dutch; see P.F.J. Obbema, "Brinckinck en Jan van Schoonhoven," in: *Codex in Context*, ed. Chr. De Backer-A.J. Geurts-A.G. Weiler (Nijmegen 1985), 277-87. *Dicta* ascribed to him, and still unedited, are found in an earlier quire of this same MS B

[7] Cum uenisset semel dominus Henricus de Alberghen[8] ad domum domini Florencii, et conuocatis fratribus dixisset eis aliquid boni cum fuisset collocatio facienda, dixit ad eum dominus Pe[trus] eiusdem domus frater: Domine Henrice, ex quo, ut scitis, incertum est an redeatis, rogo ut dimittaris fratribus nostris aliquod memoriale per quod possent uestri recordari, et sic si mortuus fueritis pro uobis instancius deum deprecari. At ille primo humiliter se ut decuit excusans, dicens in se parum esse uirtutis, tandem precum instancius et importunitate deuictus, ita respondit: Verbum memoria dignissimum, in Christo karissimi, hoc uobis memoriale relinquo. Quia ultra uiginti-unum annos domui nostri in Albergen prefui, et nec usque hodie placcam uel minus exposui uel expendi quam non uellem fratribus meis in computacione latem ubi quando et qua de causa eam expendimus. In quo laudabili uerbo fratres nostri domus domini Florencii edificati sunt non modice.

<Dominus Henricus Albergen // de fideli dispensacione // nota>

[8] Item, uolens dominus G[odefridus] pater noster fratres nostros hortari ad oracionis instanciam et frequenciam, dixit eis inter cetera: Secundum sentire meum firmiter credo quod nunquam aliquis, cum bene orauerit et cordialiter se in oracione deo commiserit, uacuus ab oracione recedit, quin acquirat sibi aliquid gracie, quamuis ipse orans hoc ignorauerit. Quod non fit sine occulta dei dispensacione, ut non extollatur ipse. Quod faciliter fieret si sentiret uel pro certo sentiret sibi graciam tunc infundi.

<Oracio non reddit uacua>

[9] Item, conuenientibus semel in unum fratribus domus nostre domini Florencii, dixit eis dominus Godefridus: Dico uobis, fratres uel sorores, quoniam cordialiter ita sentio. Vellem me ambobus oculis esse exsecatum et sic usque ad mortem mansurum, nec et sic umquam uenissem ad presbiterium. Item dixit: Cum deberem ordinare, fui fere medius cecus; utinam totus excecus fuissem. Quam bene [michi[9]] fuisset. Item dixit: Milleseis plus timeo de actis in gradibus quam extra ordines, et si deberem iam mori, nulla me tam terrerent sicud illa[10] que egi postquam sum effectus presbiter. Item dominus G[odefridus]: Contra consilium meum est ut, quandocumque potest aliquis aliquo modo abesse, nullomodo aggrediatur ut uel presumaret ut fiat presbiterus.

<contra anhelantes ad presbiterium>

[10] Item dixit idem dominus Godefridus: Quandocumque moritur quis confessus mee filius, inuadat me horror quidam. Timeo enim ne sit ali-

---

[8] On this figure, see pp. 290-91 above.

[9] michi *add. supra lin.*

[10] *illa...presbiter.* was written in the top margin of the following folio (68r), then the next saying, *Item...presbiterus,* written above it in that same margin.

quid neglectum uel minus diligenter actum circa eum quod posset esse sibi causa periculi.

[11] Item, conuenerunt quandoque fratres domus nostre in die sacramenti, et dixit eis dominus Godefridus pater noster: Nichil ita obstare profectui nostro spirituali sicud indigna sumpcio sacramenti, quod scilicet nos non condignie preparamus.

<De sacramento>

[12] Item, uenerunt aliquando ad domum nostram dominus Theodricus Hirsen, dominus Henricus rector congregacionis in Alberghen, et dominus Henricus Huusdanien. Et conuenientibus eis in unum una cum fratribus nostris, motum est inter cetera que esset perfecta mortificacio uel abrenunciacio. Et dixit inter ceteros dominus Henricus Albergen: Audite me. Dicam uobis quod sencio. Ista michi uidetur esse perfecta mortificacio, ut oportet quis uilis et despectus et contemptus mori et uiuere et nullius reputacionis apparere. Ac addidit: Vellem me tales quatuor hic posse reperire. Spero tamen quod omnes scitis.[11] Sed heu in monasteriis et congregacionibus paucos ualde tales inuenio.

<quid sit perfecta mortificacio>

[13] Item, uenit aliquando frater aliquis ad dominum Godefridum dicens: Domine Godefride, grauat me multum tedium in scriptura ita quod multum tedet me scribere. Cui ille: Frater karissime, scribere feruenter et cum desiderio orare est apud deum. Cogita igitur figens in corde tuo quod sedes sit equus, pergamenum ante te clipio, penna lancea. Hiis armis diabolo scripturus et resiste; et quanto forcius scripseris et feruencius, tanto ille longius fugiet a te. Timeo tamen quod sis inordinatus in scribendo, ut quando importunus nimis ... tibi bene succedit, quando uero male nimis, tristaris. Sed tu niteraris esse equanimis.

<De scriptura>

[14] Item, dixit frater aliquis[12] domino Godefrido: Puto in corde meo quod plus placeret deo orare, legere, cantare, psalmos ruminare quam scribere. Cui ille: Quid uis accepcius deo agere quam scribere sacram scripturam? Licet autem scribere in se non ita religiosum ut apparet, caritas tamen et obediencia faciunt ipsum multum meritorium.

[15] Item, dixit dominus Godefridus cuidam fratre: Mane, frater, in uocacione qua uocata es, quoniam horribile ualde audiui narrante domino Henrico de Haes in Diepenveen[13] de quodam. Hic cum esset in quadam

---

[11] scitis: sitis? MS A emends to read 'tales estis'.

[12] idem *add. supra lin.*

[13] This is probably Henry of Harderwijk, a canon regular of Windeshim, who served as father-confessor at Diepenveen during the years 1427-39, and died in 1447.

deuota congregacione, suadente ut putandum est diabolo, exiit et ad uomitum canis rediens, scilicet se uanitatibus rursum substrauit. Quod quantum deo displicuit, et rei exitus patefecit. Nam cum dominus malicie ipsius finem ponere decreuisset, ad mortem usque languore correptus, ad extrema peruenit. Agonizanti autem illi quidam secularis litteratus cum nomine Helias astitit, et mortis eius consummacionem exspectauit. Cum autem iam spiritus exitum minaretur excurrere, hic undique pre dolore inexplicabili sudoris guttis, alta cepit et horribili uoce eiulare dicens: Heu, me miserum quoniam eterna morte multandus iure sum ...dampnatus. Cui Helius astans admirans respondit[14]: Cur sic frater loqueris? Que nam est causa dampnacionis? Cur esse possit? Cui ille: Eram miserante deo in congregacione bona in qua si perstitassem, ab eterna me morte gracia dei preseruassem. Sed quoniam apostatans gracie uocacione dei ingratus extiti, ad hanc quam uides miserabilem mortem diabolo id ductore per- ueni. Et hiis dictis tradidit spiritum–heu horrendis tortoribus perpetuo cruciandum. Quo uiso Helias ille qui pacientibus affuit, salutis proprie modo immemor, postponitis cunctis ne simile precipicium experiretur timens, imperante domino, deuotum quendam et uenerabilem patrem dominum Henricum rectorem congregacionis in monasterio adiit. Et eius consilio et auxilio perpetuo dei seruicio sub institucione et regula fratrum cruciferorum in quodam monasterio se mancipauit.

<Exemplum notabile de inconstancia>

[16] Rediens quandoque dominus Godefridus de Noerthoirn, cum dominice die fratres conuenissent, dixit eis inter cetera quoniam retulit ei pater in Noierthoirn, quod raptus fuit aliquando frater aliquis laicus. Et in uisione uisum est sibi quod beata uirgo Maria, quam ipsi ibi summo uen- erantur affectu, ei affuit assidens ei cum filio suo, induta uestibus totaliter candidis et mundassis. Cumque eius pulchritudinem et uestium nitorem frater ille curiosius intueretur, uidit quod uestis beate fuit in parte aliqua sanguine aspersa et bene maculata. De quo cum frater ille miraretur, sta- tim ad genua prouolutus coram eius se geri pedibus prostrauit, interro- gans eam suppliciter et dicens: O sancta Maria, quis maculauit ita uestem tuam? At illa tacens nichil respondit. Tunc ille secundo quesiuit ut primus, et illa adhuc tacuit secundo. Cumque tercio frater ille diceret: O sancta Maria maculaui ego uestem tuam? Tunc illa illo respondit, dicens: Non tu sed ille, ostendens quendam de laicis qui die precedenti forte uel certiter iuxta[15] monasterium in uilla propinqua oberrauerat, et usque ad ebrietatem potatus in fornicacionem ceciderat. Cumque frater ille priori hanc uisionem retulisset, ille mane fratrem predictum adiit et eum quo- modo se res haberent sollicite inquesiuit. Cumque nullomodo interroga- tus ueritatem confiteri noluisset, tandem prior dixit quia talem uisionem frater aliquis habuisset, et ergo sibi qualiter se res haberent manifestaret.

---

[14] ait *er.*
[15] iuxta *scripsit bis* (folio change).

Tunc ille rubore ductus, uidens ueritatem latem non posse, confessus est quia ebrius in adulteriam cecidisset. Qui postmodum monasterium exiens et ad seculum rediens, uxorem duxit–et qua morte finiendus sit dominus nouit. Et adiunxit dominus Henricus: Videamus ergo et nos fratres, ne eciam nos maculemus uestem[16] beate uirginis passionibus nostris ac uiciis.
<De aspersione uestis beate uirginis>

[17] Item, dixit dominus Godfridus eodem tempore quoniam passiones nostre sunt nobis quodammodo ligamen uel uinculum quo coniuncti tenamur et nobisinuicem substernimur. Quis enim nostrum iam uel aliquando se audet alii preferre? Quoniam possumus uere dicere, hebrei sunt et ego, passionati sunt et ego, etcetera.
<Quomodo presunt nobis pasiones>

[18] Item, facta collacione de generibus meditabilium, cum motum esset de contemplacione, dixit dominus G[odefridus]: Si sciremus uiriliter resistere passionibus, expellemur paulatim passiones nostras et uicia. Tunc successiue per se sine nostro labore ergo ad illam induceremur nobis contemplacionem. Quoniam primo uiciosi adhuc et passionati, laborantes pro epugnacione uiciorum sumus puri actiui, tandem euictis aliqualiter passionibus et purificato pro parte corde efficimur ex utraque uita uniri. Tercio, ad plenum purificato corde efficimur contemplacionem; quoniam beatitudo illa est de mundicia cordis, presupponit omnes alios beatitudines. Quartum, ipsa est ad premium. Mundicia enim cordis, inquit, finis est uite actiue.
<Quomodo peruenimur ad contemplacionem>

[19] Item, dixit idem quoniam nulla michi uidetur apcior uia ad contemplacionem quam oracio assidua.

[20] Item, facta aliquando minucione sanguinis ...cum uenissent fratres ante prandium propter uentum in pistrino,[17] ubi recreacionis causa caritatiue simul loquebantur de scripturis, inter loquendum Rodolphus mouit per enigma edifacatorium ualde dicens: Quis nobis dicet[18] quid istud significet? Quoniam legi in rapiario quod erat scriptum rudiis litteris ante inicium alicuius capituli, quoniam docuit quis aliquem alium dicens, 'Hic et non alibi, sic et non aliter, nunc et non alias'. Cumque singuli ut apparuit de huius intellectu haberent, ipse exposuit ad monitam sic. Qui dixit–quoniam Frater Henricus solet dicere, 'qui dedit concilium, fecerat et auxilium'–dicens: Quando uenit frater aliquis ad locum aliquem ubi proposuit deo seruire, si audierit, 'Ecce ibi in tali loco sunt tales fratres tam deuoti' etcetera, utputa ibi Carthusienses, ibi regulares, dicet homo

[16] uestem *add. in marg.*
[17] This would take place at their farmsite called Ter Steghe just outside Deventer.
[18] nobis dicet *scripsit bis.*

cursim in corde suo sibi 'hic debeo deo seruire et non alibi'. 'Sic', idest secundum exercicium domus istius, 'et non aliter', idest secundum exercicia illorum uel in illorum que homini diuersa occurrunt. 'Nunc et non alias', hoc est, non est[19] crastinando, utputa dicere cras me emendabo, uel si ad hoc uel ad hoc uenissem, tunc me bene emendarem.

<dixit ipse teutonice>

[21] Conuenimus aliquando et facta collacione de tribus inimicis, cum de carne loqueremur, affuit dominus Godefridus et dixit quia, cum fuerimus octoginta annorum et baculo innitentes, terram matrem nostram incuruus capitis inclinari, tunc possimus habere spem de uictoria carnis. Et allegauit pro exemplo quia noui, inquiens, hominem ultra ut presumo octaginta uel nonaginta annorum, qui tum post hoc cecidit. Unde dixit nobis quod non esset presumendus de multitudine annorum ad uicendum uicium carnis. Unde dixit quomodo sedit semel dominus Henricus van Goude Arnem ad mensam cum quodam quondam multum seculari et actiuo sed iam conuerso. Erat uero in tempore illo quo incipiebamur congregacio sororum in Arnem. Cum ergo de sororibus loquerentur, dixit ille secularis quod libencius uideret sororem pulchram quam deformem. Et respondit dominus Henricus, percuciens more solito manum ad pectus: Et ego uobis dico, nominans eum ex nomine, Een bedelaer die ghewoen waer te bedelen worde, hi bluit; sii solde bedelen van ghewonte. Ad quod alius intelligens eum: Estimatis sic, domine Henrice? Dixit eciam quia audiui aliquando senem aliquem loquentem: Unum uicium perdidi, quod me ultra omnia peniteo. Et hoc erat quia defecto corpore iam non posset explere libidinem suam.

<De castitate>

[22] Item dixit: In omnibus sorores sustineo dummodo castitatem saluam inuenio. Et adiunxit libencius: Habeo quod sorores inter se litigantes false percuciendo blauium oculum faciant, quin quod aliqua carnalitate uiciate in aliquo castitatem fedent.

[23] Item dixit: Multum deberemus niti trahere iuuenes ad castitatem, quia, inquit, paucissimi[20] et paucissime inueniuntur casti et caste–et tam pauci quod communis homo hoc non crederet.

[24] Item, nacta occasione dixit de domino Johanne Brinkerinc quod fuisset multa gracia preditus in considerandis personis, et quomodo dixisset semel cuidam sorore quod adhuc non contentaretur centum uiris. Quod postea verum patuit, quia publica meretrix in Daventria est effecta. Hoc uero, scilicet, quod dominus Johannes sibi hoc dixisset, ipsa reuelauit postea cuidam custodi iuuenorum ciuitatis, qui ulterius dixit michi.

---

[19] non *add. et er.*
[20] paucissimi *scripsit bis.*

[25] Item dixit: Hec est uera custodia castitatis, ut homo nunquam se habeat securum sed semper suspectum, et quamuis se longo tempore se senciit non fuisse hac tempore uexatum, non tum liber sit. Sed ita semper se habeat in cautela et custodia sui[21] quasi maxime temptaretur, uisum utique et alios sensus interiores et exteriores custodiendo.

<Nota pro castitate>

[26] Item dixit: Quoniam castitas est dulcissima uirtus, que ceteras quodammodo uirtutes reddit sapiosas, et magnum donum a deo accepit cui datam est sapere ea que sunt castitatis, quia fundamentum quodammodo est ceterarum uirtutum, et est secundum sanctum Thomam fundamentum contemplacionis.

[27] Item retulit michi Petrus Amsterdammis quomodo dixisset dominus Godefridus quod, non multum curaret si inter audiendum confessiones fratrum domus nostre dormiret, dummodo hec duo, scilicet castitatem et caritatem fraternam salua inueniret.

[28] Item, dixit dominus G[odefridus] pater noster: Estimo quod non maior causa quare ita multi deficimus in uia dei et quod non magis proficimus quam quod minus digne preparamus nos ad sumpcionem [huius[22]] sacramenti uenerabilis, et quod ficte confitemur et ex consuetudine. Insuper quod tam tepide persoluimus horas domino deo nostro.

<de sacramento>

[29] Item, dixit aliquando dominus Henricus de Alberghen in communi conuenta fratrum, quoniam aliud non sentiret quam si aliquis usque mortem in domo nostra in Daventria perseueraret, et esset communis bonus. Adiunxit dominus G[odefridus]: Qui affuit in omni obediencia sine purgatorio auolaret.

[30] Item, idem tunc dixit quomodo cum uenisset et esset in domo magistri Gherardi, rogauit eum Rodolphus ut diceret sororibus aliquid boni. Et respondit: Quid uolo multum uexare communitatem? In tribus michi uideretur omnia consistere. Primum, ut frater uel soror nichil occultum in corde retineat quod non reuelet suo superiori in confessione et extra. Secundum, ut nichil de se presumat facere absque scitu et consensu et uidere rectoris. Tercium, ut in omnibus homo purificet intencionem, quia si intencio fuere mala, nichil de sequentibus ualet. Hec tria, inquit, dixit sororibus, et quod dominus addendum dedit.

[31] Item, dixit quod armonia et cantus etcetera diuersos diuersimode mouet. Talia inquit cum hic frequentarem, me solent commonere de

---

[21] ut *add. et er.*
[22] huius *er.*

morte. Sed quondam rector in Swollis dominus G[erardus] Kalkar[23] talia tam eger tulit, quod solebat tempore carius primi recedere de Swollis in Windesim.

[32] Item, dixit quoniam quando solebam hic frequentare, tunc ualde delectabile michi erat exire portam et uidere post Sutzvaniam et Ysalam. Sed in hoc ordinati michi exercicium adduxi in consuetudinem cogitare in corde mea: Ecce ista iam aliquid apparent, et ultra breue tempus omnino non erunt. Et sic ammonebamur de uanitate mundi contempnanda.

[33] Cum conuenissemus aliquando in dominica quadam quadragesima et tractassemus de arcioribus exerciciis tempori illi congruis, et alius istud alius illud proposuisset agendum, dixit dominus G[odefridus]: Sic hoc nostrum commune exercicium, ut unusquisque omne quod sibi sinistrum paciendum euenire in tota ista quadragesima equo animo sufferat, et nullius ammonitus eciam iniuste se excuset.

<in ieiunio>

[34] Item, dixit in alia quadam dominica quadragesimali: Unusquisque se iam studeat ad interiora conuertere et se ad internitatem dare. Discedat omnis rancor et suspicio de corde nostro. Et studeamus per unitatem mutuam cordialiter uniri. In hiis enim est uerus fructus, et cetere exteriores obseruancie in tantum bone sunt in quantum nobis ad ista deseruiunt.

[35] Facta minucione aliquando, cum conuenissemus in Stegha, recitauit nobis dominus G[odefridus], quia dixisset sibi prior de Thabor, quod prior de Windesim moriturus tria reliquerit fratribus suis pro testamento: primum, ne uterentur uasis stanneis, secundum, ne utentur carnibus assatis, tercium ut bene peciarent tunicas suas.[24]

[36] Item, uenit aliquando ad nos dominus Henricus de Nimgen, et humiliter dixit nobis, quoniam semper soleo magis compungi de illis[25] uiciis meis que possunt in publico ab aliis notari, quamuis eciam parua sunt, quam in illis que latent et non apparent ante homines, quamuis magna sint.

[37] Item, idem dixit: Quando ego ueni ad Dauentriam et steti hic, uidi fratres domus istius tam mature humiliter et auctoritatiue incedere, ut quando uidissem eos omnia interiora mea me mouerentur, et pre illorum

---

[23] Gerardus Scadde van Kalkar, rector at Zwolle, 1396-1409.

[24] The intermediary may be the same Henry of Harderwijk, a canon of Windesheim, who served as prior of Thabor near Sneek (Friesland) for a time before 1428. The names of priors in the 1430s and 1440s are not known to historians.

[25] de illis *scripsit bis*.

reuerencia manemur foris ante pistrinum uel in pistrino, et uero uidemur
uenire in eorum conspectu ad palacium.
<mores fratrum>

[38] Item, dixit michi frater Theodricus quod dixisset aliquando dominus
Floris: Tota res nostra nichil est nisi studuerimus humilitatem.
<humilitas>

[39] Item, dixit aliquando nobis dominus Rodolphus: Tota res patrum
nostorum precedencium stabat in mortificacione. Iam uero nos querimus
nostra commoda. Et si mouemus aliquid, solemus dicere de commoditate
et conueniencia rerum. Quod est eorum sentire contrarium.

[40] Item, quesiuit aliquando frater aliquis a domino Rodolpho: Quis est
optimus modus quo se aliquis habeat ad[26] ista exteriora ut cibos et uestimenta, etcetera? Et dixit, ut omnia homo sumat cum graciarum actione,
siue bona siue mala.

[41] Item, motum est aliquando de tunicis peciandis uel lauandis. Et dixit
Rodolphus quoniam dixit sibi semel Johan Kalkar quod dixisset sibi
semel dominus Floris: Dicant omnes quod uelint. Vos autem lapt mi cleder wel ende suuerlic. Et addidit Rodulphus causam: Quando uestes sunt
competenter accurate peciate, tunc lauencius et diucius portamus; quando uero multum et notabiliter habesse, tunc certe mouemur ad nouas
uestes.
<De peciandis uestibus>

[42] Item, dixit nobis dominus Godefridus: Tempore minucionis, tunc
debemus simul conferre de laudabilibus dictis et factis precedencium
patrum nostorum.

[43] Item dixit michi aliquando frater noster Theodricus quia recitasset
sibi semel dominus Johannis Haerlem in Zutvania quomodo dominus
Florencius aliquando dixit fratribus, quod possent seipsos aliquando
exhortari ad bonum, dicens sibiipsis: Nonne fortis est et sanus, et deus
misericors[27] qui libenter dat graciam tibi? Et iam habes aptum tempus!
Cur ergo non facis quod bonum est, etcetera, uel similiter.

[44] Quesiui aliquando a certo: Si iam essetis sanus et iuuenis, quomodo
et ad quod uellitis uos magis dare? Et dixit mihi: Ego pauper et infirmi
capitis sum. Sed patres nostri multum dabant se ad frangendam propriam
uoluntatem.

---

[26] ad] in *er.*
[27] et deus *add. et er.*

[45] Item, dixit aliquando Tricus de domino Henrico Bruyn, quia habebat multas bonas consuetudines que ualde bene deseruirent fratribus nostris. Primo, quia multum dilexit cameram et assiduus erat in camera. Cum autem uenisset aliquando aliquis ad cameram eius et uidens picturas dixisset ei, 'Frater Henrice, habetis hic bonam cameram,' respondit: Hec camera est mea Hollandia, Brabancia, Dyocesis, Gelria, etcetera. Secundo, quia ualde deditus erat sacris scripturis, et in tantum ut aliquando dicit michi dominus Rudolphus ut penne nichil nisi de sacris scripturis loqui et uellet et sciret. Und eciam consueuit dicere quia plus diligeret librum bonum quam magnum caballam, quale legitur de sancto Thoma de Aquino. Tercio, quia libenter solebat hominibus aliquid boni dicere et collacionem facere. Quarto, quia libenter et sepius consueuit celebrare. Quinto, quod nulli timendum erat quod aliquid diceret de eo in priuato uel absencia quod non uoluisset eum presentem audiuisse, et nichil detractionis umquam audire potuit. Sexto, quod libenter consueuit sacram scripturam scribere. Quantum scripsit apparet in scriptis et quaternis suis.

<hoc dixit de Henrico dees>

[46] Item, dixit Rodolphus quod deberemus nobis cauere ab amaritudine cordis et sic frequenter ammonere. Item, addidit quomodo dominus Lubbertus[28] fuisset ualde sollicitus in ammonendo, et quia dixisset in extrema infirmitate quod quando periret in nobis ammonicio, tunc periret domus nostra. Item, dixit Rodolphus quomodo nos habemus ammonicionem loco capittuli.

<Ammonicio>

[47] Item, dixit Rodolphus frater: Quando haberetis de sero multum temporis, tunc possitis quandoque legere septem psalmos uel partem uigiliarum, quia melius est quod homo faciat aliquod boni in camera, quamuis sit insipidum, quam quod uagetur foris inutiliter occupatus extra cameram.

[48] Item dixit, quoniam concilium sanctorum patrum est quod homo ante prandium deberet orare et post prandium laborare.

[49] Item, dixit idem Rodolphus: Quando non habemus conscienciam in aliquo die de rancorosis amaris uel carnalibus cogitacionibus, tunc spero quod sufficit de aliis uanis irrumpentibus infra horas uel alias habitis confiteri in generali. Et simile possimus obseruare de sero quando notauimus defectus.

<De notandis cogitacionibus et confite....>

---

[28] Lubbert was one of the founding brothers, who died already in 1398.

[50] Item dixit: De sero non nimis diu deduceremus tempus in notandis defectibus, quia, dixit, euenit michi aliquando tempus tantum pro hoc deducere, quod melius fuisset non notasse omnino.

[51] Item, dixit dominus Godefridus: Estimo et nichil aliud scio me audiuisse a domino Geraerdo Stuerman, qui tunc forte erat clericus et portabat sereum ante sacramentum quando dominus Florenus debebat uel iniungi uel communicare, quod dominus Floris tunc in extrema infirmitate conquestus fuit quod unquam tegisset calicem. Et addidit: quid tunc nos pueri facimus qui adhuc deberemus a tergo mundari.
<De presbiterio>

[52] Item dixit dominus Godefridus: Nisi quis uiolenti et magna fortitudine et precipuo dono spiritus sancti se exercitauerit in uirtutibus et spiritualibus exerciciis, postquam effectus est presbiter, de die in diem deficiet in uirtutibus, siue senciat ipse siue non. Et addidit quia presbiterium est res consumptiua uirtutis, et multa presupponit et multa requirit et ualde consumit, quia trahit post se longam et rufam caudam.[29]
<Contra affectum presbiterii>

[53] Item, dixit idem alio tempore quia cum ipse semel solus esset cum domino Amilio in extrema infirmitate, et familiariter cum eo loqueretur, quod dixit sibi dominus Amilius in sacerdocii inicio esset frequenter paragraphus emendacionis.

[54] Item, conuenientibus nobis semel in camere domini G[odefridi] in die dedicacionis ecclesie, dixit idem dominus Godefridus: Hec esset iam dedicacio nostra, ut unusquisque nostrum reuocaret nunc ad memoriam quomodo ab inicio dominus uocasset eum ad suum seruicium, et quam benigne prouidisset sibi de congruis loco tempore statu et confratribus, et quibus uoluntati eius posset deseruire. Et reuolueret in animo suo quantum per instrumenta sibi prouisa operatus esset, et quanto profectu spirituali tantis beneficiis dei respondisset. Et si inueniret se hucusque ingrate et negligenter egisse, pulsaret tunc campanas cordis sui deuotis et compunctis cordis suspiriis, de multa sua negligencia adeo remissionem et indulgenciam implorando, proposita ad emendam innouando et firmiter in corde statuendo. Et consimiliter totus in communi populus faceret de uocacione prima ad fidem per spirituales patrones et apostolos nostros Willibrordum et Lebuinum et ceteros eorum pro nostra conuersione collaboratores. Et dixit Rodolphus quod ad hoc bene congrueret quod nunc habemus patronum nostrum presentem et quod sanctorum relique iam processione deferuntur. Si uero inuenerimus nos competenter egisse, deberemus nunc deum de uocacione nostra et profectu nostro benedicere et laudere et

---

[29] causam *er, et scripsit* caudam.

nobisipsis congaudere. Et hec esset spiritualis materia de leticia et gaudio huius festiuitatis.

<In dedicacione>

[55] Fui aliquando solus cum domino Godefrido in Diepeueen, et cognaui in animo meo interrogare ipsum de futuro successu domus nostre. Cumque mouissem sibi, inde respondit: Et ego iam actu de hoc cogitaui. Et inter cetera que michi tunc familiariter reuelauit, dixit: Ego uellem me iam actu carere ambabus manibus meis et quod nunquam uenissem ad gradum sacerdocii, et ambobus pedibus meis et nunquam uenissem ad regimen domus nostre.

* * *

Quedam dicta patrum

[I] [C]³⁰onuenerunt aliquando fratres et dixit dominus Godefridus: Non queramus multa priuilegia in communibus consuetudinibus nostris; hoc modo bone consuetudines solent perire, unde et priuilegium dicitur quasi 'priuans legem'.

[II] Dixit dominus Rodolphus: Duo debemus attendere in nouiciis suscipiendis. Primum, ut sint fortes et apti in corpore. Unde idem ait: Nullo modo acceptandum esse illum qui non sufficit ad exercicia domus nostre et communes labores, quia illi tales non sunt contenti sua indulta indulgentia, sed etiam alios aut totam communitatem conantur ad talia priuilegia in cibis et aliis inducere, et sic ex tali acceptatione immineret domui nostre graue periculum. Secundum, ut sint apti in anima, ut scilicet sint inclinati ad despectum statum humilitatis nostre et ad tractum puerorum et sint in uoluntate emendandi mores, etcetera.

[III] Dixit dominus Rodolphus³¹: O quid putatis, fratres, imminebit tunc domui domini Florencii cum ad hoc peruenirent fratres, ut abiciant *Profectus religosorum, Horologium eterne sapiencie, Meditaciones beati Bernardi* et similes deuocionis libros, et paruipendant tales, sed sermones uel consimiles intellectuales materias et predicatorias assumant? Puto uere quod continget ei sicud pater sanctus Franciscus uidit de statua ei ostensa habente caput aureum et collum argenteum, etcetera. Et ipse fratribus suis predixit. Unde idem dominus Rodolphus ait quod pater noster dominus Amilius habuit in uoto (nescio quociens in anno) studere *Profectus religiosorum.*

[IV] Dixit dominus Rodolphus: Puto quod tunc aliquis bene studet quando ita studet ut accendatur ad compunctionem et orationem, et uix potest ultra studere quin oporteat eum prius orare.

---

³⁰ Space left for an initial, two lines high, which was never added.
³¹ At this point the scribe inserted: Illud dictum beati Bernardi semper recolens, Doctrina spiritus non curiositatem acuit sed charitatem accendit.

[V] Dixit dominus Otgerus Hoern: Quando modicum studui et post hoc dedi me ad orationem ad tempus aliquod, uel quando me excercitaui ad aliquam deuotionem, tunc paratus sum loqui cum pueris uel aliis de quacumque materia spirituali, sicut michi occurrerit. Quando uero obrui intellectum multis scripturis et diutini studio, non affectatus oratione uel aliqua devotione, uix inuenio quid dicam, etiam in multis preuisus.

[XI] Dixit dominus Godfridus: Nichil ita obstat profectui nostro spirituali sicut indigna sumptio uenerabilis sacramenti, quod scilicet nos non diligenter preparamus.

[XII] Venerunt aliquando ad domum domini Florencii dominus Theodricus Herxen et dominus Henricus rector in Albergen et dominus Henricus Huesden. Et conuenientibus nobis in unum, mota est questio que esset perfecta mortificatio. Et dixit inter cetera dominus Henricus de Albergen: Ista michi uidetur perfecta mortificatio, ut optet quis uilis et despectus uiuere et mori et nullius reputationis apparere. Et addidit: Vellem me hic quatuor tales inuenire. Spero tamen quod omnes tales estis. Sed heu in congregationibus et monasteriis paucos ualde tales inuenio.

[XIII] Venit quandoque frater aliquis ad dominum Godfridum dicens: Grauat me multum tedium in scribendo. Cui ille ait: Frater charissime, scribere feruenter et cum desiderio orare, milicia est apud Deum. Cogita igitur figens in corde tuo quod sedes sit equus, pergamenum ante te clypeus, penna lancea. His armis diabolo scripturus resiste, et quanto fortius scripseris et fervencius, tanto longius fugiet a te. Timeo tamen quod sis inordinatus in scribendo, scilicet nimis importunus quando bene succedit, et nimis deiectus quando male. Sed stude esse modestus et equanimis.

[XVII] Dixit dominus Godfridus: Passiones nostre sunt nobis uincula, quibus coniuncti tenemur inuicem, et inuicem substernimur. Quis enim nostrum iam in aliquo audebit se alii preferre, quoniam possumus uere dicere Hebrei sunt et ego, passionati sunt et ego.

[XX] Mouit dominus Rodolphus questionem dicens: Quis nobis ista exponet? Legi in libello quodam antiquo, quod docuerit quis alium dicens: Hic et non alibi, sic et non aliter, Nunc et non alias. Tandem ipse qui proposuit enigma, sic exposuit. Si audierit frater aliquis, Ecce in tali loco sunt boni religosi, Carthusienses ibi, regulares illic, etcetera, dicet in corde suo: Hic debeo seruire Deo et non alibi. Sic secundum exercicia domus istius et non aliter, idest secundum exercicia illorum, quia homini uaria occurrunt. Nunc et non alias, hoc est non protrahendo, utputa dicere cras me emendabo.

[XXI] Dixit dominus Godfridus: Cum fuerimus octoginta annorum, et baculo innitentes, terram matrem nostram recuruato dorso et collo inspexerimus, tunc poterimus habere spem de uictoria carnis. Et allegauit pro exemplo: Noui, inquit, hominem ultra octoginta annos habentem (ut presumo) uel nouaginta, qui tamen post hos annos cecidit. Unde, ait, non est presumendum de multitudine annorum ad uincendum uicium carnis.

[XXII] Dixit dominus Henricus Goude: In omnibus sorores sustineo, dummodo castitatem saluam inuenio. Et adiunxit: Libentius sustineo quod sorores inter se litigantes percuciendo liuidum oculum faciant cuiquam quam quod aliqua carnalitate uiciate sint.

[XXIII] Item dixit: Multum debemus niti trahere iuuenes ad castitatem, quia, inquit, paucissimi inueniuntur casti, et tam pauci quod communis homo hoc non crederet.

[VI] Dixit dominus Rodolphus de Johanne Arnem, qui dixit nunquam se aliquid scripsisse pro collationibus aliis faciendis sed solum propter se, quamuis ipse ualde multa scripsisse cognoscitur.

[VII] Dominus Henricus pater in Albergen multum rogatus a fratribus nostris ut memoriale aliquod relinqueret eis, ait: Ultra uiginti-unum annos domui nostre prefui, et nec usque hodie placcam uel minus exposui uel expendi quam uellem latere fratres meos in computacione ubi quando et qua de causa eam expenderim. In hoc laudabili uerbo fratres nostri multum edificati sunt.

[VIII] Volens dominus Godfridus pater noster fratres hortari ad studium oracionis, dixit inter cetera: Secundum sentire meum firmiter credo quod nunquam aliquis, quando bene orauerit et cordialiter se deo in oracione commiserit, uacuus ab oracione recedat, quin acquirat sibi aliquid gracie, quamuis orans hoc ignorauerit. Quod non fit sine occulta dei dispensatione, ut non extollatur ipse, quod facile fieret si pro certo sciret sibi tunc graciam infundi.

[IX] Dixit dominus Godfridus fratribus congregatis: Dico uobis, fratres, quod cordialiter ita sencio. Vellem me ambobus oculis esse excecatum, et sic usque ad mortem mansurum, quod nunquam uenissem ad sacerdotium. Item ait: Ego ordinandus fuit semicecus. Utinam totus fuissem excecatus, quam bene michi esset. Item dixit: Millies plus timeo de actibus meis in gradu sacerdotali quam quos feci extra ordines. Et si iam oporteret me mori, nulla me tantum terrerent quantum illa que egi in sacerdocio meo.

[XXV] Dixit dominus Henricus Goude: Hec est uera custodia castitatis, ut homo nunquam sit securus sed semper sit suspectus. Et quamuis longo tempore non senserit se uexatum hac tempatatione, tamen semper ita se habeat in custodia et cautela quasi maxime temptaretur, uisum et alios sensus interiores et exteriores custodiendo.

[XXVI] Item dixit: Castitas est dulcissima uirtus, que ceteras uirtutes quodam modo reddit saporosas. Et magnum donum a deo accepit cui datum est sapere ea que sunt castitatis, quia secundum Thomas fundamentum est contemplationis.

[XXVII] Solet dicere dominus Godfridus quod interdum non multum curaret si inter confessiones fratrum domus nostre dormiret, dummodo hec duo, scilicet castitatem et fraternam charitatem, salua inueniret.

[XXVIII] Dixit dominus Godfridus pater noster: Estimo quod non maior causa sit quare multi deficimus in uia dei et non proficimus, quam quod minus digne nos preparamus ad sumptionem uenerabilis sacramenti, et quod ficte confitemur et ex consuetudine. Insuper quod tam tepide persoluimus horas domino deo nostro.

[XXX] Dixit dominus Henricus pater in Albergen ex rogatu domini Rodolphi sororibus domus magistri Gerardi: Quid multum loquar? In tribus uidentur michi omnia consistere. Primum est, quod soror nichil occultum in corde retineat quod non reuelet suo superiori in confessione et extra. Secundum est, ut nichil de se presumat facere absque scitu et consensu rectoris. Tercium est, ut in omnibus homo purificet intencionem, quia si intencio mala fuerit, de sequentibus nichil ualet.

[XXXIII] Cum conuenissemus quadam dominica quadragesime, et colloquium fieret de mortificatione uiciorum, dixit dominus Godfridus rector: Sit hoc nostrum exercicium commune, ut unusquisque nostrorum omne quod sibi contrarium occurrerit, tota ista quadragesima equo animo sufferat. Et nullus ammonitus etiam iniuste se excuset.

[XXXIV] Item quadam alia dominica dixit: Unusquisque studeat se iam ad interiora conuertere. Discedat omnis rancor et suspicio de corde nostro, et studeamus per charitatem uniri. In his enim uerus fructus consistit. Et cetere obseruancie exteriores in tantum bone sunt in quantum nobis ad ista deseruiunt.

[XXXV] Dixit dominus Godfridus quadam die minucionis, quod prior in Wyndesim reliquit moriturus pro testamento hec tria: Primum, ne uterentur uasis stanneis; secundum, ne uterentur carnibus assis; tercium, ut bene repetiarent uestimenta sua et tunicas.

[XXXVIII] Dixit dominus Florencius: Tota res nostra nichil est nisi humilitati studerimus.

[XXXIX] Dixit dominus Rodolphus: Tota res patrum nostrorum stabat in mortificatione. Iam uero nos querimus nostra commoda. Et si aliquid mouerimus in communi, hoc fit propter commoditatem rerum temporalium. Quod est sentire eorum contrarium.

[XL] Interrogatus dominus Rodolphus: Quis est optimus modus uti temporalibus istis ut cibis, uestibus et ceteris. Dixit: Ut homo omnia sumat cum graciarum actione que illi subministrantur, siue bona fuerint siue mala.

[XLI] Motum est aliquando de tunicis repetiandis, et dixit dominus Rodolphus: Audiui a Iohanne Kalcker, dixit michi dominus Florencius, Dicant omnes quid uelint, Vos autem lapt myn cleder ual ende suuerlick.

[XLII] Dixit nobis dominus Godfridus: Tempore minutionis debemus simul conferre de laudabilibus dictis et factis precedentium patrum nostrorum.

[XLIII] Dixit dominus Florencius quandoque fratribus quod possent seipsos hortari contra tedium ad bonum, dicentes sibiipsis: Nonne fortis est et sanus? Et Deus misericors est, qui libenter dat graciam? Et iam habes aptum tempus. Cur ergo non facis quod bonum est?

[XLV] Dixit Theodricus frater noster de domino Henrico Bruyn quod habebat multas bonas consuetudines, que ualde etiam deseruirent fratribus nostris. Primo quod multum dilexit cameram, et assiduus erat in ea. Cum enim uenisset aliquando quidam in camera eius, ait ei:

Frater Henrice, habetis hic bonam et pulchram cameram. Respondit: Hec camera est mea Hollandia, Brabancia, Gelria, Dyocesis, etcetera. Secundo, quod deditus erat ualde sacris scripturis, et in tantum quod (sicut michi dixit dominus Rodolphus) pene nichil sciret et uellet loqui nisi de sacris scripturis. Unde etiam consueuit dicere, quod plus diligeret librum bonum quam magnum caballum, quale etiam legitur de sancto Thoma Aquinensi. Tercio, quod libenter solebat hominibus aliquid boni dicere et collationem facere. Quarto, quod libenter et sepius solet celebrare missam. Quinto, quod nulli timendum erat quod aliquid diceret de eo in priuato quod noluisset ipsum presentem audiuisse, et nichil detractionis unquam audire potuit. Sexto, quod libenter solebat sacram scripturam scribere, et quantum scripsit patet in scriptis et quaternis eius.

[XLVI] Dixit dominus Rodolphus: Caueamus nobis solum ab amaritudine cordis, et sic frequenter ammoneamus inuicem. Item, ait quod dominus Lubbertus fuerat ualde sollicitus in ammonendo, qui etiam ait in extrema infirmitate sua: Quando perit inter nos ammonicio, tunc peribit domus nostra. Dixit dominus Rodolphus: Nos habemus ammoniciones mutuas loco capituli religiosorum.

[XLVII] Dixit dominus Rodolphus: Quando quis uesperi habuerit multum temporis, tunc legeret septem psalmos, aut partem de uigiliis, quia melius est, ait, quod homo faciat aliquid boni in camera, quamuis non sapiat ei, quam uagetur extra cameram.

[XLVIII] Idem ait: Consilium sanctorum patrum est ante prandium orare et post prandium laborare.

[L] Idem dixit: Vespertino tempore non nimis diu deducemus tempus in notandis defectibus, quia euenit michi, ait, aliquando tantum temporis pro hoc deducere quod melius fuisset non notasse omnino.

[LI] Dixit dominus Gotfridus: Audiui a domino Gerardo Stuerman, qui portauit candelam ceream ante uenerabile sacramentum in extrema unctione domini Florencii, quod dominus Florencius conquestus est se unquam tetigisse calicem. Et addidit Stuerman: Quid ergo nos pueri faciemus, quibus opus esset a tergo lauari et mundari?

[LII] Dixit dominus Gotfridus: Nisi quis uiolenti et magna fortitudine et precipue dono spiritus sancti se exercitauerit in uirtutibus et spiritualibus exerciciis, postquam fuerit ordinatus sacerdos de die in diem deficiet, siue ipse hoc sentiat siue non. Et addidit: Sacerdotium est res consumptiua uirtutis, et multa requirit et ualde consumit, et trahit post se caudam longam.

[LIII] Item ait quod dominus Amilius dixit ei in extrema infirmitate: Sacerdocii inicium frequenter est paragraphus emendationis.

[LV] Dixit dominus Gotfridus cuidam fratri familiariter: Ego uellem me carere ambobus manibus meis, quod nunquam uenissem ad sacerdocium, et ambobus pedibus meis, quod nunquam uenissem ad regimen domus nostre.

[IX] Dixit Gotfridus: Consilium meum est ut quandocumque potuerit homo aliquo iusto modo abesse, non aggrediatur sacerdocium.

[X] Idem ait: Quandocumque moritus aliquis filiorum confessionis mee, inuadit me horror quidam, et timeo ne sit aliquid per me neglectum aut minus actum quod possit ei cedere in damnum aliquod salutis.

BETWEEN SEVERITY AND MERCY. THREE MODELS OF PRE-REFORMATION URBAN REFORM PREACHING: SAVONAROLA — STAUPITZ — GEILER

Berndt Hamm*

I. *Urban 'dirigenti religiosi' of the Reformation and Late Middle Ages[1]*

(1.) The success of the Reformation in the cities of Germany and Switzerland is generally considered to be inconceivable apart from the key role played by urban preachers. It was through such preachers, their compelling and stirring sermons, not least also through the pamphlets they composed, that the teaching of the Reformation received its decisive popular impetus among urban communities and the peasant population of the surrounding countryside. At the same time, these preachers influenced the religious politics of civic, noble and princely authorities in a normative way.

Yet the influence which the urban preachers exercised on the introduction and implementation of local or territorial reformations after about 1522, can be properly understood only in the context of late medieval developments. My *first thesis* is this: the principal reason why the preachers of the Reformation were able to acquire such enormous authority in their cities and beyond, was that before and after 1500, learned and respected urban preachers, pastors and devotional writers had already gained a high level of spiritual leadership among the urban public, especially where influential elements of that public were already striving for spiritual reform.

The offices held by such spiritual leaders were diverse. Some were secular priests in endowed preaching positions in cathedrals or

---

* Professor of History and Historical Theology, Friedrich-Alexander-Universität, Erlangen-Nürnberg. (Translated by Helen Heron and Gotthelf Wiedermann)
    [1] This essay is an expanded form of a lecture given at the international Savonarola-Conference in Ferrara, Italy, in Spring 1998. The main focus of this conference was the significance and the influence of religious leaders (*dirigenti religiosi*) in European cities during the 15th and 16th centuries. – I shall restrict myself in the bibliographical references in the footnotes mostly to lists of sources. More extensive material on urban piety and preaching in the 15th and 16th centuries can be found in my book *Bürgertum und Glaube. Konturen der städtischen Reformation*, Göttingen 1996.

other city churches; others, more commonly, were preachers at mendicant churches. Additionally, there were the itinerant penitential and indulgence preachers who visited the towns and cities for a period of days or weeks only, such as during Lent, and who drew the crowds with their eloquence. Compared to the preachers of the early Reformation the urban preachers of the late middle-ages may appear less spectacular, because they operated within the framework of the approved doctrine of the church and did not challenge the ecclesiastical hierarchy, but they already fulfilled to a degree the function of urban *dirigenti religiosi* in the full sense of the word *"dirigere"*: guidance, orientation, regulation, direction, standardisation, control, criticism and correction. The preachers of the urban pulpit were prominent and, at times, controversial figures among the civic communities. Their drive for an ecclesiastical and ethical reform of the community was often frustrated by obstacles, in particular those posed by the political authorities, and yet their influence on the formation of a community's norms and conscience should not be underestimated. The new ideas of the Reformation's preaching could therefore slip into an existing, tried and tested form.

(2.) Even in terms of their message there is a certain continuity between the preachers of the Reformation and the spiritual objectives of the late medieval *dirigenti religiosi*. The stirring effect of urban Reformation preaching derived directly from the special nature of its message. By declaring Scripture an exclusive norm for the life of the church and the individual believer, that preaching met two essential needs: the longing for the liberating experience of forgiveness and peace of conscience on the one hand, and the need for a binding communal order and discipline on the other. Reformation preachers, the *dirigenti religiosi* of the cities, seized this dual opportunity of guidance by interpreting the Bible on the one hand as the comforting message of God's mercy, liberating believers from the need to justify themselves through religious works as well as from the demands of church imposed obligations, and on the other hand by interpreting it as the binding message of a holy God, who wishes to sanctify his liberated congregation in the spirit of love and remove the leaven of vice from it.

It is worth emphasizing that the auditors of these urban sermons were not only attracted by the promise of God's unheard-of grace, but also by the proclamation of a new severity in the fight against sin and vice. With regard to the latter, the various classes of the communities had differing views of a Christian order of love and discipline. While the governing elite were mainly concerned with securing their subjects' obedience and willingness to bear burdens, the less well-to-do wished to see the greed, extravagance and indulgence of the rich checked, economic pressures relieved and social misery alleviated. Thus the polarity of grace and severity, mercy and justice, Gospel and Law, freedom and discipline, comfort and admonition, promise and menace determined the message of Reformation preaching as well as the expectations of the believers. Christ reigns over the city as the crucified saviour, but also as law-giver and judge. Between these poles range the various types of *dirigenti religiosi* and of urban Reformations.

(3.) The theological dialectic of the inviting mercy of the reconciled God and the impelling severity of the divine law-giver, so central to the character of the diverse types of Reformation, is incomprehensible apart from an awareness of the tensions within late medieval theology. It presupposes a polarity which is at the same time different from and analogous to that of the preachers and pastors of the late medieval cities. In this respect, too — and this is my *second thesis* — the influence and attraction of urban Reformation preaching can be adequately grasped only if note is taken of the way in which the various positions of the pre-Reformation *dirigenti religiosi* were continued and, at the same time, changed. A closer look at the urban reform preachers before and after 1500 reveals that they, too, find their individual positions within a field of tension between the poles of God's infinite mercy for the sake of Jesus Christ, and of his relentless strictness as the heavenly law-giver, judge and avenger. The comforting call to throw oneself completely on God's saving mercy stands alongside the menacing warning that only those will reach salvation who truly repent of all their sins, make satisfaction for their transgressions and follow God's law.

The sermons and devotional writings of these spiritual leaders therefore demonstrate in an exemplary way how the spirituality of the late Middle Ages was caught between two dominating perspectives and, depending on the individual author, tended to the one or the other direction. One perspective stresses the strictly judging, rewarding and punishing justice of God which through encouragements, warnings or terrifying threats compels the believer — who is considered capable of religious achievements and merits — to earn his salvation with good intentions and works. On the other hand there is the perspective of mercy: it conveys an awareness of human weakness and of the insufficiency of good works, directing the believer to the saving mercy of God the Father, Christ, Mary and the saints. It is to their compassion, mediation and intercession that weak and afflicted sinners are encouraged to entrust themselves with full hope. In the following I shall attempt to investigate how these two perspectives are accentuated and combined, for it is this that determines the character of the theology and spirituality preached in each case. How does the respective preacher relate to each other the strictness of the Law and the leniency of the Gospel? How does he define justice (or righteousness) and mercy, and what kind of compromise determines their relationship? Is the category of retributive justice the prevailing norm dominating his discourses on mercy, or is divine mercy his point of departure, seeing even the retributive justice of God in the light of his saving grace? Such questions indicate how diverse, even contradictory, the spiritual orientation of the late medieval urban *dirigenti religiosi* was. The components of threats, warnings, encouragement and consolation are mixed in all possible proportions.

(4.) On the basis of such criteria the urban *dirigenti religiosi* before and after 1500 may be divided into three main types: first, we note the type of preachers who strike predominantly a menacing key, terrifying their listeners by preaching the wrath of a punishing God, the relentless severity of a *deus iudex*. The objectives of a complete change of life-style, of Christian perfection and of the spiritual purification of the individual as well as the community are central to their sermons. Second, we encounter a contrasting type of preaching, in which the leniency and comfort of God's mercy dominate over all the terrifying aspects of his justice and punishment. Such preaching unfolds before the listener above all the boundless treasures of divine mercy, in particular of Christ's suffering and its vicarious atonement. Such preachers of the *misericordia Dei* tend to play down the demands made on the spiritual capabilities of the believer and the notion of the sinner's indispensible co-operation for his salvation, maximizing instead the believer's hope in the manifold forms of assistance offered by God and the Church. Finally, a third type of preachers display no clear prevalence of either menacing severity or comforting mercy. These are the preachers who attempt to strike a balance between retributive justice and generous mercy, between threat and comfort, between moral exertion and trust. Depending on circumstances and audience they may emphasize more strongly the seriousness of divine judgement, the urgency of penitence and the necessity of good conduct for salvation; at other times their sermons will highlight the saving power of grace based on vicarious atonement or merits, of intercessions, sacraments and indulgences, which compensate for the believer's moral failures and spiritual weakness.

In the following I intend to illustrate these three main types of spiritual counselling by reference to the examples of three prominent *dirigenti religiosi* in cities of the late middle-ages: Girolamo Savonarola (1452-1498) in Florence, Johannes von Staupitz (ca. 1468-1524) in Nuremberg and Johannes Geiler von Kaysersberg (1445-1510) in Strasbourg. As preachers and spiritual writers all three made an extraordinary impact. All of them provoked a lively response in the cities mentioned and enjoyed enormous respect and veneration among the political elite. All of them subjected the prevailing secular circumstances to a focused spiritual perspective. All of them aimed at reform and at the spiritual renewal of the believer, monastic life and the church, in particular at true penitence and a love of God which radiates throughout the whole life of a Christian; and all of them had in view the urban community which they wanted to provide with religious guidance.

(5.) There is a close connection between the preachers' attitude and the political, social, cultural and religious climate of the cities in which they operated. Of course, their attitudes were also influenced to a large degree by their respective ecclesiastical status: as prior of a Dominican convent closely connected with the rule of the Medici (Savonarola), as head (Vicar-General) of a congregation of observant monasteries of the Augustinian order in Germany and the Netherlands (Staupitz), and as someone commissioned by the Chapter to serve as Cathedral Preacher (Geiler von Kaysersberg). Yet, whatever differences there are in their manner of preaching and in the specific character of their spirituality, these cannot be explained adequately by reference to their ecclesiastical status or to the differing urban situations alone.

Admittedly, Savonarola's style of preaching is inconceivable apart from the particular social and political context of upper Italy and the city republic of Florence with its highly developed Renaissance culture; and Geiler's and Staupitz' very different styles of delivery are, no doubt, also determined by the fact that they did not preach from a pulpit in the heated and polarized atmosphere of the city on the Arno, but in the more moderate, peaceful and conservative climates of Strasbourg and Nuremberg. But it would be wrong to see these contexts as inevitably determinative: In Savonarola's Florence there were other preachers who did not share the menacing tone of his sermons, just as one should not necessarily deduce Geiler's individual style of preaching at Strasbourg or Staupitz' at Nuremberg from the peculiar characters of these cities. No doubt the Dominican Savonarola was heavily influenced by the Thomist teaching of his order, but at the same time he stood in the tradition of the penitential preachers from various orders of northern Italy. Staupitz, the Augustinian friar, was naturally loyal to the theology of the (alleged) founder of his order, yet his interpretation of St. Augustine was also considerably influenced by medieval theological traditions outside his order. Conversely, Geiler adopted as his model Jean Gerson, a secular cleric like himself, but at the same time felt drawn to the monastic ideal of withdrawal from the world.

Each of the three therefore displays his own dynamic of theology, spirituality and personal character, which transcends his local and social context and his form of ecclesiastical life — just as the way that the writings of each found reception beyond the boundaries of local circumstances or theological traditions. We are therefore dealing with three individually conditioned, yet quite exemplary types of urban *dirigenti religiosi*, who may be compared in spite of their geographical distance. I view their individual originality as an accentuation or illustration of the generally typical. A comparison thus affords us an impression of the variety of type and the range of message in reform preaching before the Reformation.

II. *Girolamo Savonarola: Preacher of God's Severity*

(1.) With his stirring sermons Girolamo Savonarola, prior of the Dominican convent of San Marco in Florence from 1491, represents the menacing and terrifying type of penitential preaching which announces the relentless strictness of God's punishing justice. In the same way that Savonarola himself in his pulpit felt an enormous pressure which, as he declared, almost burst the arteries in his breast[2], so he subjected his listeners to a shocking eschatological and moral pressure. Long before he appeared in public with his claim of a prophetic vision of future terrors and a prophetic interpretation of political events, his preaching style already possessed the character of a *terrifica praedicatio* (terrifying preaching). This is how he himself described one of his sermons which he delivered in the Florentine cathedral of S. Maria del Fiore on 27 April 1491.[3] In it he harshly chastised the greed, extravagance and vanity of the clergy, the hardheartedness of the rich and powerful who imposed unbearable taxes on the poor, and the sexual vices of the licentious. Throughout the nineties he continued with an untiring, pounding monotony to criticise the superficiality of monastic life, the excessive finery of women, the pernicious preference for pagan books by humanist scholars, and above all the unholiness of gamblers and blasphemers, of the indifferent and of sceptics, the so-called "lukewarm", condemning again and again the secularisation of the clergy, the exploitation of the poor and the perversity of the "sodomites" (i.e. homosexuals). God's wrath, Savonarola threatened in his sermon of 1491, will visit all such people of vice with terrible plagues; a new flood of retribution will come over them and only a small number, he himself and those faithful chosen by God, will escape the horrifying destruction.

This terrifying tone, alarming the listeners in a partly fascinating, partly shocking way, was maintained by Savonarola throughout the following years: the wrath of God at the Florentines' disobedience, his approaching punishment in the shape of natural catastrophes, the imminent flood and eternal condemnation in hell, the call to conversion and penitence, the promise of salvation for the few who repent in time and serve God in holy simplicity and pure love, renouncing all worldly affluence.[4] After 1492 Savonarola intensified the menac-

---

[2] Savonarola: 3rd. sermon on the Psalms, 13th. Januar 1495, in: *Prediche sopra i Salmi*, ed. Vincenzo Romano, Vol. 1, Rome 1969 (Edizione nazionale delle opere di Girolamo Savonarola), p. 56.12-15. Cf. also Savonarola's testimony: "I should like to say nothing and be silent but I can not; for the Word of God is like a fire in my heart, and if I did not beat out the flames they would consume me entirely." Cf. Jer. 20.9; 1st sermon on Amos and Zechariah from 17th February 1496, in: *Prediche sopra Amos et Zaccaria*, ed. Paolo Ghiglieri, Vol. I, Rome 1971, pp. 20.28 – 21.1.

[3] Savonarola: *Compendium revelationum* (October 1495), in: *Compendio di rivelazioni* [...], ed. Angela Crucitti, Rome 1974, p. 136.5f: "Quamobrem eodem mane terrificam praedicationem egi"; cf. the earlier Italian version (August 1495), ibid. p. 10.9f: "feci una spaventosa predicazione".

[4] On the subject of 'simplicity' cf. Savonarola's treatise of August 1496: *De simplicitate christianae vitae*, ed. Pier Giorgio Ricci, Rome 1959 (Edizione nazionale delle

ing and terrifying character of his penitential sermons through new types of prophetic visions. The most important of these was the vision of the sword, to which he returned again and again[5]: He saw a hand in heaven holding a sword with the inscription: "The sword of the Lord will come over the earth shortly and swiftly" (*Gladius Domini super terram cito et velociter*[6]), while above the hand it read: "True and just are the judgements of the Lord" (*Vera et iusta sunt iudicia Domini*; Revelation 19.2). A loud voice sounded over the whole earth: "Hear ye, all dwellers of the earth, thus speaks the Lord: I, the Lord, speak in my holy wrath. Behold, the days are approaching when I will wield my sword over you. Return to me, before my wrath blazes up; for then misery will come over you; you will seek peace and not find it." Following this, angels floated down to earth to offer a white garment and a cross to every human being. The repentant accepted this gift of grace and cleansing; most, however, rejected it full of scorn. But then God's sword turned against the earth: The sky filled with dark clouds and thunder, swords, hail, arrows and fire all at once rained down, plagues, famines and innumerable afflictions erupted on earth. Only those dressed in the white garments and carrying the crosses in their hands were rescued by the angels. The vision ended with an appeal to the Florentines: "Therefore heed the word of God: The Lord desires to have mercy on you. Return to the Lord, for he is merciful and compassionate and shows righteousness to all who call on him. But if you refuse, I will avert my eyes from you for ever." Soon, it will be "too late": Then the sinners will ask for an opportunity to repent but receive none.

---

opere di Girolamo Savonarola). Gundolf Gieraths (*Savonarola: Ketzer oder Heiliger?*, Freiburg-Basel-Vienna 1961, p. 181) aptly summarises the content of the five books: ... back to simplicity, back to the original love. Savonarola addresses the individual ranks and professions and shows that Christian love does not consist in wealth, external acts, parroted prayers, magnificent church buildings, gold-embroidered robes and splendid vessels, nor in indulgences, pilgrimages and the veneration of relics, but in purity of heart, in sincerity of attitude and in authentic love. Genuine Christians trust in God's providence and expect the highest bliss in the hereafter.

[5] Savonarola only later described the vision he had in 1492 ("in the night before my last Advent sermon") in his *Compendio di rivelazioni/Compendium revelationum* (Aug./Oct. 1495), ed. Crucitti (as in n. 3): report of the vision pp. 12.10 – 14.15 (Italian) and pp. 138.7 – 140.14 (Latin).

[6] In this famous statement about the Sword, Savonarola combines the Vulgate terminology "gladius Domini" (cf. Isaiah 34.6) with the phrase "cito et velociter" (Joshua 23.16 and Joel 3.4). In his 1st sermon on Haggai (1st Nov. 1494) Savonarola states that it is not quite two years since he prophesied to Florence: "The Sword of the Lord will come over the earth soon and speedily!" Cf. below, p. 329 with n. 7.

For the prophetic visionary Savonarola this terrible moment of judgement in which the sword of divine wrath would strike arrived in the autumn of 1494. The French King Charles VIII, whom Savonarola saw as the Lord's instrument of punishment against godless Italy, stood at the borders of Tuscany with his army, ready to move against Florence. On 1 November Savonarola announced to his anxious listeners that events were proving him right. Less than two years ago he had announced to them for the first time that the sword of the Lord would come shortly and swiftly over them. Not he, but the Lord had predicted it to them. Now this prophecy has come true: The sword has arrived![7] And yet there still is a chance to turn to God. In this politically desperate situation, in which the city's government is confused and without sense of direction, Savonarola's preaching becomes an impassioned entreaty to repent: "I speak to you, Florence, and have but one desire: to shout to you with a loud voice: Repent!"[8] "Repentance is the only remedy."[9] "You sinners, you obstinate and lukewarm people, all you who always delay your repentance: Repent now, do not delay any further — the Lord is still waiting for you and calls you to himself."[10]

(2.) Even though this sermon contains massive threats by identifying current events as the sword of God and by announcing to his listeners that, not least for spatial reasons, they are already much closer to hell, which is at the centre of the earth, than to the much more distant heavenly paradise[11], one cannot fail to notice how powerfully Savonarola can combine such a message with an element of comfort and with a reference to God's welcoming mercy. He woos the Florentines by calling to them: "Repent! See how good and merciful the Lord is; he wants to lead you to the ark and save you. Come therefore, you sinners, come, for God is calling you."[12] Even though the flood will come, the saving ark has been built. This is the image to which Savonarola returns again and again. The sword of the Lord and infernal condemnation are, indeed, imminent; but "the heavenly

---

[7] Savonarola: 1st sermon on Haggai, 1st Nov. 1494, in: *Prediche sopra Aggeo*, ed. Luigi Firpo, Rome 1965 (Edizione nazionale delle opere di Girolamo Savonarola), p. 12.13-17.

[8] *Prediche sopra Aggeo*, ibid, p. 11.19-21.

[9] Ibid. p. 11.4.

[10] Ibid. p. 4.21-25.

[11] Ibid. p. 2.6-11.

[12] Ibid. p. 4.27-30

kingdom is close at hand" as well. To enter into the ark of divine mercy, all that is required is a sincerely penitent heart.[13]

From November 1494 Savonarola accentuates the theme of mercy more strongly than in previous sermons. His own words reveal that he is fully aware of this shift, as we see for example in a sermon in which he addresses God: "Lord, I did indeed consider you to be the greatest good and your mercy to be boundless. But the true greatness of your mercy was beyond my powers of comprehension."[14] Previously, he had directed his attention above all to the hardheartedness of the sinners and their impending doom, expecting "that the earth would certainly open up to devour the godless and obstinate, seeing that no more mercy was to be expected from you"[15], but now God let him know that in his abundant mercy he is still inviting sinners to turn to him[16], that the door of the ark is still open. It may not stay open for much longer, and few only will turn to God while the great majority will be consigned to hell; but thanks and praise are due to God's boundless mercy, that a small part of humanity at least will be saved.[17] Savonarola explains to his disturbed listeners: "We should not marvel at the small number of the righteous, for we must not forget that it is no little thing when God raises human beings, who had fallen so low, to such lofty heights."[18] After all, only a small number of sinners are capable of showing a genuine penitence which flows from an attitude of true love; the majority can only muster an inferior, pretended penitence.[19]

This last statement already indicates where Savonarola sees the limits of God's mercy. The Dominican prior and preacher of penitence is an impressive example of the way in which the infinite mercy of God could be exalted even by those late-medieval preachers of penitence who terrified their listeners out of their wits with their prophecies of doom. The entire preaching activity of Savonarola, especially after the end of 1494, could be presented as a mission in the name of divine mercy; he himself characterises his mission occa-

---

[13] Ibid. p. 3.6-8.
[14] Ibid. pp. 3.30-4.3.
[15] Ibid. p. 4.12-15.
[16] Cf. ibid. p. 18.12f: "See, my beloved, how great is the love of God ...!"
[17] *Prediche sopra Aggeo*, ibid. p. 2.20-27.
[18] Ibid. p. 2.27-30.
[19] Ibid. pp. 2.30-3.3. On the characteristics of true repentance cf. ibid. p. 3.8-22.

sionally as such, and in 1496, evaluating his own preaching, he judged that he had kept "to the side of mercy."[20] There is a pronounced trend in more recent Savonarola research to interpret the caesura of the year 1494 in this way: the gloomy prophet of doom, who announced his city's destruction, became instead a prophet of salvation, a herald of divine mercy and the harbinger of a time of blessing in this world. Florence, it is maintained, now came to represent not the Babylon of Rome but a heavenly Jerusalem on earth.[21] We may, indeed, register a change in Savonarola: To the same degree that he turned into a political prophet and saw the first fruits of the realization of his ideas of political, social and religious change in Florence — through a *rapprochement* with the French king, the expulsion of the Medici, the introduction of a republican constitution and the reform of public morality —, to the same degree, therefore, to which he was politically and socially successful, allowing himself to be drawn into the reform of urban society, there took shape before his visionary eye the possibility of a purified and holy community on earth, a new Jerusalem. It is for this hoped-for Florence that he predicted a bright future, a millenium of good fortune as it were, of fame and wealth based on its ethical renewal, its existing virtues and a pure, divine love that would unite all citizens. This is the vision of a theocracy in which Christ is king of Florence, in which everyone lives in accordance with Christ's law and in which Savonarola, as the authorised prophet of the divine will, guides this republic of Christ through the dangers of this world.

(3.) Savonarola arrived at his theocratic vision of a holy Florence in effect as late as November 1494, during Charles VIII's Italian campaign. In my view, however, the change in the Dominican is misrepresented if we focus exclusively on this shift from prophecy of doom to one of salvation, of his preaching of wrath and the flood to one of mercy and the ark. Careful reading of his sermons between 1494 and 1498, the year of his execution, reveals how the themes of

---

[20] Savonarola: 1st sermon on Amos and Zechariah, 17th Febr. 1496, in: *Prediche sopra Amos et Zaccaria* (as in n. 2), p. 17.14: "alla parte della misericordia".

[21] This interpretation of Savonarola is particularly represented by Donald Weinstein: *Savonarola and Florence. Prophecy and Patriotism in the Renaissance*, Princeton 1970, especially Chapter IV: Florence, the New Jerusalem (pp. 138-158), e.g. p. 145: "It was a fundamental transformation of Savonarola's eschatology. [...] The preacher of repentance had become a prophet of the millenium, exchanging his earlier radical pessimism for an even more radical optimism."

menace and terror continue to prevail without interruption; by the same token his preaching before 1494 had already contained announcements of divine mercy. Savonarola's way of preaching remains a *praedicatio terrifica* (terrifying preaching) — the difference is that he has changed the aim of his threatening: Whereas he previously wanted to save a small number from the general corruption in church and society, he now sees the chance of a city cleansed from the wicked, which will become a centre of church renewal (*renovatio ecclesiae*) radiating throughout Italy and Europe, and of mission among the heathens throughout the world. That the Florentines have been offered this unique opportunity in spite of the continuing immorality of their private and public lives, is for him evidence of God's incomprehensible mercy. But the way in which he presents the chance of repentance and self-cleansing is imbedded in an undiminished barrage of threats predicting the most horrendous plagues as well as individual and political ruin.

An example of this can be seen in a sermon delivered by Savonarola on 13th January 1495. Here he combines the possibility of a renewal of the Church spreading out from Florence with the proclamation of terrible divine sanctions if the Florentines do not mend their ways. He takes up his earlier vision of the Sword and adjures his listeners: "Believe, then, and change your ways! Do not think that the punishment has passed you by; for I observe how the Sword is turning back."[22] "Its point is not yet turned down. God is still waiting for you to do penance."[23] The wrath of God is still enflamed, his Sword will shortly be drawn.[24] "Do penance while the Sword is still sheathed and not yet dipped in blood!"[25] God's punishment, his scourge and chastisement is near; if they do not change their ways soon, it will be too late. This tenor runs through the whole sermon. It gives the passages where Savonarola speaks of God's offer of mercy[26] the character of an urgent, sombre ultimatum. This is true even in Savonarola's well-known comparison of the offer of salvation with an apple: "Do not forget, Florence, that I told you I had given you an apple, as a mother gives a crying child an apple to soothe it.

---

[22] Savonarola: 3rd Sermon on the Psalms, 13th January 1495, in: *Prediche sopra i Salmi* (as in n.2), p. 42.7-9.

[23] *Prediche sopra i Salmi*, ibid. p. 54.8-10.

[24] Ibid. p. 56.24-27.

[25] Ibid. p. 62.10-12.

[26] E.g. ibid. p. 52.10-13.

But if the child continues crying and does not quiet down, she takes the apple away and gives it to another of her children. Therefore I tell you, Florence, God has given you the apple — i.e. he has chosen you as his own. If you will not repent and return to God, he will take the apple from you and give it to others. This will happen as surely as I stand here in the pulpit."[27]

(4.) The character of this sermon is typical of Savonarola's style of preaching and his political and moral proposals for reform in the following years. His view of the possibility of renewal and salvation is always determined by the perspective of the avenging righteousness and punitive militancy of the wrathful God. This change in the city to which he aspires and which he partially achieves is also characterised by a spirit of unrelenting strictness, cleansing militancy and punitive severity. Among his favourite biblical passages are Jesus' words in Matthew 10.34: "I have not come to bring peace but a sword." For him this means that God's righteousness will and must extirpate the wicked from the city and send them to hell.[28] Savonarola repeatedly challenges the political leadership of the city to tighten policing measures, practise a relentless criminal justice, track down the depraved and sentence them to physical punishment and even execution. God desires a devout Florence, cleansed of the irresponsible ungodly. Only in this way can his wrath be appeased.[29] God's true righteousness and true mercy are, in Savonarola's eyes, complementary in that they are uncompromising, even cruel, in their dealings with the depraved and political enemies. Consequently in May 1495 he demanded vigilance against adversaries within the city walls, justifying this with the claim that "[m]ercilessness has meantime become a great mercy."[30] In the same sense two months later he can describe a lenient sentence as a particular kind of ruthlessness: "for

---

[27] Ibid. p. 58.4-12.

[28] Savonarola: 1st Sermon on Haggai, 1st Nov. 1494, in: *Prediche sopra Aggeo* (as in n. 7), pp. 9.29-10.5.

[29] Cf. Pierre Antonetti: *Savonarola: Ketzer oder Prophet? Eine Biographie*, Zürich 1992 (Original French edition: *Savonarole. Le prophète désarmé*, Paris 1991), p. 196. Among the many biographies of Savonarola, Antonetti's stands out because it remains close to the sources and is soberly objective in its analysis, avoiding both the hagiographic and apologetic tendencies of Savonarola-enthusiasts and the opposite tendencies of his critics.

[30] Cf. Antonetti (as in n. 29), p. 147, on a sermon delivered by Savonarola on 8th May 1495: On 8th May he again prophesied the *renovatio Ecclesiae* at a time unspecified, but unavoidable since it is desired by God. This will take place violently ("with the Sword" he says); he also prophesies the conversion of the unbelievers and the

an indulgent justice is *de facto* a 'ruthless compassion' when it tolerates violation of the divine Law."[31] Hence: One must simply be ruthless in the proper — i.e. radically severe — way to convey God's true compassion, his aim to save and renew the Church. Anyone who is compassionate in the wrong way by being lenient to iniquity is in reality bringing God's dreadful avenging righteousness into play. Hence Savonarola's intention to purify Florence is the project of a terrifying, judgmental and where necessary, devastating compassion, a *terrifica misericordia*.

It is not *that* Savonarola — like all preachers of repentance in the Middle Ages — talks of God's mercy but *how* he does so that is definitive for the character of his preaching. The fact that God elects people at all and is prepared to save them is a sign of mercy. But this mercy is discharged according to the yardstick of punishing and rewarding justice. It exalts to salvation only those who have put on the "white robe" — i.e. those who in loving devotion to God have done penance and cleansed themselves from sin "till their conscience is completely clean and white."[32] A mercy like this must simultaneously be relentless because it must destroy the unclean, remove them even now from the sanctified community within the city. Savonarola demonstrated this kind of mercy and purification when, on Palm Sunday 1496, he sent a procession led by a thousand white-robed children through the streets of Florence crying

---

expansion of Florentine territory through the recovery of lost cities. He pleads for vigilance against internal enemies, against the lukewarm, and against those who oppose the republican constitution; the latter he desires to be punished as an example to others, for "Mercilessness has meantime become a great mercy" and even Jesus Christ was not sent "to bring peace, but the sword" into the world.

[31] Cf. Antonetti (as in n.29), p. 161, summarising Savonarola's sermon of 12th July 1495 impressively: On 12th July a further attack on the lukewarm whom God abhors, for "it is better to be a prostitute, a soldier or a boor than a lukewarm person". He also battles with those who are "cold" i.e. content with a religion reduced to ceremonial, hymns and music. Florence must awaken and weed out its sinners, the city must live with a pure heart, for God will give them wealth and power, even at the price of "two or three plagues" and an inexorable justice which must forget any tolerance; this too is shown in the Old Testament. As an example he mentions the punishment of the Israelites for their whoring with the daughters of the Moabites (Numbers 25.1-13) and the penalty for desecrating the Sabbath (Numbers 15.32-36). The new political order must be supported by a "strict dispensation of justice", for an indulgent justice is *de facto* a "ruthless compassion" if it tolerates violation of the divine Law.

[32] Savonarola: 3rd Sermon on the Psalms, 13th January 1495, in: *Prediche sopra i Salmi* (as in n. 2), p. 53.25-27.

"Long live Christ the King and Queen Mary![33]

(5.) In the last days of his life, when the eloquent preacher of repentance was in prison awaiting his execution he wrote the famous interpretation of and meditation on Psalm 51 (Vulgate 50) "Be merciful to me, O God, a Sinner"[34], which was printed and widely distributed after his death. The text is full of the self-abasement of the supplicant who cries for God's saving mercy and puts his hope in it. There is no trace of fear and threat because the central theme is exclusively the personal relationship between the penitent and his God. But even in this prayer the main concern is the cleansing of the penitent. It is the tears of repentance that cleanse the heart of the sinner.[35] Since it is God's mercy which makes this loving repentance possible, Savonarola can pray: "Wash me, I beseech you, with the water of your mercy!" as well as "Wash me with the water of my tears!"[36] This cleansing comes about through the intensity of union with Christ: "If you pour over me the power of his blood, if Christ dwells in me through faith, if I am united with him through love and emulate him in humility and suffering, I shall be cleansed of all my sinfulness and you will wash me with the tears I weep through love of Christ."[37] In this way, on the day of his execution, Savonarola (as he

---

[33] Cf. Antonetti (as in n. 29), p. 200. For a precise description of the procession (in which, after the children, came all the orders in the city, the secular priests with the suffragan bishop, the civil authorities and a incalculable number of adults, likewise in white robes) see Joseph Schnitzer: *Savonarola. Ein Kulturbild aus der Zeit der Renaissance*, Vol. I, Munich 1924, pp. 332-334.

[34] Savonarola: Expositio in psalmum *Miserere mei Deus*; critical edition of the Latin original in: *Operette spirituali*, ed. Mario Ferrara, Vol. 2, Rome 1976 (Edizione nazionale delle opere di Girolamo Savonarola), pp. 195-234. On the reception in the first decades cf. Josef Nolte: "Evangelicae doctrinae purum exemplum. Savonarolas Gefängnismeditationen im Hinblick auf Luthers theologische Anfänge", in: J. Nolte, Hella Tompert, Christof Windhorst (eds.): *Kontinuität und Umbruch. Theologie und Frömmigkeit in Flugschriften und Kleinliteratur an der Wende vom 15. zum 16. Jahrhundert*, Stuttgart 1978 (= Spätmittelalter und Frühe Neuzeit 2), pp. 59-92.

[35] Savonarola already set forth these ideas, for example, in his 1st sermon on Haggai on 1st November 1494, in: *Prediche sopra Aggeo* (as in n. 7), p. 9.4-11 (in an exegesis of Vulgate Psalm 136.1: "By the rivers of Babylon we sat down and wept"): "O Florence, sit down, too, by the rivers of your sins. Weep so that your tears turn into rivers to wash them away. Think of your heavenly Fatherland, the source of your soul. Endeavour to return there through repentance as the Israelites did. In a foreign country one cannot sing but merely weep — i.e. you in yourself, where you have distanced yourself from God through your sins."

[36] Savonarola: Expositio in psalmum *Miserere mei Deus* (as in n. 34), Latin edition p. 202.12f: "Lava me, inquam, aqua gratiarum tuarum"; p. 202.15f: "Lava me aqua lacrimarum mearum", with the continuation: "lava me aqua Scripturarum tuarum".

[37] Ibid. pp. 210.29-211.5: "[...] quando virtutem sanguinis eius effundes super

prays at the end of the document) will become, through conformity to the suffering Christ of Golgotha, a pure offering which God will accept for salvation: "Take me as a sacrifice of righteousness, as an offering of devout purity, as a burnt offering from the life of my order and as a sacrificial beast on the altar of your Cross!"[38]

Thus Savonarola remains true to his principles to the end. He appeals to a divine mercy that is at the same time righteousness in that it accepts as a spotless offering the human life purified by penitence and modelled on Christ. The category of righteousness which demands purity and rewards purity is the higher criterion which determines Savonarola's discourse on and supplication for mercy.

III. *Johannes von Staupitz: Preacher of God's Mercy*

(1.) Without exaggerating the contrast, one can say that the direct antithesis to Savonarola's prophetic, apocalyptic and threatening preaching and to his correlation of God's mercy and righteousness can be seen in the sermons delivered by Johannes von Staupitz, Vicar-General of the German Observant order of Augustinians, in Advent 1516[39] and in Lent 1517[40] to a Nuremberg public.[41] Luther's

---

me, quando per fidem habitabit Christus in me, quando per dilectionem ei coniunctus fuero, quando humilitatem eius et passionem imitabor, tunc mundabor ab omnibus immunditiis meis, tunc lavabis me lacrimis meis a Christi amore fluentibus."

[38] Ibid. p. 234.16-18: "[...] suscipias me in sacrificium iustitiae, in oblationem sanctimoniae, in holocaustum religiosae vitae et in vitulum crucis tuae", with the continuation: "per quam transire merear ab hac valle miseriae ad gloriam illam, quam praeparasti diligentibus te. Amen." The preceding final section of the document is determined by the thought that the people freed of guilt by being totally consumed by the fire of love of God bring God an "offering of righteousness" (sacrificium iustitiae); ibid. pp. 233.18-234.14.

[39] Staupitz immediately translated the Nuremberg Advent sermons of 1516, delivered in the vernacular, into a Latin tract which appeared at the beginning of 1517: *Libellus De exsecutione aeternae praedestinationis*, ed. Lothar Graf zu Dohna, Richard Wetzel, Berlin – New York 1979 (= *Johann von Staupitz: Sämtliche Schriften* 2 = Spätmittelalter und Reformation 14).

[40] Staupitz' German Nuremberg Lenten sermons in 1517 have been preserved in the form of the so-called *Nürnberger Predigtstücke*. This is a selection of high-quality transcripts from the pen of Nuremberg humanist Lazarus Spengler, who served as secretary to the city council. He had the writing ability and theological training necessary to convey Staupitz' thoughts and words adequately so that we may quote the transcripts as Staupitz' text filtered through Spengler's sympathetic reception. Compared with the documents written and published by Staupitz himself (especially in

superior, teacher, father confessor and fatherly friend fascinated his listeners both male and female by the vividness with which — looking at Christ's vicarious expiatory suffering — he proclaimed the greatness and omnipotence of God's mercy. In these sermons there is no trace of a threatening or terrifying note. Only very marginally is there a suggestion of the possibility of damnation and the torments of hell. The whole focus of these sermons is on love and faith, not on intimidation and fear. Where he speaks of the righteousness of the Judge, it is depicted as the leniency of the merciful Father: "Hence we should love God as the most benevolent, most merciful Father, and fear him as a righteous, mild judge — not as a slave fears his master but as a child his father."[42] This childlike fear of God, as Staupitz repeatedly explains, has nothing to do with a transgressor's fear of the executioner but is humble reverence and loving faith in God's infinite, paternal loving-kindness[43]. Hence the pain of a true repentance for one's own sins is not to be likened to a shabby "gallows repentance" which is only thinking fearfully of avoiding punishment[44]. A person who is truly repentant regrets far more that he has violated the Commandments of God, his beloved Father, and thereby offended and angered him[45].

(2.) Admittedly there are in Staupitz, too — very restrained and cautious — echoes of the wrath of God, but that wrath does not, as in Savonarola, become a theme in its own right. The Augustinian monk does not wish to proclaim to his Nuremberg congregation that God rages against them and threatens them with afflictions, but that God ever and again pardons them if they confess their sins and call

---

comparison with the temporally close *Libellus De exsecutione aeternae praedestinationis*) there are no noticeable differences, but throughout there is a high level of theological and terminological correspondence. Edition of the *Nürnberger Predigtstücke* in: Joachim Karl Friedrich Knaake (ed.): *Johann von Staupitzens sämmtliche Werke, Vol. 1: Deutsche Schriften*, Potsdam 1867, pp. 15-42.

[41] My planned edition of Staupitz' letters will give detailed information on Staupitz' many contacts with Nuremberg before 1516/17, his sojourns in the Free City and his followers there. Cf. for the present Berndt Hamm: "Humanistische Ethik und reichsstädtische Ehrbarkeit in Nürnberg", in: *Mitteilungen des Vereins für Geschichte der Stadt Nürnberg*, 76 (1989), pp. 65-147, here 133-143.

[42] "Dorumb sollen wir Got lieben als den allerfreuntlichsten, parmherzigsten vater und forchten als einen gerechten, milten richter, nicht mit ainer knechtlichen, sonder ainer kindtlichen forcht." Staupitz: *Nürnberger Predigtstücke*, ed. Knaake (as in n. 40), p. 26.

[43] Cf. e.g. ibid. p. 44.

[44] Ibid. p. 16.

[45] Ibid. p. 17.

on him full of trust for merciful forgiveness: "For his mercy is boundless and infinite and of such a kind that it cannot be denied to one who craves it sincerely and reverently."[46] Hence God is not only the one who graciously effects all that is good in mankind, prompting human hearts and stirring them to good works. He is also the gracious God who accepts them by grace, particularly at the end of their earthly existence, even when their devotion is fragile and the quality of their repentance imperfect.[47] With the boundless worth of his Passion, Christ acts vicariously for sinners everywhere where their own sanctity remains a pitiful fragment. Staupitz' theme is not the purity and perfection of a pious life, a renewed Church, a reformed Order or a converted community, important though the serious sanctifying of life in the spirit of love is for him. What he is chiefly concerned about is God's mercy to those who are elect yet unclean, loving yet imperfect, those who have been showered with blessings yet are still needy, those sanctified but not yet unambiguously saints.

Staupitz returns again and again to this ambivalence, even at table in the Augustinian monastery, when dining with distinguished citizens of Nuremberg, proclaiming his sometimes serious, sometimes humorous thoughts about everything under the sun.[48] It is difficult and problematical, he says, to pass judgement on man's devoutness and spiritual nature, for holiness is something hidden: "No one knows where God the Almighty lives or on whom He desires to work the greatest grace"[49], and it often happens that there is more virtue, devotion and divine influence hidden under the robe of a middle-

---

[46] "Dann sein parmherzigkait ist unmessig und unendtlich und der aigenschafft, wan der mensch die hertzlich begert, das die keinem rechtbegerenden kan versagt werden." Ibid. p. 24.

[47] On the deficits of human repentance, which are compensated for by the merit of Christ's Passion cf. ibid. pp. 16-19.

[48] These so-called *Nürnberger Tischreden*, delivered by Staupitz, are also handed down in the records of city council secretary Lazarus Spengler (cf. n. 40). They date from Advent and Lent 1516/17 (perhaps only from Lent) when Staupitz preached in Nuremberg and occasionally invited some patricians and reputable burghers to communal repasts in the Augustinian monastery. On the people who belonged to Staupitz' circle of friends – among them the leading city councillors – cf. Hamm (as in n. 41), pp. 133-135; Edition of the German *Nürnberger Tischreden* in: Knaake (as in n.40), pp. 42-49. Like the *Predigtstücke*, the *Tischreden* reproduce the Augustinian cleric's particular body of thought in a remarkably authentic way.

[49] "Nymandt wais, wo Got der almechtig wonen, bey welchem er auch am hochsten gnad wurcken will." Staupitz: *Nürnberger Predigtstücke*, ed. Knaake (as in n. 40), p. 33 (under the title: "Do not judge others").

class woman than under the habit of monks or nuns.[50] In God's eyes a reverent Christian soul is one moment sick and leprous, the next clean and pure.[51] In statements such as these the Augustinian expresses his reserve with regard to extreme ideals of sanctity and purity and human appraisals of the sanctity and purity of others. He cautions the people of Nuremberg against judging the depths of the human heart, which cannot be seen from the outside but can only be known by God.[52] When someone told him while dining that he had heard that the Emperor Maximilian had expressed the hope that one day after his death people would pray to him: "Holy Maximilian, intercede for us!" Staupitz answered: I would not object if his Majesty were to be sanctified — but I should dearly like to know what sort of nature and essence one must have to become sanctified (i.e. to enter Paradise).[53] This idea of not knowing and not being able to judge, so characteristic of Staupitz, is strikingly different from the attitude of Savonarola who asserts an exact knowledge of what holiness is and which people in Florence and Rome are candidates for hell.

(3.) We see exactly the same contrast in the way in which Savonarola and Staupitz react to the political events and radical changes taking place in their time. Savonarola, convinced of his own prophetic authority, claims that he has an unequivocal, apocalyptic divinely-revealed knowledge of certain future earth-shaking events and of the hidden meaning of the current political situation. He lays open and interprets history. Thus, for example, he knows that the French king Charles VIII carries the prophesied Sword of God[54] and that he as a new Cyrus is bringing about the renascence of the Church and the perdition of the ungodly.[55] Staupitz, too, declares to his hearers in Nuremberg his firm belief that all earthly events occur within God's administration and rule (*verwaltung und regirung*).[56] But he

---

[50] Ibid.: "[...] und beschicht gar zu vil malen, das undter ainer samaten schauben mere tugent, beschwerlikait [perhaps better improved by 'beschawlikait' than Knaake's suggested 'bestendigkait'] unnd gots wurckung dann unter der kutten verporgen ligt."

[51] Staupitz: *Nürnberger Tischreden*, ed. Knaake (as in n. 48), p. 45.

[52] Ibid.

[53] Ibid. p. 47: "Ich mocht gar wol leiden, das sein mjt. heilig wurd, allain das ich doch wist, was schicklikait und wesens ainer sein must, der doch heilig wurd."

[54] Cf. above p. 329 with n.7. Cf. Savonarola: 3rd Sermon on the Psalms, 13th January 1495, in: *Prediche sopra i Salmi* (as in n. 2), pp. 55.12-56.27.

[55] Cf. e. g. Savonarola: *Compendio di rivelazioni/Compendium revelationum*, ed. Crucitti (as in n. 3), pp. 14.28-15.8 (Italian) and pp. 140.29-141.9 (Latin).

[56] Staupitz: *Nürnberger Predigtstücke*, ed. Knaake (as in n. 40), p. 29.

believes that this all happens contrary to any human conjecture or calculation — to the great astonishment of humankind who time after time are amazed at how rapidly events unfold quite differently from their expectations. God does not show his hand. His wisdom is awesome and awe-inspiring. While Savonarola's prophetic knowledge uncovers things alarming and threatening, Staupitz' deliberations on the impossibility of foreknowing the future work towards the reassuring advice to see God's merciful omnipotence — *sein macht, sein krafft und parmherzigkait* (his might, his power and mercy) — in everything that may happen unexpectedly or inexplicably.[57] The hidden God is the amazingly loving God.

It is the same basic attitude of trust in God which will also lead us in troubled times not — as with Savonarola — to fear the wrath of God but to feel the rod of a loving Father and love him in return.[58] For God "desires to be loved rather than feared by us, his creatures, therefore humankind should love him more than fear him."[59] Whatever happens apparently to our detriment, we can firmly believe that it happens by the will of God for our benefit.[60] As Christians, says Staupitz, we have the assurance that nothing can separate us from the love of God (Rom. 8.39) — not even the sword, "because we are anointed with the oil of mercy".[61] Here Staupitz's use of the sword as metaphor follows the manner not of Savonarola, but of St. Paul; it is not intended to conjure images of divine retribution, but rather to stand as shorthand for the afflictions, temptations and persecutions which, though they must come, cannot shake the Christian's faith in God's loving care.

(4.) The Augustinian preacher's attitude to individual and collective crises corresponds to the kind of political instruction that he dispenses from the pulpit and at the tables of the ruling classes of the Free City. The nucleus of his political ethics lies in the maxim: A ruler should behave in such a way that he is more loved than feared by his subjects; for love and trusting affection serve far more than

---

[57] Ibid. p. 29f.

[58] Ibid. p. 25f.

[59] "Also wil auch Got von unns, seinen creaturen, mer geliebt dann geforcht werden, dorumb ine der mensch mer lieben dann forchten soll." Ibid. p. 25.

[60] Staupitz: *De exsecutione aeternae praedestinationis*, ed. Dohna, Wetzel (as in n. 39), § 195: "[...] quaecumque contra se facta pro se facta firmiter credit" (allusion to Rom. 8.28,31); cf. ibid. § 93, § 174 and § 237f.

[61] Ibid. § 240: "[...] an gladius? non, quia uncti sumus oleo misericordiae" (cf. James 5.14f).

fear, harshness and cruelty to uphold a system of government.[62] How rulers deal with the opprobrious weaknesses and transgressions of their subjects should also be determined on this principle. Staupitz challenges a fanaticism of purification: "*Man kann die posen von den guten nit ganz sondern*" (One cannot completely separate the evil from the good). A god-fearing, righteous and prudent regime will rather, by its own honourable conduct, cover up the defects and disgrace of the *reudigen Schafe* (mangy sheep).[63] In principle, even in the case of wrongdoers in prison, far more can be achieved in a city through friendliness and a manner that inspires confidence than through cruel, terrifying stringency.[64] Those who commit public misdemeanours ought to be subject to public punishment, but this should be undertaken sensitively, "on a just scale, at a suitable time and without harming the public good."[65]

(5.) While Savonarola pursues a very inflexible, consistent theocratic vision, what Staupitz expects from the members of his order, the faithful in the Church and the political community is certainly determined by a fundamental spiritual perspective. At the same time it is modified by a certain tolerance, equanimity and spiritual and clerical self-restraint. This goes so far that he can say: "I would be happier and less worried to be ruled by a clever, shrewd rogue than by a pious fool."[66] For Staupitz human piety, religiosity and saintliness are, in any case, surrounded by many question marks, as we have seen. It is very difficult to assess spiritual quality and morality. There is the danger of self-confident arrogance or apprehensive

---

[62] Staupitz: *Nürnberger Predigtstücke*, ed. Knaake (as in n. 40), pp. 38f and 25. On the maxim that a ruler should so behave towards his subjects that they love him more than fear him (also ibid. p. 36f) cf. Cicero: *De officiis* 2.23: "omnium autem rerum nec aptius est quicquam ad opes tuendas ac tenendas quam diligi nec alienius quam timeri". On the contrary maxim of the Nuremberg Humanists e.g. Konrad Celtis, cf. Hamm (as in n. 41), p. 139 n. 297.

[63] Staupitz: ibid. p. 37 with the central statement: "Ein fromer, erlicher regirer und oberer ist allain ein schandtfleck- oder schandendecker, dann ein vernunfftiger, frommer regent bedeckt die schandt der underthanen." (A pious, honest ruler or authority only covers over blemishes or disgraces, for a rational, pious regent compensates for the disgraceful acts of his subjects.)

[64] Ibid. p. 38 f.

[65] "[...] mit ainer rechten mass, zu bequemer zeit und on zurruttung gemains nutz." Ibid. p. 42; on Staupitz' ideas of a consistent criminal justice (which is in no way lax) cf. also p. 35.

[66] "Ich will dannocht lieber und mit mynder beschwert regirt werden von ainem geschickten, vernunfftigen puben dann ainem fromen narren." Staupitz: *Nürnberger Tischreden*, ed. Knaake (as in n. 48), p. 49 (end of the text).

despair with regard to one's own situation. Decisive here, as Staupitz
tirelessly preaches, is that we put our whole trust solely in God's mercy and love, run to him again and again in order "to crave a new
mercy and grace every time."[67]

Mercy and trust are the key concepts in his preaching. He gives
clear expression to this pastoral conception when he comes out energetically against the intimidating preachers of his time who are dri-
ving sinners to despair and sets up against them his picture of consolation.[68] It is much easier to throw someone into water than to pull
him out[69]: "Therefore every preacher, as a guide appointed by God,
should direct his teaching toward showing the sinners a comforting
right path so that, liberated from the burden of their consciences and
scrupulous feelings and freed from sin, they may be receptive to
God's grace and mercy and the merit of his Passion."[70] Staupitz
instructs those who are free from sin (or who think they are) to confess their need before God in like manner and to seek the mercy and
help of the Crucified. God derives little pleasure from one who com-
mits no sin and consequently no longer cries to him for mercy and
compassion.[71] Thus the whole preaching style of the Augustinian
flows into the praise of the *summa misericordia* (supreme mercy) of God
which meets the *summa miseria* (supreme misery) of humanity.[72]

(6.) Staupitz recognizes the vulnerability of his position. He
expressly deals with the accusation that he speaks "too mildly and too

---

[67] "[...] allemal ain newe parmherzigkait und gnaden zu begern." Staupitz: *Nürnberger Predigtstücke*, ed. Knaake (as in n. 40), p. 23, under the title (p. 22): "Wie der
mensch durch ain vertrewlich gemute und hoffen Got dem almechtigen verainigt
werden und aus menig seiner sunden an Gotes parmherzigkait nit verzweiffeln sol."
(How man will be united with God the Almighty through a confident disposition and
hope and should not doubt in God's mercy because of the great number of his sins.)

[68] Ibid. p. 27f.

[69] Ibid: "Es ist nit schwer, ainen in ain wasser zu werffen; das ist aber nit gering
und vil grosser, ainen im wasser lebendig zu behalten und dovon zu entledigen." (It
is not difficult to throw someone into water, but it is no small task, and indeed a
much greater thing, to keep a person alive in water and to remove him from it.)

[70] "Deshalb auch ain yder prediger als von Got aingesetzter weglaiter seine leer
dohin ergrunden solt, den sundern ainen trostlichen rechten wege anzuzaigen,
dodurch sie von beschwerung ires gewissens und ainem scrupulosischen gemute
entledigt, von sunden entpunden, auch gots gnad und parmherzigkait und der ver-
dienstnus seins leidens vehig sein mocht(en)." Ibid. p. 27.

[71] Ibid. p. 24.

[72] Staupitz: *De exsecutione aeternae praedestinationis*, ed. Dohna, Wetzel (as in n. 39), §
64: "Admirantur theologi unionem hypostaticam divinae naturae cum humana,
immortalitatis cum morte, impassibilitatis cum dolore. Ego admiror coniunctionem
summae misericordiae cum summa miseria."

familiarly" (*zu milt und vil vertrewlich*) about God's mercy. That, one might allege, would reduce God's wisdom and righteousness to nothing[73]. Then God would react to the continually new insult of a sinner's misdeeds with continually new pardon; he would behave like a foolish man who is constantly slapped in the face and who constantly allows himself to be persuaded to react good-naturedly.[74] Staupitz answers: God does behave in just such a foolish way — according to earthly standards — as we can see in the innocent, submissive suffering of Christ: Christ allowed himself, without resisting, to be mocked by Herod and his followers as the "greatest fool".[75] Staupitz continues: "By enduring such foolishness Christ made the fountain of mercy so vast and plentiful for us that he will always give man a share in his mercy if he heartily sighs and begs, so often as he comes when he has fallen, yes even if he came thus a thousand times a day." [76]

Certainly God is just and wise, but there, in Christ's Passion, "justice and wisdom are made to obey and serve mercy", as Staupitz says, echoing Psalm 144.9 in the Vulgate: "God's mercy surpasses all his other works."[77] This clearly demonstrates how for Staupitz the relationship between God's righteousness and mercy is the reverse of what Savonarola preached. In Savonarola's sermons mercy and salvation are spoken of solely in the framework of a severe avenging justice which demands purity and pursues the path of threat, fear and harshness. Staupitz, however, shows God's righteousness — even in its punitive aspect — totally in the light of a mercy that showers blessings upon impure, imperfect sinners. Hence he preaches a confidence in God's mercy which is at the same time a love of his justice.

---

[73] Staupitz: *Nürnberger Predigtstücke*, ed. Knaake (as in n. 40), p. 24.

[74] Ibid. p. 24f.

[75] Cf. Luke 23.11.

[76] "Mit solcher geliten thorhait hat er unns den prunnen der parmherzigkait so weit und reichlich gemacht, das er dem menschen uff ain hertzlich erseuffzen und bitten, so offt er komet und gefallen ist, ja ob er den tag tausent mal der gestalt keme, seiner parmherzigkait allweg tailhafftig machen will." Staupitz: *Nürnberger Predigtstücke*, ed. Knaake (as in n. 40), p. 25.

[77] "[...] ist gerechtigkait und weishait der parmherzigkait gehorsam und underthenig worden; und nach den worten des propheten <ubertrifft> die parmherzigkait Gotes alle andere seine werck." Ibid. Cf. Vulgate Psalm 144.9: "[...] miserationes eius super omnia opera eius"; instead of using the verb "surpasses" (ubertrifft) we could amend the text by using "is above" or "is greater than".

IV. *Johannes Geiler von Kaysersberg: Preacher between Severity and Mercy*

(1.) In the manner of their preaching Savonarola and Staupitz represent opposite extremes on the scale of late medieval options for giving spiritual guidance from an urban pulpit. Their exceedingly emphatic emphases on God's punitive, purifying strictness or on his inviting mercy were breathtaking and intriguing — though Savonarola polarised while Staupitz integrated, with no sign of turbulent excitement and division among his listeners. Even where they were seriously endeavouring to reform the life of the individual, Church and city, both before and after 1500 the pastoral of the urban *dirigenti religiosi* was characterised by the attempt to forge a "moderate" *via media* between the foci of the strict justice of the judgmental God and the gentle compassion of the merciful God, between threat and solace, between fear and hope. This attempt was apparent already at the beginning of fifteenth century in Jean Gerson who had insisted on both mankind's capacity and ability for meritorious works, and on the necessity for humble readiness to trust unreservedly in the mercy of God, Christ, Mary and the saints. One of the best-known preachers before the Reformation who adopted Gerson's pastoral conception was Johannes Geiler von Kaysersberg. From 1478 to 1510 he enthralled the people of Strasbourg with his sermons as official preacher in the cathedral as well as in other churches and particularly in the nuns' convents of the city.

(2.) If we want to define his type of preaching and pastoral care, his medial position as a secular priest between the Dominican Savonarola and the Augustinian recluse Staupitz, we must take account of two points in particular: first, his theological mould; and second, the pastoral problem he saw facing him. The shape of his understanding of justification, grace, penitence and merit is striking. In his teaching on mankind's way to salvation he inclines decidedly to the later Franciscan direction as it was represented by William of Ockham, handed down by Gerson and, towards the end of the fifteenth century, exemplified particularly by the Tübingen professor (and onetime Cathedral preacher in Mainz) Gabriel Biel.[78] This gives his whole style of preaching from the outset a cast totally different from that of a "theo-

---

[78] On Geiler's personal and theological attachment to Gabriel Biel cf. E. Jane Dempsey Douglass: *Justification in Late Medieval Preaching. A Study of John Geiler of Keisersberg*, Leiden 1966 (= Studies in Medieval and Reformation Thought 1), p. 7 and 37.

logy of grace" Augustinianism such as is characteristic of Staupitz. We shall return to this later.

From a pastoral point of view Geiler, as preacher and pastor of Strasbourg, sees the main problem as spiritual presumption: people fail to take God's Commandments seriously, they sin heedlessly and then put their trust in God's mercy, Christ's vicarious suffering and their own Baptism.[79] The devil whispers to them: "God has made a covenant with us. Come then, the devil says, sin bravely, for however great your sins may be, God's mercy is still greater!"[80] Geiler describes his difficulty as a preacher in the following manner: "The whole world in our time is so corrupt that it is quite dangerous to preach about God's mercy. For where there is one who despairs there are 100, nay 1,000 and ten times 100,000 overconfident people; and yet they are all mistaken."[81]

This quotation, very characteristic of Geiler, shows that he defined the main spiritual problem of the citizens differently from Savonarola and Staupitz in their urban contexts. Savonarola disapproves particularly of the attitude of the — as he sees it — godless "lukewarm", i.e. the indifferent, the sceptical and frivolous who practise a blend of values from church piety and from secular culture, and who abhor him as a sinister, fanatical zealot. Staupitz is concerned about the easily swayed weaklings but particularly about the earnestly pious — i.e. on the one hand the spiritually proud and on the other those with an over-anxious, timorous, fainthearted conscience. Geiler's particular complaint, however, is about an ethos of cheap grace, the attitude of the lax who rely too much on God's mercy without being willing to take up the hard work of a life of penitence.

When considering these differing attitudes of the three preachers we must not forget that they are dealing with different cities and peo-

---

[79] Cf. the quotation from Geiler in Dempsey Douglass, ibid. p. 173, n. 6.

[80] "[diabolus ...] dicit deum pactum nobiscum fecisse. Eya, inquit, pecca audacter, quia quantumcunque magna sint peccata tua, maior est misericordia sua." Geiler von Kaysersberg: *De xii fructibus spiritus sancti*; cited by Dempsey Douglass, ibid. p. 174, n. 3.

[81] "Sic infectus est hac tempestate mundus totus, ut periculosum admodum sit de misericordia dei predicare. Ubi unus enim reperitur desperans, centum inveniuntur, immo mille et decies centena milia presumptuosi; et tamen omnes decipiuntur. Dominus enim etsi misericors, iustus tamen iudex nemini facit igitur iniuriam per sententiam, sibi quod eius est auferendo." From the same work, following the quotation in n. 80; cited by Dempsey Douglass, ibid. p. 174, n.4.

ple; but at the same time the way they perceive the urban population is characteristically different. Savonarola's outlook is considerably influenced by the confrontation of the Dominican, set on reform and oriented above all to the ideal of poverty, with the glittering Renaissance culture of Florence. Staupitz, frequently although only for short periods in Nuremberg, sees the city with the eyes of an outsider, the Superior of a monastic order who is more used to dealing with the pastoral problems of monks and nuns than with those of burghers and their wives. Geiler on the other hand, who served for decades as chief preacher in the city Cathedral, is directly bound up with the life of Strasbourg's citizens. But he does not set his sights only on the worldly (to his mind, all too worldly) citizenry. He also has his eye on the reformed nunneries, particularly the "Reuerinnen" (Penitents) to whom he also preaches and who present him with other pastoral challenges than the worldly, challenges requiring more consolation than strictness.

(3.) Geiler's view of the spiritual carelessness and credulity of the men and women of Strasbourg moves him to put strong emphasis on the importance of keeping God's Commandments, on the severity of the divine Judgement and on the relentlessness of God's righteousness, which judges according to works. Typical, for example, is the admonitory, even threatening tone in which he tells the story of two monks: After one of them died he appeared to the other in a lamentable state and with distressed expression. When the other asked him why he appeared to him in such a state the dead monk answered three times with the words: "No one believes, no one believes, no one believes." When the living monk asked what it was that no one believed, the other replied, "how strictly God judges and how severely he punishes". Having uttered those words he vanished and left the living brother in a state of fear and trembling.[82] Again and again Geiler points to the impending eternal death of damnation and the tribunal "of the stern judge, where we must account for everything even to the last farthing" (cf. Mt. 5.26).[83]

---

[82] "[...] Respondit defunctus tribus vicibus: 'Nemo credit, nemo credit, nemo credit.' Quaesivit vivus, quid esset, quod nemo credit. Respondit defunctus: 'quam districte iudicat deus et quam severe punit'. His dictis disparuit et viventem fratrem magno timore concussum dereliquit, ut dicitur in speculo exemplorum." Geiler von Kaysersberg: *Navicula poenitentiae*, cited by Dempsey Douglass, ibid. p. 172, n. 2.

[83] "[...] des strengen richters, da wir muessen rechnung tuon biß auf den lesten quadranten." Geiler von Kaysersberg: *18 Eigenschaften eines guten Christenpilgers* =

It is interesting to see how Geiler, as compared to Savonarola, speaks in this connection about God's punitive sword of judgement. Geiler admonishes those who are unwilling to forsake the house of their sins for fear of the contempt, ridicule and defamation of their fellows. They should disregard such gossip as the gabbling of geese and be less intimidated by the *rauschenden laub* (rustling leaves) than by the *außgezognen schwert Gottes* (unsheathed sword of God).[84] In contrast to the prophetic and apocalyptic Savonarola, who expected the coming of an historical apocalyptic cataclysm with the sword of God, in Geiler's conventional eschatology the sword symbolises God's judgmental action immediately after death, when God the Father assigns the soul, separated from the body[85], its place either in Hell, Purgatory or Paradise — as so many pictures from the late Middle Ages depict this individual judgement, showing God the Father with his sword of judgement unsheathed.[86]

It is in keeping with this pastoral style of admonitory strictness that Geiler continuously calls attention to the standard against which every person is to be measured in the divine Judgement. The first and foremost requirement for the Christian pilgrim in order that he may ultimately reach the goal of his earthly pilgrimage, eternal life, is a pure love with which he loves God above all else for his own sake. As a ship is closed below to the water and open to heaven above, so must the heart of the Christian, in love and yearning for its heavenly home, shut itself off from all earthly desires and pleasures.[87] For

---

Deutsche Predigten 1508, Nr. II, in: Gerhard Bauer (ed.): *Johannes Geiler von Kaysersberg: Sämtliche Werke, Teil 1: Die deutschen Schriften, Abt 1: Die zu Geilers Lebzeiten erschienenen Schriften, Bd. 2*, Berlin – New York 1991, p.151.20-22.

[84] Ibid. p. 149.17-150.1. Cf. Geiler von Kaysersberg: *Der Pilger mit seinen Eigenschaften*, in: *Sämtliche Werke* (as in n. 83), Bd. 1, Berlin – New York 1989. p. 63.24-29: "[...] sunder fürcht mer das schwert Gottes des herrn, des dir leib und sel wirt von ain ander teilen in ewige verdamnuß, und das schwert und den man fürcht mer, den das yederman iber dich spottet!" (Be more afraid of the sword of God the Lord that will separate body and soul into eternal damnation, and fear the sword and man more than that someone mocks!)

[85] Cf. the quotation in n. 84. In the so-called particular or individual judgement immediately after death where God the Father is the judge, the soul is judged separate from the body, while in the universal or Last Judgement Jesus Christ judges the soul reunited with the body, together with all mankind.

[86] Cf. e.g. the votive picture of Ulrich Schwarz painted by Hans Holbein the Elder (ca. 1508) in the National Gallery in Augsburg; illustrations and commentary in Bruno Bushart: *Hans Holbein d. Ä.*, 2nd edition, Augsburg 1987, pp. 102-105; cf. also Hartmut Boockmann: *Die Stadt im späten Mittelalter*, Munich 1986, p. 168f, Nr. 264.

"strait is the gate and narrow is the way" (Mt. 7.14).[88] While for Staupitz (and also for the Thomistic speculation of Savonarola) Christian love of God and of one's neighbour is a gift of the electing grace moving the heart of the elect, Geiler, in accordance with his Ockhamist approach, sees in love the supreme principle of human achievement. The sinner must, on the basis of his own natural rational capacity, spur himself on to virtue, extract what there is in his native abilities (*facere quod in se est*) and in this way attain to a true love of God and his neighbour. Like his contemporary Gabriel Biel, Geiler also believes that people can and must, by virtue of their own innate, reasoned morality, bring forth even the pain of true contrition from their love of God. Geiler's guidance for the soul achieves its particular character of strictness against the background of an anthropology of the moral freedom, sensibility and potentiality of the individual, still persisting after the Fall. The ethical standard is no higher than that of Staupitz, for the Augustinian is even more radical and consistent in making love of God the sole criterion of Christian spirituality and ethics. But Geiler appeals to man's ability and obligation to acquire salvation through his own efforts. It is true that the sinner can only have a claim to eternal life and make amends for the punishment for sin because God has conferred on him justifying grace. But it is the person himself, the human as a moral character who — with the contribution of his own free will — brings forth acceptable and commendable works of pure love of God and his neighbour in order to withstand the Judgement. It is true that salvation is impossible without the fundamental contribution of Christ's Passion or without Christ's subsequent acceptance of the sinner for Justification and Redemption. However, it is characteristic of Geiler's theological outlook and pastoral aspirations that he commences from this principle: Neither for the transmission of justifying grace nor for the opening of the Kingdom of Heaven and admission to the heavenly glory is the Passion of Christ the sole and complete ground of merit (*"Numquam tamen est sola et totalis causa meritoria"*).[89] God desires that we gain eternal life through our own free actions — i.e. we receive it

---

[87] Geiler von Kayserberg: *Navicula poenitentiae*; cited by Dempsey Douglass (as in n. 78), p. 39 column 2.

[88] "Der weg ist schmal unnd das thor ist eng." Geiler von Kayersberg: *18 Eigenschaften* (as in n. 83), p. 142.5f with the context on Christian virtue which one must acquire "with strict practice" (p. 142.1).

[89] "Respondeo breviter, quod, licet passio Christi sit principale meritum, propter

not simply as a gift but as something purchased — and consequently we take possession of it with a kind of legal right (*"quasi iustitiae titulo"*).[90] The admonitory and urgent insistence with which Geiler impresses the fulfilling of God's Commandments upon the people of Strasbourg is always directed at this eschatological obligation and opportunity, at the necessity and possibility of gaining Heaven as Christian "purchasers".[91]

(4.) However this is only the one side of Geiler's pastoral goals, the judgmental aspect which I spoke of earlier.[92] Other than for Savonarola the aspect of mercy achieves a significance of its own in Geiler's preaching and devotional writings. The *misericordia Dei* as the focus of consolation and exhortation confronts the focus of the awe-inspiring righteousness of the Judge. On the one hand, when he shows the *misericordia Dei* to advantage Geiler von Kaysersberg has an eye on the despondent sinners who apprehensively doubt their own religious efficacy – indeed, who tend to despair. Here he is probably thinking, as we have seen, less of the lay citizens than of those in religious orders, particularly nuns.[93] On the other hand God's mercy must be magnified to those who presumptuously put their trust in their own spiritual superiority and probity. The first group must be encouraged to hope by being shown the boundlessness of God's mercy and forgiveness, the second must be educated in humility by being made aware that in God's verdict, even their best deeds would merely be sewage if God in his limitless mercy did not descend to their level and accept their works as meritorious.

As pastoral advice Geiler formulated the maxim: "Before the Fall (into sin) mankind should reflect on the divine righteousness, but after the Fall he should always pay heed to the divine mercy. For

---

quod confertur gratia, apertio regni et gloria, numquam tamen est sola et totalis causa meritoria." Geiler von Kaysersberg: *Navicula poenitentiae*; cited by Dempsey Douglass (as in n. 78), p. 183, n. 2 (with a reference to a verbatim passage in Gabriel Biel's 'Collectorium', ibid. n. 3).

[90] "Vult nos Dominus vitam aeternam mereri et propriis actibus quasi iustitiae titulo possidere pro soluto, titulo honorabili et pro empto et non solum pro donato." Ibid. (Geiler von Kaysersberg: *Navicula poenitentiae*) p. 183, n 2.

[91] Cf. e.g. a letter written around 1500 by the Nuremberg provost Sixtus Tucher in which he describes the Christian life as a "blissful business" through which one may "win eternal profit and gain with temporal possessions"; quoted in Hamm (as in n. 41), p. 129.

[92] Cf. above under I/3.

[93] Cf. above p. 345, n. 81 with the following text.

God's mercy is so great that it would never condemn a person laden with all the sins of the world who felt pain that he had, in committing them, arrogantly offended so good a lord, his God, and who firmly resolved to refrain [from such sins] in the future."[94] To those who are worried, frightened and overzealous, Geiler characteristically stresses: God is not as strict as you think. You have a God who is lenient and generous.[95] In this sense Geiler asks for compassionate ("süße") father confessors[96]; and with this compassion he ministers to the Christian pilgrim who feels himself deprived of the spiritual virtues — patience, hope and love.[97] He invites the pilgrim to turn like a beggar full of trust, in beseeching prayer, to God, to all the good angels and saints and "to crave from them spiritual alms and ask with an assured hope for all that he needs".[98] The steadfast hope of the tempted Christian should be focused on the promised fact that in the judgement after death, he will have powerful advocates: Christ will show his Father the wounds of his Passion and Mary will show her son the breasts with which she devotedly nursed him. Thus emerges an effective stairway of salvation.[99] Sinners should place their hope above all on Mary who, herself human, is closest to them.[100] Neither the Son nor the Father can or will deny her loving advocacy.[101] Mary's pure compassion, her special position before God and the certainty that

[94] "Ante casum igitur cogitet divinam iustitiam, sed post casum divinam misericordiam semper attendat. Misericordia enim Dei tanta est, ut, si homo haberet omnia peccata mundi super se et doleret, quod cum eis tam bonum dominum Deum suum superbe offendisset, et firmiter proponeret amplius abstinere, Deus talem nunquam damnaret." Geiler von Kaysersberg: *Navicula poenitentiae*; cited by Dempsey Douglass (as in n. 78), p. 175f, n. 4.

[95] About the Christian pilgrim who takes on too heavy a burden of spiritual discipline he writes: "Er entzücht Got sein glorij, wann es scheynett vor andern menschen, als ob Got so streng sey, das sich der mensch also eroeßen mueß. Du hast ainen milten, reilichen Got." (He takes away God's glory, for it makes it seem to others, as if God were so strict that man must exhaust himself to an extreme degree. You have a lenient, generous God.) Geiler von Kaysersberg: *18 Eigenschaften* (as in n. 83), p. 155.14-17.

[96] "Ipse [sacerdos] erit tibi dulcis, sicut et debet." Geiler von Kaysersberg: *Navicula poenitentiae*; cited by Dempsey Douglass (as in n. 78), p. 154, n. 1.

[97] Geiler von Kaysersberg: *18 Eigenschaften* (as in n. 83), p. 159.23-31.

[98] "[...] von inen tzuo begeren der gaystlichen allmuoßen und alles, das er nottürfftig ist, mit ainer unzweifelichen hoffnung da haischen." Ibid. p. 160.3-8.

[99] Cf. Dempsey Douglass (as in n. 78), p. 191.

[100] Cf. ibid. pp. 191-195.

[101] Cf. the quotation from Geiler's *Navicula poenitentiae* in Dempsey Douglass, p.193, n. 3.

she will hear them gives human hope a kind of personal assurance of salvation.[102]

With his comforting pastoral advice Geiler forges ahead to the point where — exactly like Gerson — he commends even despair and despondency as a means of salvation to the faithful who have uneasy consciences. He advises anyone who doubts whether his virtuous deeds are well pleasing to God "that you despair and lose trust in all your good works and count them worthless."[103] He should not despair of God's mercy but of the efficacy of his own emotions and deeds.[104] If the sinner is troubled as to whether he has made sufficient confession or is adequately prepared to receive the Eucharist, he should humbly despair of his pious endeavours, turn his gaze from them and put all his trust in God's mercy alone.[105] He may joyfully "have complete confidence and trust that through the merit of our dear Lord he will be blessed and possess the joy of eternal life."[106] In the same sermon he goes on to say that God did not 'make the Kingdom of Heaven for geese': "He did not suffer in vain. It is his desire that we be blessed."[107] Thus for Geiler, Christ's Passion can become the supporting foundation of hope and trust. Because all of this is particularly relevant for the dying, Geiler formulated guidelines to teach how one should behave in the hour of death: "Bend and abase

[102] On the characteristic conception of the Christian certainty of hope (which, to be sure, can be based on different ideas – e. g. more mystic, christological or mariological) of Jean Gerson and those 'Frömmigkeitstheologen' who come from his tradition cf. Sven Grosse: *Heilsungewißheit und Scrupulositas im späten Mittelalter*, Tübingen 1994 (= Beiträge zur historischen Theologie 85); Berndt Hamm: "Warum wurde der Glaube für Luther zum Zentralbegriff des christlichen Lebens", in: Stephen E. Buckwalter, Bernd Moeller (eds.): *Die frühe Reformation in Deutschland als Umbruch*, Gütersloh 1998 (= Schriften des Vereins für Reformationsgeschichte 199), pp. 103-127, here 107-113.
[103] "[...] daz du verzwifelst und verzagst an allen dinen guoten wercken und nit dovon haltest." Geiler von Kaysersberg: *Von den zwölf schefflin*, ed. Luziam Pfleger, in: *Archiv für elsässische Kirchengeschichte* 6 (1931), pp. 206-216, here 212; cf. ibid: "daz du gantz uff din eigenen fliß verzwiffelst" (that you despair totally of your own diligence).
[104] "Pridie desperationem de Dei misericordia vituperavi; hodie autem desperationem de propriis meritis laudo. Et sic non est contradictio." Geiler von Kaysersberg: *De dispositione ad felicem mortem*; cited by Dempsey Douglass (as in n. 78), p. 171f, n. 5.
[105] Cf. the texts quoted in Dempsey Douglass, p. 168-170 with their punch-line "sola misericordia Dei" (e. g. p. 169 n. 1 and 169f n. 4).
[106] "[...] ein gantz hoffen und vertruwen haben, daz er durch daz verdienen unsers lieben herren selig sol werden und die freid des ewigen lebens besitzen." Geiler von Kaysersberg: *Von den zwölf schefflin* (as in n. 103), p. 216.
[107] "Er het nit vergebens gelitten. Sin will ist, daz wir selig werden." Ibid.

yourself humbly in total despair of your own merits and strengths. Beware in the hour of your death of arrogance, presumption and proud satisfaction in your good works, but put all your hope and trust in the suffering, death and merit of our dear Lord Jesus Christ. For all our righteousness is false and like a stained, filthy rag in the eyes of God." (cf. Isa. 64.6 Vulgate.)[108]

(5.) In the same context, however, at the end of a sermon in which Geiler advises his female audience[109] to put their whole trust in the vicarious agency of Jesus Christ, he urges them to continue *"mit allem fliß"* (with all diligence) to employ their spiritual powers and emotions so that Christ's bitter suffering and death may bring forth fruit, and that they may in this way become blessed.[110] The advice to humbly doubt their own capabilities and not to rely on them leads into the exhortation to harness their own spiritual virtue with all diligence (*facere quod in se est*).[111] It is precisely this humble turning away from oneself, precisely this total trust in Christ, Mary and the saints, which is the highest achievement of one who loves God. For love reaches its highest intensity and real meritoriousness when it has become so humble that it no longer thinks about its own merit. At the same time this is a warning to those who incline to spiritual pride: Strive for the Kingdom of Heaven in such a way that you do not expect anything from your own achievements but everything from God's mercy! As Geiler sees it only so will they be meritorious. When Geiler encourages them to humility, to despair of self and to total faith in God's mercy, he is thinking of the maximum development of a human being's religious capacity.

Hence in Geiler the perspective of mercy does not nullify the per-

---

[108] "Tucken und sich demuetecklichen trucken durch ein gantze verzwyfelung an synen verdiensten und krefften. Huot dich in der stund dynes sterbens vor hochfart, vermessenheit und üppigem wolgefallen dyner guoten werck, sunder all din hoffnung und vertrüwen setz in das lyden, sterben und verdienst unsers lieben herren Jesu Christi. Wann alle unser gerechtikeiten falsch sind und vor der angesicht gottes als eyn befleckt, unrein tuoch (Isa. 64.6 Vulgate)." Geiler von Kaysersberg: *Sterbe-ABC*, in: *Sämtliche Werke, Bd.* 1 (as in n. 84), p. 107.12-20 (19th Rule).

[109] According to Pfleger (as in n. 103, p. 206) Geiler's sermon 'Von den zwölf schefflin' which we have already quoted three times (cf. n. 103, 106 and 107) was apparently delivered in a Strasbourg nunnery (probably St. Margaret and Agnes) on 21st January 1500.

[110] Geiler von Kaysersberg: *Von den zwölf schefflin* (as in n. 103), p. 216.

[111] On 'facere quod in se est' (i. e. the maximum exertion of one's own spiritual capacities as a provision for grace and salvation) in Geiler von Kaysersberg cf. Dempsey Douglass (as in n.78), Index p. 236 column 2.

spective of justice; it is simply another method the preacher uses to motivate those in need of orientation to develop their moral excellence to the full. Of course it is not simply a pastoral method; it is also a dogmatic position, for in Geiler's theology of piety, God's avenging justice stands in a balanced relationship with his mercy, which is based on vicarious atonement and intercession. This gives Geiler's sermons and devotional writings as a whole a character of moderate balance and sound sense. It would be hard to imagine him making the sort of statements Staupitz makes, stating for example that the merciful God behaves like a "naive fool" with regard to sinners.[112] God's mercy as described by Geiler always takes account of man's free will and his diligent efforts to show honour and obedience to God's Commandments. But the preacher must constantly encourage the people energetically to these efforts. That, according to Geiler's self-understanding, is his primary duty. In this respect ethical strictness is the Alpha and Omega of his spiritual guidance in the city.

(6.) This may be confirmed by considering how Geiler von Kaysersberg behaved as the religious and political conscience of the city council of the Free City of Strasbourg — with all the independence which the office of Cathedral preacher (appointed by the cathedral chapter, not by the city council) bestowed on him. Savonarola's apocalyptic rigorism was foreign to him. He had no desire to change the city's constitution or to set up a theocracy under the control of the clergy. He, like Staupitz, took as a matter of course the pragmatic juxtaposition of spiritual and secular areas of authority, of ardent otherworldly piety and sober political and commercial calculation, and he did nothing to shake it. But unlike Staupitz he could make vigorous attack on the city authorities when he thought it was a matter of the validity of God's Commandments as the highest legal norm in the city. When in 1481 there was a substantial increase in the price of grain and provision for the poor was endangered, he encouraged the poor, should the need arise, to break open the granaries of the rich with axes and take what they needed. He did, however, add the reservation that the time had not yet come; when it did, he would tell them. As a result the council requested that in future he refrain in his sermons from *"solicher swerer rede"* (such ominous talk).[113] Several years

---

[112] Cf. above under III/6.

[113] Uwe Israel: *Johannes Geiler von Kaysersberg (1445-1510): der Straßburger Münsterprediger als Rechtsreformer*, Berlin 1997 (= Berliner historische Studien 27), p. 240f.

later, towards the end of the century, he challenged his listeners from
the pulpit to depose their rulers if they did not take measures against
blasphemy: "If they refuse to do it, one should elect others who do
love God."[114]

In 1500 Geiler's displeasure at the behaviour of the city council
reached such a pitch that in a sermon he said of the councillors, "they
are all on the devil's side, like their ancestors and progeny". A council
delegation asked Geiler why he had said this, assuring the preacher
that the council did not want to do anything improper. Geiler
promised the council a written catalogue of charges that he himself
would present at the Town Hall. This took place in January 1501.[115]
In these "21 Articles of Complaint"[116] Geiler lists a series of civic practices and regulations which in his view transgressed "against Christian
Law and God's Commandments".[117] He warned that the city might
suffer serious damage because of this blatant spiritual disobedience –
perhaps not in temporal matters but certainly in spiritual.[118] The souls
of the magistrates and the community would fall into God's disfavour
and consequently become eternally corrupt.[119] Here Geiler is revealed
as the threatening herald of God's strict justice. His recommendations
for reform are admittedly on the whole moderate, and fit in principle
into the existing legal structure so that in the following years the council did indeed take up some of these proposals.

Corresponding to the balance between justice and mercy as
depicted above, Geiler sometimes advocates greater strictness,
sometimes greater leniency and care in his Articles. Thus he
demands that the city impose harsher penalties for killing a
stranger, blasphemy and violation of virgins.[120] Homicide calls for

---

[114] "Wolten sie es aber nit thuon, so sol man von allem volck andere erwelen, die
got lieb hetten." Ibid. p. 262 and 289.

[115] "[...] sye weren alle des teüfels, und ir vorfahren und ir nachkomen." Cf. the
report Geiler gives in his prologue to the '21 Articles'. It is edited together with the
'Articles' in L. Dacheux: *Die ältesten Schriften Geilers von Kayserberg*, Freiburg i. Br. 1882
(Reprinted, Amsterdam 1965), pp. 1f (prologue), 3-42 (21 Articles) and 43-76 (notes).

[116] On the formation, transmission, construction and content of the '21 Articles'
cf. the judicious account in Israel (as in n. 113), pp. 178-267.

[117] "[...] wider christeliche gäsatz und Gottes gebote." Introductory comment of
Geiler to the '21 Articles', ed. Dacheux (as in n. 115), p. 3.

[118] Geiler's postscript to the '21 Articles', ibid. p. 40.

[119] Introductory comment of Geiler to the '21 Articles', ibid. p. 3: "fallen in
ungenoden Gottes und ewige irer selen verdamnisz" (fall into God's disfavour and
the eternal damnation of their souls).

[120] Geiler treats the three cases ("schlecht ein burger ein fremden zu tod" [if a

punishment by hanging or beheading: the existing legislation, which provides merely for a fine, is not sufficient deterrent – indeed may be said to be an invitation to capital offences. The council should also take stronger measures against games of chance[121] and heathen or secular behaviour in the Cathedral that profanes the sacred place.[122] On the other hand Geiler advocates that the council should be more restrained in the use of torture, in particular that they should not without sufficient suspicion *aufziehen* (strappado) or *marteren* (torment) and consequently damage the person and reputation of the accused.[123] In the preceding years Geiler had continually tried — finally with success — to abolish the practice of refusing those condemned to death confession, last communion and Christian burial.[124] It is also remarkable how emphatically Geiler desires in his Articles to see that the right of asylum of ecclesiastical institutions is respected[125] and the care of the sick, homeless[126] and poor[127] assured. By his standards of social ethics this is a fundamental public responsibility of sharing the mercy demanded by God.[128] In this context he also strives for tax relief for those with smaller incomes and for the destitute. It is not acceptable for the poor to be more heavily encumbered than the rich; rather that the principle of justice should be in force: "Those who have much should give a lot, those with little should give little and thus they are equal, each according to his state."[129] At the end of his 21st Article which he wrote to 'warn' those who ruled the city Geiler sets as a maxim the Vulgate quotation from Ecclesiastes 12.13: "'Fear God and keep

---

citizen beats a stranger to death], "gotslesterung" [blasphemy] and "geschendung der jungkfrouwen" [violation of a virgin]) in Article 18, ed. Dacheux (as in n. 115), p. 36. Cf. Israel (as in n. 113), pp. 261-267.

[121] Cf. Article 7, 8 and 9 (ed. Dacheux, pp. 21-25) and Israel, pp. 218-221.

[122] Cf. Article 16 and 14 (ed. Dacheux, pp. 31f. 33-35) and Israel, pp. 232-235.241-247.

[123] Cf. Article 16 and 14 (ed. Dacheux, pp. 31f. 33-35) and Israel, pp. 232-235.241-247.

[124] Cf. Israel (as in n. 113), pp. 264-267.

[125] Cf. Article 15 (ed. Dacheux, p. 32) and Israel, p. 250.

[126] Cf. Article 12 on the Hospice (ed. Dacheux, pp. 26-30) and Israel, pp. 238-241.

[127] Cf. Article 13 (ed. Dacheux, p. 30f) and Israel, pp. 227-231.

[128] On the norm of mercy cf. Article 12 (ed. Dacheux, p. 29f); cf. also the norm of "mönschlicheit" (humanitas) in Article 13 (ed. Dacheux, p. 31 with p. 67, n. 2).

[129] "Wer viil gutz hat, sol viil geben, wer wenig hat, soll wenig geben und also die burger glich sin, ieder nach syner macht." Article 20 (ed. Dacheux, p. 38) and Israel (as in n. 113), p. 256.

his Commandments; that is every man' — i.e. each person is created for this purpose."[130]

(7.) Shortly after Geiler's death in 1510 his friend the Humanist
Jacob Wimpfeling wrote an obituary in which he praised the moderate position of the Cathedral preacher, neither too strict nor too
lenient: "He made sins neither too small nor too great."[131] As we
have seen, this is a fitting characterisation of Geiler's preaching and
pastoral work. Like Gerson and Biel[132] he strove for a balance
between consolation and warning and for a balance in the proclamation of the strict justice and gracious mercy of God. Hence he represents a third kind of urban preacher, located between a style of
preaching which predominantly threatens and inculcates God's re-
tributory justice and one which predominantly comforts and extols
God's omnipotent mercy. As we have seen, Savonarola fit his statements about mercy into the pattern of divine justice which demands
purity and punishes impurity; Staupitz held that both rewarding and
punishing justice derive from God's overriding mercy. In Geiler we
find the attempt to see the features of God's gracious mercy in the
process of his justice, and the features of his avenging justice in the
workings of his mercy.

V. *Looking on to the Reformation*

The contrast between the extremes of Savonarola and Staupitz
gives an impression of the breadth of the religious spectrum that was
shaped by the preaching of the urban *dirigenti religiosi* of the late Middle Ages. Geiler von Kaysersberg on the other hand shows the potentiality of the nuances and hybrid forms that determined the middle
area of the spectrum. This moderate, accommodating, balancing
mediation of God's severity and mercy, of threat and consolation was

---

[130] Geiler's postscript to the '21 Articles', ed. Dacheux, p. 41: "'Time Deum et
mandata eius observa: hoc est omnis homo', id est ad hoc factus est omnis homo."

[131] "Nulli blandus adulator, non peccata nimium attenuans nec plus aequo exag-
gerans, in dicenda veritate nullius timens potentiam." Cited by Israel (as in n. 113),
p. 284.

[132] On Gabriel Biel as cathedral preacher in Mainz cf. the recent publication of
Wilfrid Werbeck: "Gabriel Biels fünfter Predigtjahrgang (1463/64). Ein Bericht über
die Gießener Hs. 838", in: Ulrich Köpf, Sönke Lorenz (eds.): *Gabriel Biel und die
Brüder vom gemeinsamen Leben. Beiträge aus Anlaß des 500. Todestages des Tübinger Theologen,*
Stuttgart 1998, pp. 93-135.

presumably typical of everyday pastoral life in the majority of European towns around 1500.

At the beginning of this article I drew attention to the relationship between the preaching of the late Middle Ages and that of the Reformation. I should like to take up that thread again at the conclusion. The Reformation would in fact substantially alter the coordinates in that it made a structural break with the conceptual framework of ideas of the late Middle Ages — affirmed even by theologians such as Staupitz — that viewed human merit, satisfaction, and morality as relevant to salvation. Reformation theology would go on to assign what is in principle a new kind of autonomous efficacy and dominance to divine grace and mercy. But as I have already stressed, the work of the reforming *dirigenti religiosi*, their commitment to preaching, spiritual welfare, instruction, church order and urban discipline in the face of rulers and local authorities, were kept in motion by the tension between compassion and strictness, between liberating Gospel and commanding Law. The *foci* of mercy and justice would permit ideas of consolation and severity, tolerance and rigor, freedom and control to emerge again in Reformation preaching, ideas that in many respects call to mind late medieval models. Again and again we can see how contemporary the theological and pastoral alternatives of Savonarola, Staupitz and Geiler remain.

On a new level — shunted, so to speak, by a religious kind of tectonic fault — we can detect three analogous types of *dirigenti religiosi* in the Reformation: 1. The apocalyptic type of Girolamo Savonarola with his vision of the imminent sword and an Italy cleansed of godlessness can be found again, for example, in the work of Thomas Müntzer from Zwickau to Mühlhausen or in the leaders of the so-called "Anabaptist Kingdom of Münster". 2. In contrast, the model typified by Johannes von Staupitz is brought to mind by the way in which Luther and — deriving from him (although also contested by him) — the Antinomianism of Johann Agricola no longer regard the life of the justified Christian in the positive leading perspective of divine Law. The mercy of Jesus Christ received through the Gospel becomes the fully sufficient principle of the new ethics of the Christian life. 3. The mediating type of a Johannes Geiler von Kaysersberg, with his balance between mercy and strictness, has its Reformation analogy in urban *dirigenti religiosi* such as Ulrich Zwingli, Johannes Oekolampad, Ambrosius Blarer, Martin Bucer or John Calvin — i.e. in the typical "Reformed" (some-

times called the "Upper German/Swiss") incorporation of the directing divine Law and strict ecclesiastical discipline in the field newly
ordered by the Gospel.[133]

Thus in certain respects the Reformation shifts back into the context of the late Middle Ages — or should we say: The tensions of the
late Middle Ages transmute themselves into the new context of the
Reformation?

*I should like to thank my translators, Rev. Helen Heron and Dr. Gotthelf Wie-
dermann for their sensitivity and Dr. Petra Seegets for her care in proofreading.*

---

[133] Cf. Heiko A. Oberman: *Masters of the Reformation*, Cambridge 1981, pp. 277-78:
"In the struggle against the unbearable burden of church law, Summenhart aimed
not to liberate the Christian conscience from the law but rather to trim to a theologically valid compass a body of legislation bloated by canonists and their canons. The
urban reformers restricted that scope of validity even more narrowly, identifying it
with the canon of scripture. But like Summenhart they had no intention of abolishing the law entirely; rather they endeavoured to proclaim, to preach for the first time
an authentic law-making it all the more binding on the individual and, in view of the
threat of divine penalty, upon the community. At the same time they introduced a
major difference, teaching that, although obedience to God might indeed often turn
away divine wrath, God's loving attention no longer came in response to human
merit.
    The process is thus better described as a 'reorientation of church law toward the
word of God and a whetting of Christian consciences', than with the image of liberation at the hands of [...] 'freedom fighters'. The believer's conscience, that formerly
left the confessional burdened by innumerable stipulations of the church's canon
law, now merely exchanged that load in the south German urban Reformation for a
new and absolute obligation to observe God's law recorded in the canon of scripture."

"SUFFER THE LITTLE CHILDREN TO COME UNTO ME, AND FORBID THEM NOT": THE SOCIAL LOCATION OF BAPTISM IN EARLY MODERN GERMANY[1]

Susan C. Karant-Nunn*

Changes made in the rituals of infant baptism after the introduction of the Reformation brought the sacramental acts into conformity with the social as well as the theological convictions of the innovators. Whereas the theology of baptism has been much studied — I shall refer to concepts that are already well known — I want to investigate the societal context of reformed rites in an effort to ascertain how the alterations that were made attempted to bring baptism "up to date" and to impose upon congregations a moralized universe. I want, in other words, to describe the "social location" of post-Reformation baptism.

I. *Late Medieval Catholicism*

Baptism has long been regarded as, together with much else, an act of incorporation into the Body of Christ. In the early church, this commitment was made largely by adults after some consideration.[2] Undergoing baptism at the end of the catechumenate now set the new Christian apart from the pagan community. One left the old world and adhered to the figurative flesh of the Savior. This being

* Associate Professor of History and Assistant Director, Division for Late Medieval and Reformation Studies The University of Arizona.

[1] A German version of this paper, "'Lasset die Kinderlein zu mir kommen, und wehret ihnen nicht': Taufe, der Leib Christi, und die Gemeinde," was presented at the Max-Planck-Institut für Geschichte, Göttingen, Germany, in March 1998. I gave an earlier English version in September 1998, at the Institute of Sacred Music, Yale Divinity School, Yale University; and yet another, very abbreviated one at the meetings of the American Society of Church History, Chicago, Illinois, January 2000. I have benefited from the suggestions made on each of those occasions.

[2] See P. Burkhard Neunheuser, *Taufe und Firmung*, Handbuch der Dogmengeschichte 4, Faszikel 2 (Freiburg/Breisgau: Herder, 1956).

joined to Christ's flesh was more concretely effected by participation in the Eucharist. Nevertheless, baptism, too, symbolized a new union, both in earthly and heavenly terms; the Church, after all, composed of the living, dead, and yet unborn faithful, was the metaphorical bride of Christ; as a further manifestation of this metaphor of intimate kinship, brides and grooms at their nuptials, according to Judeo-Christian teaching, became one flesh.[3]

On the eve of the Reformation, Catholic baptism, as a series of gestures, hardly conveyed this doctrine any longer. The sacrament had long since transferred predominantly to infants, who were thought to be barred from heaven if they should die without receiving it. For this reason, midwives, and *in extremis* other persons, however polluted by gender or unbelief, might administer the saving word-formula. In such emergencies, the scene of the rite was an isolated one, most frequently the birthing chamber.

Even if the newborn were in no danger, baptism was often a hasty and private affair. The midwife, accompanied in many instances by one or two other godparents selected by the infant's father, bore her small charge to the church at any convenient time of the day. Only richer citizens could risk the gathering in of distant kindred, whose tardy arrival might postpone the rite by several days. The party was ideally greeted at the door, and the still speechless nursling inquired of, as though it were competent to reply, "What do you seek?" From beginning to end of the baptismal dialogue, the godparents played the role of the baptisand, saying the Creed on his behalf and answering questions as though they were he: "Do you renounce the Devil and all his minions?"[4] Although now quite archaic in its symbolism, the paramount feature of late medieval baptism was its alleged ability to save from evil. Neither parent was present. The godparents themselves had no visible sense of representing the Christian Church. Rather, they straightforwardly behaved as what in reality they were: relatives, midwife, close friends, patrons. In giving the child an earthly name, they collectively embodied the hopes of the family for the

---

[3] On the development of baptismal theology in the Middle Ages, Peter Cramer, *Baptism and Change in the Early Middle Ages, c. 100–c. 1150* (Cambridge, England: Cambridge University Press, 1993). On the history of the ritual, Alois Stenzel, *Die Taufe, eine genetische Erklärung der Taufliturgie*, Forschungen zur Geschichte der Theologie und des innerkirchlichen Lebens 7/8 (Innsbrück, Austria: Felizian Rauch, 1957).

[4] Adolph Franz, ed., *Das Rituale des Bischofs Heinrich I. von Breslau* (Freiburg/-Breisgau, Germany: Herder, 1912), 19, for example.

wellbeing of their child in the mundane present, not in some posthumous future.[5]

The Catholic ritual reveals, then, these two emphases: that the child should be qualified to enter heaven and afforded some protection against evil in this world by means of acts and sacramental objects and substances; and that via the godparents, he or she should gain some benefit in the social realm, that advantage varying greatly with the wealth and inclinations of these spiritual relations. The metaphor of the Body of Christ has nearly disappeared. Baptism occurs in a corner of an empty sanctuary or a separate chapel; the world is contextually, gesturally excluded.

The baptismal rite also conveyed to the newborn, often from within the hour of its birth, the gendering of society. If in Christ there were no male and female, this certainly did not apply in the telluric sphere. In this world people took note instantly of the sex of the infants and acted in different and prescribed ways. If two infants, one a boy and one a girl, came to baptism at the same time, the boy had to be ministered to first.[6] The rubrics normally prescribed specific prayers for girls and others for boys — even though these scripts sometimes disagreed as to which text was which. The manual of the diocese of Breslau offers the following for little boys:

> "God of Abraham, God of Isaac, God of Jacob, God who didst appear to thy servant Moses on Mount Sinai, and didst lead thy children Israel out of the land of Egypt, appointing for them the angel of thy mercy, who should guard them by day and by night, we beseech thee, Lord, that thou wouldst vouchsafe to send thy holy angel from heaven, that he may likewise guard this they servant N. and lead him to the grace of thy baptism."[7]

---

[5] On the history of name-giving, see Michael Mitterauer, *Ahnen und Heilige: Namengebung in der europäischen Geschichte* (Munich: C. H. Beck, 1993), which provides valuable background for the Middle Ages. However, Mitterauer leaps from the high Middle Ages to the modern era and does not refer to changes in naming introduced by the Reformation. This shows his orientation toward Catholic continuity.

[6] On gendered aspects of the late medieval rituals, see Hermann Josef Spital, *Der Taufritus in den deutschen Ritualien von den ersten Drucken bis zur Einführung des Rituale Romanum*, Liturgiewissenschaftliche Quellen und Forschungen 47 (Münster/Westfalen: Aschendorff, 1968), 35-37. Spital says that at the end of the Middle Ages, not all rubrics prescribed the standing places of males and females, but the majority did. In any case, they consistently provided prayers and exorcisms differentiated by sex.

[7] J. D. C. Fisher, *Christian Initiation: Baptism in the Medieval West, a Study in the Disintegration of the Primitive Rite of Initiation*, Alcuin Club Collections 47 (London: SPCK, 1965), 160-61; Franz, *Das Rituale*, 17; Spital, *Der Taufritus*, 70-71.

The following is to be said over girls:

> "God of heaven, God of earth, God of angels, God of archangels, God of patriarchs, God of prophets, God of apostles, God of martyrs, God of confessors, God of virgins, God of all that live good lives, God whom every tongue confesses and before whom every knee bows, of things in heaven and things in earth and things under the earth, I invoke thee, Lord, upon this thine handmaid N. that thou mightest vouchsafe to lead her to the grace of thy baptism."[8]

Exorcisms, too, were sex-specific. The following was said over males:

> "Therefore, accursed devil, hearken to thy sentence, and give honor to the living and true God: give honor to Jesus Christ his Son and to the Holy Spirit, and depart from this servant of God N. because our God and Lord Jesus Christ has vouchsafed to call him to himself by the gift of the Holy Spirit to his holy grace and blessing and to the fount of baptism."[9]

The priest was to proclaim over females:

> "I exorcise thee, unclean spirit, by the Father and the Son and the Holy Ghost, that thou come out and depart from this handmaid of God N. for he himself commands thee, accursed one, damned and to be damned, who opened the eyes of the man that was born blind, and on the fourth day raised Lazarus from the tomb."[10]

The Breslau rubric prescribed in all, three prayers and four exorcisms for male children, and two prayers and three exorcisms for female children, in itself a sign of the lower valuation of the latter sex in the ecclesiastical schema.[11] Clergy expended more time and effort in relation to the male. On the other hand, the ideological content of the prayers and exorcisms does not lend itself to clear differentiation between masculine and feminine.

This gendering of children virtually from the hour of their birth was quite a consistent feature of liturgical life. Even in the early church, females stood or sat on the north — the tainted — side of the sanctuary and males on the south. Males were to receive the eucharist first, and females second, though in the late Middle Ages

---

[8] Fisher, *Christian Initiation*, 162; Franz, *Das Rituale*, 18; Spital, *Der Taufritus*, 70-71.
[9] Fisher, *Christian Initiation*, 161; Franz, *Das Rituale*, 17; Spital finds that this formula was sometimes used with boys and sometimes with girls, even in gender-differentiated liturgies (*Der Taufritus*, 76).
[10] Fisher, *Christian Initiation*, 163; Franz, *Das Rituale*, 18; Spital, *Der Taufritus*, 78.
[11] Franz, *Das Rituale*, 66.

this was not always enforced. Brides stood at their nuptials on the inferior side, sometimes construed as the groom's left, sometimes as the priest's left — but the left side nonetheless.[12]

II. *The Reformation*

The changes that Martin Luther proposed in the administration of baptism left a recognizable skeleton of the Catholic precedent intact.[13] His "Taufbüchlein Deutsch" of 1523 departed only in small ways from past practice, for, as he notes in a postscript,

> "I haven't yet wanted to change anything in particular in the baptismal booklet ... To spare weak consciences I let it stay almost as it is, so that they don't complain that I want to bring in a new baptism and find fault with those who have been baptized up till now, as though they weren't properly baptized."[14]

His major addition was the "Great Flood Prayer," in which he draws an analogy between the deluge of Noah's time and the washing clean of and holding secure (as in the Ark) of Christian souls.

Three years later, however, Luther was less concerned with sparing weak consciences. Pressed by Nicolaus Hausmann, he curtailed the old ceremony considerably by taking out several exorcisms — yet keeping some — and two of the medieval prayers. He removed exsufflation, touching the infant's ears and nose with saliva, anointing the child with oil, and placing a burning taper in its hand. But he retained his innovative prayer. For Luther, baptism cleansed the individual of original sin. His passage explaining baptism in the

---

[12] Gendering practices endured in Roman Catholic baptism at least up till the Second Vatican Council. See Hermann A. P. Schmidt, *Introductio in liturgicam occidentalem* (Freiburg/Breisgau: Herder, 1960), esp. 265-76. On the gender meanings of the right and left sides, see Joan Cadden, *Meanings of Sex Differences in the Middle Ages: Medicine, Science, and Culture* (Cambridge, England, and New York: Cambridge University Press, 1993), passim.

[13] On Luther's early theology concerning baptism, see W. Jetter, *Die Taufe beim jungen Luther. Eine Untersuchung über das Werden der reformatorischen Sakraments- und Taufanschauung*, Beiträge zur historischen Theologie 18 (Tübingen, Germany, 1954). On his baptismal theology overall, see Lorenz Grönvik, *Die Taufe in der Theologie Martin Luthers*, Acta Academiae Aboensis, ser. A, vol. 36, no. 1 (Åbo, Finland: Åbo Akademi, 1968).

[14] "Das Taufbüchlein," *D. Martin Luthers Werke, Kritische Gesamtausgabe*, 68 vols. (Weimar: H. Böhlau, 1883-1999) (hereafter WA) 12: 48, my translation.

greater catechism of 1529 reveals his emphasis upon the saving power of the sacrament: "No greater jewel can adorn our body or soul
than baptism; for through it perfect holiness and salvation become
accessible to us, which are otherwise beyond the reach of man's life
and energy."[15] The Wittenberg reformer does not *refer* to baptism as
the rite of entry into the body of Christians, of engraftment onto the
body of Christ. He does urge godparents' prayers for the wellbeing of
their spiritual progeny. In the main, Luther adhered to the medieval
pattern of baptism as a means of overcoming the Old Adam. It bore,
like the Catholic ritual, on the relationship between the individual
soul and God. It was a private act, carried out with all due haste after
birth, unwitnessed by neighbors other than the godparents.

It is noteworthy that Luther's rubrics omit gendered exorcisms and
prayers.[16] One could perhaps take this as evidence of the female's rising position within incipient Protestantism. However, the visitation
protocols reveal Lutheran churchmen's continual concern that gender differences be strictly observed in the ritual life of the parish.[17]
These gentlemen regarded Catholic practice as having become too
lax.

The retention of emergency baptism underscores the Lutheran
sense of the urgency of this initiation. Theology aside, permitting the
midwife to administer this sacrament to a child whose hold on life
was precarious told every simple parishioner that baptism was a prerequisite of salvation. The principal distinction between Lutheran
and Catholic practice was the evangelicals' insistence upon the
baby's being fully emerged from the birth canal. Pastors across Germany were to ensure that no midwife reached into the womb and
christened a child. Baptism, church authorities said, was "the new
birth," and how could one who had never been born undergo a figurative new birth? The governors of the church in the Duchy of Prussia declared in 1568 that the "old women" could not perform emergency baptism on a child "unless it were whole and completely born

---

[15] This translation is from the "Large Catechism," *The J. N. Lenker Edition of
Luther's Works*, 14 vols. (Minneapolis: Luther Press, 1903-1910), 14: 165.

[16] Andreas Osiander's 1524 baptismal rubric for Nuremberg retained the features
of late medieval Catholic baptism, including differential prayers and exorcisms for
the genders, but he distributed them equally: three of each for boys and for girls.
Ordnung wie man Tauffet, bißher in Latein gehalten, verteütscht (Nuremberg: n. p., 1524), no
pagination.

[17] See my comment on this in *The Reformation of Ritual: An Interpretation of Early Modern Germany* (London and New York: Routledge, 1997), 53.

into the world; baptism is a new birth, and if the child has not yet been entirely born into the world the first time, then how can it be reborn?"[18]

Communal impulses in the Southwest of Germany played a major part in shaping post-Reformation baptism there. While it would be impossible to prove a connection between the more pronounced communal sentiments of the Southwest and the rise of a congregational setting for the baptism of infants, I would assert that this is more than a coincidence. Peter Blickle has attempted to demonstrate the applicability of his notion of "communal Reformation" throughout Germany, but not without some qualification by other scholars.[19] One of the striking aspects of baptism in the Southwest is that men like Ulrich Zwingli, Martin Bucer, and John Calvin removed every part of the ceremony that could be regarded as superstitious or idolatrous. In Zurich and Geneva — less consistently in Strasbourg — ecclesiastical spaces in general were cleansed of images and other concrete bearers of sanctity, among them baptismal fonts. Fonts were objectionable as symbolic references to the womb of Holy Mother Church.[20] Infants were now baptised over simple basins. In latitudinarian Strasbourg, much was removed, but some familiar artifacts remained, including some baptismal fonts. God's physical presence was drastically reduced; as in other rituals, God became a spiritual presence, and likewise His interaction with human beings impalpable and beyond mortal influence. Bucer writes,

"We pay no heed to the teaching about chrism, oil, salt, clay and candles, nor do we use them. The reason for this is that they are human

---

[18] Emil Sehling, comp., *Die evangelischen Kirchenordnungen des 16. Jahrhunderts*, 15 vols. (1-5, Leipzig: O. R. Reisland, 1902-1913; 1-15, Tübingen: J. C. B. Mohr [Paul Siebeck], 1955-77) (hereafter KOO), vol. 4 (reprinted Aalen, Germany: Scientia Verlag, 1970), 92. This was official Catholic teaching during the Middle Ages but was not observed. See Anneliese Sprengler-Ruppenthal, "Das kanonische Recht in Kirchenordnungen des 16. Jahrhunderts," in Richard H. Helmholz, ed., *Canon Law in Protestant Lands*. Comparative Studies in Continental and Anglo-American Legal History 11 (Berlin: Duncker & Humblot, 1992), 50-121, here at 70-73.

[19] See the varying positions taken by the contributors to Peter Blickle, ed., *Landgemeinde und Stadtgemeinde in Mitteleuropa: Ein struktureller Vergleich*, Historische Zeitschrift, Beiheft 13 (Munich: R. Oldenbourg, 1991). These treat the period from 1300-1800 and thus sometimes identify communal structures in an earlier century that had already considerably weakened by the age of the Reformation.

[20] Walter M. Bedard, *The Symbolism of the Baptismal Font in Early Christian Thought*, Studies in Sacred Theology, 2nd series, 45 (Washington, D. C.: Catholic University of America Press, 1951), 56-57.

inventions without warrant in God's Word, which have been the cause
of much superstition. Hence it has come to pass that this chrism and
oil can be consecrated only by a bishop and only on Maundy Thurs-
day. So also many people have not been allowed to bathe their children until the priest has been paid a penny or a groat to wipe off the
chrism and oil. Such magic tricks ill become intelligent and rational
Christians, who ought to pay heed to the Word of their Lord and follow it alone."[21]

In each of these settings, baptism now came before the entire congregation. The rite was drastically simplified, and it was performed in
the presence of the *Gemeinde*. In villages under these cities' control or
influence, that *Gemeinde* was made up not just of householders but
also of lords, rural officials, and the poor who hired themselves out
but did not possess the concrete stake of ownership in the local
arable. In the cities, baptism occurred increasingly in the presence of
the residents of an infant's neighborhood, which is to say its parish. A
larger city might be made up of two or more parishes. Church leaders, through the communal context of baptism, revivified the ancient
metaphor of baptism as engraftment onto the body of Christ, symbolized by the body of believers.

Luther's fledgling Christian was nearly alone before God, but
Bucer's was not. In 1524, Bucer's *Grund und ursach auss gotlicher schrifft
der neüwerungen an dem nachtmal des herren, so man die Mess nennet, Tauff,
Feyrtagen, bildern und gesang in der gemein Christi, wann die zusamenkompt,
durch und auff das wort gottes zu Strassburg fürgenomen* appeared, setting out
in detail the liturgical modifications that had been made.[22] The
reformer mentions "the sponsors, together with the other brethren,"
who are admonished to love these children as fellow members of the
body of Christ ... ."[23] The rite is to be carried out in the presence of
the congregation, which is emblematic of the divine body. Baptism
not being essential to salvation, the sacrament can wait at least until
the next regular service of worship. This text contains the idea that

---

[21] Translation of J. D. C. Fisher, *Christian Initiation, the Reformation Period*, Alcuin
Club Collections 51 (London: S. P. C. K., 1970), 34. Original in Robert Stupperich,
ed., *Martin Bucers Deutsche Schriften*, vol. 1, *Frühschriften 1520-1524* (Gütersloh, Germany: Gerd Mohn; simultaneously Paris: Presses universitaires de France, 1960),
258.
[22] Stupperich, *Bucers Deutsche Schriften*, 1: 185-278. See also Hughes Oliphant Old,
The Shaping of the Reformed Baptismal Rite in the Sixteenth Century (Grand Rapids, Michigan: Eerdmans, 1992), 54-62.
[23] Stupperich, *Bucers Deutsche Schriften*, 1: 258.

the *congregation*, rather than the godparents, is the baptismal sponsor; and those present are admonished that they have the duty to see that the child is raised as a Christian.[24] Johannes Oecolampadius adopted a similar pattern in Basle.[25]

In Zurich, Zwingli employed particularly pointed language in stressing that with baptism, the infant was engrafted into the body of Christ. He inserted this statement for the officiant in his rubric of 1525:

> "Inasmuch as you have heard that the Lord desires people to bring the little children to Him — for he is also the Savior of children — we want to bring Him this [particular] infant; that is, through baptism [we want to] receive it into His community and give it the sign of the communion and the people of God."[26]

He goes on to use the accusative case, asserting that the child is baptized *into* the name of the Father, Son, and Holy Ghost.

> "*In* hat die ard, daß man's brucht, da man von ußen hinynkumpt; als wenn man spricht: 'Er gadt in das huß,' ist gewüß, daß er ußerhalb was, und ist hinyn ggangen [sic]. *Im* hat die ard, das man's brucht, da man schon dinnen [sic] ist; also so man spricht: 'Er gadt im hus,' so verstat man wol, das er vor unnd ee er anhub zu gon, er imm hus was. So nun Paulus spricht: 'Wir alle, die in Christum Jesum getoufft sind, muß ie sin, das er sagen wil, das wir, die ußerhalb Christo Jesu warend, mit dem touff in inn tretten sygind.'" ("It is in the nature of the word *into* [as a preposition requiring the accusative] that a person uses it when he comes in from outside, as when we say, 'He goes into the house'; it is certain that he was outside and has gone in. [By contrast] the word *in* [as a preposition requiring the dative object], as used in [the sentence], 'He walks within the house', gives us clearly to understand that before he began to walk, he was [already] inside the house. It must be that when Paul says, 'All of us who are baptized in Jesus Christ,' he means that we, who were outside of Jesus Christ, upon being baptized have stepped *into* Him.")[27]

In addition, observers unrelated to the tiny baptisand benefited from

---

[24] Old, *Shaping*, 61.

[25] Old, *Shaping*, 69-70.

[26] Quoted in Fritz Schmidt-Clausing, *Zwingli als Liturgiker: Eine liturgiegeschichtliche Untersuchung* (Göttingen, Germany: Vandenhoeck & Ruprecht, 1952), 161.

[27] Schmidt-Clausing, *Zwingli als Liturgiker*, 69; taken from *Corpus Reformatorum* 4: cols. 243-44.

the reminder of their own baptism and of God's care for them. Their shared identity as God's children was underscored by their unison recitation of the Lord's Prayer.[28]

Later in the sixteenth and seventeenth centuries, more christening rites included the saying of the complete Creed. Even though this was mainly to compel the laity finally to memorize it, the speaking in one voice (una voce) may be seen as having a unifying effect.

After Luther's death, a more communally centered baptism spread into other parts of Germany. This occurred earliest in other parts of the Southwest, as in Augsburg in 1537[29] and Württemberg in 1555.[30] But thereafter it is visible in the North as well. In his ecclesiastical ordinance of 1569, Duke Julius of Braunschweig provided that baptism should be carried out only in "public general assembly" (öffentlicher gemeiner Versammlung), and in order to make its celebration visible to all, the font should be set one or two steps above the floor level of the sanctuary.[31] Perhaps this trend is aptly symbolized by the positioning of the baptismal font (Sophientaufe) directly in the nave aisle in Wolfenbüttel's main parish church, completed in the early seventeenth century.[32]

Another respect in which the Swiss and Southwest German baptismal liturgies may manifest the more pronounced communal tendencies in that region is in their inclusion of parents in the rite. While in much of the rest of Germany, at least at this early date, mothers

---

[28] The inclusion of the Lord's Prayer in the baptismal liturgy dates at least to the eighth century and probably earlier. See "The Gelasian Sacramentary," E. C. Whitaker, *Documents of the Baptismal Liturgy*, 2nd ed. (London: S. P. C. K., 1974), 177-79. Here, however, it is recited by the priest rather than the congregation or the body of catechumens.

[29] Sehling, KOO, 12: 57, 63.

[30] *Kirchenordnung, Wie es mit der Lehre vnd Ceremonien im Fürstenthumb Würtemberg* [sic] *angerichtet vnd gehalten werden soll* (Tübingen, Germany: Vlrich Morharts Witfraw, 1555), esp. Bii.

[31] Wilhelm Rauls, "Die Taufe in der Geschichte der Evangelisch-lutherischen Landeskirche in Braunschweig," *Jahrbuch der Gesellschaft für niedersächsische Kirchengeschichte* 73 (1975), 58. For the original texts, see Sehling, KOO, 6: 125-26, 156, 554, 664. Cf. the Saxon ordinance of 1580, Sehling, KOO, 1: 426; for Henneberg, 1582, 2: 304; the Welf lands of Wolfenbüttel and Lüneburg and the cities of Braunschweig and Lüneburg, 1560s and 1570s, 6: 156, 554, 664; County of Oldenburg, 1573, 7/2: 1100.

[32] Peter Königfeld and Rolf-Jürgen Grote, "Altar, Raum und Ausstattung der Hauptkirche Beatae Mariae Virginis: Restaurierung und Geschichte," in D*ie Hauptkirche Beatae Mariae Virginis in Wolfenbüttel*, Forschungen der Denkmalpflege in Niedersachsen 4 (Hameln, Germany: C. W. Niemeyer, 1987), 117-68, here see fig. 103, p. 139; the notes, pp. 279-81.

were definitively excluded and fathers lurked in the background as hosts, Zwingli, Bucer, and Oecolampadius sought to bring fleshly progenitors to the fore as those closest to a child and most appropriately to be charged with seeing to its spiritual development. Godparents might still be featured in the *dramatis personae*, but alongside them was at least the father. John Calvin followed this pattern in Geneva.[33] Although Calvin's "Form of Administering Baptism" does not say so explicitly, he wrote to Caspar Olevianus, "Unless they are impeded by business, fathers are ordered to attend."[34] In John Knox's *Genevan Service Book*, the rubric Knox used while in Geneva with the Marian exiles from 1556-1559, the infant's father comes with his child and the godparents to the place where the sacrament is to be performed, exclusively in front of the entire congregation. The officiating clergyman assures those present that it is not necessary "that all those that receive this Sacrament have the use of understanding and faith, but chiefly that they be contained under the name of God's people, so that the remission of sins in the blood of Jesus Christ doth appertain unto them by God's promise, which thing is most evident by St. Paul, who pronounceth the children begotten and born (either of the parents being faithful) to be *clean* and *holy*."[35]

Fathers and godparents likewise brought their babies forward in the congregation of Dutch Calvinists led by Johann à Lasco in London during the reign of Edward VI.[36]

The growing concept that children were not impure but indeed provisionally a part of the Christian community owing to the faith of their parents, helps to explain the requirement that at least the father

---

[33] Karen Spierling, a doctoral student of Robert Kingdon at the University of Wisconsin, is writing her dissertation on baptism in Calvin's Geneva. She was kind enough to allow me to see unpublished papers based on her research: "Water: The Baptismal Role of Parents in Perceval Roguet's Geneva," presented at the meetings of the Renaissance Society of American, Los Angeles, California, March 1999; and "Baptism in Calvin's Geneva: At the Crossroads of Church and City," read at the meetings of the Sixteenth Century Studies Conference, St. Louis, Missouri, October 1999.

[34] *Corpus Reformatorum*, vol. 33: Ioannis Calvini opera quae supersunt omnia, vol. 5, ed. Wilhelm Baum, Eduard Cunitz, and Eduard Reuss (Braunschweig, Germany: C. A. Schwetschke und Sohn, 1866), cols. 185-92; letter to Olevian, CR 46, Ioannis Calvini, vol. 18 (Braunschweig, 1878), cols. 235-36.

[35] Peter J. Jagger, *Christian Initiation 1552-1969: Rites of Baptism and Confirmation since the Reformation Period*, Alcuin Club Collections 52 (London: S. P. C. K., 1970), 163-64.

[36] Rubric reproduced in Sehling, KOO, 7/1: 610.

attend baptism. As a faithful man, he is already a bond between Christ and his child, and he now logically brings the infant forward for the formal, public declaration of that bond through the act of external washing that testifies to God's internal cleansing. In Lutheran lands, mothers nevertheless did not appear at christenings much before the eighteenth century, for until their churching, they were *confined.* That the mother's faith, too, could be instrumental for her offspring is seen in the Calvinist, and by the end of the century in many Lutherans', insistence that a mother's own faith provisionally signaled her dead baby's membership among the people of God.[37] Thus, infants who died before they could be baptized were to be buried in consecrated ground or the regular cemetery, and, within Lutheranism (where ritual burial was performed), with full solemnities. Nevertheless, the much reprinted foreword to Luther's second *Taufbüchlein* announced that up until its baptism, an infant was "possessed by the devil and a child of sin and lacking in grace."[38]

The idea that in particular fathers ought to play an active part in their babies' Christian initiation was occasionally introduced into other parts of Germany. In Augsburg at mid-century, the rubric has the officiant request the parents and godparents to step forward.[39] Likewise, in Oberland in Franconia in 1558, fathers are admonished to be present, to pray for their children, and to sign the baptismal register themselves.[40] The magistrates of Regensburg declare in 1572, "Because it is in every way proper that the father personally appear at his child's baptism, present his offspring to God Almighty, and pray that in a fatherly manner He receive it into the communion of the faithful," the pastor must so instruct the people and make them comply.[41] Fathers did sometimes resist. In 1586, the villagers of Sara near Weimar refused to attend their own children's baptismal ceremonies. The fathers protested to the parish visitors that this was an innovation of the pastor.[42] As a general principle, private baptism

---

[37] Luther himself briefly expressed the view that Christian mothers' deep desire to have had their deceased babies baptised would be taken into account by God (WA 53: 206). On the shift among Protestants toward full Christian burial of unbaptised infants, see Irmgard Wilhelm-Schaffer, *Gottes Beamter und Spielmann des Teufels: Der Tod in Spätmittelalter und Früher Neuzeit* (Cologne and Weimar: Böhlau, 1999), 132-37.

[38] WA 19: 537.

[39] Sehling, KOO, 12/2: 98. The mother, however, will hardly have been present.

[40] Sehling, KOO, 11: 45.

[41] Sehling, KOO, 13: 508-509. See also the County of Hohenlohe, 1558 and 1579, 14: 126, 370.

attended only by godparents remained possible in Lutheran Germany.[43] A late-seventeenth-century pastor complained that for the most part, parents (meaning fathers) seldom attended their babies' christening.[44] Nevertheless, the practice became very widespread in the sixteenth and seventeenth centuries of baptizing infants in the presence of the congregation, and of verbally associating the child with the larger body of Christians. To an increasing extent, their fathers were at least within the church.[45]

Even within the lands of godparental preeminence, authorities insisted that the father nominate prospective sponsors to the pastor in advance of christening and that the pastor had the right, if not the duty, to interview these and ensure that they were Christians in good standing, of mature age, morally upright, and well-informed on the precepts of their faith. Only then could the ceremony proceed as planned. During the sixteenth and seventeenth centuries, this pattern came to prevail. It represents — especially when contrasted with the lackadaisical supervision of godparents in the late Middle Ages — one more small aspect of those practices collectively called confessionalization and social disciplining. A godparent had to understand what it meant to be an adherent of whatever creed was established in his or her parish, for only then could the sponsor sincerely take up the obligation of instructing the spiritual child. A godparent must be of sober and responsible life style, for if not, he or she could hardly provide a proper model of Christian deportment or take the duties of godparenthood seriously.[46] Under no circumstances could a person of another religious persuasion stand with a child at its christening, a convic-

---

[42] Thüringisches Hauptstaatsarchiv Weimar, Reg. Ji 67, "Kirchen- und Schul-Visitations-Acta. 1586," fol. 369.

[43] The ongoing Lutheran practice of the use of godparents is interestingly explained in Michael Pharetratus, *Von der Gevatterschafft, So bey vnnd zu der heiligen tauff vor Alters her gestifftet, ein nützlicher, nöhtiger, nicht vnlustiger Sermon, Vnterricht vnd Vnterrede. Dem Einfeltigen, vnnd insonderheit dem deutschen Mann zu besserer Nachrichtung in bekanter Sprach Frag- vnd Antworts weise verfasset* (Jena: Johan Weidner, 1617). This pastor in Neustadt an der Orla regards godparenthood as a theologically indifferent matter but an entrenched custom.

[44] Georg Grabow, *Aller Gevattern Schuldige Pflicht, so wol bey, als nach der Tauff ...* (Leipzig: Johann Wilhelm Krüger, 1683), 44.

[45] For example, in Augsburg (among Lutherans) from at least 1537 (Sehling, KOO, 12/2: 72).

[46] The Calenberg-Göttingen ecclesiastical ordinance of 1542 contains an explicit charge to godparents (Sehling, KOO, 6/1: 802); likewise, the Kasseler Kirchenordnung of 1566, which contains a long, detailed description of the qualifications and duties of godparents (Sehling, KOO, 7/2/1: 272-74).

tion that families along religio-political boundaries did not always share. The clergymen who administered this sacrament within any denomination were able to bar nonmembers from baptismal patronage. By the eighteenth century, nevertheless, the crossing of denominational lines was sometimes allowed, even though regretted.[47]

One of the accusations leveled against Anabaptists was that they did not care for their children. In fact, such an accusation would have resonated among the common laity, who in general adhered to the pre-Reformation view that the ritual was a prerequisite of mundane safety and eternal bliss. We might well consider the alterations made in baptismal rituals in thinking about the old historiographic question, raised by Philippe Ariès, as to whether the early modern period saw a rise in parental affection.[48] In his *Grund und ursach* of 1524, Bucer provides the following manner of proceeding. The pastor should perform the ritual, "... after a short explanation of what baptism is and signifies, and also congregational prayer that Christ should baptize the child through His Spirit and that the godparents together with other brethren might love it as their fellow member in Christ and, as soon as possible, by means of healing doctrine, lead it to Christ. We have grounds in Scripture for doing this and nothing further."[49]

---

[47] I take up the subject of religious border-crossing in "Confessional Ambiguity along Borders: Popular Contributions to Religious Tolerance in Sixteenth-Century Germany," Seventeenth Annual Skotheim Lecture, published as a pamphlet (Walla Walla, Washington: Whitman College, 1998).

[48] Ariès, *Centuries of Childhood: A Social History of Family Life* (New York: Knopf, 1962), which has given rise to no end of scholarly debate: Barbara Beuys, *Familienleben in Deutschland: Neue Bilder aus der deutschen Vergangenheit* (Reinbek bei Hamburg: Rowohlt, 1980); Barbara Hanawalt, *The Ties that Bound: Peasant Families in Medieval England* (New York: Oxford University Press, 1986); idem, *Growing Up in Medieval London* (New York: Oxford University Press, 1993); Linda Pollock, *Forgotten Children: Parent-Child Relations from 1500 to 1900* (Cambridge, England: Cambridge University Press, 1983); Lawrence Stone, *The Family, Sex and Marriage in England, 1500-1800* (New York: Knopf, 1977); Philip J. Greven, *The Protestant Temperament: Patterns of Childrearing, Religious Experience, and the Self in Early America* (New York: Knopf, 1977); Michael Mitterauer and Sieder in passing agree on growing affect within the family: *Vom Patriarchat zur Partnerschaft: Zum Strukturwandel der Familie* (Munich: C. H. Beck, 1977), translated into English as *The European Family: Patriarchy to Partnership from the Middle Ages to the Present* (Oxford, England: Blackwell, 1982).

[49] "... nach kurtzer verklerung, was der tauff sey und bedeut, auch gemein gepett, das Christus wolle das kind durch sein geist taüffen und sye den pfettern sampt andern brudern befelhen, das sye solche wollen als ire glider in Christo lieben und, so bald moglich, durch die heilsam lere zu Christo furen. Des haben wir grund in der schrifft und nit weiters." *Bucers Deutsche Schriften*, vol. 1, *Frühschriften 1520-1524*, 258.

The Strasbourg order of baptism contains an evocative prayer, imploring God to grant the benefits of baptism to the child and through it even to its neighbors.

> "Almighty and eternal God, merciful Father, inasmuch as the just live through faith alone and it is impossible for a person without faith to please You, so we ask You to grant faith to this child whom You have created, and that in accordance with Your Son's promise, you seal and enclose that faith in its heart through the Holy Spirit as evidence of Your work of true inner renewal. As in the manner of the death of Christ Jesus, may the [former, i.e., the Old Adam] child be buried with Him and through Him [the new person] be awakened from the dead so that it may live a new life in praise of the glory of God and to the uplifting of its neighbor. Amen."[50]

In his Basel rubric of 1526, Oecolampadius asks the entire congregation to pray with him: "Now in particular I ask you to pray truly with me, as I baptize the child with water and bring it into the body of Christians, that God baptize it inwardly with His Spirit and preserve it in the number of His elect ... ."[51]

Clearly all these instructions and prayers emphasize the entrance of the child upon baptism into the Christian community. They support my contention, above, that the metaphor has been restored. But there is another dimension, one of collective *concern* for the wellbeing of the child. This shows itself as collective prayer and attention during the service, and it is to continue afterward as an ongoing effort to lead the young person into Christian conviction and way of life within society. I am suggesting, in short, that the manner in which the sacrament was carried out and the words employed expressed

---

[50] "Almechtiger, ewiger got, barmhertziger vatter, dieweyl der gerecht lebt allein ym glauben und unmüglich ist, das dir etwas on glauben gefall, so bitten wir dich, das du disem kindt, das da ist dein creatur, die gab des glaubens, verluhen wellest, in welchem du sein hertz mit dem heylgen geist noch deins suns verheissung versiglen und vericheren wollest, uff das dein innerliche ernewerung warhafftiglich bedeutet werde, und das es als in den todt Christi Jesu getaufft mit ym begraben und durch yn von den todten vfferweckt sy, zu wandeln in eim newen leben zu lob der herrlicheit gots und zu vffbauwung seiner nechsten, Amen." Friedrich Hubert, *Die Strassburger liturgischen Ordnungen im Zeitalter der Reformation* (Göttingen: Vandenhoeck & Ruprecht, 1900), 40-41.

[51] "Jetzt in sonderheit bitt ich eüch, das jr mit mir bittet trewlich, das, so ich das kind mit dem wasser tauff, und nem es in die zal der Christen, das es gott mit dem geist innerlich tauff, und halt es in der zal seyner ausserwelten ... ." *Form und gstalt*, fol. A v v.

increased interest in the infant's development on earth.

No one could credibly maintain that Martin Luther cared less than Zwingli, Bucer, or Oecolampadius about children. Certainly Luther was taken with his own offspring, and not just with Magdalena, whose death as a teenager in 1542 nearly undid Katharina and him. Veit Dietrich recorded the following utterance at Luther's dining table:

> "To the baby whom he held in his hands he spoke thus: 'How have you deserved, or why should I love you so much that I make you an heir of all I have? [Besides] shitting, peeing, [and] crying, you fill the whole house with screaming — [and yet] I have to have so much concern for you?'"[52]

When we read through the Reformer's *Das Taufbüchlein aufs Neue zugerichtet. 1526*, we see, however, that his focus remains upon the threat presented by the Devil. In his foreword, he exhorts the godparents to pray sincerely that God ". . . not only help him get out of the Devil's power, but also strengthen him so that he may withstand him [the Devil] in living and in dying.[53] The attendants should pray along with the priest, "unified in their hearts."[54] The rite, as Luther recommends it, does not emphasize love of the child or communal watchfulness. Here, at least, Luther left unreiterated the traditional obligations of the baptismal sponsors.

After Luther's death, as prominent a role as his *Taufbüchlein* continued to play in Lutheran christening rituals, church authorities increased the affective and communal strains by means of added prayers and admonitions. In the Kassel church ordinance of 1566, we find:

> "Faithful Father, grant the parents of these children, the godparents, and all of us who are gathered together, Your entire congregation, that in true faith we may receive this Your so gracious promise and work and take it up in right thankful spirit; that we may serve these

---

[52] Ad infantulum, quem in manibus gestabat, sic dixit: Wie hastus verdienet, oder warumb sol ich dich so lieb haben, das ich dich zum erben mache illius, quod habeo? Mit scheissen, binckeln, weinen, vnd das du das gantze hause mit schreien erfullest, das ich so sorgfeltig mus fur dich sein? WA, *Tischreden*, 1, no. 1004, p. 505.

[53] "yhm ... nicht allein von des teuffels gewalt helffe, sondern auch stercke, das es müge widder yhn ritterlich ym leben und sterben bestehen." WA 19: 531-41, here at 537.

[54] Ibid., 538.

children, who are supposed to be *Your* children and heirs, faithfully and enthusiastically [and] raise them in such a way that through them Your name is further hallowed ... ."[55]

A collect used during baptism in Augsburg in 1619, and perhaps reaching back to 1555, begins, "Grant, o merciful God and Father, that with true thankfulness we praise this Your unspeakable favor [*Gnad*] and good deed to this child, whom you have given to your congregation."[56] Earlier liturgies had not been quite this outspokenly grateful for the gift of children. At the end of the seventeenth century, a Frankfurt school rector explains to his readers,

> "Even the heathens and Turks love their [children], but only with a natural love. Christians have to look further and regard their off-spring [*Ehepflantzen*] not just as their own but also as God's. They [the children] are a precious treasure especially with regard to their immortal souls; God has entrusted them to you, and in due course He will demand them back from you. Therefore, you are the soul-shep-herds and the treasurers of God and have pressing reasons to be diligent, so that nothing will be wasted or lost through your neglect."[57]

It is important to recall that we are dealing here with normative literature. It may be possible to show the directions in which authorities' convictions were developing without these necessarily corresponding to changes within society. This is a wholly other question. In the seventeenth century, Lutheran clergymen's wedding sermons, though still harshly critical of women, nevertheless strove to encourage within the couples standings before them a strong sentimental and even an erotic tie.[58] Could this indeed accompany a growing offi-

---

[55] "So gib nu, getreuer Vatter, den eltern dieser kinder, den gevattern und uns allen miteinander, deiner ganzen gemein, daß wir alle diese deine so gnedige ver-heißung und werk in warem glauben und mit recht dankbarem gemüt aufnemen und an diesen kindern, die nu deine kinder und erben sein sollen, treulich und mit lust dienen, sie also aufziehen, daß auch durch sie dein göttlicher nam mehr geheiliget ... ." Sehling, KOO, 7/2/1: 276.

[56] *Forma. Wie vom heyligen Tauff, vnd dem heyligen sacrament deß Leibs vnd Bluts Christi ... zu reden sey ... Wiederumb von newem getruckt* (Augsburg: David Francken, 1619), would be p. Bvi. Although this is a Lutheran rubric, it is noteworthy that the godparents (or one of them) no longer lift the infant out of the font. The officiant now holds the baby alone. The godparents are allowed to lay a hand on the child immediately after its christening, as a sign of their commitment (would be p. Bviii).

[57] Georg Grabow, *Treuhertzige Erinnerung Von den Pflichten Aller Christlichen Eltern* (Frankfurt am Main: Johann David Zunner, 1688), 109.

[58] See my "'Fragrant Wedding Roses': Lutheran Wedding Sermons and Gender Definition in Early Modern Germany," *German History* 17, 1 (1999), 25-40.

cial sense of the importance of an emotional tie between parents and children? We need to revisit this question, and along with it the more interesting one of people's actual behavior.

The regional upheaval over the elimination of exorcism might be viewed as a manifestation of simple parents' keen desire for their children's wellbeing. Even though baptismal exorcism ceased in Saxony at the end of the sixteenth century, it was retained in other territories.[59] This was probably more than a concession to the world view of the unlettered, for as we see in the Great Witch Hunt, many prominent people, too, feared the alleged powers of the Devil.

A final dimension of baptismal observances in early modern Germany were the meals and other festivities that fathers gave for godparents, relatives, and friends immediately after the liturgy. These meals should not be seen as separable from the ecclesiastical procedure, for in the eyes of the people they were not. Whether in the parents' home or in a public place such as a tavern, the father provided the most generous repast, including inebriating beverage, that he could afford. Here he demonstrated his gratitude for the responsibilities that the godparents had just assumed by his willingness to be free in his gifts to them. He gave evidence of the reciprocity that he understood to be at the heart of spiritual patronage. Leaders of church and state took great exception to these celebrations. They objected to their cost, which, they claimed, undermined the budgets of too many families. They especially took exception to the excessive drinking and lascivious behavior that resulted from this entertainment. Pastors saw their flocks emerge from what was to have been a deeply spiritual and consequential observance and immediately manifest behavior at the opposite end of the moral spectrum. Wedding and police regulations as well as the ecclesiastical ordinances of the entire period strove to curtail, and in Calvinist areas to eliminate, these practices. Lutheran rulers did not succeed in abolishing them, for they were rooted in traditions of sociability and family life that were indispensable to many people.

---

[59] Bodo Nischan, "The Exorcism Controversy and Baptism in the Late Reformation," *Sixteenth Century Journal* 18, 1 (1987), 31-51; reprinted in idem, *Lutherans and Calvinists in the Age of Confessionalism* (Aldershot, Eng.: Ashgate, 1999), 31-50; summarized for Brandenburg in idem, *Prince, People and Confession: The Second Reformation in Brandenburg* (Philadelphia: University of Pennsylvania Press, 1994), 141-43.

III. *Conclusion*

In view of the militancy of the Reformation and post-Reformation eras, it may be surprising to remember that Catholic, Evangelical (Lutheran), Reformed (Calvinist), and Anglican Christians all recognized each others' services of baptism as fundamentally valid. This was so even though their reciprocal critiques were often severe. The Anabaptists as a group were the principal exception to this rule, for their departure from the established core was too drastic — and they, in turn, rejected the prevalent pedobaptism. Among the emerging "main-line denominations" including Catholicism, the ritual patterns of the Middle Ages remain at least detectable, and in the Lutheran case are thoroughly recognizable through the seventeenth century. The devastation of the Thirty Years' War may have thrown parishes back even more upon tradition, for oversight of the churches very nearly came to an end. After the war, however, the same paradigms were reinstated, with ongoing changes in prayers, a subject that warrants further study. Among all European Christians, baptism remained an essential rite of induction into the godly sphere.

Along with every other ecclesiastical rite of passage, governors of the churches included baptism in their drive to confessionalize and morally improve the populace. Women and men were to be kept separated within the churches; reformed ceremony continued to underscore gender differences. Pastors were to maintain careful records of who was baptized and who the godparents were. Where infants were illegitimate, this was noted and the authorities informed so that they could investigate the circumstances of conception. These mothers could not undergo churching. By controlling admission to the office of godparent, pastors oversaw their parishioners' knowledge of the faith and their standing in the church. Those who were ineligible to receive Communion could not serve as sponsors.

Confirmation is a wholly other subject, a ritual performed upon the older child or the young adolescent; it took place years after baptism. Nevertheless, it marked the completion of the initiatory process. Among Lutherans, this second rite was indispensable. By means of it, young people took up for *themselves* the vows that others had made on their behalf at their baptism. They demonstrated their mastery of essential doctrine, and they were admitted to the Communion table and thus more completely into the spiritual collectivity. Henceforward, as grownup Christians they bore the weight of their own transgressions. As practical creeds, rooted in the vicissitudes of life, both the Lutheranism and the Reformed denominations of the late sixteenth century manifest tensions between the teaching of justification by faith as an abstraction and the need for people to conform their behavior to an orderly standard. The liturgical life of the churches must be seen against this dual background.

LATE MEDIEVAL RELIGIOSITY AND THE RENAISSANCE OF CHRISTIAN MARTYRDOM IN THE REFORMATION ERA

Brad S. Gregory*

The sixteenth century witnessed a stunning renaissance of Christian martyrdom. Across Western Europe some five thousand men and women in all — Protestants, Anabaptists, and Roman Catholics — were judicially tried and executed as either heretics or religious traitors over the course of the sixteenth century.[1] At first sight, martyrdom's reappearance seems unexpected in the 1520s, a sudden resurgence after a medieval dormancy that had lasted several centuries. Martyrdom had waned with the advance of European Christianization. The chances of shedding one's blood for Christ had all but vanished in a world where the liturgical calendar framed the flow of time, where dioceses and parishes formed the geography of Christendom, and where non-ecclesiastical institutions wielded power to protect the Church against its enemies. Martyrdom, once a fundamental mode of Christian sanctity under hostile Roman emperors, migrated to the margins: by the high Middle Ages almost the only real candidates for martyrdom were crusaders or, from the thirteenth century, missionary friars to Asia, northern Africa, or the Middle East. To be sure, medieval Christians who ran afoul of the Church, such as Waldensians, Lollards, and Hussites, were executed

---

* Assistant Professor of History, Stanford University
    [1] The round figure of five thousand should be taken as an approximation, like so many sixteenth-century statistics. It is compiled from data given in William Monter, "Heresy Executions in Reformation Europe," in *Tolerance and Intolerance in the European Reformation*, ed. Ole Peter Grell and Bob Scribner (Cambridge: Cambridge University Press, 1996), pp. 48-65; Geoffrey F. Nuttall, "The English Martyrs 1535-1680: A Statistical Review," *Journal of Ecclesiastical History*, 22 (1971), 191-197; and É. De Moreau, *Histoire de L'Église de Belgique*, vol. 5 (Brussels: L'Édition universelle, 1952), pp. 172-206. The term "religious traitors" refers to those Roman Catholics executed as traitors in the British Isles for their refusal to disavow allegiance to the papacy. The only English Catholic executed as a heretic in the early modern period was the Franciscan John Forest. See Peter Marshall, "Papist as Heretic: The Burning of John Forest, 1538," *Historical Journal*, 41 (1998), 351-374.

as heretics with ecclesiastical cooperation even as they honored their slain fellow believers as martyrs. The few famous martyrs within the Church, however, above all St. Thomas (Becket) of Canterbury (d. 1170) and St. Peter Martyr (d. 1252), make clear that only unusual circumstances could produce Catholic martyrs in Europe. With good reason, then, Richard Kieckhefer has written that by the fourteenth century, "the fantasy of dying for the faith was seldom more than a fantasy except for the missionaries."[2] In his monumental study of late medieval sanctity, André Vauchez has noted that between 1254 and 1481, popes canonized no one who had died a violent death. Vauchez adds that "at the end of the Middle Ages, the identification of sanctity with martyrdom is no more than a memory."[3]

If this were the whole story, it would be difficult to make sense of the response to the first executions of the Reformation. On July 1, 1523, Hendrik Vos and Johann van den Esschen were burned as heretics beneath the Gothic spire of the city hall in Brussels, several months after the suppression of their monastery in Antwerp. Members of the Observant Augustinians, the same religious order to which Martin Luther belonged, these two had repeatedly refused to recant their unquestionably Lutheran views.[4] After their deaths, the two men were immediately, widely, and clearly seen by sympathizers as the first two martyrs for restored Christian truth. By the year's end, there appeared sixteen editions of a vernacular pamphlet about their deaths "for the sake of evangelical truth," published by at least eight different printers working in no fewer than seven different Ger-

---

[2] Richard Kieckhefer, *Unquiet Souls: Fourteenth-Century Saints and Their Religious Milieu* (Chicago: University of Chicago Press, 1984), p. 66.

[3] André Vauchez, *La sainteté en occident aux derniers siècles du moyen age d'après les procès de canonisation et les documents hagiographiques*, 2nd ed. (Rome: École Française de Rome, 1988), pp. 482, 484, quotation on 484.

[4] For documents pertaining to the suppression of the monastery in Antwerp and the treatment of the monks prior to the executions of Vos and van den Esschen, see *Corpus documentorum inquisitionis pravitatis neerlandicae* [hereafter *CDN*], ed. Paul Fredericq, vol. 4 (Ghent: J. Vuylsteke; and The Hague: Martinus Nijhoff, 1900), pp. 136-139, 141-142, 156-159, 160, 163-172, 173-177, 183-184, 191-192. The Observant Augustinian houses in Antwerp, Ghent, and Dordrecht were among the first channels by which Luther's teachings reached the Low Countries. See Alphonsus de Decker, *Les Augustins d'Anvers et la Réforme* (Antwerp: A. de Decker, 1884); Julius Boehmer, "De Beschaffenheit der Quellenschriften zu Heinrich Voes und Johann van den Esschen," *Archiv für Reformationsgeschichte*, 28 (1931), 130; Alastair Duke, "The Origins of Evangelical Dissent in the Low Countries," in *Reformation and Revolt in the Low Countries* (London: Hambledon Press, 1990), pp. 15-16; *CDN*, vol. 4, 138-142.

man towns.[5] Another pamphlet, this one in eloquent Latin, described their heroic deaths, enumerated the sixty-two articles that they refused to recant, and at length encouraged others to remain steadfast amid persecution, even in the face of death.[6] One Martin Reckenhofer defended each of these sixty-two articles in yet a third *Flugschrift*, aiming thereby to show, as the title put it, that Vos and van den Esschen were "martyred in Brussels for the sake of the Gospel."[7] Luther himself, in his *Letter to the Christians of the Low Countries*, written within weeks of the executions, praised God for having produced two men who had shed their blood for Christ. The witness of his fellow Augustinians also inspired the reformer to write his very first hymn, in which he rendered their interrogations and deaths in a rhyming narrative.[8] The swift reaction to these executions shows that the reemergence of Christian martyrological interpretation required no incubation period whatsoever.

Indeed, even *before* any evangelicals or Anabaptists were executed, martyrological awareness was in the air. After Luther was "kidnapped" from the Diet of Worms in the spring of 1521, Albrecht Dürer heard rumors of his murder, likened him to Christ, and hoped that Erasmus might "attain the martyr's crown."[9] Luther remained very much alive, however, busily translating the New Testament into German from the sanctuary of the Wartburg castle. There, early in 1522, he wrote a published letter of consolation to those who suffered persecution for the sake of God's word. Suffused with his theology of the cross, his letter linked the papacy's fifteenth-century Hussite victims to forebodings that he too might

---

[5] *Der actus vnd handlung der degradation vnd verprennung der Christlichen Ritter vnd merterer Augistiner ordens geschehen zu Brussel* ... [Speyer: Johann Eckhart, 1523], repr. in *Bibliotheca Reformatoria Neerlandica* [hereafter *BRN*], vol. 8, ed. Frederik Pijper (The Hague: Martinus Nijhoff, 1911), p. 15. For the editions, see Hildegard Hebenstreit-Wilfert, "Märtyrerflugschriften der Reformationszeit," in *Flugschriften als Massenmedium der Reformationszeit*, ed. Hans Joachim-Köhler (Stuttgart: Klett-Cotta, 1981), pp. 432-436.

[6] *Historia de dvobvs Avgvstinensibvs, ob Euangelij doctrinam exustis Bruxellae* ... [n.p., 1523], repr. in *BRN*, vol. 8, pp. 35-54.

[7] Martin Reckenhofer, *Dye histori, so zwen Augustiner Ordens gemartert seyn tzü Bruxel yn Probant, von wegen des Euangelij* ... [Erfurt: Wolfgang Stürmer, 1523], repr. in *BRN*, vol. 8, pp. 66-114.

[8] See Martin Luther, *Ein Brief an die Christen im Niederland* (1523), in *D. Martin Luthers Werke. Kritische Gesamtausgabe*, 60 vols. (Weimar: H. Böhlau, 1883-1980) [hereafter *WA*], vol. 12, pp. 77.6-9, 78.2-8, and idem, *Eynn hubsch Lyed von denn zcweyen Marterern Christi, zu Brussel von den Sophisten zcu Louen verbrandt*, in *WA* 35, pp. 411-415.

[9] Quoted in Jane Campbell Hutchison, *Albrecht Dürer: A Biography* (Princeton: Princeton University Press, 1990), pp. 164-165, quotation on 165.

soon be killed.[10] Similarly, before Conrad Grebel carried out the first adult baptisms in Zurich, he made clear what true Christians could expect at the hands of "the world": "Genuine, believing Christians are sheep in the midst of wolves, sheep for the slaughter," he wrote, who "must be baptized in anxiety and distress, sadness, persecution, suffering, and death, tried in the fire, and must obtain the fatherland of eternal rest not by strangling bodily, but rather spiritual, enemies."[11] At the time Grebel wrote this to Thomas Müntzer in the late summer of 1524, not a single Anabaptist had even been baptized, let alone killed. The expectation of persecution and the prospect of death for Christ preceded the renaissance of martyrdom itself.

It is not impossible that Luther, Grebel, and other reformers in the 1520s derived their martyrological awareness solely from the Bible. By returning to scripture as the sole source of God's revelation, they were reminded, for example, that "precious in the sight of the Lord is the death of his faithful ones" (Ps. 116:15) and that, as Paul had written to Timothy, "all who want to live a godly life in Christ Jesus will be persecuted" (2 Tim. 3:12).[12] The Bible is laced with passages about the inevitable persecution of the righteous and the blessedness of those who persevere through suffering. Still, central as scripture was to early evangelicals and Anabaptists, and relevant as such views were to their experience, there is no reason to assume that, since martyrdom had been dormant for centuries on the eve of the Reformation, martyrological sensibility was reconstituted solely from the Bible. The earliest evangelicals and Anabaptists had not ceased to be late medieval Christians. It seems fitting in an article honoring Heiko Oberman, who perhaps more than any other scholar has traced profound continuities as well as undeniable changes between late medieval and Reformation Christianity, to explore the indebtedness of the sixteenth-century renaissance of martyrdom to the late Middle Ages.

Oberman has shown that Luther did not come to his assertions *ex*

---

[10] Luther, *Missive an Hartmutt von Cronberg geschrieben* (1522), in WA 10.II, p. 59.25-34.

[11] Conrad Grebel to Thomas Müntzer, 5 September 1524, in *Quellen zur Geschichte der Täufer in der Schweiz*, vol. 1, *Zürich*, ed. Leonhard von Muralt and Walter Schmid (Zurich: S. Hirzel, 1952), p. 17.

[12] Biblical quotations are from the *New Revised Standard Version*. Biblical quotations and paraphrases from late medieval and sixteenth-century texts have been translated directly from the sources.

nihilo as a man inexplicably "ahead of his time," standing outside history as a herald of the modern world.[13] Similarly, it is doubtful whether the sudden sprouting of martyrdom in the 1520s would have occurred without fertile late medieval soil. This article seeks to show ways in which this ground nourished martyrdom in the sixteenth century. To discern the texture and composition of this soil, we need to examine not (the lack of) active martyrdom in the generations prior to the Reformation, but rather religious attitudes and practices relevant to martyrdom — those aspects of late medieval Christianity that help to account for its resurgence in the sixteenth century. In so doing, we shall excavate continuities between "late medieval" and "early modern" that might otherwise remain buried beneath the religious upheavals of the sixteenth century.

Above all, it was a drastically changed religio-political situation, not any novel or newly rediscovered values, that precipitated the sudden rebirth of martyrdom. A cluster of religious convictions and devotional practices central to late medieval Christianity were adopted and adapted in the early Reformation and beyond. By the 1520s late medieval Christians had been exhorted for more than a century to embrace and embody the virtue of patient suffering. Similarly, they had been schooled in the imitation of their crucified martyr-savior and in the affective meditation on his passion and death, events that they imagined and memorialized in multiple media. The hugely popular *Ars moriendi* had taught them how to prepare for their own deaths and to die well. And they prayed to the saints, God's friends and the most exalted members of Christ's mystical body, many of whom were ancient martyr-saints. All these interrelated convictions and activities bore directly on martyrdom, should the circumstances for it reemerge, which is precisely what happened in the 1520s. Far from scrapping everything in the late medieval inheritance, Protestant and Anabaptist leaders, with their insistence on *sola scriptura*, intensified widespread dispositions pertinent to martyrdom and applied them to persecuted fellow believers. In England, Roman Catholics who rejected Henry VIII's claims to be supreme head of the Church of England inaugurated a new era of martyrdom among those loyal to Rome. Clearly, only small minorities of devout men and women enacted the willingness to die for their beliefs. For just

---

[13] Heiko A. Oberman, *Luther: Man between God and the Devil*, trans. Eileen Walliser-Schwartzbart (New Haven: Yale University Press, 1989).

that reason, however, we need not be much concerned here with whether or not many late medieval Christians were spiritually indifferent conformists. The point is that their seriously committed contemporaries, like the sixteenth-century martyrs, were not. Across the confessional divides that martyrdom itself was helping to create, late medieval religious sensibilities influenced both Christians who were willing to die for their convictions and fellow believers who recognized them as martyrs.

Nearly a thousand years before the Reformation, Gregory the Great had written that "if, with the help of the Lord, we strive to observe the virtue of patience, even though we live in the peace of the Church, nevertheless we bear the palm of martyrdom."[14] Martyrdom was reborn so easily in the early sixteenth century because medieval Christianity had sublimated rather than eliminated it in the first place. From a certain perspective, the willing endurance of violent death for Christ was only the limiting case of the patient endurance of tribulation, an extremely broad category in pre-industrial Europe. Beginning even before Constantine's conversion, the theology and practice of "spiritual" or "white" martyrdom sustained notions integral to martyrdom itself.[15] Depending on political circumstances, not all Christians could be martyrs. Still, as Gregory the Great and other patristic and medieval writers insisted, they could all exercise the virtue of patience in their ordinary lives. Out of love for Christ, all could willingly embrace suffering and accept hardships as a spiritual discipline, submitting patiently to God's providence and the unfolding of his will.[16]

Late medieval Christians heard this message repeatedly, right up into the sixteenth century. The *Golden Legend*, for example, despite its thirteenth-century origins, was by far the most widespread hagiographical collection in late medieval Europe, with over two

---

[14] Gregory the Great, *Homiliae in evangelia*, 2.35.7, quoted in Alfred C. Rush, "Spiritual Martyrdom in St. Gregory the Great," *Theological Studies*, 23 (1962), 580. On the importance of spiritual martyrdom for Gregory, see also Carole Straw, *Gregory the Great: Perfection in Imperfection* (Berkeley: University of California Press, 1988), pp. 187-188.

[15] See Rush, "Spiritual Martyrdom," pp. 574-575; Robert Markus, *The End of Ancient Christianity* (Cambridge: Cambridge University Press, 1990), pp. 70-72; Louis Gougaud, *Dévotions et pratiques ascétiques du moyen age* (Paris: Desclee de Brouwer, 1925), pp. 200-219.

[16] On the importance of patience as a virtue in the fourteenth century, see the treatment by Kieckhefer, *Unquiet Souls*, pp. 50-88, to which my analysis is indebted.

hundred printed editions in the half-century before the Reformation.[17] It linked patience with martyrdom in its entry for the Feast of All Saints (November 1). Referring to Gregory the Great as well as to other Church fathers, the entry describes spiritual martyrdom as patience in adversity, compassion toward the needy, and the endurance of injustice along with love of one's enemy. The sublimation of martyrdom was fertile, fostering a host of Christian virtues in its stead. A person who enacted them "beareth the cross in his thought" and "is a martyr secretly in his mind."[18] The early fifteenth-century collection of sermons by the English priest John Mirk was printed twenty-three times between 1483 and 1532. In the sermon on St. Lawrence, famous for his taunts to the torturers who were grilling him on a gridiron, Mirk exclaimed "what joy and merit it is to suffer tribulation and persecution and disease patiently." Likewise, to suffer injustice while thanking God and praying for one's enemies "devoutly in clean charity" made a person "a martyr though he shed not his blood."[19]

The brothers and sisters of the *devotio moderna*, the voluntary religious movement that flourished especially in the Low Countries and the Rhineland in the late fourteenth and fifteenth centuries, embraced the joyful endurance of suffering. Late in his life Geert Grote (1340-1384), for example, the founder of the movement, consoled a young monk in a letter that counseled patience and the imitation of Christ through reflection on the scriptures. "Rejoice, rejoice, my beloved," he wrote, "when you fall into various temptations and trials because after you have stood the test you will receive the crown

---

[17] This figure is derived from Robert Francis Seybolt, "Fifteenth Century Editions of the *Legenda aurea*," *Speculum*, 21 (1946), 327-338; Sherry L. Reames, *The Legenda aurea: A Reexamination of Its Paradoxical History* (Madison: University of Wisconsin Press, 1985), pp. 27-29; and Brenda Dunn-Lardeau and Dominique Coq, "Fifteenth- and Sixteenth-Century French Editions of the *Légende dorée*," *Bibliothèque d'Humanisme et Renaissance*, 47 (1985), 88-93.

[18] [Jacques de Voragine], *The Golden Legende*, trans. Wynkyn de Worde (London: Wynkyn de Worde, 1512), fol. 310. In order to preserve a period sense of language, I have used early sixteenth-century English translations of the *Legenda aurea*, the *Imitatione Christi*, and the *Ars moriendi*, even though they are not always especially close translations of the Latin. Spelling and punctuation have been modernized in sources from the period.

[19] [John Mirk], *The festyuall* (London: Wynkyn de Worde, 1519), fols. 131, 71. For the editions, see *A Short Title Catalogue of Books Printed in England, Ireland, Scotland and Wales, 1475-1640*, 2nd ed. [hereafter *STC*], ed. A. W. Pollard, G. R. Redgrave, et al., vol. 2 (London: Bibliographical Society, 1976), pp. 156-157.

of life (Jas 1:2, 12)."[20] Grote amassed many of the same biblical citations about the patient endurance of tribulation that persecuted
Christians in divergent traditions would read, hear, and internalize in
the sixteenth century. Likewise, Dirk van Herxen (1381-1457), probably the most influential leader in the second generation of the movement, left a collection of his own spiritual counsels. They included,
"In adverse and difficult times, show a broad back through patient
strength and tranquillity of soul. Preserve a good heart through trust
in God. He will have great peace of heart who despises the prosperity
of this world and fears none of its adversities, nor indeed is there anything there to be feared."[21] By far the most famous and influential
work to emerge from the *devotio moderna* was *The Imitation of Christ*. It
survives in more than 800 manuscripts and was printed in more than
120 editions in seven languages between 1470 and 1520.[22] The
work's title articulated a late medieval spiritual ideal, while its content
stipulated how to pursue it. Patient steadfastness through suffering
was indispensable: "There is nothing more profitable for thyself and
acceptable to God than to be patient and glad to suffer for the love of
him. And if prosperity and adversity were put in thy election thou
shouldest rather choose adversity, than desire to be recreate with
many consolations. For by adversity thou art made conformable unto
Christ and all his saints."[23]

According to late medieval *dévots*, the authoritative genealogy of
patient suffering was what made it virtuous. Christ himself had told
would-be disciples to deny themselves, warning them that "whoever
does not take up the cross and follow me is not worthy of me" (Matt.
10:38). Hence tribulation was not merely to be endured with
clenched fists and gritted teeth, but joyfully welcomed and even
desired. The savior of humanity was no hypocrite: he himself had

---

[20] Geert Grote, "Letter [62]: On Patience and the Imitation of Christ," in *Devotio
Moderna: Basic Writings*, ed. and trans. John Van Engen (New York and Mahwah,
N.J.: Paulist Press, 1988), p. 84.

[21] "Certain Exercises of Lord Dirk of Herxen Found after His Death," in *Devotio
Moderna*, ed. and trans. Van Engen, pp. 212 (quotation), 52.

[22] These figures are derived from Roger Lovatt, "The *Imitation of Christ* in Late
Medieval England," *Transactions of the Royal Historical Society*, 5th ser., 18 (1968), 113;
Augustin De Backer, *Essai bibliographique sur le livre "De imitatione Christi"* (1864; reprint,
Amsterdam: Desclee de Brouwer, 1966), pp. 1-9, 34-35, 107-111, 127-129, 149,
155-156, 174; *STC*, vol. 2, pp. 393-394.

[23] [Thomas à Kempis], *A full deuoute and gostely treatyse of the Imytacyon and folowynge
the blessed lyfe of our moste mercyfull Sauyour cryste* ... (London: Richard Pynson, 1517),
2.12, fol. [F6r-v].

walked where he had commanded others to follow. Perseverance through adversity shaded into voluntary ascetic practice, based on the Lord's own admonitions and example. Grote waxed evocative about the mimetic desire of Christian asceticism: "When a holy mind begins to love the humanity of Christ powerfully, even beyond every delight in this world, and to suck upon the wounds of Christ, as oil from a rock and honey from the hardest crag (Dt 32:13), and to draw near the inner acts of Christ — oh, how much will he then yearn to be vexed, tried, and reproached so as to be made both like and pleasing to his lover."[24] Christ's infinite love, manifest above all in his passion and death, elicited love from those who sought to imitate him in turn. Especially considering the Lord's promise of eternal life, this love would find its fulfillment, not an obstacle, in the willingness to die for him. In the words of *The Imitation of Christ,* Jesus "hath gone before thee bearing the cross, and thereupon for thy love suffered death. Then take the cross of tribulation, sickness or other diseases and desire to suffer death for his love, if thou will be assembled to him in patiently suffering pain, tribulation and death, then thou shalt be a partner of his pleasure, consolation and perpetual life and joy." Or again, "when thou comest to that degree of patience that tribulation is sweet and pleasant for thee for the love of God, then esteem thyself in good state, and that thou hast found paradise in earth."[25] However remote the prospect of martyrdom, the desire for it never wholly died, because it followed from an ardent love for Christ. So too did the impulse to imitate the patient suffering for which his passion was the paradigm.

The fundamental image in late medieval Christianity was the crucifix, the focus of collective worship space from the tiniest chapel to the largest cathedral. It depicts a horrific martyrdom — especially in the exaggerated realism of so many fifteenth- and early sixteenth-century exemplars, of which Grünewald's *Isenheim Altarpiece* is perhaps the most famous. Yet crucifixes were only one among dozens of ways in which the martyr-savior's passion and death were recalled in the decades preceding the Reformation. This variety of forms catered to

---

[24] Grote, "Letter [62]," in *Devotio Moderna,* ed. and trans. Van Engen, p. 88. On ascetic desire and identification with Christ among saintly men and women in the fourteenth century, see Kieckhefer, *Unquiet Souls,* pp. 118-121.

[25] [à Kempis], *Imytacyon of cryste,* 2.12, sigs. F3v, F5v. For the same sensibilities in Bonaventure, see E. Randolph Daniel, "The Desire for Martyrdom: A *leitmotiv* of St. Bonaventure," *Franciscan Studies,* 32 (1972), 74-87.

Christians across the spectrum of religious commitment from the
indifferent to the intense. On the eve of the Reformation, the lackadaisical might limit themselves to watching passion plays during
Holy Week or, on Good Friday, to shuffling along urban routes modeled on Jerusalem's *via dolorosa*, listening to preachers' harangues,
seeking maximum indulgences for minimum effort. Those with more
initiative might buy a cheap woodcut of Christ's crucifixion, or of a
cognate image such as the beaten and bloody Man of Sorrows. Hundreds of such woodcuts were churned out in the century before the
Reformation.[26] Or they might endow Masses in honor of Christ's five
wounds (hands, feet, and side) in their wills, a common practice in
England.[27] Still further along the devotional spectrum, men and
women might recite the Hours of the Cross, a standard part of the
Books of Hours that were published for lay use in huge quantities in
the decades before the Reformation.[28] Or they might recite the
evocative prayers from pamphlets like the Flemish *Devout Meditation
upon the Passion*, which was written in the late fifteenth century and
printed five times between ca. 1518 and 1525.[29] Committed clergy,
religious, and laity might enter into the passion scenes in the pseudo-
Bonaventuran *Meditations on the Life of Christ*, which was translated into
English by the Carthusian Nicholas Love in the early fifteenth century and widely dispersed thereafter.[30] Or if one happened also to be

---

[26] For examples, see the reproductions in Max Geisberg, *The German Single-Leaf
Woodcut: 1500-1550*, 4 vols. (New York: Hacker, 1974), and in Richard S. Field, *Fif-
teenth Century Woodcuts and Metalcuts from the National Gallery of Art, Washington, D.C.*
(Washington, D.C., n.d.).

[27] Eamon Duffy, *The Stripping of the Altars: Traditional Religion in England, c. 1400-c.
1580* (New Haven: Yale University Press, 1992), pp. 243-244. On devotion to
Christ's passion in late medieval England, see ibid., pp. 238-248 and, more extensively, Ellen M. Ross, *The Grief of God: Images of the Suffering Jesus in Late Medieval England* (New York: Oxford University Press, 1997).

[28] Roger S. Wieck, *Time Sanctified: The Book of Hours in Medieval Art and Life* (New
York: George Braziller, 1988), pp. 89-90. For the large number of published editions–at least 114 Latin editions in England or on the Continent for sale in England
between 1477 and the 1530s, and 760 dated editions in France between 1485 and
1530–see, respectively, Duffy, *Stripping of the Altars*, p. 212, and Albert Labarre,
"Heures (Livres d'Heures)," in *Dictionnaire de spiritualité ascétique et mystique* [hereafter
DSAM], vol. 7, pt. 1 (Paris: Beauchesne, 1969), col. 420.

[29] *Dit is een devote meditacie op die passie ons liefs heeren ...* , repr. in *Bijdragen voor de
geschiedenis van het Bisdom van Haarlem*, 11 (1884), pp. 324-343. For the dates of composition and publication, see Michel-Jean Picard, "Croix (chemin de)," *DSAM*, vol. 2,
cols. 2584-2585.

[30] See Michael G. Sargent, ed., *Nicholas Love's "Mirror of the Blessed Life of Jesus
Christ"* (New York: Garland, 1992). According to Eamon Duffy, Love's translation,

the king of England, one might order that Christ's five wounds be represented at every royal meal, as Henry VI did.[31] In his classic treatment of late medieval Burgundian culture, Johan Huizinga criticized this "overabundance of devotional content" in which "consciousness was entirely permeated and saturated with Christ and the Cross."[32] According to Grote, however, this was just as things should be: "This cross of Christ should therefore ever be raised before us in meditation; his passion, his contumely, derision, injury, and sorrow should ever move our affections."[33] The redemptive suffering and death of their Lord greeted Christians in plays and processions, poems and pamphlets, hymns and woodcuts, sculptures and paintings, treatises and prayer books, whether they were at home, in church, or passing roadside shrines in their travels. The often graphic depictions sought to impress upon them the price paid for the possibility of their salvation, the staggering reality of the son of God's immeasurable love and painful martyrdom. If he had suffered like *that* for love of them, could not they at least bear their own daily tribulations for love of him?

And so the *passio Christi* elicited the *patientia Christianorum*, a message evident in a popular sermon published first in 1519. "If a pain or sickness burdens you," the author wrote, "consider how trifling this is compared to Christ's thorny crown and nails. ... If sadness or any bodily or spiritual adversity afflicts you, strengthen your heart and say, 'Why should I not also suffer a little affliction, seeing that my Lord sweated blood in the garden because of his anxiety and affliction? It would be a lazy, shameful servant who wants to lie in bed when his master has to struggle amidst the dangers of death."[34] These thoroughly late medieval admonitions were written by none other than Martin Luther, who reworked the meaning of Christ's passion accord-

---

which survives in fifty-six complete or originally complete manuscripts, "was probably the most popular vernacular book of the fifteenth century" in England. Duffy, *Stripping of the Altars*, p. 235. See also Sargent, "Introduction" to *Nicholas Love's "Mirror,"* p. lxiii.

[31] John W. McKenna, "Piety and Propaganda: The Cult of Henry VI," in *Chaucer and Middle English Studies in Honour of Rossell Hope Robbins*, ed. Beryl Rowland (London: Allen and Unwin, 1974), p. 74.

[32] Johan Huizinga, *The Autumn of the Middle Ages*, trans. Rodney J. Payton and Ulrich Mammitzsch (Chicago: University of Chicago Press, 1996), pp. 221, 220.

[33] Grote, "Letter [62]," in *Devotio Moderna*, ed. and trans. Van Engen, p. 89.

[34] Luther, *Ein Sermon von der Betrachtung des heiligen Leidens Christi* (1519), in *WA* 2, p. 141.14-15, 25-29. This sermon was published twenty-four times between 1519 and 1524. Ibid., pp. 131-134.

ing to his own theology without rejecting the traditional imperatives to patience. This was no idiosyncracy of the "more medieval" Luther, in contrast to Protestants less beholden to the Middle Ages or the monastery. Later Protestants, too, including those in the Reformed tradition, would use similar language in urging their persecuted fellow believers to steadfastness, much in keeping with late medieval sensibilities.[35]

Whereas martyrdom was a remote fantasy for late medieval Christians, death was an unavoidable certainty. Pre-modern Europe was beset by high infant mortality, peopled by women for whom childbirth was a recurrent danger, threatened with fires and floods and, after the mid-fourteenth century, swept by waves of plague and other infectious disease. All contributed to "the raw insecurity of life," to use James Tracy's felicitous phrase.[36] The skeletons who alternated with living souls in the *danse macabre* reminded everyone, regardless of their wealth and status, of what awaited them, "and so the end of every man in this world is death, and the life of man in this world as a shadow vanish away."[37] Sudden death was especially fearsome,

---

[35] Such views permeate the abundant Reformed Protestant anti-Nicodemite writings of the 1540s and 1550s. Consider, for example, the language and content in the following examples from George Joye and Pierre Viret, so similar to what we have seen in the *devotio moderna*. According to the English Protestant refugee Joye, writing in 1544, persecuted Christians should "give our selves over into [Christ's] hands to fashion us by his cross, to exercise, whet, hew, square and polish us at his benign will, to make us like his son our saviour." J[oye], *A present consolation for the sufferers of persecucion for rughtwysenes* ([Antwerp: Steven Mierdman], 1544), sig. [C8]. In the words of John Calvin's colleague Viret, "My dear brothers, since we are members of Jesus, it must be neither remarkable nor astonishing if we are participants in his cross and sufferings. For if we want to reign with him, we must suffer together with him. Since he is our head, we are his members; the head cannot proceed by one path and the members by another, but rather the entire body and the members follow the head who guides and governs them. If therefore our head was crowned with thorns, we cannot be part of the body without feeling their sting and without grief piercing our heart. If our king and sovereign master has been hoisted and hung on wood completely naked, completely bloodied, completely burdened with reproaches, insults, and blasphemies, it cannot be that we wait in this world to sleep always at our leisure, to be exalted with honors and dignities, being dressed in purple, velour, and silk . . ." Viret, *Epistre consolatoire, envoyée aux fideles qui souffrent persecution pour le Nom de Jesus et Verité evangelique* (Geneva: Jean Girard, 1541), partially repr. in *Correspondance des Réformateurs dans les pays de langue française*, ed. A.-L. Herminjard, vol. 6 (Geneva: H. Georg, 1883), p. 430, translation mine.

[36] James D. Tracy, *Europe's Reformations, 1450-1650* (Lanham, Md.: Rowman and Littlefield, 1999), p. 33.

[37] [à Kempis], *Imytacyon of cryste*, 1.23, sig. C4v. On the *danse macabre*, see Huizinga, *Autumn of the Middle Ages*, pp. 164-172; Philippe Ariès, *The Hour of Our Death*, trans. Helen Weaver (New York: Vintage, 1982), pp. 116-118.

since it would prevent the opportunity to confess one's sins and to receive the Eucharist en route to the afterlife. It makes perfect sense that something like the "art of dying well" would appear and proliferate in such a world, as it did in the fifteenth century. It stood to reason that people should prepare for what they could not avoid. Accordingly, the longer of the two texts known collectively as the *Ars moriendi* was "composed in short terms for to teach every man well to die" while he still "hath understanding, health and reason."[38]

To die well presupposed proper understanding, sound preparation, and an awareness of the ordeal of dying itself. Jesus had comforted the penitent thief crucified with him — "Truly I tell you, today you will be with me in paradise" (Luke 23:43) — and rightly disposed Christians also faced death with a hope, yet not a presumption, of heavenly reward. Death was not annihilation, but rather "none other thing but the issue or going out of prison and exile," indeed "the breaking of all the bonds of this cursed and evil world ... and entry into joy and glory." Well prepared, a penitent and hopeful Christian would not fear death but rather "receive it without any contradiction but also joyously, as he should abide the coming of his good friend."[39] All the same, death would remain the consummate ordeal of one's life. The devil would seek to subvert the dying Christian with deathbed temptations, trying to wrest him or her from God. As the *Ars* warned, the devil might endeavor to pry one from the faith, the foundation without which "it is impossible to please God"; he might foment despair for one's sins, even though "a person ought to have all hope and confidence in God" and "the pity and mercy of God is much more than any iniquity or wickedness"; Satan could affront God's providence by inciting impatience, seduce the spiritually ambitious to a prideful complacency, or lure one to preoccupation with worldly concerns, including one's family.[40] At this time, as one lay dying, perseverance in the virtue of patient suffering was both most imperiled and most important. It would be no different for persecuted Christians facing execution in the sixteenth century.

Mercifully, God had provided: late medieval men and women faced death not alone, nor surrounded merely by their family and

[38] *Here begynneth a lityll treatise shorte and abredged spekynge of the arte and crafte to knowe well to dye,* trans. William Caxton (London: William Caxton, 1490), sig. A1.
[39] Ibid., sigs. A1v, A2.
[40] Ibid., sigs. A2-A4v, quotations on A2, A2v, A3.

friends, but together with the powerful members of Christ's own body, the saints, interceding with God on their behalf. According to the *Ars moriendi*, "When it shall please God, the right splendant company of angels be at thy departing and meet thee. The right clear senate of apostles will defend thee, the victories of martyrs may meet thee. The company adorned with shining confessors will environ thee. The assembly of right joyous virgins take and receive thee. And the bosom of the blessed rest of patriarchs will open to thee, and join them with thee."[41] Throughout their lives and as those lives ebbed away, late medieval Christians sought in every sort of saint intercessors who, because joined to Christ himself, could help allay their maladies and supply their needs. In his *Festival*, Mirk aimed to inspire Christians to "have the more devotion in good saints," that they might "come unto the church to serve God and pray his holy saints of their help."[42]

The ubiquity and importance of the saints is one of the most striking features of late medieval Christianity. Many of them were (or were believed to have been) ancient martyr-saints. Their violent deaths were significant not because late medieval Christians needed models in the face of persecution, but because God had made them efficacious intercessors on the basis of their heroic deaths. Men and women needed the specialized help that martyr-saints could provide. At the end of the story about St. Dorothy in the *Golden Legend*, for example, one is urged to "devoutly pray to this blessed Saint Dorothy that she be our special protectress against all perils of fire, of lightning, of thundering, and all other perils, and that at our end may receive the sacraments of the church, that after this short life we may come unto bliss in heaven."[43] Whether they had been martyrs or not, saints were God's helpers. So it was that in 1505, a young law student named Martin Luther prayed to St. Anne for protection during a terrifying thunderstorm, vowing to become a monk if she preserved him.

At the same time, neither the exemplary virtues nor the violent deaths of the martyrs had receded entirely behind their intercessory role. Their sufferings were vividly imagined and the stories of their travails widely dispersed: of the principal saints in the *Golden Legend*,

---

[41] Ibid., sig. B4.
[42] [Mirk], *Festyuall*, fol. 2.
[43] *Golden Legende*, fol. 361.

two-thirds are martyrs, many of whose tortures and deaths are recounted in graphic detail.[44] The martyrs best embodied those strands of late medieval religiosity explored here: they had enacted the patient suffering for love of Christ most dramatically, had imitated his own passion most closely, and had epitomized the art of dying well under the most intimidating circumstances. Thus a regimen of prayer from the early years of the *devotio moderna* prescribed "conversion to the saints" as a daily part of its weekly cycle, with martyrs highlighted on Thursdays: "turn your attention to the holy martyrs who so lovingly poured out their blood for the love of God and so willingly gave themselves over to death for eternal life. Call upon them also for patience and in every tribulation plead with them for victory, particularly those, as mentioned earlier, for whom you have a special devotion."[45] Like the martyr-savior to whom they were bound in love, the martyr-saints also inspired patience and provided strength in adversity.

Considered together — and we should consider them together, because they were closely intertwined — the virtue of patience, devotion to Christ's passion, the *Ars moriendi*, and the importance of martyr-saints comprised a large part of Christian life on the eve of the Reformation. Remove them and we would hardly recognize late medieval Christianity; pull them apart and we would sunder what late medieval Christians had conjoined. All men and women could be spiritual martyrs by willingly bearing adversity, despite the unlikelihood of actual martyrdom. In so doing they were imitating their Lord, who out of love and in obedience to his Father's will himself suffered martyrdom by crucifixion, reminders of which were everywhere. In facing their own inevitable deaths, Christians were to persevere patiently against Satan's temptations to make them renounce faith or despair of salvation, confident of God's mercy and his promises of heavenly reward, looking to their Lord's own passion for strength and inspiration. And in both living and dying, men and women were aided by the intercession of male and female saints, themselves exemplary imitators of Christ and, in the case of martyr-saints, paragons of patience and extraordinary trust in God. It is most

---

[44] Reames, *Legenda aurea*, pp. 98, 256 n. 44.

[45] "On the Life and Passion of Our Lord Jesus Christ, and Other Devotional Exercises," in *Devotio Moderna*, ed. and trans. Van Engen, p. 194. On the character and provenance of this work, see ibid., pp. 49-51.

unlikely that as the 1510s became the 1520s, these central aspects of late medieval Christianity simply vanished. On the contrary, depending on where one stood and what else one believed, they acquired a dramatic new relevance against an apocalyptic horizon.

Beginning in the early 1520s, as the Reformation movement gained momentum and encountered resistance, martyrdom again became a real prospect. Evangelicals and Anabaptists applied to threatened fellow believers late medieval notions that they tweaked with their own readings of scripture. The virtue of patient suffering might now demand perseverance that encompassed actual martyrdom, and yet God's word counseled, "Do not fear what you are about to suffer.... Be faithful unto death, and I will give you the crown of life" (Rev. 2:10). The art of dying well might mean the steadfast acceptance of being burned alive or beheaded for the refusal to forsake God's truth, still "Do not fear those who kill the body but cannot kill the soul; rather fear him who can destroy both soul and body in hell" (Matt. 10:28). Although the intercessory role of martyr-saints was rejected, their heroic deaths were not, since even in biblical times holy men and women had born witness with their lives: "They were stoned to death, they were sawn in two, they were killed by the sword; they went about in skins of sheep and goats, destitute, persecuted, tormented" (Heb. 11:37). With such biblical predecessors behind them, persecuted evangelicals and Anabaptists had good reason to look "to Jesus the pioneer and perfecter of our faith, who for the sake of the joy that was set before him endured the cross, disregarding its shame" (Heb. 12:2). In this context, God's word did not oppose but rather *clarified* late medieval sensibilities. It equipped persecuted Christians to triumph over the temptations to recant their faith and patiently to endure even the terrors of execution, just as it had helped previous generations with their everyday hardships and their ordinary deaths. The contextual shift from protection to persecution unsublimated martyrdom.

Across political and linguistic divides, early evangelical leaders told fellow believers to persevere and publicized slain fellow believers as martyrs. A pamphlet by the pseudonymous "Nicodemus Martyr," for example, counseled people to reject self-indulgent penances and to accept instead the true cross of affliction in their lives: "out of his fatherly will the Lord applies the cross to you, as he commonly does with his children, so accept it gladly, as a good child, receive it in a friendly way and kiss it, and it will become for you blessed and good. It is truly a watchword and a sign from Christ our Lord ... through which his followers, servants, and children are recognized. He says, 'The servant is not greater than the lord; if they persecuted me, they will not spare you.'"[46] In the Low Countries, a descriptively titled and anonymous pamphlet, *A Comforting Letter for All Who are Persecuted for the Truth and for Christ's Name,* reminded beleaguered evangelicals that "since we are members of Christ's body, we should not be surprised if we participate in his sufferings and his cross."[47] A French pamphlet about Wolfgang Schuch, an evangelical pastor killed in Nancy (Lorraine) in June 1525, noted the persecution suffered by Old Testament "holy patriarchs and prophets" as well as New Testament "apostles and disciples of Jesus Christ," inferring that "if we belong to the body of Jesus Christ, we must walk along the same path by which he and his members have walked."[48] And William Tyndale opened his *Obedience of a Christian Man,* one of the most important early evangelical works in England, with pages on the expectation of persecution for Christ's sake. In no uncertain terms, based directly on Paul in 2 Tim. 2:11-12, Christians are called "to die with Christ that we may live with him, and to suffer with him that we may reign with him. We be called unto a kingdom that must be won with suffering only, as a sick man winneth health." Indeed, "there is no other way into the kingdom of life, than through persecution and suffering of pain and of very death, after the example of Christ. Therefore let us arm ourselves with the comfort of the scriptures"[49] Such examples could be multiplied at length, drawn not only from early evangelicals but also from Protestant leaders in subsequent decades.

The same phenomenon is to be observed among Anabaptists, for

---

[46] "Nicodemus Martyr," *Von dem warhafftigen Creutz Christi, wo man dasselbig finden, wie man auch solche eeren, tragen vnd erheben sol.* . . . (n.p., 1528), sig. A4. The biblical verse paraphrased is John 15:20.

[47] *Eenen Troostelijcken Sentbrief, voor alle die om derwaerheyt, ende om Christus naem veruolcht worden* [Antwerp: Matthias Crom, ca. 1530; reprint, Wesel: Hans de Braeker, 1558], repr. in *BRN,* vol. 8, p. 125.

[48] "Theodulus Philadelphus" [François Lambert?], *Epistre chrestiene enuoyee a tresnoble Prince monseigneur le duc de Lorayne* [Strasbourg: Jehan Preus, 1526], sigs. A2-A3, quotations on sigs. A2, A2v, A3. For the identification of Lambert as the probable author, see Bernd Moeller, "Inquisition und Martyrium in Flugschriften der frühen Reformation in Deutschland," in *Ketzerverfolgung im 16. und frühen 17. Jahrhundert,* ed. S. Seidel Menchi (Wiesbaden: Harrassowitz, 1992), p. 24 n. 10.

[49] William Tyndale, *The Obedience of a Christen man and how Christen rulers ought to governe* . . . ([Antwerp: Jacob Hoochstraten], 1528), fols. 6, 9v.

whom the Bible was no less foundational than it was for Protestants. Therefore biblical admonitions about suffering were no less authoritative. Conrad Grebel's premonitions of persecution were amply confirmed in the decade after 1525. Indeed, Anabaptists were so vulnerable in Germanic lands after the Peasants' War, and in the Low Countries after the Kingdom of Münster, that scriptural views about suffering applied to them even more thoroughgoingly than they applied to evangelicals. Like Grebel, Michael Sattler, for example, a watershed figure among the early Swiss Brethren, saw the way of true Christians in the world as one of "sheep among wolves." Nonetheless, the truth remained "the sure-footed and living way of Christ," as Sattler wrote from prison to fellow believers, which led "through the cross, distress, imprisonment, self-renunciation, and in the end through death." On this path, embattled Anabaptists were to "proceed ahead, firm and unwavering, in all patience, not abolishing or putting aside the cross that God has applied to you."[50] Likewise, when in 1534 Jakob Huter, the founder of Hutterite Anabaptism in Moravia, wrote to followers in Hohenwart, Austria, he told them not to despise the chains and sufferings of Christ, "but rather be glad about them with all your hearts," for they are "a true sign and seal of all the devout children of God," seen also among "all holy prophets and patriarchs" as well as among Christ's followers. Huter went on to apply to Anabaptists facing martyrdom some of the same biblical passages with which Geert Grote had consoled his monastic friend a century and a half earlier.[51] Circumstances had changed, but not the truth of God's word or the value of patient suffering. Like a host of other early Anabaptist leaders, both Sattler and

---

[50] [Michael Sattler], "An die gemeynd Gottes zü Horb," in [idem], *Brüderlich vereynigung etzlicher kinder Gottes, sieben Artickel betreffend. Item, eyn sendtbrieff Michael Sattlers* ... ([Strasbourg: Jacob Cammerlander], 1533), ed. Walter Köhler, repr. in *Flugschriften aus den ersten Jahren der Reformation*, ed. Otto Clement, vol. 2 (Leipzig: Rudolf Haupt, 1908), pp. 318, 319. On Sattler, see C. Arnold Snyder, *The Life and Thought of Michael Sattler* (Scottdale, Pa.: Herald Press, 1984).

[51] In Hans Fischer, *Jakob Huter: Leben, Froemmigkeit, Briefe* (Newton, Kansas: Mennonite Publication Office, 1956), pp. 22-24, quotation on 22. For Huter and Grote, compare ibid., p. 24, with Grote, "Letter [62]" in *Devotio Moderna*, ed. and trans. Van Engen, pp. 84-85, 86-87. The particular Anabaptists to whom Huter was writing in this instance were led by Bastel Glaser, who would himself be executed in January 1538. See Jacob Hutter, *Brotherly Faithfulness: Epistles from a Time of Persecution* (Rifton, N.Y.: Plough Publishing, 1979), p. 49; Werner O. Packull, *Hutterite Beginnings: Communitarian Experiments during the Reformation* (Baltimore: The Johns Hopkins University Press, 1995), pp. 270, 392 n.75.

Huter were themselves executed for their beliefs.

Finally, the Roman Catholic martyrs who refused to swear the oath of supremacy under Henry VIII inherited the same late medieval sensibilities, as we might well suspect. For Catholics the Bible was also God's authoritative word — although they claimed that its proper understanding was inseparable from the authoritative tradition of the visible Church. Among the Henrician martyrs, Thomas More's prison writings, packed with biblical quotations and paraphrases, are the most famous and richly revealing sources. The final chapter title in his *Dialogue of Comfort Against Tribulation* might have been taken straight from *The Imitation of Christ* (a text More knew extremely well): "The consideration of the painful death of Christ, is sufficient to make us content to suffer painful death for his sake." Consistent with the counsel of the *Ars moriendi*, More too sought the proper balance between hope and humility: "When we feel us too bold, remember our own feebleness, when we feel us too faint, remember Christ's strength. In our fear let us remember Christ's painful agony, that himself would for our comfort suffer before his passion, to the intent that no fear should make us despair, and ever call for his help, such as himself list to send us."[52] Like More, John Fisher, the bishop of Rochester, was deeply devoted to Christ's passion. In prison before his own death, he wrote about how, lifted by Christ's love, "martyrs innumerable both men and women have shed their blood, and have endured every kind of martyrdom were it never so cruel, were it never so terrible."[53] The practical imperative was clear for persecuted Catholics in the present. It would remain equally obvious for the Elizabethan clerical missionaries two generations later.

Even this cursory treatment shows that late medieval attitudes related to martyrdom were taken up and applied by Protestants,

[52] Thomas More, *A Dialogue of Comfort Against Tribulation*, vol. 12 in *The Complete Works of St. Thomas More*, ed. Louis L. Martz and Frank Manley (New Haven and London: Yale University Press, 1976), pp. 312.1-3, 318.25-29.

[53] John Fisher, *A spirituall consolation, written by Iohn Fyssher Bishoppe of Rochester, to hys sister Elizabeth, at suche tyme as hee was prisoner in the Tower of London* ... [London: Thomas East, 1578], sigs. F5v-[F6], [D8v], quotation on [D8v]. For More's anatomically detailed description of the crucified Christ, which underlies the devotional thrust of the entire final chapter of his *Dialogue of Comfort*, see ibid., pp. 312.10-313.1. On Fisher's devotional sensibilities in general, see Eamon Duffy, "The Spirituality of John Fisher," in *Humanism, Reform and the Reformation: The Career of Bishop John Fisher*, ed. Brendan Bradshaw and Eamon Duffy (Cambridge: Cambridge University Press, 1989), pp. 205-231.

Anabaptists, and Roman Catholics once the prospect of martyrdom reemerged in the sixteenth century. According to some late medieval Christians, however, including Waldensians, Hussites, and Lollards, the renaissance of martyrdom for Christian truth was underway more than a century before the German Reformation began. If any further evidence were needed to demonstrate the intimate relationship between late medieval religious sensibilities and martyrdom itself, the prison correspondence of John Hus provides it in eloquent abundance. From Constance during the month before he was burned on 6 July 1415, Hus averaged a letter a day to his followers, sharing with them his afflictions and aspirations. He evinced repeatedly the value of patience and suffering in imitation of Christ, who "suffered for us, leaving us an example that we should follow in His steps. He had to suffer, as He Himself said; and it behoves us to suffer, so that the members would suffer along with the head. He says: 'If anyone would come after me, let him deny himself and take up his cross and follow me.'"[54] Hus looked to biblical and early Christian martyr-saints, including Eleazar, the Maccabees, John the Baptist, and Catherine, not only for intercessory aid but as paradigmatic models in martyrdom. Referring especially to Peter and Paul, Hus prayed, "may those glorious martyrs thus joined with the king of glory be pleased to intercede for us, so that being strengthened by their help, we may be partakers of their glory, patiently suffering whatever the omnipotent Lord God decrees that we suffer for our greater good."[55] Here the saints, joined with Christ, are both intercessors and inspiration, which fit Hus's circumstances perfectly. Martyrdom crystallized late medieval — and biblical — religious

---

[54] *The Letters of John Hus*, trans. Matthew Spinka (Manchester: Manchester University Press, 1972), to John of Chlum, 23 June 1415, no. 86, p. 187. The biblical verse quoted is Matt. 16:24. See also, for example, a letter written shortly after he arrived in Constance to his supporters from Prague who had accompanied him there: "Let the Day of Judgment be terrible before your eyes, that you sin not; and the eternal joy, that you may long for it; and the suffering of the Saviour, that you may gladly suffer along with Him. For if you keep His suffering in mind, you will gladly undergo opposition, reviling, slander, beating, and imprisonment, and, should it be His will, even bodily death for His holy truth." Ibid., 16 November 1414, no. 52, p. 134.

[55] Ibid., ca. 20 June 1415, no. 78, p. 174 (Eleazar and Maccabees); ca. 20 June 1415, no. 80, p. 176 (Eleazar, Maccabees, and "many saintly men and women of the New Law"); 26 June 1415, no. 91, p. 196 (St. Catherine); 27 June 1415, no. 94, pp. 200-201 ("saints of the New and Old Testaments"); and 29 June 1415, no. 97, pp. 204-205 (Peter and Paul, quotation).

sensibilities, whether in Hussite Bohemia, Reformation Germany, or Henrician England.

It is clear that although active martyrdom had dwindled along with European Christianization, late medieval Christianity was permeated by values, virtues, and practices closely connected to it. Martyrdom had not died with the ancient martyrs — it was living alternative lives in medieval Christianity. Prefigured by the late medieval executions of Hussites, Lollards, and Waldensians, the sudden rebirth of martyrdom in the 1520s stemmed from fertile soil indeed, considering the spiritual intensity that devotion to Christ's passion or the ascetic desire to suffer for the Lord could inspire. Yet scripture *by itself* signaled continuity between the late Middle Ages and the Reformation era; it was the insistence on "scripture alone" that made martyrdom germinate anew. Geert Grote and Thomas à Kempis had known the biblical passages about persecution and suffering no less intimately than did Martin Luther or Michael Sattler or Thomas More. The questions in the sixteenth century concerned not whether God's word was authoritative — all agreed that it was — but rather *what it said*, how its meaning was determined, and how its authority was preserved. The ways in which Protestants and radical Protestants answered these questions led to their literal departures from the late medieval Church. Hence Protestant, Anabaptist, and Roman Catholic martyrs held many late medieval and biblical religious sensibilities in common, but they died for mutually incompatible views of Christian truth. In so doing, they unwittingly helped to create a world of Christian pluralism that very few of them would have welcomed or approved. Still less would they have esteemed the secularism that would eventually fill the cracks of a fractured Christendom. Not the Reformation itself but the consequent religio-political conflicts, the disagreements that fed more than a century of religious wars, heralded the modern world. Christian martyrdom in Europe faded again, only this time it was not sublimated. Instead, in the long run, the secular state anesthetized it and the religiosity from which it derived with new values and practices of its own.[56]

---

[56] For a full-length treatment of Christian martyrdom in the Reformation era, including its relationship to the late medieval inheritance, see my *Salvation at Stake: Christian Martyrdom in Early Modern Europe* (Cambridge, Mass., and London: Harvard University Press, 1999).

PSALMS BEFORE SONNETS: THEODORE BEZA AND THE *STUDIA HUMANITATIS*

Scott M. Manetsch*

Theodore Beza was profoundly shaped by the intellectual program of Renaissance humanism.[1] As a boy, Beza received an education befitting his noble heritage. Under the tutelage of the Hellenistic scholar Melchior Wolmar, he was trained in classical philology and literature, and read most of the canonical Greek and Latin authors.[2] In his early twenties, Beza rejected the legal career envisioned by his father and, drunk on the writings of Cicero and the poetry of Catullus, resolved instead to devote himself to the *bonnes lettres* and the pursuit of literary fame. Moving to Paris, Beza became a member of a sodality of young humanists, rubbing shoulders with some of the most influential poets and grammarians of his generation. His personal library included works by Cicero, Catullus, Virgil, Pliny, Varro, Livy, Terence, Ovid, and Quintilian.[3] The publication of a collection of Beza's Latin love poems entitled *Poemata* (1548) seemed to assure his place among the humanist elite of France. He was, in the words of Jacques Peletier, "well-regarded, valued, and honored" by everyone in Paris; a man "happy in the gifts of grace, nature, and fortune."[4]

In 1548 a crisis of body and conscience altered the trajectory of

* Assistant Professor of Religion, Northwestern College

[1] I wish to thank Richard Muller, Don Sinnema, and Mike Kugler for reading and commenting on early drafts of this article. In addition, I am grateful for the generous financial support provided by the H. Henry Meeter Center for Calvin Studies (Calvin College and Calvin Theological Seminary, Grand Rapids, MI).

[2] Three decades later, Beza will note in a letter to Melchior Wolmar: "Hoc enim vere possum affirmare, nullum esse nobilem vel graecum vel latinum scriptorem quem ego intra septennium quo apud te vixi non degustarem...." 12 March 1560, in *Correspondance de Théodore de Bèze*, vol. 3 (Geneva: Librairie Droz, 1963), 45.

[3] Beza addresses his beloved books in his poem *Ad bibliothecam*: "Salvete, incolumnes mei libelli / Meae deliciae, meae salutes / Salve, mi Cicero, Catulle, salve / Salve, mi Maro, Pliniumque uterque, / Mi Cato, Columella, Varro, Livi, / Salve, me quoque Plaute, tu Terenti, / Et tu salve, Ovidi, Fabi, Properti." Cited in Henri Meylan, "La Conversion de Bèze, ou les longues hésitations d'un humaniste chrétien," in *D'Erasme à Théodore de Bèze* (Geneva: Librairie Droz, 1976), 151.

[4] Jacques Peletier, *Ortografe*, cited in Natalie Davis, "Peletier & Beza Part Company," *Studies in the Renaissance* XI (1964): 193.

Beza's future plans. Bed-ridden with a serious illness, the young poet contemplated how literary aspirations and a clandestine marriage had distracted him from weightier spiritual matters. Thus, in October of that year, the young humanist renounced his benefices and the Catholic religion, and with his wife fled to Protestant Geneva. In the preface to his tragedy *Abraham sacrifiant*, written two years later, Beza likened his decision to that of the patriarch Abraham: just as Abraham was willing to sacrifice his son Isaac in obedience to the divine command, so Beza had sacrificed his homeland, his family, and his literary ambitions for the sake of the evangelical faith. At the same time, Beza scolded his friends back in Paris: instead of indulging in the vain fantasies of classical learning, they should rather glorify God. It would be far better for humanists "to sing a psalm to God, than to write sonnets in the style of Petrarch."[5]

Was Beza's conversion to the Protestant religion, then, a decisive departure from his commitment to humanism? The question is of some importance, given the larger issues it raises regarding the relationship between the Renaissance and the Reformation, or humanism and Calvinism.[6] Beza's attitude toward humanism after his con-

---

[5] "... en lieu de s'amuser à ces malheureuses inventions ou imitations de fantaisies vaines et deshonnnestes, (si on en veult juger à la verité) regardassent plustost à magnifier la bonté de ce grand Dieu, duquel ils ont receu tant de graces, qu'à flatter leurs idoles, c'est à dire leurs seigneurs our leurs dames, qu'ils entretiennent en leurs vices, par leurs fictions et flatteries. A la verité il leur seroit mieux seant de chanter un cantique à Dieu, que de petrarquiser un Sonnet, et faire l'amoureux transy, digne d'avoir un chapperon à sonnettes: ou de contrefaire ces fureurs poëtiques à l'antique, pour distiller la gloire de ce monde, et immortaliser cestuy cy ou ceste là...." *Abraham sacrifiant*, ed. Keith Cameron, Kathleen Hall, Francis Higman (Geneva: Librairie Droz, 1967), 47-48. Beza says very much the same thing in his epistolary introduction to *Les Psaumes en vers français avec leurs mélodies*: "Seulement que le monde soit si bien advisé, qu'au lieu de chansons en partie vaines et frivoles, en partie sottes et lourdes, en partie sales et vilaines et par conséquent mauvaises et nuisibles, dont il a usé par ci devant, il s'accoustume ci-après à chanter ces divins et celestes cantiques avec le bon Roy David." Cited in Mario Richter, "A propos des 'Chrestiennes Méditations' de Théodore de Bèze. Essai de définition," in *La Méditation en prose à la Renaissance*, ed. Centre V. L. Saulnier (Paris: Presses de l'École Normale Supérieure, 1990), 62.

[6] The literature on these subjects is immense. I have particularly benefited from Quirinus Breen, "Humanism and the Reformation," in Jerald C. Brauer, ed., *The Impact of the Church Upon its Culture* (Chicago: University of Chicago Press, 1968); William Bouwsma, *John Calvin, A Sixteenth-Century Portrait* (Oxford: Oxford University Press, 1991); Robert Linder, "Calvinism and Humanism, The First Generation," *Church History* 44 (1975): 167-81; Lewis Spitz, "Humanism and the Reformation," in *Transition and Revolution, Problems and Issues of European Renaissance and Reformation History*, ed. Robert M. Kingdon (Minneapolis, MN: Burgess Publishing Co., 1974), 153-67; Lewis Spitz, *The Northern Renaissance* (Englewood Cliffs, NJ: Prentice-Hall, Inc., 1972).

version continues to be debated by historians of early-modern Europe. Natalie Davis has asserted, for example, that Beza's inner turmoil preceding his flight from Paris was "whether to be a humanist or a Reformer."[7] Mario Richter has drawn a similar conclusion, noting that after his conversion, Beza became sharply critical of pagan poetry that celebrated human reason and was conceived for aesthetic pleasure rather than for spiritual edification. Richter notes a radical contrast "between the attitude of a humanist" like Ronsard, and "that of a reformer" like Beza.[8] Other scholars, however, disagree. Paul Geisendorf has noted Beza's substantial role in the development of the Genevan Academy, an institution with a distinctly humanistic curriculum. Concludes Geisendorf: "More than a theologian ... Beza is in fact a humanist."[9] Robert Linder agrees with this assessment. Examining the reformer's method, rhetorical style, and attitude toward the classical languages and pagan authors, he concludes that Beza at mid-life may well be called a "Christian humanist." Linder admits, however, that Beza apparently became more critical of humanism during the final years of his life, a consequence of the "hardening of his theological arteries."[10] Kirk Summers, in a recent study of Beza's use of the Greek and Latin authors, shares Linder's conclusion: following his Protestant conversion Theodore Beza remained a "Christian classical humanist."[11]

This brief survey of scholarly opinion suggests a general weakness of research on Beza's relation to humanism: historians have largely ignored the last three decades of the reformer's life, drawing instead

---

[7] Davis, "Peletier and Beza Part Company," 194.

[8] "Appelant Bèze au combat, Ronsard était donc parfaitement conscient qu'il s'adressait à un homme qui avait composé des oeuvres cohérentes, des modèles admirés d'une poétique conçue pour le salut et non pour le plaisir esthétique.... Nous nous trouvons là en présence de l'opposition radicale entre l'attitude d'un humaniste et celle d'un réformateur." Richter, "A propos des 'Chrestiennes Méditations,'" 62.

[9] "Plus qu'un théologien et tout autant qu'un politique, Bèze est en effect un humaniste." *Théodore de Bèze* (Geneva: Labor et Fides, 1949), 261. Beza's oration at the founding of the Genevan Academy (1559) has been held up as a model of humanist eloquence, richly ornamented with statements from classical authors and filled with the praises of humane studies. For an English translation of the *Oratio Bezae in solenni actu inaurationis academiae Genevensis*, see Lewis Spitz's "Humanism and the Reformation," 176-79.

[10] Linder, "Calvinism and Humanism," 173.

[11] Summers, "Theodore Beza's Classical Library and Christian Humanism," *Archiv für Reformationsgeschichte* 82 (1991): 193-207.

broad generalizations from a handful of texts and letters written shortly after Beza's religious conversion in 1548.[12] This lacuna is troubling given that more than one-half of Beza's literary corpus and nearly two thousand extant letters date from *after* 1572. This article will correct this imbalance by outlining Beza's attitude toward humanistic studies between 1572 and his death in 1605. Specifically, I will gauge the reformer's commitment to the cultural and educational program of Renaissance humanism — the *studia humanitatis* —, paying particular attention to Beza's published writings and unpublished correspondence during the last three decades of his life.

What, then, do we mean by the *studia humanitatis* and how did the "old" Theodore Beza view them? Paul Oskar Kristeller has shown that the *studia humanitatis* comprised a "cultural and educational program" in which a cycle of scholarly disciplines — including grammar, rhetoric, history, poetry, and moral philosophy — was taught through the use of classical Latin and Greek literature.[13] By encouraging the collection, translation, and careful analysis of ancient texts, this educational program held up classical antiquity as the standard for learning and the model for culture. The goal of this program of study in Quattrocento Italy was to train young men of the ruling elite to make wise moral choices and to speak and write persuasively. Although not conceived as a philosophy *per se*, the *studia humanitatis* did have certain philosophical implications: the humanistic curriculum presupposed the value of responsible participation in the political community; so too, in teaching young men to make wise practical decisions on the basis of probability, humanism constituted a significant departure from the pursuit of metaphysical certitude championed by medieval Aristotelian philosophy. Thus, the *studia humanitatis* was more concerned to train young men to live and govern well than to impart knowledge of religious or scientific truth.[14] In northern lands, a distinctive "Christian humanism" flourished which sought to reform the ills of church and society by the critical study of classical literature — including the scriptures and the books of Christian antiquity — in their original languages. Christian humanists such as Erasmus envisioned that the recovery of the writings and wisdom of

---

[12] Richter's study of Beza's *Chrestiennes meditations* (1582) is a notable exception.

[13] Paul Oskar Kristeller, *Renaissance Thought, The Classic, Scholastic and Humanist Strains* (New York: Harper and Row, 1961), 9-10.

[14] Charles Nauert, *Humanism and the Culture of Renaissance Europe* (Cambridge: Cambridge University Press, 1998), 14-19.

classical antiquity and the early Christian Church would produce a
more just and peaceful society in Europe and would foster inward
spirituality and genuine religious devotion.[15] Like their Italian counterparts, therefore, the Christian humanists of the north believed that
the ultimate goal of the *studia humanitatis* was as much the formation
of the soul as the training of the rational faculties.

To the end of his life, Beza remained committed to the *studia
humanitatis* and retained great admiration for the scholars who championed Christian humanism. As with Luther and Calvin before him,
he believed that the recovery of the knowledge of the biblical languages in the sixteenth century was a divine gift that was dispelling
the darkness of medieval superstition and spreading the light of the
Gospel throughout Europe.[16] The return *ad fontes* — to early manuscripts of the scriptures as well as to the books of classical pagan and
Christian authors — was a necessary precondition for spiritual
reform and renewal. The close connection that Beza perceived
between the classical languages, the *studia humanitatis*, and the advent
of religious reformation is seen most clearly in his book *Icones*.[17] Pub-

---

[15] See Nauert's helpful survey of the character and progress of 'Christian humanism' in northern Europe, in *Humanism and the Culture of Renaissance Europe*, 95-123. In
the dedicatory epistle of his *Novum Instrumentum* (1516), Erasmus stated several of the
Christian humanists' central beliefs: "For one thing I found crystal clear: our chiefest
hope for the restoration and rebuilding of the Christian religion ... is that all those
who profess the Christian philosophy the whole world over should above all absorb
the principles laid down by their Founder from the writings of the evangelists and
apostles, in which that heavenly Word which once came down to us from the heart
of the Father still lives and breathes for us and acts and speaks with more immediate
efficacy, in my opinion, than in any other way. Besides which I perceived that that
teaching which is our salvation was to be had in a much purer and more lively form
if sought at the fountain-head and drawn from the actual sources than from pools
and runnels. And so I have revised the whole New Testament (as they call it) against
the standard of the Greek original...." Cited in Cornelis Augustijn, *Erasmus, His Life,
Works, and Influence* (Toronto: Toronto University Press, 1991), 89.

[16] In the letter preface of his *Psalmorum Davidis et aliorum prophetarum, libri quinque*
(Geneva, 1579), Beza writes: "Immensum est igitur illud Dei Opt. Maxi. beneficium
nostris temporibus in Ecclesiam Dei collatum, quod restituta sit Hebraei sermonis
cognitio, & quasi coelitus rursum in Ecclesiam effusum linguarum trium donum, ex
quibus fontibus hauriri sacra, & puri rivuli in omnes regiones diduci possint" (*3).
Note also Beza's comments in his *Sermons sur l'histoire de la resurrection de nostre Seigneur
Iésus Christ* (Geneva, 1593): "... à grand peine y a-il quatre vingts ans, qu'il a pleu à
nostre Dieu de renvoyer comme du ciel le dons des langues, & susciter avec l'art de
l'impression, tant plusieurs Princes que quelques excellens personnages, par le
moyen desquels ces horribles ruines ont esté peu à peu, & sont encores, redressée, &
ceste lumiere a commencé de reluire, voire avec tresgrande splendeur" (416).

[17] Originally appearing under the title *Icones, id est verae imagines virorum doctrina*

lished in 1580, this work contained a brief biographical sketch, a portrait, and an epitaph honoring more than forty (deceased) churchmen, martyrs, princes, and princesses who had been sympathetic to the cause of "true religion" in Europe. The *Icones* called special attention to French and German humanists such as Guillaume Budé, Jacques Lefèvre d'Etaples, Robert Estienne, Julius Caesar Scaliger, Joachim Camerarius, Melchior Wolmar, Johannes Reuchlin, Beatus Rhenanus, Ulrich von Hutten, and Conrad Gestner who had mastered the biblical languages and promoted ancient learning, and by doing so, dissipated the shadows of religious ignorance and superstition.[18] In addition, the *Icones* praised Protestant reformers for their facility with the biblical languages and their knowledge of classical literature: Wolfgang Capito, Sebastian Munster, Emmanuel Tremellius, and Conrad Pellican were well-versed in Hebrew; Peter Martyr Vermigli was a *homotrilinguis* who from childhood had been eager to study humane letters; Abraham Musculus wrote erudite commentaries on the scriptures and classical Greek authors; Leo Jud executed learned translations of the sacred text. To this constellation of religious "heroes" Beza even added the names of Erasmus and the French king Francis I. Although Erasmus had clung to Catholic tradition and rejected true religion, Beza chose to honor him because "he more than anyone else is responsible for the revival of the humane letters (*bonnes lettres*)" in sixteenth century Europe.[19] Similarly, even though Francis I had been "an enemy of pure doctrine,"

---

simul et pietate illustrium (Geneva, 1580), this work was translated by Simon Goulart and republished the following year under the title *Les vrais portraits des hommes illustrés*. I am relying on a modern reproduction of this French edition (Geneva: Slatkine Reprints, 1986).

[18] In his sketch of Beatus Rhenanus, for example, Beza comments: "Mais au reste, tous ceux qui aiment les bonnes lettres doivent beaucoup à ce personnage, qui d'un adresse & diligence notable a si bien descouvert l'antiquité, qu'il faut confesser que c'est un des premiers qui a remarqué beaucoup de choses non entendues au paravant: & qui ouvrant le chemin enveloppé d'espaisses tenebres au paravant, a monstré l'entrée pour parvenir à la conoissance du reste, par lui non assez bien entendu. Nous avons pour tesmoins de cela ses trois livres de l'estat des afaires d'Alemagne, ses doctes annnotations & observations sur Tertullian, Cornelius Tacitus, Pline, Tite Live, Seneque & Velleius Paterculus." *Icones*, 72.

[19] Beza writes of Erasmus: "... quand il a esté question de Religion, il s'est contenté de taxer & brocarder les superstitions, & refusant de profiter en la connoissance du principal, encor qu'il eust assez de iugement pour y attaindre, & de moyen par les doctes qui vivoyent de son temps, au lieu d'y penser à bon escient il se rendit advocat d'une tresmauvaise cause. Toutesfois puis que les bonnes lettres à leur retour au monde lui sont autant redeuables qu'à autre quelconque d'alors, ie suis content de lui donner place en cest endroit, & la louange que s'ensuit." *Icones*, 25.

Beza nevertheless praised him for "restoring to a position of honor the Hebrew, Greek, and Latin languages as well as humane studies (*bonnes sciences*)." Thanks to the patronage of this Catholic king, humanistic studies had served as "the doorkeepers to the temple of the true religion, which has chased away the ignorance that was preventing the truth from progressing."[20]

Beza's literary corpus during the final decades of his life bears further witness to his abiding love for classical philology and commitment to the humanistic educational program. His private correspondence was regularly adorned with Greek phrases and allusions from classical literature. He took an active interest in the pronunciation of ancient Hebrew as well as sixteenth-century French.[21] He delighted in writing Latin poems, and took strong exception to criticisms of their style or meter.[22] In 1579, he completed a new Latin translation of the Psalter with a brief commentary prefixed to each psalm.[23] In the years that followed, Beza devoted himself to the study of the Hebrew language in his translation of the Song of Songs in Latin verse (1584), his sermon series on the books Song of Songs (1586) and Ecclesiastes (1588), and his commentary on the book of Job (1589).[24] Perhaps the reformer's enthusiasm for the Hebrew tongue is most evident in a project that was apparently never executed. In his seventy-ninth year, Beza requested a wealthy patron to underwrite the cost of publishing an ancient copy of the Pentateuch in Hebrew, with parallel translations in Greek, Persian, Arabic, and Spanish. Beza noted:

---

[20] "Ne sois marri, ô Roy trespuissant ... de ce que tu es, & non plustost, mis en ce livre, dedié seulement à ceux ausquels tu as esté tant contraire en ta vie: & toy, lecteur chrestien, ne te fasche point de voir ici cest adversaire de la pure doctrine. Certainement il m'a semblé que ie ne devois laisser en arriere ce Prince, ci qui a remises en honneur les langues Hebraique, Grecque[,] Latine, & les bonnes sciences, pour estre les portieres du temple de la vraye Religion, & qui a chassé l'ignorance laquelle empeschoit la verité de venir en avant." Beza, *Icones*, 133.

[21] For Beza's comments on the correct pronunciation of Hebrew, see his letter to Johann Piscator, 8/18 March 1586, published in Cyprian, *Catologus Codicum Manuscriptorum Bibliothecae Gothanae* (Leipzig, 1714), 44-45. Likewise, in 1584, Beza published *De francicae linguae recta pronuntiatione* (Geneva, 1584).

[22] In 1586, for example, Beza wrote an impassioned defense of his translation in trochaic verse of the Song of Solomon against the Hebraicist Gilbert Genebrard who preferred an iambic meter. See *Ad Gilberti Genebrardi accusationem...* (Geneva, 1586).

[23] *Psalmorum sacrorum libri quinque, vario carminum genere Latine expressi, & argumentis atque paraphrasi illustrati* (Geneva, 1580). This work went through five Latin editions and one French edition during the next decade.

[24] For bibliographical information on these works, see Frédéric Gardy, *Bibliographie des Oeuvres Théologiques, Littéraires, Historiques et Juridiques de Théodore de Bèze* (Geneva: Librairie Droz, 1960).

"The Lord has truly equipped us with strength to produce this book ... so that God's law might always remain in Israel."[25]

But Beza's lifelong commitment to the classical languages and the humanistic educational program is most evident in his *Annotationes* of the New Testament.[26] First published in 1556, the *Annotationes* went through three major revisions after 1580. Each of these revisions contained in three columns the Greek text, Beza's Latin translation of the Greek text, and Jerome's Vulgate text. At the bottom of each page, Beza added copious exegetical and theological notes, which defended reformed doctrine and debated points of grammar and syntax with biblical scholarship ancient and modern. Here we see clearly Beza's immense debt to Christian humanism. Verse by verse, Beza consulted — and regularly praised, criticized, or corrected — Erasmus's biblical annotations, Greek New Testament, and Latin translation.[27] The reformer also drew extensively from the Targum studies of John Mercier (*doctissimus vir sanctae memoriae*), the commentaries of Guillaume Budé (*Budaeus ille Graecae linguae doctissimus*), the linguistic insights of Emmanuel Tremellius (*doctissimus Hebraeus Emanuelus Tremelius beatae memoriae*), the critical editions of Robert Estienne (*noster Stephanus*), the numismatic studies of Joachim Camerarius (*doctissimus Camerarius*), and the chronological research of Joseph Scaliger (*amicissimus meus*).[28] Though of secondary importance, Beza also consulted the work of the humanists Lefèvre d'Etaples and Lorenzo Valla, as well as the Hebrew scholar David Kimhi.

The *Annotationes* provides ample evidence of Beza's prodigious knowledge of classical and Christian antiquity. The list of pagan Roman and Greek authors who find a place in the notes is impressive:

---

[25] "Dominus vero accinscit nos robore ad excudendum hunc librum, et purificavit nos ad imprimendos multos libros, ut lex resideat penes Israelem." Beza to Wenceslas Morkowsky of Zastrisell, 10/20 July 1598, Paris, Bibliothèque Ste. Geneviève, ms. 1455, fol. 287v-88.

[26] I have consulted the 1594 edition of the *Annotationes*, entitled *Theodori Bezae annotationes maiores in Novum dn. nostri Iesu Christi Testamentum* (n.p., 1594). This work stands more in the tradition of the philological annotations of Erasmus than in the commentary tradition of John Calvin. Hence, Beza comments: "Caterum etsi neque mei est propositi commentaria scribere, neque libens quenquam reprehendo, in hoc praesertim scribendi genere, in quo non dubito quin ipse in varias reprehensiones incurram; tamen monendum esse putavi lectorem, ut quaedam ab Erasmo scripta in hunc locum de iureiurando..." *Annotationes*, I, 36b-37a.

[27] For a survey of Erasmus's immense contribution to sixteenth-century biblical scholarship, see Augustijn, *Erasmus*, 89-106.

[28] Beza, *Annotationes*, I, 44b, 79a, 144a, 131b, 90b, 144a.

the poets Homer, Virgil, Catullus, Ovid, Horace, and Lucan; the philosophers Plato, Aristotle, and Seneca; the dramatists Euripides, Sophocles, Aristophanes, Terence, and Plautus; the orators Demosthenes, Cicero, and Quintilian; the historians Xenophon, Herodotus, Plutarch, Livy, Suetonius, Pliny the Younger, Sallust, and Tacitus. Of these authors, Cicero, Homer, and Virgil are named most frequently.[29] In his annotations on the Gospel of Matthew alone, Beza cites no fewer than fifteen different Ciceronian orations. Although Beza's knowledge of these classical authors is sometimes derivative, gleaned from the writings of contemporary humanists such as Erasmus, Budé, or Camerarius, most of his citations appear to be drawn directly from the original works themselves.[30] In addition to these pagan authors, the *Annotationes* makes frequent reference to early Christian writers such as Tertullian, Jerome, Chrysostom, Cyprian, Augustine, Origen, Justin Martyr, and Eusebius. Of these churchmen, Beza appears to place particular confidence in Tertullian and Augustine.

What function do these classical authorities serve in the *Annotationes*? First, Beza cites the ancient authors most frequently in order to clarify the meaning of Greek and Latin words or to explain ancient customs. For example, he looks to the writings of Cicero to define the words *fidem* and θυμὸν and approves of Plato's conclusion that magi were wise men from Persia.[31] In a similar fashion, he consults passages in Homer, Virgil, Herodotus, and the Talmud to explain the symbolic act of the Jewish high priest tearing his clothes during Jesus' trial (Matthew 26:65).[32] Second, in his *Annotationes*, Beza marshals the authority of classical authors to correct interpretations or doctrines that he deems erroneous. Thus, after criticizing non-Christian

---

[29] In his annotations on the Gospel of Matthew alone, Beza appeals to Cicero more than 50 times, Homer more than 25 times, and Virgil more than 20 times. The names of Herodotus, Pliny, Demosthenes, Aristotle, and Terence appear at least 10 times each.

[30] Thus, for example, Beza notes: "Fuisse vero hanc assentiendi formulam apud Graecos etiam usurpatam docet D. Camerarius, prolatis ex Euripide & Xenophonte exemplis." *Annotationes*, I, 149b. Beza had access to the writings of almost all of the classical authors listed above through the holdings of the library of the Genevan Academy. See Alexandre Ganoczy, *La Bibliothèque de l'Académie de Calvin. Le Catalogue de 1572 et ses Enseignements* (Geneva: Librairie Droz, 1969), 118-33.

[31] *Annotationes*, I, 129b, 14b-15a, 9b. Regarding Cicero, Beza writes: "Fidem, τὼν πίστιν, id est, dictorum & conventorum constantiam ac veritatem, ut recte definit Cicero: quod explicandum putavi ad vitandam homonymiam." Again, "Cicero θυμὸν excandescentiam interpretatur, quem sequuti sumus."

[32] *Annotationes*, I, 150a.

philosophers of antiquity, Beza affixes a passage from Cicero's *De natura deorum* in which the Roman orator himself condemned the superstition of the ancient philosophers.[33] Likewise, the reformer regularly solicits the opinions of early Church fathers such as Tertullian, Augustine, Jerome, and Chrysostom to demonstrate the 'errors' of his Catholic opponents. Third, less frequently Beza cites ancient authors in order to refute their beliefs or teachings. He judges as 'crazy' Plato's defense of communism and condemns the 'hallucinations' of Origen who "shamefully profanes the chief tenets of our religion."[34] Even Augustine is criticized from time to time for faulty exegesis or careless argumentation.[35] Finally, it is clear that Beza regularly amasses classical authorities and cites pithy maxims and quotations in order to ornament his annotations. In a discussion of pagan feasts and sacrifices (1 Corinthians 10), for example, Beza quotes from eight lines of Virgil's *Aeneid* and notes that the Latin poet has described the matter "beautifully."[36] In the *Annotationes*, the texts of classical antiquity are not only a resource for philological study or an arsenal for theological debate; they also serve to "garnish" and "decorate" the work, making it aesthetically pleasing and persuasive. Wedding exegesis with eloquence, biblical study with classical scholarship, the *Annotationes* reflect Beza's commitment to the program of Christian humanism.

Having said this, however, an important qualification must be made: whereas Beza looked to classical Greek and Latin texts as models of eloquence and sources for practical knowledge, he nonetheless did not invest them with moral authority. In his *Sermons sur l'histoire de la passion* (1592), Beza put the matter bluntly: We cannot expect to discover true religion or divine wisdom from the classical authors. Plato, for example, foolishly claimed that animals have immortal souls, and Aristotle rejected the doctrines of creation and providence. Although "some traces of supernatural wisdom may be found in the ancients," it is invariably "mixed with an infinite amount of mud and mire."[37] Beza echoed these criticisms in his

---

[33] *Annotationes*, II, 19a-b.

[34] "Sed hic quoque hallucinatum esse Origenem nemo mirabitur, qui ipsius in Epistolam ad Romanos commenta legerit, quibus praecipuum religionis nostrae caput vir ille foedissime profanavit." *Annotationes*, I, 113a. The reference to *Platonis delirium* is found at ibid., I, 463a.

[35] See, for example, *Annotationes*, I, 11a, 42b-43a.

[36] *Annotationes*, II, 208b.

[37] "Tels sont ceux-là qui veulent apprendre de Platon, ou d'Aristote la religion, en

Commentary on Job: "there are more substantial and certain guidelines for a godly and righteous life" found in Job 31 alone, Beza believed, "than in all the books of the Philosophers or Historians."[38] The Genevan reformer was equally critical of the moral vices of Cato and Cicero; even the civic virtues that they promoted "can be considered no better than sins, because the Holy Spirit declares that any deed not done in faith is sin."[39] Cicero himself was in fundamental error in his opinions about human nature, the origins of evil, and the nature of the good life.[40] Thus, whereas the classical Greek and Latin authors could teach an eager student how to speak well, reason carefully, and rule wisely, they were unreliable guides to spiritual enlightenment.

Despite these criticisms, the old Beza did not altogether renounce the *studia humanitatis* in practice. At the Genevan Academy, he remained a staunch advocate of studying the classical languages and

---

quoy ils se trompent doublement.... Car ces grands philosophes sont devenus vain en leurs discours, & se disans estre sages sont devenus fols. Et qu'ainsi soit, si nous croyons Aristote, ce monde n'aura iamais esté creé, & la providence de Dieu ne s'estend point aux choses particulieres. Si nous croyons Platon, les ames des bestes seront par mesmes arguments aussi bien immortelles, que celles hommes, & passeront, de corps en corps.... Bien est-il vray qu'en quelques bien anciens il se trouve quelques traces de la sapience supernaturelle, & qui sont comme les restes de la doctrine des anciens Patriarches. Mais ce qu'il y a de pur en cela, se trouve meslé d'une infinité de fange, & de bourbe." *Sermons sur l'histoire de la passion et sepulture de nostre Seigneur Iésus Christ.* (Geneva, 1592), 324-25. Note also Beza's comment in *Sermons sur l'histoire de la resurrection*: They are "fols & insensés qui cerchent une Theologie en un Platon & en un Aristote, & en general es discours de leurs foles cervelles, soit en tout, soit en partie" (358).

[38] "Hoc enim vere mihi liceat affirmare, Christiane lector, plura hoc uno capite comprehendi pie & vere iuste vita praecepta ... non in nuda contemplatione, sed certissimo exemplo & usu confirmata proponi, quam in ullis vel Philosophorum vel historicorum libris extent." Beza, *Iobus Theodori Bezae partim commentariis partim paraphrasi illustratus* (Geneva, 1579), 195.

[39] "Sic Catones ebriosissimi fuerunt, & maximi foeneratores, quorum etiam unus uxorem suam locat, alius vero vel prorsus furiosus vel magnanimitatis gloriam affectans moritur αὐτόχειρ. Sic magnae fuerunt Ciceronis virtutes, sed quid illo per universam vitam vanius & ambitiosius? Pro patria sese devoverunt Decii. Esto, ut ambitiose istud non fecerint, sed amore patrae: mens tamen illorum ultra patriae amorem non est progressa. At id demum recte diligitur, quod propter Deum diligitur. Sed nolo in istis peculiaribus exemplis diutius immorari. Illud autem omnino fatendum est peccara fuisse illa omnia, quum quicquid ex fide non sit peccatum esse pronuntiet Spiritus Sanctus, non tamen, ut quae directe contra legem naturae & honestatem fiunt." Beza, *Iobus*, 12-13.

[40] See Beza's epistolary preface to *Solomonis concio ad populum habita, de vita sic instituenda, ut ad veram aeternamque felicitatem perveniatur: Theodori Bezae paraphrasi illustrata* (Geneva, 1588) where he debates Cicero at length on foundational questions of Christian anthropology.

reading the ancient authors.[41] The reformer was instrumental in drawing to the academy several of Europe's top philologists: most notably, Joseph Scaliger (the son of Julius Caesar Scaliger), Matthew Beroald, Cornelius Bertram, and Isaac Casaubon. Nonetheless, Beza insisted, the study of classical philology must not be divested from Christian spiritual formation. From the pulpit in Geneva, Beza cajoled his congregation in the early 1590s: "You students, whether old or young, never separate your studies and the humane letters from the true knowledge of salvation.... And you fathers and mothers, be very careful and diligent to teach your children their catechisms as much as their humane letters..."[42] Likewise, Beza insisted, ministers of the Gospel should be trained in the *studia humanitatis*. But, if one had to choose between a humanistic education and Christian piety, there was little doubt as to which was more important: better to have an unlearned but godly pastor, than a wicked minister who was well-versed in the classics.[43] Clearly, in Beza's mind, a classical education — and knowledge of the ancient languages—did not necessarily assure moral virtue.

In addition, during the final fifteen years of his life, Beza grew increasingly critical of some of the books in the humanists' canon — books which, whether ancient or modern, were held up as models of rhetorical and stylistic excellence. From his pulpit in the early 1590s, the reformer sadly noted that many youth were exposed to terrible

---

[41] For a discussion of the liberal arts curricula at the Genevan Academy during the second-half of the sixteenth century, see Charles Borgeaud, *Histoire de l'Université de Genève*, vol. 1 (Geneva: Georg & Co., 1900), 42-47, 175-220; Karin Maag, *Seminary or University? The Genevan Academy and Reformed Higher Education, 1560-1620* (Brookfield, VT: Scolar Press, 1995), 35-102; Marvin Anderson, "Theodore Beza: Savant or Scholastic," *Theologische Zeitschrift* 43 (1987): 320-32; and Pierre Fraenkel, "De l'Écriture à la Dispute. Le cas de l'Académie de Genève sous Théodore de Bèze," in *Cahiers de la Revue de Théologie et de Philosophie* (Lausanne: Revue de Théologie et de Philosophie, 1977).

[42] "Et vous escoliers grands & petis, ne separez iamais vos estudes & bonnes lettres, d'avec la vraye science de salut.... Et vous peres & meres soyez autrement soigneux & diligens de faire instruire vos enfans, tant es bonnes lettres (veu qu'il ne vous couste rien que de les envoyer au college) que sur tout es Catechismes." *Sermons sur l'histoire de la resurrection*, 418.

[43] "Combien donc que tant qu'il est possible on doive eslire personnages qui ayent cognoisance des bonnes letres avec la pieté: si est ce que la pieté avec le zele & saincte simplicité doivent aller devant: & tel manie un instrument de quelque estat mechanique, qui est toutesfois plus digne de manier le glaive de la parole de Dieu, que ceux la mesmes qui auront estudié toute leur vie: comme l'evenement le monstre, quand il plaist à Dieu." *Response aux cinq premieres et principales demandes de F. Jean Haye, moine Jesuite aux ministres Escossois* (Geneva, 1586), 43.

obscenities by reading certain of the ancient Greek and Latin poets. Indeed, Beza complained, "most of the high schools and universities are no better than whore-houses" in that they train their students "to read and interpret such stinking writings."[44] The reformer voiced similar concerns in a published letter to Christians in the Low Countries in 1593. To preserve the legacy of the Reformation, magistrates should insure that young men are carefully taught the biblical languages. At the same time, the curricula at Dutch academies must be carefully supervised so that "the reading of so many scandalous and detestable books — whether ancient or modern — should be explicitly forbidden..." Though vulgar books have long been recommended reading on account of their antiquity, nonetheless they provoke the wrath of God and expose students to dangers no less real than "the most infected whorehouse."[45] Beza's arresting comparison of humanist colleges to brothels of promiscuous ideas suggests the ambivalence with which he viewed classical learning at the end of his life. While affirming the values of Christian humanism and promoting the *studia humanitatis* in principle, he nonetheless recognized the powerful — and potentially dangerous — enticements of classical literature. The eloquence and literary brilliance of scandalous authors (is Beza perhaps thinking of Aristophanes, Juvenal, and Martial?) could easily

---

[44] "Que dirons nous aussi de ces puantes cloaques de bouches, pleines de paroles pourries & infectes, qu'elles vomissent, & de ces plumes tant sales, & maquerelles de toute infection, de tant d'escrivans, & sur tout de ces vilains estalons de bourdeaux, polluans la saincte poesie, Grecs, Latins, François, & anciens & nouveaux de toutes nations, dont tout le monde est auiourd'huy infecté plus que iamais? & nous esbahissons-nous si des la tendre ieunesse les esprits sont infectés de telles ordures, tellement que la plus part des Colleges & Universités sont autant de bordeaux, voire de Sodomes & de Gomorrhes, estant la ieunesse instruite en la lecture & interpretation mesme de tels & si puans escrits?" *Sermons sur l'histoire de la passion*, 313-14.

[45] "... i'ai pensé ne pouvoir estre à bon droict repris plus que tresrecommandable soin que Vous avez de dresser des pepinieres, sur tout, comme ie presuppose, pour peupler la Cité de Dieu de ce qui y est le plus requis, il Vous plaise de donner ordre, voire bien exactement, que la Saincte langue, en premier lieu, y soit fidelement & diligemment enseignee: & secondement, que la lecture de tant de plus qu'infames & abominables livres anciens & nouveaux (desquels la terre mesme deust estre tenue pour polluee, & par la lecture desquels la ieunesse est introduite & eslevee comme en un bordeau le plus infect qui se puisse trouver) soit severement defendue, forclose, & bannie des estudes, qui doivent estre purs & sacrés à toute chasteté & pureté: estant vray que s'il y a chose au monde qui provoque l'ire de Dieu sur la Chrestienté, c'est le remuement trop infame de telles souillures, chose toutesfois non seulement par trop longe continuation tolerees, mais recerchee & prisee sous pretext d'apprendre ie ne say quelles antiquités, desquelles la memoire n'a que trop duré." Beza to the Christian States of the Provinces of Holland, Zeeland, etc., 1/11 January 1593. Letter-preface in *Sermons sur l'histoire de la resurrection*, ¶¶¶.vi.

infatuate and disarm unwary students, rendering them vulnerable to moral perversion. Hence, Beza insisted, the humane letters must be carefully scrutinized and sanitized; they are to be fully in the service of the cause of religious reform.

In light of jeremiads such as these, we may well be tempted to conclude that by the end of his life, Beza the "religious reformer" had almost entirely supplanted Beza the "Christian humanist." Such a conclusion would be inaccurate. As we have seen above, Beza's 1594 edition of the *Annotationes* reveal him to be a devotee of classical literature and the ancient languages. Likewise, his abiding love for poetry suggests that a strict dichotomy between "reformer" and "humanist" is unwarranted. By the 1580s, Beza had grown increasingly tired of theological debate and longed for more tranquil studies.[46] He regretted that he had so little time to write poetry.[47] Given his failing strength, he wished that he could devote himself more completely to the Psalms and to his annotations of the New Testament. He longed for an opportunity to engage in "a more peaceful genre of writing," to consider "Christian things" rather than "Aristotelian things."[48] For the "old" Beza, works of poetry and songs of praise to God had become far more satisfying than rational theological disputation. During the last decade of his life, Beza finally found some leisure to

---

[46] Beza writes to Bartholomew Chaericus: "Et fateor me nunc invitum ad hoc scribendi genus accedere [i.e. theological treatises]: quod nullum esse videam istiusmodi scriptionum finem, et in hac externa aetate mea, tranquillioribus studiis dedere meipsum percupiam: sic tamen, ut numquam, Deo favente, defensioni veritatis sim defuturus." 27 August/6 September 1584, Paris, Bibliothèque Ste. Geneviève, ms. 1455, fols. 31-33.

[47] Responding to a request to compose a French poem in honor of the Count of Würtemberg's vineyard, Beza notes with regret: "Sur quoy je vous prie de croire et assurer mondit Seigneur qu'à son retour il n'y a chose au monde à moi possible en quoy je ne prenne très grand plaisir de m'employer de très bon coeur quand il luy plaira m'honorer de ses commandements: mais en ce faict je suis si mal habile que j'auroy honte de présenter à son Excellence (à Wirtemberg) chose de ma façon en rime françoise, le pouvant assurer que jamais depuis le Psaumes je ne me suis addonné à rime françoise, et ne fis jamais sonnet. Et quant aux vers latins, combien que dès longtemps j'en aye entrepris l'exercice, toutes fois j'y pourroy bien peut-être faire quelque chose, mais vous ne me demandez point que vous en ayez à faire." Beza to Jean Bouhin, 26 July/5 August 1586, published in *Bulletin de la société de l'histoire du protestantisme français* 31 (1882): 61-62.

[48] "Nam haec etiam aetas ac valetudo mea postulant, ut vel istas scribendi partes aliis resignem, vel certe ad placidius aliquod scriptionis genus me totum convertam, unde consolationem maiorem capiam, περὶ τῆς ἀναλυσεως, non illa aristotelica, sed christiana cogitans. Itaque me superioribus mensibus in scribenda brevi psalmorum paraphrasi exercui...." Beza to André Dudith, 2 June 1579, Paris, Bibliothèque Ste. Geneviève, ms. 1456, fols. 247-49.

return to his beloved poetry. In 1595, he completed a collection of biblical songs — put into French rhyme — which had been commissioned by the French National Synod of Montauban the previous year.[49] Two years later he published a final edition of his *Poemata*.[50] Shorn of its youthful indiscretions, in this collection of poetry, epigrams, and epitaphs Beza celebrated the lives of Protestant "heroes" while delivering a scathing attack on the Catholic religion.[51] The imprint of a Christian humanist is clearly visible: here we find a translation of Virgil's account of Queen Dido's death (*Aeneid*, IV), poems commemorating the life of the Scottish humanist George Buchanan and the death of Beza's wife Claudine Denosse, epitaphs (in Latin, Greek, and Hebrew) honoring deceased Protestant reformers, and epigrams recounting the defeat of the Spanish Armada as well as recalling events from the lives of Emperor Charles V, King Francis I, King Henri III, and Queen Elizabeth of England.

Beza's delight in poetry is further witnessed in his private correspondence. The reformer frequently appended short Latin poems and epitaphs to his letters in order to honor friends or revile theological opponents.[52] Oftentimes tragedy wrenched from Beza short poems, which expressed sorrow and offered consolation. Thus, receiving word that the son of a close friend in Germany had died, Beza wrote a poignant letter in which he expressed his condolences and attached a poem: "I have been deeply touched by this very great sorrow you are experiencing and ... I am sending to you some verses in honor of your son. Although the Muses have not been favorable in

---

[49] The minutes of the National Synod of Montauban read: "Monsieur de Beze sera prié, au nom de la Compagnie, de traduire en Rime Françoise les Cantiques de la Bible, pour les chanter dans l'Eglise avec les Pseaumes." Jean Aymon, *Tous les Synodes Nationaux des Églises réformées de France* (The Hague, 1710), 185. Two years later, the National Synod of Saumur noted: "Il a été remis au prochain Synode National de resoudre, si le chant des Cantiques nouvellement mis en Rime par Mr. de Beze, sera introduit dans l'Eglise, surquoi les Provinces y viendront prêtes" (ibid., 200).

[50] This revision of the *Poemata* is a partial reproduction of the 1569 and 1588 editions of this work. The new materials added to this edition of the *Poemata* are described in Gardy, *Bibliographie*, 8-9.

[51] Because of its strong confessional orientation, Paul Geisendorf has concluded that "le Réformateur a définitivement supplanté le poète" in this 1597 edition. Geisendorf, *Théodore de Bèze*, 394-95. Nonetheless, as noted, the mark of the Christian humanist is still evident.

[52] See, for example, Beza to Johannes Glychius, 27 March/6 April 1590, Gotha, Forschungsbibliothek, ms. A 404, fol. 187; Beza to Paladius, 13/23 November, 1596, ibid., fols. 194-95; Beza to Daniel Fabivus, 13 October 1601, Paris, Bibliothèque Ste. Geneviève, ms. 1455, fols. 403-5.

inspiring this poem, nonetheless please accept this reminder of our mutual friendship."[53] Beza also wrote poetry to mark important personal milestones. On the occasion of his own seventy-seventh birthday, Beza penned these verses to a good friend:

> "A hen that I bought for a very small sum,
> Bore fifteen chicks before one month was done.
> But to you, kind Christ, what fruit have I given,
> During the seventy-seven years I have been living?
> ...
> Forgive me Lord, and to my humble prayer attend,
> That I may be your chick, and you to me a hen."[54]

The pleasure that Beza drew from writing poems is also evident in his correspondence with Catherine de Bourbon, sister of the French king Henri IV. In early 1596, Catherine sent several samples of her religious poetry to Beza, asking for his comments and support.[55] In his response, the Genevan reformer expressed delight that the poetic gift of Marguerite d'Angoulême had been resurrected in her grand daughter. After suggesting stylistic improvements, he concluded with these words of encouragement: "If you continue to write poetry, your soul will receive consolation from it, and it will lift you higher and more devoutly toward heaven than you could have imagined possible."[56] To the

---

[53] "Ut autem intelligas ista sic a me scribi ut tamen non mediocriter hoc tuo iustissimo dolore commovear, atque adeo communem in hoc casu iacturam totius Ecclesiae, ac praesertim Germaniae deplorem, mitto ad te versiculos quibus filio tuo parentavi. Quos, etsi non admodum faventibus Musis effusos, velim tamen ut tanquam certum mutuae nostrae coniunctionis μνημόσυνον accipias." 17/27 October 1587, Paris, Bibliothèque Ste. Geneviève, ms. 1455, fols. 590-91. Although employed as a poetic convention, Beza's reference to the Greek Muses (effectively pagan deities) provides additional evidence of the degree to which he has internalized humanistic style and thought.

[54] "Ter quinos Gallina mihi dedit unica pullos / Mesne uno, denis assibus empta prius. / Ast ego septenis decies, sexque insuper annis / Quos retuli fructus, Christe benigne tibi? / .... / Sed quorsum haec? unum hoc tribuas, peto, Christe, roganti: / Sis gallina mihi, sim tibi pullus ego!" Theodore Beza to Jean-Jacques Grynaeus, 24 June/4 July 1595, published in *Bulletin de la société de l'histoire du protestantisme français* 3 (1855), 146-47.

[55] Catherine de Bourbon to Beza, 26 January 1596, Geneva, ms. Tronchin, vol. 2, fol. 24. For samples of Catherine's poetry, see *Bulletin de la société de l'histoire du protestantisme français*, 2 (1854): 142-44.

[56] "Voilà, Madame, ce que j'ay pu observer en ceste vostre poésie, en l'exercice de laquelle si vous continuez, vostre esprit en recevra consolation, s'eslevant par manière de dire plus haut et plus dévotieusement vers le ciel par une telle manière d'escrire qui a cela de son naturel...." Beza to Catherine de Bourbon, [1596], Geneva, ms. Tronchin, vol. 5, fols. 305-7.

end of his life, Theodore Beza the religious reformer, remained a poet
— and a Christian humanist — at heart.

The disjunction commonly drawn between "humanist" and
'reformer' fails to capture adequately the complexity of Theodore
Beza. In Beza's *Annotationes* and private correspondence we find biblical quotations and classical allusions existing comfortably side by
side. The reformer delighted in composing poetry and citing Virgil,
yet was scandalized by the writings of several other ancient poets. If
sharply critical of Erasmus, the "prince" of the humanists, Beza
nonetheless drew extensively from his biblical scholarship and celebrated the genius and achievements of many other Christian humanists in Germany and France. Theodore Beza recognized the limitations and dangers of the humane letters. Though he believed that the
studia humanitatis were of real value in training the minds and tongues
of young men, he insisted that these studies be carefully supervised
lest they mislead and corrupt impressionable students. The impulse
ad fontes that had been instrumental in the recovery of the biblical languages and reforming the church could, if unchecked, become a
courtesan luring youth to her "whorehouse." Notwithstanding these
dangers, the reformer of Geneva remained committed to the central
convictions of Christian humanism: the rediscovery of the biblical
languages and the study of classical literature were instrumental in
religious reform. Although they were unable to teach young men
how to be virtuous or righteous, nonetheless the *studia humanitatis*
served an important role as "doorkeeper" to spiritual reformation.

LIFE, DEATH, AND RELIGION DURING THE THIRTY YEARS' WAR

Sigrun Haude*

"On 8 October [1632] there remained, oh destitution, only one little cow in Unteregg. Elisabeth Fröhlich von Rappen (Mindelheim) was shot at home by a cavalryman, the same with Johann Rauch; the very old Johann Bischleger died of the beatings and wounds inflicted by Swedes. Blind Johannes Korknicher was miserably bludgeoned to death with an axe or a rod. Widow Maria Elsler died of the fright and pain inflicted by cavalrymen. Widower Georg Micheler was first tortured many times by cavalrymen, then brutally stabbed to death by a musketeer. Michael Kiebeler was shot in the head at Eßmühle (Windesheim). In Rappen five of ten houses were burned down, in Willoss (Oberdorf) fourteen, in Rohr (Oberdorf) three. During the years 1634 and 1635, pestilence and starvation added to these horrors ..."[1]

Many personal accounts of the Thirty Years' War resemble these graphic descriptions by Stephan Mayer, minister in Unteregg, Bavaria. Mayer and his congregations were luckier than some because the war did not hit their region until 1632, but when it finally did come, the horrific impact made up for the earlier period of grace. Other territories situated in the corridor of troop movements were overrun time and again, while the war touched still other areas only once or twice. Nevertheless, although some regions saw more military action than others,[2] the war's by-products — forced contributions, quartering of soldiers, plundering, disease,

---

* Associate Professor of History, University of Cincinnati
[1] "Am 8. Oktober gab es, o Armuth, in Unteregg nur noch ein einziges Kühlein. Elisabeth Fröhlich von Rappen (Mindelheim) wurde daheim von einem Reiter erschossen, ebenso Johann Rauch; der greise Johann Bischleger starb an den von den Schweden empfangenen Schlägen und Wunden. Der blinde Johannes Korknicher wurde von einem Soldaten mit einer Axt oder Prügel erbärmlich totgeschlagen, Witwe Maria Elsler starb an den Folgen der von den Reitern verursachten Schrecken und Schmerzen. Witwer Georg Micheler dortselbst wurde zuerst von Reitern vielfach geplagt, sodann von einem Musketier mit einem Messer erbärmlich erstochen. Michael Kiebeler ward zu Eßmühle (Mindelheim) durch den Kopf geschoffen. In Rappen wurden von zehn Häuser fünf niedergebrannt, in Willoss (Oberdorf) vierzehn, in Rohr (Oberdorf) drei. Zu diesem Schrecken gesellte sich im Jahre 1634 und 35 noch Pest und Hungersnoth." M. Stephan Mayer, "Kurze Aufzeichnungen aus den Zeiten des Schwedenkrieges, 1625-45," *Deutsche Gaue* 11 (1910): 26-31, here 26-27.

inflation, starvation, and fear — affected the population much
more broadly. This article investigates how people in Germany
dealt with a war that lasted three decades, how they coped with
painful, repeated, sometimes catastrophic losses and everyday hardships.[3]

In the past, research has focused on the war's origins, phases,
major battles, and iridescent military leaders, such as Albrecht Wal-
lenstein and Gustavus Adolphus. The 350th anniversary of the
Peace of Westphalia produced further studies on Germany's distinctive constitutional history.[4] A few contributions pursued questions of
a different kind, concerning the *Alltagsgeschichte* and cultural history
of the war. In military history, the relatively new emphasis on everyday life has meant a much greater differentiation among the military
and a shift of focus from military leaders to soldiers and their experiences of the war.[5] In other areas, historians have begun investigating

---

[2] On how regions are differently affected by traumatic events, see Arthur E.
Imhof, *Die Verlorenen Welten. Alltagsbewältigung durch unsere Vorfahren – und weshalb wir uns
heute so schwer damit tun* (Munich: Beck, 1985), 100-101.

[3] On the Thirty Years' War in general, see Ronald G. Asch, *The Thirty Years'
War: The Holy Roman Empire and Europe, 1618-1648* (New York: St. Martin's Press,
1997); Günter Barudio, *Der Teutsche Krieg 1618-1648* (Frankfurt a. M.: Fischer,
1985); Johannes Burkhardt, *Der Dreißigjährige Krieg* (Frankfurt a. M.: Suhrkamp,
1992); Helmut Lahrkamp, *Dreißigjähriger Krieg – Westfälischer Frieden* (Münster:
Aschendorff, 1997); Herbert Langer, *Kulturgeschichte des 30jährigen Krieges* (Leipzig:
Kohlhammer, 1978); Geoffrey Parker (ed.), *The Thirty Years' War* (London: Rout-
ledge, 1987); Josef Polisenský, *Der Krieg und die Gesellschaft in Europa 1618-1648*
(Prague: Academia, 1971); Theodore Rabb (ed.), *The Thirty Years' War: Problems of
Motive, Extent and Effect* (Boston: Heath and Company, 1964); Konrad Repgen (ed.),
Krieg und Politik 1618-1648. Europäische Probleme und Perspektiven (Munich: Oldenbourg,
1988); Bernd Roeck, *Als wollt die Welt schier brechen. Eine Stadt im Zeitalter des
Dreißigjährigen Krieges* (Munich: Beck, 1991); Hans Ulrich Rudolf (ed.), *Der Dreis-
sigjährige Krieg. Perspektiven und Strukturen* (Darmstadt: Wissenschaftliche Buchge-
sellschaft, 1977); Georg Schmidt, *Der Dreissigjährige Krieg* (Munich: Beck, 1996); S. H.
Steinberg, *The Thirty Years' War and the Conflict for European Hegemony 1600-1660* (New
York: Norton & Company, 1966); C. V. Wedgwood, *The Thirty Years' War* (London:
Anchor Books, 1961). John C. Theibault, *German Villages in Crisis: Rural Life in Hesse-
Kassel and the Thirty Years' War, 1580-1720* (Atlantic Highlands: Humanities Press,
1995) is a good example of a local study.

[4] See, for example, Klaus Bussmann, Heinz Schilling (eds.), *1648: War and Peace in
Europe*, 3 vols. (Munich: Veranstaltungsgesellschaft 350 Jahre Westfälischer Friede,
1998).

[5] See, for example, Peter Burschel, *Söldner im Nordwestdeutschland des 16. und 17.
Jahrhunderts. Sozialgeschichtliche Studien* (Göttingen: Vandenhoeck & Ruprecht, 1994;
Bernhard R. Kroener, Ralf Pröve (eds.), *Krieg und Frieden. Militär und Gesellschaft in der
Frühen Neuzeit* (Munich: Ferdinand Schöningh, 1996); and Wolfram Wette (ed.), *Der
Krieg des kleinen Mannes. Eine Militärgeschichte von unten* (Munich: Piper, 1995).

how civilians managed during the war.[6]

The following analysis is part of a larger study on the cultural history of the Thirty Years' War. It uses published autobiographical accounts (*Selbstzeugnisse*) to find some initial answers as to how people lived through the war.[7] Broadly defined, *Selbstzeugnisse* include autobiographies, diaries, family chronicles *(Hausbücher)* and chronological records, church registers (*Kirchenbücher*), and recording calendars, i.e., calenders especially designed for short record keeping (*Schreibkalender*). In sum, they comprise, as James Amelang has noted, "any literary form that expresses lived experience from a first person point of view."[8] In the first half of the seventeenth century, the lines between the literary forms of autobiographies, diaries, and other chronological accounts were fluid.[9] Autobiographies, unlike their later counterparts, focused little on self-reflection or the construction of an individual personality. Rather than confidently arranging one's personal history from hindsight, these texts frequently merely listed events or experiences chronologically, without explanatory connections or transitions. With the adoption of such a *Reihungsstruktur*, seventeenth-century autobiographies were still indebted to the medieval recording tradition.[10]

---

[6] See, for example, Benigna von Krusenstjern, Hans Medick (eds.), *Zwischen Alltag und Katastrophe. Der Dreißigjährige Krieg aus der Nähe* (Göttingen: Vandenhoeck & Ruprecht, 1999).

[7] My research for this project profited greatly from the recent interest in autobiographical texts as a historical source, which produced, among other works, Benigna von Krusenstjern's valuable catalog of printed *Selbstzeugnisse der Zeit des Dreißigjährigen Krieges*, Selbstzeugnisse der Neuzeit, vol. 6 (Berlin: Akademie Verlag, 1997).

[8] James S. Amelang, "*Vox populi*: popular autobiographies as sources for early modern urban history," *Urban History* 20 (1993): 30-42, here 33. See also Kaspar von Greyerz's assessment of autobiographical sources (in this case autobiographies and diaries) in "Religion in the Life of German and Swiss Autobiographers (Sixteenth and Early Seventeenth Centuries)," in idem (ed.), *Religion and society in early modern Europe 1500-1800* (Winchester, Mass.: Allen & Unwin, 1984), 223-41. Winfried Schulze, following the Dutch scholars Jacob Presser and Rudolf Decker, prefers the term "Ego-Dokumente" to "Selbstzeugnisse." The argument is that "Ego-Dokumente" include both free and forced testimonies. Thus, tax records, interrogations, visitations, and court records can also be utilized as documents pointing toward the self. See his "Vorbemerkung" and his "Ego-Dokumente: Annäherung an den Menschen in der Geschichte?" in idem (ed.), *Ego-Dokumente: Annäherung an den Menschen in der Geschichte* (Berlin: Akademie Verlag, 1996), 9-30. I see no reason why the term "Selbstzeugnisse" cannot embrace the same range of documents.

[9] Kaspar von Greyerz, *Vorsehungsglaube und Kosmologie: Studien zu englischen Selbstzeugnissen des 17. Jahrhunderts* (Göttingen: Vandenhoeck & Ruprecht, 1990), 16.

[10] Ingrid Schiewek, "Zur Manifestation des Individuellen in der frühen deutschen Selbstdarstellung. Eine Studie zum Autobiographen Bartholomäus Sastrow (1520-1603)," *Weimarer Beiträge* 13 (1967): 885-915, here 893.

Often the autobiographer stepped back, while he or she recounted events of the day and other facets of life around him or her.[11] Early modern German autobiographies until the end of the seventeenth century, therefore, narrated personal facts in their external contexts.[12] Diaries were most often written out of the spontaneity of the moment, as were recording calenders; nevertheless, one does find instances where authors erased or added comments later.[13]

What might be a disadvantage for the literary scholar, who prefers texts to fit neatly into certain literary categories, becomes a window of opportunity for the historian. The Thirty Years' War produced a plethora of autobiographical accounts, most of which were variations on chronological records. The authors listed and observed, informed and commented, wailed and cheered; in short, these texts are a unique source on attitudes and behaviors during these three decades.

By the seventeenth century, diaries and family chronicles were no longer the sole domain of the upper classes, although popular autobiographies still accounted for only a small portion of the overall yield. Even so, as Benigna von Krusenstjern points out, these numbers are relative and need to be taken with caution.[14] For example, diaries of abbots and parish registers maintained by ministers, both benefiting from institutional protection, were much more likely to survive than the recording calendars of the lower classes.

Autobiographical texts, often viewed with suspicion by early modern historians because of their mixture of facts and interpretation, are immensely valuable for studying a society's culture since they reflect people's perceptions of events, their thoughts and opinions, and how they dealt with the experiences.[15] These works do not tell the whole

---

[11] See Stephan Pastenaci's pithy comment: "Die Lektüre frühneuhochdeutscher Autobiographien ist aufgrund der Heterogenität der Texte, oberflächlich betrachtet, gewiß kein Lesevergnügen. Intimes, Persönliches wechselt mit unpersönlichen Berichten aus der Ereignisgeschichte, es werden Anekdoten aus der Stadt, Biographien von anderen Persönlichkeiten breit ausgemalt. Private Briefe wechseln mit der ausführlichen Wiedergabe zeitgenössicher Dokumente. Es dominiert das Faktische vor der Reflektion." "Probleme der Edition und Kommentierung deutsch-sprachiger Autobiographien und Tagebücher der Frühen Neuzeit, dargestellt anhand dreier Beispiele," in Jochen Golz (ed.), *Edition von autobiographischen Schriften und Zeugnissen zur Biographie*, Beihefte zu Editio, vol. 7 (Tübingen: Niemeyer, 1995), 10-26, here 11.

[12] Amelang, "*Vox populi*," 33.

[13] Pastenaci, "Probleme der Edition," 20.

[14] Krusenstjern, *Selbstzeugnisse*, 11.

[15] See Keneth D. Barkin's assessment of the positive value of autobiographies for social and comparative history in "Autobiography and history," *Societas* 6 (1976): 83-108, here 86.

history of the Thirty Years' War; nonetheless, they reveal vital aspects of it. Eventually, they need to be read in conjunction with other documents produced during the war.[16]

This discussion focuses on the most widespread and enduring affliction of the war: the passage and quartering of soldiers and what it entailed — plundering, violence, starvation, the spread of disease, and dislocation. Accounts reveal patterns of behavior as well as individual and unique responses to these adversities. People encountered the war on a pragmatic and a psychological or ideological level. Modes of behavior, however, differed according to local situations.

Among the pragmatic steps taken to survive the rampage of war, flight constituted one of the most prominent choices. In the case of the passage and quartering of troops, this meant most often a temporary escape to a safer haven, until the danger passed, rather than permanent emigration.[17] Pastor Mayer in the Bavarian village Unteregg had to flee ten times from his parsonage. On one occasion imperial soldiers stripped him of his shoes and socks and, as he added with grim humor, "machten also aus einem Pfarrer einen Barfüßer" ("turned a minister into a barefooted monk").[18] Another time, Mayer was luckier and escaped the soldiers by hiding in the cesspool.[19]

To put walls between themselves and the plundering troops, many peasants fled to a nearby city.[20] One can imagine that staying in these more fortified places was only the lesser of two evils. Rarely were cities prepared to accommodate thousands of peasants complete with

---

[16] This is the goal of my larger project on the Thirty Years' War.

[17] Walter Kürschner, "Aus dem Kirchenbuch von Reichensachsen (und Langenhain) von 1639-1653," *Archiv für hessische Geschichte und Alterthumskunde* N.F. 9 (1913): 48-55, here 51 and 54; Hanna Kappus-Wulsow, "Trübe Jahre im Ried nach dem ältesten Kirchenbuch Altenheims," *Die Ortenau* 14 (1927): 140-54; "Rudimenta Chronologiae Imp. Civ. Friedbergensis in Wetteravia. Das ist Anfang und kurzer Begriff zu einer Chronik der kais. Freien Reichsstadt Friedberg i. d. W.," *Chroniken von Friedberg* 1 (1937): 90-143, here 126.

[18] Mayer, "Kurze Aufzeichnungen," 29.

[19] Ibid., 30.

[20] Johann Morhard, *Haller Haus-Chronik* (Schwäbisch Hall: Eppinger Verlag, 1962), 133; Kürschner, "Aus dem Kirchenbuch von Reichensachsen," 52-53; "Aus der Chronik von Colmar," *Jahrbücher für die Landeskunde der Herzogthümer Schleswig, Holstein und Lauenburg* 2 (1859): 268-75, here 272; Elisabeth Erdmann, "Der Dreißigjährige Krieg im Spiegel der Tagebücher des Thomas Mallinger. Handlungsweisen der Bevölkerung," *Zeitschrift für die Geschichte des Oberrheins* 143/N. F. 4 (1995): 515-27, here 523; Gerd Zillhardt, *Der Dreißigjährige Krieg in zeitgenössischer Darstellung: Hans Heberles 'Zeytregister' (1618-1672). Aufzeichnungen aus dem Ulmer Territorium* (Ulm: Kommissionsverlag Kohlhammer, 1975); "Rudimenta Chronologiae Imp. Civ. Friedbergensis," 128.

their beds, precious belongings, and whatever farm animals they could salvage. Some refugees were able to rent a room in a burgher's house, but the rest had to contend with the streets. Others took refuge in neighboring castles or abbeys.[21] These were so cramped, particularly during the winter season, that people could find standing room only.[22]

The almost inevitable result of the invasions from the countryside was price increase, hunger, and pestilence.[23] Ulm, a city particularly hard hit by the passage of troops since it lay strategically at the point of departure to upper Swabia, tried to keep abreast of such developments by admonishing the refugees to cleanliness and to caution when using fire.[24] But eventually the heavy influx of desperate people subjected Ulm to the same consequences of overpopulation. Hans Heberle, shoemaker in a village near Ulm, kept a *Zeytregister* in which he recorded a total of twenty-eight flights into Ulm over a period of eighteen years (1631-1648). During his third flight he noted: "There is distress and misery, starvation and death. There we lay on top of each other in great wretchedness. Then price increase and hunger broke in on us, after these the evil disease, pestilence. Many hundreds of people died during this year, 1634."[25] Heberle lost his second son as well as three of his sisters and a brother on this flight.

When pestilence struck, it was difficult to maintain the traditional ceremonies and rituals. The large number of fatalities in 1635 prompted Ulm's council to mandate that those who died of disease would not receive a funeral sermon.[26] When in 1629 the epidemic hit Hamburg, which housed thousands of additional people from the countryside, Pastor Marcus Frisius of the nearby village Colmar related that a number of clergy had been "honorably and well

---

[21] Zillhardt, *Der Dreißigjährige Krieg*, 158; Maurus Friesenegger, *Tagebuch aus dem 30jährigen Krieg*, edited by P. W. Mathäser (Munich: Süddeutscher Verlag, 1974); Wilhelm Krämer (ed.), "M. Johann Daniel Mincks Chronik über den 30jährigen Krieg nach den Aufzeichnungen im Gross-Bieberauer Kirchensaalbuch," *Beiträge zur Hessischen Kirchengeschichte*, N. F. 2 (1905): 1-38, here 17.

[22] Krämer, "Daniel Mincks Chronik," 17-18.

[23] "Aus der Chronik von Colmar," 272-73; "Rudimenta Chronologiae Imp. Civ. Friedbergensis," 129.

[24] Zillhardt, *Der Dreißigjährige Krieg*, 53.

[25] Ibid., 152.

[26] Ibid., 155. Heberle reported that some 15,000 people died in Ulm during the year 1635; ibid., 162.

buried" (*ehrlich und wohl beerdigt*).[27] The explicit mention that the common ritual had been observed suggests that most of the inhabitants did not have this privilege.

Hunger and thirst drove people to extreme measures. During famine, eating dogs and cats was the least outrageous practice. Selling dog meat, mice, and rats reaped good profits.[28] More gruesome were the reports of cannibalism that appear in many autobiographical accounts.[29] Thirst threatened to kill Ulm's inhabitants when imperial troops blocked off the water supply. It got to the point that "almost everybody drank their own urine or the urine of their children, and even regarded it as good ... The thirst grew so intense that they did not care about being hungry."[30] When the peasants finally made ready to bring in the harvest, they faced a massive plague of mice. Ulm's peasants, however, met the scourge head on and dug up the gigantic mouse burrows which stored enough food to feed them for half a year.[31] People in the area of Hamburg fished for pike and perch in the ditches of the fields and with the profits were able to put some bread on the table.[32]

Over the years, Ulm's councilmen tried to alleviate the strain on the city by forcing the peasantry to return home. The government threatened to fine those who did not obey their order. From 1643 on, those seeking refuge had to pay a fee in order to be admitted into the city. These were desperate measures designed to establish order and to keep both city and countryside functioning. The government was by no means oblivious to the plight of its peasantry: during what proved to be Heberle's twenty-seventh and penultimate flight, the magistrates sent lieutenants with muskets to accompany the villagers on their flight into the city because several of them had been overtaken and robbed by French soldiers.[33]

Magistrates attempted to counteract the devastation in the countryside to secure food for the city's inhabitants as well as for the peasantry. After fields and villages had been destroyed by troops, Ulm's

---

[27] "Aus der Chronik von Colmar," 272. See also Krämer, "Daniel Mincks Chronik," 19.

[28] Zillhardt, *Der Dreißigjährige Krieg*, 176.

[29] See, for example, Zillhardt, *Der Dreißigjährige Krieg*, 176-77, and Mayer, "Kurze Aufzeichnungen," 28.

[30] Zillhardt, *Der Dreißigjährige Krieg*, 158.

[31] Ibid., 159.

[32] "Aus der Chronik von Colmar," 273.

[33] Zillhardt, *Der Dreißigjährige Krieg*, 219, n. 454.

council handed out seeds to its destitute subjects to plant the spring crop.[34] In Gross-Bieberau, Hesse, peasants combined their efforts, and in pairs, under the promise of future payment, borrowed horses from Jews so they could work the fields. And, indeed, a year later almost everyone reportedly owned a horse again.[35]

Peasants also fled to larger villages and collectively defended themselves against attacks.[36] Yet another frequently chosen alternative was for villagers to hide in forests in order to escape persecution, robbery, and torture.[37] In the words of Maurus Friesenegger, abbot of the Benedictine monastery in Andech, Bavaria: "The villages are deserted and the forest populated."[38] Pastor Lorenz Ludolph of Reichensachsen in Lower Saxony and his parishioners withdrew into the mountainous wilderness, where they built huts to evade roaming soldiers and escalating contributions. Once things had sufficiently calmed down, they returned on Sundays to gather in their church for worship. They did not dare ring the church bell but instead hit it briefly three times to summon the parishioners. For half a year, the troops misread the signal as a secret sign among the villagers to warn against approaching troops so that everyone could get out of the way.[39] Instead the opposite was the case.

Negotiations represent a second strategy of cities and territories trying to cope with the hardships inflicted upon them. The bargaining over the amount of contributions and provisions and where troops ought to be quartered run constant through the records. While providing food and money for the armies was inevitable, the extent of this burden was often negotiable.[40] Several men distinguished themselves during the war as expert mediators, as did *Stättmeister* Georg Friedrich

---

[34] Ibid., 163-64.

[35] Krämer, "Daniel Mincks Chronik," 25.

[36] Zillhardt, *Der Dreißigjährige Krieg*, 203. This was also a practice strongly recommended by Ulm's city council. Ibid., 219, n. 455.

[37] J. Rullmann (ed.), "Die Einwirkungen des 30jährigen Krieges auf die Stadt Schlüchtern und ihre Umgegend, aus Kirchenbüchern zusammengestellt," *Zeitschrift des Vereins für hessische Geschichte und Landeskunde*, N. F. 6 (1875): 201-50, here 248; Friesenegger, *Tagebuch*, 24, 34.

[38] Friesenegger, *Tagebuch*, 24.

[39] Krüschner, "Aus dem Kirchenbuch von Reichensachsen," 52.

[40] Otto Stemmler, "Die Ortenau in Abt Gaissers Tagebüchern (1621-1655)," *Die Ortenau* 29 (1949) [= N. F. 1]: 43-68, here 58-59; Johannes Rosa, "Chronikalische Notizen (1618-34)," *Chroniken von Friedberg* 1 (1937): 151-85, here 181; Zillhardt, *Der Dreißigjährige Krieg*, 121.

Seufferheld, after 1644 the most important negotiator for Schwäbisch Hall.[41] Besides his rhetorical skills Seufferheld used bribes to ward off the passage and quartering of soldiers and to reduce the requested sums of contribution. A pair of riding boots or a bottle of wine went a long way to win the goodwill of officers.

Some cities tried to avoid quartering soldiers in their area by paying contributions, but they were not always successful.[42] The villagers around Schlüchtern in Hesse felt relatively fortunate because they only had to suffer the hardship of providing for cavalrymen quartered in Schlüchtern and Steinau. As Pastor Martin Feilinger noted in his parish register: "If [the cavalrymen] had been divided among the villages as well, things would have been much more miserable than [having them] in the restricted towns. There one could contain them more easily."[43]

A particularly intriguing case of negotiations has been preserved by a Dominican nun of Bamberg, Maria Anna Junius.[44] The sisters had refused to abandon their convent during the Swedish war, even though it lay dangerously exposed. Instead they wound their way unharmed through the war by being friendly with the [Protestant] Swedes and by using their charm and the preserves of their pantry. Whenever they did run into problems, they immediately turned to the highest ranking officer to plead their case — and always succeeded. Maria Junius summed it up in her chronicle: "And even though the Swedes were frequent visitors to our house, they nevertheless always behaved modestly and honorably toward us. Although sometimes they came upon us like fierce lions and bears, they turned into patient and gentle lambs once they saw us and talked to us."[45] Negotiations were conducted on every level, whether by a renowned mediator like Seufferheld for Schwäbisch Hall or by villagers who asked for an extension or a lowering of the demands.

---

[41] Gerd Wunder, "Georg Friedrich Seufferheld. Stättmeister der Reichsstadt Schwäbisch Hall, 1613-1686," in Max Miller and Robert Uhland (eds.), *Lebensbilder aus Schwaben und Franken*, vol. 9 (Stuttgart: Kohlhammer Verlag, 1963), 56-68, here 60.

[42] Zillhardt, *Der Dreißigjährige Krieg*, 118-19, n. 112.

[43] Rullmann, "Einwirkungen des 30jährigen Krieges auf die Stadt Schlüchtern," 222.

[44] Friedrich Karl Hümmer (ed.), "Bamberg im Schweden-Kriege. Nach einem Manuscripte (Mittheilungen über die Jahre 1622-1634)," *Bericht über Bestand und Wirken des historischen Vereins zu Bamberg* 52 (1890): 1-168; 53 (1891): 169-230.

[45] Hümmer, "Bamberg im Schweden-Kriege," 222.

Sometimes one paid whatever one could and prayed that the officers would be satisfied.[46]

Armed resistance, particularly by the peasants — the hardest hit among the population — marks a third way of [en]countering the onslaught of troops. This was not an isolated phenomenon but permeated accounts of the war.[47] Burghers, too, fought cavalrymen who mistreated them.[48] Cities tried to channel this violence into more controlled venues. Ulm organized its own defensive guard made up of eligible men of Ulm's domain to carry out missions assigned by the city council.[49] Probably fearing that defiance by the villagers would make the troops even more aggressive, the government ordered its subjects to hand over their weapons. When, however, soldiers threatened the countryside, the council secretly provided the villagers with muskets so they could defend themselves.[50] Both magistrates and high-ranking military were determined to maintain a certain standard of discipline among troops.[51] Even though they were unable to stop or substantially reduce violence, marauding soldiers who were caught met with harsh justice. Officers who did not keep order among their troops were executed as well.[52] Thus, contemporaries took a variety of pragmatic measures to deal with the damage wrought by the war.

Practical and ideological responses overlapped when magistrates began mandating days of prayer and penance to avert God's wrath. In 1628 the council of Ulm ordered its city and territory to conduct an hour of prayer, a practice kept alive until 1650.[53] Other cities initiated similar practices whenever their regions became involved in the

[46] Rosa, "Chronikalische Notizen," 174.

[47] "Rudimenta Chronologiae Imp. Civ. Friedbergensis," 123; Stemmler, "Die Ortenau," 56, 59; Hümmer, "Bamberg im Schweden-Kriege," 170. See also Adolf Schmid, "Georg Gaisser (1595-1655). Prior von St. Nikolaus und Herr im Klosterbad Rippoldsau," Die Ortenau 61 (1981): 87-102, here 98.

[48] "Eine Potsdamsche Pfarrchronik aus der Zeit des großen Krieges," Zeitschrift für Preußische Geschichte und Landeskunde 20 (1883): 207-34, here 222.

[49] Zillhardt, Der Dreißigjährige Krieg, 114, 134, 137, 143, 145, 151. For the organization of Schaffhausen's guard, see Karl Schmucki, "Georg Michael Wepfer," Schaffhauser Biographien, Part 5, 68 (1991): 225-42, here 227.

[50] Zillhardt, Der Dreißigjährige Krieg, 119.

[51] "Rudimenta Chronologiae Imp. Civ. Friedbergensis," 127, 138.

[52] "Rudimenta Chronologiae Imp. Civ. Friedbergensis," 129.

[53] Elisabeth Erdmann, "Der Dreißigjährige Krieg im Spiegel der Tagebücher des Thomas Mallinger. Handlungsweisen der Bevölkerung," Zeitschrift für die Geschichte des Oberrheins 143/N. F. 4 (1995): 515-27, here 524.

war.[54] To remove what seemed the prime obstacle to regaining God's grace, governments took measures to establish a stricter discipline. In 1638 Ulm's council issued a mandate against cursing.[55] Most astounding was the rigor with which Strasbourg tried to cleanse its city of immorality. In his *Schreibkalender*, Hans Michael Moscherosch detailed the strong action Strasbourg's council took in 1620 against the "whores' nests."[56] Within a month, their chief was beheaded and another implicated person hanged. Every Wednesday and Saturday prostitutes and rogues were pilloried. In the midst of lamentations about the end of the world, the city told three high-ranking politicians to stay home on account of whoring and informed them that they had lost their honor. Strasbourg beheaded another female whoremaster and moved against further culprits.[57]

On a psychological and ideological level, religion proved a strong anchor for those afflicted.[58] Their faith provided a way to deal with the sheer endless misery.[59] People firmly believed that God governed their lives and that he sent bad times as well as brief respites from grief. Authors bear witness to an overwhelming confidence in God's design, to a conviction that the torments brought on by war represented God's just punishment for men's sins and ingratitude, but that in the end he would not abandon them. It was comforting to know that he, if no one else, had a plan and knew the way out of this nightmare. Some were unfailing in their faith — at least according to their autobiographical accounts — and felt justly punished for their sins, not asking why they had to suffer such pain. Others like Hans Heber-

---

[54] Adolf Schmidt, "Moscheroschs Schreibkalender," *Jahrbuch für Geschichte, Sprache und Litteratur Elsass-Lothringens* 16 (1900): 139-90, here 160; "Rudimenta Chronologiae Imp. Civ. Friedbergensis," 122, 141; Karl Schmucki, "Georg Michael Wepfer," 226; Krämer, "Daniel Mincks Chronik," 9-16, 24-33.

[55] Zillhardt, *Der Dreißigjährige Krieg*, 174.

[56] Schmidt, "Moscheroschs Schreibkalender," 160.

[57] Schmidt, "Moscheroschs Schreibkalender," 162-65.

[58] On the importance of religion, see also Bernd Roeck, "Der Dreißigjährige Krieg und die Menschen im Reich. Überlegungen zu den Formen psychischer Krisenbewältigung in der ersten Hälfte des 17. Jahrhunderts," in: Bernhard R. Kroener and Ralf Pröve (eds.), *Krieg und Frieden. Militär und Gesellschaft in der Frühen Neuzeit* (Munich: Ferdinand Schöningh, 1996), 265-79, here 277-79; Schiewek, "Manifestation des Individuellen," 895; von Greyerz, *Vorsehungsglaube und Kosmologie*.

[59] That parish records and diaries of abbots would hold this viewpoint is not so surprising, but it is also evident in other, non-ecclesiastical records, e.g. the diaries of Schaffhausen's secretary Georg Michael Wepfer. Schmucki, "Georg Michael Wepfer," 234.

le, after having endured repeated flights, the loss of most of his family, and many hardships through pillaging soldiers, cried out: "O God, why do the heathen rage! We can only second what dear David has to say in Psalm 2: O Lord, do not let us perish completely because we are called after your name."[60] He ended, however, by expressing his hope that God would let the sun shine again after this storm.

If the autobiographical accounts are trustworthy gauges, this powerful trust in God helped people cope with the tortures of war. However, it did not eradicate the fear generated by the excruciating experiences.[61] Every regiment sweeping through the country aroused new horror and trepidation.[62] According to the Dominican nun Maria Junius, fear was a factor contributing to the high death toll in 1634, when "the city of Bamberg buried more than 1600 people, who died only because of the great fright, misery, and hunger."[63] Fear could lead to desperation, insanity, and suicide.[64] A chronicler of Friedberg reported that "Johann Bolhard, at this time burgomaster and butcher by profession, stabbed himself to death during the sermon on account of the sadness of the war and his melancholy during the morning."[65] Although the autobiographical accounts frequently mention instances of suicide — Moscherosch reported five suicides in Strasbourg for the years 1620 to 1626; similarly, city minister Wolfgang Ammon related three cases for Marktbreit — the documents examined for this study do not yield conclusive evidence that the Thirty Years' War led to a higher number of suicides. Rarely did authors discuss the motives for these actions, which may or may not have been connected to experiences related to the war.[66] The picture is further complicated by the possibility that several recorded deaths may well have been suicides, but were not designated as such. For

---

[60] Zillhardt, *Der Dreißigjährige Krieg*, 154.

[61] "Potsdamsche Pfarrchronik," 225.

[62] Zillhardt, *Der Dreißigjährige Krieg*, 154.

[63] Hümmer, "Bamberg im Schweden-Kriege," 208.

[64] Pastor Bartholomaus Dietmar of Franconia describes a case of insanity most likely caused by the heavy burden of contributions in "Aus der Chronik des Bartholomäus Dietmar (1592-1670)," in Marianne Beyer-Fröhlich (ed.), *Selbstzeugnisse aus dem Dreissigjährigen Krieg und dem Barock* (Darmstadt: Wissenschaftliche Buchgesellschaft, 1970), 81-93, here 90-91.

[65] "Rudimenta Chronologiae Imp. Civ. Friedbergensis," 127.

[66] Schmidt, "Moscheroschs Schreibkalender"; Franz Hüttner (ed.), "Selbstbiographie des Stadtpfarrers Wolfgang Ammon von Marktbreit (d. 1634)," *Archiv für Kulturgeschichte* 1 (1903): 284-325.

example, Moscherosch narrated the find of a drowned woman, but did not indicate whether she had caused her own death.[67]

Writing down one's experience and attempting to create mental order in the midst of chaos was another powerful psychological way of coping with the misery engendered by the war. As mentioned earlier, the war produced a flood of autobiographical texts. Recording events and impressions was a means to make sense of one's life.[68] Similarly to the reliance on God's providence, these testimonies describe an effort and a desire to believe in some order that was still available. In this case, authors attempted to produce such order by recording the episodes. "Processing" (*Verarbeiten*) the experiences also created a sense of distance between oneself and the events. The ordeal was not bottled up inside but placed outside oneself, on the paper, to be looked at. Several authors — like Heberle, Mayer, and Friesenegger — used irony and sarcasm to relate conditions and occurrences. Here, humor or cynical detachment became buffers to protect oneself from the calamitous effects of the war. Amazingly, in many autobiographical accounts descriptions of gloom stand side by side with expressions of joy over a good wine, a rich harvest, or a sunny day. Not losing sight of the beauty that remained may have been the most powerful weapon against succumbing to the very real destruction of the war.

Flights into cities and forests; negotiations between the populace and the troops; peasants' resistance to pillaging soldiers; confidence in God's plan; attempts to create mental order in the midst of chaos — all of these reactions describe patterns of behavior during the Thirty Years' War. The form and success of these steps, however, depended largely on local conditions. Certainly, such external manifestations of coping with life during the war can only partially explain how people endured its ordeals. Some were worn so thin by its costs that, as Pastor Feilinger of Hesse put it, "they were willing to leave this Egyptian darkness."[69] Others, like Abbot Friesenegger, perse-

---

[67] Schmidt, "Moscheroschs Schreibkalender," 184.

[68] See also Jan Peters, "Wegweiser zum Innenleben? Möglichkeiten und Grenzen der Untersuchung popularer Selbstzeugnisse der Frühen Neuzeit," in: *Historische Anthropologie* 1 (1993): 235-49.

[69] Rullmann, "Einwirkungen des 30jährigen Krieges auf die Stadt Schlüchtern," 232; see also 246 and Uwe Jens Wandel (ed.), *Lebens- und Leidensweg des M. Johann Gerhard Ramsler, Specials zu Freudenstadt. Die Lebenserinnerungen eines württembergischen Landpfarrers (1635-1703)* (Stuttgart: W. Kohlhammer Verlag, 1993), 24.

vered by adjusting to the reality of war and by growing accustomed
to the misery it brought.[70] And then there were people like the shoemaker Heberle who, on his twelfth flight into Ulm, exclaimed that all
the problems and poverty in the city could have been borne, had
they been able to sow the spring corn. When he had to flee the invad-
ing imperial troops for the fourteenth time, he concluded that this
way they would never get on in life.[71] These people showed an enormous resilience and dared to keep their eyes focused squarely on a
(better) future.

---

[70] Friesenegger, *Tagebuch*, 111.
[71] Zillhardt, *Der Dreißigjährige Krieg*, 172, 180

HEIKO AUGUSTINUS OBERMAN

BIBLIOGRAPHY

BOOKS

Archbishop Thomas Bradwardine, a Fourteenth Century Augustinian. A Study of His Theology in Its Historical Context (Utrecht, 1957; revised edition: 1958).

Christianity Divided. Protestant and Roman Catholic Theological Issues, with Daniel J. Callahan and Daniel J. O'Hanlon, S.J., eds. (New York, 1961; London, 1962). French: *Catholiques et Protestants. Confrontations théologiques sur l'Écriture et la Tradition, l'interprétation de la Bible, l'Église, les Sacrements, la Justification* (Paris, 1963).

The Harvest of Medieval Theology. Gabriel Biel and Late Medieval Nominalism (Cambridge, MA, 1963; revised edition: Grand Rapids, 1967; 3rd edition: Durham, NC, 1983). German: *Der Herbst der mittelalterlichen Theologie, Spätscholastik und Reformation,* 1 (Zürich, 1965).

Gabrielis Biel Canonis Misse expositio, 4 volumes, with William J. Courtenay, eds., Veröffentlichungen des Instituts für Europäische Geschichte Mainz, Abteilung für Abendländische Religionsgeschichte, 31-34 (Wiesbaden, 1963-67).

Forerunners of the Reformation. The Shape of Late Medieval Thought (New York, 1966; London, 1967; Philadelphia, 1981).

[Gabrielis Biel] Defensorium obedientiae apostolicae et alia documenta, with Daniel E. Zerfoss and William J. Courtenay, eds. (Cambridge, MA, 1968).

Ketters of voortrekkers. De geestelijke horizon van onze tijd. Vier gesprekken tussen G. C. Berkouwer, E. Schillebeeckx and H. A. Oberman, ed. (Kampen [1970]).

De dertiende apostel en het elfde gebod. Paulus in de loop der eeuwen, with G. C. Berkouwer, eds. (Kampen, 1971).

Editor, with introduction, *Ockham, the Conciliar Theory, and the Canonists,* by Brian Tierney, Facet Books, Historical Series, 19 (Philadelphia, 1971).

Contra vanam curiositatem. Ein Kapitel der Theologie zwischen Seelenwinkel und Weltall, Theologische Studien, 113 (Zürich, 1974).

Karikatuur van de tijdgeest (Kampen, 1974).

The Pursuit of Holiness in Late Medieval and Renaissance Religion. Papers from the University of Michigan Conference, with Charles Trinkaus, eds., Studies in Medieval and Reformation Thought, 10 (Leiden, 1974).

Luther and the Dawn of the Modern Era. Papers for the Fourth International Congress for Luther Research, Studies in the History of Christian Thought, 8, ed. (Leiden, 1974).

Deutscher Bauernkrieg 1525, Zeitschrift für Kirchengeschichte 85 (1974), ed. Sonderheft.

Itinerarium Italicum. The Profile of the Italian Renaissance in the Mirror of its European Transformations. Dedicated to Paul Oskar Kristeller on the occasion of his 70th birthday, with Thomas A. Brady, Jr., eds., Studies in Medieval and Reformation Thought, 14 (Leiden, 1975).

Werden und Wertung der Reformation. Vom Wegestreit zum Glaubenskampf, Spätscholastik und Reformation, 2 (Tübingen, 1977; 2nd edition: 1979; 3rd edition: 1989). English: *Masters of the Reformation. The Emergence of a New Intellectual Climate in Europe* (Cambridge, 1981). Italian: *I maestri della Riforma. La formazione di un nuovo clima intellettuale in Europa* (Bologna, 1982).

Wurzeln des Antisemitismus. Christenangst und Judenplage im Zeitalter von Humanismus und Reformation (Berlin, 1981; 2nd edition: 1983). Dutch: *Wortels van het antisemitisme. Christenangst en jodenramp in het tijdperk van humanisme en reformatie* (Kampen, 1983). English: *The Roots of Anti-Semitism in the Age of Renaissance and Reformation* (Philadelphia, 1984).

Die Kirche im Zeitalter der Reformation, Kirchen- und Theologiegeschichte in Quellen, 3, ed. (Neukirchen-Vluyn, 1981; 2nd edition: 1985; 3rd edition: 1988).

Gregor von Rimini. Werk und Wirkung bis zur Reformation, Spätmittelalter und Reformation, Texte und Untersuchungen, 20, ed. (Berlin, 1981).

Luther. *Mensch zwischen Gott und Teufel* (Berlin, 1982; 2nd edition: 1983; Paperback: dtv, München, 1986; 3rd edition: Berlin, 1987; Siedler Paperback, Berlin, 1987; Doubleday Paperback, New York, 1992). Italian: *Martin Lutero. Un uomo tra Dio e il diavolo* (Roma-Bari, 1987). Dutch: Luther. *Mens tussen God en duivel* (Kampen, 1988). English: *Luther. Man between God and the Devil* (New Haven, 1989). Spanish: *Lutero. Un hombre entre Dios y el diablo* (Madrid, 1993). Fontana paperback: Luther. Man between God and the Devil (London, 1993)

Maarten Luther. Feestelijke herdenking van zijn vijfhonderdste geboortedag (Amsterdam, 1983).

Die Reformation von Wittenberg nach Genf (Göttingen, 1986) — hereinafter cited as *Die Reformation*. Italian: *La Riforma protestante da Lutero a Calvino* (Roma-Bari, 1989).

The Dawn of the Reformation. Essays in Late Medieval and Early Reformation Thought (Edinburgh, 1986) — hereinafter cited as *The Dawn*.

Die Wirkung der Reformation. Probleme und Perspektiven, Institut für Europäische Geschichte Mainz, Vorträge, 80 (Stuttgart, 1987).

De erfenis van Calvijn. Grootheid en grenzen (Kampen, 1988).

Rapport van de Verkenningscommissie, 2 volumes, with A.H. Smits, J. Emerton, A. van der Kooij (Ministerie van Onderwijs en Wetenschappen, Den Haag, 1989).

Initia Calvini: The Matrix of Calvin's Reformation, Koninklijke Nederlandse Academie van Wetenschappen (Amsterdam, 1991). Also published as: *Initia Calvini: Die Matrix van Calvyn se Hervorming* (Pretoria, 1991).

Reformiertes Erbe. Festschrift für Gottfried W. Locher zu seinem 80. Geburtstag, Editor with Ernst Saxer, Alfred Schindler and Heinzpeter Stucki, Vol. I, (Zurich, 1992); Vol. II (Zurich, 1993).

Anticlericalism in Late Medieval and Early Modern Europe, Editor with Peter A. Dykema, 2nd ed., SMRT (Leiden, 1994 [1992])

Handbook of European History 1400-1600. Late Middle Ages, Renaissance and Reformation, Editor with Thomas A. Brady, Jr. and James D. Tracy, Vol. 1, (Leiden, 1994).

Handbook of European History 1400-1600. Late Middle Ages, Renaissance and Reformation, Editor with Thomas A. Brady, Jr. and James D. Tracy, Vol. 2, (Leiden, 1995).

The Impact of the Reformation, (Grand Rapids, 1994).

The Reformation. Roots and Ramifications, (Edinburgh, 1994).

ARTICLES

1958

'Thomas Bradwardine.' *Theologisch Woordenboek*, vol. 3 (Roermond, 1958): cols. 4574-4575.

"Op weg naar de Voordagen." *Kleine kampdogmatiek*, N.C.S.V. (1958): 22-29.

"The *sermo epinicius* ascribed to Thomas Bradwardine (1346)," with James A. Weisheipl, O.P. *Archives d'Histoire Doctrinale et Littéraire du Moyen Age 33ᵉ année*, 25 (1958): 295-329.

1960

"Thomas Bradwardine. Un précurseur de Luther?" *Revue d'Histoire et de Philosophie Religieuses* 10 (1960): 146-151.

"Some Notes on the Theology of Nominalism, with Attention to its Relation to the Renaissance." *The Harvard Theological Review* 53 (1960): 47-76.

"De Praedestinatione et Praescientia. An Anonymous 14th-Century Treatise on Predestination and Justification." *Nederlands Archief voor Kerkgeschiedenis* 43 (1960): 195-220.

"The Preaching of the Word in the Reformation." *The Harvard Divinity Bulletin* 25, no. 1 (1960): 7-18. Also published as: "Preaching and the Word in the Reformation." *Theology Today* 18, no. 1 (1961): 16-29. Revised: "Reformation, Preaching, and *ex opere operato.*" *Christianity Divided* (New York, 1961; London, 1962): 223-239 (See BOOKS). French: "Réforme, prédication et 'ex opere operato'." *Catholiques et Protestants* (Paris, 1963): 211-227 (See BOOKS).

1961

"Bibliografie der Nederlandse Kerkgeschiedenis 1957," with J. W. Schneider, J. F. Hoekstra and G. H. M. Posthumus Meyjes. *Nederlands Archief voor Kerkgeschiedenis* 44 (1961): 101-119.

"Gabriel Biel and Late Medieval Mysticism." *Church History* 30 (1961): 259-287.

"Protestant Reflections on Church and State." *Theology and Life* 4, no. 1 (1961): 60-65.

"Unity as a Gift and Goal." *Unity is to Fulfill, is to Forgive*, SCM in New England (Cambridge, MA, 1961): 6-7.

1962

"Quo Vadis, Petre? The History of Tradition from Irenaeus to *Humani Generis*." *The Harvard Divinity Bulletin* 26, no. 4 (1962): 1-25. Also published as: "Quo Vadis? Tradition from Irenaeus to Humani Generis." *Scottish Journal of Theology* 16, (1963): 225-255. Also in *The Dawn*: 269-296 (See BOOKS).

"Facientibus quod in se est Deus non denegat gratiam. Robert Holcot, O.P. and the Beginnings of Luther's Theology." *The Harvard Theological Review* 55 (1962): 317-342. Also in *The Reformation in Medieval Perspective*, ed. Steven E. Ozment (Chicago, 1971): 119-141. Also in *The Dawn*: 84-103 (See BOOKS).

1963

"The Ecumenical Council. Vatican II and the Dialogue in America." *Harvard Alumni Bulletin* 65, no. 8 (1963): 348-349. Dutch: Vaticanum II en de controverse in Amerika." *Reformatorische Orientatie* 1 (1963): 12-14.

1964

"De driehoek: Late Middeleeuwen — Rome — Reformatie." (Radio lectures) *Reformatorische Orientatie* 2 (1964): 1-12. Also in *Rondom het Woord* 6, no. 1 (1964): 15-18 (Summary).

"Observations on Vatican II, Second Session." *The Current* 5 (1964): 52-64.

"The Virgin Mary in Evangelical Perspective." *Journal of Ecumenical Studies* 1 (1964): 271-298. Also in Facet Books, Historical Series, 20 (Philadelphia, 1971). German: "Schrift und Gottesdienst. Die Jungfrau Maria in evangelischer Sicht." *Kerygma und Dogma* 10 (1964): 219- 245. Dutch: "Reformatorische ruimte voor de mariologie." *Uit tweeen één. Tussentijdse balans van het gesprek Rome — Reformatie*, eds. H. M. Kuitert and H. A. M. Fiolet (Rotterdam, 1966): 183-209.

"Das tridentinische Rechtfertigungsdekret im Lichte spätmittelaltcrlicher Theologie." *Zeitschrift für Theologie und Kirche* 61 (1964): 251-282. Also in *Concilium Tridentinum*, ed. Remigius Bäumer, Wege der Forschung, 313 (Darmstadt, 1979): 301-340 (with Addendum).

"Holy Spirit — Holy Writ — Holy Church. The Witness of the Reformation." *The Hartford Quarterly* 5 (1964): 43-71.

"Catholics and Jews." *From ... The Pulpit*, Congregation Rodeph Shalom (Philadelphia, Autumn 1964): [3-12].

1965

"Eenzame Paus of Eerste der Broeders." Derde zitting Vaticanum. *Woord en Dienst* 14 (1965): 5-6. Also in *De Paus van Rome. Opvattingen over een omstreden ambt*, ed. Michel van der Plas (Utrecht, 1965): 140-146. German: "Der 'einsame Papst' — oder der Erste unter den Brüdern." *Orientierung* 29 (1965): 7-9. English: "Lonely Pope or First of the Brethren?" *TheChristian Century* 82 (1965): 835-837.

"De Maagd Maria — hoeksteen of struikelblok," "Ark van Noach of Arc de Triomphe." Vaticanum II: de derde zitting. *Woord en Dienst* 14 (1965): 21-23, 39-40.

"Vaticaans Concilie en Nieuwe Theologie." (Radio lecture) *Woord en Dienst* 14 (1965): 28-29.

"Infinitum capax finiti. Kanttekeningen bij de theologie van Calvijn." *Vox Theologica* 35, no. 6 (1965): 165-174.

"Fides Christo formata. Luther en de Scholastieke theologie." *Ex Auditu Verbi. Theologische opstellen aangeboden aan G. C. Berkouwer*, eds. R. Schippers, et al. (Kampen, 1965): 157-175. English revised version: "'Iustitia Christi' and 'Iustitia Dei'. Luther and the Scholastic Doctrines of Justification." *The Harvard Theological Review* 59 (1966): 1-26. Also in *The Dawn:* 104-125 (See BOOKS). German: "'Iustitia Christi' und 'Iustitia Dei'. Luther und die scholastischen Lehren von der Rechtfertigung." *Der Durchbruch der reformatorischen Erkenntnis bei Luther*, ed. Bernhard Lohse, Wege der Forschung, 123 (Darmstadt, 1968): 413-444.

"Duns Scotus, Nominalism, and the Council of Trent." *John Duns Scotus, 1265-1965*, eds. John K. Ryan and Bernardine M. Bonansea, Studies in Philosophy and the History of Philosophy, 3 (Washington, D.C., 1965): 311-344. Also in *The Dawn:* 204-233 (See BOOKS).

1966

"Die 'Extra'-Dimension in der Theologie Calvins." *Geist und Geschichte der Reformation. Festgabe Hanns Rückert zum 65. Geburtstag*, eds. Heinz Liebing and Klaus Scholder, Arbeiten zur Kirchengeschichte, 38 (Berlin, 1966): 323-356. Also in *Die Reformation:* 253-282 (See BOOKS). English: "The 'Extra' Dimension in the Theology of Calvin." *The Journal of Ecclesiastical History* 21 (1970): 43-64. Also in *The Dawn*: 234-258 (See BOOKS).

"Theologie des späten Mittelalters. Stand und Aufgaben der Forschung." *Theologische Literaturzeitung* 91 (1966): cols. 401-416.

"Prof. dr. Maarten van Rhijn. Tussen herinnering en hoop." *Woord en Dienst* 15 (1966): 389.

1967

"From Ockham to Luther — Recent Studies." *Concilium* (London) vol. 7 (Church History). Part I: 2 (1966): 63-68; Part II: 3 (1967): 67-71.

"Simul gemitus et raptus: Luther und die Mystik." *Kirche, Mystik, Heiligung und das Natürliche bei Luther.* Vorträge des Dritten Internationalen Kongresses für Lutherforschung, ed. Ivar Asheim (Göttingen, 1967): 20-59. Also in *Die Reformation:* 45-89 (See BOOKS). English original: *"Simul Gemitus et Raptus:* Luther and Mysticism." *The Reformation in Medieval Perspective,* ed. Steven E. Ozment (Chicago, 1971): 219-251. Also in *The Dawn:* 126-154 (See BOOKS).

"Wir sein pettler. Hoc est verum. Bund und Gnade in der Theologie des Mittelalters und der Reformation." Antrittsvorlesung, Tübingen, June 1, 1967. *Zeitschrift für Kirchengeschichte* 78 (1967): 232-252. Also in *Die Reformation:* 90-112 (See BOOKS).

"Roms erste Antwort auf Luthers 95 Thesen. Bemerkungen zum 450. Jahrestag der Reformation." *Orientierung* 31 (1967): 231-233.

"The Reformation: Proclamation of Grace." *Review and Expositor* 64 (1967): 161-169. Also in *God and Man in Contemporary Christian Thought.* Proceedings of the Philosophy Symposium held at the American University of Beirut, ed. Charles Malik (Beirut, 1970): 55-64.

"The Protestant Tradition." *The Convergence of Traditions. Orthodox, Catholic, Protestant,* ed. Elmer O'Brien, S.J. (New York, 1967): 67-135.

1968
Preface, *Christianity and Humanism. Studies in the History of Ideas,* by Quirinus Breen. Collected and published in his honor, ed. Nelson Peter Ross (Grand Rapids, 1968): VII-VIII.

"Wittenbergs Zweifrontenkrieg gegen Prierias und Eck. Hintergrund und Entscheidungen des Jahres 1518." *Zeitschrift für Kirchengeschichte* 80 (1969): 331-358. Also in *Die Reformation:* 113-143 (See BOOKS).

1969
"De rechtvaardigingsleer bij Thomas en Luther. Twee zielen één gedachte?" *Kerk en Theologie* 20 (1969): 186-191.

1970
"Luther contra Thomas." *Kerk en Theologie* 21 (1970): 295-301.

1971
"Paulus in de spiegel van de kerkgeschiedenis," "Paulus en Luther." (Radio lectures) *Rondom het Woord* 13, no. 1 (1971): 1-4, 62-70 . Also in *De dertiende apostel en het elfde gebod* (Kampen, 1971): 7-10, 68-76 (See BOOKS).

"'Et tibi dabo claves regni caelorum'. Kirche und Konzil von Augustin bis Luther. Tendenzen und Ergebnisse," I. *Nederlands Theologisch Tijdschrift* 25 (1971): 261-282 (II: See 1975).

1972

"Das neue Gebot." Predigt über Johannes 13, 34-36, gehalten am 19. Januar 1972 in St. Johannes, Tübingen. *Theologische Beiträge* 3 (1972): 49-56.

"Einleitung zur Reihe Spätmittelalter und Reformation, Texte und Untersuchungen." *Der Physikkommentar Hugolins von Orvieto OESA,* ed. Willigis Eckermann, Spätmittelalter und Reformation, Texte und Untersuchungen — hereinafter cited as SuR — 5 (Berlin, 1972): XVII-XXVI. Reprinted in *Bibliographie zur Geschichte und Theologie des Augustiner-Eremitenordens bis zum Beginn der Reformation,* ed. Egon Gindele, SuR 1 (Berlin 1977): V-XIII.

1973

"The Shape of Late Medieval Thought: The Birthpangs of the Modern Era." *Archiv für Reformationsgeschichte* 64 (1973): 13-33. Also in *The Pursuit of Holiness in Late Medieval and Renaissance Religion* (Leiden, 1974): 3-25 (See BOOKS). Also in *The Dawn:* 18-38 (See BOOKS).

"Mystiek als daad. Thomas Müntzer: Mystiek en revolutie." (Radio lectures) *Rondom het Woord* 15, no. 2 (1973), 5868. Also in *Mystiek in de westerse kultuur,* eds. G. C. Berkouwer, R. Hensen and G. H. M. Posthumus Meyjes (Kampen, 1973): 58-68. Revised: "Thomas Müntzer: van verontrusting tot verzet." In memoriam Gerrit Cornelis van Niftrik. *Kerk en Theologie* 24 (1973): 205-214.

1974

"Headwaters of the Reformation. *Initia Lutheri — Initia Reformationis." Luther and the Dawn of the Modern Era* (Leiden, 1974): 40-88 (See BOOKS). Also in *The Dawn:* 39-83 (See BOOKS).

"Tumultus rusticorum: Vom 'Klosterkrieg' zum Fürstensieg. Beobachtungen zum Bauernkrieg unter besonderer Berücksichtigung zeitgenössischer Beurteilungen." *Deutscher Bauernkrieg 1525, Zeitschrift für Kirchengeschichte* 85 (1974): 301-316, Sonderheft (See BOOKS). Also in *Der deutsche Bauernkrieg von 1525,* ed. Peter Blickle, Wege der Forschung, 460 (Darmstadt, 1985): 214-236. Also in *Die Reformation:* 144-161 (See BOOKS). English expanded version: "The Gospel of Social Unrest: 450 Years after the so-called 'German Peasants' War' of 1525." *The Harvard Theological Review* 69 (1976): 103-129. Also in *The German Peasant War of 1525 - New Viewpoints,* eds. Bob Scribner and Gerhard Benecke (London, 1979): 39-51. Also in *The Dawn:* 155-178 (See BOOKS).

"Kapers op de Goede Hoop. Een oproep tot ommekeer." *Kerk en Theologie* 25 (1974): 221-230. German: "Kap ohne gute Hoffnung. Beobachtungen zur Lage in Südafrika." *Evangelische Kommentare* 8 (1975): 156-158, 163.

"De erfenis van Thomas van Aquino. Uitstraling en grenzen." *Woord en Dienst* 23 (1974): 229-230.

1975

"Quoscunque tulit foecunda vetustas. Ad Lectorem." *Itinerarium Italicum* (Leiden, 1975): IX-XXVIII (See BOOKS).

"Reformation and Revolution: Copernicus' Discovery in an Era of Change." *The Nature of Scientific Discovery.* A Symposium Commemorating the 500th Anniversary of the Birth of Nicolaus Copernicus, ed. Owen Gingerich, Smithsonian International Symposia Series, 5 (Washington, D.C., 1975): 134-169. Expanded version in *The Cultural Context of Medieval Learning.* Proceedings of the first International Colloquium on Philosophy, Science, and Theology in the Middle Ages, eds. John Emery Murdoch and Edith Dudley Sylla, Boston Studies in the Philosophy of Science, 26 (Dordrecht, 1975): 397-429; Discussion: 429- 435. Also in *The Dawn:* 179-203 (See BOOKS).

"'Tuus sum, salvum me fac'. Augustinréveil zwischen Renaissance und Reformation." *Scientia Augustiniana. Studien über Augustinus, den Augustinismus und den Augustinerorden.* Festschrift Adolar Zumkeller OSA zum 60. Geburtstag, eds. Cornelius Petrus Mayer and Willigis Eckermann, Cassiciacum, 30 (Würzburg, 1975): 349-394.

"'Et tibi dabo claves regni caelorum'. Kirche und Konzil von Augustin bis Luther. Tendenzen und Ergebnisse," II. *Nederlands Theologisch Tijdschrift* 29 (1975): 97-118 (I: See 1971).

"Theologe der Revolution oder der Reformation? Thomas Müntzer nach 450 Jahren," with Reinhold Mokrosch. *Evangelische Kommentare* 8 (1975): 279-282.

"Van agitatie tot revolutie: De boerenoorlog als Europees fenomeen." (Radio lectures) *Rondom het Woord* 17, no. 3 (1975): 30-38, 60.

1976

"Het kruis van het antisemitisme." (Radio lectures) *Rondom het Woord* 18, no. 2 (1976): 53-62.

"Calvin's critique of Calvinism." *Christian Higher Education. The Contemporary Challenge.* Proceedings of the First International Conference of Reformed Institutions for Christian Scholarship, Institute for the Advancement of Calvinism, Wetenskaplike Bydraes van die PU vir CHO, Series F, 6 (Potchefstroom, 1976): 372-381.Also in *The Dawn:* 259-268 (See BOOKS).

1977

"Reformation: Epoche oder Episode." *Archiv für Reformationsgeschichte* 68 (1977): 56-111.

"Via moderna — Devotio moderna: Tendenzen im Tübinger Geistesleben 1477-1516. Ecclesiastici atque catholici gymnasii fundamenta." *Theologen und Theologie an der Universität Tübingen. Beiträge zur Geschichte der Evangelisch-Theologischen Fakultät,* ed. Martin Brecht (Tübingen, 1977): 1-64.

"Die Anfänge der Tübinger Theologie und die Reformation." *"... helfen zu graben den Brunnen des Lebens.*" Historische Jubiläumsausstellung des Universitätsarchivs Tübingen, eds. Uwe Jens Wandel, et al., Ausstellungskataloge der Universität Tübingen, 8 (Tübingen, 1977): 33-37.

"Die deutsche Tragödie im Zeitalter der Reformation. Böse Weisheit aus Tübinger Sicht." *Heute von Gott reden,* eds. Martin Hengel and Rudolf Reinhardt (München, Mainz, 1977): 113-137.

1978

"Fourteenth-Century Religious Thought: A Premature Profile." *Speculum* 53 (1978): 80-93. Also in *The Dawn:* 1-17 (See BOOKS). Also published as: "The Reorientation of the Fourteenth Century." *Studi sul XIV secolo in memoria di Anneliese Maier,* eds. A. Maierù and A. Paravicini Bagliani, Storia e Letteratura, 151 (Roma, 1981): 513-530.

1979

"Der moderne Wanderpapst." *Evangelische Kommentare* 12 (1979): 663-664.

"De aangevochten God. De betekenis van de reformatie voor onze tijd." (Radio lecture) *Rondom het Woord* 21, no. 1 (1979): 30-34.

Preface, *Johann Arndt. True Christianity,* ed. Peter Erb, The Classics of Western Spirituality (New York, 1979): XI-XVII.

Preface, *Gregorii Ariminensis OESA Lectura super Primum et Secundum Sententiarum,* ed. A. Damasus Trapp, OSA — hereinafter cited as *Gregorii Ariminensis OESA Lectura* vol. 4, SuR 9 (Berlin, 1979): V-IX.

Preface, *Gregorii Ariminensis OESA Lectura,* vol. 5, SuR 10 (Berlin, 1979): V-VI.

"Zum Geleit. Ziel der Staupitz-Gesamtausgabe." *Johann von Staupitz. Sämtliche Schriften, Lateinische Schriften,* vol. 2: *Libellus de exsecutione aeternae praedestinationis,* eds. Lothar Graf zu Dohna, Richard Wetzel and Albrecht Endriß, SuR 14 (Berlin, 1979): V-X.

1980

"Dichtung und Wahrheit. Das Wesen der Reformation aus der Sicht der Confutatio." *Confessio Augustana und Confutatio. Der Augsburger Reichstag 1530 und die Einheit der Kirche.* Internationales Symposion der Gesellschaft zur Herausgabe des Corpus Catholicorum, ed. Erwin Iserloh, Reformationsgeschichtliche Studien und Texte, 118 (Münster, 1980): 217-231. Also in *Materialdienst des Konfessionskundlichen Instituts Bensheim* 32 (1981): 14-19. Also in *Die Reformation:* 223-237 (See BOOKS).

"Werden und Wertung der Reformation. Thesen und Tatsachen." *Reformatio Ecclesiae. Beiträge zu kirchlichen Reformbemühungen von der Alten Kirche bis zur Neuzeit.* Festgabe für Erwin Iserloh, ed. Remigius Bäumer (Paderborn, 1980): 487-503. Also in *Die Reformation:* 15-31 (See BOOKS).

"Willem Cornelis van Unnik 1910-1978. 'Novi foederis scriptorum interpres'." *The Library of the late Dr. W. C. van Unnik.* Book auction catalogue (Utrecht, 1980): 3-4.

Preface, *Gregorii Ariminensis OESA Lectura,* vol. 6, SuR 11 (Berlin, 1980): V-VIII.

"Vom Protest zum Bekenntnis. Die Confessio Augustana: Kritischer Maßstab wahrer Ökumene." *Blätter für württembergische Kirchengeschichte* 80/81 (1980/1981): 24-37. Also in *In Reutlingen gesagt.* Rückblick auf die landeskirchliche Festwoche aus Anlaß der 450 Jahrfeier des Augsburger Bekenntnisses vom 17. bis 22. Juni 1980, ed. Christoph Duncker [Reutlingen, 1980]: 50-63. Also in *Die Reformation:* 208-222 (See BOOKS). Also in *450 Jahre Reformation. Schorndorf im Spätmittelalter und in der Reformationszeit,* eds. Reinhold Scheel and Uwe Jens Wandel, Schriftenreihe des Stadtarchivs Schorndorf, 2 (Schorndorf, 1987): 29-37.

1981

"Die Bedeutung der Mystik von Meister Eckhart bis Martin Luther." *Von Eckhart bis Luther. Über mystischen Glauben,* ed. Wolfgang Böhme (Karlsruhe, 1981): 9-20. Also in *Die Reformation:* 32-44 (See BOOKS). Also in *Begegnung mit Gott. Über mystischen Glauben,* Bücher mystischer Lebensdeutung, ed. Wolfgang Böhme (Stuttgart, 1989): 83-101.

"Zwischen Agitation und Reformation: Die Flugschriften als 'Judenspiegel'." *Flugschriften als Massenmedium der Reformationszeit.* Beiträge zum Tübinger Symposion 1980, ed. Hans-Joachim Köhler, Spätmittelalter und Frühe Neuzeit, 13 (Stuttgart, 1981): 269-289.

"Stadtreformation und Fürstenreformation." *Humanismus und Reformation als kulturelle Kräfte in der deutschen Geschichte.* Ein Tagungsbericht, ed. Lewis W. Spitz, Veröffentlichungen der Historischen Kommission zu Berlin, 51 (Berlin, 1981): 80-103; Discussion: 174-187.

Preface, *D. Martin Luther. Operationes in Psalmos 1519-1521, vol. 2: Psalm 1 bis 10 (Vulgata),* eds. Gerhard Hammer and Manfred Biersack, Archiv zur Weimarer Ausgabe der Werke Martin Luthers, 2 (Köln, 1981): V-VI.

Preface, *Gregorii Ariminensis OESA Lectura,* vol. 1, SuR 6 (Berlin, 1981): V-X.

1982

"Martin Luther. Vorläufer der Reformation." *Verifikationen.* Festschrift für Gerhard Ebeling zum 70. Geburtstag, eds. Eberhard Jüngel, Johannes Wallmann and Wilfrid Werbeck (Tübingen, 1982): 91-119. Also in *Die Reformation:* 162-188 (See BOOKS).

Preface, *Gregorii Ariminensis OESA Lectura,* vol. 2, SuR 7 (Berlin, 1982): V-VI.

1983

"Luther, Israel und die Juden. Befangen in der mittelalterlichen Tradition." *Das Parlament,* no. 3 (January 22, 1983): 12. Also in *Martin Luther heute,* ed. Bundeszentrale für politische Bildung, Themenheft, 3 (Bonn, 1983): 65-71. Also published as: "Luther, Deutschland und die Juden." *Die Reformation geht weiter. Ertrag eines Jahres,* eds. Ludwig Markert and Karl Heinz

Stahl (Erlangen, 1984): 159-169. Dutch: "Luther, Israel en de Joden." *Luther na 500 jaar Teksten, vertaald en besproken*, eds. J. T. Bakker and J. P. Boendermaker (Kampen, 1983): 145-167. English: "Luther, Israel and the Jews." *Colloquium. The Australian and New Zealand Theological Review* 16, no. 2 (1984): 21-27.

"'Hier stehe ich, ich kann nicht anders'. Martin Luther, der Christ zwischen Mittelalter und Endzeit." *Die Presse* (March 26/27, 1983): Spectrum, I-II.

"Luthers Beziehungen zu den Juden: Ahnen und Geahndete." *Leben und Werk Martin Luthers von 1526 bis 1546*. Festgabe zu seinem 500. Geburtstag, ed. Helmar Junghans (Berlin, Göttingen, 1983): 519-530, 894-904. Also published as: "Die Juden in Luthers Sicht." *Die Juden und Martin Luther — Martin Luther und die Juden. Geschichte, Wirkungsgeschichte, Herausforderung*, ed. Heinz Kremers (Neukirchen-Vluyn, 1985): 136-162.

"Three Sixteenth-Century Attitudes to Judaism: Reuchlin, Erasmus and Luther." *Jewish Thought in the Sixteenth Century*, ed. Bernard Dov Cooperman, Harvard Judaica Texts and Studies, 2 (Cambridge, MA, 1983): 326-364.

"Le combat de Luther pour l'Église: La chrétienté entre Dieu et le diable." *Luther et la Réforme allemande dans une perspective oecuménique*, ed. Centre Orthodoxe du Patriarcat Oecuménique, Les Études Théologiques de Chambésy, 3 (Chambésy-Genève, 1983): 427-446.

"Van wierook tot caricatuur. De nationale toe-eigening van Maarten Luther." *Kerk en Theologie* 34 (1983): 177-184. English: "The Nationalist Conscription of Martin Luther." *Piety, Politics, and Ethics.* Reformation Studies in Honor of George Wolfgang Forell, ed. Carter Lindberg, Sixteenth Century Essays & Studies, 3 (Kirksville, MO, 1984): 65-73.

"Luther — tussen wieg en sterfbed," "Luther — tussen revolutie en reformatie," "Luther — tussen begin en einde," "Luther — tussen God en chaos," "Luther — tussen goddelijke gave en menselijke keuze," "Luther — tussen hoop en haat." (Radio lectures) *Rondom het Woord* 25, no. 3 (1983): 62-102.

Preface, *Johannes von Paltz. Werke*, vol. 1: *Coelifodina*, eds. Christoph Burger and Friedhelm Stasch, SuR 2 (Berlin, 1983): V-VIII.

Preface, *Johannes von Paltz. Werke*, vol. 2: *Supplementum Coelifodinae*, ed. Berndt Hamm, SuR 3 (Berlin, 1983): V-VI.

"Zürichs Beitrag zur Weltgeschichte. Zwinglis Reformation zwischen Erfolg und Scheitern." *Neue Zürcher Zeitung*, no. 94 (April 21/22, 1984): 65; Fernausgabe, no. 93 (April 20/21, 1984): 37. Also in *Die Reformation:* 238-252 (See BOOKS). Dutch: "Zürichs bijdrage aan de wereldgeschiedenis — Zwingli's reformatie tussen slagen en falen." *In de Waagschaal* 13 (1984): 388-392.

1984

"'Immo'. Luthers reformatorische Entdeckungen im Spiegel der Rhetorik."

Lutheriana. Zum 500. Geburtstag Martin Luthers von den Mitarbeitern der Weimarer Ausgabe, eds. Gerhard Hammer and Karl-Heinz zur Mühlen, Archiv zur Weimarer Ausgabe der Werke Martin Luthers, 5 (Köln, 1984): 17-38.

"Thesen zur Zwei-Reiche-Lehre." *Luther und die politische Welt.* Wissenschaftliches Symposion in Worms, eds. Erwin Iserloh and Gerhard Müller, Historische Forschungen, 9 (Stuttgart, 1984): 27-34.

"Martin Luther: Zwischen Mittelalter und Neuzeit." *"Gott kumm mir zu hilf." Martin Luther in der Zeitenwende. Berliner Forschungen und Beiträge zur Reformationsgeschichte,* ed. Hans-Dietrich Loock, Jahrbuch für Berlin-Brandenburgische Kirchengeschichte, Sonderband (Berlin, 1984): 9-26. Also published as: "Martin Luther: Mensch zwischen Gott und Teufel." *Werden und Wirkung der Reformation.* Ringvorlesung an der Technischen Hochschule Darmstadt im Wintersemester 1983/84. Eine Dokumentation, eds. Lothar Graf zu Dohna and Reinhold Mokrosch, THD-Schriftenreihe Wissenschaft und Technik, 29 (Darmstadt, 1986): 117-137. Also in *Die Reformation:* 189-207 (See BOOKS).

"University and Society on the Threshold of Modern Times: The German Connection." *Rebirth, Reform and Resilience. Universities in Transition 1300-1700,* eds. James M. Kittelson and Pamela J. Transue (Columbus, OH, 1984): 19-41.

Preface, *Gregorii Ariminensis OESA Lectura,* vol. 3, SuR 8 (Berlin, 1984): V-VII.

1985

"Klaus Scholder 1930-1985." *Zeitschrift für Kirchengeschichte* 96 (1985): 295-300.

"Die Reformation als theologische Revolution." *Zwingli und Europa.* Referate und Protokoll des Internationalen Kongresses aus Anlaß des 500. Geburtstages von Huldrych Zwingli, eds. Peter Blickle, Andreas Lindt and Alfred Schindler (Zürich, 1985): 11-26. Also published as: "Eine Epoche — Drei Reformationen." *Die Reformation:* 283-299 (See BOOKS).

"From Confrontation to Encounter: The Ugly German and the Ugly American." *German-American Interrelations. Heritage and Challenge,* ed. James F. Harris (Tübingen, 1985): 1-5.

1986

"Reformator wider Willen. Erinnerung an Erasmus von Rotterdam." *Evangelische Kommentare* 19 (1986): 478-480.

"'Mensen als ik komen eeuwenlang zelden voor'." [Erasmus:] Een intellectueel portret. *NRC Handelsblad* (November 6, 1986): Bijlage, 1-2.

"*Via antiqua e via moderna*: preambolo tardo medievale alle origini teoriche della Riforma." *Sopra la volta del mondo. Onnipotenza e potenza assoluta di Dio tra medioevo e età moderna,* ed. Angela Vettese (Bergamo, 1986): 57-77. English original: "*Via Antiqua and Via Moderna*: Late Medieval Prolegomena to

Early Reformation Thought." *Journal of the History of Ideas* 48 (1987): 23-40. Also in *From Ockham to Wyclif*, eds. Anne Hudson and Michael Wilks, Studies in Church History, Subsidia, 5 (Oxford, 1987): 445-463.

Preface, *D. Martin Luthers Werke. Kritische Gesamtausgabe*, vol. 62: *Ortsregister* (Weimar, 1986): IX-XI.

"Martin Luther: Mensch zwischen Gott und Teufel" in *Werden und Wirkung der Reformation*. Ringvorlesung im WS 83/84, eds. Von Lothar Graf zu Dohna and Reinhold Mokrosch (Darmstadt, 1986): 117-137.

1987

"The Impact of the Reformation: Problems and Perspectives." *Politics and Society in Reformation Europe*. Essays for Sir Geoffrey Elton on his Sixty-Fifth Birthday, eds. E. I. Kouri and Tom Scott (Houndmills, 1987): 3-31.

Preface, *Johann von Staupitz. Sämtliche Schriften, Lateinische Schriften*, vol. 1: *Tübinger Predigten*, ed. Richard Wetzel, SuR 13 (Berlin, 1987): 1-2.

1988

"Osiander an Joachim Rheticus," "Osiander an Copernicus," "Osiander an Joachim Rheticus," "Vorrede zu: Nicolaus Copernicus, De revolutionibus." First critical edition of Osiander-Copernicus-acta. *Andreas Osiander d. Ä. Gesamtausgabe*, vol. 7: *Schriften und Briefe 1539 bis März 1543*, eds. Gerhard Müller and Gottfried Seebaß (Gütersloh, 1988): no. 262, pp. 278-280; no. 275, pp. 333-336; no. 276, pp. 337-338; no. 292, pp. 556-568.

"Teufelsdreck: Eschatology and Scatology in the 'Old' Luther." *The Sixteenth Century Journal* 19 (1988): 435-350.

"Gli ostinati Giudei: mutamento delle strategie nell'Europa tardo-medioevale (1300-1600)." *Ebrei e Cristiani nell'Italia medioevale e moderna: conversioni, scambi, contrasti*. Atti del VI Congresso internazionale dell'AISG, eds. Michele Luzzati, Michele Olivari and Alessandra Veronese, Associazione Italiana per lo Studio del Giudaismo, Testi e Studi, 6 (Roma, 1988): 123-140. English original: "The Stubborn Jews. Timing the Escalation of Antisemitism in Late Medieval Europe." Introduction to *Year Book XXXIV* of the Leo Baeck Institute (London, 1989): XI-XXV.

Preface, *Devotio Moderna. Basic Writings*, ed. John Van Engen, The Classics of Western Spirituality (New York, 1988): 1-3.

1989

"Captivitas Babylonica: Die Kirchenkritik des Johann von Staupitz." *Reformatio et reformationes*. Festschrift für Lothar Graf zu Dohna zum 65. Geburtstag, eds. Andreas Mehl and Wolfgang Christian Schneider, THD-Schriftenreihe Wissenschaft und Technik, 47 (Darmstadt, 1989): 97-106.

"*Duplex misericordia*: Der Teufel und die Kirche in der Theologie des jungen Johann von Staupitz." *Festschrift für Martin Anton Schmidt zum 70. Geburtstag, Theologische Zeitschrift* 45 (1989): 231-243.

"'Met tabellen tegen taboes'. Mijmeringen over de toekomst van de theologie in Nederland." *Kerk en Theologie* 40 (1989): 309-314.

"*Die Gelehrten die Verkehrten:* Popular Response to Learned Culture in the Renaissance and Reformation." *Religion and Culture in the Renaissance and Reformation,* ed. Steven E. Ozment, Sixteenth Century Essays & Studies, 10 (Kirksville, MO, 1989): 43-63.

"Luther and the Devil." *Luther and the Devil, Lutheran Theological Seminary Bulletin* 69, no. 1 (1989): 4-11; Discussion: 11-15.

Preface, *Johannes von Paltz. Werke,* vol. 3: *Opuscula,* eds. Christoph Burger, et al., SuR 4 (Berlin, 1989): V-VI.

1992

"The Discovery of Hebrew and the Discrimination against the Jews: The 'Veritas Hebraica' as Double-Edged Sword in Renaissance and Reformation." *Germania Illustrata: Essays on Early Modern Germany Presented to Gerald Strauss,* eds. Andrew C. Fix and Susan C. Karant-Nunn (Kirksville, Missouri, 1992): 19-34.

"Ignatius of Loyola and the Reformation: The Case of John Calvin." *Ignacio de Loyola y su Tiempo.* Congreso Internacional de Historia (9-13 Scticmbre 1991) ed. Juan Plazaola (Bilbao, 1992): 807-817.

"John Calvin: The Mystery of his Impact." *Calvin Studies VI.* Presented at a Colloquium on Calvin Studies at Davidson College and Davidson College Presbyterian Church Davidson, North Carolina, ed. John H. Leith (January 1992): 1-14.

"Europa afflicta: The Reformation of the Refugees." *Archiv für Reformationsgeschichte,* Jahrgang 83 (1992): 91-111.

1993

Foreword, *The Bolsec Controversy on Predestination, from 1551-1555,* Philip C. Holtrop (New York and Toronto, 1993): xvii-xix.

"Subita Conversio: The Conversion of John Calvin." *Reformiertes Erbe.* Festschrift für Gottfried W. Locher zu seinem 80. Geburtstag, vol. II, eds. Heiko A. Oberman, Ernst Saxer, Alfred Schindler and Heinzpeter Stucki (Zurich, 1993): 279-295.

Preface "Anticlericalism as an Agent for Change" p.ix-xi in *Anticlericalism in Late Medieval and Early Modern Europe,* ed. Peter A. Dykema and Heiko A. Oberman (Leiden, 1993): xi + 704

"The Pursuit of Happiness: Calvin Between Humanism and Reformation." *Humanity and Divinity in Renaissance and Reformation.* Essays in Honor of Charles Trinkaus, eds. John W. O'Malley, Thomas M. Izbicki and Gerald Christianson (Leiden, 1993): 251-283. Also in *Studia Historiae Ecclesiasticae* 19 (December 1993): 1-34.

"Johannes Reuchlin: Von Judenknechten zu Judenrechten." *Reuchlin und die Juden,* eds. Arno Herzig and Julius H. Schoeps with Saskia Rohde (Sigmaringen, 1993): 39-64.

"Wessel Gansfort: *Magister contradictionis*." Wessel Gansfort (1419-1489) and Northern Humanism, eds. F. Akkerman, G.C. Huisman and A.J. Vanderjagt (Leiden, 1993): 97-121.

"'Maastricht' mist mythische dimensie" and "Een nieuw transatlantisch manifest is nodig" in *Het Financieele Dagblad*, August 6, 1993, p. 9; August 7 and 9, 1993, p. 7.

1994

"Gansfort, Reuchlin and the 'Obscure Men': First Fissure in the Foundations of Faith." *Studien zum 15. Jahrhundert*. Festschrift für Erich Meuthen, eds. Johannes Helmrath, Heribert Müller with Helmut Wolff (Munich, 1994): 717-735.

"Via Calvini. Zur Enträtselung der Wirkung Calvins." *Zwingliana*, vol. 21, (1994): 29-57.

1996

"The Travail of Tolerance: Containing Chaos in Early Modern Europe" in *Tolerance and Intolerance in the European Reformation*, eds. Ole Peter Grell and Bob Scribner (Cambridge, 1996): 13-31.

"Reuchlin and the Jews: Obstacles on the Path to Emancipation" in *The Challenge of Periodization. Old Paradigms and New Perspectives*, ed. Lawrence Besserman (New York and London, 1996): 67-93.

"Curiosi te Salutant: A Premature Assessment," in *Biblical Interpretation in the Era of the Reformation*, Essays Presented to David C. Steinmetz in Honor of His Sixtieth Birthday, eds. Richard A. Muller, John L. Thompson, (Grand Rapids: William B. Eerdmans, 1996): x-xiii.

1997

"The Devil and the Devious Historian: Reaching for the Roots of Modernity," in *KNAW/Heineken Lectures, 1996*, (Amsterdam, 1997): 33-44.

"Hus und Luther. Der Antichrist und die zweite reformatorische Entdeckung," in *Jan Hus. Zwischen Zeiten, Völkern, Konfessionen*, Vorträge des internationalen Symposions in Bayreuth vom 22. Bis 26. September 1993, ed. Ferdinand Seibt, (Munich: R. Oldenbourg Verlag, 1997): 319-346.

1998

"Calvin and Farel: The Dynamics of Legitimation in Early Calvinism," in *Journal of Early Modern History*, vol.2, No. 1 (February 1998): 32-60. Also in Reformation and Renaissance Review, No. 1, (June 1999): 7-40.

"Zwinglis Reformation zwischen Erfolg und Scheitern: Zürichs Beitrag zur Weltgeschichte," in *Vivat Helvetia. Die Herausforderung einer nationalen Identität*, ed. Jattie Enklaar and Hans Ester (Amsterdam: Rodopi, 1998): 89-103.

1999

"Hus and Luther. Prophets of a Radical Reformation," in *The Contentious Triangle. Church, State, and University*, A Festschrift in Honor of Professor George Huntston Williams, ed. Rodney L. Petersen and Calvin Augustine Pater, vol. LI Sixteenth Century Essays and Studies (Kirksville: Thomas Jefferson University Press, 1999): 135-166.

2000

"Nachsinnen und Bewerten Tübinger Befund aus transatlantischer Perspektive," in *Relationen–Studien zum bergang vom Spätmittelalter zur Reformation*, Festschrift zu Ehren von Prof. Dr. Karl-Heinz zur Mühlen, ed. Athina Lexutt, Wolfgang Matz (Münster: Lit Verlag, 2000): 11-13.

INDEX OF PERSONS

INDEX OF PLACES

INDEX OF SUBJECTS